THIRD EDITION

GATEWAYS
TO DEMOCRACY
an Introduction to
American Government

THE ESSENTIALS

John G. **Geer**
Vanderbilt University

Wendy J. **Schiller**
Brown University

Jeffrey A. **Segal**
Stony Brook University

Richard **Herrera**
Arizona State University

Dana K. **Glencross**
Oklahoma City Community College

CENGAGE
Learning·

Australia • Brazil • Mexico • Singapore • United Kingdom • United States

***Gateways to Democracy: An Introduction to American Government, The Essentials,* Third Edition**
John G. Geer, Wendy J. Schiller,
Jeffrey A. Segal, Richard Herrera,
Dana K. Glencross

Product Team Manager: Carolyn Merrill

Content Developer: Naomi Friedman

Managing Developer: Joanne Dauksewicz

Associate Content Developer: Amy Bither

Product Assistant: Abigail Hess

Senior Media Developer: Laura Hildebrand

Marketing Manager: Valerie Hartman

Content Project Manager: Cathy Brooks

Art Director: Linda May

Manufacturing Planner: Fola Orekoya

IP Analyst: Alexandra Ricciardi

IP Project Manager: Farah Fard

Production Service and Compositor:
MPS Limited

Text Designer: Studio Montage

Cover Designer: Rokusek Design

Cover Image: Building: © Black Russian Studio/
Shutterstock.com; Man: © Joana Lopes/
Shutterstock.com

Library of Congress Control Number: 2014949551

Package ISBN: 978-1-285-85291-1

Text-only student edition ISBN: 978-1-285-85857-9

Loose-leaf edition ISBN: 978-1-305-63401-5

Cengage Learning
20 Channel Center Street
Boston, MA 02210
USA

Cengage Learning is a leading provider of customized learning solutions with office locations around the globe, including Singapore, the United Kingdom, Australia, Mexico, Brazil, and Japan. Locate your local office at **www.cengage.com/global**

Cengage Learning products are represented in Canada by Nelson Education, Ltd.

To learn more about Cengage Learning Solutions, visit **www.cengage.com**

Purchase any of our products at your local college store or at our preferred online store **www.cengagebrain.com**

KP-LLF
Printed in the United States of America
Print Number: 03   Print Year: 2016

Brief Contents

Chapter 1   Gateways to American Democracy   3
Chapter 2   The Constitution   29
Chapter 3   Federalism   59
Chapter 4   Civil Liberties   87
Chapter 5   Civil Rights   119
Chapter 6   Public Opinion and the Media   155
Chapter 7   Interest Groups   199
Chapter 8   Political Parties   231
Chapter 9   Elections, Campaigns, and Voting   265
Chapter 10   Congress   309
Chapter 11   The Presidency   349
Chapter 12   The Bureaucracy   387
Chapter 13   The Judiciary   419
Chapter 14   Economic, Domestic, and Foreign Policy   455

Appendix

A. The Declaration of Independence   494
B. The Constitution of the United States   498
C. *Federalist Papers* 10 and 51   514

Contents

CHAPTER 1: Gateways to American Democracy 3

Gateways: Evaluating the American Political System 4

Democracy and the American Constitutional System 6

Liberty and Order 6

The Constitution as Gatekeeper 7

American Political Culture 11

Responsiveness and Equality: Does American Democracy Work? 13

The Demands of Democratic Government 16

Self-Interest and Civic Interest 18

Politics and the Public Sphere 18

Your Gateway to American Democracy 21

What you need to know about your text and online study tools to study efficiently and master the material 22

CHAPTER 2: The Constitution 29

Before the Constitution 30

The British Constitution 30

Toward Independence 31

The Declaration of Independence 33

The Articles of Confederation 33

The Constitutional Convention 35

Large versus Small States 35

Nation versus State 36

North versus South 36

Gates against Popular Influence 38

The Ratification Process 38

Government under the Constitution 40

The Structure of Government 40

The Amendment Process 41

The Partition of Power 42

The Ratification Debates 45

Federalists and Antifederalists 46

Consolidation of Federal Authority 46

The Scope of Executive Authority 46

The Scope of Legislative Authority 47

The Lack of a Bill of Rights 47

The Responsive Constitution 48

The Bill of Rights 48

The Civil War Amendments 50

Amendments That Expand Public Participation 50

Constitutional Interpretation 50

The Constitution and Democracy 54

CHAPTER 3: Federalism 59

Why Federalism? 60

Why Unify? 60

Confederal, Unitary, and Federal Systems 61

Constitutional Framework 64

Grants of Power 64

Limits on Power 65

Groundwork for Relationships 68

The Changing Nature of American Federalism 70

Nationalization in the Founding Generation (approximately 1789–1832) 71

The Revolt against National Authority: Nullification, Slavery, and the Civil War (approximately 1832–65) 71

Dual Federalism (approximately 1865–1932) 74

Cooperative Federalism: The New Deal and Civil Rights (approximately 1932–69) 74

The New Federalism (approximately 1969–93) 75

Summing Up: Were the Antifederalists Correct? 78

State and Local Governments 79

State Executive Branches 79

State Legislative Branches 79

State Judicial Branches 79

Local Governments 80

Direct Democracy 80

Federalism and Democracy 82

CHAPTER 4: Civil Liberties 87

What Are Civil Liberties? 88

Civil Liberties and Civil Rights 88

Balancing Liberty and Order 89

Constitutional Rights 90

The Bill of Rights and the States 90

Civil Liberties in Times of Crisis 92

The World Wars 92

The War on Terror 93

Civil Liberties and American Values 96

The First Amendment and Freedom of Expression 96

Freedom of Speech 96

Freedom of the Press 100

Religious Freedom 103

Free Exercise 103

The Establishment of Religion 104

The Right to Keep and Bear Arms 106

Criminal Procedure 106

Investigations 107

Trial Procedures 109

Verdict, Punishment, and Appeal 109

The Right to Privacy 111

Birth Control and Abortion 111

Homosexual Behavior 113

The Right to Die 114

Civil Liberties and Democracy 114

CHAPTER 5: Civil Rights 119

What Are Civil Rights? 120

Civil Rights and Civil Liberties 120

The Constitution and Civil Rights 120

Legal Restrictions on Civil Rights 121

Slavery 122

Restrictions on Citizenship 123

Racial Segregation and Discrimination 125

Ethnic Segregation and Discrimination 127

Women's Suffrage 127

Continued Gender Discrimination 129

The Expansion of Equal Protection 132

State Action 132

Judicial Review 133

The End of Legal Restrictions on Civil Rights 134

Dismantling Public Discrimination Based on Race 134

Dismantling Private Discrimination Based on Race 137

Dismantling Voting Barriers Based on Race 138

Dismantling Public Discrimination Based on Ethnicity 139

Dismantling Voting Barriers Based on Ethnicity 140

Dismantling Private Discrimination Based on Ethnicity 141

Dismantling Discrimination Based on Gender 142

Frontiers in Civil Rights 146

Sexual Orientation and Same-Sex Marriage 146

Disability Rights 149

Undocumented Immigrants 149

Civil Rights and Democracy 150

CHAPTER 6: Public Opinion and the Media 155

The Power of Public Opinion 156

What Is Public Opinion? 157

The Public's Support of Government 157

Public Opinion Polls 159

Scientific Polling and the Growth of Survey Research 159

Types of Polls 160

Error in Polls 162

The Shape of Public Opinion 163

Partisanship 164

Ideology 164

Is the Public Informed? 165

Is the Public Polarized? 167

Group Differences 170

Socioeconomic Status 170

Age 171

Religion 171

Gender 171

Race and Ethnicity 172

Education 174

The Political News 175

What Are the Mass Media? 175

The Functions of the News 175

The Law and the Free Press 176

The Mass Media in the Twenty-First Century 177

The Changing Media Environment 178

The Decline of Newspapers 179

The Durability of Radio 180

The Transformation of TV News 181

Infotainment 181

Blogs 182

Social Networking 183

The News Media and Latino Voters 184

The News and the Millennials 185

The Impact of the News Media on the Public 186

The Propaganda Model 186

The Minimal Effects Model 187

The Not-So-Minimal Effects Model 187

Evaluating the News Media 189

Are the Media Biased? 189

Quality of Information 190

Implications of the Internet 192

The Era of Media Choice 193

Public Opinion, the Media, and Democracy 193

CHAPTER 7: Interest Groups 199

Interest Groups and Politics 200

What Are Interest Groups? 200

The Right to Assemble and to Petition 201

The History of Interest Groups 202

Types of Interest Groups 204

Economic Interest Groups 204

Ideological and Issue-Oriented Groups 207

Foreign Policy and International Groups 208

What Interest Groups Do 210

Inform 210

Lobby 210

Campaign Activities 215

The Impact of Interest Groups on Democratic Processes 219

Natural Balance or Disproportionate Power 219

Self-Service or Public Service 220

Open or Closed Routes of Influence 222

Characteristics of Successful Interest Groups 224

Leadership Accountability 224

Membership Stability 224

Financial Stability 226

Influence in the Public Sphere 226

Interest Groups and Democracy 227

CHAPTER 8: Political Parties 231

The Role of Political Parties in American Democracy 232

What Are Political Parties? 232

What Political Parties Do 233

The Party Nomination Process 237

The Dynamics of Early Party Development 241

Political Factions: Federalist versus Antifederalist 241

Thomas Jefferson, Andrew Jackson, and the Emergence of the Democratic Party 242

The Antislavery Movement and the Formation of the Republican Party 243

Party Loyalty and Patronage 244

Reform and the Erosion of Party Control 245

The Effects of a Two-Party System 246

Limited Political Choice 246

The Structural Limits 247

The Role of Third Parties 247

The Tea Party 250

Obstacles to Third Parties and Independents 251

Challenges to Party Power from Interest Groups 254

Party Alignment and Ideology 254

The Parties after the Civil War 254

The New Deal and the Role of Ideology in Party Politics 255

Civil Rights, the Great Society, and Nixon's Southern Strategy 256

The Reagan Revolution and Conservative Party Politics 257

The Modern Partisan Landscape 258

Political Parties and Democracy 260

CHAPTER 9: Elections, Campaigns, and Voting 265

The Constitutional Requirements for Elections 266

Presidential Elections 266

Congressional Elections 271

The Presidential Campaign 273

Evolution of the Modern Campaign 273

The Caucuses and Primaries 274

The National Convention 274

Issues in Presidential Campaigns 275

Fundraising and Money 275

Swing States 277

Microtargeting 278

Campaign Issues 279

Negativity 279

Issues in Congressional Campaigns 280

Fundraising and Money 281

The Role of Political Parties 281

Incumbency Advantage 281

The Practice and Theory of Voting 283

The Constitution and Voting 283

Competing Views of Participation 283

The History of Voting in America 284

Who Votes? 287

Turnout 290

The Demographics of Turnout 291

Why Citizens Vote 293

An Economic Model of Voting 293

A Psychological Model of Voting 294

An Institutional Model of Voting 295

Is Voting in Your Genes? 296

Assessing Turnout 296

Is Turnout Low? 296

Do Turnout Rates Create Inequality? 299

Voting Laws and Regulations 300
  Reforms to Voting Laws in the 1890s 300
  The National Voter Registration Act 301
  New Forms of Voting 301
Elections, Campaigns, Voting, and Democracy 303

CHAPTER 10: Congress 309

Congress as the Legislative Branch 310
  Representation and Bicameralism 310
  Constitutional Differences between the House
    and Senate 311
The Powers of Congress 316
  Taxation and Appropriation 316
  War Powers 317
  Regulation of Commerce 317
  Appointments and Treaties 317
  Impeachment and Removal from Office 319
  Lawmaking 319
  Authorization of Courts 320
  Oversight 320
The Organization of Congress 322
  The Role of Political Parties 322
  The House of Representatives 323
  The Senate 325
  The Committee System 326
  Advocacy Caucuses 329
The Lawmaking Process 330
  The Procedural Rules of the House and Senate 330
  Legislative Proposals 333
  Committee Action 334
  Floor Action and the Vote 334
  Conference Committee 335
  The Budget Process and Reconciliation 335
  Presidential Signature or Veto, and the Veto
    Override 337
The Member of Congress at Work 337
  Offices and Staff 337
  Legislative Responsibilities 340
  Communication with Constituents 342
  The Next Election 342
Congress and Democracy 344

CHAPTER 11: The Presidency 349

Presidential Qualifications 350
  Constitutional Eligibility and Presidential Succession 350
  Background and Experience 352
  The Expansion of the Presidency 354

Presidential Power: Constitutional Grants
and Limits 355
  Commander in Chief 355
  Power to Pardon 355
  Treaties and Recognition of Foreign Nations 356
  Executive and Judicial Nominations 357
  Veto and the Veto Override 359
  Other Powers 361
  Congress's Ultimate Check on the Executive:
    Impeachment 361
The Growth of Executive Influence 363
  Presidential Directives and Signing Statements 363
  Power to Persuade 365
  Agenda Setting 367
The President in Wartime 368
  Power Struggles between the President and
    Congress 369
  Power Struggles between the President and the
    Judiciary 374
The Organization of the Modern White House 375
  The Executive Office of the President 375
  The Office of the Vice President 376
Presidential Greatness 377
  Franklin Delano Roosevelt (1933–45): The New Deal and
    World War II 377
  Lyndon Baines Johnson (1963–69): The Great Society
    and Vietnam 379
  Ronald Reagan (1981–89): The Reagan Revolution and
    the End of the Cold War 380
The Presidency and Democracy 382

CHAPTER 12: The Bureaucracy 387

The American Bureaucracy 388
  What Is the Bureaucracy? 389
  Constitutional Foundations 390
  The Structure of the Bureaucracy 390
Core Components of the Bureaucracy 396
  Mission 396
  Hierarchical Decision-Making Process 396
  Expertise 397
  Bureaucratic Culture 397
The Historical Evolution of the Bureaucracy 399
  The Expansion of Executive Branch Departments 399
  The Growth of Regulatory Agencies and Other
    Organizations 400
  From Patronage to the Civil Service 401
  Career Civil Service 404
  Political Appointees 405
  Diversity in the Federal Bureaucracy 406

Private-Sector Contract Workers 407

Bureaucrats and Politics 408

Accountability and Responsiveness in the Bureaucracy 410

The Roles of the Legislative and Judicial Branches 410

Efficiency and Transparency 411

Whistleblowing 414

Bureaucratic Failure 414

The Bureaucracy and Democracy 415

CHAPTER 13: The Judiciary 419

The Role and Powers of the Judiciary 420

English Legal Traditions 420

Constitutional Grants of Power 421

State and Lower Federal Courts 423

State Courts in the Federal Judicial System 423

The District Courts 426

The Courts of Appeals 428

The Supreme Court 430

Granting Review 430

Oral Arguments 431

The Decision 431

Judicial Decision Making 433

Judicial Restraint: The Legal Approach 434

Judicial Activism: The Extralegal Approach 435

Restraint and Activism in Judicial Decision Making 437

The Impact of Court Rulings 437

The Appointment Process for Federal Judges and Justices 438

The District Courts 440

The Courts of Appeals 441

The Supreme Court 441

Demographic Diversity on the Court 443

Historical Trends in Supreme Court Rulings 444

Expansion of National Power under the Marshall Court 446

Limits on National Power, 1830s to 1930s 446

Strengthened National Power, 1930s to the Present 447

The Judiciary and Democracy 450

CHAPTER 14: Economic, Domestic, and Foreign Policy 455

Public Policy under a Constitutional System 456

The Process of Policy Making 457

The Regulatory Process 459

Blocking Implementation 460

State Governments and Public Policy 460

Domestic Policy 462

Entitlement Programs, Income Security, and Health Care Overview 463

The Affordable Care Act (ACA) 465

Immigration Policy Overview 467

Energy, Environmental Policy, and Climate Change Overview 469

Economic Policy 472

An Overview: Intervention in the Economy 472

Fiscal Policy 473

Monetary Policy 473

Trade Policy 477

Foreign Policy 482

An Overview: International Relations and U.S. Foreign Policy Goals 482

Foreign Policy Tools 485

Public Policy and Democracy 490

Appendix

A. The Declaration of Independence 494
B. The Constitution of the United States 498
C. *Federalist Papers* 10 and 51 514

Glossary 522
Endnotes 532
Index 555

 **MindTap™**

1. To get started, navigate to: **www.cengagebrain.com** and select "Register a Product".

A new screen will appear prompting you to add a Course Key. A Course Key is a code given to you by your instructor - this is the first of two codes you will need to access MindTap. Every student in your course section should have the same Course Key.

2. Enter the Course Key and click "Register."

If you are accessing MindTap through your school's Learning Management System such as BlackBoard or Desire2Learn, you may be redirected to use your Course Key/Access Code there. Follow the prompts you are given and feel free to contact support if you need assistance.

3. Confirm your course information above, and proceed to the log in portion below.

If you have a CengageBrain username and password, enter it under "Returning Students" and click "Login." If this is your first time, register under "New Students" and click "Create a New Account."

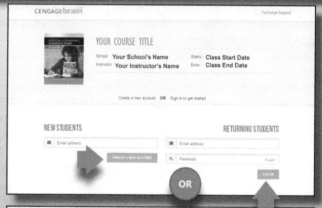

4. Now that you are logged in, you can access the course for free by selecting "Start Free Trial" for 20 days, or enter in your Access Code.

Your Access Code is unique to you and acts as payment for MindTap. You may have received it with your book or purchased separately in the bookstore or at **CengageBrain.com**. Enter it and click "Register."

NEED HELP?

For CengageBrain Support: Login to **Support.Cengage.com**. Call **866-994-2427** or access our **24/7 Student Chat!** Or access the **First Day of School PowerPoint Presentation** found at cengagebrain.com.

Letter to Instructor...

Dear *Introduction to American Government* Instructor:

As teachers and scholars of American government, we have come together to write a textbook that would engage students in both the process and the policy outcomes of U.S. government. The book presents an updated lens through which we can examine the theoretical and structural foundations of American democracy and the resulting political process that demands an active and informed citizenry. To help students understand American democracy and see how they can be involved in their government, we peel back the layers of the political system to expose its inner workings and to examine how competing interests can both facilitate and block the people's will. In doing so, we use the conceptual framework of gateways. We contend that there are gates—formal and informal—that present obstacles to participation and empowerment. But there are also gateways that give students a chance to influence the process and to overcome the obstacles. The gateways framework helps students conceptualize participation and civic engagement—even democracy itself. Our book is both realistic and optimistic, contending that the American system can be open to the influence of students and responsive to their hopes and dreams—if they have information about how the system works. But we avoid cheerleading by also pointing out the many gates that undermine the workings of government. Although the size and complexity of the American constitutional system is daunting, it is imperative to prepare for the demands of democratic citizenship. This has never been truer than today, when we have a rapidly changing demographic balance within our population. Today groups that were formerly underrepresented in American politics and society, such as second- and third-generation Latinos, are a powerful force in government. It is our hope that this textbook can awaken students and motivate them not only to learn about politics but to also participate actively throughout every stage of their lives.

In keeping with the theme of gates and gateways in American politics, we also open each chapter with a **vignette** that tells the story of people who have successfully navigated their own way in politics. The important role of the vignette for the instructor is to show the students how people like them have made a difference in American political and social life; our vignette subjects vary by historical era, career choice, gender, race, ethnicity, and party affiliation. We also include landmark **Supreme Court cases** related to every chapter's subject to show students the continuous and vital role it plays in both upholding and knocking down gates to policy implementation and political participation. We include **policy features** in each chapter to illustrate how the chapter's core content operates in a real-time, real-life basis. To round out our emphasis on how the core structure of a political system can encourage or discourage participation, we include a **Global Gateway feature** in each chapter, which informs students about politics around the globe and how it compares to what they see in the American context.

New to This Edition

- A new dedicated focus on Latino politics and participation reflects the changing demographic infrastructure in America today by providing new coverage of the politics and issues affecting Latinos in every chapter of the book:
  - New sections on the history of Latino civil rights, including a time line of significant events in Latino political history
  - New Supreme Court cases of significance to Latino constitutional and voting rights
  - New section on Latino political leaders and grassroots organizations
  - New chapter vignettes highlighting the gateways used by Latinos
  - Expanded discussion of the Latino vote and its implications for elections and governing
- New freestanding chapter on domestic, economic, and foreign policy making
- New freestanding chapter which combines the chapters on Public Opinion and the Media into one comprehensive chapter
- Revamped policy features embedded in each chapter that reflect the most current issues related to each chapter's subject

- Updated opening vignettes, Global Gateways, and new Supreme Court cases to incorporate the changes in American politics since the publication of the second edition
- Streamlined learning objectives and outcomes
- New coverage of the impact of the changes in campaign spending that arose from recent Supreme Court decisions
- Revamped discussion of microtargeting in light of the success of the Obama campaign in 2012
- New coverage of social media and its role in forging opportunities for participation
- Up-to-date coverage of the 2014 midterm elections examining the impact of the Tea Party, turnout trends, and the role of money in 2014 campaigns

Mindtap

As an instructor, MindTap is here to simplify your workload, organize and immediately grade your students' assignments, and allow you to customize your course as you see fit. Through deep-seated integration with your Learning Management System, grades are easily exported, and analytics are pulled with just the click of a button. MindTap provides you with a platform to easily add in current events videos and RSS feeds from national or local news sources. Looking to include more currency in the course? Add in our KnowNow American Government Blog link for weekly updated news coverage and pedagogy.

Teaching American government remains a vitally important but constantly challenging task for all of us. We know that there are many books to choose from to use in your course. We believe that *Gateways* is a book that has an innovative approach in reaching and engaging students across a range of backgrounds and enables instructors to more easily achieve their pedagogical goals in American government courses. We have seen it work for our students, and we know it will work for yours.

Sincerely,

John G. Geer, john.g.geer@vanderbilt.edu
Wendy J. Schiller, Wendy_Schiller@Brown.edu
Jeffrey A. Segal, jeffrey.segal@stonybrook.edu
Richard Herrera, Richard.Herrera@asu.edu
Dana K. Glencross, dglencross@occc.edu

Letter to Student...

Dear Student:

Our book begins with a simple question: How does anyone exert political influence in a country of more than 318 million people? Students in American government classrooms across the country are grappling with this question as they develop an appreciation of their role in American public life. In our own classrooms, students ask us, What is my responsibility? Can I make a difference? Does my participation matter? How can I get my opinions represented? These are gateway questions that probe the opportunities and limits on citizen involvement in a democracy. For that reason, we not only provide you with essential information about the American political system but also show you how to become a **more powerful advocate for yourself** within that system. It is not enough to know what you want your government and society to be—you must learn how to make it happen. This book shows you how people from all walks of life have opened gates to influence public policy, and it shows you the relevance of government in your life. It is our hope that this textbook motivates you not only to learn about politics but also to participate actively throughout every stage of your life.

In keeping with the theme of gates and gateways in American politics, we open each chapter with a vignette that tells the story of people who have successfully navigated their own way in politics. These are people like you who have different gender, ethnic, racial, and partisan backgrounds, and who have made a difference in American political and social life. We also include other features focusing on the Supreme Court, public policy, and global governance that show you how politics plays out in the United States and around the world. All of these special features are designed to relate specifically to you—the student—to give you a blueprint with which to navigate the political system. What makes our book different?

- Streamlined learning objectives and outcomes help you better understand the material and prepare for the graded assignments that go with the class. We have checkpoint questions at the end of each main section, as well as key terms study guide questions throughout each chapter.

- Latino politics and participation coverage reflect the changing demographic infrastructure in America, especially among young people by providing new coverage of the politics and issues affecting Latinos in every chapter of the book.

- Updated accounts are included of people who are changing American politics today.

- Current policy case studies are included on issues such as voting participation, environmental protection, military conflict, and personal privacy.

- A comprehensive chapter which discusses public opinion and the media.

- A comprehensive chapter on elections, campaigns, and voting.

As a student, the benefits of using MindTap with this book are endless. With automatically graded practice quizzes and activities, automatic detailed revision plans on your essay assignments offered through Write Experience, an easily navigated learning path, and an interactive eBook, you will be able to test yourself inside and outside the classroom with ease. The accessibility of current events coupled with interactive media makes the content fun and engaging. On your computer, phone, or tablet, MindTap is there when you need it, giving you easy access to flashcards, quizzes, readings, and assignments.

As teachers, our main goal both in this book and in the classroom is to empower you as active participants in American democracy. We know that you balance a lot of competing demands for your time, from other classes, to work, to family responsibilities. This book provides you with the core information you need to succeed in your American government classes, and just as important, to knock open the gates that may stand in your way to achieve your goals within the political system.

Sincerely,

John G. Geer, john.g.geer@vanderbilt.edu
Wendy J. Schiller, Wendy_Schiller@Brown.edu
Jeffrey A. Segal, jeffrey.segal@stonybrook.edu
Richard Herrera, Richard.Herrera@asu.edu
Dana K. Glencross, dglencross@occc.edu

Resources for Students and Instructors

Students

Access your Gateways to Democracy, Essentials, *3e, resources via*
www.cengagebrain.com/shop/isbn/9781285852911.

If you purchased MindTap or CourseReader access with your book, enter your access code, and click Register. You can also purchase the book's resources here separately through the Study Tools tab or access the free companion website through the Free Materials tab.

Instructors

Access your Gateways to Democracy, Essentials, *3e, resources via*
www.cengage.com/login.

Log in using your Cengage Learning single sign-on user name and password, or create a new instructor account by clicking on New Faculty User and following the instructions.

Gateways to Democracy, Essentials, 3e *– Text Only Edition*

ISBN: 978-1-285-85857-9

This copy of the book does not come bundled with MindTap.

MindTap for *Gateways to Democracy, Essentials,* 3e

Instant Access Code: 978-1-305-07863-5

Printed Access Code: 978-1-285-85859-3

MindTap for American Government is a fully online, personalized learning experience built upon Cengage Learning content. MindTap combines student learning tools—readings, multimedia, activities, and assessments—into a singular Learning Path that guides students through their course. Through a wealth of activities written to learning outcomes, it provides students with ample opportunities to check themselves for understanding, while also providing faculty and students alike with a clear way to measure and assess student progress.

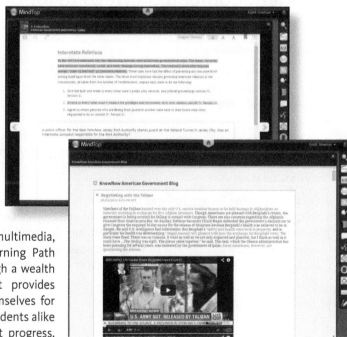

Faculty can use MindTap as a turnkey solution or customize it by adding YouTube videos, RSS feeds, or their own documents directly within the eBook or within each chapter's Learning Path. The product can be used fully online with its interactive eBook for *Gateways to Democracy* or in conjunction with the printed text.

Instructor Companion Website for *Gateways to Democracy, Essentials*, 3e

ISBN: 978-1-285-86567-6

This Instructor Companion website is an all-in-one multimedia online resource for class preparation, presentation, and testing. Accessible through Cengage.com/login with your faculty account, you will find available for download: book-specific Microsoft® PowerPoint® presentations, a test bank compatible with multiple Learning Management Systems, an Instructor's Manual, Microsoft® PowerPoint® Image Slides, and a JPEG Image Library.

The test bank, offered in Blackboard, Moodle, Desire2Learn, Canvas, and Angel formats, contains learning objective-specific multiple-choice, short answer, and essay questions for each chapter. Import the test bank into your Learning Management System to edit and manage questions, as well as to create tests.

The Instructor's Manual contains chapter-specific learning objectives, an outline, key terms with definitions, and a chapter summary. Additionally, the Instructor's Manual features a critical thinking question, lecture launching suggestion, and an in-class activity for each learning objective.

The Microsoft® PowerPoint® presentations are ready-to-use visual outlines of each chapter. These presentations are easily customized for your lectures and offered along with chapter-specific Microsoft® PowerPoint® Image Slides and JPEG Image Libraries. Access the Instructor Companion Website at www.cengage.com/login.

Student Companion Website for *Gateways to Democracy, Essentials*, 3e

ISBN: 978-1-285-86566-9

This free companion website for *Gateways to Democracy, 3e,* is accessible through cengagebrain .com and allows students access to chapter-specific interactive learning tools, including flashcards, glossaries, and more.

Cognero for *Gateways to Democracy, Essentials*, 3e

ISBN: 978-1-305-08130-7

Cengage Learning Testing Powered by Cognero is a flexible, online system that allows you to author, edit, and manage test bank content from multiple Cengage Learning solutions, create multiple test versions in an instant, and deliver tests from your Learning Management System, your classroom, or wherever you want. The test bank for *Gateways to Democracy* contains learning objective-specific multiple-choice, short answer, and essay questions for each chapter.

CourseReader for
American Government

CourseReader 0-30 Instant Access Code: 978-1-111-47997-8

CourseReader 0-30 Printed Access Code: 978-1-111-47995-4

CourseReader: American Government allows instructors to create your reader, your way, in just minutes. This affordable, fully customizable online reader provides access to thousands of permissions-cleared readings, articles, primary sources, and audio and video selections from the regularly updated Gale research library database. This easy-to-use solution allows you to search for and select just the material you want for your courses. Each selection opens with a descriptive introduction to provide context and concludes with critical-thinking and multiple-choice questions to reinforce key points. CourseReader is loaded with convenient tools such as highlighting, printing, note-taking, and downloadable PDFs and MP3 audio files for each reading. CourseReader is the perfect complement to any political science course. It can be bundled with your current textbook, sold alone, or integrated into your Learning Management System. CourseReader 0-30 allows access to up to 30 selections in the reader. Instructors can contact their Cengage Learning consultant for details. Students should only purchase CourseReader if assigned by their instructor.

Election 2014 Supplement

ISBN: 978-1-305-50018-1

Written by John Clark and Brian Schaffner, this booklet addresses the 2014 campaigns and elections, with real-time analysis and references.

Acknowledgments

Writing the third edition of an introductory textbook requires a dedicated and professional publishing team. We are thrilled that Richard Herrera, associate professor of political science at Arizona State University, has joined our team and brought with him his deep and rich understanding of Latino politics. We were also extremely fortunate to continue to work with a number of excellent people at Cengage Learning, including Carolyn Merrill. Carolyn has been a rock-steady foundation, and her choice of Naomi Friedman as our development editor was outstanding. Naomi has guided us through a comprehensive revision of the book to focus more on the vital role that traditionally underrepresented groups, such as Latinos, play in knocking down the gates that stand in the way of participation. Edward Dionne and Jill Traut have been vigilant managers of the copyedit process, and Reba Frederics has been terrific in updating our photo and images in the book. We also want to thank the entire sales force at Cengage Learning for their tireless efforts to promote the book.

Our gratitude goes to all of those who worked on the various supplements offered with this text, especially the test bank author, Nate Vanden Brook from Oklahoma City Community College, and the Instructor's Manual author, Adam Newmark from Appalachian State University.

By definition, an American government textbook is a sweeping endeavor, and it would not be possible to succeed without our reviewers. They provided truly constructive input throughout the review and revision process, especially on our new comprehensive policy chapter. We list their names on the following page, and we are grateful to them for their contributions to the development of this textbook.

Each of us would also like to thank the individuals who supported us throughout the project.

John G. Geer: I would like to thank Carrie Roush and Marc Trussler for their help with revising this textbook. Special mention goes to Drew Engelhardt for his amazing efforts in pulling together new material for this third edition. I owe many thanks to Jeff, Rick, and Wendy. They are fabulous collaborators and even better friends. I am lucky to know them and to have the chance to work with them on this project. My deepest and most heartfelt appreciation goes to Beth Prichard Geer. Beth has made possible a new edition of my life that I will be forever grateful for.

Wendy J. Schiller: I would also like to express my appreciation for the opportunity to work with John, Jeff, and Rick—each excellent scholars and colleagues. For her support on this edition, I would like to give a big thanks to Kaitlin Sidorsky for all her research assistance. I would also like to thank my husband, Robert Kalunian, who provides an endless supply of patience, support, and perspective.

Jeffrey A. Segal: I thank my previous co-authors, John and Wendy, for once again making the endeavor of the new edition a totally enjoyable experience; Naomi Friedman for her fresh look at the materials; Rick Herrera for joining the "Gater" team; and Carolyn Merrill for the foresight of asking him aboard. For the second straight edition, Justine D'Elia has provided invaluable research assistance. My professional colleagues, both at Stony Brook and beyond, have cheerfully answered innumerable queries from me. I appreciate their assistance.

Richard Herrera: I would like to thank John, Wendy, and Jeff for inviting me to join the author team. They are an exciting group of scholars with whom to work. The creative process that produced this edition has been a wonderful experience. Their support, along with Naomi Friedman's, has been most valuable as I navigated my way through the revision process. I would also like to thank Marian Norris for her support, patience, and encouragement throughout this new adventure.

Dana K. Glencross: My deepest appreciation and admiration goes to this tremendous team of authors for allowing me the opportunity to work with them yet again. My husband Carl deserves my thanks for his support and patience, as does Annalyn Gill who provides great insights and challenges to my questions. Reagan the basset hound earns recognition for providing companionship during many late hours spent working on this fantastic new edition.

Reviewers

We would also like to thank the instructors who have contributed their valuable feedback through reviews of the second edition in preparation for this third edition:

Martin Adamian, *California State University, Los Angeles*
Lynn Brink, *North Lake College*
Jeffrey Christiansen, *Seminole State College*
Monte Freidig, *Santa Rosa Junior College*

Lori Han, *Chapman University*
Sally Hansen, *Daytona State College*
Debra St. John, *Collin County Community College*

We also thank the reviewers of the previous editions:

Steve Anthony, *Georgia State University*
Wayne Ault, *Southwestern Illinois College*
Jane Bryant, *John A. Logan College*
Jared Burkholder, *Grace College*
David Dulio, *Oakland University*
Joshua Dyck, *University of Massachusetts, Lowell*
Matthew Eshbaugh-Soha, *University of North Texas*
Jeff Fine, *Clemson University*
Charles Finocchiaro, *University of South Carolina*
James Goss, *Tarrant County College, Trinity River*
Rhonda Gunter, *Maryland Community College*
Bill Horner, *University of Missouri, Columbia*
Amy Jasperson, *Rhodes College*
Mark Jendrysik, *University of North Dakota*
Aaron Knight, *Houston Community College, Northeast*
Lyn Maurer, *Southern Illinois University at Edwardsville*
Heather Myabe, *University of West Georgia*

James McCann, *Purdue University*
John Mercurio, *San Diego State University*
Michael Moore, *University of Texas at Arlington*
Jonathan Morris, *East Carolina University*
James Newman, *Idaho State University*
Mark Peplowski, *College of Southern Nevada*
Jamie Pimlott, *Niagara University*
Dave Price, *Santa Fe Community College*
Narges Rabii, *Saddleback College*
Tim Reynolds, *Alvin Community College*
David Ross, *Stark State College*
Margaret Scranton, *University of Arkansas at Little Rock*
John Shively, *Longview Community College*
Alec Thomson, *Schoolcraft College*
Nate Vander Brook, *Oklahoma City College*
Laura Wood, *Tarrant County College, Northwest Campus*
Davis Woodward, *Clemson University*

About the Authors

John G. Geer

(PhD, Princeton University) is the Gertrude Conaway Vanderbilt Professor of Political Science and co-directs the Vanderbilt Poll. Geer has published widely, including *In Defense of Negativity*, which won the Goldsmith Prize from the Shorenstein Center at Harvard University. Geer has been a visiting scholar at Harvard University and Princeton University. Geer teaches Introduction to American Politics, as well as specialty courses on elections and campaigns. His teaching has drawn much note, winning numerous teaching awards at both Arizona State University and Vanderbilt University. Geer is a frequent commentator in the press, with appearances on all the major networks (e.g., Fox News, CBS Evening News, CNN), and he has been quoted in newspapers ranging from *The New York Times* to *The Washington Post* to the *LA Times*. He has done interviews for major international outlets as well, such as BBC and Al Jazeera.

Wendy J. Schiller

(PhD, University of Rochester) is an Associate Professor of Political Science and Public Policy at Brown University (Twitter acct @profwschiller). She was legislative assistant for Senator Daniel P. Moynihan, a federal lobbyist for Governor Mario M. Cuomo, a Guest Scholar and PhD Fellow at the Brookings Institution, and a post-doctoral fellow at Princeton University. She has published *The Contemporary Congress* (2003, 2005) with Burdett Loomis, *Partners and Rivals: Representation in U.S. Senate Delegations* (2000), and *Electing the Senate: Indirect Democracy before the Seventeenth Amendment* (2014) with Charles Stewart III. She teaches courses on a wide range of American politics topics, including Introduction to the American Political Process, The American Presidency, Congress and Public Policy, Parties and Interest Groups, and The Philosophy of the American Founding. Professor Schiller is a political analyst for local and national media outlets, including CNN.com, Bloomberg Radio, NPR, and WJAR10, the local NBC affiliate in Providence.

Jeffrey A. Segal

(PhD, Michigan State University) is SUNY Distinguished Professor and Chair of the Political Science Department at Stony Brook University. He has served as Senior Visiting Research Scholar at Princeton University and held a Guggenheim Fellowship. Segal is best known, with Harold Spaeth, as the leading proponent of the attitudinal model of Supreme Court decision making. Segal has twice won the Wadsworth Award for a book (with Spaeth) or article 10 years or older with lasting influence on law and courts. He has also won the C. Herman Pritchett Award (again with Spaeth) for best book on law and courts. His work on the influence of strategic factors on Supreme Court decision making won the Franklin Burdette Award from APSA. With Lee Epstein, Kevin Quinn, and Andrew Martin, he won Green Bag's award for exemplary legal writing. He has also won a national award sponsored by the American Bar Association for innovative teaching and instructional methods and materials in law and courts.

Richard Herrera

(PhD, University of California Santa Barbara) is Associate Professor of Political Science and Associate Director for the School of Politics and Global Studies at Arizona State University. He directs the ASU Capital Scholars Washington, DC, Summer Internship program for ASU and coordinates the ASU-McCain Institute for International Leadership Internship Program. He has contributed articles to the *American Political Science Review*, *Journal of Politics*, *Legislative Studies Quarterly*, and *State Politics and Policy Quarterly*. His current research interests are focused on U.S. governors, their ideology, policy agendas, and representative functions. He teaches courses in American Politics, American Political Parties, and American Politics and Film.

Dana K. Glencross

(MA, Oklahoma State University) is a Professor of Political Science at Oklahoma City Community College, where she has served as Chair of the Department for History, Political Science, Geography, and Medical Terminology, and as Chair of the Faculty Association. Professor Glencross was a governor's appointee to the Oklahoma Commission for Teacher Preparation and a member of the the Faculty Advisory Council to the Oklahoma State Regents for Higher Education. She was elected as the national chairwoman of the Association of Chapter Advisors to the Phi Theta Kappa Honor Society. She co-authors a chapter on "Public Policy" in *Oklahoma Government and Politics: An Introduction* (2007, 2012, 2014). She teaches courses including American federal government, state and local government, comparative politics, and law. She is a regular guest on local television and radio broadcasts, discussing elections and current events. She received the OCCC President's Award for Excellence in Teaching and twice has been recognized as the Oklahoma Political Science Association's Teacher of the Year.

Career Opportunities: Political Science

Introduction

It is no secret that college graduates are facing one of the toughest job markets in the past fifty years. Despite this challenge, those with a college degree have done much better than those without since the 2008 recession. One of the most important decisions a student has to make is the choice of a major; many consider future job possibilities when making that call. A political science degree is incredibly useful for a successful career in many different fields, from lawyer to policy advocate, pollster to humanitarian worker. Employer surveys reveal that the skills that most employers value in successful employees—critical thinking, analytical reasoning, and clarity of verbal and written communication—are precisely the tools that political science courses should be helping you develop. This brief guide is intended to help spark ideas for what kinds of careers you might pursue with a political science degree and the types of activities you can engage in now to help you secure one of those positions after graduation.

Careers in Political Science

LAW AND CRIMINAL JUSTICE

Do you find that your favorite parts of your political science classes are those that deal with the Constitution, the legal system, and the courts? Then a career in law and criminal justice might be right for you. Traditional jobs in the field range from lawyer or judge to police or parole officer. Since 9/11, there has also been tremendous growth in the area of homeland security, which includes jobs in mission support, immigration, travel security, as well as prevention and response.

PUBLIC ADMINISTRATION

The many offices of the federal government combined represent one of the largest employers in the United States. Flip to the bureaucracy chapter of this textbook and consider that each federal department, agency, and bureau you see looks to political science majors for future employees. A partial list of such agencies would include the Department of Education, the Department of Health and Human Services, and the Federal Trade Commission. This does not even begin to account for the multitude of similar jobs in state and local governments that you might consider as well.

CAMPAIGNS, ELECTIONS, AND POLLING

Are campaigns and elections the most exciting part of political science for you? Then you might consider a career in the growing industry based around political campaigns. From volunteering and interning to consulting, marketing, and fundraising, there are many opportunities for those who enjoy the competitive and high-stakes electoral arena. For those looking for careers that combine political knowledge with statistical skills, there are careers in public opinion polling. Pollsters work for independent national organizations such as Gallup and YouGov, or as part of news operations and campaigns. For those who are interested in survey methodology there are also a wide variety of non-political career opportunities in marketing and survey design.

INTEREST GROUPS, INTERNATIONAL AND NONGOVERNMENTAL ORGANIZATIONS

Is there a cause that you are especially passionate about? If so, there is a good chance that there are interest groups out there that are working hard to see some progress made on similar issues. Many of the positions that one might find in for-profit companies also exist in their non-profit interest group and nongovernmental organization counterparts, including lobbying and high-level strategizing. Do not forget that there are also quite a few major international organizations—such as the United Nations, the World Health Organization, and the International Monetary Fund, where a degree in political science could be put to good use. While competition for those jobs tends to be fierce, your interest and knowledge about politics and policy will give you an advantage.

FOREIGN SERVICE

Does a career in diplomacy and foreign affairs, complete with the opportunity to live and work abroad, sound exciting for you? Tens of thousands of people work for the State Department, both in Washington D.C. and in consulates throughout the world. They represent the diplomatic interests of the United States abroad. Entrance into the Foreign Service follows a very specific process, starting with the Foreign Service Officers Test—an exam given three times a year that includes sections on American government, history, economics, and world affairs. Being a political science major is a significant help in taking the FSOT.

GRADUATE SCHOOL

While not a career, graduate school may be the appropriate next step for you after completing your undergraduate degree. Following the academic route, being awarded a Ph.D. or Master's degree in political science could open additional doors to a career in academia, as well as many of the professions mentioned earlier. If a career as a researcher in political science interests you, you should speak with your advisors about continuing your education.

Preparing While Still on Campus

INTERNSHIPS

One of the most useful steps you can take while still on campus is to visit your college's career center in regards to an internship in your field of interest. Not only does it give you a chance to experience life in the political science realm, it can lead to job opportunities later down the road and add experience to your resume.

SKILLS

In addition to your political science classes, there are a few skills any number of which will prove useful as a complement to your degree:

Writing: Like anything else, writing improves with practice. Writing is one of those skills that is applicable regardless of where your career might take you. Virtually every occupation relies on an ability to write cleanly, concisely, and persuasively.

Public Speaking: An oft-quoted 1977 survey showed that public speaking was the most commonly cited fear among respondents. And yet oral communication is a vital tool in the modern economy. You can practice this skill in a formal class setting or through extracurricular activities that get you in front of a group.

Quantitative Analysis: As the Internet aids in the collection of massive amounts of information, the nation is facing a drastic shortage of people with basic statistical skills to interpret and use this data. A political science degree can go hand-in-hand with courses in introductory statistics.

Foreign Language: One skill that often helps a student or future employee stand out in a crowded job market is the ability to communicate in a language other than English. Solidify or set the foundation for your verbal and written foreign language communication skills while in school.

STUDENT LEADERSHIP

One attribute that many employers look for is "leadership potential" which can be quite tricky to indicate on a resume or cover letter. What can help is a demonstrated record of involvement in clubs and organizations, preferably in a leadership role. While many people think immediately of student government, most student clubs allow you the opportunity to demonstrate your leadership skills.

Conclusion

Hopefully reading this has sparked some ideas on potential future careers. As a next step, visit your college's career placement office, which is a great place to further explore what you have read here. You might also visit your college's alumni office to connect with graduates who are working in your field of interest. Political science opens the door to a lot of exciting careers, have fun exploring the possibilities!

GATEWAYS

TO DEMOCRACY an Introduction to American Government

THE ESSENTIALS

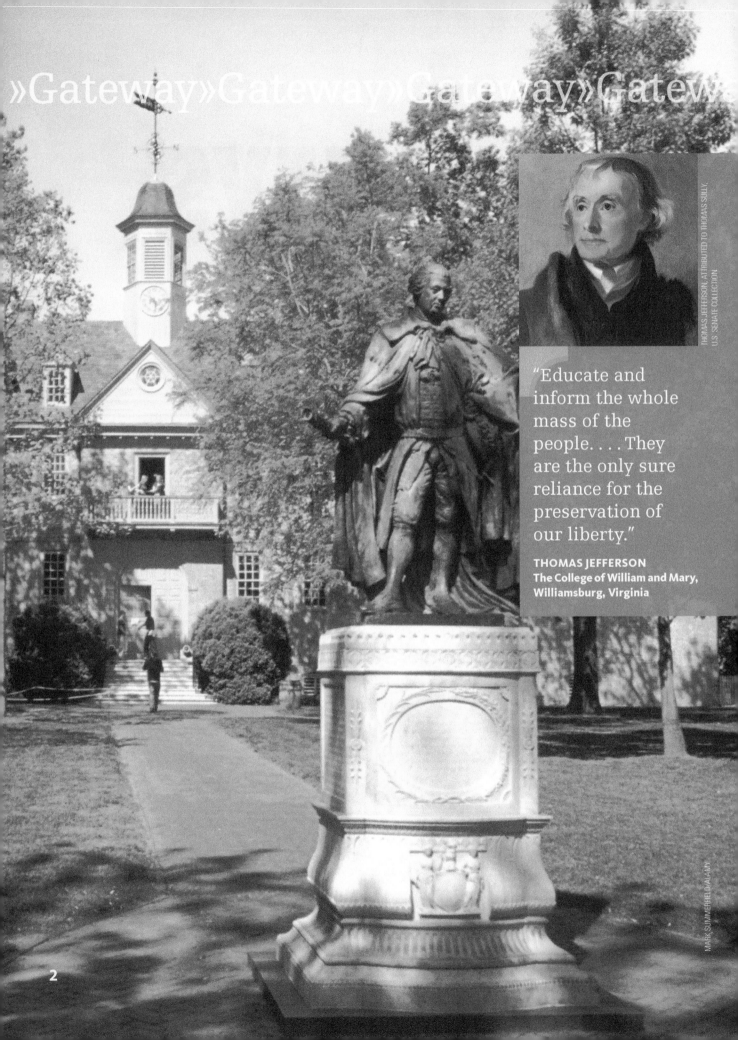

"Educate and inform the whole mass of the people. . . . They are the only sure reliance for the preservation of our liberty."

THOMAS JEFFERSON
The College of William and Mary, Williamsburg, Virginia

1

Gateways to American Democracy

In 1760 Thomas Jefferson left his boyhood home in the hills of Piedmont, Virginia, to attend the College of William and Mary in the colonial capital of Williamsburg. There were only six colleges in the American colonies at that time, and Jefferson was fortunate to have the opportunity to pursue his education. At William and Mary, he studied mathematics, physics, ethics, and the law. He described himself as a "hard student," and, according to family tradition, he studied fifteen hours a day, rising at dawn and reading far past midnight. "Determine never to be idle," he later told his daughter. "It is wonderful how much may be done if we are always doing." His family's position in Virginia gave rise to expectations. Jefferson's father, Peter Jefferson, owned a considerable amount of land and, like his grandfather and great-grandfather, was involved in colonial politics.

Despite his family's wealth, however, Jefferson faced personal hardships. His father died unexpectedly in 1757, making him the head of the family at age 14. Once he turned 21, he would inherit most of his father's wealth and land, but until then, he had to pursue his education while assisting his seven siblings. He managed to fulfill his family responsibilities and complete his studies, staying in Williamsburg after graduating from William and Mary in 1762 to study law with one of the colony's leading lawyers. In 1769, at age 26, he won election to the House of Burgesses—the legislative assembly for the colony of Virginia.

Thomas Jefferson entered politics at a time of great upheaval in America. Discontent with British rule was rising, and Virginia was a hotbed of opposition. When the House of Burgesses began considering various measures in opposition to British rule, the colonial governor—a representative of the

British Crown—dissolved it. This act closed an avenue—or what we call in this textbook a "gateway"—for participation. With no legitimate way to express grievances, the colonists began to talk of independence. Independence was a radical step; it meant revolution, and revolution would mean the end of colonial government and the creation of new institutions of government. Jefferson understood the connection between the people and their government as a social contract; if a government did not serve the people, the people should end it. In the Declaration of Independence, he speaks of revolution as a right of self-governing men:

"We hold these truths to be self-evident: That all men are created equal; that they are endowed by their Creator with

Need to Know

1.1 Identify the successes we have achieved and the obstacles we face in establishing a "more perfect union"

1.2 Analyze how the constitutional system balances liberty and order

1.3 Describe the political values and ideologies Americans share

1.4 Evaluate American democracy in terms of responsiveness and equality

1.5 List the responsibilities of individuals in a democracy

 WATCH & LEARN MindTap® for American Government
Watch a brief "What Do You Know?" video summarizing The Democratic Republic.

certain unalienable rights; that among these are life, liberty, and the pursuit of happiness; that, to secure these rights, governments are instituted among men, deriving their just powers from the consent of the governed; that whenever any form of government becomes destructive of these ends, it is the right of the people to alter or to abolish it, and to institute new government, laying its foundation on such principles, and organizing its powers in such form, as to them shall seem most likely to effect their safety and happiness."

This passage from the Declaration of Independence is famous. Most Americans know the ringing statement on equality with which it begins. But it is also important to note Jefferson's statement that government not only derives its power "from the consent of the governed," but that if government is not responsive to the governed, the people have the right "to alter or to abolish it." In other words, it is the people's right—and responsibility—to ensure that the "gateways to democracy" are always open and available to them in their pursuit of life, liberty, and happiness. Jefferson and the other Founders in effect sought to replace the British Crown and build effective and meaningful institutions (or gateways) whereby the people of the new nation could enjoy a responsive government while retaining their individual freedoms. These themes of the Declaration of Independence—equality and responsiveness—were present at the creation of the new government. They continue to shape the government as each generation of Americans has sought to make them a reality.

The questions we put before you are fundamental. How does American government work? Is our system of government really democratic? Does it foster equality and responsiveness?

These are not easy questions to answer, but they are important and enduring. The Founders wrestled with them more than 200 years ago. We hope this book helps you wrestle with them as well. Our goal is not to answer the questions for you. Rather, it is your responsibility to draw your own conclusions. The central aim of this book is to give you the information and the analytical tools you need to judge the Founders' democratic experiment for yourself.

1.1 Gateways: Evaluating the American Political System

> ❯ Identify the successes we have achieved and the obstacles we face in establishing a "more perfect union"

LISTEN & LEARN
MindTap for American Government

Access Read Speaker to listen to Chapter 1.

This textbook, *Gateways to Democracy*, explains how citizen involvement has expanded American democracy and how each of you can also influence the political system. We call the avenues of influence, as noted previously, "gateways." This book serves as a handbook for democratic citizenship by peeling back the layers of American government to reveal the ways you can get involved and to explain the reasons you should do so. The American political system is complicated, large, and sometimes frustrating. As the term *gateways* implies, there are also *gates*—obstacles to influence, institutional controls that limit access, and powerful interests that seem to block the people's will. We describe these as well because to be a productive and influential member of American society, you need to understand how American government and politics work.

Through citizen involvement, American democracy has achieved many successes:

- The nation and its institutions are amazingly stable. The United States has the oldest written constitution in the world.
- The government has weathered severe economic crises, a civil war, and two world wars; yet it still maintains peaceful transitions of power from one set of leaders to the next.
- Citizens are able to petition the government and to criticize it. They can assemble and protest the government's policies.
- The American economy has created an excellent standard of living, among the highest in the world.

- American society has attracted millions of immigrants, giving many of them a gateway to citizenship.
- Americans exhibit more commitment to civic duty than do citizens in nearly all other major democracies.[1]
- Americans show more tolerance of different political views than do citizens in other major democracies.[2]

These successes do not mean that there are not problems:

- Inequality persists, and government is sometimes slow to respond.
- Even with the election and reelection of President Barack Obama, racial tensions continue to haunt the country.
- The gap between the rich and the poor continues to grow, with increasing numbers of people living in poverty.[3]
- The public's trust in the institutions of government has never been so low.[4]
- The rate of turnout in elections is among the lowest of the major democracies.
- Despite a high level of religious tolerance, there is also persistent distrust of some religious minorities, such as Muslims and Mormons.[5]
- Despite being proud of our nation of immigrants, at times the country seeks to erect gates to certain groups as they seek to become citizens.
- Political polarization continues to increase, as reflected in staggering partisan differences in the public's judgment of President Obama.[6]
- The U.S. national debt is $17.7 trillion as of September 15, 2014, and growing every day.[7]

Social scientists have been measuring the gap between the rich and the poor since the 1930s, and that gap has grown in the past few decades. Reports in 2013 indicated that the incomes of the top 1 percent rose 20 percent, while the remaining 99 percent's income rose only 1 percent. The wealthiest 1 percent in 2012 earned 19 percent of all income in the United States. The wealthiest 10 percent earned nearly 50 percent of total earnings.[8]

To solve these and other problems and achieve the "more perfect Union" promised in the Constitution, the nation's citizens must be vigilant and engaged. We have framed our book with the goal of demonstrating the demands and rewards of democratic citizenship. As we explore the American political system, we place special emphasis on the multiple and varied connections among citizenship, participation, institutions, and public policy. Our focus is on the following gateway questions:

- How can you get yourself and your opinions represented in government?
- How can you make government more responsive, and responsible, to citizens?
- How can you make American democracy better?

The laws that regulate the American economy, social issues, and even political participation are examples of **public policy**—the intentional action by government to achieve a goal. In the arena of public policy, we determine who gets what, when, and how, and with what result. In each chapter of this book, we will examine a major public policy issue related to the chapter topic. You will find that the public policy process is often divided into stages: identification of the problem; placing the problem on the agenda of policy makers;

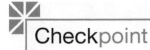
formulating a solution; enacting and implementing the solution; and finally evaluating the solution to make sure that it solves the problem and revising the solution to improve it. These stages combine to form an ideal model of the process; however, this process does not always unfold so neatly. You will also find that individuals, organizations, and political institutions all work together to determine public policies: Congress, the president, the executive branch agency that deals with the issue, the courts, political parties, interest groups, and interested citizens. In each chapter, you will learn about an important public policy, analyze who the stakeholders are and how the policy is formed, evaluate the policy, and, finally, construct your own solution (see Public Policy and Gateways to Democracy).

1.2 Democracy and the American Constitutional System

❯ Analyze how the constitutional system balances liberty and order

Democracy is the kind of government to which the people of many nations aspire, but it has not always been so. Only in the past two centuries—partly through the example of the United States—has democracy gained favor. Let us sketch some of the fundamental aspects of American democracy.

Liberty and Order

Literally and most simply, **democracy** is rule by the people, or **self-government**. In a democracy, the citizens hold political authority, and they develop the means to govern themselves. In practice, that means rule by the majority, and in the years before American independence, **majority rule** had little appeal. In 1644 John Cotton, a leading clergyman of the colonial period, declared democracy "the meanest and worst of all forms of government."[9] Even after American independence, Edmund Burke, a British political philosopher and politician, wrote that a "perfect democracy is . . . the most shameless thing in the world."[10] At the time democracy was associated with mob rule, and mobs were large, passionate, ignorant, and dangerous. If the mob ruled, the people would suffer. There would be no **liberty** or safety; there would be no **order**. Eighteenth–century mobs destroyed private property, burned effigies of leaders they detested, tarred and feathered their enemies, and threatened people who disagreed with them. In fact, such events occurred in the protests against British rule in the American colonies, and they were fresh in the minds of those who wrote the Declaration of Independence and the Constitution.

John Adams, a signer of the Declaration of Independence and later the nation's second president (1797–1801), was not a champion of this kind of democracy. "Democracy," he wrote, "is more bloody than either aristocracy or monarchy. Remember, democracy never lasts long. It soon wastes, exhausts, and murders itself. There is never a democracy that did not commit suicide."[11] Adams knew about mobs and their effects firsthand. As a young lawyer before the Revolution, he agreed to defend British soldiers who had been charged with murder for firing on protesters in the streets of Boston. The soldiers' cause was unpopular, for the people of Boston detested the British military presence. But Adams believed that, following British law, the soldiers had a right to counsel (a lawyer to defend them) and to a fair trial. In later years, he considered his defense of these British soldiers "one of the best pieces of service I ever rendered my country."[12]

Why? In defending the soldiers, Adams was standing up for the **rule of law**, the principle that could prevent mob rule and keep a political or popular majority under control so it could not trample on **minority rights**. An ancient British legal principle, the rule of law holds that all people are equal before the law, all are subject to the law, and no one is above it. Adams and the others who wrote America's founding documents believed in a **constitutional system** in which the people set up and agree on the basic rules and procedures that will govern them. A constitutional system is a government of laws, not of men. Without a constitution and rule of law, an unchecked majority could act to promote the welfare of some over the welfare of others, and society would be torn apart.

The American constitutional system, therefore, serves to protect both liberty and order. The Constitution sets up a governmental structure with built-in constraints on power (gates) and multiple points of access to power (gateways). It also has a built-in means for altering the basic rules and procedures of governance through amendments. As you might expect, the procedure for passing amendments comes with its own set of gates and gateways.

The Constitution as Gatekeeper

"If men were angels," wrote James Madison, a leading author of the Constitution and later the nation's fourth president (1809–17), "no government would be necessary. . . . In framing a government which is to be administered by men over men," he continued, "the great difficulty lies in this: You must first enable the government to control the governed; and in the next place oblige it to control itself" (see *Federalist* 51 in the Appendix). Madison and the other **Framers** of the Constitution recognized that the government they were designing had to be strong enough to rule but not strong enough to take away the people's rights. In other words, the Constitution had to serve as a gatekeeper, both allowing and limiting access to power at the same time.

James Madison, Thomas Jefferson, John Adams, and the other **Founders** had read many of the great political theorists. They drew, for example, on the ideas of the British political philosophers Thomas Hobbes and John Locke in perceiving the relationship between government and the governed as a **social contract**. If people lived in what these philosophers called a state of nature, without the rule of law, conflict would be unending, and the strong would destroy the weak. To secure order and safety, individuals come together to form a government and agree to live by its rules. In return, the government agrees to protect life, liberty, and property. The right to life, liberty, and property, said Locke, are **natural** or **unalienable rights**—rights so fundamental that government cannot take them away.

But these ideas about government as a social contract were untested theories when Madison and others began to write the Constitution. There were no working examples in other nations. The only model for self-government was ancient Athens, where the people had

Public Policy and Gateways to Democracy: Raising the Minimum Wage

The first federal minimum wage requirement was signed into law by President Franklin Delano Roosevelt in 1938 as part of the Fair Labor Standards Act; it set the minimum wage at 25 cents per hour and established a 44-hour workweek. States could mandate pay levels above the federal minimum wage, but they could not go below it. While he was lobbying Congress and the public on behalf of the bill, President Roosevelt said that the United States should give "all our able-bodied working men and women a fair day's pay for a fair day's work."[13] Others have also argued that individuals, families, and communities must be able to earn a living wage in order to rise above the poverty level, which would in turn give them more time and energy to participate in the democratic process.

Today the federal minimum wage is set at $7.25, although twenty-one states require employers to pay more than that wage (see Table 1.1). Still, even at that wage, working full time leaves workers 40 percent below the poverty level.[14] Some states, such as California and Connecticut, are considering proposals to raise the minimum wage to more than $10 an hour over a period of several years. However, there are also states that either have no state-mandated minimum wage or a minimum wage lower than the federal standard; in both cases, businesses earning more than $500,000 per year in revenues are required to meet the federal standards.[15]

Table 1.1 Minimum Wage (MW) by State

Greater Than Federal MW		Equals Federal MW of $7.25		Less Than Federal MW	No MW Required
AK–$7.75	MO–$7.50	DE	NH	AR–$6.25	AL
AZ–$7.90	MT–$7.90	HI	OK	GA–$5.15	LA
CA–$8.00	NJ–$8.25	IA	PA	WY–$5.15	MS
CO–$8.00	NM–$7.50	ID	SD		SC
CT–$8.70	NV–$8.25	IN	TX		TN
DC–$8.25	NY–$8.00	KS	UT		
FL–$7.93	OH–$7.95	KY	VA		
IL–$8.25	OR–$9.10	MD	WV		
MA–$8.00	RI–$8.00	NC	WI		
ME–$7.50	VT–$8.73	ND			
MI–$7.40	WA–$9.32	NE			
MN–$8.00*					

*scheduled to rise to $9.50 by 2016

Source: http://www.dol.gov/whd/minwage/america.htm#Washington

TITLE IMAGE: © ISTOCK.COM/SAPFIRR

In February 2014, President Barack Obama echoed FDR's sentiment in his annual State of the Union address to Congress, when he announced that he would raise the minimum wage by executive order for all federally funded employees to $10.10 per hour. In his words, "if you cook our troops' meals or wash their dishes, you shouldn't have to live in poverty."[16] He went on to ask that Congress formally raise the federal minimum wage for all workers to that same level.[17]

The central argument against raising the minimum wage to $10.10 or even higher is that most of these types of jobs are located in small businesses that cannot afford to pay the higher wages. Opponents of higher minimum wages fear these employers will not hire more workers, and they may even fire existing workers, in order to keep their businesses profitable. Those who oppose raising the minimum wage also argue that open trade policies have given an unfair advantage to foreign manufacturers that can hire workers at very low wages and so produce and sell goods for less. However, it is difficult to assess the impact of raising the minimum wage on job growth or trade imbalances because there are so many other factors that affect the economy. For example, the last raise in the federal minimum wage occurred in 2009 in the midst of a major recession caused by a crash in the housing market. How many jobs were lost due to the recession, and how many resulted from the hike in minimum wage? It is possible that the increased minimum wage contributed to a decline in jobs, but it is also possible that the increase had no effect at all in the larger context of an economic downturn. Economists and other experts have not reached a consensus on this question.

In terms of policy choices then, society must judge what FDR called a "fair day's pay for a fair day's work." In the context of the American democracy, the minimum wage debate raises fundamental questions about the government's role in guaranteeing equality of economic opportunity.

CONNECT WITH YOUR CLASSMATES
MindTap™ for American Government

Access The Democratic Republic Forum: Discussion—Rule of Law and the Constitution.

Construct Your Own Policy

1. Using the table, figure out what the minimum wage is in your state. Do you think it is reasonable given the cost of living in your area? If you wanted to change the minimum wage laws in your area, what level of government would you have to lobby—local, state, federal, or a combination?

2. Construct a minimum wage policy that takes into account a worker's age, education, and family circumstance.

governed themselves in a **direct democracy**. In Athens, citizens met together to debate and to vote. That was possible because only property-owning males were citizens, and they were few in number and had similar interests and concerns.[18]

But the new United States was nothing like the old city-state of Athens. It was an alliance of thirteen states—former colonies—with nearly 4 million people spread across some 360,000 square miles. Direct democracy was impractical for such a large and diverse country, so those who wrote the Constitution created a **representative democracy** in which the people elect representatives who govern in their name. Some observers, including the Framers, call this arrangement a **republic**, a form of government in which power derives from the citizens, but their representatives make policy and govern according to existing law.

Could a republic work? No one knew, certainly not the Framers. The government they instituted was something of an experiment, and they developed their own theories about how it would work. Madison, for example, rejected the conventional view that a democracy had to be small and homogeneous so as to minimize conflict. He argued that size and diversity were assets because competing interests in a large country would balance and control—or check—one another and prevent abuse of power. Madison called these competing interests **factions**, and he believed that the most enduring source of faction was "the various and unequal distribution of property. Those who hold, and those who are without property, have ever formed distinct interests in society," he wrote. (See *Federalist 10* in the Appendix.)

In a pure democracy, where the people ruled directly, Madison expected that passions would outweigh judgments about the common good. Each individual would look out for himself, for his self-interest, and not necessarily for the interests of society as a whole, which is what we might call **civic interest**. In a republic, however, the people's representatives would of necessity have a broader view. Moreover, they would, Madison assumed, come from the better educated, a natural elite. The larger the republic, the larger the districts from which the representatives would be chosen, and thus the more likely that they would be civic-minded leaders of the highest quality. More important, in a large republic, it would be less likely that any one faction could form a majority. Interests would balance each other out, and selfish interests would actually be checked by majority rule.

Balance, control, order—these values were as important to the Framers as liberty. So while the Constitution vested political authority in the people, it also set up a governing system designed to prevent any set of individuals, any political majority, or even the government itself from becoming too powerful. The Framers purposely set up barriers and gates that blocked the excesses associated with mob rule.

Consequently, although the ultimate power lies with the people, the Constitution divides power both vertically and horizontally. Within the federal government, power is channeled into three different branches—the **legislature** (Congress), which makes the laws; the **executive** (the president and the government departments, or bureaucracy), which executes the laws; and the **judiciary** (the Supreme Court and the federal courts), which interprets the laws (see Figure 1.1). This vertical division of power is referred to as the **separation of powers**. To minimize the chance that one branch will become so strong that it can abuse its power and harm the citizenry, each branch has some power over the other two in a system known as

Legislative Branch	Executive Branch	Judicial Branch
	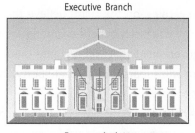	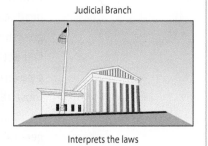
Makes the laws	Executes the laws	Interprets the laws

Figure 1.1 The Three Branches of Government

Within the federal government, power is divided into three separate branches.

checks and balances. The Constitution also divides power horizontally, into layers, between the national government and the state governments. This arrangement is known as **federalism**. In a further division of powers, state governments create local governments.

The American constitutional system thus simultaneously provides gateways for access and gates that limit access. The people govern themselves, but they do so indirectly and through a system that disperses power among many competing interests. This textbook explores both the gateways and the gates that channel and block the influence of citizens.

Checkpoint

CAN YOU:

- Make a connection between minority rights and democratic rule
- Define social contract
- Analyze how the Constitution divides power

1.3 American Political Culture

> Describe the political values and ideologies Americans share

As an experiment, the American republic has been open to change in the course of the nation's history. Despite their theorizing, the Framers could not have anticipated exactly how it would develop. Madison was right, however, about the enduring influence of factions. The people quickly divided themselves into competing interests and shortly into competing **political parties**, groups organized to win elections. The process by which competing interests determine who gets what, when, and how is what we call **politics**.[19]

Madison was right, too, about the sources of division, which are often centered in the unequal distribution of property and competing ideas about how far government should go to reduce inequality. Public opinion about such matters is sometimes described as falling on a scale that ranges from left to right, and when people have a fairly consistent set of views over a range of policy choices, they are said to have a **political ideology**, that is, a coherent way of thinking about government—a philosophy so to speak. In contrast, **party identification**, or partisanship, is a psychological attachment to a particular party. This attachment is related to political ideology, but it is more personal than philosophical.

A person's ideology can be a strong clue as to what he or she thinks about politics. On the left end of the scale are **liberals** who favor government efforts to increase equality, including higher rates of taxes on the wealthy than on the poor and greater provision of social benefits, such as health care, unemployment insurance, and welfare payments to support those in need. **Conservatives**, on the right, believe that lower taxes will prompt greater economic growth that will ultimately benefit everyone, including the poor. Thus, liberals support a large and active government that will regulate the economy, while conservatives fear that such a government will suppress individual liberty and create a dependency that actually harms those it aims to help.

The left–right division is not just about economics, however. For social issues, liberals generally favor less government interference, while conservatives favor rules that will uphold traditional moral values (see Figure 1.2). Conservatives are, therefore, more likely to support laws that ban abortion and same-sex marriage, while liberals are more likely to favor a woman's right to make decisions over reproductive matters as well as the right of same-sex couples to wed.

Although terms such as *conservative* and *liberal* are often used to label American political attitudes, most Americans are not very ideological in their orientation to politics. They are likely to take independent positions on various issues, leaning left on some and right on others. In fact, most Americans are **moderates**, not seeing themselves on one end of the

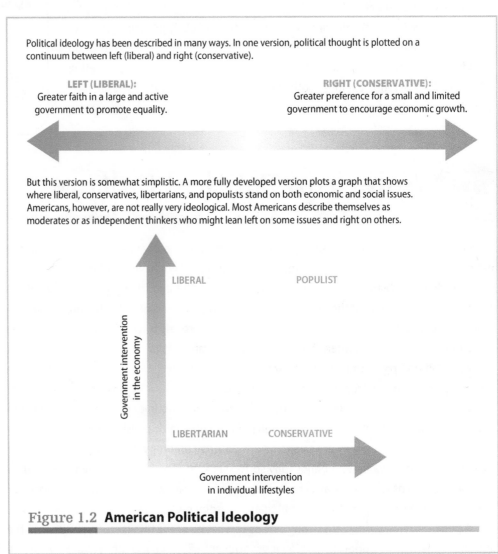

Political ideology has been described in many ways. In one version, political thought is plotted on a continuum between left (liberal) and right (conservative).

LEFT (LIBERAL):
Greater faith in a large and active government to promote equality.

RIGHT (CONSERVATIVE):
Greater preference for a small and limited government to encourage economic growth.

But this version is somewhat simplistic. A more fully developed version plots a graph that shows where liberal, conservatives, libertarians, and populists stand on both economic and social issues. Americans, however, are not really very ideological. Most Americans describe themselves as moderates or as independent thinkers who might lean left on some issues and right on others.

LIBERAL   POPULIST

Government intervention in the economy

LIBERTARIAN   CONSERVATIVE

Government intervention in individual lifestyles

Figure 1.2 **American Political Ideology**

scale or the other. A sizable number of Americans also describe themselves as **libertarians**, believing that government should not interfere in either economic matters or social matters. Others take a **populist** perspective, opposing concentrated wealth and adhering to traditional moral values.

Despite its many perspectives, American **political culture** as a whole generally favors **individualism** over communal approaches to property and poverty, especially in comparison to the industrialized democracies of Europe and elsewhere in the world (see Global Gateways: Social Welfare, Public Debt, and Free Enterprise). The United States spends less on government programs to help the less-well-off than many other countries, and it has historically refrained from assuming control of business enterprises, such as railroads and banks, except in times of crisis. The United States tends to favor **capitalism**, an economic system in which business enterprises and key industries are privately owned, as opposed to **socialism**, in which they are owned by government. Yet, to prevent the worst abuses of capitalism, which can arise as businesses pursue profit to the detriment of citizens, Congress has passed laws that regulate privately owned businesses and industries. For example, government monitors banks and financial markets, ensures airline safety, and protects workers from injury on the job.

In a republic, policy making should reflect the will of the people expressed through their elected representatives and interest groups. Madison envisioned that the people's representatives managing the policy-making process would be an elite—well-educated people of "merit." But if the people divide into different classes, as Madison also envisioned, there is a danger to democracy if the people's representatives are an elite who represent only their own interests and not civic-minded leaders who consider the common good. In the 1950s, the sociologist C. Wright Mills in fact wrote about a narrow **power elite** made up of leaders from corporations, government, and the military that controlled the gates and gateways to power. But in the 1960s, the political scientist Robert Dahl took issue with Mills and argued that policy making has a more **pluralist** basis, with authority held by different groups in different areas. In this view, coal companies, as stakeholders, have a large say in coal policy, and farmers, as stakeholders, have a large say in farm policy, rather than a single power elite controlling both policy areas.

> ## Checkpoint
>
> **CAN YOU:**
> - Explain the importance of political ideology
> - Distinguish between liberalism and conservatism
> - Identify the political values that most Americans share

1.4 Responsiveness and Equality: Does American Democracy Work?

> ❯ Evaluate American democracy in terms of responsiveness and equality

Does American democracy work? That is a question we will be asking in every chapter of this book, and we invite you to start working on an answer. As citizens, you have both a right and a responsibility to judge the government because it is *your* government.

globalgateways

Social Welfare, Public Debt, and Free Enterprise

Throughout this book, we look at American democracy from a global perspective, comparing aspects of the U.S. government and civic life to those similar aspects elsewhere in the world. We begin with three related items: the extent to which the United States and other countries provide social welfare benefits, the relative size of government debt, and the extent to which the economies of the United States and other countries are controlled by the government, shown as an economic freedom score.

The first column in the table shows that the United States allocates a smaller percentage of its budget to social welfare programs than do the industrial democracies of Western Europe. These democracies, however, have higher tax rates to pay for these benefits. France, for example, spends 13 percentage points more of its GDP (gross domestic product—the general measurement of the value of a nation's economy) on social welfare programs than does the United States. Democracies in Asia and Eastern Europe generally provide lower levels of benefits. The second column shows government debt as a percentage of its GDP. The debt ratio of the United States is higher than that of France or Germany but much lower than that of Japan or Greece. The third column presents the amount of control a nation exerts over its economy. Here the United States is fairly typical among the Western industrial democracies. In contrast, North Korea and Cuba, both nondemocratic, exercise much greater government control. There are no examples of nations that have exercised complete or nearly complete control over economic matters that have not simultaneously exercised complete or nearly complete control over political matters. Also note that nations with extensive social welfare systems can be both democratic and free market oriented. There is, in short, no easy formula for promoting both the economic health and social welfare of a country.

Table 1.2 Social Welfare Spending, Government Debt, and Economic Freedom: Fifteen Nations Compared

Nation	Social Welfare Spending (as a % of GDP), 2009	Debt (as a % of GDP), 2012	Economic Freedom Score, 2014 (lowest [0.0] to highest [100.0])
Cuba	NA	19	28.7
Denmark	30.2	45.4	76.1
Estonia	20	9.8	75.9
France	32.1	90.2	63.5
Germany	27.8	81	73.4
Greece	23.9	156.9	55.7
Ireland	23.6	117.4	76.2
Japan	22.192	211.7*	72.4
Mexico	8.2	42.85	66.8
New Zealand	21.2	35.9	81.2
North Korea	NA	NA	1
Portugal	25.6	55.6	63.5
Spain	26	86	67.2
Turkey	12.8	36	64.9
United States	19.2	101.6	75.5

* Data from 2011

NA = not available

Sources: Organization for Economic Co-Operation and Development, "Social Expenditure – Aggregated data, http://stats.oecd.org/Index.aspx?QueryId=4549; "Government Debt to GDP, List by Country," Trading Economics, 2012, http://www.tradingeconomics.com/government-debt-to-gdp-list-by-country; The Heritage Foundation, "2014 Index of Economic Freedom," http://www.heritage.org/index/ranking, all accessed January 17, 2014.

1. Why do countries that have free market economies also tend to be democratic?

2. On what dimension does the United States stand out in comparison to other countries?

To guide your thinking, we focus on two basic themes, **responsiveness** and **equality**. Is government responsive to the needs of its citizens? Do all citizens have an equal chance to make their voices heard? We ask you to keep these themes in mind as you learn about the U.S. political system. Throughout this textbook, we present the latest data that speak to these broad issues. It is important to remember that we are not offering our opinions about government; instead, we are putting forward the most important evidence and theories, from a variety of perspectives, over the past fifty or so years. It is up to you to consider them and form your own conclusions.

One way to begin to evaluate American democracy, and to appreciate it, is to look briefly at alternative models of government. In a **monarchy**, an **autocracy**, and an **oligarchy**, a single person or a small elite rules society. Such systems are by definition undemocratic. Rulers in these systems have little need to be responsive to the people. They hold most of the power and are not generally accountable to those they rule. They may try to satisfy the people with programs that meet basic needs for food and safety, but they do so to ensure submission. Rulers in such systems are overthrown when dissatisfaction rises to a level at which citizens are willing to risk their lives in open revolt, as they did in the Ukraine in 2014, or when the army or police conspire to replace one ruler with another.

In contrast, a democracy asks its citizens to be actively engaged in their own governance, for the benefit of all. As the preamble to the U.S. Constitution states, the people create government (agree to a social contract) to "establish Justice, insure domestic Tranquility, provide for the common defence, promote the general Welfare, and secure the Blessings of Liberty to ourselves and our Posterity." The American system of government fundamentally provides protection from foreign enemies and from internal disorder; it also strives to meet the common needs of all citizens.

To promote the general welfare, the government develops public policy, as we have seen. Through incentives, it can alter the actions of individuals that lead collectively to bad outcomes.

The government often has a stake in pursuing what economists call **public goods**: goods from which everyone benefits. The core idea is that no one can be excluded. We all get the benefits of clean air, even if we have been driving cars and not taking buses. The fact that

people cannot, by definition, be denied access to public goods creates disincentives for people to contribute to their provision. Government can require people to contribute to public goods through taxation. This is a primary justification for government. **Private goods**, by contrast, can be extended to some individuals and denied to others. When a government awards a contract to build a new library, the firm that wins the contract gets private goods (that is, money) from the government. The firms that lost the bid are denied that chance.

Who determines what goods, whether private or public, the government should provide, at what levels, and how to pay for them? These are core public policy problems. There are competing interests at every point in determining who gets what, when, and how. Politics

EMMANUEL DUNAND/GETTY IMAGES

Citizens gathering to hear presidential candidate Rick Santorum in a classic town hall format. The candidate and these citizens get a chance to express their opinions.

is the process by which the people determine how government will respond. And it is in evaluating the basic fairness of government's response, and the basic equality of the people's general welfare that is thus secured, that we see whether American democracy is working.

Representative democracy succeeds when there is constant interaction between the people and the government. Government must be responsive to the needs and opinions of the people, and the public must find ways to hold government accountable.

For a government to respond fairly to citizens, all citizens must have an equal opportunity to participate in it. Each citizen must have a chance to have his or her voice heard, either by voting or by participating in the political process and public life. These ideas form the basis of **political equality**. If citizens are not treated equally, with the same degree of fairness, then the foundation of democratic government is weakened. Simply put, democracy requires political equality, and political equality requires democracy. One way to evaluate American democracy is to evaluate the degree to which political equality has been achieved.

There are other aspects of equality. **Equality of opportunity** is one aspect—the expectation that citizens will be treated equally before the law and have an equal opportunity to participate in government. Does equality of opportunity also mean that citizens have an equal opportunity to participate in the economy (to get a job, to get rich) and in social life (to join a club, to eat at a restaurant)? And what about **equality of outcome**, the expectation that incomes will level out or that standards of living will be roughly the same for all citizens? What can, or should, government do to ensure equality of opportunity, or equality of outcome? These questions are hotly contested (see Supreme Court Cases: *Plyler v. Doe*), especially efforts to forge equality of outcome. We return to these issues in the final section of this introductory chapter.

In President Obama's first inaugural address, he said, "I stand here today humbled by the task before us, grateful for the trust you have bestowed, mindful of the sacrifices borne by our ancestors."[20] Those ancestors include the millions of Americans who over more than two centuries have worked to make American democracy more responsive and to make America more equal. We challenge you to join them. This textbook will give you the information you need to understand the way American government works and to recognize the gates and the gateways. We also invite you to think critically about American democracy, to engage in a class-wide and nationwide conversation about how well it is working, to offer ideas for making it work better, to influence the decision makers who make public policy, and even to become one of them.

Checkpoint

CAN YOU:

- Identify the functions of government as defined by the Preamble
- Identify the roles individuals play in a democracy
- Explain the differences between equality of opportunity and equality of outcome

1.5 The Demands of Democratic Government

> List the responsibilities of individuals in a democracy

American democracy is not a spectator sport. It does not mean choosing sides and rooting for your team from the sidelines or from the comfort of your living room. It requires more than being a fan; you need to get into the game. But politics is more than a game. It shapes your life on a day-to-day basis. As a result, you have both rights and responsibilities. While the specific reasons to be involved in public life may vary, the need to participate does not.

supreme court cases

Plyler v. Doe (1982)

QUESTION: Does the equal protection clause prohibit states from charging children of undocumented workers tuition in order to attend public school?

ORAL ARGUMENT: December 1, 1981 (listen at http://www.oyez.org/cases/1980-1989/1981/1981_80_1538)

DECISION: June 15, 1982 (read at http://caselaw.lp.findlaw.com/cgi-bin/getcase.pl?court=us&vol=457&invol=202)

OUTCOME: Texas violates the equal protection clause when it charges tuition to public school students who cannot prove U.S. citizenship (5-4).

In response to the increasing costs of educating children who were not citizens of the United States, Texas passed a law in 1975 stating that it would not reimburse local school districts for any of those costs. The law also relieved local school districts of any obligation to educate such children.

The parents of certain unnamed Mexican American school children who were denied access to the Tyler Independent School District filed suit, claiming that the law deprived their children of the equal protection of the law as guaranteed by one of the clauses of the Fourteenth Amendment to the Constitution.

The Supreme Court ruled with the parents, noting first, that while the subjects filing the lawsuit were not citizens of the United States, the Fourteenth Amendment prohibits states from denying the equal protection of the law to all "persons" under its jurisdiction, a term that does not distinguish between citizens and aliens. In reaching this part of the decision, the Court relied on a speech by Congressman John Bingham, one of the authors of the Fourteenth Amendment: "Is it not essential to the unity of the Government and the unity of the people that all persons, whether citizens or strangers, within this land, shall have equal protection in every State in this Union in the rights of life and liberty and property?"

The Supreme Court's equal protection decisions set different standards of review depending on the group being discriminated against in the law. The toughest standard, "strict scrutiny," applies to laws that discriminate on account of race or discriminate against aliens who are legally in the country. The parents bringing the suit admitted that they could not establish that the children were in the country legally. This distinction meant that the Court would only apply its lowest standard of review, "minimal scrutiny." Under strict scrutiny, Texas would have to show that it had a vital or "compelling interest" in passing the law, a difficult hurdle to pass. However, under minimal scrutiny, Texas only had to show a rational justification for the law.

Texas argued that it had a rational justification for the law, protecting the state's budget. It argued that without such a rule, undocumented workers would flood Texas, and the state's citizens would be required to pay more in taxes to educate them.

A majority of justices rejected that argument, noting that the law places a lifetime hardship on the children, that undocumented workers come to Texas for a variety of reasons, and that prohibiting the employment of undocumented workers would be far more effective in protecting Texas's budget than denying education to their children.

A public education is a gateway for individuals to a higher paying job, a fuller life, and a more active role in the democratic system. Providing equal access to education is one of the central ways we ensure equality of opportunity in the United States.

1. Can you identify reasons unrelated to prejudice that would lead Texas to want to deny education funds to the students in this case?

2. Should the Supreme Court treat cases involving legal immigrants (strict scrutiny) differently from cases involving undocumented residents (minimal scrutiny)?

Self-Interest and Civic Interest

The first reason to be involved is **self-interest**. You want government to serve your needs. Those needs, of course, range widely, depending on your stage of life, personal circumstances, and values. Some individuals prefer that the government stay out of people's lives as much as possible, and others prefer governmental assistance for the causes they hold dear. Whatever way you define your self-interest, by getting involved you send signals to elected officials, and if enough people agree with you, the government will likely act.

The second reason, what we call civic interest, is more complex. The idea is that people get involved in the process because they want to be part of the voluntary organizations that make up the **civil society** which enables communities to flourish. They want to help others, improve their neighborhoods, and create an even better nation. Groups of interested people can accomplish things that individuals acting alone cannot. By working together, people can encourage greater responsiveness from government. In so doing, they are better able to communicate their needs to a government that, in turn, becomes more responsive.

You are more likely to be civic-minded than college students in previous generations. If you were born between 1982 and 2003, you are part of the generation that social science researchers have identified as the **Millennials**. In reaction to the idealistic and ideological baby boomer generation born between 1946 and 1964, and the more cynical Generation X born between 1964 and 1982, Millennials are more likely to be optimistic and practical, to value consensus and community building, to solve problems through compromise, to be committed to political involvement, to be concerned for the welfare of others, and to want to strengthen the political system.[21]

Participation in the public sphere serves the larger civic interest. Voting is the most obvious political act. Those who control the levers of power need to know your views so they can respond. With all the new technologies, the interface between people and politicians is now easier than ever.

COMPARE WITH YOUR PEERS
MindTap for American Government

Access The Democratic Republic Forum: Polling Activity—Defining Marriage in California.

Politics and the Public Sphere

Your generation has the power to shape the future in which you will live. Will America continue to be a land of opportunity? The following issues represent some of the important concerns that you and the nation face. Working on these problems is reason enough to take part in the nation's civic life.

Educational Opportunity. Because you are in college, education policy affects you every day and is important to your future. Education has long been considered both a fundamental component of democratic society and a stepping-stone to economic advancement. But what does it take to get a college degree, and who should bear the burden?

These are important questions because the cost of a college education continues to rise. Private colleges are increasingly expensive, and during times of economic decline, as states and local governments have faced budget cuts, public institutions of higher learning have also raised tuition (see Figure 1.3). The consequence of these increases is that students are taking on more and more debt to pay for these higher costs. This debt imposes a greater financial burden on you and begins to hurt just when you may also be thinking about having a family and buying a house.

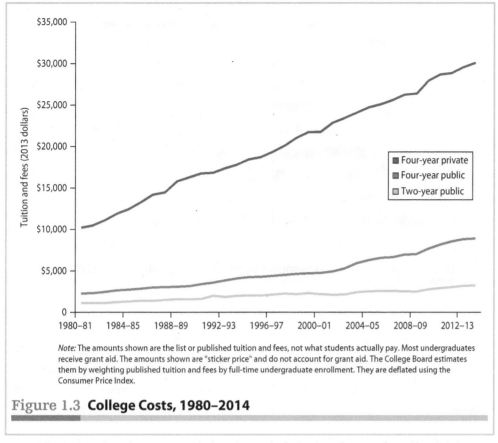

Note: The amounts shown are the list or published tuition and fees, not what students actually pay. Most undergraduates receive grant aid. The amounts shown are "sticker price" and do not account for grant aid. The College Board estimates them by weighting published tuition and fees by full-time undergraduate enrollment. They are deflated using the Consumer Price Index.

Figure 1.3 College Costs, 1980–2014

Source: College Board compilation of average tution and fee charges http://trends.collegeboard.org/college-pricing/figures-tables/published-prices-national

If an educated public is necessary to democracy, and if the entire nation benefits from the contributions of college-educated individuals, does the federal government have an obligation to promote educational opportunity? Congress has decided it does and authorizes the Department of Education to spend some $32 billion annually to fund financial aid for higher education, including Pell Grants, work-study programs, and supplemental education opportunity grants. In response to deficit concerns, however, Pell Grants in general have been decreasing—from $41 billion in 2012 to $30 billion in 2014.[22]

College affordability is a concern of all college students and deserves to be a concern for the nation generally (see Figure 1.4). Yet Americans do not hear much discussion about education in the news media. A recent study by the Brookings Institution indicates that only 1.4 percent of coverage by television, websites, and radio deals with issues in education.[23] Does the lack of media attention pose a barrier to getting

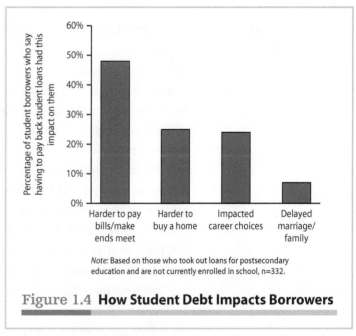

Note: Based on those who took out loans for postsecondary education and are not currently enrolled in school, n=332.

Figure 1.4 How Student Debt Impacts Borrowers

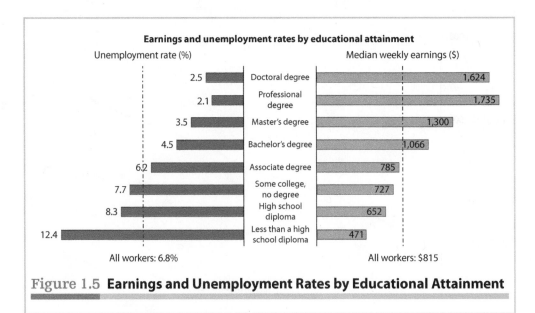

Figure 1.5 Earnings and Unemployment Rates by Educational Attainment

Source: U.S. Census Bureau, Current Population Survey, Pew Research Center, p. 6.

educational opportunity on the policy agenda? What can you do to make government responsive to concerns about education? Education policy is examined in more detail in Chapter 3, Federalism.

Economic Opportunity.　Educational opportunity is linked to economic opportunity because the more education you have, the more you are likely to earn. And the differences over the course of a lifetime can be millions of dollars in personal income (see Figure 1.5). But with the economic problems of late, will you be able to find a good job after graduation? In recent years college graduates have not fared as well as they have in the past. This should change as the economy improves.

An educated public with jobs that pay well and make a contribution to society is surely good for the entire nation. But does the government have an obligation to create economic opportunity? Should it intervene in business and the marketplace to equalize opportunity or to preserve competition, or should government allow the economy to be shaped by market forces? Throughout this book, we examine the role of government in the economy by taking a hard look at its obligations as well as at federal and state budgets, deficit spending, the national debt, and tax policy. These concerns are currently at the top of the policy agenda because in recent years, the federal government has run historically high deficits (has spent more than it receives in revenue) that have produced a huge jump in the national debt. Just twenty years ago, the national debt was about 5 trillion. In 2014, the national debt was more than $17.7 trillion—a more than three-fold increase. To put this 2014 figure in a global context, consider that the United States has the seventh highest national debt, as a proportion of GDP, in the world (see Global Gateways on page 14).

Paying off this debt will take generations; your great-grandchildren might very well still be paying for it when they reach adulthood. For you, now, the size of this debt means that the federal government has less funding and limited flexibility for investing in programs that might create economic opportunity, such as education, job training, and infrastructure.

How the government pays off this debt affects you, too, especially changes in the tax system that may alter your future income and job prospects. Thus the federal budget and its ability to expand economic opportunity will directly affect your quality of life and standard of living in both the short run and the long run.

As individuals and groups make their voices heard with energy and commitment, they fulfill a vital role in democratic government.

Your Gateway to American Democracy

James Madison, whom we have quoted extensively in this introductory chapter, offers one final thought: "Knowledge will forever govern ignorance; and a people who mean to be their own governors, must arm themselves with the power which knowledge gives."[24] To govern yourself, you will need to understand your government, to be informed about issues you care about, to participate in politics, and to be engaged in the nation's civic life. As Madison and all those who wrote the nation's founding documents understood, an engaged public is the best check on excesses of power that threaten fair and just government. If the people do not meet the demands of democratic citizenship, if they do not fulfill their responsibilities, they will lose the freedoms they cherish.

We have written this book to give you the information you need to understand your government—its gates and gateways. We hope it will also push you to evaluate whether government is working for you and for all the nation's citizens. How democratic are we? How can we be better? One thing is certain: We will not be better unless you are involved. The only way to make American democracy more responsive and more equal is by participating.

JUSTIN SULLIVAN/GETTY IMAGES

We, therefore, invite you—actually, we urge you—to enter the gateways to democracy. These gateways are open to you as an American. They empower you, as a citizen, to play an important role in American civic life, and they enable you to experience the amazing arena of American politics. We look forward to sharing the journey with you.

What you need to know about your text and online study tools to study efficiently and master the material

Learning about American government can be your first step through the gateway. Each chapter of *Gateways to Democracy* is built to maximize efficient studying and help you get the most out of your course in American government. But these study materials are just part of the guidance for learning that *Gateways to Democracy* provides. Study aids start on the first page of every chapter, with a "Need to Know" list of learning objectives. Each objective is keyed to a major section of the chapter, and at the end of that section, you'll find a "Checkpoint"—a list of questions that will allow you to test yourself to see if you've mastered specific content before moving on to the next section. Then at the end of the chapter, you'll find the "Need to Know" objectives, a summary of the main ideas associated with each objective, and the "Checkpoint" questions repeated with an application for participating in American democracy. Use this Learning Outcomes chart as a chapter review.

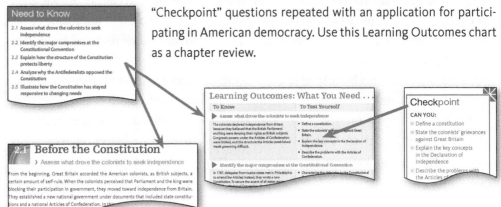

"Key Concepts" are boldfaced in the chapter text, defined on the page, and amplified at the end of the chapter with questions that will let you test your comprehension. In Chapter 1, however, definitions are consolidated to serve as essential vocabulary that you can refer to throughout the course.

Understanding the workings of American government and your role as a citizen involves more than mastering content. Throughout the chapter, margin questions—called Key Questions—ask you to think for yourself about the role and responsiveness of government, the meaning of citizen equality, and the gates and gateways in American democracy.

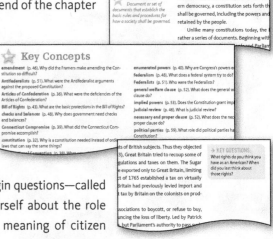

Gateways to Democracy also offers an online learning package called Mindtap. Through interactive assignments, including videos, graphs, and political cartoons mapped to the "Need to Know" learning objectives, you can master the essential concepts of American government and understand how they apply to real life. With Mindtap, you learn more, are better prepared to participate in class, and improve your grade. Mindtap also includes an eBook. Get instant access via CengageBrain (http://www.cengagebrain.com) or via a printed access card in your bookstore.

Master the Concept
of The Democratic Republic with MindTap™ for American Government

 REVIEW MindTap™ **for American Government**
Access Key Term Flashcards for Chapter 1.

 STAY CURRENT MindTap™ **for American Government**
Access the KnowNow blog and customized RSS for updates on current events.

 TEST YOURSELF MindTap™ **for American Government**
Take the Wrap It Up Quiz for Chapter 1.

 STAY FOCUSED MindTap™ **for American Government**
Complete the Focus Activities for The Democratic Republic.

Key Concepts

Use the list of key concepts for this chapter as a glossary for this course. Each of the following entries includes the page numbers on which a particular concept is introduced, and most list later chapters in which the concept is discussed. A full glossary of key concepts is also included at the back of the book.

autocracy: System of government in which the power to govern is concentrated in the hands of an individual ruler. (p. 15)

capitalism: Economic system in which businesses and key industries are privately owned and in which individuals, acting on their own or with others, are free to create businesses. (p. 13)

checks and balances: Government structure that authorizes each branch of government (executive, legislative, and judicial) to share powers with the other branches, thereby holding some scrutiny of and control over the other branches. (p. 11, Chapter 2)

civic interest: Concern for the well-being of society and the nation as a whole. (p. 10, Chapter 9)

civil society: Voluntary organizations that allow communities to flourish. (p. 18)

conservatives: Individuals who distrust government, believing that free markets offer better ways than government involvement to improve people's livelihood. In the social sphere, conservatives have more faith in government's ability to enforce traditional values. (p. 12, Chapters 6, 8)

constitutional system: System of government in which people set up and agree on the basic rules and procedures that will govern them. (p. 7, Chapter 2)

democracy: System of government in which the supreme power is vested in the people and exercised by them either directly or indirectly through elected representatives. (p. 6, Chapters 2, 9, 14)

direct democracy: Form of democracy in which political power is exercised directly by citizens. (p. 10, Chapter 3)

equality: Idea that all individuals are equal in their moral worth and so must be equal in treatment under the law and have equal access to the decision-making process. (p. 15, Chapters 5, 14)

equality of opportunity: Expectation that citizens may not be discriminated against based on race, gender, or national background and that every citizen should have an equal chance to succeed in life. (p. 16, Chapters 5, 13, 14)

equality of outcome: Expectation that equality is achieved if results are comparable for all citizens regardless of race, gender, or national background or that such groups are proportionally represented in measures of success in life. (p. 16, Chapters 5, 13)

executive branch: The branch of the federal government that executes the laws. (p. 10, Chapters 2, 11)

faction: Defined by Madison as any group that places its own interests above the aggregate interests of society. (p. 10, Chapters 7, 8)

federalism: System of government in which sovereignty is constitutionally divided between national and state governments. (p. 11, Chapters 2, 3)

Founders: The people who were involved in establishing the United States, whether at the time of the Declaration of Independence or the writing of the Constitution. (p. 7, Chapters 2, 14)

Framers: The people who were involved in writing the Constitution. (p. 7, Chapter 2)

individualism: Set of beliefs holding that people, and not government, are responsible for their own well-being. (p. 13)

judicial branch: The branch of the federal government that interprets the laws. (p. 10, Chapters 2, 13)

legislative branch: The branch of the federal government that makes the laws. (p. 10, Chapters 2, 10)

liberals: Individuals who have faith in government to improve people's lives, believing that private efforts are insufficient. In the social sphere, liberals usually support diverse lifestyles and tend to oppose any government action that seeks to shape personal choices. (p. 11, Chapters 6, 8)

libertarians: Those who generally believe that government should refrain from acting to regulate either the economy or moral values. (p. 13, Chapter 8)

liberty: Political value that cherishes freedom from an arbitrary exercise of power that constricts individual choice. (p. 6, Chapter 2)

majority rule: Idea that a numerical majority of a group should hold the power to make decisions binding on the whole group; a simple majority. (p. 6, Chapters 9, 10)

Millennials: Generation born between 1982 and 2003. (p. 18, Chapters 6, 7)

minority rights: Idea that majority should not be able to take certain fundamental rights away from those in the minority. (p. 7, Chapter 5)

moderates: Individuals who are in the middle of the ideological spectrum and do not hold consistently strong views about whether government should be involved in people's lives. (p. 12, Chapters 6, 8)

monarchy: System of government that assigns power to a single person who inherits that position and rules until death. (p. 15, Chapter 2)

natural (unalienable) rights: Rights that every individual has and that government cannot legitimately take away. (p. 7, Chapter 4)

oligarchy: System of government in which the power to govern is concentrated in the hands of a powerful few, usually wealthy individuals. (p. 15)

order: Political value in which the rule of law is followed and does not permit actions that infringe on the well-being of others. (p. 6, Chapters 2, 4)

party identification: Psychological attachment to a political party; partisanship. (p. 11, Chapters 6, 8, 9)

pluralism: Political system in which competing interests battle over the direction and content of important policy making. (p. 13, Chapter 7)

political culture: A shared way of thinking about community and government and the relationship between them. (p. 13)

political equality: The idea that people should have equal amounts of influence in the political system. (p. 16, Chapters 5, 14)

political ideology: Set of coherent political beliefs that offers a philosophy for thinking about the scope of government. (p. 11, Chapters 6, 8)

political parties: Broad coalitions of interests organized to win elections in order to enact a commonly supported set of public policies. (p. 11, Chapter 8)

politics: Process by which people make decisions about who gets what, when, and how. (p. 11, Chapter 8)

populists: Those who oppose concentrated wealth and adhere to traditional moral values. (p. 13, Chapters 3, 9)

power elite: Small handful of decision makers who hold authority over a large set of issues. (p. 13, Chapters 6, 7, 9)

private goods: Goods or benefits provided by government in which most of the benefit falls to the individuals, families, or companies receiving them. (p. 15, Chapter 7)

public goods: Goods or benefits provided by government from which everyone benefits and from which no one can be excluded. (p. 15, Chapters 7, 9)

public policy: Intentional actions of government designed to achieve a goal. (p. 5, Chapter 12)

representative democracy: Form of democracy in which citizens elect public officials to make political decisions and formulate laws on their behalf. (p. 10, Chapters 2, 3, 9, 10)

republic: Form of government in which power derives from citizens, but public officials make policy and govern according to existing law. (p. 10, Chapter 2)

responsiveness: Idea that government should implement laws and policies that reflect the wishes of the public and any changes in those wishes. (p. 15, Chapters 2, 10, 12, 14)

rule of law: Legal system with known rules that are enforced equally against all people. (p. 7, Chapter 4)

self-government: Rule by the people. (p. 6, Chapter 3)

self-interest: Concern for one's own advantage and well-being. (p. 18, Chapters 6, 7, 9)

separation of powers: Government structure in which authority is divided among branches (executive, legislative, and judicial), with each holding separate and independent powers and areas of responsibility. (p. 10, Chapter 2)

social contract: Theory that government has only the authority accorded it by the consent of the governed. (p. 7)

socialism: Economic system in which the government owns major industries. (p. 13)

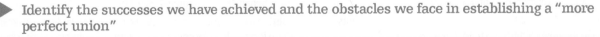

Learning Outcomes: What You Need . . .

To Know	To Test Yourself	To Participate

▶ Identify the successes we have achieved and the obstacles we face in establishing a "more perfect union"

To Know	To Test Yourself	To Participate
American democracy offers many gateways to participation because, at its core, American government is about individuals and self-governance. There are also gates against public participation—obstacles to influence, institutional controls that limit access, and powerful interests that seem to block the people's will. To be an engaged and productive citizen, you need to take advantage of the gateways but also know how to navigate around the gates.	• List the successes of American democracy. • Identify challenges we face in achieving "a more perfect union."	• Begin evaluating American democracy based on the concepts you have learned in this chapter.

▶ Analyze how the constitutional system balances liberty and order

To Know	To Test Yourself	To Participate
Democracy is self-government. In the American constitutional system, the people set up and agree on the basic rules and procedures that will govern them. The American constitutional system works to protect both liberty and order. The Constitution sets up a governmental structure with built-in constraints on power (gates) and multiple points of access to power (gateways). Power in American government is divided among three branches (executive, legislative, and judicial) and between the national government and the states.	• Make a connection between minority rights and democratic rule. • Define social contract. • Analyze how the Constitution divides power.	• Understand the tension that surrounds issues related to government responsiveness and citizen equality.

▶ Describe the political values and ideologies Americans share

To Know	To Test Yourself	To Participate
American political culture favors individualism, and the U.S. economic system favors capitalism. American citizens may lean conservative or liberal, but most are moderates. With a government designed to constrain power and the popular will, and a citizenry divided into different perspectives and prizing individualism, the development of public policy is difficult and complex.	• Assess the importance of political ideology. • Distinguish between liberalism and conservatism. • Identify the political values that most Americans share.	• Figure out what political beliefs you hold and where you stand within the spectrum of political ideologies.

To Know	To Test Yourself	To Participate

▶ **Evaluate American democracy in terms of responsiveness and equality**

To Know	To Test Yourself	To Participate
One way to evaluate whether public policy is serving the people of the United States and to judge whether American democracy is working is to measure government responsiveness and citizen equality.	• Identify the functions of government as defined by the Preamble. • Contrast the role of citizens in a democracy to their role in other forms of government. • Explain the differences between equality of opportunity and equality of outcome.	• Consider what political goals you think the government should set for itself regarding responsiveness and equality.

▶ **List the responsibilities of individuals in a democracy**

To Know	To Test Yourself	To Participate
Civic interest pushes people to help others and become active participants in a democracy. Education is a fundamental component of democratic society and a stepping-stone to economic advancement.	• Compare self-interest to civic interest. • Describe public policies that encourage you to participate in American democracy.	• Recognize all the options for participation and their importance.

"In New York, in Washington, they don't understand our problems. They don't know about the 3 million Mexicans who live in the Southwest. Let us pray to God that we triumph, that the nation's Supreme Court agrees with us."

GUS GARCIA
University of Texas at Austin

The Constitution

Gus Garcia, high school valedictorian and star of the debate team at the University of Texas at Austin, grew up observing the social and legal discrimination against Latinos in Texas. It was the 1940s. Like Thurgood Marshall, the famed civil rights attorney and the first African American on the Supreme Court, Garcia wanted to fight for the rights of his people. Garcia followed his undergraduate years at the University of Texas with law school there. After serving in the Judge Advocate General Corps in the military, Garcia returned to Texas where he worked as legal counsel for the League of United Latin American Citizens (LULAC) and helped create the American GI Forum, a veterans group for Latinos, in 1948.

He also ran for the Board of Education in San Antonio, Texas, in 1948, joining forces with a local African American businessman. Their white opponents took out an ad in the local paper on the day before the election declaring, "It is your duty to keep racial and sectional strife out of your schools by electing experienced people who can work together in harmony.... Among the other candidates is a Negro undertaker [and] an active member of LULAC"[1] (i.e., Garcia). Garcia won the election, becoming the first Latino to serve on the San Antonio School Board.

In 1948, Garcia won a federal district (trial) court case on behalf of Minerva Delgado and others seeking to deny the state of Texas the authority to segregate Latino public school students as a violation of the Fourteenth Amendment, which guarantees equal protection of the law.[2] This decision, without recognition from higher courts, was largely ignored within the state of Texas. Thurgood Marshall, though, requested access to the *Delgado* case file from the attorneys in that case as part of his battle against racial

discrimination.[3] Yet Garcia continued the struggle for Latino civil rights.

In 1952 Garcia began work on the case of *Hernandez v. Texas*,[4] which would arguably become the most important constitutional decision by the Supreme Court regarding the Latino community in the United States.

The *Hernandez* case involved the murder conviction of Pedro Hernandez by an all-white jury in Texas. It was the first time that the Supreme Court dealt with a case involving issues related to Latinos as well as the first time a Latino attorney had argued before the Supreme Court. Texas argued that the equal protection clause only applied to African Americans, not other ethnic groups. Garcia, alternatively, argued that within

Need to Know

2.1 Assess what drove the colonists to seek independence

2.2 Identify the major compromises at the Constitutional Convention

2.3 Explain how the structure of the Constitution protects liberty

2.4 Analyze why the Antifederalists opposed the Constitution

2.5 Illustrate how the Constitution has stayed responsive to changing needs

WATCH & LEARN MindTap for American Government
Watch a brief "What Do You Know?" video summarizing The Constitution.

Texas, Mexican Americans were treated as "a class apart" from the white community and should receive the protections of the equal protection clause of the Fourteenth Amendment. The fact that Latinos still had separate schools and bathrooms, and did not sit on juries, convinced a unanimous Supreme Court that "the constitutional guarantee of equal protection of the laws is not directed solely against discrimination between whites and Negroes."[5] The justices were convinced that under the social and legal system in Texas, Mexican Americans were treated as "a separate class"[6] and as such deserved full constitutional protection from the equal protection clause, and that Texas denied Hernandez that protection by excluding Latinos from serving on juries. The Court, which had already heard, but not yet decided, the *Brown v. Board of Education* case, was interested enough in Garcia's argument that it gave him unscheduled extra time during oral argument, an extremely rare gesture. The Supreme Court reversed the conviction of Hernandez. That reversal allowed Texas to retry Hernandez by a jury that did not exclude Latinos. Hernandez was found guilty again.

Nevertheless, Gus Garcia's legal victory led to a fundamental change in how the U.S. Constitution is interpreted with regard to discrimination against Latinos, granting them legal security under the equal protection clause of the Fourteenth Amendment. Garcia used the constitutional system of the United States to create new rights for the Latino community. Moreover, just two weeks after the *Hernandez* decision, the Supreme Court struck down segregated schools in *Brown v. Board of Education*, a case in which Garcia had been a supporter.

In this chapter, we examine the governing documents prior to the Constitution, particularly the Articles of Confederation and its deficiencies. We also track the debates at the Constitutional Convention and afterward, as the people of the United States decided whether to ratify the new Constitution. They did ratify it, but almost immediately they amended it. After we examine the structure and philosophy behind the new Constitution, we consider its responsiveness, through both amendment and less formal procedures, to changing times.

The information from this vignette comes from the Salinas article cited in the first footnote as well as A Class Apart: A Mexican American Civil Rights Story, PBS Home Video, 2009, from which we pulled the opening quote.

 # 2.1 Before the Constitution

❯ Assess what drove the colonists to seek independence

From the beginning, Great Britain accorded the American colonists, as British subjects, a certain amount of self-rule. When the colonists perceived that Parliament and the king were blocking their participation in government, they moved toward independence from Britain. They established a new national government under documents that included state constitutions and a national Articles of Confederation. In this section, we trace that process.

The British Constitution

constitution:
Document or set of documents that establish the basic rules and procedures for how a society shall be governed.

A **constitution** is the fundamental law undergirding the structure of government. In a modern democracy, a constitution sets forth the basic rules and procedures for how the people shall be governed, including the powers and structure of the government, as well as the rights retained by the people.

Unlike many constitutions today, the British constitution is not a single document but rather a series of documents. Beginning with the Magna Carta in 1215, the British constitution defined the rights of the people and Parliament and limited the powers of the king. Following the so-called Glorious Revolution of 1688–89, Parliament asserted the power to suspend the law, to levy taxes, and to maintain a standing army. By the eighteenth century, British subjects believed that the British constitution guaranteed them certain rights, including the right not to be taxed without their consent and the right to be tried by a jury of their peers.

Toward Independence

The American colonists believed they had all the rights of British subjects. Thus they objected when, following the French and Indian War (1754–63), Great Britain tried to recoup some of the costs of defending the colonies by imposing regulations and taxes on them. The Sugar Act of 1764 set forth a long list of items that could be exported only to Great Britain, limiting competition for the colonists' goods. The Stamp Act of 1765 established a tax on virtually all forms of paper used by the colonists. Although Britain had previously levied import and export taxes on the colonies, this was the first direct tax by Britain on the colonists on products made and sold in America.

The colonists reacted angrily, forming trade associations to boycott, or refuse to buy, British goods. They also published pamphlets denouncing the loss of liberty. Led by Patrick Henry, they challenged not just the taxes themselves, but Parliament's authority to pass such measures. "Give me liberty," proclaimed Henry before the Virginia House of Burgesses, "or give me death." Soon enough, riots broke out against Stamp Act collectors, making enforcement impossible.

Britain repealed the Stamp Act in 1766 but replaced it with the Townshend Acts, which imposed new taxes on imports. The colonists mobilized against these new import taxes. Led by Samuel Adams, the Massachusetts legislature issued a letter declaring the Townshend Acts unconstitutional because they violated the principle of "no taxation without representation." The colonists thus began to insist that they had the right to participate in the political decisions that affected them.

The British justified their lack of representation by claiming that all English citizens were represented by all members of Parliament, who purportedly acted in the common good. As political thinker and politician Edmund Burke wrote, "Parliament is a *deliberative* assembly of *one* nation, with *one* interest, that of the whole."[7] The colonists, however, rejected this view.

> → KEY QUESTIONS:
> What rights do you think you have as an American? When did you last think about those rights?

> → KEY QUESTIONS:
> How does the American view of representation differ from the British view?

THE STAMP ACT RIOTS AT BOSTON.

American Colonists protest the British Stamp Act.

NORTH WIND PICTURE ARCHIVES/ALAMY

Table 2.1 **Events Leading to the Revolution**

Year	Event	Description
1764	Sugar Act	Required colonists to export certain items only to Britain
1765	Stamp Act	Imposed taxes on almost all paper products; boycotts and riots followed
1766	Townshend Act	Imposed new taxes on imports; led to rallying cry "no taxation without representation"
1770	Boston Massacre	Five colonists killed by British soldiers; led Parliament to repeal all Townshend Act taxes except for tea tax
1773	Boston Tea Party	Colonists dump taxed tea into Boston Harbor
1774	Coercive Act	Restricted political freedoms in Massachusetts
1774	Quartering Act	Required colonists to house British soldiers in their homes
1774	1st Continental Congress	Rejected Reconciliation with Britain and sent grievances to King George III
1775	2nd Continental Congress	Acted as the national government of states, 1775–1781; approved Declaration of Independence and appointed George Washington as commander of the army

© CENGAGE LEARNING®

→ KEY QUESTIONS:
What does today's Tea Party have in common with the Boston Tea Party?

Aggrieved by taxation without representation, the colonists continued to resist the Townshend Acts through boycotts of taxed goods. Britain responded by dissolving the Massachusetts legislature and seizing a ship belonging to John Hancock, one of the leaders of the resistance. Britain also sent troops to quell the resistance, but the presence of soldiers during peacetime aggravated tensions. British soldiers fired on a threatening crowd in 1770, killing five colonists and wounding six others in what became known as the Boston Massacre. With boycotts of British goods costing Britain far more than the taxes raised, Parliament rescinded all of the Townshend Act taxes except the one on tea. In 1773 Parliament granted the East India Company the exclusive right to sell tea to the colonies, and the company then granted local monopolies in the colonies. Angered by both the tax and the monopoly, colonists once again took action. Disguised as Indians, they dumped a shipload of tea in Boston Harbor.

In 1774 Britain responded to the Boston Tea Party with the Coercive Acts, which, among other things, gave the royal governor the right to select the upper house of the Massachusetts legislature. The Coercive Acts also denied Massachusetts the right to try British officials charged with capital offenses. Further legislation, the Quartering Act, required colonists to house British soldiers in their private homes, even during times of peace.[8] These acts convinced many colonists that their liberty was at stake and that rebellion and independence were the only alternatives to British tyranny.

In an attempt to present a more united front about colonial grievances, Benjamin Franklin proposed a congress, or assembly of representatives. The First Continental Congress, with delegates chosen by the colonial legislatures, met in Philadelphia in 1774. It rejected a reconciliation plan with England and instead sent King George III a list of grievances. It also adopted a very successful compact among the colonies not to import any English goods. Finally, it agreed to meet again as the Second Continental Congress in May 1775. This Second Continental Congress acted as the common government of the states between 1775 and 1781.

In April 1775, following skirmishes with British troops in Lexington and Concord, outside of Boston, the Second Continental Congress named George Washington commander of a new Continental Army. In 1776, with hostilities under way, Thomas Paine penned his influential pamphlet *Common Sense*, which called for independence from Britain. "There is something very absurd, in supposing a continent to be perpetually governed by an island," he argued.[9] *Common Sense* was the most widely distributed pamphlet of its time, and it helped convince many Americans that independence was the only way they could secure their right to self-government.

→ KEY QUESTIONS:
Was the American Revolution really about taxation, or was it about something else?

The Declaration of Independence

In June 1776, the Continental Congress debated an independence resolution but postponed a vote until July. Meanwhile, it instructed Thomas Jefferson and others to draft a **Declaration of Independence**. Congress approved the Declaration of Independence on July 4. Jefferson's Declaration relied in part on the writings of John Locke in asserting that people had certain natural (or unalienable) rights that government could not take away, including the right to life and liberty (see Chapter 1, Gateways to American Democracy). For Locke's reference to property, Jefferson substituted "the pursuit of happiness."

The Declaration listed grievances against King George III, including suspending popularly elected colonial legislatures, imposing taxes without representation, and conducting trials without juries. It then declared the united colonies to be thirteen "free and independent states." (The full text of the Declaration of Independence is in the Appendix.)

Even before the Declaration, the Continental Congress advised the colonies to adopt new constitutions "under the authority of the people." Reacting against the limitation on rights imposed by the British monarch and by royal governors in the colonies, these new state constitutions severely limited executive power but set few limits on legislative authority. At the same time, Americans made little effort to establish a national political authority, as most Americans considered themselves primarily citizens of the states in which they lived. Nevertheless, the Continental Congress needed legal authority for its actions, and, in 1777, its members proposed a governing document called the **Articles of Confederation**.

Declaration of Independence: *The 1776 document declaring American independence from Great Britain and calling for equality, human rights, and citizen participation.*

Articles of Confederation: *Initial governing authority of the United States, 1781–88.*

The Articles of Confederation

The Articles required unanimous consent of the states for adoption, which did not occur until 1781, just a few months before American victory in the Revolutionary War. They formally established "the United States of America," in contrast to the Declaration, which was a pronouncement of "Thirteen United States of America." According to the Declaration, each of the thirteen independent states had the authority to do all "acts and things which independent states may of right do," such as waging war, establishing alliances, and concluding peace. These were thirteen independent states united in a war of independence. With the Articles, the states became one nation with centralized control over making war and foreign affairs. But due to the belief that Great Britain had violated fundamental liberties, the Articles emphasized freedom from national authority at the expense of order. Thus the states retained all powers not expressly granted to Congress under the Articles.

Moreover, those expressly granted powers were extremely limited. Congress had full authority over foreign, military, and Indian affairs. It could decide boundary and other disputes between the states, coin money, and establish post offices. But Congress did not have the authority to regulate commerce or, indeed, any authority to operate directly over citizens of the United States. For example, Congress could not tax citizens or products (such as imports) directly; it could only request (but not demand) revenues from the states.

In addition to limiting powers, the Articles made governing difficult. Each state had one vote in Congress, with the consent of nine of the thirteen required for most important matters, including borrowing and spending money. Amending the Articles required the unanimous consent of the states. In 1781 tiny Rhode Island, blocking an amendment that would have set a 5 percent tax on imports, denied the whole nation desperately needed revenue. Moreover, the Articles established no judicial branch, with the minor exception that Congress could establish judicial panels on an ad hoc basis to hear appeals involving disputes between states and to hear cases involving crimes on the high seas. There was no separate executive branch, but Congress had the authority to establish an executive committee along with a rotating president who would manage the general affairs of the United States when Congress was not in session.[10]

→ KEY QUESTIONS:
Why didn't the Articles of Confederation work as a governing document?

These deficiencies led to predictable problems. With insufficient funds, the nation's debts went unpaid, hampering its credit. Even obligations to pay salaries owed to the Revolutionary War troops went unfulfilled. Without a centralized authority to regulate commerce, states taxed imports from other states, stunting economic growth. Lack of military power allowed Spain to block commercial access to the Mississippi River. Barbary pirates off the shores of Tripoli captured American ships and held their crews for ransom.

While the government of the United States suffered from too little authority, James Madison, Thomas Jefferson, and others came to believe that the governments of the states possessed too much authority. Popularly elected legislatures with virtually no checks on their authority passed laws rescinding private debts and creating trade barriers against other states. They also began taking over both judicial and executive functions.

With the United States in desperate financial straits, James Madison proposed a convention of states to consider granting the national government the power to tax and to regulate trade. Only five states showed up at this 1786 Annapolis Convention, preventing it from accomplishing much.

As the Annapolis Convention took place, word spread of a revolt in western Massachusetts that made the weakness of the national government all too clear.

BETTMANN/CORBIS

Daniel Shays led a protest movement of debt-ridden farmers facing foreclosures on their homes and farms. Demanding lower taxes and the issuance of paper money, they engaged in mob violence to force the Massachusetts courts to close.

Revolutionary War hero Daniel Shays and several thousand distressed farmers forced courts to close and threatened federal arsenals. Not until February 1787 did Massachusetts put down Shays's Rebellion. The revolt helped convince the states that, on top of the Articles' other problems, the document provided for too much freedom and not enough order. The Annapolis Convention thus issued an invitation to all thirteen states to meet in Philadelphia in May 1787 to consider revising the Articles of Confederation. This time only Rhode Island declined the invitation.

Checkpoint

CAN YOU:

- Define a constitution
- State the colonists' grievances against Great Britain
- Explain the key concepts in the Declaration of Independence
- Describe the problems with the Articles of Confederation

2.2 The Constitutional Convention

> Identify the major compromises at the Constitutional Convention

The delegates who met in Philadelphia were charged with amending the Articles of Confederation so that the national government could work more effectively. Almost immediately, however, they moved beyond that charge and began debating a brand new constitution. To complete that newly proposed constitution, the delegates needed to reach compromises between large and small states over representation, between northern and southern states over issues related to slavery, and between those who favored a strong national government and those who favored strong state governments. The Convention's rules granted each state one vote, regardless of the size of the state or the number of delegates it sent. The document they created, which was then sent to the states for ratification, is, with subsequent amendments, the same Constitution we live by today. (The full text of the Constitution of the United States is in the Appendix.)

Large versus Small States

Upon the opening of the Philadelphia Convention in May 1787, Edmund Randolph of Virginia presented the delegates with James Madison's radical proposal for a new government. Known as the Virginia Plan, Madison's proposal included a strong central government that could operate directly on the citizens of the United States without the states acting as intermediaries. The legislative branch would consist of two chambers: a lower chamber elected by the people and an upper chamber elected by the lower chamber. Each chamber would have representation proportional to the populations of the states: the larger the population, the more representatives a state would have. The legislature would have general authority to pass laws that would "promote the harmony" of the United States and could veto laws passed by the states. The Virginia Plan proposed a national executive and a national judiciary, both chosen by the legislature. A council of revision, composed of the executive and judicial members, would have final approval over all legislative acts.

Madison's proposals astonished many of the delegates from the smaller states and some from the larger states as well. To counter the Virginia Plan, on June 15 William Patterson of New Jersey presented the Convention with the New Jersey Plan, which strengthened the

Articles by providing Congress with the authority to regulate commerce and to directly tax imports and paper items. It also proposed a national executive chosen by the legislature and a national judiciary chosen by the executive.[11] Each state would retain equal representation in Congress.

The question of proportional or equal representation generated enormous controversy. Madison insisted that proportional representation for both chambers was the only fair system, and the small states insisted that they would walk out if they lost their equal vote. Roger Sherman of Connecticut proposed what became known as the **Connecticut Compromise**. The makeup of the lower chamber, the House of Representatives, would be proportional to population, but the upper chamber, the Senate, would represent each state equally.

Connecticut Compromise: *Compromise on legislative representation whereby the lower chamber is based on population, and the upper chamber provides equal representation to the states.*

Nation versus State

While the question of representation threatened the Convention, there was substantial agreement over the role of the national government. The delegates rejected the New Jersey Plan, which would have continued government under the Articles.

The delegates also did not approve the Virginia Plan in full, but the plan substantially influenced the proposed Constitution. Under the new Constitution, the government had the authority to operate directly on the citizens of the United States. Congress was not granted general legislative power, but rather **enumerated powers**, that is, a list of powers it could employ. Among its enumerated powers were the authority to tax to provide for the general welfare; to regulate commerce among the states and with foreign nations; to borrow money; to declare war, raise armies, and maintain a navy; and to make all laws "necessary and proper for carrying into Execution the foregoing Powers." The tax and commerce powers were among those missing from the Articles.

enumerated powers: *Powers expressly granted to Congress by the Constitution.*

Congress did not receive the authority to veto state laws, but the Constitution declared that national law would be supreme over state law, bound state judges to that decision, and created a national judiciary that would help ensure such rulings. Moreover, the Convention set explicit limits on state authority, prohibiting the states from carrying on foreign relations, coining money, and infringing on certain rights. Finally, the Convention approved a national executive (that is, the president) who could serve as a unifying force throughout the land. Table 2.2 presents the components of the Virginia Plan, the New Jersey Plan, and the proposed Constitution.

→ KEY QUESTIONS:
Were the delegates to the Constitutional Convention more concerned about liberty or about order?

North versus South

Resolving the question of nation versus state proved less difficult than resolving the question of representation. More difficult still were questions related to slavery. Although slavery existed in every state except Massachusetts, the overwhelming majority of slaves, nearly 95 percent, were in the southern states, from Maryland to Georgia.[12] As Madison put it, "The States were divided into different interests not by their difference of size, but principally from their having or not having slaves."[13] Not all northern delegates at the Convention opposed slavery, but those who were abolitionists wanted an immediate ban on importing slaves from Africa, prohibitions against the expansion of slavery into the western territories, and the adoption of a plan for the gradual freeing of

Table 2.2 The Virginia and New Jersey Plans Compared to the Constitution

Issue	Virginia Plan	New Jersey Plan	Constitution
Operation	Directly on people	Through the states	Directly on people
Legislative structure	Bicameral and proportional	Unicameral and equal	Bicameral, with lower chamber proportional and upper chamber equal
Legislative authority	General: power to promote the harmony of the United States	Strict enumerated powers of the Articles of Confederation, plus power to regulate commerce and limited power to tax	Broad enumerated powers
Check on legislative authority	Council of revision	None	Presidential veto, with possibility of a two-thirds override
Executive	Unitary national executive chosen by legislature	Plural national executive chosen by legislature	Unitary national executive chosen by Electoral College
Judiciary	National judiciary chosen by legislature	National judiciary chosen by executive	National judiciary chosen by president with advice and consent of Senate

© CENGAGE LEARNING®

slaves. Delegates from Georgia and South Carolina, whose states would never accept the Constitution on these terms, wanted guaranteed protections for slavery and the slave trade and no restrictions on slavery in the territories. To secure a Constitution, compromises were necessary.

Many supporters of slavery recognized the horrors of the foreign slave trade, and by 1779 all states except North Carolina, South Carolina, and Georgia had banned it. Leaving the authority to regulate the foreign slave trade to Congress would inevitably have resulted in its being banned everywhere and probably would have kept those three states from joining the union. Thus, a slave trade compromise prohibited Congress from stopping the slave trade until 1808.

A second compromise involved how slaves should be counted when calculating population for purposes of representation. Madison's Virginia Plan based representation on the number of free inhabitants of each state, whereas the southernmost slave states wanted slaves to be fully counted for purposes of representation. Delegates from the northern states, on the other hand, argued that slave states, which by definition denied the humanity of slaves, should not benefit by receiving extra representation based on the number of slaves that they had. Under the Articles, taxes requested of the states were based on the population of each state, with five slaves counting as three people. The Convention agreed to use this **three-fifths** formula not just for representation but also for whatever direct or population taxes the national government might choose to levy. This compromise had a significant impact on representation in the House of Representatives.[14]

A third compromise involved slavery in the western territories, and it came not from the Convention but from the government under the Articles, which passed the Northwest

> → KEY QUESTIONS:
> Were the delegates right or wrong to compromise on slavery?

 three-fifths compromise:
Compromise over slavery at the Constitutional Convention that granted states extra representation in the House of Representatives based on their number of slaves at the ratio of three-fifths.

Ordinance in July 1787. This ordinance, which established the means for governing the western lands north of the Ohio River (eventually the states of Ohio, Indiana, Illinois, Michigan, and Wisconsin, and parts of Minnesota), prohibited slavery in this territory but also provided that fugitive slaves who escaped to the territory would be returned to their owners. The Constitution incorporated these provisions.

With the precedent of prohibiting slavery in the Northwest Territory established in the Northwest Ordinance, the Convention gave Congress the right to regulate the territories of the United States without mentioning whether slavery could be allowed or prohibited.

Gates against Popular Influence

Compared to the British constitutional system, the 1787 Constitution provided direct and indirect gateways for popular involvement (see Figure 2.1). Nevertheless, the Framers did not trust the people to have complete control over choosing the government. In two important ways—the election of the president and the election of the Senate—the Constitution limited popular control.

Originally, state legislatures selected U.S. senators. The Framers feared that a Congress elected directly by the people would be too responsive to the popular will. The indirect election of senators was thus intended to serve as a check on the popular will. In 1913, the Seventeenth Amendment granted the people the right to elect senators directly.

Another gate against the people's participation was the election of the president through the **Electoral College**. Rather than directly electing the president through a popular vote, the Constitution established an Electoral College, in which electors actually choose the president. Each state receives a number of electors equal to its number of representatives plus senators, and each state legislature chooses the manner for selecting the electors from its state—by popular vote, legislative selection, or some other mechanism. State legislatures used to select electors. Today, each state legislature allows the people of the state to choose that state's electors, but in the early days of the **republic**, many state legislatures kept that right for themselves. Yet, the Electoral College remains in effect as a gate against direct popular control.

The Ratification Process

With agreements reached on representation in Congress, federal or national power, and slavery, the delegates made a few final decisions. First, despite the urging of George Mason of Virginia, the delegates chose not to include a **Bill of Rights**—a listing of rights retained by the

→ KEY QUESTIONS:
What compromises made the Constitution possible? Is compromise, as a political strategy, good or bad for democracy? Why is it out of favor today?

→ KEY QUESTIONS:
Why did the delegates set up gates against citizen participation? Whose participation did they not consider at all?

Electoral College: *The presidential electors, selected to represent the votes of their respective states, who meet every four years to cast the electoral votes for president and vice president.*

republic: *Form of government in which power derives from citizens, but public officials make policy and govern according to existing law.*

→ KEY QUESTIONS:
Did the delegates trust the people?

Bill of Rights: *First ten amendments to the Constitution, which provide basic political rights.*

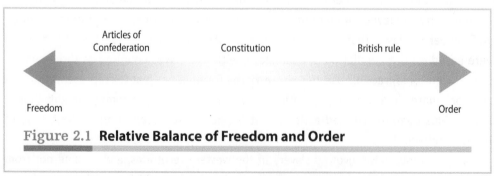

Figure 2.1 Relative Balance of Freedom and Order

© CENGAGE LEARNING®

people that Congress did not have the authority to take away, such as freedom of speech and freedom of religion. Because Congress had enumerated powers only, and because the authority to regulate speech, religion, and other freedoms was not among the powers granted to Congress, delegates believed there was no need to prohibit Congress from abridging such rights.

→ KEY QUESTIONS:
Do the people today retain the right to institute new government?

Second, the delegates needed a method for ratifying, or granting final approval of, the Constitution. Fortunately, the states had already established a precedent for ratifying constitutions in state conventions, rather than through state legislatures.

Similarly, the delegates at the Constitutional Convention chose to send the proposed Constitution to the states for approval via special ratifying conventions to be chosen by the people. The Constitution would take effect among those states approving it when nine of the thirteen states ratified it. The Articles had required that all state legislatures approve a proposed amendment for it to pass, but the Constitutional Convention sought approval from a higher authority: the people of the United States. This process for ratification followed the statement in the Declaration of Independence that "it is the right of the people...to institute new government." Hence, the Constitution's preamble establishes the Constitution in the name of "We the People of the United States."

In September 1787, with these final steps taken, delegates to the Constitutional Convention believed they had produced a constitution that remedied the deficiencies of the Articles (see Table 2.3), and they voted on the final document. Some of the delegates had left by September, but thirty-nine signed the document, with only three refusing to do so. Crucially, given Convention rules, a majority of the delegates from each of the states voted yes.

Checkpoint

CAN YOU:

- Characterize the delegates to the Constitutional Convention
- Explain how the interests of large and small states differed
- State why the Convention rejected the Virginia Plan
- Explain how the interests of the northern states and the southern states differed
- Describe how the 1787 Constitution protected against too much popular influence
- Recall who would ratify the new constitution

Table 2.3 **Deficiencies of the Articles of Confederation and Constitutional Remedies**

Deficiency in the Articles of Confederation	Remedy in the Constitution
Legislative branch could not regulate commerce	Congress can regulate commerce "among the states"
Legislative branch could only request taxes from states	Congress can directly raise taxes from individuals
Approval of nine of thirteen states needed for passage of major legislation	Approval of a majority of both legislative chambers needed for passage of all legislation; a two-thirds majority needed to override presidential vetoes
No permanent executive branch	A "President of the United States"
No permanent judicial branch	A Supreme Court plus other inferior courts that Congress can establish
Unanimity for constitutional amendments	Approval of two-thirds of each chamber plus three-fourths of the states
Few limits on state authority, mostly over foreign affairs	States limited in foreign affairs, plus could not suppress certain rights through bills of attainder, *ex post facto* laws, and so on

© CENGAGE LEARNING®

2.3 Government under the Constitution

> ❯ Explain how the structure of the Constitution protects liberty

The final document sent to the states for ratification laid out a structure of democratic government and proposed mechanisms whereby the Constitution could be amended. It also reflected the Framers' attempt to establish a government powerful enough to ensure public order yet containing enough gateways to guarantee individual liberty.

The Structure of Government

The Constitution established three branches of government: the legislative, the executive, and the judicial.

The Legislative Branch. The legislative branch, as explained in Chapter 1, makes the laws. The Constitution established a bicameral Congress, consisting of two chambers. The lower chamber, the House of Representatives, is proportioned by population (until the Thirteenth Amendment, the slave population was added to the free population according to the three-fifths formula described previously). Members of the House are elected for two-year terms directly by the people, with voting eligibility determined by each state. Representatives have to be at least 25 years old, residents of the state they serve, and U.S. citizens for at least the previous seven years.

The upper chamber, the Senate, consists of two senators from each state, regardless of size. Designed to serve as a check on the popular will, which would be expressed in the House of Representatives, state legislatures chose senators until 1913 when the Seventeenth Amendment granted the people of each state the exclusive right to do so.[15] A six-year term also serves to limit responsiveness to popular whims, and an age minimum of 30 presumably provides more mature and levelheaded thinking. Senators also have to be residents of the state in which they serve and U.S. citizens for nine years or more.

Bills to levy taxes have to originate in the House, but other bills may originate in either chamber. To become law, a bill has to pass each chamber in identical form and is then presented to the president for his signature. If the president signs the bill, it becomes law, but if he disapproves, he can **veto** the bill. Congress can then override the veto by a two-thirds majority in each chamber.

Article I, Section 8, of the Constitution limits Congress's authority to an eighteen-paragraph list, or enumeration, of certain powers. The first paragraph grants Congress the authority "to Collect Taxes…to pay the Debts and provide for the common Defence and general Welfare of the United States." Paragraphs 2 through 17 grant additional powers such as borrowing and coining money, regulating commerce, and raising an army. Then paragraph 18 grants Congress the authority to pass all laws "necessary and proper for carrying into Execution the foregoing Powers."

Additionally, the Constitution gives the House the authority to impeach—to bring charges against—the president and other federal officials. The Senate has the sole authority to try cases of impeachment, with a two-thirds vote required for removal from

CONNECT WITH YOUR CLASSMATES
MindTap® for American Government

Access The Constitution Forum: Discussion—The Constitution and Law Making.

veto: *Authority of the president to block legislation passed by Congress. Congress can override a veto by a two-thirds majority in each chamber.*

office. The Senate also has the sole authority to ratify treaties, which also require a two-thirds vote, and to confirm executive and judicial branch appointments by majority vote.

The Executive Branch.

The executive branch of government consists of a unitary president, chosen for a four-year term by an Electoral College. The Electoral College itself is chosen in a manner set by the legislature of each state. Eventually, every state gave the people the power to vote for its electors (as discussed earlier).

A president must be at least 35 years of age, a resident of the United States for the previous fourteen years, and either a natural-born citizen of the United States or a citizen of the United States at the time of the adoption of the Constitution.

Because the Framers believed that the legislative branch would naturally be stronger than the executive branch, they did not feel the need to enumerate the executive powers as they did the legislative powers. Recall that Congress does not have a general legislative authority, but only those legislative powers granted under the Constitution. In contrast, the Constitution provides the president with a general grant of "the executive Power" and certain specific powers, including the right to veto legislation and grant pardons. The president also is commander in chief of the armed forces. With the advice and consent of the Senate, the president makes treaties and appoints ambassadors, judges, and other public officials. The president leads the executive branch of government, being charged with taking care that the laws are faithfully executed.

The Judicial Branch.

The Constitution vests the judicial authority of the United States in one Supreme Court and other inferior courts that Congress might choose to establish. The president appoints judges with the advice and consent of the Senate. They serve "during good Behaviour," which, short of impeachment, means a life term.

→ KEY QUESTIONS:
Why did the delegates establish three branches of government?

The Constitution extends the authority of the federal courts to hear cases involving certain classes of parties to a suit—cases involving the United States, ambassadors, and other public ministers; suits between two or more states or citizens from different states—and certain classes of cases, most notably cases arising under the Constitution, laws, and treaties of the United States. In the historic case *Marbury v. Madison* (1803), the Supreme Court took this authority to hear cases arising under the Constitution of the United States to establish the power of **judicial review**, the authority of the Court to strike down any law passed by Congress when the Court believes the law violates the Constitution (see Supreme Court Cases: *Marbury v. Madison*).[16]

judicial review: *Authority of courts to declare laws passed by Congress and acts of the executive branch to be unconstitutional.*

The Amendment Process

The Constitution provides two paths for changing the Constitution via **amendment**. The first path requires a two-thirds vote in each chamber of Congress, followed by the approval of three-fourths of the states. That statewide approval can be attained either through the state legislatures or through state ratifying conventions, as directed by Congress. The second path allows two-thirds of the states to request a national constitutional convention that could propose amendments that would go into effect when approved by three-fourths of the states (see Figure 2.2). Again, this approval could be obtained through state legislatures or through state ratifying conventions. Additionally, the Constitution prohibits amendments that would

amendment: *Formal process of changing the Constitution.*

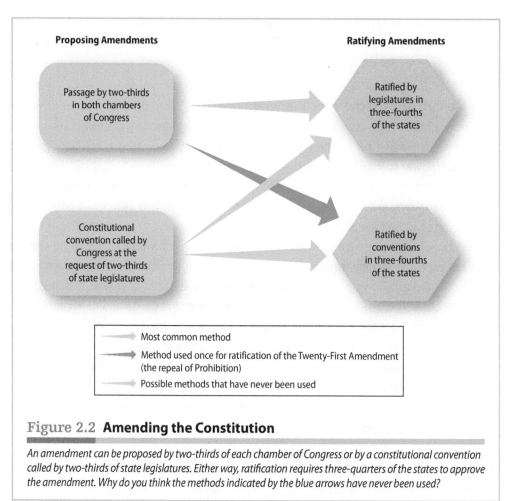

Proposing Amendments

Passage by two-thirds in both chambers of Congress

Constitutional convention called by Congress at the request of two-thirds of state legislatures

Ratifying Amendments

Ratified by legislatures in three-fourths of the states

Ratified by conventions in three-fourths of the states

→ Most common method

→ Method used once for ratification of the Twenty-First Amendment (the repeal of Prohibition)

→ Possible methods that have never been used

Figure 2.2 Amending the Constitution

An amendment can be proposed by two-thirds of each chamber of Congress or by a constitutional convention called by two-thirds of state legislatures. Either way, ratification requires three-quarters of the states to approve the amendment. Why do you think the methods indicated by the blue arrows have never been used?

deny any state an equal vote in the Senate or any amendment that would have allowed a banning of the foreign slave trade before 1808. Both paths for amending the Constitution are complex and difficult, which has kept the Constitution from being modified over popular but short-lived issues.

The Partition of Power

In attempting to explain and justify the constitutional structure, James Madison wrote of "the necessary partition of power among the several departments as laid down in the constitution" (see *Federalist* 51 in the Appendix). He acknowledged that elections serve as the primary means of ensuring that the government is responsive to the wishes of the people. If it is not, the people can vote for a new government. Under the Constitution, the people have direct authority to elect the House of Representatives. But to prevent the majority from imposing oppressive laws on the minority, the rest of the government was chosen indirectly, as we have seen.

Lest the people not be sufficient to keep government under control, however, the Constitution had built in "auxiliary precautions," as Madison called them, to make sure government could not concentrate power. Thus, **federalism** splits power between nation and state, **separation of powers** divides the powers that remained with the national government among the three branches of government, and **checks and balances** give each branch some

federalism: *System of government in which sovereignty is constitutionally divided between national and state governments.*

separation of powers: *Government structure in which authority is divided among branches (executive, legislative, and judicial), with each holding separate and independent powers and areas of responsibility.*

checks and balances: *Government structure that authorizes each branch of government (executive, legislative, and judicial) to share powers with the other branches, thereby holding some scrutiny of and control over the other branches.*

supreme court cases

Marbury v. Madison (1803)

QUESTION: Does Congress have the authority to expand the Supreme Court's original jurisdiction beyond that granted by the Constitution?

ORAL ARGUMENT: February 10, 1803

DECISION: February 23, 1803 (read at http://www.law.cornell.edu/supremecourt/text/5/137)

OUTCOME: No, thus establishing the power of judicial review (4–0)

It is hard to imagine a more momentous decision resulting from what the historian John A. Garraty called, this "trivial squabble over a few petty political plums."* In the closing days of President John Adams's administration, the Federalist Adams nominated William Marbury to the position of justice of the peace for the District of Columbia, and the Federalist Senate confirmed the nomination. But in the hectic final hours of Adams's administration, Secretary of State John Marshall neglected to deliver the commission. When Democratic-Republican Thomas Jefferson became president, his new secretary of state, James Madison, refused to deliver the commission, thus keeping Marbury from assuming his office.

Marbury filed suit at the Supreme Court, believing that the Judiciary Act of 1789 expanded the Court's original jurisdiction to give the Court the authority to hear cases involving writs of *mandamus* (orders to government officials to undertake specific acts) as an original matter, that is, as a trial, and not just as an appeal.

The Supreme Court declared that because the Constitution precisely specified which types of cases the Supreme Court could hear as an original matter, the section of the Judiciary Act that expanded the Court's original jurisdiction conflicted with the Constitution. Moreover, if a law conflicts with the Constitution, either the law is supreme over the

Constitution, or the Constitution is supreme over the law. The Court ruled that it must be the case that the Constitution is supreme over the law. Finally, the Court declared that the judiciary would decide such issues. "It is emphatically the province and duty of the judicial department to say what the law is," wrote Marshall, who in the closing days of the Adams administration had been nominated and confirmed as chief justice of the United States. The Supreme Court would not order Madison to deliver the commission to Marbury. Marbury presumably had the right to get the commission from a different court but never sought to do so. Instead, he returned to his highly successful banking career.

The Court in *Marbury* granted itself the momentous authority of judicial review, the power to strike down laws passed by Congress and state legislatures on the grounds that those laws violate the Constitution. Although the Court did not frequently use this power in the early days of the republic, citizens filing lawsuits would later use it to get the Court to strike down, among other things, segregated schools (*Brown v. Board of Education*, 1954), anti-abortion statutes (*Roe v. Wade*, 1973), and federal refusal to recognize same sex marriages (*U.S. v. Windsor*, 2013).

1. How does judicial review provide a gateway to participation in the political system?
2. Why is it the judiciary's job to determine whether a law is unconstitutional?

*"The Case of the Missing Commissions," in John A. Garraty, ed., *Quarrels That Have Shaped the Constitution* (New York: Harper and Row, 1964, p. 13.

authority over the powers of the other branches. Even after all this, the Constitution places additional limits on both federal and state powers.

Federalism.   The first means of preventing a concentration of power was to divide authority between the national and state governments. Rather than provide Congress with a general power to legislate in the national interest, the Constitution granted Congress enumerated powers. All powers not granted to Congress remained with the states. This division of power is made explicit in the Tenth Amendment to the Constitution: "The powers not delegated to the United States by the Constitution, nor prohibited by it to the States, are reserved to the States respectively, or to the people."

Separation of Powers.   Madison believed that "the accumulation of all powers, legislative, executive, and judiciary, in the same hands, whether of one, a few, or many, and whether hereditary, self-appointed, or elective, may justly be pronounced the very definition of tyranny."[17] Thus, after dividing power between the national and state governments, the Constitution separates those powers that it grants to the national government among the three branches. Under the Constitution, all legislative powers granted belong to Congress, the executive power vests in the president of the United States, and the judicial authority resides in a Supreme Court, plus any lower courts Congress might choose to establish. Moreover, because the "legislative authority . . . necessarily, predominates" in a republican government (*Federalist* 51), legislative power was further separated into two distinct chambers— a House and a Senate—each with different manners of election and terms of office.

Checks and Balances.   Under the Constitution, balance among the branches was achieved by giving each one some authority to counteract, or check, the authority of the other two (see Figure 2.3). Thus the president has the authority to propose legislation to Congress and to veto bills passed by Congress; Congress can override that veto by a two-thirds majority of each chamber. The president has the authority to pardon people convicted of crimes. The president also nominates federal judges, subject to the advice and consent of the Senate. The Senate also advises and consents to high-ranking executive branch appointments, such as ambassadors and cabinet officials. The House can impeach executive and judicial appointees, and the Senate can convict and remove impeached officials from office by a two-thirds majority. Congress, subject to presidential veto, has the authority to establish lower courts and set their jurisdiction (decide what cases they can hear). It also has the authority to set the Supreme Court's appellate jurisdiction. The appellate jurisdiction is the Supreme Court's authority to hear cases on appeal from lower courts and is the heart of the Supreme Court's judicial power. Congress has this authority over the courts; the courts, on the other hand, can decide the constitutionality of laws passed by Congress. While the Constitution does not explicitly grant this power of judicial review to courts, judicial review has been largely unchallenged since announced by the Supreme Court in *Marbury v. Madison*. The courts also have the authority to review the legality of actions taken by executive branch officials.

Limits on Powers.   The delegation of powers to Congress, and the reservation of all remaining powers to the states, would have given states the same authority to pass oppressive laws that they had under the Articles. To prevent that, the Constitution limits state authority in several ways. First, it makes federal law supreme over state law. Second, it guarantees that the states establish a republican form of government. Third, the Constitution sets limits on the sort

→ KEY QUESTIONS:
Why does the Constitution divide and separate power?

→ KEY QUESTIONS:
Has the division of power between the national government and the states hindered or advanced democracy?

→ KEY QUESTIONS:
What is the purpose of checks and balances?

COMPARE WITH YOUR PEERS
MindTap™ for American Government

Access The Constitution Forum: Polling Activity—Raising the Debt Ceiling.

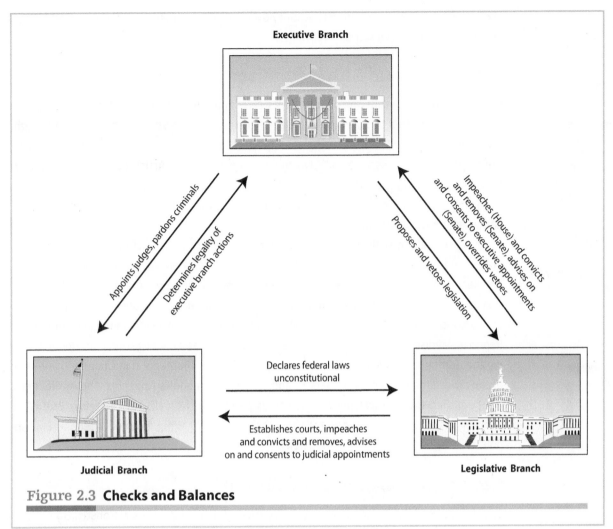

Executive Branch

Appoints judges, pardons criminals

Determines legality of executive branch actions

Impeaches (House) and convicts and removes (Senate), advises on and consents to executive appointments (Senate), overrides vetoes

Proposes and vetoes legislation

Declares federal laws unconstitutional

Establishes courts, impeaches and convicts and removes, advises on and consents to judicial appointments

Judicial Branch

Legislative Branch

Figure 2.3 **Checks and Balances**

of legislation states can pass. They also cannot pass bills of attainder (legislative acts declaring people guilty of crimes) or prosecute individuals under *ex post facto* laws, which make behavior illegal after individuals have engaged in it.

The Constitution also expressly limits the authority of Congress. Like the states, Congress can pass neither bills of attainder nor *ex post facto* laws. It also cannot suspend the writ of *habeas corpus*—a guarantee that incarcerated people can go before a judge to have the legality of their confinement determined—except in cases of invasion or rebellion.

Checkpoint

CAN YOU:

▪ Describe the basic structure of the U.S. Constitution

▪ Explain how amendments get proposed and ratified

▪ Evaluate why power is partitioned

2.4 The Ratification Debates

> Analyze why the Antifederalists opposed the Constitution

With the proposed Constitution to be accepted or rejected by the people of the various states, the state ratification debates largely ignored the question of representation that led to the Connecticut Compromise and the Three-Fifths Compromise. Instead, most of the debate concerned the extent of national power under the Constitution, with many expressing fears about the consolidation of federal authority over the states, the scope of executive and legislative power, and the lack of a bill of rights.

Federalists and Antifederalists

By the time the state ratifying conventions started meeting, two distinct camps had formed. Those who supported the Constitution cleverly named themselves **Federalists**, even though they were really more nationalist than federalist. ("Federal," according to Madison, meant "a Confederacy of sovereign states,"[18] which better described the Articles of Confederation, or even the New Jersey Plan, than the new Constitution.) Those who opposed the Constitution, whose leaders included the outspoken Revolutionary leader Patrick Henry of Virginia, became known as the **Antifederalists**.

Madison, along with John Jay, who later became the first chief justice of the United States, and Alexander Hamilton, who later founded the Federalist Party and served as the first secretary of the treasury, wrote eighty-five essays, today known as the *Federalist Papers*, that attempted to convince the citizens of New York to ratify the Constitution. They wrote anonymously under the pen name "Publius," taken from an early leader in the ancient Roman Republic. Madison's essays, especially, are still read today as a leading source for understanding the Constitution. We quoted from them earlier in this chapter and in Chapter 1, and two of the most famous essays, numbers 10 and 51, are in this book's Appendix. The Antifederalists published their attacks under anonymous pen names as well, most notably "Brutus"—another leader of the ancient Roman Republic—and "Old Whig," named after the English political party that opposed the monarchy.

Consolidation of Federal Authority

The Antifederalists found much to disapprove of in the proposed Constitution. They argued that the Constitutional Convention had violated the Articles by moving beyond mere amendment and proposing a new government, one that did not require the unanimous consent of the states. They worried that because sovereignty, the ultimate lawmaking authority, could not be split, and because national law was supreme over state law, a national government under the Constitution would inevitably consolidate its authority over the state governments.

The Federalists answered both of these charges by claiming that sovereignty rested not in the legislature, as had typically been believed, but in the people, as the preamble to the Constitution suggested. Therefore the people could propose any new form of government they wished. And if the people were sovereign, they could split their grant of lawmaking authority between the national and state governments as they saw fit.

The Scope of Executive Authority

Other concerns centered on the scope of executive authority. With no term limits on the executive in the original Constitution, the Antifederalists feared that the president would turn into a monarch, and of the worst type—an elected one. Alexander Hamilton responded in *Federalist* 69 with an explanation of the limits on the executive: elections, whereby the president could be voted out of office; impeachment, whereby the president could be removed from office for "high crimes and misdemeanors"; and the limited

Federalists: *Initially, those who supported the Constitution during the ratification period; later, the name of the political party established by supporters of Alexander Hamilton.*

Antifederalists: *Those who opposed the new proposed Constitution during the ratification period.*

→ KEY QUESTIONS:
Were the Antifederalists more concerned about liberty or about order?

veto power, which could be overridden. The president of the United States, Hamilton concluded, was much closer in power to the governor of New York than to the king of England.

The Scope of Legislative Authority

Two provisions in Article I, Section 8, of the Constitution, which specified the powers of Congress, particularly alarmed the Antifederalists: the **general welfare clause** and the **necessary and proper clause**. This section of the Constitution begins by stating that "Congress shall have Power to lay and Collect Taxes…to…provide for the…general Welfare of the United States." It concludes by stating that Congress has the power "to make all Laws which shall be necessary and proper for carrying into Execution the foregoing Powers." Antifederalist Brutus contended that "the legislature under this constitution may pass any law which they may think proper."[19]

Madison responded in *Federalist* 41 that the power to tax "to provide for the general Welfare" was not a general grant of power to tax for any purpose whatsoever but, rather, a power to tax for the enumerated powers that followed. "Nothing is more natural nor common than first to use a general phrase, and then to explain and qualify it by a recital of particulars."[20] To Madison, Article I, Section 8, granted the right to tax to provide for the general welfare and then listed various other powers that defined the full scope of the general welfare clause.

Similarly, the Federalists argued that the necessary and proper clause was not a general grant of authority to pass all laws that were necessary and proper, but rather, as the clause explicitly stated, the authority to pass all laws that were "necessary and proper for carrying into Execution the foregoing [that is, previously listed] Powers." Thus, if a law is necessary and proper for borrowing money, or raising an army, or establishing a post office, Congress may pass such a law, for those powers are among the "foregoing Powers" granted Congress. This explicit restriction of the necessary and proper clause to the other powers was absent, however, in the general welfare clause. To Madison, the restriction was obviously implied; to the Antifederalists, it was a threat to limited government.

Nevertheless, to clarify that the Constitution did not provide general powers to Congress, the Federalists agreed to an amendment to the Constitution declaring that "The powers not delegated to the United States by the Constitution, nor prohibited by it to the States, are reserved to the States respectively, or to the people." Interestingly, the amendment parallels a similar provision from the Articles that declared that the states retained all powers not "expressly delegated" to the national government. By limiting congressional authority to those powers delegated to it, rather than the stricter standard of those powers expressly delegated to it, the Constitution creates a somewhat greater authority for **implied powers**.

The Lack of a Bill of Rights

The most serious charge against the Constitution was that it did not contain a bill of rights. The Federalists argued that a bill of rights was not necessary because

LIBRARY OF CONGRESS PRINTS AND PHOTOGRAPHS DIVISION WASHINGTON, D.C[LC-DIG-PPMSCA-17522]

1787 engraving depicting the conflict between the Federalists and Anti-Federalists in Connecticut. The Federalists are portrayed as representing trading interests while the Anti-Federalists are shown as favoring farming interests.

→ KEY QUESTIONS:
Was the Bill of Rights necessary in 1787? Is it necessary today?

Congress had only those powers granted by the Constitution. If Congress was not granted the authority to, say, abridge freedom of the press, it was unnecessary to say that Congress could not abridge freedom of the press. The Federalists, specifically Alexander Hamilton in *Federalist* 84, went further to claim that a bill of rights could be dangerous because listing some rights but not others could imply that the rights not listed could be abridged.

It is hard to imagine people concluding from the Federalist argument that rights would be safer without a bill of rights. Not only is this a complicated argument, but combining the necessary and proper clause with the broad powers granted Congress under the Constitution—such as regulating interstate commerce and taxing to provide for the general welfare—probably means that Congress could have found ways to pass laws abridging freedom of assembly, freedom of speech, and other freedoms. The Federalists eventually gave in to the Antifederalist argument, agreeing that amending the Constitution to provide a bill of rights would be among the first items of business under a newly ratified Constitution. To prevent the listing of certain rights to create an assumption that Congress could abridge other rights not listed, the Bill of Rights included the Ninth Amendment: "The enumeration in the Constitution, of certain rights, shall not be construed to deny or disparage others retained by the people."

Despite the Antifederalist arguments about excessive national power, the lack of a bill of rights, and a too-powerful executive, states began ratifying the new Constitution. By June 1788, ten states had ratified, one more than needed to establish the new Constitution.

Checkpoint

CAN YOU:

- Characterize the Federalists and Antifederalists
- Compare competing arguments over who was sovereign under the Constitution
- Explain why the Antifederalists believed the president had too much power
- Explain why the Antifederalists believed Congress had too much power
- Recall which problem in the proposed Constitution the Federalists agreed to correct

2.5 The Responsive Constitution

> Illustrate how the Constitution has stayed responsive to changing needs

The government the Framers devised has lasted more than two hundred years. As in 1787, it still has three branches of government, Congress still consists of two chambers, and the Electoral College still chooses the president. But other parts of the U.S. constitutional system have changed substantially, some to fix flaws and some to respond to new circumstances and developing ideas about the nature of equality. Some of these changes, such as the Bill of Rights, came through the formal amendment process. Others were the result of changing interpretation by the Supreme Court about what the Constitution means. Still others are what some call "extraconstitutional." That is, they affect the way the constitutional system operates even though the Constitution itself has not been amended to reflect them. Most prominent is the development of political parties (see Chapter 8, Political Parties).

The Bill of Rights

As part of the fight over ratification, the Federalists agreed that they would propose a Bill of Rights after the new Constitution was ratified, and some state ratifying conventions forwarded proposals for specific amendments. The states then ratified ten of the amendments

globalgateways

The English Bill of Rights

In 1689, Parliament won the long power struggle with the monarch by making the acceptance of a written Declaration of Rights a condition for ascending the throne. King William III and Queen Mary agreed. They became lawful sovereigns, and the English people—including those who lived in Britain's colonies—were confirmed in their belief that they possessed "undoubted Rights and Liberties." These rights, recorded on parchment, included the following (in the original English):

- That levying money for or to the use of the Crowne by pretence of Prerogative without Grant of Parliament for longer time or in other manner than the same is or shall be granted is illegal
- That it is the right of the Subjects to petition the King and all Commitments and prosecutions for such petitioning are illegal
- That the raising or keeping a Standing Army within the Kingdome in time of Peace unlesse it be with Consent of Parliament is against Law
- That the Subjects which are Protestants may have Armes for their defence suitable to their Conditions and as allowed by Law
- That the Freedome of Speech and Debates or Proceedings in Parliament ought not to be impeached or questioned in any Court or Place out of Parliament
- That excessive Bayle ought not to be required nor excessive Fines imposed nor cruell and unusuall Punishments inflicted
- That Jurors ought to be duely impannelled and returned and Jurors which passe upon men in Tryalls for high Treason ought to be Freeholders

Read this list of rights carefully. They were written almost exactly a century before the American Bill of Rights. The language and spelling are certainly different, but the content is familiar.

1. Which of these rights did the American colonists believe the British had violated before the Revolution?
2. Which of these rights did the citizens of the new United States write into their Bill of Rights?

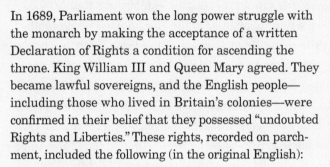

PARLIAMENTARY ARCHIVES

The English Bill of Rights is preserved at Britain's National Archives in London.

TITLE IMAGE: © KLETR/SHUTTERSTOCK.COM

in 1791 as a Bill of Rights that became part of the Constitution. Many of these amendments stated rights that had been guaranteed under British law or had been abridged by the British during the decade before the Revolution, causing the Americans to demand independence (see Global Gateways: The English Bill of Rights).

The First Amendment guarantees major political rights, including freedom of speech, press, and assembly, and the free exercise of religion. It also prohibits establishing a national religion or, more precisely, any law "respecting an establishment of religion." The Second Amendment protects the right to bear arms; the Third Amendment prohibits the quartering of soldiers in one's home in times of peace. The Fourth, Fifth, Sixth, and Eighth Amendments protect rights relating to criminal procedure, including the right at trial to the assistance of an attorney and the right to a trial by jury (Sixth). (The Seventh Amendment protects the right to a trial by jury in civil cases over $20.) The criminal procedure amendments also prohibit unreasonable searches and seizures (Fourth); compulsory self-incrimination (Fifth); double jeopardy, or being tried a second time for a crime after one is found not guilty (Fifth); and cruel or unusual punishments (Eighth). The Fifth Amendment also prohibits deprivations of life, liberty, or property without due process of law, and it prohibits the government from seizing private property for a public use without fair or "just" compensation. We examine the meanings of these amendments in Chapter 4, Civil Liberties.

The Civil War Amendments

Following the Civil War, Congress proposed and the states ratified three amendments. The Thirteenth Amendment (1865) prohibits slavery. The Fourteenth Amendment (1868), aimed at protecting the newly emancipated slaves, makes all people born in the United States citizens of the United States. It also prohibits states from denying anyone due process of law, the equal protection of the law, and the privileges or immunities of citizens of the United States. The Fifteenth Amendment (1870) prohibits states from denying anyone the right to vote on account of race or prior status as slaves. All three amendments give Congress the authority to enforce the measures by appropriate legislation, thus adding to Congress's enumerated powers. These amendments radically changed the structure of the federal government by giving the national government authority over internal matters of the states. We deal with these civil rights more extensively in Chapter 5, Civil Rights.

Amendments That Expand Public Participation

→ KEY QUESTIONS:
How has the Constitution changed, and why?

Other amendments have further extended the gateways to public participation in government by giving the people the right to vote for their senators directly (Seventeenth, 1913), guaranteeing women the right to vote (Nineteenth, 1920), allowing residents of the District of Columbia to vote in presidential elections (Twenty-Third, 1961), prohibiting states from setting poll taxes as a requirement of voting in federal elections (Twenty-Fourth, 1964), and guaranteeing the right to vote for those age 18 or older (Twenty-Sixth, 1971). For a summary of all the amendments, see Figure 2.4.

Constitutional Interpretation

The Constitution has also changed through interpretation by the Supreme Court (see Public Policy and the Constitution: The Death Penalty). Following the explicit establishment of

Figure 2.4 **The Amendments to the Constitution**

Following the specific protections of the first eight amendments to the Constitution, many subsequent amendments have corrected structural problems in the operation of government. Others have expanded participation and equality.

Color Code: Criminal procedure | Participation | Equality | Structure | Miscellaneous

First	1791	Prohibits abridging freedoms of religion, speech, press, assembly, and petition
Second	1791	Prohibits abridging the right to bear arms
Third	1791	Prohibits involuntary quartering of soldiers in one's home during peacetime
Fourth	1791	Prohibits unreasonable searches and seizures
Fifth	1791	Affirms the right to indictment by a grand jury and the right to due process; protects against double jeopardy, self-incrimination, and taking of property without just compensation
Sixth	1791	Affirms rights to speedy and public trial, to confront witnesses, and to counsel
Seventh	1791	Affirms right to jury trials in civil suits over $20
Eighth	1791	Prohibits excessive bail, excessive fines, and cruel and unusual punishments
Ninth	1791	Declares that the enumeration of certain rights does not limit other rights retained by the people
Tenth	1791	Reserves the powers not granted to the national government to the states or to the people
Eleventh	1798	Prevents citizens from one state from suing another state in federal court
Twelfth	1804	Requires that electors cast separate votes for president and vice president and specifies requirements for vice presidential candidates
Thirteenth	1865	Prohibits slavery in the United States
Fourteenth	1868	Makes all persons born in the United States citizens of the United States and prohibits states from denying persons within its jurisdiction the privileges or immunities of citizens, the due process of law, and equal protection of the laws; apportionment by whole persons
Fifteenth	1870	Prohibits states from denying the right to vote on account of race
Sixteenth	1913	Grants Congress the power to tax income derived from any source
Seventeenth	1913	Gives the people (instead of state legislatures) the right to choose U.S. senators directly
Eighteenth	1919	Prohibits the manufacture, sale, or transportation of intoxicating liquors
Nineteenth	1920	Guarantees women the right to vote
Twentieth	1933	Declares that the presidential term begins on January 20 (instead of March 4)
Twenty-First	1933	Repeals the Eighteenth Amendment
Twenty-Second	1951	Limits presidents to two terms
Twenty-Third	1961	Grants Electoral College votes to residents of the District of Columbia
Twenty-Fourth	1964	Prohibits poll taxes
Twenty-Fifth	1967	Specifies replacement of the vice president and establishes the position of acting president during a president's disability
Twenty-Sixth	1971	Guarantees 18-year-olds the right to vote
Twenty-Seventh	1992	Sets limits on congressional pay raises

© CENGAGE LEARNING®

judicial review in *Marbury v. Madison*, the Court has exercised the authority to determine what the Constitution means. Under that authority, the powers of Congress have grown enormously. During the Great Depression of the 1930s, the Court began to interpret Congress's power to tax to provide for the general welfare as extending beyond the enumerated powers. Rather, in line with the interpretation of the general welfare clause that the Antifederalists feared, the Court now holds that Congress can tax and spend for virtually any purpose that is not expressly prohibited.

Public Policy and the Constitution:
The Death Penalty

The Constitution contains some degree of ambiguity about the death penalty. In several places, it seems to allow capital punishment. The Fourteenth Amendment's due process clause says that states may not deprive people of life, liberty, or property without due process of law, thus suggesting that life, liberty, and property may be taken so long as the states follow due process. Similarly, the Fifth Amendment declares that no person shall be held for a capital crime without indictment by a grand jury. In contrast, the Eighth Amendment prohibits "cruel and unusual" punishments.

Before 1972, most states allowed capital punishment and did so by declaring crimes for which capital punishment could be imposed (usually murder, but sometimes also rape) and then leaving it up to the jury to decide whether capital punishment should be inflicted in a specific case. In 1972, the Supreme Court put a temporary halt to capital punishment, declaring that the process of complete jury discretion was cruel and unusual in that it led to an arbitrary and unequal imposition of the death penalty.[21] According to one justice in this sharply divided case, who received the death penalty and who did not was as arbitrary as who gets hit by lightning. (Figure 2.5 shows the fluctuations in the number of executions per year.)

Various states responded to this decision by requiring juries to follow certain guidelines before imposing the death penalty. In 1976, the Supreme Court ruled 7–2 that the death penalty with such guidelines did not constitute cruel and unusual punishment under the

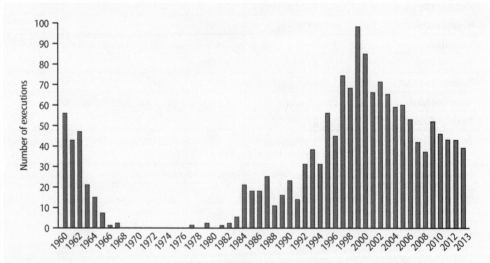

Figure 2.5 Annual executions in the United States, 1960–2013

Annual executions dropped significantly in the years before the Supreme Court's temporary halt of capital punishment in 1972, but public support for capital punishment remained high. After the Court reinstituted capital punishment in 1976, the number of executions rose. The number later dipped, as DNA evidence revealing that some death row inmates had been wrongly convicted made the public wary about the death penalty.

Source: Annual Executions, 1960–2013. Death Penalty Information Center, 2013.

Constitution.[22] Currently, thirty-two states permit capital punishment.[23] Given strong public approval for the death penalty—nearly 2-1 in an October 2013 Gallup poll[24]—Congress allows it for certain federal crimes, including terrorist acts that result in death, murder for hire, kidnappings that result in murder, and murder related to the smuggling of aliens.[25] The United States is seeking the death penalty in the case of Dzhokhar Tsarnaev, the accused Boston Marathon bomber, even though Massachusetts does not allow capital punishment.[26]

Although the Supreme Court has attempted to limit the unequal application of the death penalty, one clear finding from studies is the effect of the race of the victim: Juries are far more likely to impose the death penalty when the victim is white than when the victim is black.[27] The Supreme Court has ruled that, even if this were the case overall, someone challenging a death sentence based on such statistics would have to prove that the jury intentionally discriminated in the particular case.[28]

The Supreme Court has put limits on who can be sentenced to death. Offenders who were under the age of 18 when their crimes were committed and those convicted of rape, even the rape of a child, cannot receive the death penalty.[29]

Some states have begun to limit their own use of this punishment. The Innocence Project, a group dedicated to reversing convictions of people who were innocent, reports 312 death penalty cases in which DNA testing demonstrated that the wrong person was convicted of the crime.[30] This finding has led many states to reduce the number of death penalty sentences. It has also led many, but not all, states to allow convicted criminals access to DNA evidence, though the Supreme Court does not require them to do so.[31] Illinois was the first state to suspend the use of the death penalty because the evidence in several death penalty cases was shown to be insufficient in establishing guilt, and the newest scientific methods using DNA exonerated several death row inmates.

In considering how well policy making works in the constitutional system, it is worth noting the inconsistent use of the death penalty across states. If two individuals commit the same crime in different states, one criminal might be put to death, and the other might be allowed to live. Should states have their own policies on capital punishment, or should the federal government impose a uniform policy on them? The inconsistent use of the death penalty raises questions about equality under the constitutional system and serves as one of the most important examples of the unintended consequences of constitutional design.

Construct Your Own Policy

1. Draft a constitutional amendment that would eliminate the death penalty in all fifty states, and include an alternative sentence for crimes that might otherwise qualify for the death penalty.
2. Draft a set of five requirements for the imposition of the death penalty that would apply in all fifty states.

Checkpoint

CAN YOU:

- List the major rights protected by the Bill of Rights
- List the major rights protected by the Civil War amendments
- Explain how amendments have expanded the gateways to public participation
- Describe how the meaning of the Constitution can change without formal amendments

→ KEY QUESTIONS:
What is the significance of judicial review?

Additionally, Congress's authority to regulate commerce between the states is now so grand that it covers virtually all commercial activity, including wheat grown by a farmer for consumption by livestock on that farmer's land because of the effect that all similarly situated wheat could have on national grain markets.[32] But in 2012, the Supreme Court held that the commerce clause did not give Congress the right to mandate that individuals purchase health insurance, upholding that requirement under the taxing part of the general welfare clause.[33]

The Constitution and Democracy

Government under the 1787 Constitution would today be considered severely lacking in both democracy and equality. The government allowed some of the people, mostly white males with property, to choose one chamber of the legislative branch of their government but did not grant the people a direct vote for the other chamber of the legislature or for the chief executive. And a government that allowed slavery would today be a pariah, an outcast, among the nations of the world.

Moreover, in 1787, states regulated the right to vote. Slaves were not allowed to vote, but states differed as to whether women, free blacks, and men without property could vote. Yet, compared to the despots and monarchs who had long ruled other countries, the government of 1787 allowed for a remarkable degree of participation by the common person. By giving voters a direct say in their state legislatures and at least indirect influence in all branches of the national government, the 1787 Constitution was a striking break with the past, even if it did not live up to the Declaration's statement that "all men are created equal."

Today participation is much more widespread than in 1787. Although the Electoral College continues to play its role every four years, each state allows the people to choose their electors. In addition, amendments to the Constitution have widened the gateways to democracy. Due to the Seventeenth Amendment, the people today directly choose their senators, making that body directly responsive to public wishes. Moreover, voting equality is guaranteed in various ways: Poll taxes are illegal (Twenty-Fourth Amendment), and voting rights, which are now guaranteed to those 18 years old and older (Twenty-Sixth Amendment), may not be abridged due to race (Fifteenth Amendment) or sex (Nineteenth Amendment).

Although the 1787 Constitution allowed the national government to exercise direct control over the citizenry, the tiny size of the national government left the people with far more control over their daily lives than they have today. But it is also the case that today the people have more control over the government. In addition to new constitutional gateways, opportunities for participation are greater than ever, with the Internet relaying information virtually instantly. It is much easier for representatives to be responsive to their constituents' desires when they can easily learn what their constituents believe, and constituents can readily learn what their representatives have done.

Master the Concept
of The Constitution with MindTap™ for American Government

 REVIEW MindTap™ **for American Government**
Access Key Term Flashcards for Chapter 2.

 TEST YOURSELF MindTap™ **for American Government**
Take the Wrap It Up Quiz for Chapter 2.

 STAY CURRENT MindTap™ **for American Government**
Access the KnowNow blog and customized RSS for updates on current events.

 STAY FOCUSED MindTap™ **for American Government**
Complete the Focus Activities for The Constitution.

Key Concepts

amendment (p. 41). Why did the Framers make amending the Constitution so difficult?

Antifederalists (p. 46). What were the Antifederalist arguments against the proposed Constitution?

Articles of Confederation (p. 33). What were the deficiencies of the Articles of Confederation?

Bill of Rights (p. 38). What are the basic protections in the Bill of Rights?

checks and balances (p. 42). Why does government need checks and balances?

Connecticut Compromise (p. 36). What did the Connecticut Compromise accomplish?

constitution (p. 30). Why is a constitution needed instead of ordinary laws that can say the same things?

Declaration of Independence (p. 33). What are the basic principles of the Declaration of Independence?

Electoral College (p. 38). Why does the Constitution provide for an Electoral College?

enumerated powers (p. 36). Why are Congress's powers enumerated?

federalism (p. 42). What does a federal system try to do?

Federalists (p. 46). Who were the Federalists?

general welfare clause (p. 47). What does the general welfare clause do?

implied powers (p. 47). Does the Constitution grant implied powers?

judicial review (p. 41). What is judicial review?

necessary and proper clause (p. 47). What does the necessary and proper clause do?

republic (p. 38). What distinguishes a republic from other forms of government?

separation of powers (p. 42). Why do governments chosen by the people still need a separation of powers?

three-fifths compromise (p. 37). What were the problems of the three-fifths compromise?

veto (p. 40). Why is the president given veto power?

Learning Outcomes: What You Need . . .

To Know	To Test Yourself	To Participate

 Assess what drove the colonists to seek independence

The colonists declared independence from Britain because they believed that the British Parliament and king were denying their rights as British subjects. Congress's powers under the Articles of Confederation were limited, and the structure the Articles established made governing difficult.	• Define a constitution. • State the colonists' grievances against Great Britain. • Explain the key concepts in the Declaration of Independence. • Describe the problems with the Articles of Confederation.	• Appreciate American political culture. • Formulate grievances you might have about the government today. • Evaluate the impact of governing documents.

 Identify the major compromises at the Constitutional Convention

In 1787, delegates from twelve states met in Philadelphia to amend the Articles; instead, they wrote a new Constitution. To secure the assent of all states represented at the Constitutional Convention, the delegates reached compromises between large and small states over representation, between northern and southern states over issues related to slavery, and between those who favored a strong national government and those who favored strong state governments in the balance of power between the two. This newly proposed Constitution was then sent to the states for ratification, and it is, with subsequent amendments, the same Constitution Americans live by today.	• Explain how the interests of the large and small states differed. • State why the convention rejected the Virginia Plan. • Explain how the interests of the northern states and the southern states differed. • Describe how the 1787 Constitution protected against too much popular influence. • Recall who would ratify the new Constitution.	• Characterize the people who hold power today. • Justify (or critique) equal representation in the Senate. • Evaluate compromise as a tool for governing.

To Know	To Test Yourself	To Participate

▶ **Explain how the structure of the Constitution protects liberty**

The Constitution lays out the structure of democratic government and the means by which the Constitution can be amended. It reflects the Framers' attempt to establish a government powerful enough to ensure public order yet restrained enough to guarantee individual liberty.	• Describe the basic structure of the U.S. Constitution. • Explain how amendments get proposed and ratified. • Evaluate why power is partitioned.	• Evaluate whether the Constitution provides gateways for, or gates against, public participation. • Determine whether the amendment process is too difficult. • Evaluate the dangers of unified power.

▶ **Analyze why the Antifederalists opposed the Constitution**

Debates over the ratification of the Constitution centered on a fear of consolidated federal authority over the states, the scope of executive and legislative power, and the lack of a bill of rights. To achieve ratification, the Federalists gave in to Antifederalist demands for a bill of rights, passing one as the first ten amendments to the Constitution.	• Characterize the Federalists and Antifederalists. • Compare competing arguments over who was sovereign under the Constitution. • Explain why the Antifederalists believed the president had too much power. • Explain why the Antifederalists believed Congress had too much power. • Recall which problem in the proposed Constitution the Federalists agreed to correct.	• Identify these positions in politics today. • Argue whether the national government or the people are sovereign today. • Evaluate the extent of presidential power. • Evaluate the extent of congressional power.

▶ **Illustrate how the Constitution has stayed responsive to changing needs**

Subsequent amendments ended slavery, protected the rights of African Americans, and generally extended public participation in government while also expanding federal authority over the states. The constitutional system established in 1787 has also been changed by constitutional interpretation and its operation altered by the development of political parties.	• List the major rights protected by the Bill of Rights. • List the major rights protected by the Civil War amendments. • Explain how amendments have expanded the gateways to public participation. • Describe how the meaning of the Constitution can change without formal amendments. • Identify the informal practices that have changed how the Constitution operates.	• Propose new rights that you would like to see constitutionally protected. • Contrast the gateways to public participation that exist today and those that existed in 1787. • Examine the evolution of constitutional meaning, and judge whether it is valid.

"Whenever you feel something could be better, you should step up and do it or help someone who can. Many of the greatest achievements came as a result of people volunteering their time towards making a positive impact."

BRIAN MAUGHAN
Oklahoma City
Community College

3

Federalism

The impacts of federal, state, and local government decisions are not just theory to Brian Maughan. They first got his attention when he was a student at Oklahoma City Community College (OCCC), and now, in his job as county commissioner, they are daily fare.

Maughan grew up in the community he now serves. His commitment to his community developed in high school, when his principal used community service to instill self-worth in at-risk students. For college, Maughan remained close by, where he could stay in touch with Ben, his best friend, who was a quadriplegic as the result of a car accident and who faced a difficult situation. The state program that supplemented federal funding for his in-home health care was being defunded, and it looked like he would be removed from his home and placed in a state care facility. The federal program—Social Security Disability Insurance (SSDI)—would not pay for a family member to provide in-home health care at the advanced level Ben's condition required. If state funding could be restored, however, Ben could remain at home, and the family member who cared for him would receive compensation. Obviously, this arrangement was preferred. Maughan took on Ben's cause as his own. While keeping up with his classes and holding down a job to pay his tuition, Maughan researched funding options and learned that the Oklahoma Developmental Disability Council could provide the aid Ben needed. For two years, he actively sought the governor's support. Because of his commitment, the governor appointed Maughan to the council, and shortly after Maughan's graduation, funding for Ben's situation was restored. Ben was able to remain at home where his family cared for him until his death, a short

time later. Maughan's success on behalf of his friend demonstrates the gateways for influence at the state and local levels that are often easier to access than the federal level.

Recognizing that active citizenship can change policies that have negative effects, Maughan decided to make government and community service his career. Today, as a county commissioner, he navigates the multiple layers of government. An accidental fire, propelled by raging winds and severe drought conditions, consumed many homes in his district. Then a tornado caused more property loss and raised public safety concerns. Maughan's job was to oversee federal disaster assistance in the removal of debris so that homeowners could begin to clean up and rebuild. But federal and county disaster aid funded only the removal of trees and natural materials; the removal of other debris was the responsibility of the homeowner and the insurance company.

Need to Know

3.1 Explain why the Framers chose a federal system

3.2 Summarize how the Constitution institutes the federal system

3.3 Outline how U.S. federalism has changed over time

3.4 Compare and contrast national and state governments

 WATCH & LEARN MindTap® **for American Government**
Watch a brief "What Do You Know?" video summarizing Federalism.

Frustrated homeowners leveled criticism at Maughan. He found an innovative solution: He mobilized more than a thousand volunteers, who donated more than ten thousand hours assisting homeowners.

Maughan does not ask more of others than he asks of himself. In a snowstorm, when snow removal resources were limited, he helped plow, sand, and salt the 177 lane miles in his district. To clean up blight, he enlists college students and offenders sentenced to community service in a program he founded called SHINE (Start Helping Impacted Neighborhoods Everywhere). The National Association of Counties recognized the program with its "2014 Achievement Award." SHINE's success also led to the passage of a state law, the "Safari McDoulett Community Service Act" (SB 1875), authorizing similar community service programs to be adopted by all counties in the state (McDoulett was the staff person responsible for administering the program but was killed in an automobile accident). The program has been modeled by

the capital city of Rwanda in Africa and presents yearly awards to students who complete 100 hours of community service. Maughan likes to tell volunteers the "broken window" story that political scientist James Q. Wilson made famous—how one unattended broken window can invite trash, graffiti, and an opportunity for more serious crimes. Volunteer labor helps Maughan stretch tight budgets and inspires civic engagement that improves the community as a whole.[1]

In federal political systems where national, state, and local governments wield power, the interplay of responsibilities is often complex and overlapping or may leave areas unfunded, as Maughan's experiences reveal. But they also offer multiple gateways to participation, policy change, and government office. In this chapter, we examine the federal system of government, including the authority of national, state, and local governments; how that authority has shifted over time; and how federalism can both enhance and impede American democracy.

LISTEN & LEARN

MindTap™ for American Government

Access Read Speaker to listen to Chapter 3.

3.1 Why Federalism?

> Explain why the Framers chose a federal system

The delegates to the 1787 Constitutional Convention in Philadelphia recognized that the system of government established by the Articles of Confederation was failing. Congress did not have the authority to regulate commerce or to raise money by taxing citizens or imports; it could only request revenues from the states. Thus, the nation's debts went unpaid, and its credit was sinking. Moreover, trade barriers erected by states against other states impeded commerce. Something had to be done. If the delegates were not able to fix the problems caused by the Articles, James Madison and others feared that the union could disintegrate.[2]

Benjamin Franklin published this political cartoon in his *Pennsylvania Gazette* on May 9, 1754, shortly after hostilities began in the French and Indian War. The earliest depiction of the need for union among Britain's American colonies, it shows New England as one segment and leaves out Delaware and Georgia altogether. Later, during the Revolution, it was a powerful symbol of American unity.

THE GRANGER COLLECTION, NYC

Why Unify?

Federalism presupposes some form of union, so the answer to the question "why federalism?" first requires an answer to the question "why unify?"

The primary answer to the unification question is that some form of union allows smaller political entities to pool their resources to fight a common enemy. The colonists could not have won the Revolutionary War if they had not banded together to fight the British. Benjamin Franklin published his famous "Join or Die" cartoon to represent the need for the colonists to stick together in military battles in the French and Indian War (1754–63).[3] By the late 1760s, though, the cartoon had come to symbolize the need for united action against British rule. After the Revolution, common threats remained not only from England but also from France and various Native American tribes.

Beyond military necessity, the colonists considered themselves to be part of a common nation with Americans in the other states. A nation is said to exist when people in a country have a sense of common identity due to a common origin, history, or ancestry, all of which the colonists shared. This sense of common identity made some form of union not only a military necessity but also a political advantage. The American people, however, also had strong loyalties to their states, an attachment that would have made eliminating states politically impossible. How strong the national government would be was the subject of heated debate at the Constitutional Convention.

→ KEY QUESTIONS:
Today the people of the United States no longer share a common origin, history, or ancestry. Does it matter?

Confederal, Unitary, and Federal Systems

A **confederal system** had existed under the Articles of Confederation. In a confederal system, independent states grant powers to a national government to rule for the common good in certain limited areas such as defense. The independent states that make up the confederation usually have an equal vote, and the confederation might require unanimous consent or other supermajorities (for example, two-thirds or three-quarters) to pass legislation. The confederal organization usually acts through the states that constitute it rather than acting directly on the citizens of those states.

confederal system: *System of government in which ultimate authority rests with the regional (for example, state) governments.*

But the Framers who met in Philadelphia in 1787 were not inclined to continue the confederal system. A majority of the delegates believed that the New Jersey Plan, which would have strengthened the national government but still granted each state one vote and still required a supermajority to pass most important issues, did not go far enough. They knew that the United States needed a stronger national government.

If a confederal system gives hardly any power to the national government, a **unitary system** of government gives it virtually every power. State or regional governments might still exist under a unitary system, but their powers and, in fact, their very existence, are entirely up to the national government. The authority of a state or regional government in a pure unitary system is similar to the relationship between a state government today and the cities and counties that exist under the state's jurisdiction. Counties can make local decisions, but they exist only because their state established them, and a county has only the authority the state grants to it.

unitary system: *System of government in which ultimate authority rests with the national government.*

A confederal system was too weak for the United States, and an overly strong central government would pose its own set of problems. The Framers particularly feared that too much power in any government could lead to tyranny. Freedom would be better guaranteed by dividing governmental powers, rather than by concentrating them in a central government.

The Framers thus established a new system of government, **federalism**. A federal system, like that of the United States, mixes features of confederal and unitary governments. The Constitution created one legislative chamber chosen by the people and based on population, and another chosen by the states and based on equal representation. Within the states' areas of authority—those areas not granted to the national government—their

federalism: *System of government in which sovereignty is constitutionally divided between national and state governments.*

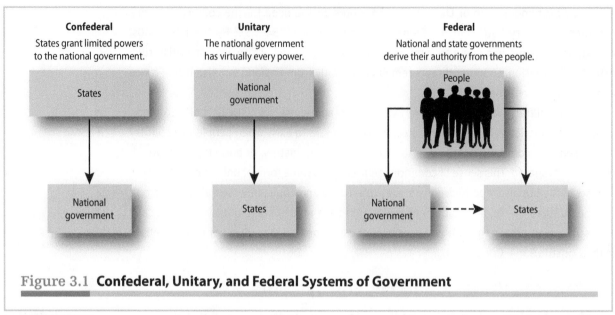

Figure 3.1 Confederal, Unitary, and Federal Systems of Government

decisions are final and cannot be overturned by the national government. Moreover, the existence of states in a federal system does not depend on the national government; rather, the states derive their authority directly from the people. Nevertheless, within areas of authority granted to the national government, or areas of authority shared by the states and the national government, the national government reigns supreme. Political scientist William Riker defines federalism as a system of government in which there exists "a government of the federation [that is, a national government] and a set of governments of the member units [that is, the states] in which both kinds of governments rule over the same territory and people, and each kind has the authority to make some decisions independently of the other" (see Figure 3.1).[4]

A federal system not only reduces the risks of tyranny; it promotes self-government. While any representative democracy involves **self-government**, or government by the people, self-government is enhanced when the decisions that affect the citizens' lives are made by representatives who are local, closer to them, and more similar to them, rather than by representatives who live far away and are dissimilar. Thus self-government is enhanced when people in Massachusetts, to the extent possible, make rules for the people who live in Massachusetts, while people in Texas make rules for the people who live in Texas.

The Framers' choice of a federal system of government was innovative because virtually all of the world's governments at the time were either unitary or confederal. Madison's original Virginia Plan did not propose a pure unitary system—Congress could not eliminate the states. However, by giving Congress a complete veto over laws passed by the states and by granting Congress the general authority to pass laws that would promote "the harmony" of the United States,[5] it would have moved the United States in that direction. The American system was an experiment, and its evolution has been shaped by the tensions, even conflicts, inherent in a system in which power is both divided and shared. Since 1787, about two dozen other nations have ordered themselves as federal systems (see Global Gateways: Federal Political Systems).

→ KEY QUESTIONS:
Which government has the biggest impact on you—the federal government or your state government?

 self-government:
Rule by the people.

→ KEY QUESTIONS:
In addition to federalism, in what other ways was the Constitution of 1787 innovative, even experimental?

Check**point**

CAN YOU:

▪ Explain why the Founders chose to unify

▪ Compare the alternatives to federalism

▪ Consider how we might know if the Framers' experiment with federalism was successful

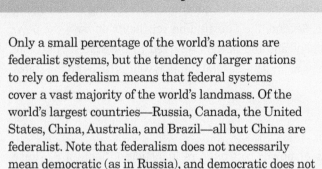

globalgateways

Federal Political Systems

Only a small percentage of the world's nations are federalist systems, but the tendency of larger nations to rely on federalism means that federal systems cover a vast majority of the world's landmass. Of the world's largest countries—Russia, Canada, the United States, China, Australia, and Brazil—all but China are federalist. Note that federalism does not necessarily mean democratic (as in Russia), and democratic does not necessarily mean federalist (as in the United Kingdom).

Within federal political systems, there are many variations. With the recent devolution of power to Scotland, Wales, and Northern Ireland, however, the United Kingdom is not quite as unitary as it once was. Scotland held a vote for independence in September 2014. The UK promised Scotland and other member states greater local authority if Scotland voted to stay in the UK, which it did. India, a multilingual nation, has a federal system with twenty-eight states and seven territories. Its federal system has a stronger national government as compared with the government of the United States, with reserve powers belonging to the national government and the states' powers enumerated. South Africa is another multilingual nation with a federal system.

The constitution divides the country into nine provinces and delegates certain powers to the national government and others to the provincial governments. Unlike the United States, the provinces do not retain reserve powers. Mexico is a federal system with thirty-one states plus a federal district. The Mexican constitution limits the form of those state governments in ways that the U.S. Constitution does not.

Those governing multilingual and multiethnic nations around the globe perceive a greater need to provide the local autonomy that comes with federalism. Sudan, which has seen its southern region secede and become South Sudan, is, along with Iraq, in the process of transitioning toward federalism. These countries hope that providing greater autonomy to different regions will keep the nation from falling apart.

1. Why have certain nations chosen a federal system?
2. Why have most nations not chosen a federal system?

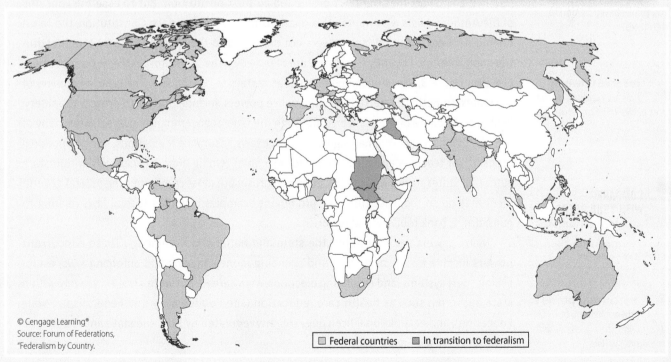

© Cengage Learning®
Source: Forum of Federations, "Federalism by Country.

☐ Federal countries   ☐ In transition to federalism

TITLE IMAGE: © KLETR/SHUTTERSTOCK.COM

3.2 Constitutional Framework

> Summarize how the Constitution institutes the federal system

The Constitution lays the framework of the U.S. federal system in a variety of ways. First, the Constitution grants specified powers to the national government, reserving all remaining powers to the states or the people. Second, the Constitution sets limits on both the powers granted to the federal government and the powers reserved to the states. Third, the Constitution lays out the relationships among the several states as well as between the states and the federal government.

Grants of Power

The Constitution lists the grants of power to Congress in Article I, Section 8. These **enumerated powers** include several powers that could only lie in a national government: raising armies, declaring war, and establishing rules for citizenship. The enumerated powers also grant powers that the central government under the Articles of Confederation did not have, including the power to tax to provide for the general welfare, to borrow money, and to regulate interstate and foreign commerce. To the list of powers in Article I, Section 8, the Framers added one final power that would substantially strengthen the national government: the power to make all laws that are "necessary and proper" for carrying out the enumerated powers.

Although the Antifederalists who opposed the ratification of the Constitution claimed otherwise, this **necessary and proper clause** does not grant Congress the authority to pass any law that it desires. Rather, the clause requires that the law be necessary and proper to one of the listed powers, such as collecting taxes or regulating commerce.

The original Constitution does not list the powers of the state governments, as the states retained all powers that were not prohibited by the Constitution. But to ease the concerns of the Antifederalists who wanted this relationship spelled out in the Constitution, the Tenth Amendment declares that "the powers not delegated to the United States by the Constitution, nor prohibited by it to the States, are reserved to the States respectively, or to the people" (see Figure 3.2 for the amendments that pertain to federalism). The **reserve powers** of the states, sometimes referred to as the police powers, include powers to protect the safety, health, and welfare of their citizens, although the federal government now regulates many of these activities. However, marriage and divorce laws, insurance regulations, and professional licensing (of teachers and electricians, for example) remain almost exclusively within state authority. States have authority to define and prosecute most crimes, but the federal government may do so too, with the most prominent examples including federal laws relating to guns, drugs, bank robbery, and terrorism.

Many powers belong to both the state and national governments. These **concurrent powers** include taxing, borrowing and spending money, making and enforcing laws, establishing court systems, and regulating elections. Many areas that were once exclusively within state authority, such as health care, education (see Public Policy and Federalism: Public Education), and occupational licensing, are now regulated by both the state and the federal governments (see Figure 3.3).

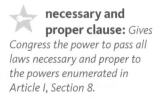

enumerated powers: *Powers expressly granted to Congress by the Constitution.*

necessary and proper clause: *Gives Congress the power to pass all laws necessary and proper to the powers enumerated in Article I, Section 8.*

→ KEY QUESTIONS:
Are there any state powers you think the federal government should have? Are there any federal powers you think should belong to the states?

reserve powers: *Powers retained by the states under the Constitution.*

COMPARE WITH YOUR PEERS
MindTap for American Government

Access the Federalism Forum: Polling Activity—State Income Tax.

concurrent powers: *Powers held by both the national and state governments in a federal system.*

Figure 3.2 Constitutional Amendments That Pertain to Federalism

Color Code: Criminal procedure Participation Equality Structure Miscellaneous

Fifth	1791	Affirms the right to indictment by a grand jury and right to due process; protects against double jeopardy, self-incrimination, and taking of property without just compensation
Tenth	1791	Reserves the powers not granted to the national government to the states or to the people
Eleventh	1798	Prevents citizens from one state from suing another state in federal court
Thirteenth	1865	Prohibits slavery in the United States
Fourteenth	1868	Makes all persons born in the United States citizens of the United States and prohibits states from denying persons within its jurisdiction the privileges or immunities of citizens, the due process of law, and equal protection of the laws; apportionment by whole persons
Fifteenth	1870	Prohibits states from denying the right to vote on account of race
Sixteenth	1913	Grants Congress the power to tax income derived from any source
Seventeenth	1913	Gives the people (instead of state legislatures) the right to choose U.S. senators directly

© CENGAGE LEARNING®

Limits on Power

The Constitution grants only specified powers to the national government, but even those powers are limited. The Constitution prohibits Congress from suspending the writ of *habeas corpus*, the right of individuals who have been arrested and jailed to go before a judge who determines whether their imprisonment is legal. The Constitution also bars the passage of any law that declares an individual guilty of a crime (a bill of attainder) and any law that makes an act illegal after the fact (an *ex post facto* law).

Following concerns expressed by Antifederalists during the state ratification debates that the proposed Constitution granted the national government too much power, one of the first

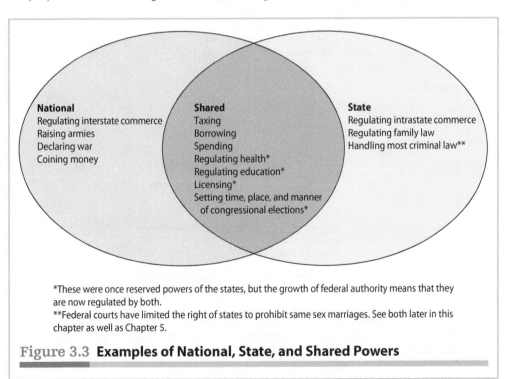

National
Regulating interstate commerce
Raising armies
Declaring war
Coining money

Shared
Taxing
Borrowing
Spending
Regulating health*
Regulating education*
Licensing*
Setting time, place, and manner
   of congressional elections*

State
Regulating intrastate commerce
Regulating family law
Handling most criminal law**

*These were once reserved powers of the states, but the growth of federal authority means that they are now regulated by both.
**Federal courts have limited the right of states to prohibit same sex marriages. See both later in this chapter as well as Chapter 5.

Figure 3.3 Examples of National, State, and Shared Powers

© CENGAGE LEARNING®

Public Policy and Federalism:
Public Education

Despite the fact that federally elected politicians talk frequently about the importance of education, the federal government itself funds about 12 percent of all elementary and secondary education spending.[6] The primary reason for this minimal funding is the federal structure. With education among the reserved powers left to the states, state and local governments developed the responsibility for educating the populace. Originally, states set education policy that local communities then implemented through locally elected school boards.[7] Depending on the state, local school boards had differing amounts of power to establish the curriculum, support extracurricular activities, hire and fire teachers, negotiate salaries for school district employees, and set standards for graduation. Over time, funding for elementary and secondary education became based on local property taxes, with some additional assistance from state governments. Just as the overall wealth of local communities and states varies, so does the amount of funding available for education.

The federal government has intervened in public education for two main reasons: to overcome the denial of equality of educational opportunity by the states and to improve the quality of education. The Supreme Court has struck down segregated schools for black students in *Brown v. The Board of Education*[8] and for Mexican Americans in *Cisneros v. Corpus Christi*[9]; however, despite these legal restrictions on segregation, many African American and Latino students continue to attend schools that are predominantly minority as shown by Figure 3.4.

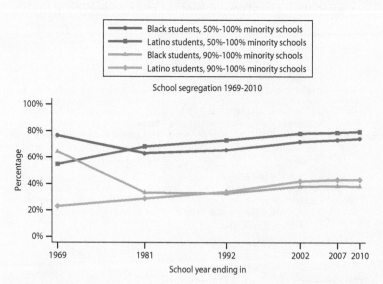

Figure 3.4 **Percent of African American and Latino Students Attending Highly Segregated Schools 1969-2010**

The percent of African American students attending highly segregated schools (greater than 90 percent minority) dropped sharply between 1969 and 1981 but has slowly risen since then. The percent of Latino students attending highly segregated schools has been increasing as well. That number is now greater for Latino students than for African American students.

Source: Adapted from Gary Orfield, John Kucsera, and Genevieve Siegel-Hawley, "E Pluribus Separation," 2012, The Civil Rights Project. Available at http://civilrightsproject.ucla.edu/research/k-12-education/integration-and-diversity/mlk-national/e-pluribus...separation-deepening-double-segregation-for-more-students/orfield_epluribus_revised_omplete_2012.pdf.

Today the federal government has numerous programs to provide equal access to education across income level, race, and level of disability. These programs are under the jurisdiction of a variety of agencies. For example, the Department of Health and Human Services (HHS) oversees the Head Start and Early Head Start programs for low-income children, while the Department of Education has programs for homeless children, remedial education programs for disadvantaged children, and programs for children with disabilities under the Individuals with Disabilities Education Act.

The federal government has also intervened to improve the quality of education. Congress originally played almost no role in public school (K–12) education, but its role increased after World War II. In 1958, it passed the National Defense Education Act, which provided grant money for increased math and science education in elementary and secondary schools. In 1965, Congress passed the Elementary and Secondary Education Act and the Higher Education Act. Each of these programs widened the gateway of access to quality education by increasing federal responsibility to fund specific programs ranging from remedial reading and writing for elementary school children to subsidized loan programs for students in college and graduate school.

Presidents have also initiated educational programs. No Child Left Behind, President George W. Bush's effort in this area, tried to impose stricter performance and accountability standards for education. President Barack Obama, while seeking to set higher standards for the No Child Left Behind program, in 2012 granted partial or full waivers to thirty-three states to give them more flexibility in achieving goals.[10] His administration has also supported the "common core," a controversial program that ties some federal spending to states that move toward a national curriculum and greater use of student testing.

States were persuaded into adopting these common standards as part of Obama's Race to the Top initiative, which allowed states to apply for extra federal funds for education provided that they agreed to adopt these standards. Of the fifty states, forty-six applied to compete for the federal funds under the Race to the Top program.[11] President Obama's 2014 budget contains $750 million for states that strengthen their early learning systems through preschool expansion or other mechanisms.[12]

Despite the stronger federal role, however, education under a federal system still permits inequality by allowing a vast disparity in how much states and local communities choose to spend on it.

> ## Construct Your Own Policy

1. Draft a federal law that would equalize funding for elementary and secondary education within states and across states. Be sure to state the role of the federal government in implementing this change in education funding.
2. Draft legislation that would design national universities directly funded by the federal government in order to improve access to higher education for more students.

orders of business for the First Congress was a proposed bill of rights. The first ten amendments to the Constitution created associational freedoms (speech, press, assembly, and religion) that Congress could not abridge; limited the authority of governmental prosecutions against alleged criminals by restricting searches and seizures and guaranteeing the right to counsel and to public trials; and protected certain additional rights, including the right to bear arms and the right to jury trials in civil suits over $20 (see Chapter 4, Civil Liberties, for more details on these rights). The Bill of Rights originally applied only to the national government, not to the states.

The Constitution contains its own set of limits on the state governments. Like the national government, states cannot pass bills of attainder or *ex post facto* laws or create titles of nobility. Moreover, states cannot coin money or enter into treaties or alliances with foreign nations. The Constitution also limits the authority of states to tax imports and exports.

direct democracy:
Form of democracy in which political power is exercised directly by citizens.

The guarantee clause of the Constitution (Article IV, Section 4) guarantees that states shall have a "Republican Form of Government," meaning that a state cannot establish a pure **direct democracy** (although New England towns sometimes run along these lines), a monarchy, or a dictatorship (here the term *republican* has nothing to do with the Republican Party but refers to representative democracy). In *Federalist* 39, Madison defined a republican form of government as one that "derives all its powers directly or indirectly from the great body of the people; and is administered by persons holding their offices during pleasure, for a limited period, or during good behavior."[13] That is, as long as the people who run the government are selected directly (as in the House of Representatives) or indirectly (as in the Electoral College) by the people, and those officeholders either have limited terms of office (as do the president and members of Congress) or can be removed for not meeting the standards of "good behavior" (as in the judiciary), the government can be considered republican.

The Fourteenth (1868) and Fifteenth Amendments (1870) limit state authority further. The Fourteenth Amendment prohibits the states from denying "any person" due process of law and the equal protection of the laws, and the Fifteenth Amendment prohibits states from denying voting rights on account of race, color, or previous condition of servitude. The Supreme Court later used the due process clause of the Fourteenth Amendment to require the states to follow most of the provisions of the Bill of Rights (see Chapter 4). Thus states must protect the same liberties as the federal government does, resulting in a nationalizing of the country's most basic rights. Both the Supreme Court and Congress have used the Fifteenth Amendment to protect equal voting rights in the states and the equal protection clause of the Fourteenth Amendment to protect other civil rights (see Chapter 5, Civil Rights).

Groundwork for Relationships

In the U.S. federal system, where both the states and the federal governments have the final say over different matters, the Constitution lays out the powers of the national government and restrictions on the powers of both the national and the state governments. In addition, it lays out the groundwork for the relationship between the national government and the state governments and for relationships among the state governments.

supremacy clause:
Makes federal law supreme over state laws (Article VI).

Relationships between the Nation and the States. The Constitution regulates the relationship between the national government and the states through three main clauses: the supremacy clause, the Tenth Amendment, and the sovereign immunity provision of the Eleventh Amendment. The **supremacy clause** (Article VI) makes the Constitution of the United

States, plus all laws and treaties made under the Constitution, supreme over state law. Thus, if federal law conflicts with state law, the federal law (assuming it is within the powers of Congress) is supreme. Moreover, because state and federal courts might differ about whether state law and federal law actually conflict in a particular case, the ultimate decision rests with the U.S. Supreme Court.[14]

National unity can be difficult to obtain. While soccer riots are usually fought by fans of different nations, here Montenegro fans fight among themselves.

As noted earlier, the Tenth Amendment states that all powers not delegated to the national government under the Constitution are reserved to the states or to the people. The Articles of Confederation had a similar clause, but it included the word *expressly* before the word *delegated*. Because the Tenth Amendment omits the word *expressly*, the implication is that the national government retains the sort of **implied powers** granted by the necessary and proper clause.

★ **implied powers:** *Powers not expressly granted to Congress but added through the necessary and proper clause.*

If the government illegally harms an individual or seizes the person's property, that person might be inclined to sue the government. The doctrine of sovereign immunity, however, means that a government cannot be sued without its permission. In a federal system with both state and federal courts, however, a state can prevent suits against itself in its own courts simply by passing a law preventing such suits. It cannot necessarily prevent lawsuits against it in federal court. Thus, in 1793, the Supreme Court allowed the lawsuit of a South Carolina man against the state of Georgia.[15] Following this decision, Congress proposed and the states quickly ratified the Eleventh Amendment, which prohibits federal courts from hearing suits against a state by citizens of another state. The Eleventh Amendment is not absolute: Congress can allow suits based on provisions in constitutional amendments passed after the Eleventh, such as the due process and equal protection clauses of the Fourteenth Amendment.

★ **commerce clause:** *Gives Congress the power to regulate commerce with foreign nations, with Indian tribes, and among the various states (Article I, Section 8).*

Relationships among the States. One of the many problems of governance under the Articles of Confederation was that the states could establish trade barriers against one another, thus limiting economic growth. Therefore, in the **commerce clause** (Article I, Section 8), the Constitution established Congress's exclusive authority to regulate commerce among the states. Thus states may not establish trade barriers against goods from other states. A state may tax goods from other states equal to the amount that it taxes goods produced in its own state, but it cannot charge extra taxes on goods that are made out of state. Congress cannot establish trade barriers in interstate commerce either because Article I, Section 9, prohibits Congress from taxing exports from any state.

The Constitution also requires agreements between two or more states to receive the approval of Congress. States that share rivers, lakes, or other natural resources frequently

Same-sex marriage is a contentious issue related to federalism. Regulating family law has been a state power, and some states have approved same-sex marriage. The federal Defense of Marriage Act affirms that neither the United States nor other states have to recognize these marriages. But in 2013, the Supreme Court ruled that the United States must recognize lawfully performed same-sex marriages.

→ KEY QUESTIONS:
Should all states be required to recognize same-sex marriages that are valid in one state?

→ KEY QUESTIONS:
Should out-of-state students pay higher tuition at state universities? Why?

make agreements over the use of their shared resources so that no one state overuses or overpollutes those resources.[16]

Article IV of the Constitution establishes additional rules that guide relationships among the states. The full faith and credit clause generally requires states to accept court decisions made in other states. What happens in Vegas does not necessarily stay in Vegas, as couples who are married (or divorced) there, are married (or divorced) throughout the United States. This seemingly simple constitutional rule is now controversial, as some states have recognized same-sex marriages as valid. Under the full faith and credit clause, same-sex marriage performed in Massachusetts would presumably be valid throughout the nation. But the clause allows Congress to create exceptions. Congress passed and President William Jefferson (Bill) Clinton (1993–2001) signed one such exception into law with the Defense of Marriage Act (1996), which relieves the federal government and the states of the obligation of accepting the validity of same-sex marriages performed in other states. President Barack Obama, however, believing the law unconstitutional, in 2011 ordered the Justice Department not to defend it. In 2013, the Supreme Court declared that the provision of the Act that prevented the federal government from recognizing same-sex marriages legally performed in other states unconstitutional.[17] While the United States must recognize such marriages, the Supreme Court has not yet ruled on whether one state must accept same-sex marriages performed in another state. In 2014, a federal judge in Kentucky, however, has decided that while Kentucky could continue its ban on same-sex marriage, the state did have to recognize same-sex marriages performed in other states.[18] Similar decisions have also been handed down in Ohio, Tennessee, and Oregon.[19]

Through its privileges and immunities clause, Article IV also requires states to treat people from other states as equal to their own residents. Thus a state may not limit the right to practice law to residents, nor may it require people to live in the state for a set amount of time to receive welfare benefits. The courts, however, have allowed certain exceptions to this constitutional guarantee, the most notable being the higher tuition that out-of-state residents pay at state universities.

Checkpoint

CAN YOU:

- ◾ Describe the different types of powers in the Constitution
- ◾ State the limits on powers established in the Constitution
- ◾ Explain how the Constitution helps set the relationship between the national and federal governments

3.3 The Changing Nature of American Federalism

> ❯ Outline how U.S. federalism has changed over time

The ratification of the Constitution pitted the state-centered Antifederalists against the nation-centered Federalists, and pro-state and pro-nation interests have contested the relative balance between the two ever since. Because a federal system presupposes separate states with guaranteed rights, tension between the layers of government is built in and inevitable. People who believe in relatively more national power contend that the national government does not derive its powers from the states, but from the people. They cite as evidence the statement in the Preamble that the Constitution was established by "We, the People of the United States." Others believe in greater state power, a view that considers the national government to be an agreement by thirteen independent states (the original colonies) to delegate certain limited powers that they had held to a national government.

From the origins of a two-party system during George Washington's presidency (1789–97) through the expansion of national authority over health care under Barack Obama, politicians and citizens have fought over the proper role of the national and state governments. Different eras show a dominance of one view over the other, but even when one side dominates, the other side pushes back. The nation began with a period of nationalization that lasted until around 1835, followed by the movement toward secession and civil war. Following the Civil War, the states and the federal government had clearly separate powers. In the era following the Great Depression and the election of Franklin Delano Roosevelt (1933–45) in 1932, national power grew enormously, only to retreat slightly following the election of Richard M. Nixon (1969–74) in 1968.

Nationalization in the Founding Generation (approximately 1789–1832)

In the 1789 and 1792 elections, the Electoral College unanimously elected George Washington as president. Washington did not run as the candidate of any political party, and his administration had no organized opposition. Within his administration, however, divisions over the extent of the authority of the national government split Secretary of the Treasury Alexander Hamilton and his allies from Secretary of State Thomas Jefferson and his allies. Hamilton favored a nation-centered federalism. He sought expansive federal power, and in 1790 proposed that Congress establish the National Bank of the United States under a broad reading of the necessary and proper clause. Jefferson, who favored a state-centered federalism, unsuccessfully opposed the bank, which Congress created with a twenty-year charter. Jefferson's allies, however, were able to limit Hamilton's plan to promote manufacturing.

The debate over national authority to establish a bank resurfaced after the first National Bank charter expired, and Congress chartered a Second National Bank. The Supreme Court resolved this issue in **McCulloch v. Maryland** (1819) in an opinion written by Federalist Chief Justice John Marshall.[20] Marshall stated that Congress had the explicit authority to coin money and collect taxes and declared that the creation of a bank helped reach those goals. Thus creating a bank was an implied power that fell within the scope of authority granted by the necessary and proper clause (see Supreme Court Cases: *McCulloch v. Maryland*).

McCulloch v. Maryland: *1819 Supreme Court decision upholding the right of Congress to create a bank.*

Five years later, the Court, in another opinion by Marshall, established a broad construction, or interpretation, of Congress's enumerated power to regulate interstate commerce. In *Gibbons v. Ogden* (1824), the Court ruled that Congress's authority to regulate commerce among the states gave it, rather than the states, the authority to manage the licensing of steamboats traveling between New York and New Jersey. Marshall further declared that the authority of Congress to regulate commerce between the states did not begin or end at state boundaries but necessarily included commercial activities interior to each state.[21] Between the decisions in *McCulloch* and *Gibbons*, the Supreme Court under Marshall supported the Federalist Party position of a strong national government with expansive powers.

The Revolt against National Authority: Nullification, Slavery, and the Civil War (approximately 1832–65)

As Marshall's Supreme Court pushed the United States in a national direction, the precedent set by the Virginia and Kentucky Resolutions led some states to claim the right to disregard national laws that they believed were unconstitutional or merely unwise. Several New

supreme court cases

McCulloch v. Maryland (1819)

QUESTION: May the federal government establish a bank? If so, does a state have the right to tax that bank?

ORAL ARGUMENT: February 22, 1819

DECISION: March 6, 1819 (read at http://www.law.cornell.edu/supremecourt/text/17/316)

OUTCOME: Yes, the bank is constitutional, and no, Maryland may not tax it (6–0).

Following the decision of Congress to establish the Second National Bank, the state of Maryland imposed a tax on the Maryland branch. The bank manager, James McCulloch, refused to pay the tax, and Maryland brought suit. The Maryland Supreme Court ruled that the bank was unconstitutional because the Constitution does not grant Congress the specific authority to create a bank. McCulloch appealed to the Supreme Court.

Attorney Daniel Webster, who had served in the House and would later serve in the Senate and as secretary of state, represented McCulloch before the Supreme Court. Among the most famed litigators of his day, Webster also represented the nationalist position before the Supreme Court in a District of Columbia lottery case and a New York steamboat case.*

The Supreme Court's decision, written by Chief Justice John Marshall, began by accepting the nation-centered view of the Constitution's founding: Rather than a compact of states, the government established by the Constitution "proceeds directly from the people; is 'ordained and established,' in the name of the people."

Regarding the power to establish a bank, Marshall noted that while the Constitution makes no reference to a bank, it does provide for coining and borrowing money, paying government debts, and levying taxes. It also allows Congress to pass all laws that are "necessary and proper" to any of the enumerated powers. Declaring

that "necessary and proper" does not mean "absolutely necessary," Marshall read the necessary and proper clause to mean "ordinary and appropriate."

In explaining the scope of the necessary and proper clause, Marshall declared, "Let the end be legitimate, let it be within the scope of the Constitution, and all means which are appropriate, which are plainly adapted to that end, which are not prohibited, but consist with the letter and spirit of the Constitution, are constitutional." Thus, creating a bank was an appropriate means of legitimate ends: regulating money and collecting taxes.

As for state taxation of the bank, Marshall based his response on the supremacy clause, observing that "the power to tax involves the power to destroy." Because states cannot destroy creations of the federal government, neither can they tax them.

The *McCulloch* decision created a broad scope for implied powers under the Constitution—powers that are not explicitly in the Constitution but are related to powers that are. Without this broad set of implied powers, Congress could not establish criminal laws for most offenses, investigate executive wrongdoing, provide student loans, establish administrative agencies, or conduct many of the other activities it routinely engages in today.

1. If Congress does not have the express authority to establish a national bank, by what authority may it do so?

2. What is the harm to federalism if a state can tax a national bank?

* *Gibbons v. Ogden*, 22 U.S. 1 (1824).

England states threatened to ignore the Embargo Act of 1807, and, in 1828, Vice President John C. Calhoun insisted on South Carolina's right to nullify a federal tariff. As the union was merely a compact among the states, Calhoun argued, dissenting states even had the right to **secede**. Against such claims, Senator Daniel Webster insisted that the union was not a compact of states, but a compact among the people of the United States.

secede: *To formally withdraw from a nation-state.*

Because nothing in the Constitution suggested that Congress had the power to limit slavery in the states, the most heated contests over congressional authority to regulate slavery involved the territories. This debate split abolitionists who wanted to ban slavery in the territories, states' rights supporters such as John C. Calhoun who thought that slave owners had the right to take their slaves into any territory, and those who favored compromises that would allow slavery in some territories but not in others. In 1857, the Supreme Court sided with the states' rights supporters, declaring in *Dred Scott v. Sandford* that Congress had no authority to regulate slavery in the territories (see Chapter 5).[22]

When Abraham Lincoln (1861–65), who favored federal efforts to prohibit slavery in the territories, won the presidential election of 1860, South Carolina seceded. Virtually every grievance listed by South Carolina involved slavery.[23] Other southern states followed, with most noting the question of slavery,[24] and they soon established their own constitution.

During the Civil War, Lincoln used his power as commander in chief to issue the Emancipation Proclamation, which prohibited slavery in states under rebellion, as slave labor was an asset to the Confederate army. Slaves in some of these states were not emancipated until ratification of the Thirteenth Amendment, which prohibited slavery throughout the nation as of December 18, 1865.

The Congresses that followed the Civil War tried to exert federal power over the states to promote equality between freedmen and whites, but President Andrew Johnson (1865–69) vetoed a civil rights bill, claiming it represented a trend toward "centralization and the concentration of all legislative power in the National Government."[25] The bill granted former slaves the rights to make contracts; sue; give evidence; and inherit, purchase, lease, and convey real and personal property. In 1866, Congress passed it over Johnson's veto. But as part of the effort to ensure that all such laws would be constitutional, Congress proposed and the states ratified the Fourteenth Amendment (1868) and the Fifteenth Amendment (1870). These greatly expanded the authority of the national government over the states. The Fourteenth Amendment requires states to provide each person due process of law (see Chapter 4) and the equal protection of the laws (see Chapter 5). The Fifteenth Amendment prevents states from abridging the right to vote on account of race. Like the Thirteenth Amendment, the Fourteenth and Fifteenth Amendments granted Congress the authority to enforce their provisions by appropriate legislation, thus adding to Congress's enumerated powers.

In 1883, however, the Supreme Court decided in the *Civil Rights Cases* to keep Congress's powers within the words of the amendments: Congress could prevent states from denying people equality, but it could not prevent private businesses or individuals from doing so, for example, by refusing to hire former slaves or to serve them at inns or restaurants. The Court thus invalidated Congress's Civil Rights Act of 1875, which had prohibited this type of private discrimination. This era, covering the period before and after the Civil War, saw the defeat of the most strident (secessionist) state-centered views, but with the Supreme Court's interpretation of the Civil War amendments, state authority remained strong.

Layer cake

Marble cake

Figure 3.5 Dual Federalism and Cooperative Federalism

Dual federalism has been likened to a layer cake (left), and cooperative federalism has been likened to a marble cake (right).

dual federalism: *Doctrine holding that state governments and the federal government have almost completely separate functions.*

Dual Federalism (approximately 1865–1932)

Although the supporters of state-centered federalism lost the Civil War, the viewpoint of a national government with limited powers did not disappear. A new viewpoint, **dual federalism**, recognized that while the national government was supreme in some spheres, the state governments remained supreme in others, with layers of authority separate from one another; political scientists later compared this arrangement to a "layer cake"[26] (see Figure 3.5). Thus the national government would be supreme over issues such as foreign affairs and interstate commerce, and the states would be supreme in matters concerning intrastate commerce and police powers.

In 1913, Congress passed and the states ratified the Sixteenth Amendment, which granted Congress the power to tax income from whatever source derived, giving the national government access to millions (and later billions and even trillions) of dollars in revenue. The increase in federal authority over areas once left to the states was aided that same year by the ratification of the Seventeenth Amendment, which took the selection of U.S. senators out of the hands of state legislatures and required that they be directly elected by the people of each state. Before 1914, state legislatures hoped senators would be responsive to the needs of the states, but with direct elections, senators had to be responsive to the needs of the people.[27]

Cooperative Federalism: The New Deal and Civil Rights (approximately 1932–69)

With the onset of the Great Depression following the stock market crash of 1929, the people wanted national action to aid the economy, and the nation-centered federalism signaled by the Sixteenth and Seventeenth Amendments strengthened considerably the ability to be responsive to those wishes. In 1932, voters elected Franklin Roosevelt as president. During his campaign, Roosevelt had promised a "New Deal" to Americans who had lost their jobs, their homes, and their savings. Following Roosevelt's inauguration, Congress passed a series of laws designed to lift the ailing economy. As before, Congress asserted its authority under the commerce clause to regulate American industry. As before, the Supreme Court rejected such legislation, claiming in one case that the mining of coal by a company with operations in several states was production and not interstate commerce.[28]

Court-packing plan: *President Franklin Roosevelt's proposal to add new justices to the Supreme Court so that the Court would uphold his policies.*

Despite vast support from Congress and the American people for his New Deal policies, Roosevelt saw the Supreme Court strike down one law after another, often by 5–4 or 6–3 votes. In response, Roosevelt proposed in 1937 to increase the number of justices on the Supreme Court. He would then be able to pack the Court with his own appointees. This controversial **Court-packing plan** met with fierce opposition in Congress. The Supreme Court, however, made passage of the plan unnecessary, for shortly after Roosevelt's proposal, the Court reversed itself and started accepting the broad authority of Congress to regulate the economy.

On taxing and spending, the Court accepted the view that virtually any taxing or spending plan that Congress believed supported the general welfare would be acceptable.

On commerce, the Court began by accepting the regulation of a giant steel company with operations throughout the United States as an appropriate regulation of interstate commerce.[29] Congress could also use the commerce clause to regulate employment conditions, said the Court, rejecting the Tenth Amendment as a limit on federal power.[30] The Court's definition of what constituted interstate commerce grew to include anything that affected interstate commerce, whether over several states or confined to one state. Roosevelt's nation-centered federalism was said by political scientists to more closely resemble a "marble cake," with specific powers under both national and state authority, than the layer-cake structure of dual federalism.[31]

Nation-centered federalism continued to dominate dual federalism through World War II and beyond. President Lyndon Baines Johnson's (1963–69) Great Society program expanded national authority even further, with federal aid to public schools—traditionally a state duty—and health care coverage to the poor (Medicaid) and elderly (Medicare). The Johnson administration gave money to the states for its programs through categorical grants—money for the states to use on what the national government wanted.

The Johnson administration also expanded national power to ensure greater equality, pushing for passage of the Civil Rights Act (1964), which prohibited job discrimination and segregation in public accommodations, and the Voting Rights Act (1965), which regulated voting rules that had largely been left to the states since the adoption of the Constitution (see Chapter 5).

State-centered federalism gained some traction, though, in opposition to the push toward equality and civil rights. In 1954 in *Brown v. Board of Education*, the Supreme Court struck down school segregation, which had been legally mandated or permitted in twenty states plus the District of Columbia. This Supreme Court decision helped put the federal government at the forefront of the fight for equality.

The New Federalism (approximately 1969–93)

In one of the last challenges to integration, segregationist Governor George Wallace of Alabama ran for president in 1968. His party, the American Independent Party, condemned what it considered to be the unconstitutional use of federal power to desegregate schools and enforce voting rights.[32] Wallace received more than 9 million votes and won the electoral votes of five states. Although Wallace ultimately lost the race, the strength of his campaign signaled a degree of wariness among voters about the powers of the national government. Other politicians, starting with Richard Nixon, the winner of the 1968 election, responded to these concerns.[33]

Presidents, Congress, and the New Federalism.   The Nixon administration began the trend, labeled New Federalism, of shifting powers back to the states.[34] The Nixon administration began a general revenue-sharing program that gave the states greater leeway about how the funds could be spent. The main idea behind Nixon's federalism was that states could more efficiently spend governmental resources than the enormous federal bureaucracy could.

Republican President Ronald Reagan (1981–89) sought to reduce the power of government in general and, as an avid supporter of the New Federalism, of the federal government

→ KEY QUESTIONS:
Why do citizens look to the federal government in times of crisis?

→ KEY QUESTIONS:
Was the Johnson administration right to use federal power to ensure equality?

→ KEY QUESTIONS:
Was Reagan right in stating that "government is the problem"?

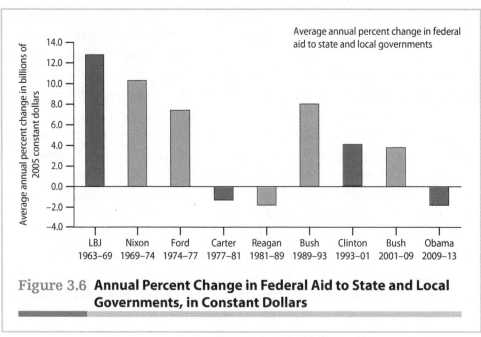

Figure 3.6 **Annual Percent Change in Federal Aid to State and Local Governments, in Constant Dollars**

Source: Derived by authors from the White House, Office of Management and Budget, Historical Tables, Table 12.1, accessed April 5, 2014, http://www.whitehouse.gov/omb/budget/historicals. The data for Obama appear low due to the stimulus spending by George W. Bush in the 2008 fiscal year.

in particular. In his first inaugural address, he declared, "Government is not the solution to our problem; government is the problem."[35] He thus cut back on categorical grants, replacing them with fewer, more flexible block grants, which set fewer restrictions on how the money could be spent. He also eliminated federal aid to state and local governments (see Figure 3.6). Nevertheless, Reagan did sign the National Minimum Drinking Age Act, which withheld a percentage of federal highway funds from states that did not increase their drinking age to 21.

The Modern Era (1993–present). During President Bill Clinton's administration, Congress moved to shift the balance of power toward the states in several ways. First, it limited unfunded mandates—legal requirements Congress imposes on the states (for example, to provide clean air, disability access, or health benefits to poor people under Medicaid) without supplying the resources to accomplish those activities. Congress did not eliminate such mandates, but it did make them harder to impose. Second, Clinton and Congress overhauled the federal welfare system, ending the federal guarantee of welfare to poor families with children, leaving final say on welfare spending with the states. Third, Congress abandoned national speed limits that had been established at the time of the 1973 Arab oil embargo and allowed states to set whatever speed limits they desired.

Although Republicans have typically supported state authority over that of the national government since the New Deal, President George W. Bush (2001–09) oversaw an administration that strengthened national authority, sometimes at the expense of the states.[36] His most prominent actions in this regard included the No Child Left Behind Act (2002), which increased federal involvement in public education, and his prescription drug plan for Medicare, which increased federal involvement in health care.[37]

Following the terrorist attacks of September 11, 2001, Congress and the Bush administration expanded national power in various ways, including the establishment of national standards for driver's licenses and new powers to monitor electronic communications.

On the other hand, the Obama administration has endorsed state-centered federalism, at least where the policies support Democratic Party positions: support for permitting states to set higher standards than the federal government on fuel economy and tailpipe emissions and a reversal of the Bush administration's crackdown on state medical marijuana programs.[38] The Obama Administration is choosing not to use federal authority to prosecute people in Colorado and Washington who legally, under the state laws thereof, use marijuana for recreational or medical purposes. In supporting national policies, President Obama has reminded Americans of the historic relationship between federalism and the oppression of minority rights in the United States.

The Supreme Court and the New Federalism.

By nominating William Rehnquist to be chief justice in 1986, Reagan hoped to move the Court toward state-centered federalism. He was not disappointed. As an associate justice (1972–86), Rehnquist had pressed, often alone on the Court, for what the Supreme Court once labeled "Our Federalism."[39] As chief justice (1986–2005), he further advanced New Federalism, now aided by a Republican bloc that grew to include seven justices. The Rehnquist Court put together pro-state majorities in decisions involving interstate commerce and sovereign immunity.

When terrorists hijacked planes and crashed them into the World Trade Center Towers in New York City on September 11, 2001, most Americans said their lives changed forever. As with all national crises, following the terrorist attacks, the national government took a greater share of power because only the national government can protect against foreign adversaries. On October 26, 2001, President George W. Bush signed the USA PATRIOT Act, which granted the federal government increased powers over financial transactions, immigration, and domestic criminal activity.

Concerning interstate commerce, for the first time since 1937, the Court rejected national laws as beyond Congress's authority to regulate under the commerce clause. In one case, the Court struck down congressional legislation banning the possession of guns near schools, declaring that the possession of a gun near a school is not an economic activity.[40] Similarly, the Court rejected a central provision of the Violence Against Women Act, which gave victims of gender-based violence the right to sue their attackers in federal court. A Virginia Tech student who had allegedly been raped by members of the football team sued her attacker and Virginia Tech, a state university, in federal court after the state chose not to bring criminal charges. The Court rejected congressional findings on the effect of such violence on commerce, and it ruled that the section of the act that allowed the lawsuits was beyond Congress's authority either under the commerce clause or under its authority to enforce the equal protection of the laws under the Fourteenth Amendment.

Although these decisions stand in contrast to the decidedly pro-national decisions of the Court since the New Deal, most questions of federal authority still are decided in favor of the national government. The Court allowed Congress to condition highway funds on states having a drinking age of 21, as the small amount of funds at risk (5 percent) made the condition a "pressure" to comply and not a "compulsion."[41] And while it did not allow Congress to take away all federal Medicaid dollars for states rejecting the growth in Medicaid under the Affordable Care Act, it did allow Congress to keep states that rejected the expansion from receiving any new Medicaid money under the Act.[42] The Court also affirmed that Congress

→ KEY QUESTIONS:
Do you tend to support nation-centered federalism or state-centered federalism? Which is more responsive? Which ensures citizen equality?

→ KEY QUESTIONS:
Should guns be allowed in or near schools and college campuses? Who should decide?

CONNECT WITH YOUR CLASSMATES
MindTap° for American Government

Access the Federalism Forum: Discussion—Patient Protection and Affordable Care Act.

can criminalize home-grown marijuana production and use even if state law allows it for medical purposes.[43] (Nevertheless, the Obama administration used its discretion not to prosecute such cases when state laws allow such use for medicinal purposes.) Indeed, the Supreme Court continues to uphold Congress's authority to regulate commercial activity.

And while the Roberts Court (2005–present) did not uphold the health care law on commerce grounds, it did uphold the law through the taxing clause, thus allowing the further nationalization of health care policy in the United States.[44]

Summing Up: Were the Antifederalists Correct?

The people of the United States ratified the Constitution over the protests of Antifederalists, who claimed that the Constitution gave virtually unlimited powers to the national government. Nevertheless, until the New Deal, either because of congressional inaction or Supreme Court reaction when Congress did act, the powers exercised by the national government were clearly limited. Today, however, due to the popular belief in the need to regulate a complex economy, the historical role that states' rights advocates have played in supporting slavery and segregation, and the Supreme Court's interpretation of the Constitution, Congress has vast powers. The fact that Congress can spend money on virtually anything as long as it is not specifically prohibited by the Constitution, and that the "necessary and proper clause means "ordinary and appropriate" leads to the conclusion that as far as the powers of the national government are concerned, the Antifederalists were correct: The federal government's powers have few limits. However, in 2013, a majority of Americans reported that they thought the federal government had too much power (see Figure 3.7). In the 2014 midterm congressional elections, voters were again asked to choose between candidates of two parties with very different views about the balance of the nation-state relationship. Thus in the U.S. federal system, the voters get to decide on that balance.

→ KEY QUESTIONS:
Were the Antifederalists right to fear the power of the national government?

Checkpoint

CAN YOU:

- Describe the role that federalism played in the run-up to the Civil War
- Explain the "layer-cake" analogy in dual federalism
- Compare dual federalism with cooperative federalism
- Explain what led to the New Federalism
- Find Antifederalist arguments in today's political debates

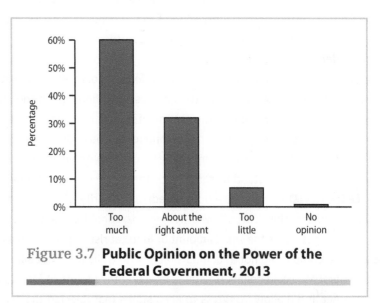

Figure 3.7 Public Opinion on the Power of the Federal Government, 2013

Source: Gallup Poll, September 2013, retrieved April 5, 2014, from the iPOLL Databank, The Roper Center for Public Opinion Research, University of Connecticut.

3.4 State and Local Governments

> Compare and contrast national and state governments

The Constitution requires that the states maintain a republican form of government, and all have done so by patterning their structure after the national government, with separate legislative, judicial, and executive branches. With the exception of procedures that allow citizens to place proposed laws directly on the ballot, state governments look remarkably similar to the federal government. Local governments, however, use a greater range of organizational options.

State Executive Branches

All fifty states choose the head of the executive branch by direct election. Most states have four-year gubernatorial terms, limit their governors to two consecutive terms, and provide for succession by the lieutenant governor.

The governors of all fifty states have the authority to veto laws subject to override by the state legislatures. Most states further grant their governors a line-item veto, the ability to veto certain parts of a spending bill without vetoing the entire bill. The president does not have this power, so when Congress passes spending bills, it usually does so by combining tens of thousands of separate spending items in an omnibus bill. The president's choice is to sign the entire bill or to veto it; he cannot veto only the appropriations he disfavors. Governors in forty-four states do have that authority, however, giving them a much stronger tool to control spending than the president has. Every state except Vermont requires a balanced budget. Unlike the federal government, which can borrow money to pay for spending programs, typically popular spending increases in the states have to be matched by typically unpopular tax increases.

The Twenty-Second Amendment (ratified in 1947) limits the president of the United States to two terms in office. Similarly, thirty-five states limit governors to two terms, Virginia limits governors to one consecutive term, and fourteen states allow unlimited terms.

→ KEY QUESTIONS:
What would happen if the president had a line-item veto?

State Legislative Branches

On the legislative side, forty-nine of the fifty states have bicameral (two-chamber) legislative branches; Nebraska has only a single chamber. Nebraska also has nonpartisan elections, meaning that candidates for election are not listed under a party banner. Most states have four-year terms for their upper chambers and two-year terms for their lower chambers.

State Judicial Branches

The greatest differences between the national and the state governments appear at the judicial level. Federal judges are nominated by the president and confirmed by the Senate. States have various procedures for selecting judges: Nearly half use an appointment process for judges on their highest court, while the rest use elections. For states that use appointments, most grant the governor the right to make appointments (usually with the consent of the state senate).

→ KEY QUESTIONS:
What effects do judicial elections have on judges' decisions? What effects should they have?

The New England town meeting, like this one in Strong, Maine, is an example of direct democracy at the local level. New England town meetings allow residents to vote directly on budgets and taxes without the election of representatives as intermediaries.

Local Governments

Local governments are far more diverse in function and design than state governments. First, there can be several different layers of local governments, with residents regulated by villages, cities, and towns or townships at the most local level and by counties above that. Some local governments run all local services, including police, schools, and sanitation. Many states, however, delegate specialized activities to special jurisdiction governments, such as school boards, water districts, fire districts, library districts, and sewer districts. The United States contains more than 38,000 special jurisdiction governments plus another 13,000 school boards. Overall, there are nearly 90,000 governmental units in the United States[45] providing hundreds of thousands of citizens a ready gateway for citizen involvement in public affairs, as Brian Maughan's story illustrates at the beginning of this chapter.

Second, local governments, unlike state governments, do not necessarily consist of three separate branches. One reason is that criminal and civil trials are usually handled in state courts, leaving little need for a local community to have its own judicial branch. Many local governments have elected leaders of the executive branch—mayors for villages and cities, county executives for counties, and supervisors for townships—but many use a city-manager system in which the legislative branch appoints a professional administrator to run the executive branch.

Direct Democracy

People also possess the ability to govern. Direct gateways to democracy in American federalism include the use of recall, initiatives, and referendums (see Figure 3.8). Recall allows citizens who gather enough petition signatures to force a special vote to remove state or

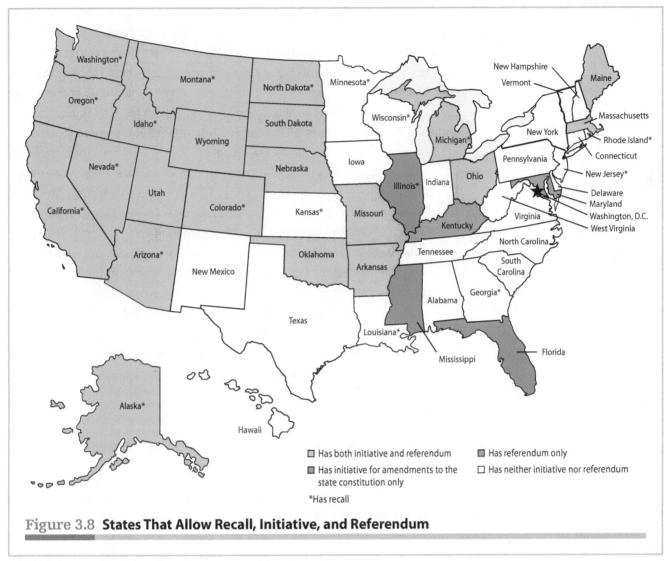

Figure 3.8 States That Allow Recall, Initiative, and Referendum

Legend:
- ☐ Has both initiative and referendum
- ■ Has initiative for amendments to the state constitution only
- ■ Has referendum only
- ☐ Has neither initiative nor referendum
- *Has recall

Source: © Cengage Learning®; data from Council of State Governments, *The Book of the States,* 2013.

local elected officials before their terms expire. Permitted in eighteen states, recall allowed a recall in Arizona of State Senator Russell Peirce, notably the author of SB 1070, the anti-immigration legislation.[46] Wisconsin voters in 2012 reconsidered the tenure of Governor Scott Walker, who had supported legislation that severely curtailed the collective bargaining rights of public employees. Walker won.

Initiative is a process that allows citizens who collect the required number of petition signatures to place proposed laws directly on the ballot for the state's citizens to vote on. Referendum allows legislatures to put certain issues on the ballot for citizen approval and requires legislatures to seek citizen approval for certain actions. Depending on the state, these actions could be proposals to borrow money, increase taxes, or approve constitutional amendments. All fifty states require referenda on some issues. Only twenty-four states allow initiatives.[47] Both procedures enable well-organized citizens to bypass the elected representatives in their state. The U.S. Constitution, in setting specific terms for senators, representatives, and presidents, prohibits recall of federal officials, and in granting all legislative powers to Congress, similarly prohibits initiative and referendum at the national level.

> → **KEY QUESTIONS:**
> The last time you voted, were there any initiatives or referenda on the ballot? Did you know enough about them to make an informed choice?

The number and importance of initiatives have grown in more recent years. In 2008, California voters passed Proposition 8, which banned same-sex marriages in the state. The Supreme Court later upheld a lower court decision striking down that initiative and restoring the right to same-sex marriage in California.[48] Since then, thirty-four states have enacted same-sex marriage (see Chapter 5). In 2014, voters in Alaska, Oregon, and Washington D.C. approved initiatives legalizing recreational use of marijuana, while voters in Alaska ($9.75), Arkansas ($8.50), Illinois ($10.00), Nebraska ($9.00) and South Dakota ($8.50) approved increases in the minimum wage above the federal rate of $7.25 to the amounts in parentheses.[49]

Direct democracy is not without its critics. As are other aspects of American government, initiatives are heavily influenced by money. Although socialists and populists originally pushed for direct democracy to expand the influence of ordinary citizens, the cost of gathering enough signatures to get on the ballot means that initiatives are limited largely to those with great financial resources. For example, almost $4 million was spent in the successful fight to legalize marijuana in Colorado, with 80 percent spent by pro-legalization groups. One group supporting legalization raised almost $1.3 million while the largest opponent raised $433,000.[50] Additionally, opposed doctors and insurance groups have already pledged to spend more than $30 million to defeat the medical malpractice reform initiative that will be on California's ballot in 2014.[51]

Checkpoint

CAN YOU:

- Compare the general features of state governments to their national counterparts
- Compare the features of local governments to their national counterparts
- Weigh the advantages and disadvantages of direct democracy

Federalism and Democracy

A federal system has more gateways than a confederal or unitary system. In confederal systems, citizens can influence their local governments, but there is little value in influencing the national government given its limited scope. Alternatively, in unitary systems, the national level has a lot of authority, but citizens cannot work their way through more localized structures to influence it. Federal systems create multiple gateways. However, they also make it less clear who is responsible if policies are not well run. If health care falters, for example, is that the fault of the national government or the state government?

Under a unitary system, there is little doubt about who is responsible if a policy fails. A unitary system also means that diverse state laws are replaced with one set of laws on issues such as medical marijuana, gay marriage, divorce, and gun control. Given that Americans have different views on these issues, the strength of a federal system is that it allows people in, say, Arizona, to live under laws created by other people in Arizona, rather than by people throughout the United States. Citizens in states with conservative majorities can obtain conservative government by electing conservative representatives, and citizens in states with liberal majorities can elect liberal representatives.

A unitary system also increases so-called conformity costs by increasing the number of people who disagree with the policies of the government. Conformity costs are not financial; they represent the dissatisfaction that people feel when they live under laws they do not like. Consider medical marijuana, for example. Under a unitary system, the nation would have a single set of medical marijuana laws. Either medical marijuana supporters or opponents would not get their way, regardless of local public opinion. With federalism, each state gets to choose for itself whether to allow the use of medical marijuana. Federalism does not eliminate conformity costs, but it does lower them. Overall, federalism allows the people who live in the most conservative states to have local rules that favor conservative values, and those who live in the most liberal states to choose local rules that favor liberal values. These citizens can also obtain results they desire through direct governing procedures such as the initiative and referendum. Although initiative procedures presumably provide for greater democratic responsiveness than does filtering preferences through elected representatives, initiatives may be too responsive to citizen desires. Madison, although not referring to the initiative itself, feared direct democracy, believing that citizens were prone to factions that would put self-interest over the best interests of society. Thus, Madison and the Framers preferred a large-scale republic over local democracies, fearful that local majorities would infringe the rights of local minorities (see *Federalist* 10 in the Appendix).

One disadvantage of federalism in the United States has been that people opposed to equality for blacks have used arguments about states' rights to protect slavery and limit civil rights. Alternatively, the nation-centric view of federalism has been used to create a more equal society for minorities subject to discrimination.

Overall, though, federalism enhances democracy by enabling more people to live under laws that are made locally, rather than forcing everyone in the nation to live under all of the same rules. State experiments with direct democracy procedures such as the initiative and referendum give citizens a gateway to influence that they do not have with the national government.

Master the Concept
of Federalism with MindTap™ for American Government

 REVIEW MindTap™ **for American Government**
Access Key Term Flashcards for Chapter 3.

 STAY CURRENT MindTap™ **for American Government**
Access the KnowNow blog and customized RSS for updates on current events.

 TEST YOURSELF MindTap™ **for American Government**
Take the Wrap It Up Quiz for Chapter 3.

 STAY FOCUSED MindTap™ **for American Government**
Complete the Focus Activities for Federalism.

 # Key Concepts

commerce clause (p. 69). How has the Supreme Court's interpretation of the commerce clause changed over time?

concurrent powers (p. 64). Why do concurrent powers exist?

confederal system (p. 61). What are the likely problems of confederal systems?

Court-packing plan (p. 74). How would this plan have impacted the independence of the judiciary?

direct democracy (p. 68). What forms of direct democracy exist in the United States?

dual federalism (p. 74). Can dual federalism work in a modern nation?

enumerated powers (p. 64). Why are Congress's powers enumerated?

federalism (p. 61). What type of nation is more likely to adopt a federal system?

implied powers (p. 69). What are some examples of implied powers?

McCulloch v. Maryland (p. 71). Does Congress need to establish a national bank?

necessary and proper clause (p. 64). How has the Supreme Court interpreted "necessary and proper"?

reserve powers (p. 64). What does it mean that states have reserve powers?

secession (p. 73). Should there ever be a right to secede from a national government?

self-government (p. 62). If you were to rank personal liberties, where would you rank self-government?

supremacy clause (p. 68). What would happen to the U.S. constitutional system without the supremacy clause?

unitary system (p. 61). What is the effect of unitary systems on gateways to participation?

Learning Outcomes: What You Need . . .

To Know	To Test Yourself	To Participate
▶ **Explain why the Framers chose a federal system**		
In writing a new Constitution in 1787, the Framers established a new system of government—federalism—in which state and national governments share power.	• Explain why the Founders chose to unify. • Compare the alternatives to federalism.	• Appreciate why you are a citizen of the nation and of a state.
▶ **Summarize how the Constitution institutes the federal system**		
The Constitution grants specified powers to the national government, reserving all remaining powers to the states and to the people. It also limits both federal and state powers and lays out the relationships among the states and between the states and the federal government.	• Describe the different types of powers in the Constitution. • State the limits on powers established in the Constitution. • Explain how the Constitution helps set the relationship between the national and federal governments.	• Propose additional limits that you would like to see on governmental power.
▶ **Outline how U.S. federalism has changed over time**		
The American system was an experiment, and its evolution has been shaped by the tensions, even conflicts, inherent in a system in which power is both divided and shared. From the beginning, nation- and state-centered interests have been pitted against each other. One recurring substantive theme in the federalism debate has involved slavery, race, and equality, with nation-centered federalism used generally to advance equality for minorities subject to discrimination. Over the years, nation-centered federalism has generally expanded through legislation and court interpretation, although there have been eras in which the Court held Congress back, and elections in which the people indicated that they thought the national government had too much power.	• Describe the role that federalism played in the run-up to the Civil War. • Explain the "layer cake" analogy in dual federalism. • Compare dual federalism with cooperative federalism. • Explain what led to the New Federalism. • Find Antifederalist arguments in today's political debates.	• Evaluate whether the federal government is too powerful. • Detect friction in your community between state and federal powers. • Decide whether the Antifederalists were correct.
▶ **Compare and contrast national and state governments**		
All fifty states have separate legislative, executive, and judicial branches that look remarkably similar to those of the federal government, while local governments use a greater range of organizational options. The structure of the federal system has a profound effect on public policy, allowing states to learn from each other but sometimes forcing them into competition with each other. The federal system also allows for vast disparities among the states, particularly in the quality of elementary and secondary education. Benefits of federalism include multiple gateways to influence, including methods of direct democracy such as the initiative and referendum. Federalism also enhances democracy by enabling more people to live under laws that are made locally, rather than forcing nationwide conformity.	• Compare the general features of state governments to their national counterparts. • Compare the features of local governments to their national counterparts. • Weigh the advantages and disadvantages of direct democracy.	• Lobby a state representative on a state issue that is important to you. • Lobby a local official on a local issue that is important to you. • Draft a referendum you would like to see your state vote on.

"My greatest regret is that rather than believing in myself, I allowed someone else's opinion to postpone my dreams."

R. STEPHANIE GOOD
Stony Brook University,
Stony Brook, New York

4

Civil Liberties

R. Stephanie Good started her college career later in life than many people, waiting until she was in her mid-thirties before enrolling first at Nassau Community College on Long Island in New York and then at nearby Stony Brook University. She graduated from both schools with highest honors, but she was as well known for her political activism as she was for her academic excellence. During her college years, she campaigned for public officials, demonstrated on behalf of environmental issues, and got arrested at Stony Brook as part of a "tent-city" protest over housing for graduate students. Committed to the idea that justice is served only when citizens take action on their own behalf, she went on to law school, earning a law degree at Hofstra University and, ten years later, a master's degree in law.

While practicing law, Good started writing. Her first book, *Law School 101,* presents survival techniques for law school and life as an attorney. Her next two books (both coauthored) uncovered corruption in notorious criminal proceedings. *Aruba: The Tragic Untold Story of Natalee Holloway and Corruption in Paradise*, a *New York Times* best seller, recounts the disappearance and presumed murder of a high school student on a school graduation trip. *A Rush to Injustice* tells the story of the Duke University lacrosse case, in which a reelection-seeking prosecutor maliciously filed felony sexual assault charges against college students whom he knew were innocent.

Good's commitment to protection of the innocent was also personal. When she was in law school, she learned that one of her sons had been subjected to inappropriate solicitations by an instructor at their local church. After she went public about this violation, other families revealed inappropriate touching by the instructor. Yet the judicial system did not consider the matter to be serious, and the instructor received only a fifteen-day sentence. Years later, when Good thought the instructor might be seeking out her son again, she decided to go online to try to find boys who also received unwarranted attention from the instructor, creating a fictitious 13-year-old girl with the AOL handle "teen2hot4u." That handle attracted interest from adult men interested in sex with an underage girl. Good then contacted the Federal

Need to Know

4.1 Identify what civil liberties are

4.2 Explain why civil liberties are limited in times of crisis

4.3 Distinguish what rights of expression the First Amendment protects

4.4 Determine what religious freedoms the First Amendment protects

4.5 Outline how the "right to bear arms" has been interpreted

4.6 Describe what protections the Bill of Rights provides to those accused of crimes

4.7 Assess what constitutes the right to privacy

 WATCH & LEARN MindTap™ for American Government

Watch a brief "What Do You Know?" video summarizing Civil Liberties.

Bureau of Investigation (FBI), which asked her to continue to play out her undercover role. Agents schooled Good on how to avoid violating the rights of the people with whom she communicated because although they may have been intent on breaking laws regarding the molestation of children, their rights as citizens also had to be protected, including their right to fair legal proceedings and their right to be considered legally innocent until proven guilty. First, she could not initiate conversations with anyone. Second, she could not be the first person to mention sex. And third, she could not be the first person to suggest a meeting. Despite these restrictions, teen-2hot4u attracted the attention of hundreds of men, more than twenty of whom tried to arrange a sexual meeting, got arrested, and then, with Good's testimony, were convicted and sentenced to prison. Good's efforts literally saved hundreds of young children from having their lives ruined. She recounted the story in her fourth book, *Exposed: The Harrowing Story of a Mother's Undercover Work with the FBI to Save Children from Internet Sex Predators*. Congressman Tim Bishop (D-N.Y.) awarded Good a certificate of commendation for her work.

In a democracy, criminal investigations must be conducted in a way that protects both the victims and society and those who are accused of crimes. Reprehensible crimes, such as sexual abuse of children, test people's willingness to recognize the rights of the accused. Yet without standard and fair criminal proceedings, citizens would be subjected to arbitrary arrest and possibly punishment, as the Duke lacrosse case shows. The tensions surrounding freedom and fair treatment in a democracy extend beyond criminal procedure. Disagreements about politics, particularly during wartime, also test people's willingness to tolerate differences in opinion. Even in peacetime, the tension between liberty, the desire to say or do what one wants, and order, the need for rules necessary for society to function, divide society. Americans want their homes to be secure against police intrusions, but they also want the police to be able to find evidence of crimes committed by others. They want freedom to follow their personal religious beliefs, but they do not want illegal practices to be allowed just because one religion might endorse them. In this chapter, we examine the balance and tension between liberty and order, with particular attention to the liberties guaranteed in the U.S. Constitution.

4.1 What Are Civil Liberties?

> Identify what civil liberties are

In 1787, the most powerful argument of the Antifederalists against the proposed constitution was that it did not protect fundamental liberties. The Antifederalist declared that these liberties, including the rights of conscience and the right of accused criminals to hear the charges against them, needed to be explicitly stated.[1] As we saw in Chapter 2, The Constitution, the Federalists eventually agreed and, to secure ratification of the Constitution, promised to amend it immediately.

Civil Liberties and Civil Rights

The **civil liberties** that were then written into the Constitution as the first ten amendments, or **Bill of Rights**, were freedoms that Americans held to be so fundamental that government may not legitimately take them away. This placed into law some of the **natural** or **unalienable rights** that Thomas Jefferson spoke about in the Declaration of Independence. These include, among others, freedom of speech and religious belief. As Supreme Court justice, Robert Jackson wrote in a 1943 case striking down a mandatory flag salute for school children that the government has no authority whatsoever over what we say or think. "If there is any fixed star in our constitutional constellation, it is that no official, high or petty, can prescribe what shall be orthodox in politics, nationalism, religion, or other

civil liberties: *Those rights, such as freedom of speech and religion, that are so fundamental that they are outside the authority of government to regulate.*

Bill of Rights: *First ten amendments to the Constitution, which provide basic political rights.*

natural (unalienable) rights: *Rights that every individual has and that government cannot legitimately take away.*

 LISTEN & LEARN
MindTap® **for American Government**

Access Read Speaker to listen to Chapter 4.

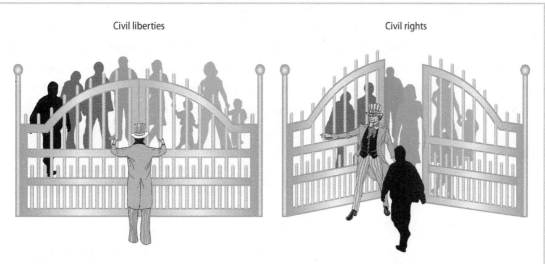

Figure 4.1 Distinction between Civil Liberties and Civil Rights

Civil liberties provide a gate or barrier that protects people against interference by the government in fundamental liberties, such as freedom of speech or religion. Civil rights often require active involvement of the government in opening gateways to full civic participation by all, regardless of race, gender, or religion.

© CENGAGE LEARNING®

matters of opinion or force citizens to confess by word or act their faith therein."[2] Civil *liberties* are outside government's authority to regulate, whereas civil *rights* are rights that government is obliged to protect (see Figure 4.1). These are based on the expectation of equality under the law and relate to the duties of citizenship and to opportunities for full participation in civic life. Civil rights are the subject of the next chapter.

Balancing Liberty and Order

The protection of civil liberties requires a governmental system designed to do so. James Madison argued in *Federalist* 10 (see the Appendix) that a representative democracy will be able to keep a minority from violating the rights of others but may not be able to hold back a majority. Thus if a majority wishes to infringe on rights, it often falls to the judiciary, which is not designed to be responsive to public desires, to protect those rights.[3] In this way, the system of separation of powers and of checks and balances would help ensure the rights of all.

While maximizing individual liberty might seem like a great idea, complete liberty could lead to a breakdown of order. As Supreme Court Justice Oliver Wendell Holmes wrote in a World War I speech case, freedom of speech does not mean that an individual has the right to falsely shout "Fire!" in a crowded theater and cause a panic.[4] Nor can liberty completely protect people from police investigations when criminal activity is suspected. Too much freedom can lead to anarchy, a state in which everyone does as he or she chooses without regard to others. Alternatively, too much order can lead to tyranny, a state in which the people are not free to make decisions about the private aspects of their lives. Protecting civil liberties thus requires a balance between individual liberty and public order.

The freedom obtained through civil liberties can conflict not only with order but also with equality. In fact, civil liberties and civil rights sometimes conflict with each other. For

→ **KEY QUESTIONS:**
Why aren't civil liberties subject to majority rule?

→ **KEY QUESTIONS:**
Which is more important to you, liberty or order?

→ KEY QUESTIONS:
Which is more important to you, liberty or equality?

example, civil rights laws that forbid businesses to refuse to serve customers because of their race limit freedom of association and infringe on property rights. Efforts at colleges to create an equal environment for all students have led to speech codes that restrict what students can say on campus. Society must decide how to strike such balances, and often that decision is a difficult one. In the case of businesses serving all customers, the nation, through its elected representatives in Congress, decided that the restriction on liberty was well worth the gain in equality. In the case of campus speech codes, students have successfully pressured many universities to rescind speech codes, and where the universities have kept the codes, students have used the gateway of the judicial system to bring lawsuits against their schools. The courts have consistently ruled that speech codes violate the First Amendment.

Constitutional Rights

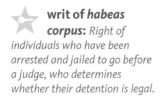

writ of *habeas corpus*: *Right of individuals who have been arrested and jailed to go before a judge, who determines whether their detention is legal.*

The main sources of civil liberties are the Constitution and the Bill of Rights. The articles of the Constitution protect the right to a **writ of *habeas corpus*,** the right of individuals to be brought before a judge to have the legality of their imprisonment determined. It also prohibits *ex post facto* laws, which make an act a crime after the act is committed, and bills of attainder, legislative acts that declare individuals guilty of a crime. The Constitution also guarantees the right to a trial by jury.

The Bill of Rights, ratified in 1791, protects additional rights, such as freedom of expression, the right to keep and bear arms, and criminal procedure (see Figure 4.2). We will examine each in detail later in the chapter.

The Bill of Rights and the States

incorporate: *Process of applying provisions of the Bill of Rights to the states.*

As originally written, the Bill of Rights limited the activities of the national government, not the state governments. Only at the end of the nineteenth century did the Supreme Court slowly begin to apply, or **incorporate**, the provisions of the Bill of Rights to the states.

Figure 4.2 **Constitutional Amendments That Pertain to Civil Liberties**

Color Code: Criminal procedure   Participation   Equality   Structure   Miscellaneous

First	1791	Prohibits abridging freedoms of religion, speech, press, assembly, and petition
Second	1791	Prohibits abridging the right to bear arms
Third	1791	Prohibits the involuntary quartering of soldiers in a person's home during peacetime
Fourth	1791	Prohibits unreasonable searches and seizures
Fifth	1791	Affirms the right to indictment by a grand jury and right to due process; protects against double jeopardy, self-incrimination, and taking of property without just compensation
Sixth	1791	Affirms rights to speedy and public trial, to confront witnesses, and to counsel
Seventh	1791	Affirms right to jury trials in civil suits over $20
Eighth	1791	Prohibits excessive bail, excessive fines, and cruel and unusual punishments
Ninth	1791	Declares that the enumeration of certain rights does not limit other rights retained by the people
Tenth	1791	Reserves the powers not granted to the national government to the states or to the people
Fourteenth	1868	Makes all persons born in the United States citizens of the United States and prohibits states from denying persons within its jurisdiction the privileges or immunities of citizens, the due process of law, and equal protection of the laws; apportionment by whole persons

© CENGAGE LEARNING®

The First Amendment is explicit about its application to the national government as it forbids certain actions by Congress. But other amendments are not explicitly tied to the national government. Thus the Fifth Amendment prohibits taking private property without just compensation. Was this a protection of citizens only against actions by the federal government or against their state governments as well?

The original answer, given by the Supreme Court in *Barron v. Baltimore* (1833), was that the Bill of Rights applied to the national government only. Under the *Barron* decision, state governments could abridge freedom of speech, the press, and religion; could conduct unreasonable searches and seizures; and more without violating the Constitution. State constitutions might protect such rights, but often they did not.

The Fourteenth Amendment (1868), which adds several restrictions on what the states can do, became a vehicle for the applications of the Bill of Rights to the states. One section declares, "No State shall make or enforce any law which shall abridge the privileges or immunities of citizens of the United States; nor shall any State deprive any person of life, liberty, or property, without due process of law." Some of those who wrote this amendment stated that one of its purposes was to overturn the *Barron v. Baltimore* decision and make the entire Bill of Rights applicable to the states.[5]

The Supreme Court never agreed with this position, known as total incorporation. But beginning in 1897, it slowly began to use the protection of "life, liberty, or property" in the Fourteenth Amendment's due process clause to incorporate some of the provisions of the Bill of Rights as binding on the states. In the 1897 case, the Court used this clause to hold that states could not deprive a railroad of its property without just compensation, a right similarly protected by the Fifth Amendment.[6] In 1925, the Court assumed that the protection of liberty in the due process clause prevented states from restricting freedom of speech, a right similarly protected by the First Amendment.[7] By 1937, the Court had settled on a process of **selective incorporation**, using the due process clause to bind the states to those provisions of the Bill of Rights that it deems to be fundamental rights.[8] This process helps equalize the protection of rights across the United States.

Today, almost all of the provisions of the First, Second, Fourth, Fifth, Sixth, and Eighth Amendments have been incorporated, with the exception of grand jury indictment and excessive fines (see Table 4.1). Thus, states can indict people, or bring them up on charges, through

→ KEY QUESTIONS:
Which government are citizens more likely to need a gate against—national or state?

selective incorporation: *Doctrine used by the Supreme Court to make those provisions of the Bill of Rights that are fundamental rights binding on the states.*

Table 4.1 Incorporated and Not Incorporated Provisions of the First through Eighth Amendments

Amendment	Provisions Incorporated	Provisions Not Incorporated
First	Religion, speech, press, assembly, petition	
Second	Keep and bear arms	
Third		Quarter soldiers
Fourth	No unreasonable searches and seizures	
Fifth	Double jeopardy, self-incrimination, due process, taking of property without just compensation	Grand jury indictment
Sixth	Speedy and public trial, right to confront witnesses, right to counsel	
Seventh		Jury trials in civil suits over $20
Eighth	Cruel and unusual punishments, excessive bail	Excessive fines

Source: © Cengage Learning®

compelling interest test: *Standard frequently used by the Supreme Court in civil liberties cases to determine whether a state has a compelling interest for infringing on a right and whether the law is narrowly drawn to meet that interest.*

Checkpoint

CAN YOU:

- Compare civil liberties to civil rights
- Contrast the problems of too much freedom to those of too much order
- Compare the importance of the rights in the 1787 Constitution with those in the Bill of Rights
- State the extent and the limits of the original Bill of Rights

the decision of judges, though charges in federal courts need the approval of a grand jury, a special jury whose sole duty is to determine whether an individual should be put on trial. The Third Amendment's protection against the quartering of soldiers in one's home during peacetime, a practice that angered the colonists, has not been incorporated but is not likely to be used today. Nor are states required, as the Seventh Amendment commands, to provide jury trials in civil suits over $20.

Once incorporated, the Court needs to determine whether that right has been violated. Generally speaking, rather than rule on each case purely on its own, the Court adopts a test to guide its decision and applies the test to the case at hand to determine whether a particular limitation of rights is acceptable. For the political rights in the Bill of Rights, such as freedom of speech, the Court most commonly uses variations of the **compelling interest test**. Under the compelling interest test, the federal government or a state can limit rights only if the Supreme Court decides that (1) the government has a compelling interest in passing the law (for example, the law is necessary for the functioning of government), and (2) the law is narrowly drawn to meet that interest. For example, the government might have a compelling interest in banning speech that might incite religious wars, but such a law would have to be narrowly drawn so as not to prevent religious speech that merely calls for struggle against oppression. However, even with such a precise definition, individuals have fought over what constitutes a compelling interest throughout American history.

→ KEY QUESTIONS:
What civil liberties are you willing to give up to ensure more protection against terrorist attacks?

4.2 Civil Liberties in Times of Crisis

> Explain why civil liberties are limited in times of crisis

Attempts to limit civil liberties are more frequent in wartime or when other threats arise as a result of the government's increased concern for order and citizens' increased concerns about security. This pattern has existed from the earliest days of the republic; it continued during the Civil War, the two world wars, and the Cold War, and following the terrorist attacks of September 11, 2001. Popular support for civil liberties usually rebounds after the crisis ends.

→ KEY QUESTIONS:
How free should you be to criticize the government? Should you be less free in wartime? Following 9/11?

The World Wars

During World War I, Congress passed the Espionage Act of 1917, which made it a crime to obstruct military recruiting, and amendments known as the Sedition Act of 1918, which banned "disloyal, profane, scurrilous or abusive language" about the Constitution or the government of the United States, as well as speech that interfered with the war effort. Subsequently, juries convicted antiwar activist Charles Schenck for circulating a flyer to draftees that compared the draft to the involuntary servitude prohibited by the Thirteenth Amendment, and Socialist Party presidential candidate Eugene V. Debs for giving a speech criticizing the war. The Supreme Court upheld both convictions, noting that greater restrictions on speech could be allowed in wartime.[9] After the war, Congress repealed the Sedition

→ KEY QUESTIONS:
Should enemy combatants have the same procedural safeguards as American citizens? What if the enemy combatant is an American citizen?

Act, and President Warren G. Harding (1921–23) pardoned Debs. In no subsequent wars has the government restricted speech as it did with the Sedition Acts of 1798 and 1918.

The War on Terror

After 9/11, Congress passed the USA PATRIOT Act. The act allowed greater sharing of intelligence information and enhancement of law enforcement's ability to tap telephone and e-mail communications. It also regulated financial transactions with overseas entities and eased the process of deporting immigrants suspected of terrorist activities. Beyond the act, President George W. Bush (2001–2009) claimed the right, as commander in chief, to detain alleged enemy combatants indefinitely, whether U.S. citizens or foreign nationals. Thus Bush declared Jose Padilla, an American allegedly involved in a plan to detonate a radioactive bomb in the United States, an "enemy combatant" and transferred him from civilian to military authority, where he would have few, if any, procedural rights. The government kept Padilla in complete isolation for more than three and a half years. Unique among those declared enemy combatants, Padilla had not been captured on the field of battle but on American soil, and, having been born in Brooklyn, he was an American citizen.

When the Supreme Court ruled that noncitizens could not be held indefinitely as enemy combatants, it became clear that the government could not hold Padilla either. So, the Justice Department removed Padilla from military custody and charged him under federal criminal law with providing material support to terrorist organizations. The government did not charge him with attempting to detonate a radioactive bomb in the United States or with conspiring to commit terrorist acts in the United States, suggesting that the original claims against him might not have held up in a court of law. His trial in Miami, with the full set of constitutional rights, required that Padilla be represented by counsel, that he be allowed to cross-examine witnesses, and that the government prove its case beyond a reasonable doubt. The government proved its case, and a jury quickly determined that Padilla was guilty. The judge then sentenced him to seventeen years in prison.

Although fewer rights exist for enemy combatants who are not U.S. citizens,[10] the Supreme Court has ruled that Congress must authorize hearings to determine the legality of the detention of even foreign enemy combatants. Such hearings must be consistent with the 1949 Geneva Conventions, an international treaty that protects the rights of prisoners of war.[11]

Beyond the enemy combatant cases, President Bush and President Obama have ordered warrantless wiretapping of conversations and interception of e-mail between American citizens and suspected foreign terrorists; normally, wiretapping requires a warrant signed by a judge or magistrate backed by probable cause that a crime is being committed. (See Public Policy and Civil Liberties: National Security Surveillance.)

BETTMANN/CORBIS

Speaking in Canton, Ohio, on June 16, 1918, Eugene V. Debs, labor organizer and three-time Socialist Party candidate for president, criticized the government for restricting free speech during wartime and declared, "If war is right let it be declared by the people." Charged with sedition, he was convicted and sentenced to prison. While in jail, he ran for president once again and received more than 900,000 votes, about 3.4 percent of all votes cast.

→ KEY QUESTIONS:
Should government have access to your phone calls and e-mail messages?

→ KEY QUESTIONS:
Should the United States obey the Geneva Conventions?

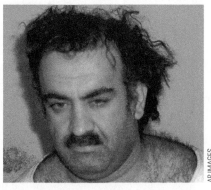

AP IMAGES

This widely circulated photograph of Khalid Sheikh Mohammed was taken on March 1, 2003, shortly after his capture during a raid in Pakistan. He is accused of masterminding the September 11, 2001, terrorist attacks on the United States and is being held at Guantanamo Bay, Cuba, awaiting trial. Local opposition prevented the Obama administration from trying him in an open criminal trial, with full legal rights, just blocks from the site of the World Trade Center attacks.

Public Policy and Civil Liberties:
National Security Surveillance

As President Obama has noted, protection against terrorist threats requires some restrictions on liberty and privacy. Though many people think of the CIA as the main intelligence agency in the United States, it is the National Security Agency (NSA) that conducts virtually all of the security-related electronic surveillance for the government, such as listening to phone calls and reading e-mails. In 1978, Congress passed the Foreign Intelligence Surveillance Act (FISA). The Act established secret FISA Courts to determine whether the United States could authorize the NSA to conduct national security wiretaps within the United States. The judges on that court are all appointed by the chief justice of the United States from among the U.S. District Courts without confirmation by the Senate. Prior to the 9/11 attacks in 2001, the FISA courts had never denied a government request for electronic surveillance.[12]

Just six weeks after the 9/11 attacks on the United States, Congress overwhelmingly passed the USA PATRIOT Act. The Act expanded the surveillance capabilities of the United States in several ways: It granted the NSA new authority to monitor e-mail, and it allowed a single warrant to cover all phones that a suspect might use.[13] President Bush ordered warrantless wiretapping (by the NSA) of conversations and interception of e-mail between American citizens and suspected foreign terrorists. Congress did endorse aspects of the president's plan after the *New York Times* published stories about the then-secret program. The program expired, but the Obama administration moved—on national security grounds—to block a lawsuit over the wiretapping brought by an Islamic charity alleged to be involved in terrorist activities.[14] In 2012, a 9th Circuit Court of Appeals panel overturned a district court ruling that the program was illegal and blocked damages claimed by the Al-Haramain Islamic Foundation.[15]

Then in 2013, Edward Snowden, a former employee of the NSA, stole and leaked tens of thousands of documents that he had access to. Those documents revealed that the NSA kept track of every phone call made in the United States, regardless of whether there was any evidence of suspicious activity. These records tracked who called whom and when, but they did not record conversations. The NSA believed that such records could help it uncover information to aid in preventing terrorist attacks.

Many Americans were outraged at what they felt to be a violation of their right to privacy. Yet the 1979 Supreme Court case *Smith v. Maryland* seemed to uphold the constitutionality of the government's warrantless use of "pen registers," devices that kept track of who called whom when without recording the conversations. Smith had robbed a woman and then began calling her. With a lead from a license plate, the police placed the pen register on Smith's phone to prove that he had been calling the robbery victim. The fact that the Court upheld the use of pen registers suggests that the NSA program is constitutional.[16] President Obama additionally defended the program by stating, "You can't have 100% security and then have 100% privacy and zero inconvenience. You know, we're going to have to make some choices as a society."[17]

Nevertheless, a lower court judge ruled that the ability of the government to obtain these records *en masse* made the violation far more serious than the individual record keeping from

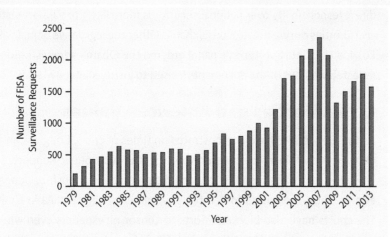

Figure 4.3 Annual Number of FISA Surveillance Requests

Note: The number of rejected surveillance applications are as follows: 2003 (4), 2006 (1), 2007 (4), 2008 (1), 2009 (1). In all other years, the number of rejected surveillance applications was 0.

Source: Adapted from the source material here: http://epic.org/privacy/wiretap/stats/fisa_stats.html

the 1979 case. The case against the NSA may become moot, however, because President Obama called for an end to the NSA's bulk collection of data in March 2014.[18] Yet, the issue may reemerge in the future until it is resolved in court.

The NSA has also filed individualized surveillance requests as shown in Figure 4.3. Between 2002 and 2012, the court rejected only eleven of nearly twenty thousand surveillance applications, about 0.05 percent.[19] Part of the reason for this is that the objects of the surveillance obviously do not get to provide evidence to counter the government's position. The director of the Administrative Office of the U.S. Courts has proposed a special advocate to promote the public's privacy interests in any particular case.[20] The ACLU filed suit against the NSA, but federal courts ruled that without evidence proving they were wiretapped, they didn't have standing to sue.

Following the 9/11 attacks, public opinion shifted strongly toward governmental efforts to increase security, even at the expense of liberty and privacy. If these programs keep future attacks from occurring, they may be very effective at keeping the freedom–order equation in balance.

Construct Your Own Policy

1. Design a policy that allows an advocate for privacy rights to rebut the government's case for surveillance.

2. Design a policy to investigate foreign and internal threats to the United States that distinguishes among postal mail, cell phone conversations, and e-mail activity.

Beyond surveillance, President Obama ordered the execution via an overseas drone air-strike of Anwar al Awlaki, a U.S. citizen who allegedly had supported al-Qaeda, the group behind the 9/11 attacks, and who had encouraged a variety of terrorist acts against the United States. Attorney General Eric Holder laid out the criteria by which the president could order the execution of a U.S. citizen, stating that "due process and judicial process are not one and the same particularly when it comes to national security."[21] The executive branch, with the most direct responsibility over national security, is more likely to support restrictions on civil liberties during times of crisis than is either the legislative or judicial branch. In 2014, a U.S. Court of Appeals panel ordered the Obama administration to release redacted versions of the documents it used to justify killing Awlaki.[22]

Checkpoint

CAN YOU:

- State the major limits on civil liberties from the Revolutionary War through the Civil War
- Identify the major targets of civil liberty restrictions during the world wars
- Describe the change and continuity in security regulations from President George W. Bush to President Obama
- Explain why wartime deprivation of rights ratchet back after the crisis ends

Civil Liberties and American Values

As these examples have demonstrated, in times of crisis, Congress and the president limit civil liberties to secure order, often with public support. The courts, however, being less responsive to public pressure, can push back against these efforts. Thus, the courts forced the government to try Padilla in civilian courts. The courts have also blocked efforts to censor newspapers even when the government has believed that the publication of certain reports would benefit wartime enemies. Nevertheless, in wartime or other times of crisis, concerns about order are at their highest, and protections for civil liberties by national and state governments typically decline. Following the emergency, a political culture that favors freedom means that public support for civil liberties, as well as the government's protections of those liberties, generally rebounds.

4.3 The First Amendment and Freedom of Expression

> Distinguish what rights of expression the First Amendment protects

The civil liberties most at risk during times of crisis are those protected by the First Amendment—freedom of speech, freedom of the press, and freedom of association. In this section, we examine each of these freedoms of expression individually. Their scope has expanded over time, despite occasional ratcheting back during wartime.

Freedom of Speech

While the First Amendment declares that "Congress shall make no law . . . abridging the freedom of speech," the Court has never taken the phrase "no law" literally. Prohibitions on speech once included blasphemy (inappropriate references to God) and defamation (speaking ill of others). States have since rescinded such laws, either legislatively or judicially. Today the Court allows limits on advocacy of unlawful activities, the use of fighting words, hate speech, and symbolic speech. The Court also allows the sort of limits imposed by time, place, and manner regulations, such as prohibitions on protests near public schools when they are in session.

Advocacy of Unlawful Activities.   When Justice Holmes wrote, in the opinion in the case of Charles Schenck, that free speech does not mean that a person can falsely shout "fire!" in a theater, he went on to explain that words spoken in wartime may have a different impact than they would in peacetime. "The question in every case," he continued, "is whether the words used are used in such circumstances and are of such a nature as to create a clear and present danger that they will bring about the substantive evils that Congress has a right to prevent." From this statement, the Court adopted the **clear and present danger test**. The Court shifted standards in subsequent decades, at one point allowing states to limit speech that merely had a tendency to cause unlawful acts. But in 1969, the Court moved back toward a stricter protection of civil liberties, ruling that speech cannot be banned unless it leads to "imminent lawless action."[23]

Fighting Words and Hate Speech.   Besides speech that imminently incites unlawful activities, the Supreme Court also allows restrictions on the basis of the fighting words doctrine. "Fighting words" are phrases that might lead the individual to whom they are directed to respond with a punch. Today, hateful racial epithets are the leading examples of fighting words, but when the Supreme Court first developed the doctrine, many milder types of words offended people. Thus, in 1942, the Court used the fighting words doctrine to uphold the conviction of a defendant for calling a town marshal a "God-damned racketeer" and a "damned Fascist."[24]

Related to fighting words is hate speech, which attacks or demeans a group rather than a particular individual. Over the past thirty years, as we noted earlier, more than 350 public colleges and universities have attempted to provide equal, nonhostile educational environments through speech codes that tell students what they are and are not allowed to say.[25] For example, Tufts University established three separate free speech zones: public areas, where speech could not be prohibited; classrooms and libraries, where derogatory and demeaning speech could be punished; and dorms, where the university placed the strictest restrictions on speech. Whereas students at many universities accepted speech codes, students at Tufts debated the issue, held public forums about freedom of speech, and physically marked off "free speech" from "non–free speech" zones.[26] Under this pressure, Tufts, a private university not legally bound by the Bill of Rights, rescinded the code.

The movement to restrict speech on college campuses has moved from public spaces and dorms into the classroom. So-called "trigger warnings" originally developed among women's rights activists to alert women who may have had traumatic experiences such as physical or sexual violence in their past that an online posting might contain material that could trigger a traumatic memory. Given the rate at which undergraduate students have suffered from these assaults, it is inevitable that any moderate-sized class will have such victims. The idea of trigger warnings in class is to give students warning that readings or classroom lectures might contain such material. For example, the student senate at U.C. Santa Barbara has resolved that trigger warnings be added to course syllabi to alert students to days in which classroom materials "might trigger feelings of emotional or physical distress." Oberlin College has issued official "trigger warning guidelines" that advise faculty to remove triggering materials from their courses entirely if not directly related to the course's learning goals.[27] Trigger warnings have grown substantially in recent years.[28]

The Supreme Court has not reviewed any of the college speech codes, but it has heard other cases related to hate speech. In one case, the Court ruled cross burning, a terrorist tactic historically used by the white supremacist Ku Klux Klan to intimidate African Americans,

→ KEY QUESTIONS:
Given the nature of terrorist attacks, is it possible to establish a "clear and present danger" before prosecuting the advocacy of unlawful activities?

clear and present danger test: *First Amendment test that requires the state to prove there is a high likelihood that the speech in question would lead to a danger that Congress has a right to prevent.*

→ KEY QUESTIONS:
How can you distinguish between fighting words and hate speech?

→ KEY QUESTIONS:
Does your college have a speech code? Should your college regulate what you can and cannot say?

supreme court cases

Snyder v. Phelps (2011)

QUESTION: May antimilitary and antigay protesters be sued for the distress they caused to the father of a marine killed in action in Iraq when they picketed at the marine's funeral?

ORAL ARGUMENT: October 6, 2010 (listen at http://www.oyez.org/cases/2010-2019/2010/2010_09_751)

DECISION: March 2, 2011 (read at http://www.law.cornell.edu/supct/html/09-751.ZS.html)

OUTCOME: The protesters are protected by the First Amendment because they are speaking out on a question of public concern.

For more than twenty years, the congregation of the Westboro Baptist Church in Topeka, Kansas, has picketed the funerals of members of the U.S. military. The church does so to show its opposition to homosexuality and the army's toleration thereof since the establishment of the "Don't Ask, Don't Tell" policy during the Clinton administration. Their pickets infamously declare that "God hates f* [pejorative for homosexuals]" and "Thank God for Dead Soldiers." These pickets at the funeral of Matthew Snyder aggravated his father, who sued the church, the minister (Fred Phelps, now deceased), and several of Phelps's daughters for intentional infliction of emotional distress. A jury awarded Snyder nearly $11 million in damages. When the U.S. Court of Appeals overturned the verdict, Snyder appealed to the Supreme Court.

The Supreme Court ruled 8–1 in favor of the protesters, declaring that the church's views on homosexuality in the military were a matter of public concern, and as such, it did not matter how crudely those concerns were expressed. They compared this intentional infliction of emotional distress to an earlier case upholding a suit dealing with an individual's credit report, which was purely a private matter. Nor did the Court find that the Westboro protests involved "fighting words," which the Court has ruled to be beyond the protections of the First Amendment. Justice Samuel Alito, in dissent, argued that the First Amendment does not give the church the right to brutalize Matthew's father while he is burying his only son. In an earlier speech case, the Court ruled that the function of the First Amendment is to "invite dispute." The boundary between "inviting dispute," which is protected, and "fighting words," which are not, is not always clear.

1. Do you believe that the Westboro Church's position on homosexuals and the military is a question of public concern? Explain.

2. Do you believe that the Westboro Church's protests at the funeral constituted "fighting words"? Explain.

to be a form of hate speech that could be banned.[29] On the other hand, the Court did not consider picketers at the funerals of U.S. soldiers to be engaged in hate speech, despite their inflammatory signs against homosexuals (see Supreme Court Cases: *Snyder v. Phelps*).

Symbolic Speech.   In the 1960s, the Des Moines school district suspended students Mary Beth Tinker, her brother John, and a third student when they wore black armbands to protest the Vietnam War. The students voiced no opinions while wearing these armbands, and no disruptions in their schools occurred. The Iowa Civil Liberties Union, an interest group that supports civil rights and liberties, brought suit against the school board, claiming that students are equal to other Americans and retain the freedom of speech rights granted by the First Amendment. The Supreme Court agreed.[30] In this instance, the armbands were considered **symbolic speech**, like other nonverbal activities that convey a political message, such as saluting the flag, burning the flag, or burning draft cards—the latter two actions also undertaken by anti–Vietnam War protesters. Alternatively, in another case, employees of a local sheriff's office "liked" the Facebook page of the person running for office against the sheriff. The sheriff fired the employees, who argued that their First Amendment rights had been violated. The court has ruled that "liking" a Facebook page is too shallow an expressive act to count as constitutionally protected speech.[31]

The Court has allowed prohibitions on the burning of draft cards because Congress has a **content-neutral** justification for requiring draft-eligible citizens to be in possession of their draft cards. That is, draft cards are essential to the smooth running of the draft,[32] and prohibiting their destruction is not intended to suppress the views of those who burn them. The Court once ruled that states also have a neutral justification for limiting protests near health care facilities, even if most of the protesters are advocating pro-life positions.[33] But in 2014 the Court reached a unanimous decision striking down a Massachusetts law limiting protests at facilities where abortions are performed. The Court has also overturned laws that require saluting the flag, as such laws do intend to instill a political viewpoint.[34] Similarly, the Court has overturned laws prohibiting flag burning, as such laws are not content neutral: They are based almost entirely on opposition to the idea being delivered by flag burning.[35] Of course, flag burners can be arrested on charges that would apply to anyone who starts a fire in public.

On the other hand, the content-neutral rule, like most constitutional rules, is not absolute. Some messages can be regulated solely because of opposition to the message, as when the Supreme Court upheld a student's suspension for unfurling a banner at a parade that declared "Bong Hits 4 Jesus" because of the banner's promotion of drug use.[36] It is easy for the Court to formulate simple rules, such as a prohibition on content-based regulations, but harder for the Court to apply those rules consistently in the unusual cases that come before it.

Time, Place, and Manner Regulations.   The fact that the First Amendment protects freedom of speech does not mean there is a right to speak wherever one wants, whenever one wants.

→ KEY QUESTIONS:
Should Americans be required to salute the flag? Should they be prevented from burning the flag?

⭐ **symbolic speech:**
Actions, such as burning the flag, that convey a political message without spoken words.

⭐ **content-neutral:**
Free speech doctrine that allows certain types of regulation of speech, as long as the restriction does not favor one side or another of a controversy.

BETTMANN/CORBIS

Mary Beth and John Tinker were teenagers in 1965 when they wore black armbands to school to protest the Vietnam War, and they were suspended. Arguing that students have free speech rights, the Iowa Civil Liberties Union sued the school district on their behalf and appealed the suspension in a series of cases that were finally appealed to the Supreme Court. In 1969, the Court ruled in the Tinkers' favor, stating: "It can hardly be argued that either students or teachers shed their constitutional rights to freedom of speech or expression at the schoolhouse gate."

In 2002, high school student Joseph Frederick unfurled this banner while his class watched the Olympic Torch relay pass through Juneau, Alaska. When the principal suspended Frederick for the banner's message about drugs, Frederick sued, saying that his free speech rights had been violated. The court of appeals, relying on the *Tinker* case, reversed the suspension, but in 2007, the Supreme Court upheld it, saying a student's free speech rights did not extend to the promotion of illegal drugs.

Regulations of the time, place, and manner of speech, such as when or where protests may take place, are generally valid as long as they are neutral or equal, that is, they do not favor one side or another of a controversy. Thus states can prohibit protests near school grounds that interfere with school activities as there is no indication that such bans favor one side of any controversy over any other side.[37]

Freedom of the Press

Thomas Jefferson, among other Founders, thought freedom of the press crucial to a free society because the press keeps the public informed about the government's activities. When the Bill of Rights was written, "the press" meant newspapers; today the term covers not only the large companies that own television and radio stations but also individually run blogs and Internet sites that anyone can create. While freedom of the press once belonged to those who owned one, today it belongs to everyone.

Like freedom of speech, however, freedom of the press is not absolute. In extraordinarily extreme cases, the government can censor items before they are published. This practice is known as **prior restraint**. In other situations, the government can punish people after the fact for what they publish.

prior restraint: *Government restrictions on freedom of the press that prevent material from being published.*

Prior Restraint. Following English law, freedom of the press in the colonies and in the early years of the United States meant freedom from prior censorship;[38] today, an extraordinary burden of proof of imminent harm is needed before the courts will shut down a newspaper before a story is printed. Even when the *New York Times* began publishing excerpts from a top-secret Pentagon analysis of U.S. involvement in the Vietnam War, the courts refused to stop the presses. The story of this case, *New York Times v. United States* (1971),[39] is told in more detail in Chapter 6, Public Opinion and the Media. One case in which the courts said that the government had met the extraordinary burden standard involved the publication of instructions on how to build a hydrogen bomb,[40] but generally, court approval of censorship by prior restraint has been so difficult to achieve that the federal government has not sought it since the 1970s. Thus even as many major newspapers published information leaked by Edward Snowden that the United States considered to be highly classified, the government did not attempt to prevent the news media from publishing it, although they did indict Edward Snowden.

First Amendment law protects the Internet and blogs from government censorship in much the same way that it protects newspapers, but the technology of the Internet makes censorship far more difficult. This was the lesson learned by a federal judge who tried to censor Julian Assange's Wikileaks website,[41] which publishes confidential documents from government, business, and religious organizations. Though the judge ordered the Wikileaks. org domain name disabled, Wikileaks already had mirror sites set up all over the world. Facing a barrage of criticism from bloggers and mainstream media groups, and given the ineffectiveness of his original decision, the judge reversed himself. But while many people may support the right of Wikileaks to publish allegations of money laundering by a Swiss bank, as in this case, what happens when Wikileaks publishes, as it has, a diagram of the first atomic bomb or secret documents about the war in Afghanistan?[42] Such cases show the difficulty of balancing freedom of the press versus censorship in a dangerous world.

Subsequent Punishment.   In certain instances, the government can engage in subsequent punishment, fining, and/or imprisoning writers and publishers after the fact for what they publish. Examples here include penalties for libel and for publishing obscenity, incitement to acts of violence, and secret military information.

The standards for convicting in a case of libel—the publishing of false and damaging statements about another person—vary according to whether that person is a public figure. The Supreme Court has made it harder for public figures than for ordinary individuals to sue for libel because public figures have access to the media and can more readily defend themselves without lawsuits. For public figures to sue, the materials must be false and damaging, and the writer or publisher must have acted with actual malice, that is, with knowledge that the material was false or with reckless disregard of whether it was true or false. Further, satire is largely exempt from libel laws. Such was in the case in *Hustler Magazine's* spoof on the "first time" for the Reverend Jerry Falwell, the founder of the conservative Christian group, Moral Majority.[43] For private figures to sue for libel, the material must be false and damaging, and there must be some degree of negligence, but the actual malice test does not apply. In democratic countries, courts can protect satire against public figures. That is less true in authoritarian countries, as the girls behind the Russian rock band Pussy Riot discovered (see Global Gateways).

Before development of the World Wide Web, only those who published printed materials could libel someone, but even then, the damage would largely be limited to those who subscribed to the publication. With the Internet, anyone can libel anyone else, and the whole world can see it. At Yale University, for example, anonymous contributors to a popular law school message board wrote derogatory comments about several female law students, including fabricated statements about their mental capacity and sexual activities. Because anyone, including potential employers, can see such statements, the potential for harm is enormous.[44] Given the anonymous nature of the posts, identifying and prosecuting the source of the statements can be difficult, if not impossible. Because freedom of speech is a fundamental right, there is no easy solution to protecting privacy in the Internet age.

Today, the government can seek subsequent punishment against individuals who publish military secrets or obscene materials. Pornographic material is not necessarily obscene, and pornography that falls short of the legal definition of obscenity receives First Amendment protection. Specifically, for materials to be obscene, they must pass all three parts of what has become known as the ***Miller* test:** (1) to the average person, applying contemporary community standards as established by the relevant state, the work, taken as a whole (not just isolated passages), appeals to the prurient (sexual) interest; (2) the work depicts in an offensive way sexual conduct specifically defined by the state law; and (3) the work lacks serious literary, artistic, political, or scientific value.[45]

→ KEY QUESTIONS:
What information on the web should the government censor?

→ KEY QUESTIONS:
How can you protect yourself from what others may say about you on the web?

Miller test: *Supreme Court test for determining whether material is obscene.*

→ KEY QUESTIONS:
Should pornography be submitted to the marketplace of ideas? Or should it be censored? On what legal grounds?

globalgateways

Pussy Riot

When the Communist Soviet Union disbanded in 1991, Boris Yeltsin became the first president of the Russian Federation, which made up the bulk of the territory, population, and military might of the former Soviet Union. Twice elected president of a burgeoning Russian democracy, Yeltsin suddenly resigned in 1999, leaving Vladimir Putin, the former director of the Soviet Secret Service (KGB) as president. Putin proved not to be a supporter of democracy and began to crack down on powerful oligarchs and powerless individuals who opposed him.

Among the powerless who opposed him was the female punk rock group Pussy Riot. In February 2012, the group, wearing masks, satirized Putin in a song they played at the main Russian Orthodox Church in Moscow. Russian authorities arrested three of the group's members, and two of them were sentenced to two years in prison. After an early release that preceded the 2014 Winter Olympics in Sochi, Russia, Amnesty International (a group that promotes freedom worldwide) brought the formerly imprisoned members, Nadezhda Tolokonnikova and Maria Alyokhina, to the United States to publicize their fight for freedom in Russia. When asked by late night talk show host Stephen Colbert why they were arrested, Alyokhina replied "We sang a fun song in a church."[46]

Before they formed Pussy Riot, Tolokonnikova and Alyokhina protested Russia's laws against homosexual behavior by kissing "forty police women."[47] When the *New York Times* asked them whether they were afraid they would be imprisoned again, Alyokhina responded, "In the two years since we were imprisoned, the situation in Russia has gotten so much worse. And if we couldn't keep quiet about it then, we certainly won't keep quiet about it now."[48] At great personal risk, the members of Pussy Riot used punk rock music as their gateway to influence their fellow citizens in a country where most of the gateways to civic influence are closed off.

1. Why would a leader such as Putin be afraid of satire?
2. Do you know musical groups that have used satire to make political points?

PHOTOXPRESS/ZUMA PRESS, INC./ALAMY

Under the *Miller* test, only "hard-core" materials could be banned.[49] The government has much greater leeway to prohibit "kiddie porn" that uses actual children[50] but not "virtual child pornography," which uses computer-simulated children.[51] Nor can the government's desire to protect children from indecent materials be used as a justification for prohibiting pornography that does not reach the level of obscenity from the Internet.[52] Similarly, the state may not ban the purchase of violent video games by minors.[53] According to a 2010 decision, under the *Miller* test, states may not ban fetish videos that, in the case at hand, showed women in high heels crushing the skulls of puppies.[54]

Checkpoint

CAN YOU:

- State the limits on the First Amendment's right to freedom of speech
- Compare prior restraint on the press to subsequent punishment

4.4 Religious Freedom

> Determine what religious freedoms the First Amendment protects

The First Amendment sets forth two distinct protections about religion. Congress, and now the states, generally may not prevent people from practicing their religious beliefs. They also cannot pass laws that establish an official religion or even favor one religion over another.

Free Exercise

Many of the first settlers in the American colonies came because of restrictions on their religious beliefs in England, where the Anglican Church was established as the official religion. When these settlers first arrived, they did not establish general freedom of religion but, rather, freedom for their religion.

Victories for religious freedom, though significant, were rare in the colonial period. In 1786, however, the Virginia General Assembly passed Thomas Jefferson's Statute for Religious Freedom, which declared freedom of religious conscience to be a natural right of mankind that governments could not restrict. Five years later, this right was affirmed in the **free exercise clause** of the Bill of Rights. Like all the provisions of the Bill of Rights, however, it originally protected individuals only against the national government, and at the time only two states—Virginia and Rhode Island—had unqualified religious freedom. So ingrained was state authority to regulate religion that when James Madison proposed an amendment that would have limited such authority, Congress rejected it.[55] Today, however, with the incorporation of the Bill of Rights, the right of individuals to the free exercise of religion is also outside of state authority to regulate.

Under the First Amendment, the government cannot criminalize an individual's private religious beliefs. Nor can the government ban specific religious activities, including student-run publications,[56] just because they are based on religious beliefs. For example, the Supreme Court struck down a ban on religious-based animal sacrifices because killing animals for other reasons was not prohibited.[57] But not all religious-based activities are protected, and states are generally free to pass laws that restrict religious practices as long as such laws have a **valid secular (nonreligious) purpose**. For example, states can ban polygamy, even though marriage with multiple wives is a central belief in some religions.[58] The state court of Utah, however, in response to a case brought by the family featured on the television show *Sister Wives*, has recently ruled that the ban on cohabitation is an unconstitutional violation

→ KEY QUESTIONS:
Should all religions get equal treatment?

⭐ **free exercise clause:** *First Amendment clause protecting the free exercise of religion.*

⭐ **valid secular purpose:** *Supreme Court test that allows states to ban activities that infringe on religious practices as long as the state has a nonreligious rationale for prohibiting the behavior.*

In 2014, the Court decided that the Hobby Lobby Corporation, which is owned by a devout Christian, did not have to abide by the requirement in the Affordable Care Act that its employee health care plan provide free access to birth control pills when the corporate owner believes that such pills can result, not just in the prevention of, but in the termination of pregnancy.

of religious freedom. Thus while the state may continue to prevent a man from having multiple marriage licenses, it cannot prevent a man from living with multiple women.[59]

In the 1960s, the Court ruled that states must have a compelling interest before they can abridge people's religious practices, even if the law restricting the practice has a valid secular purpose. Thus even though the government has a valid secular purpose in conducting a military draft, members of religious groups that oppose warfare, such as Quakers, may be exempt. In the case of former boxing champion Muhammad Ali, a Muslim, who argued that he could only fight wars declared by Allah or the Prophet, the Court overturned a conviction for draft evasion.[60]

One case that demonstrates the contest between the branches of government over what constitutes free exercise concerns the use of the hallucinogenic drug peyote in religious rituals. In 1990, when two Native American drug counselors who used peyote were fired from their jobs and denied unemployment compensation, the Supreme Court used the valid secular purpose test to uphold Oregon's decision to deny this compensation.[61] Members of Congress overwhelmingly disapproved, however, and passed legislation stating that the Supreme Court must use the compelling interest test in deciding free exercise cases. The Supreme Court responded by declaring part of the Religious Freedom Restoration Act unconstitutional repeating the statement from *Marbury v. Madison* that the province of the judicial branch is "to say what the law is."[62] Congress does have the authority, however, to declare the religious use of peyote to be legal, and it has done so. Moreover, Congress has decided that its own laws must have a compelling interest before they can limit religious freedom.

Generally, states need only have a valid secular purpose to pass laws that also happen to restrict religious practices. On the other hand, the Supreme Court has established a "ministerial exception" that frees religious organizations from having to abide by federal antidiscrimination laws—in this case, the Americans with Disabilities Act—when choosing their ministers. The Court here used the free exercise clause to limit the scope of an otherwise valid act of Congress.[63]

The Establishment of Religion

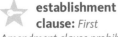 **KEY QUESTIONS:**
Can corporations have religious beliefs? If so, can they be required to provide birth control pills that some believe result in the termination of pregnancy to their employees?

establishment clause: *First Amendment clause prohibiting governmental establishment of religion.*

The **establishment clause** of the First Amendment prevents Congress from recognizing one church as the nation's official church, as Britain had done with the Anglican (Episcopal) Church. Originally, states were free to establish state religions if they chose to, and when the Constitution was adopted, nearly half the states had done so.[64] The antiestablishment movement began in Virginia, where between 1784 and 1785, James Madison fought tax assessments used to support Christian religious teachers, and Thomas Jefferson secured passage of the Disestablishment Bill in 1786, which ended Virginia's official establishment of the Anglican Church. In an 1802 letter to the Baptists of Danbury, Connecticut, Jefferson called for a "wall of separation" between church and state. The Supreme Court adopted that phrase in 1947 but declared that using taxpayer funds to provide public transportation to parochial schools did not breach the wall.[65]

The establishment clause literally prohibits not just the establishment of religion but also any law "respecting an establishment of religion." The Supreme Court has taken this phrase to mean that steps by the government favoring one religion over another, or even religion over no religion, cannot be taken, even if those steps fall far short of an official establishment of religion.

Chaplain leads American Air Force crew serving in Afghanistan in prayer.

The Supreme Court's test for determining whether laws violate the establishment clause is known as the *Lemon* test, named after a litigant in a 1971 case.[66] Under this test, a challenged law must be shown to have a secular (nonreligious) legislative purpose and a primary effect that neither advances nor inhibits religion. The law must also avoid an excessive entanglement between church and state, such as a strict monitoring of church activities. Using these standards, the Supreme Court has banned organized school prayers and devotional Bible readings.[67] The Bible can be read as part of a comparative religion course, however, and students can pray silently. The Supreme Court has also used this test to strike down laws that prohibited the teaching of evolution[68] as well as laws granting equal time for creation science—the position that scientific evidence supports the biblical view of creation—if evolution is taught.[69] Whether doctrines are called creation science or intelligent design, courts have ruled that they are religious doctrines that cannot constitutionally be taught as part of the science curricula in public schools. Nevertheless, state legislatures, presumably in an attempt to be responsive to their constituents, continue to approve creation science curricula.

It is often difficult to understand why some activities violate the establishment clause and others do not. Separationists believe, with Jefferson, that there should be a strict wall between church and state. Accommodationists, on the other hand, believe that as long as the state does not favor one religion over another, it can generally pass laws that support religion. The Supreme Court's decisions on these grounds have been mixed, with conservative justices typically supporting the accommodationist position, and liberal justices typically supporting the separationist view (see Chapter 13, The Judiciary, on ideology and the Supreme Court). The end result has been confusion: The Court allows short religious prayers by clergy at high school graduation ceremonies as long as students are not compelled to participate[70] but not by students at high school football games.[71] States may provide textbooks for secular subjects in parochial schools[72] but not instructional aids such as charts and maps.[73]

Lemon test: *Test for determining whether aid to religion violates the establishment clause.*

→ KEY QUESTIONS:
Should prayers be allowed in school? Under what circumstances? What types of prayers? Is saying a silent prayer the same as wearing an armband?

Checkpoint

CAN YOU:

■ Explain the difference between free exercise of religion and the establishment of religion

■ State the difference between separationists and accommodationists

4.5 The Right to Keep and Bear Arms

> Outline how the "right to bear arms" has been interpreted

While many if not most Americans agree about the fundamental aims of the various First Amendment rights, no such agreement exists about the fundamental aims of the Second

Amendment. The amendment declares, "A well regulated Militia, being necessary to the security of a free State, the right of the people to keep and bear Arms, shall not be infringed." Supporters of gun rights view the amendment as providing an individual right to keep and bear arms, while opponents view the "well regulated Militia" clause as limiting this right to those in organized militias.

The Supreme Court finally decided the issue in 2008, ruling that there is an individual right to possess a gun, at least for self-defense in one's home.[74] The case involved a law prohibiting the private possession of firearms by the District of Columbia, which is a "federal enclave" and, for constitutional purposes, thus considered part of the federal government rather than a state. The Court's 5–4 decision split along ideological lines, with the five most conservative justices support-

Otis McDonald, a plaintiff in *McDonald v. Chicago,* joined the suit against Chicago's handgun law because he wanted to have a handgun at home to protect himself from gangs. On June 18, 2010, the Supreme Court ruled that the Constitution incorporated the Second Amendment, declaring that states could not ban private possession of guns for self-defense.

ing an individual right to keep and bear arms for self-defense, indicating that the right can be regulated but not denied. The four most liberal justices dissented, arguing that the "well regulated Militia clause" limits whatever right of gun ownership exists to military purposes.

The conclusion that the Second Amendment protects an individual right to bear arms does not answer the question of whether that amendment is also binding on the states. The Supreme Court answered that question in 2010, declaring that the right is incorporated.[75]

Checkpoint

CAN YOU:

■ Explain why the Second Amendment is ambiguous about an individual's right to keep and bear arms

4.6 Criminal Procedure

> Describe what protections the Bill of Rights provides to those accused of crimes

Provisions in the Fourth, Fifth, Sixth, and Eighth Amendments contain the heart of the protections afforded people against arbitrary police and law enforcement tactics. They protect the manner in which the police conduct investigations, the procedures used at trial, and the punishments that may be given following conviction. The liberal Warren Court greatly expanded the rights of accused criminals, but since then, more conservative courts have trimmed those rights.

Investigations

The major limits on investigating crimes involve the authority to search for physical evidence and the warnings that must be given before questioning a suspect. The police also cannot entrap people into committing crimes they would not otherwise commit, which is why R. Stephanie Good, in her role as "teen2hot4u," could never be the first person to bring up the subject of potential sexual activity.

Searches and Seizures. The English practice of issuing writs of assistance, general warrants that allow searches of any person or place with no expiration until the death of the king, was among the causes that led to the American Revolution. Thus, the Fourth Amendment prohibits unreasonable searches and seizures. Although the amendment does not specify what makes a search unreasonable, it does specify that warrants must be backed by probable cause.

The Supreme Court has never interpreted the amendment to require warrants for all searches or seizures. If the police see illegal goods in plain view, they may seize them without a warrant. Similarly, if they observe a crime, they do not have to get a warrant before they arrest the individual. The Supreme Court has also established a broad right to search the person and the area within his or her control following an arrest and incident to it. This right now permits the police to conduct strip searches of arrestees entering the general population of a jail, even for the most minor violations, such as driving without a seat belt.[76] The Supreme Court ruled in 2014 that the police may not search the contents of a cell phone unless confiscated incident to a lawful arrest.[77]

The areas over which individuals have Fourth Amendment protections are those in which there is an **expectation of privacy**. According to the Supreme Court, there are no Fourth Amendment rights in areas over which there is no expectation of privacy, such as discarded garbage, someone else's home, a hotel room once one has checked out, or an international border. The Supreme Court has not ruled on the issue, but several state supreme courts have upheld the right of schools to search lockers used by students because students have a diminished expectation of privacy over their lockers. While students at public universities do have an expectation of privacy in their college dorm rooms, many schools require them to waive their Fourth Amendment rights when they sign their dorm contracts. (Like the First Amendment, the Fourth Amendment does not limit private parties, such as private universities.) More generally, people waive their Fourth Amendment rights whenever they grant permission for the police to search, as long as the police request is not coercive.[78]

 expectation of privacy test: *Supreme Court test for whether Fourth Amendment protections apply.*

As for biological searches, police may require Breathalyzer tests of people suspected of drunk driving, but blood tests require a warrant.[79] On the other hand, the Court recently upheld Maryland's requirement that all persons charged with certain crimes submit DNA samples for the state's database.[80] The DNA samples remain with the state even if the state later drops the charges or the person is found not guilty.

For areas over which there is an expectation of privacy, the degree of Fourth Amendment protection depends on the level of that expectation, as determined by the Supreme Court. For example, the Court has ruled that individuals have the highest expectation of privacy in their homes, nearly as much in their places of business, but substantially less in their cars.[81] There is no expectation of privacy if what is exposed is in plain view, even if, like a marijuana patch on private property, it requires a low-flying plane to view it.[82] There is no expectation of privacy over smells, allowing police to use drug-sniffing dogs to establish probable cause. Drug-sniffing dogs, however, may not enter the porch outside a home in order to sniff for illegal drugs.[83] There is, however, an expectation of privacy over the thermal (heat) signals given off by homes, thus prohibiting the police from using heat monitors to establish probable cause for indoor marijuana growing.[84]

Searches of homes almost always require a warrant (and thus probable cause). Searches of businesses usually do, but the Court allows warrantless searches of businesses that are subject to health, safety, or administrative regulations, such as restaurants, construction sites, and banks. For example, a restaurant kitchen suspected of health violations may be searched without a warrant. The police may establish, without probable cause, roadblocks to stop all cars on a road to check for licenses and registration or for drunk drivers. They may, of course, pull over any car for an observed violation, and they may search the car incident to arrest if they choose to arrest the person for that violation.[85] They may also pull a person over based on an anonymous tip.[86] The Court has ruled that police require a warrant to physically place a GPS transmitter on a car to trace a person's movements, as placing the transmitter on the car requires a physical trespass.[87] The Court explicitly left open the constitutionality of relying on cell phone towers to provide the same information, as such information does not involve a physical intrusion by the police. The Court also allows drug testing without probable cause in "special needs" cases, such as student athletes and people applying for jobs at the U.S. Customs Office, but not of politicians seeking elective office.[88]

If the police conduct a search that is later found to be in violation of the Fourth Amendment, the **exclusionary rule** holds that the evidence cannot be used in trial. Originally established by the Supreme Court in 1914, the doctrine was made binding on state and local governments, where most law enforcement takes place, by means of selective incorporation in *Mapp v. Ohio* (1961).[89] Defenders support the rule, which is not explicitly in the Constitution, as the only means of making sure that the police follow the Fourth Amendment. Police will have less incentive to violate the Fourth Amendment if they know that the evidence from illegal searches cannot be used in court. Critics complain that excluding such evidence allows guilty people to go free simply because the police made a mistake.[90] The Supreme Court has backtracked a bit on the rule, establishing a good faith exception, which allows evidence to be used if the police obtain a warrant but the warrant is later found to lack probable cause.[91] There is also an "inevitable discovery" exception, which allows illegally obtained evidence to be used if the court finds that the evidence would have been discovered even without the illegal search.[92]

Interrogations. The Fifth Amendment protects the right against self-incrimination, being forced to give testimony against oneself during criminal investigations or at criminal trials. The Supreme Court originally interpreted the self-incrimination clause to prohibit coerced confessions because they are inherently unreliable. But in the famous 1966 decision *Miranda v. Arizona*, the Court declared that the right against self-incrimination would be protected regardless of whether there was any evidence of coercion.[93] Rather, prior to police interrogation of subjects who are in custody, the subjects must be told that (1) they have the right to remain silent, (2) anything they say may be used against them, and (3) they have the right to an attorney, free if they cannot afford one. Police strenuously objected to these requirements at first, fearing that they would drastically curtail legitimate confessions. But in 2000, the Court upheld the *Miranda* decision, noting that its requirements had become so embedded in routine police practice that they had become part of the national culture.[94]

→ KEY QUESTIONS:
If the police are tracking your car's movements, does it matter if they physically touched your car to do so?

exclusionary rule:
Supreme Court rule declaring that evidence found in violation of the Fourth Amendment cannot be used at trial.

→ KEY QUESTIONS:
Why did the First Congress write so many protections regarding criminal procedure into the Bill of Rights?

Trial Procedures

The trial protections of the Bill of Rights include the right to indictment by a grand jury (Fifth Amendment), the right to counsel and an impartial jury (both Sixth Amendment), and the right against self-incrimination (Fifth Amendment), which, as noted, applies to trials as well as investigations. The Fifth Amendment also contains a general right to due process of law.

To prevent the government from bringing people to trial without sufficient cause, the Fifth Amendment requires indictment by a grand jury, which indicts by majority vote. This right has not been incorporated so it applies to the federal government only, which prosecutes only a small percentage of total criminal cases, as criminal law is mostly under the authority of the states.

The Sixth Amendment's right to counsel originally meant that defendants could have an attorney represent them if they could afford one. In *Powell v. Alabama* (1932), a case involving undoubtedly false allegations of rape filed against several black youths, the Supreme Court ruled that, in death penalty cases where the defendants were ignorant, illiterate, or the like, the government must provide an attorney if defendants cannot afford one.[95] In 1963, the Court recognized in the landmark *Gideon v. Wainwright* case how crucial counsel is in even simple felony cases.[96] Today, the rule applies to any case in which a defendant could receive as little as one day of jail time.[97]

The Sixth Amendment also guarantees the right to a trial by an impartial jury. Originally, a jury trial meant twelve people deciding unanimously, but the Court now allows juries as small as six people, and twelve-person juries need not decide unanimously.[98] The *impartial* part of the clause grants the defense and prosecutor unlimited rights to challenge potential jurors for cause. Examples include knowing other people in the case, having been a victim of a similar crime, and not having an open mind on the issue. These challenges must be approved by the trial judge. State rules also grant prosecutors and defense counsel a limited number of peremptory challenges, or challenges without cause. The substantive limit on peremptory challenges is that neither side may use the potential juror's race or gender as a reason for the challenge.[99]

The application of the self-incrimination clause to trials means that defendants cannot be compelled to be witnesses against themselves. That is, they have an absolute right not to testify, and the prosecution cannot even tell the jury that the defendant chose not to testify.

Verdict, Punishment, and Appeal

At the end of a trial, the jury must decide whether to convict or acquit the defendant. Following conviction, the judge imposes a sentence, unless it is a death penalty case, in which case the jury decides. Convicted defendants may usually appeal their convictions to a higher court.

Double Jeopardy. If the jury acquits the defendant, the double jeopardy clause prevents the person from being tried again for the same offense. But if the jury cannot reach a verdict, the government can retry the defendant. Also, if the defendant is

Booking photo of Ernesto Miranda. His case led the Warren Court to require police to give arrested suspects "Miranda Warnings."

AP IMAGES/MATT YORK

→ KEY QUESTIONS:
Is the U.S. criminal justice system too harsh? Or does it let too many criminals get off on "technicalities"?

CONNECT WITH YOUR CLASSMATES
MindTap™ for American Government

Access the Civil Liberties Forum: Discussion—Eighth Amendment Rights.

Two California police officers shown here beating a mentally ill homeless person, Kelly Thomas. After the officers were found not guilty of murder, Thomas's father filed civil charges against the officers. That suit has yet to be resolved.

JOSHUA SUDOCK-POOL/GETTY IMAGES

found guilty at trial, but the conviction is overturned on appeal, the defendant may be tried again. The Supreme Court does allow a defendant to be tried separately for the same offense by the state government and the federal government, even if the defendant was found not guilty at the state or federal trial that was held first. Because most crimes are either state offenses or federal offenses, this form of double jeopardy does not often occur.

The main exception concerns a trial for the federal crime of violating someone's civil rights, which is occasionally prosecuted after a state acquittal on the specific offense (such as murder or assault). For example, in 2012, George Zimmerman, an armed neighborhood watch coordinator, shot 17-year-old African American Trayvon Martin while Martin was walking through Zimmerman's gated community. Zimmerman approached Martin, a scuffle ensued in which Zimmerman suffered mild head injuries, and Zimmerman fatally shot Martin. Zimmerman was charged with murder but was acquitted based on Florida's Stand Your Ground Law, which does not require people in Florida to retreat in the face of a threat. Many people have called for U.S. Attorney General Eric Holder to prosecute George Zimmerman for violating the civil rights of Trayvon Martin. No charges have yet been filed, but a decision by the Justice Department is expected on the matter soon.[100]

Sentencing. Following a guilty verdict, the judge determines the sentence, except in death penalty cases, where the jury makes the determination. Sentences must not violate the Eighth Amendment's prohibition on cruel and unusual punishment. The concern of the Framers undoubtedly grew out of English punishments that included torture.[101] The phrase itself, however, is highly ambiguous, leaving courts with a fair amount of discretion about whether punishments are unconstitutional.

As for the length of the sentence imposed, the Supreme Court grants great leeway to the states. In 1980, the Court upheld the sentencing to a life term with the possibility of parole of a defendant who had committed his third felony. The first felony was fraudulent use of a credit card for an $80 purchase, the second a forged check for $28.36, and the third accepting payment of $120.75 to fix an air conditioner that he never fixed.[102] As the defendant found out, the Supreme Court rarely finds constitutional violation in the length of a sentence.

On the death penalty, however, the Supreme Court ruled in 1972 that the complete discretion given to juries as to which people are convicted of capital crimes was so arbitrary as to constitute cruel and unusual punishment.[103] Then, in 1976, the Court ruled mandatory death sentences to be unconstitutional but allowed states to impose the death penalty provided they give jurors specific guidelines to consider, such as the brutality of the crime or whether the crime was murder for hire.[104] For more on the death penalty, see Chapter 2.

Checkpoint

CAN YOU:

- Describe the limits on police investigations of crimes
- Explain the trial rights protected by the Constitution
- State the protections for those convicted of crimes

Appeals.   Convicted criminals do not have a right to appeal a trial court conviction unless a federal constitutional right has been violated. How states handle violations of state constitutional rights are largely up to the states, even if evidence is later found that the convicted criminal is factually innocent. Although the continued imprisonment or execution of a factually innocent person might appear to be a quintessential case violating due process, the Supreme Court has ruled that people convicted of crimes before DNA testing became available do not have a constitutional right to such evidence, which in many cases could definitively prove their innocence or guilt.[105] Indeed, there is no constitutional right for a factually innocent person not to be executed for a capital crime after a jury has concluded that the person is legally guilty, even if new evidence creates strong doubts as to guilt.[106]

4.7 The Right to Privacy

> Assess what constitutes the right to privacy

Although a number of constitutional provisions bear on privacy, such as search and seizure, self-incrimination, and First Amendment freedoms, none explicitly grants a general right to privacy. Nevertheless, the Ninth Amendment demands that the listing of certain rights, such as speech and religion, should not be understood as invalidating rights not listed. Since 1965, the Supreme Court has used the Ninth Amendment, the due process clause of the Fourteenth Amendment, and other privacy-related amendments to establish a general right to privacy. Subsequently the Court has faced decisions about whether to expand this privacy right to include abortion, homosexual behavior, and the right to die.

Birth Control and Abortion

In 1873, Anthony Comstock, a crusader for traditional morality, lobbied Congress to pass a law prohibiting the transportation in interstate commerce of both pornography and birth control. Many states, including Connecticut, passed their own Comstock Laws, which prohibited the use of birth control, even by married couples. In 1961, Estelle Griswold, executive director of the Planned Parenthood League of Connecticut, opened a birth control clinic in order to get arrested or fined so that she could challenge the constitutionality of the law. Her $100 fine, upheld by the Connecticut Supreme Court, allowed her to appeal to the U.S. Supreme Court. In *Griswold v. Connecticut* (1965), the Court voided what one justice called "an uncommonly silly law."[107] The case established a **right to privacy** (see Figure 4.4), and the Court soon expanded this decision to cover the right of unmarried people to use birth control.[108] Birth control as a political issue was then dormant until 2012, when the secretary of health and human services interpreted the Patient Protection and Affordable Care Act requirement that insurance plans cover birth control under the category of preventive medicine. The Catholic Church, which believes using birth control goes against church teachings, protested the application of these rules to cover employee health insurance at Church-affiliated schools and hospitals. The Obama administration then revised its policies to mandate that the insurance companies themselves cover the cost of birth control rather than the Church, or any other organization that objects to the use of birth control as part of its fundamental teachings.

right to privacy:
Constitutional right inferred by the Court that has been used to protect unlisted rights such as sexual privacy and reproductive rights, plus the right to end life-sustaining medical treatment.

No Soldier shall, in time of peace be quartered in any house, without the consent of the Owner . . . .

Third Amendment

Congress shall make no law . . . abridging . . . the right of the people peaceably to assemble . . . .

First Amendment

The right of the people to be secure in their persons, houses, papers, and effects, against unreasonable searches and seizures, shall not be violated . . . .

Fourth Amendment

The enumeration in the Constitution, of certain rights, shall not be construed to deny or disparage others retained by the people.

Ninth Amendment

No person . . . shall be compelled in any criminal case to be a witness against himself . . . .

Fifth Amendment

. . . nor shall any State deprive any person of life, liberty, or property, without due process of law. . . .

Fourteenth Amendment (section 1)

In 1965, in *Griswold v. Connecticut*, the Supreme Court overturned a Connecticut law that made it a crime for any person, including married couples, to use birth control. This landmark case drew on guarantees in the First, Third, Fourth, Fifth, Ninth, and Fourteenth Amendments to establish a general right to privacy. These guarantees are the right of association, the prohibition against quartering soldiers, the protection against unreasonable searches, the protection against self-incrimination, the rights retained by the people, and the due process of law. Justice William O. Douglas, who wrote the opinion, explained the justification with reference to "penumbras," or "zones": "Specific guarantees in the Bill of Rights have penumbras formed by emanations from those guarantees that help give them life and substance." He also stated the justification more bluntly: "Would we allow the police to search the sacred precincts of marital bedrooms for the tell-tale signs of the use of contraceptives? The very idea is repulsive."

Figure 4.4 The Right to Privacy

Even more controversial than the question of birth control is the question of abortion. Before the middle of the nineteenth century, most states followed the English practice of making abortion illegal only after "quickening," that is, noticeable movement by the fetus, usually around the sixteenth to eighteenth week of pregnancy. By the end of the nineteenth century, most states had eliminated the quickening distinction, making abortion illegal throughout pregnancy. By the 1950s, every state but Alabama banned abortion except to save the life of the mother; Alabama's broader exception included preserving the mother's health.

Following a substantial increase in birth defects caused by the sedative thalidomide (1957–61) and a German measles epidemic (1962–65), deaths from illegal abortion, and the resurgence of the women's rights movement, interest groups such as the National Association for the Reform of Abortion Laws (NARAL) organized for the loosening of antiabortion laws. Between 1967 and 1969, ten states passed laws allowing abortion if there was a "substantial risk" that the child would be born with a "grave physical or mental defect" or that continuing the pregnancy would "gravely impair the physical or mental health of the mother" and in cases of rape or incest.[109] In 1970, three states legalized pre-viability abortions, those performed before the sixth month of pregnancy, when the fetus could not survive on its own.

Then, in 1973, the Supreme Court decided **Roe v. Wade,** which established a national right to abortion.[110] Using the compelling-interest test, the Court declared that states had a compelling interest in preventing abortion in the third trimester, when the fetus could live on its own, and a compelling interest in regulating abortion during the second trimester to protect the health of the woman seeking the procedure. The state had no interest in regulating or preventing abortion in the first trimester. The Court's ruling took the issue out of state politics, where it had been located, and situated it in national politics, where it has become a perennial controversy, with presidential candidates regularly vowing to nominate Supreme Court justices who would either uphold or strike down *Roe v. Wade*. Since that time, states have sought to regulate and limit the procedure, and in the past twenty years, abortion rates have slowly declined.

Following years of debate about *Roe v. Wade*, the Court reconsidered the decision in 1992.[111] That decision upheld the basic right to abortion established in *Roe v. Wade* but replaced the compelling interest/trimester framework, declaring that states could regulate abortion prior to viability as long as those regulations did not constitute an undue burden on a woman's right to terminate her pregnancy. According to the Court, spousal notification constitutes an undue burden, but requiring doctors to provide the woman with information about the risks of abortion and a twenty-four-hour waiting period does not. Parental consent for minors is not an undue burden as long as the minor has an option of seeking a judge's approval if she cannot obtain a parent's consent.

Abortion remains a salient issue in national politics, with the Supreme Court's role front and center. While the Supreme Court continues to enforce the *Roe v. Wade* decisions, state legislatures have been very active in attempting to limit access to abortion. In 2013, twenty-two states enacted seventy abortion restrictions.

Homosexual Behavior

As of 1961, every state had laws prohibiting sodomy, and these laws were broad enough to cover virtually all sexual conduct between people of the same sex. In the next decades, some states decriminalized sodomy, and by 1986, only twenty-four states continued to outlaw sodomy between consenting adults. Georgia, one of the states that continued such laws, authorized twenty-four years of imprisonment for a single act of consensual sexual behavior that fell under its sodomy laws. In a case challenging this law, the Supreme Court declared that the right to privacy did not cover homosexual behavior.[112] At the time, more than 80 percent of Americans thought that homosexual behavior was "always" or "almost always" wrong.[113] But by 2003, with the percentage of Americans with this belief down more than 20 percentage points, the Supreme Court reversed itself, declaring in **Lawrence v. Texas** that "the liberty protected by the Constitution allows homosexual persons the right to choose to enter upon relationships in the confines of their homes and their own private lives"[114] (see Supreme Court Cases in Chapter 6, Public Opinion and the Media).

Roe v. Wade: *1973 Supreme Court case extending the right to privacy to abortion.*

→ KEY QUESTIONS:
What are the arguments for and against the right of privacy in relation to abortion? What is your opinion? Are you "pro-life" or "pro-choice"?

→ KEY QUESTIONS:
When the people disagree with a Supreme Court decision, what can they do about it?

Checkpoint

CAN YOU:

- Compare privacy rights in birth control and abortion
- Evaluate the role of public opinion on public laws toward homosexuality

→ KEY QUESTIONS:
Does government have a right to regulate who can live in the same house or apartment?

Lawrence v. Texas: *2003 Supreme Court case extending the right to privacy to homosexual behavior.*

The Right to Die

As part of the right to privacy, the Supreme Court has held that that people who make their wishes clearly known have a constitutional right to terminate life-sustaining care, such as artificial feeding or insertion of breathing tubes.[115] This right does not, however, include the right to assisted suicide, when physicians or family members provide ill people with pills or other means of ending life.[116]

Civil Liberties and Democracy

At the beginning of the chapter, we quoted Justice Jackson's opinion from the flag salute case that no government official can declare what shall be required in terms of basic beliefs and values. But what if elected officials do so anyway? Jackson responded that it was then the courts' job to protect such rights: "The very purpose of a Bill of Rights was to withdraw certain subjects from . . . political controversy, to place them beyond the reach of majorities and officials and to establish them as legal principles to be applied by the courts. One's . . . fundamental rights may not be submitted to vote; they depend on the outcome of no elections."[117]

Judicial decisions do not exist in a vacuum. Over the long run, if the Court is unresponsive to the people, new presidents will appoint new judges who better represent the people's preferences.[118] And while the Supreme Court is not accountable to the electorate in the same way that Congress and the president are, Congress and the president do have ways to try to hold the Court accountable. One way or another, the Court cannot stand alone in protecting civil liberties if popular support is not behind it. One of the difficulties in protecting civil liberties in a democracy is that although it is easy to feel sympathy for teenagers who wear black armbands to protest war, most litigants whose cases set precedents that protect all of the nation's freedoms are not as wholesome, and the causes they espouse may be racist, sexist, or violent.[119]

Unlimited liberties can also harm social order, particularly in times of crisis. Note, however, that in the period following 9/11, Congress made no attempt to criminalize antiwar speech, as it had during World War I; there was little public demand for such restrictions, as tolerance of opposing viewpoints among Americans has increased dramatically over the years. **Political tolerance**, the willingness of people to put up with ideas with which they disagree, is essential to both the marketplace of ideas and democratic stability.[120] Although critics have attacked the Supreme Court for establishing a right to privacy that is not explicitly in the Constitution, this decision remains highly popular, with 98 percent of Americans considering the right essential or important. But if the public loses its concern over civil liberties, sooner or later, the Supreme Court will as well.

political tolerance: *Willingness of people to put up with ideas with which they disagree.*

Master the Concept
of Civil Liberties with MindTap™ for American Government

REVIEW MindTap™ **for American Government**

Access Key Term Flashcards for Chapter 4.

STAY CURRENT MindTap™ **for American Government**

Access the KnowNow blog and customized RSS for updates on current events.

TEST YOURSELF MindTap™ **for American Government**

Take the Wrap It Up Quiz for Chapter 4.

STAY FOCUSED MindTap™ **for American Government**

Complete the Focus Activities for Civil Liberties.

Key Concepts

Bill of Rights (p. 88). Why is the Bill of Rights so important?

civil liberties (p. 88). What is the difference between civil liberties and civil rights?

clear and present danger test (p. 97). How much leeway does the clear and present danger test provide to dangerous speech?

compelling interest test (p. 92). What does the compelling interest test require?

content-neutral (p. 99). Why must time, place, and manner regulations be content-neutral?

establishment clause (p. 104). What were the Framers trying to prohibit with the establishment clause?

exclusionary rule (p. 108). Is the exclusionary rule fair?

expectation of privacy test (p. 107). What problems can you foresee with the expectation of privacy test?

free exercise clause (p. 103). Can the free exercise clause protect behavior, or does it just protect beliefs?

incorporate (p. 90). Why has incorporation been so important to our liberties?

Lawrence v. Texas (p. 113). Are laws that discriminate against gays or lesbians likely to continue to survive?

***Lemon* test** (p. 105). Which prong(s) of the *Lemon* test might be violated if a state prohibits the teaching of evolution?

***Miller* test** (p. 101). Does the *Miller* test go too far in regulating pornography, or does it not go far enough?

natural (unalienable) rights (p. 88). Which rights do you believe are unalienable?

political tolerance (p. 114). Why is political tolerance so essential for democracy?

prior restraint (p. 100). How does prior restraint harm the marketplace of ideas?

right to privacy (p. 111). What rights are protected under the right to privacy?

Roe v. Wade (p. 113). What would happen if the Constitution did not protect abortion rights?

selective incorporation (p. 91). How does selective incorporation differ from total incorporation?

symbolic speech (p. 99). How might one protest inequality without speaking any words?

valid secular purpose (p. 103). Why is the valid secular purpose test necessary?

writ of *habeas corpus* (p. 90). Why was this one of the few rights originally enshrined in the Constitution?

Learning Outcomes: What You Need . . .

To Know	To Test Yourself	To Participate
Identify what civil liberties are		
Civil liberties are freedoms so fundamental that they are outside the authority of government to regulate. It often falls to the judiciary to protect them. They include, among others, rights surrounding freedom of expression and criminal procedure, and they were written into the Constitution in 1791 as the first ten amendments, or the Bill of Rights. Although these protections of individual freedoms at first applied only to the federal government, Supreme Court decisions have gradually applied many of them to the states as well.	• Compare civil liberties to civil rights. • Contrast the problems of too much freedom to those of too much order. • Compare the importance of the rights in the 1787 Constitution with those in the Bill of Rights. • State the extent and the limits of the original Bill of Rights.	• Know your constitutional rights. • Decide if any constitutional rights provide too much freedom. • Consider what would happen if civil liberties were subject to majority rule.
Explain why civil liberties are limited in times of crisis		
Attempts to limit civil liberties are more frequent in wartime and during other threats, given increased government need for order and increased citizen concern about security. But support for the protection of civil liberties usually rebounds after the crisis ends. The scope of First Amendment freedoms of expression has generally expanded, although during wartime they are likely to be curtailed. Even in wartime, the courts have almost always protected the press from government censorship, but the government can prosecute newspapers for publishing obscenity, secret military information, and articles that incite violence.	• Identify the major targets of civil liberty restrictions during the world wars. • Describe the change and continuity in security regulations from President George W. Bush to President Obama. • Explain why wartime deprivation of rights ratchet back after the crisis ends.	• Consider whether dissent in wartime is unpatriotic. • Evaluate the role of the media in times of crisis. • Evaluate the threats to freedom from responses to terrorism.

To Know	To Test Yourself	To Participate
▶ Distinguish what rights of expression the First Amendment protects		
The First Amendment protects rights of speech, press, and assembly.	• State the limits on the First Amendment's right to freedom of speech. • Compare prior restraint on the press to subsequent punishment.	• Discuss whether First Amendment rights can be absolute.
▶ Determine what religious freedoms the First Amendment protects		
The First Amendment also protects freedom of religious practice and prevents the government from establishing one religion over all the others.	• Explain the difference between the free exercise of religion and the establishment of religion. • State the difference between separationists and accommodationists.	• Consider what would happen if the First Amendment granted a complete exemption from secular laws that violated one's religious beliefs. • Debate the "wall of separation" between church and state.
▶ Outline how the "right to bear arms" has been interpreted		
The Supreme Court has declared that the Second Amendment protects an individual right to bear arms for self-defense in one's home.	• Explain why the Second Amendment is ambiguous about an individual's right to keep and bear arms.	• Debate what limits should exist on gun rights and on what grounds.
▶ Describe what protections the Bill of Rights provides to those accused of crimes		
Provisions in the Fourth, Fifth, Sixth, and Eighth Amendments protect individuals accused of crimes in police investigations and regulate trial procedures and types of punishments.	• Describe the limits on police investigations of crimes. • Explain the trial rights protected by the Constitution. • State the protections for those convicted of crimes.	• List any additional limits you might like to see on police investigations or trial rights. • Debate the death penalty.
▶ Assess what constitutes the right to privacy		
Although the Constitution and its amendments do not explicitly grant a general right to privacy, the Supreme Court has used various constitutional provisions to establish this right, creating one of the most contentious areas of constitutional law and interpretation.	• Compare privacy rights in birth control and abortion. • Evaluate the role of public opinion on public laws toward homosexuality.	• Debate whether health insurance laws should require coverage for birth control. • Consider whether judicial protection of homosexual rights are necessary. • Write your own "living will" stating your preferences for medical treatment if at the time you were unable to make them known.

"I need everyone to stop pretending that nothing is wrong."

ERIKA ANDIOLA, on YouTube, following the arrest of her mother and brother by immigration police, Arizona State University*

5

Civil Rights

Escaping domestic violence, Erika Andiola's mother, came to the United States from Mexico without documentation with Erika and two of Erika's siblings when Erika was only eleven. Erika originally received a scholarship to attend Arizona State University, but a new Arizona law prohibited undocumented students from receiving scholarships, so the scholarship was rescinded. Even though her undocumented status made it difficult to find employment, Erika worked to pay for tuition, studied, and graduated from Arizona State in 2009 with a B.A. in psychology. Erika then went to work for Congresswoman Kyrsten Sinema (see the opening vignette in Chapter 9, Elections, Campaigns, and Voting). She also began lobbying to support President Obama's proposed DREAM Act, which would have granted permanent residency to undocumented immigrants if they arrived in the United States before they turned 16, received an honorable discharge from the military, or completed at least two years toward a college degree. While the bill passed the House in 2010, it never received the supermajority necessary to end the filibuster against it in the Senate. In 2012, however, President Obama directed Immigration and Customs Enforcement (ICE) to stop deporting undocumented students who met DREAM Act standards.

Despite the president's order, in 2013, agents from ICE broke into the Andiola family house, arresting Erika's mother and brother. Erika organized a huge protest against the arrests, and they were released the following day. As Marielena Hincapié, executive director of the National Immigration Law Center, put it, "Not all immigrant families have the benefit of Erika to mobilize the whole country overnight." Erika used the gateway of grassroots activism to get the government to use its discretion to not deport her family. Due to the massive support she received from around the country, her efforts succeeded.

In 2014, Andiola began a hunger strike at Immigration and Customs Enforcement (ICE) headquarters in Phoenix Arizona. One week later, Phoenix police arrested her, a move that could have led to her deportation but, perhaps due to her status as an activist for undocumented Americans, did not. She launched #not1more in an attempt to get President Obama, who has deported more undocumented residents than any other president, to end deportations. She also launched a hunger strike at the White House.

Andiola remains optimistic about the future. When asked by the *New York Times* where her activism is leading,

Need to Know

5.1 Define civil rights

5.2 Explain how the federal and state governments suppressed civil rights

5.3 Assess how equal protection has expanded

5.4 Identify the groups at the forefront of the civil rights movement

5.5 Describe the new battles for civil rights

 WATCH & LEARN MindTap™ **for American Government**
Watch a brief "What Do You Know?" video summarizing Civil Rights.

the woman who originally went to college to become a psychologist replied, "I haven't been able to think that far. At this point, I just want to be able to pass immigration reform. I want to be able to keep my mom here, and we'll see where life takes me from there."[1]

In this chapter, we look at the idea of equality, how it has changed, and how the federal government's enforcement of it has changed as well. We examine how grassroots racial, ethnic, and gender-based movements pressured the courts to protect civil rights and how Congress enforced court rulings with legislation. As with civil liberties (see Chapter 4, Civil Liberties), however, finding the right balance of rights for minority groups frequently divides members of society from one another, and divides democratically responsive legislatures from lifetime-appointed judges.

LISTEN & LEARN

MindTap for American Government

Access Read Speaker to listen to Chapter 5.

5.1 What Are Civil Rights?

〉 Define civil rights

Although the Declaration of Independence declared that "All men are created equal," the Constitution originally had little to say about equality, at least as the concept is understood today. Even the debate over the ratification of the Constitution had little to do with equality. It was much more about how much power to invest in the federal government. Today, however, equality is a hallowed principle of American political culture, but the notion and the reality evolved slowly over two centuries.

Civil Rights and Civil Liberties

civil rights: *Set of rights centered around the concept of equal treatment that government is obliged to protect.*

Civil rights are rights related to the duties of citizenship and the opportunities for participation in civic life that the government is obliged to protect. These rights are based on the expectation of equality under the law. The most important is the right to vote. In contrast to civil liberties (see Chapter 4), Americans have struggled hard to gain civil rights.

Civil rights also differ from civil liberties in that while government is the only authority that can suppress liberties—for example, by suppressing freedom of speech or forbidding a certain religious belief—both government and private entities, such as individuals or businesses, have the capacity to engage in discrimination by treating people unequally.

→ KEY QUESTIONS:
Why would a government discriminate?

public discrimination:
Discrimination by national, state, or local governments.

private discrimination:
Discrimination by private individuals or businesses.

The government can therefore take three different roles when it comes to civil rights. It can engage in state-sponsored or **public discrimination** by actively discriminating against people. It can treat people equally but permit **private discrimination** by allowing individuals or businesses to discriminate. Finally, it can try, as the U.S. government has since the 1960s, to treat people equally and to prevent individuals or businesses from discriminating. Thus it falls to government to protect individuals against unequal treatment and to citizens to ensure that the government itself is not discriminating against individuals or groups. In a democracy, the majority rules, but the gateways for minorities must also be kept open.

The Constitution and Civil Rights

Despite the statement on equality in the Declaration of Independence, the role of the government with regard to ensuring equality was not written into the Constitution, and the United States has a bleak history on civil rights. The Founders were not much concerned with equality as it is understood today. Many of them owned slaves, and they did not see a contradiction between doing so and the Declaration's statement on equality. The Constitution gave the states authority over voting, and most states restricted the right to vote to free males with a certain amount of property. Slaves could not vote, and in a few states, even free African Americans could not vote—neither could women (except in New Jersey) or Native Americans.[2] During the nation's first century and even thereafter, state laws and the national government actively discriminated against people on the basis of race, gender, and ethnic background.

Following the Civil War, the Thirteenth Amendment ended slavery, and the Fourteenth Amendment forbade states to deny any person "the equal protection of the laws." Nevertheless, the equality of African Americans was not thereby guaranteed. Some of the members of Congress who wrote the Fourteenth Amendment believed that equality was limited to "the right to go and come; the right to enforce contracts; the right to convey his property; the right to buy property" and little more.[3] The courts agreed, and the federal government made little effort to ensure equal treatment during the nation's second century.

Meanwhile, women won the right to vote (1920) but not the right to full participation in public life. Native Americans born on reservations became citizens (1924), but not until the civil rights and women's movements of the 1950s and 1960s did legal discrimination against African Americans, women, and ethnic minorities end. Today, the government actively aims to treat individuals and groups as equals before the law and to use its authority to prevent state and local governments, and individuals and businesses, from discriminating.

In the past half-century, the meaning of "all men are created equal" has been expanded to include women and all people subject to the jurisdiction of the United States. Yet Americans still debate the meaning of *equality*. Should, or can, the government ensure **equality of opportunity** for all people? Should, or can, it engineer **equality of outcome**? That is, is it enough for society to provide equality of opportunity by prohibiting discrimination? What if that still leaves members of groups that have historically been discriminated against, such as women and minorities, with fewer advanced degrees and lower incomes? As it has throughout the course of the nation's history, the meaning of equality continues to evolve.

In the next sections, we see how, as the idea of equality expanded, the federal government moved from actively treating different groups unequally under the law, to asserting equality under the law but doing little to protect it, to actively enforcing it.

> KEY QUESTIONS:
What did equality mean to the Founders?

> KEY QUESTIONS:
What is your idea of equality—equality of opportunity or equality of outcome?

 equality of opportunity: *Expectation that citizens may not be discriminated against on account of race, gender, or national background and that every citizen should have an equal chance to succeed in life.*

equality of outcome: *Expectation that equality is achieved if results are comparable for all citizens regardless of race, gender, or national background or that such groups are proportionally represented in measures of success in life.*

Checkpoint

CAN YOU:
- Compare civil rights to civil liberties
- Track changes in civil rights from the Constitution as originally ratified to today

5.2 Legal Restrictions on Civil Rights

> Explain how the federal and state governments suppressed civil rights

Slavery split the United States from the founding of the nation through the Civil War. After the Civil War, the Constitution prohibited slavery. It also prohibited the states from denying equality, but many states continued to discriminate. Both Congress and the Supreme Court had the authority to enforce equality, but neither took action. Women, African Americans, and ethnic minorities suffered under unequal laws, with denial of the right to vote and laws that limited their full participation in labor markets, professions, and public life. Discriminatory laws also affected Asians, prohibiting those who were not born in the United States from becoming citizens and later preventing them from immigrating to the United States altogether.

Slavery

→ KEY QUESTIONS:
Describe the role of compromise in American politics. Is it wise or foolish for politicians to compromise?

Slavery came to the colonies in 1619 when a Virginian purchased Africans from a Dutch shipper. Colonial Africans originally were servants, largely indistinct from indentured servants of other races who bound themselves to service for a limited number of years in return for free passage to Britain's American colonies. But African slavery soon became established in colonial law. In 1664, Maryland passed legislation declaring that all "Negroes or other slaves hereafter imported . . . shall serve for life."[4] The law also made slaves of the children of slaves.

The compromises made at the Constitutional Convention allowed the United States to form, but they also allowed slavery to grow and spread. By 1808, when Congress banned the further importation of slaves from Africa, the slave population had reached 1 million, and it continued growing through natural increase thereafter. With neither slave nor free forces dominant politically, Congress continued to compromise. The Missouri Compromise (1820) banned slavery in the territories north of the southern border of Missouri, thus keeping most of the vast lands of the Louisiana Purchase free. The Compromise of 1850 allowed territories captured in the Mexican War to decide for themselves whether to be free or slave. The Kansas-Nebraska Act (1854) undid the Missouri Compromise by allowing each territory to vote on whether to allow slavery. The Supreme Court further extended the reach of slavery in **Dred Scott v. Sandford** (1857).[5]

Dred Scott v. Sandford: *The 1857 Supreme Court decision declaring that blacks could not be citizens and Congress could not ban slavery in the territories.*

Dred Scott, a slave who had moved with his master from the slave state of Missouri to the free Wisconsin Territory and then back to Missouri, sued in federal court for his freedom based on his extended stay in free territory. The Supreme Court's decision in the case, written by Chief Justice Roger Taney, a former slave owner, declared (1) that no black—slave or free—could be an American citizen, and thus that no black could sue in a federal court; (2) that blacks were "beings of an inferior order" who had "no rights which the white man was bound to respect"; (3) that the Declaration of Independence's statement that "all men are created equal" did not include men of African heritage; (4) that Congress's authority to "make all needful Rules and Regulations respecting the Territory . . . [of] the United States" did not include the right to prohibit slavery in those territories; and (5) that slaves were the property of their owners, so freeing Scott would violate his owner's Fifth Amendment right not to be deprived of his property without due process of law. With this decision, the regulation of slavery in the territories was removed from the national authority of Congress and placed in the hands of local authorities in the territories.

The 1860 election of Abraham Lincoln (1861–65), who opposed the extension of slavery, prompted southern states to secede from the union. During the ensuing Civil War, Lincoln issued the Emancipation Proclamation, which made slavery illegal in those states in rebellion as of January 1, 1863. The Proclamation did not pertain to border states that retained slavery but remained in the Union. Slavery was finally ended in the United States following Union victory and ratification of the Thirteenth Amendment in 1865 (see Figure 5.1).

Figure 5.1 Constitutional Amendments That Pertain to Civil Rights

Color Code:	Criminal procedure	Participation	Equality

Thirteenth	1865	Prohibits slavery in the United States
Fourteenth	1868	Makes all persons born in the United States citizens of the United States and prohibits states from denying persons within its jurisdiction the privileges or immunities of citizens, the due process of law, and equal protection of the laws; apportionment by whole persons
Fifteenth	1870	Prohibits states from denying the right to vote on account of race
Nineteenth	1920	Guarantees women the right to vote
Twenty-Fourth	1964	Prohibits poll taxes

Restrictions on Citizenship

The Constitution was not explicit on birthright citizenship, but the clause requiring that presidents be natural-born citizens seemingly implies that people born in the United States are citizens.[6] Yet on the basis of ethnic background, some groups were denied the status of **citizenship** and the privileges it entailed, such as property rights and the protection of civil liberties.

citizenship:
Full-fledged membership in a nation.

The Constitution explicitly allows people not born in the United States to become citizens through naturalization by granting Congress the authority "to establish a uniform rule of naturalization." Congress's first such law, the Naturalization Act of 1790, restricted citizenship to "free white persons" who had lived in the United States for two years, swore allegiance to the United States, and had "good character." Though restrictive on race, the act allowed Catholics, Jews, and other "free white persons" to become naturalized citizens, rights that most European nations did not allow. The act also declared people born overseas to parents who were U.S. citizens to be natural-born citizens. Congress first allowed nonwhites to become naturalized citizens in 1870, when it extended naturalization to "persons of African descent."

Native Americans. In 1823, the Supreme Court declared that Native Americans were merely inhabitants, "an inferior race of people, without the privileges of citizens."[7] The legislative policy of the United States toward Native Americans included forcible removal from various territories under the Indian Removal Act of 1830 and the creation of land reserved for them (Reservations) starting with the Indian Appropriations Act in 1851. The Fourteenth Amendment's citizenship clause did not remedy this situation: The Court ruled in 1884 that the clause did not provide citizenship to Native Americans born on reservations because reservations are not fully under the jurisdiction of the United States.[8] Not until the Indian Citizenship Act of 1924 did Congress provide natural-born citizenship to Native Americans born on reservations.

Latinos. Latinos in the Southwestern United States arrived prior to American settlers. They lived in areas from Texas to California, and Tejanos, the term for people of Mexican descent living in Texas, fought alongside other Texans in battles against the Mexican Army. Perhaps due to the close affiliation with Mexico, many Tejanos, Californios, and other Latinos lost their properties after the Treaty of Guadalupe Hidalgo, which ended the Mexican-American War and resulted in Mexico ceding what is now California, Nevada, New Mexico, Arizona, Utah, Texas, Wyoming, and Colorado. After the United States annexed Texas, Anglos forcibly expelled many Tejanos. Those who remained, though formally granted citizenship, were often faced with "second-class" status with few recognized rights.[9]

→ KEY QUESTIONS:
Who should be a citizen?

The history of the treatment of Latinos by the U.S. government is a mixed one. In the late 1920s and early 1930s, approximately 2 million people of Mexican descent were deported to Mexico due to economic and political pressures stemming from the Great Depression. Roughly 60 percent of those expelled during what became known as the Mexican Repatriation were U.S. citizens. "Federal, state, and local governments working together involuntarily removed many U.S. citizens of Mexican ancestry, many of whom were born in the United States. These citizens cannot be said to have been 'repatriated' to their native land."[10] As a result of the Mexican Repatriation, ". . . the nation lost roughly one-third of its Mexican population. A similar program took place in the 1950s under the offensive name "Operation Wetback,"[11] and similar "roundups" have occurred as recently as 1997.[12] In 2005, the California Assembly passed the "Apology Act for the 1930s Mexican Repatriation Program" in recognition of the coerced removal of legal residents of Mexican descent.

The Mexican Repatriation delayed for decades the full emergence of the Latino community as a political, economic, and social force in the United States."[13] Civil rights enjoyed by Latinos today were not always recognized as such nor are they guaranteed to be so in the future. As Latinos continue to be the fastest growing ethnic group in the United States, it is clear there have been many gates to political participation placed before them, which are discussed more in depth in Chapter 9, Elections, Campaigns, and Voting.

Asian Americans.

Even after Congress allowed "persons of African descent" to become naturalized citizens in 1870, Asians still could not become naturalized citizens. Often states enacted discriminatory legislation to bar Asians from benefiting from opportunities granted to other residents. California's 1879 constitution prohibited Chinese from voting and from employment in state and local government. In 1913, California prohibited Japanese immigrants from purchasing farmland.[14]

Indeed, fear of Chinese immigrants led to an 1882 prohibition on the immigration of Chinese to America. That ban was the first significant restriction on immigration to the United States. Congress extended this ban to all Asians in 1921. The ban stayed in effect until 1943, when Congress allowed an annual quota of 105 immigrants from China, a World War II ally. The 1943 act also allowed Chinese to become naturalized citizens but did not allow other Asians to do so. Congress ended this restriction on Asian naturalization in 1952 but kept strict limits on the number of Asian immigrants until 1965.

THE 'CHINESE WALL' AROUND THE USA, PUBLISHED IN 'HARPER'S WEEKLY', 23RD JULY, COMMENTING ON THE ANTI-CHINESE IMMIGRATION MOVEMENT IN THE USA, 1970 (LITHO), NAST, THOMAS (1840-1902)/PRIVATE COLLECTION/PETER NEWARK PICTURES/THE BRIDGEMAN ART LIBRARY

Drawing of a wall depicting the exclusion of Chinese immigrants from the United States.

Beyond the setbacks of the anti-Asian immigration policies, President Franklin Delano Roosevelt (1933–45) issued an executive order for the evacuation of all 110,000 people of Japanese ancestry who resided west of the Rocky Mountains—whether citizen (most of them) or not—and their placement in relocation camps following the Japanese attack on Pearl Harbor. Congress ratified the president's order, and in 1944, the Supreme Court endorsed it in *Korematsu v. United States (1944)* ruling that the authority for relocation was within the war power of the United States.[15]

→ KEY QUESTIONS:
Does military necessity overrule civil rights? If so, under what circumstances?

Although the government justified the program on the grounds of military necessity rather than racial animosity, it did not attempt wholesale roundups of German Americans despite the existence of the German American Bund, a pro-Nazi association with about twenty thousand members before the war. That the government even rounded up Japanese American children from orphanages suggests that racial animosity was more important than security concerns.[16] The program remained in effect through the war years, although the government filed no charges of disloyalty or subversion against any person of Japanese ancestry. Many Japanese Americans valiantly served the United States in segregated military units during the war.

Immigration Limits.   Congress used immigration laws to keep out ethnic groups as well as anyone considered undesirable, including "idiots," insane people, paupers, felons, polygamists, anarchists, and people coming for "immoral purposes."[17] Immigration officials used the morality clauses to keep homosexuals from entering the country until 1979.[18]

→ KEY QUESTIONS:
What restrictions, if any, should there be on immigration?

In the early twentieth century, immigration soared, only to drop back during World War I. After the war, the Ku Klux Klan resurfaced, now targeting immigrants, Catholics, and Jews as well as blacks. With nearly 5 million members and chapters throughout the country, the Klan joined others with less violent supremacist beliefs to pressure Congress to limit immigration.[19] The Immigration Act of 1924 established quotas for ethnic groups based on the proportion of Americans from each nationality resident in 1890, thereby severely limiting the number of whites considered to be of "lower race," that is, those from southern and eastern Europe,[20] who constituted a huge proportion of immigrants from the 1890s on. Under the act, the quota for Italy, for example, dropped more than 90 percent[21] from the percentage allowed in the Immigration Act of 1921, which also established quotas but based them on the proportion of each nationality resident in 1910.

In 1952, President Harry S. Truman (1945–53), claiming that such quotas were un-American, vetoed a bill that continued the national quota system, but Congress overrode his veto. With the Immigration and Nationality Act of 1965, Congress rescinded the quota system and the especially severe restrictions on Asian immigration. Today, to apply for citizenship, one must have had legal permanent residence for five years, or three years if married to a U.S. citizen. Applicants also must be of good moral character and must be able to pass a test on questions such as "who elects the president?".

Racial Segregation and Discrimination

The end of slavery did not make former slaves equal citizens. Immediately after the war, southern states wrote new constitutions that severely limited the civil and political rights of the freedmen. These so-called black codes prevented them from voting, owning land, and

★ **Reconstruction:** *The period from 1865 to 1877 in which the former Confederate states gained readmission to the Union and the federal government passed laws to help the emancipated slaves.*

★ **equal protection clause:** *Prevents states from denying any person the equal protection of the laws (Fourteenth Amendment).*

leaving their plantations. Congress responded with the Civil Rights Act of 1866, which guaranteed the right of freedmen to make contracts, sue in court if those contracts were violated, and own property. Congress also established military rule over the former Confederate states, which would end in a state when it passed a new state constitution that guaranteed black suffrage and when it ratified the Fourteenth Amendment. With former Confederates barred from voting, blacks constituted a majority of the electorate in several states, and more than six hundred freedmen served in state legislatures during **Reconstruction**, as this era was called.

The Fourteenth Amendment (1868), in addition to guaranteeing that no state shall deny any person due process of law (see Chapter 4), prohibits states from denying any person the **equal protection** of the law. It also makes all people born in the United States citizens of the United States, overturning the Supreme Court's ruling in the *Dred Scott* case that blacks could not be U.S. citizens. In an attempt to prevent states from rescinding the right of black suffrage, the Fifteenth Amendment (1870) declared that the right to vote could not be abridged on account of race.

In segregated school systems, the schools for black children and the schools for white children were almost never equal. These insurance photographs show Liberty Hill Colored School and Summerton Graded School in Clarendon County, South Carolina, in 1948. They were used as evidence in *Briggs v. Elliott,* one of the school segregation cases decided with *Brown v. Board of Education* (1954).

Opponents of freedmen rights turned to violence. In 1866, Confederate veterans formed the Ku Klux Klan (KKK), a terrorist organization aimed at restoring white supremacy. In 1873, white supremacists massacred more than a hundred blacks in Colfax, Louisiana, as part of an ongoing election dispute. The federal government brought charges against three of the perpetrators, but the Supreme Court reversed their conviction, arguing that the Fourteenth Amendment gave Congress the authority to act only against states that violated civil rights (public discrimination), not against individuals who did so (private discrimination).[22]

Reconstruction ended with a deal over the 1876 election. A close and contested race between Republican Rutherford B. Hayes and Democrat Samuel Tilden was resolved when southern Democrats in Congress agreed to allow Hayes to become president in return for the withdrawal of federal troops from the South. Freed from military rule, white supremacist groups such as the Klan embarked on a campaign of lynching and other forms of terrorism against blacks.

State governments were not responsive to the victims because, despite the Fifteenth Amendment, southern politicians established a set of rules that kept blacks from voting. **Poll taxes** limited the voting of poor blacks (as well as of poor whites). The white primary took advantage of the fact that, with the Republican Party negatively associated with Lincoln and the Civil War, the Democratic Party completely dominated southern politics. Therefore, whoever won the local Democratic primary for an office was sure to win in the general election. Excluding blacks from voting in Democratic primaries meant that blacks had no effective vote at all. Even so, states used literacy tests to disqualify voters. These involved reading and interpreting difficult passages. To avoid disqualifying white voters as well, grandfather clauses gave exemptions to men whose grandfathers had been eligible to vote. The men who received these exemptions were, of course, always white (see Chapter 9 for further discussion of these techniques and an example of a literacy test).

These legal strategies effectively disenfranchised black men. In addition, state and local **Jim Crow laws** enforced segregation of whites and blacks in all public places. When a New Orleans civil rights organization challenged a Louisiana law requiring segregated railway cars by having Homer Plessy, who was one-eighth black, sit in the whites-only car, the Supreme Court upheld the segregation.[23] *Plessy v. Ferguson* (1896) established the **separate-but-equal doctrine**, which held that states could segregate the races without violating the equal protection clause of the Fourteenth Amendment as long as the separate facilities were equal.[24] Southern states segregated schools, libraries, and other public institutions and required the segregation of restaurants, inns, and other places of public accommodation. The facilities were almost never equal. African Americans in northern states often experienced discrimination in hiring, housing, hotels, and restaurants, though segregation was not enforced by law. African Americans could serve in the military but generally in segregated units under white officers. During the late nineteenth and early twentieth centuries, discrimination was state-sponsored in the South; elsewhere in the nation, people engaged in private discrimination without challenge.

Ethnic Segregation and Discrimination

Latinos and other ethnic groups experienced many of the same discriminatory practices as did African Americans. The separate but equal doctrine of *Plessy v. Ferguson* (1896) applied to Hispanics and other minorities. White voters instituted segregation in the South and the West. Phoenix, Arizona, ran separate schools for blacks, Indians, and Mexicans.[25] California ran separate schools for Asians as well as Mexicans,[26] while Texas kept Mexican Americans in separate classrooms.[27] In areas of the Southwestern United States, Latinos were required to sit in the back of buses, sit in movie theater balconies, and attend separate public schools. The end of segregation practices aimed at African Americans did not necessarily end them for Latinos (see Table 5.1).

Women's Suffrage

By law and by custom, women were also excluded from public life from the earliest days of the nation. In 1776, Abigail Adams had urged her husband, John Adams, to "remember the ladies" in drafting the nation's founding documents. In language similar to that later used by Jefferson in the Declaration, she warned, "if particular care and attention is not

poll taxes: *Tax on voting; prohibited by the Twenty-Fourth Amendment (1964).*

Jim Crow laws: *Southern laws that established strict segregation of the races and gave their name to the segregation era.*

separate-but-equal doctrine: *Supreme Court doctrine that upheld segregation as long as there were equivalent facilities for blacks.*

→ KEY QUESTIONS:
If some people are blocked from voting, what is the effect on government?

→ KEY QUESTIONS:
Should all citizens have the right to vote? Are there any citizens who should not have this right?

Table 5.1 Timeline of Civil Rights and Latinos[1]

Year	Event
1912	New Mexico enters the union as an officially bilingual state, with voting in both Spanish and English, as well as bilingual education.
1917	The U.S. Congress passes the Jones Act, granting citizenship to Puerto Ricans.
1921	*Orden Hijos de América* (Order of the Sons of America) organizes Mexican American workers to raise awareness of civil rights issues and fight for fair wages, education, and housing.
1928	Octaviano Larrazolo (R-NM) becomes the first Latino U.S. Senator.
1929	The League of United Latin American Citizens (LULAC) organizes against discrimination and segregation and promotes education among Latinos. It remains the largest and longest-lasting Latino civil rights group in the country.
1948	The American G.I. Forum forms in Texas to combat discrimination and improve the status of Latinos; branches eventually form in 23 states.
1954	*Hernandez v. Texas* strikes down discrimination based on class and ethnic distinctions.
1965	Congress passes the Voting Rights Act.
1965	Cesar Chavez and Dolores Huerta found the United Farm Workers association. It becomes the largest and most important farm worker union in the nation. Huerta becomes the first woman to lead such a union. The Grape Boycott becomes one of the most significant social justice movements for farm workers in the United States.
1966	*Katzenbach v. Morgan* allows Congress to prohibit English proficiency voting requirements for Puerto Ricans in New York.
1968	The Mexican American Legal Defense and Education Fund (MALDEF) is established, becoming the first legal fund to pursue protection of the civil rights of Mexican Americans. The Puerto Rican Legal Defense and Education Fund is founded in 1972.
1970	*Cisneros v. Corpus Christi Independent School District* extends the *Brown* decision to Latinos.
1973	*White v. Regester* calls for the creation of single-member election districts to prevent the dilution of Latino and African American voting strength.
1974	The first major Latino voter registration organization, the Southwest Voter Registration Education Project (SVREP) launches, registering more than two million Latino voters in the first 20 years.
1975	Congress votes to expand the Voting Rights Act to require language assistance at the polls and that election materials be available in multiple languages.
1982	*Plyler v. Doe* extends Fourteenth Amendment equal protection to children of undocumented workers.
1994	*Johnson v. DeGrandy* establishes the importance of proportionality as part of the totality of circumstances that must be considered in the redistricting process in this case from Florida involving Cuban Americans.
2001	The DREAM Act first introduced in Congress
2009	Sonia Sotomayor becomes first Latino Supreme Court Justice.
2013	*Shelby v. Holder* strikes down original formulas from the Voting Rights Act of 1965 that trigger requirements for states and local governments to obtain preclearance for changes to their election laws.

[1] Derived from "Latino Civil Rights Timeline, 1903 to 2006" in *Teaching Tolerance*, Southern Poverty Law Center. http://www.tolerance.org/latino-civil-rights-timeline
© CENGAGE LEARNING®

paid to the ladies, we are determined to foment a rebellion, and will not hold ourselves bound by any laws in which we have no voice or representation."[28] Nevertheless, neither the Declaration nor the Constitution made any provision for women's rights. Rather, the states continued the English policy of coverture, which granted married women no rights independent of their husbands. They could not own property, keep their own wages, or

During World War I, members of the National Woman's Party picketed the White House. Wearing banners announcing their colleges, they challenged President Woodrow Wilson to bring home the concern for liberty that he expressed for Europe. More than 150 women were arrested, and about 100 were sentenced to federal prisons, where some went on hunger strikes and were force-fed.

sign contracts. As for voting, each state set its own rules. In 1789, only New Jersey allowed women the right to vote (provided the women met the state's property requirements), a right it rescinded in 1807.[29]

In 1848 leaders of the **women's suffrage movement** met in Seneca Falls, New York, to organize for the right to vote. They prepared a "Declaration of Sentiments" that used the language of the Declaration of Independence to assert that "all men and women are created equal," but few results came from this meeting. Then, in 1869, Susan B. Anthony and Elizabeth Cady Stanton formed the National Woman Suffrage Association (NWSA), which lobbied for the right of women to vote and unsuccessfully opposed the Fifteenth Amendment unless it was changed to include women's suffrage. With the NWSA focused on gaining national suffrage through constitutional amendment, an alternative organization, the American Woman Suffrage Association (AWSA), formed to press for state-by-state suffrage rights.

While state control of voting gave southern states the power to disenfranchise blacks, it also gave western states the power to experiment with women's suffrage. The territory of Wyoming granted women's suffrage in 1869 and continued it upon statehood in 1890. Males in Colorado voted for women's suffrage in 1893. Utah granted women the right to vote in 1895. In 1913, Illinois granted women the right to vote for president but not for other national offices. In 1916, the people of Montana elected the first woman to serve in the U.S. House of Representatives, Jeannette Rankin (see Figure 5.2).

Suffragist amendments failed numerous times in Congress before receiving the necessary two-thirds vote in both chambers in 1919.[30] By August 1920, with effective lobbying by suffragist groups, three-quarters of the states ratified the Nineteenth Amendment, guaranteeing women the right to vote in the November 1920 presidential election (see also Chapter 9; for information on women's equality elsewhere in the world, see Global Gateways: Equal Treatment of Women).

 women's suffrage movement: *Movement to grant women the right to vote.*

→ KEY QUESTIONS:
Were Anthony and Stanton right or wrong to lobby against the Fifteenth Amendment?

→ KEY QUESTIONS:
Why was there such strong resistance to women's suffrage?

→ KEY QUESTIONS:
Should women be protected by an equal rights amendment?

Continued Gender Discrimination

Nevertheless, public law and private attitudes continued to block women from full participation in the nation's public life. Radical feminists pushed for an equal rights amendment, which

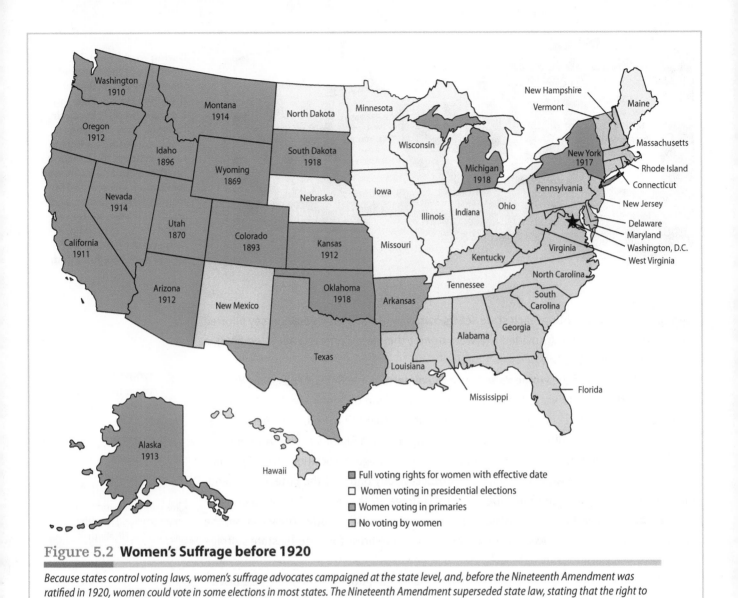

Figure 5.2 Women's Suffrage before 1920

Because states control voting laws, women's suffrage advocates campaigned at the state level, and, before the Nineteenth Amendment was ratified in 1920, women could vote in some elections in most states. The Nineteenth Amendment superseded state law, stating that the right to vote could not be denied or abridged by the United States, or by any state, on account of sex.

Source: © Cengage Learning; data from Mary Beth Norton et al., *A People and a Nation: A History of the United States,* 8th ed. (Boston: Houghton Mifflin, 2008), 608.

would have overturned protective legislation and other laws that treated men and women differently. Although introduced in Congress in 1923 and every year thereafter, it was not taken seriously. Even in 1945, only a minority of white males thought that women should be able to take jobs outside the home.[31]

Not surprisingly, the federal and state governments were responsive to these sorts of views. As late as 1972, eleven states continued to enforce coverture laws.[32] Louisiana, for example, gave a husband "as 'head and master' of property jointly owned with his wife," the complete right to dispose of such property without his wife's consent.[33] Teachers were commonly forced to retire if they got married.[34] Outside of coverture laws, Social Security provided survivors' benefits for children if their working fathers died but not if their working mothers died. It similarly provided unemployment benefits to children of unemployed fathers but not to children of unemployed mothers. Males in the military received benefits for their

globalgateways

Equal Treatment of Women

Virtually all nations formally protect equality under the law, but the degree to which women actually obtain equal treatment varies enormously, as does the degree to which women are elected or appointed to positions of authority.

India. Females suffer from legal and societal discrimination, including forced prostitution, prisoner rape, and the murder of female babies. The murder of women for bringing dishonor to their families, or their husbands' families, continues. *Sati*, the custom in which a widow kills herself on the funeral pyre of her husband, also continues. Dowry, the exchange of money or goods from the bride's family to the groom's, is also illegal, yet the press regularly reports on dowry disputes that have led to the murder of the bride. Nevertheless, a woman, Indira Gandhi, served as India's prime minister (1966–77 and 1980–84). Additionally, as of 2012, women in India also have positions as the head of several states and as the speaker of the Lok Sabha, the lower house in India's parliament.

Israel. Israel guarantees equality on account of sex, and equality is largely the case in secular society. Military service is compulsory for men and women. The nation's fourth prime minister was a woman— Golda Meir (1969–74). Today, women hold over 20 percent of the seats in the Knesset. Religious authorities, on the other hand, still have control over some civil matters, such as marriage, burial, and control of holy sites. Consequently, Jewish and Muslim women can have difficulty obtaining divorces without the consent of their husbands. However, Israeli law allows courts to fine and imprison unwilling husbands. Moreover, heterosexual and same-sex couples who do not marry in religious courts are granted legal privileges through the common law marriage.

South Africa. South Africa's constitution prohibits discrimination on account of sex, but there is pervasive violence and discrimination against women in South Africa, including violence by the military. Rape, sexual abuse, and forced marriages are very serious problems. Women have achieved some representation in South Africa's government and in fact hold a large share of seats in the National Assembly.

1. Why have other democracies elected female heads of government (prime ministers) while the United States has not had a female president?

2. Why do constitutional guarantees of equal rights for women not always translate into actual equality for women?

Source: Freedom House; U.S. Department of State.

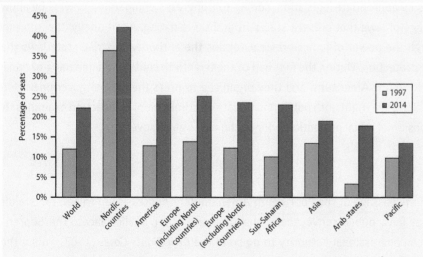

Note: The Nordic countries are Denmark, Finland, Iceland, Norway, Sweden, the Faroe Islands, Greenland, and the Åland Islands.

Source: Adapted from Inter-Parliamentary Union, 2011, "Women in Parliament in 2010: The Year in Perspective," Table 2.

WORLD AND REGIONAL AVERAGES OF WOMEN IN PARLIAMENT, 1997 AND 2014

One measure of progress for women is the percent of women in national legislatures. As can be seen from this figure, women are an increasing percentage of national legislatures in every region of the world. See the Global Gateways box in Chapter 13, The Judiciary, for the percentage of national high court judges held by women.

Checkpoint

CAN YOU:

- Describe the role of the Supreme Court in the expansion of slavery

- Enumerate ways that racial discrimination persisted after emancipation

- Track the steps in the achievement of women's suffrage

- Survey the laws that discriminated against women

- Identify the groups that have been denied rights to U.S. citizenship

- Discuss restraints on civil rights during wartime

dependents that females in the military did not receive. Idaho gave preferences to men over women in determining who would administer a dead relative's estate. Utah required parents to support sons until age 21 but daughters only until age 18. A woman could not work as a bartender in Michigan unless she was the wife or daughter of the bar's owner.[35]

Because women were treated differently than men under the law, many laws also discriminated against men. Colorado allowed females to drink beer at age 18; males had to wait until they turned 21. California, like many states, made it a crime for males of any age to have sexual relations with females under the age of 18 but had no corresponding penalty for females having sexual relations with underage males. Alabama, like many states, imposed alimony obligations on men only. New York allowed unwed mothers, but not unwed fathers, to block the adoption of their children. Florida provided property tax relief to widows but not to widowers. Even today, only males have to register for the military draft.[36] Many of these laws were based on an implicit assumption that women, viewed as the weaker sex, needed special protection by the government.[37] As late as 1961, the Supreme Court exempted women from jury duty because they were "the center of home and family life."[38]

5.3 The Expansion of Equal Protection

> Assess how equal protection has expanded

Today, Congress, constitutional amendments, and court decisions have largely put an end to public discrimination, and no clause has been as powerful in this effort as the equal protection clause of the Fourteenth Amendment, which prohibits states from denying any person the equal protection of the law. The amendment gives Congress the authority to enforce its provisions by appropriate legislation, adding to Congress's enumerated powers by allowing the passage of laws that prevent states from discriminating. Additionally, the Supreme Court, through the power of judicial review, retains the authority to strike state laws that violate equal protection. During the first half of the twentieth century, the meaning of equality changed for many Americans, and they organized to press the federal government into playing a crucial role to fight both public and private discrimination. This section examines the gradual expansion of equal protection prior to the civil rights movement.

→ KEY QUESTIONS:
If equality was not explicitly protected in the Constitution as originally ratified, how did it get to be so important today?

State Action

CONNECT
WITH YOUR CLASSMATES
MindTap® for American Government

Access the Civil Rights Forum: Discussion—Minority Rights Protection.

Shortly after the passage of the Fourteenth Amendment, Congress tried to ban private discrimination at inns, public conveyances, theaters, and other public places. The Supreme Court rejected congressional authority to do so in the *Civil Rights Cases* (1883), ruling that the Fourteenth Amendment prohibited public discrimination by the states only, not private discrimination by businesses or individuals. From the 1880s until the 1940s, the federal government remained passive with regard to discrimination, allowing states and locales to require segregation of the races and permitting public and private institutions to make their own rules regarding it.

In 1948, however, the Court ruled that private discrimination can be prohibited if it involves significant **state action**. The case involved housing. A group of homeowners signed a contract pledging never to sell their homes to blacks, but one of the homeowners did so. The neighbors sued to prevent the new owners from taking possession of the house, and the state supreme court ruled in favor of the neighbors. The U.S. Supreme Court reversed the state supreme court, ruling that judicial enforcement of the discriminatory private contract constitutes state action and thus is prohibited by the Fourteenth Amendment.[39]

→ KEY QUESTIONS:
Why is majority rule not always congruent with civil rights?

state action: *Action by a state, as opposed to a private person, that constitutes discrimination and therefore is an equal protection violation.*

Judicial Review

While the state-action doctrine allowed the Supreme Court to prohibit limited types of private discrimination, the equal protection clause of the Fourteenth Amendment is better suited to fighting public discrimination. In the next two decades, the Supreme Court actively applied the equal protection clause of the Fourteenth Amendment to do so. Congress also has the authority to enforce the equal protection clause, but democratically elected legislatures and executives are not necessarily designed to be responsive to minority groups, for they are chosen by a majority of voters. Thus civil rights organizations such as the National Association for the Advancement of Colored People (NAACP) and the League of United Latin American Citizens (LULAC) turned to the judiciary, whose members are not elected and so do not directly depend on majority support, for assistance in establishing legal equality.

→ KEY QUESTIONS:
Who should ensure citizen equality? State governments? The federal government? The president? Congress? The courts? Citizens?

As with civil liberties issues, for which the Court uses the standard of compelling interest (see Chapter 4), in civil rights cases, the Court has constructed tests to determine whether laws violate the equal protection clause. Depending upon the group whose right has been violated, the Court sets different standards of how closely it will scrutinize the law alleged to violate equal protection. There are at least three levels. The Court reserves the toughest standard of review, strict scrutiny, for laws alleged to discriminate on account of race, ethnicity, religion, or status as a legally admitted alien. It uses mid-level, or heightened scrutiny, for laws that discriminate on account of sex and the lowest level of scrutiny, rational basis, for general claims of discrimination (see Table 5.2).

Checkpoint

CAN YOU:

- Track the changing meaning of equality
- Explain why "state action" is so important to the equal protection clause
- Demonstrate that the judicial branch might be a better protector of civil rights than the legislative branch

Table 5.2 Supreme Court Scrutiny in Equal Protection Cases

Claim of Discrimination	Standard of Review	Test
Unprotected category	Lowest	Rational basis to achieve a legitimate governmental objective
Sex	Heightened	Exceedingly persuasive justification; use of sex as a governmental category must be substantially related to important governmental objectives
Race, ethnicity, religion, and legally admitted aliens	Strict	Most rigid scrutiny; use of race as a governmental category must be precisely tailored to meet a compelling governmental interest

© CENGAGE LEARNING®

5.4 The End of Legal Restrictions on Civil Rights

> Identify the groups at the forefront of the civil rights movement

The events that brought about the government's shift from enforcing discrimination to protecting against it did not begin with the government. It began with pressure from groups that were discriminated against that mobilized on their own behalf. This gateway of public pressure generally involves the use of civil liberties such as freedom of speech and of assembly to engage in protests and other activities aside from voting because minority groups, by definition, do not have the numbers to change policies through the ballot box alone.

Dismantling Public Discrimination Based on Race

 **Brown v. Board of Education:** *The 1954 Supreme Court decision striking down segregated schools.*

Among the most consequential forms of segregation from the Jim Crow era was the mandatory separation of schools for whites and blacks. Beginning in 1935, the NAACP's Legal Defense Fund embarked on a legal campaign—led by Thurgood Marshall, who would later become the first African American to serve on the Supreme Court—to dismantle the system of separate-but-equal schools in southern and border states that were always separate but rarely equal. After a series of cases in which the Supreme Court struck down specific segregated schools because they were not equal,[40] the Court ruled more generally in **Brown v. Board of Education** (1954) that separate schools were inherently unequal, even should facilities be essentially similar (see Supreme Court Cases: *Brown v. Board of Education*). Segregation in schools violated the equal protection clause of the Fourteenth Amendment. The Fourteenth Amendment only requires that states provide equal protection of the laws, but on the same day as the *Brown* decision, the Supreme Court used the due process clause of the Fifth Amendment to prohibit the national government from denying equal protection.[41]

CARL IWASAKI/TIME LIFE PICTURES/GETTY IMAGES

In 1950, when Linda Brown was entering third grade, her father Oliver Brown tried to enroll her in the Sumner School. The 10-year-old had been going to Monroe School, walking between train tracks and along streets without sidewalks to get there. Although it was closer, Sumner was for white students, and when Oliver Brown was told Linda could not attend, he took his case to the NAACP. Here the family stands in front of their home; Linda is on the left.

As historic as the *Brown* decision was, the case by itself did little to desegregate southern schools. Part of the problem was that the Court allowed local circumstances to influence the rate of integration, ambiguously requiring that local districts desegregate "with all deliberate speed."[42] Further, southern segregationists launched a massive resistance to the *Brown* decision. This campaign included "The Southern Manifesto," a document signed by 101 southern members of Congress deploring the *Brown* decision; the denial of state funds to any integrated school; and tuition grants for white students to attend segregated private schools. In addition, unruly segregationist mobs threatened black students seeking to integrate previously white schools. While neither the Supreme Court nor the Dwight D. Eisenhower administration (1953–61) could prevent every school disruption by segregationist mobs, both intervened in Little Rock, Arkansas. Eisenhower

supreme court cases

Hernandez v. Texas (1954)

Brown v. Board of Education (1954)

QUESTIONS: *Hernandez:* Does the equal protection clause allow Texas to exclude Mexican Americans from juries? *Brown:* Can states provide segregated schools for black and white schoolchildren?

ORAL ARGUMENT

Hernandez: January 11, 1954

Brown: December 7–9, 1953

DECISION:

Hernandez: May 3, 1954 (read at http://laws.findlaw .com/us/347/475.html)

Brown: May 17, 1954 (read at http://laws.findlaw.com /us/347/483.html)

OUTCOME:

Hernandez: No. The equal protection clause protects Mexican Americans (9–0).

Brown: No. Separate educational facilities are inherently unequal (9–0).

As noted in Chapter 2, The Constitution, Texas systematically excluded Mexican Americans from the murder trial of Pete Hernandez. Famed attorney and activist Gus Garcia told the Supreme Court that while the intent of the equal protection clause was to prevent racial discrimination against former slaves and their descendants, Texas treated Mexican Americans as a "class apart," and they therefore should be shielded against discriminatory laws by the equal protection clause. The Court agreed.

Two weeks later, the Supreme Court decided the *Brown* case. When Linda Brown was in third grade, her father, with the help of the NAACP, brought a suit against the Topeka school board for refusing to allow her to attend the local school that white children in their neighborhood attended.

In *Plessy v. Ferguson* (1896), the Supreme Court had ruled that the equal protection clause of the Fourteenth Amendment did not prohibit the states from establishing separate-but-equal facilities for whites

and blacks. The Court did not really begin to look at whether the facilities were equal or not until 1938, when it held that Missouri's paying for blacks to go to law school out of state was not the same as providing facilities within the state that were equal to its white law school.[*] A pair of 1950 cases declared, first, that admitting a black to an all-white school but forcing him to sit in a separate row and dine at a separate table was unconstitutional,[†] and second, that the equality of separate schools had to be compared on both objective factors that could be measured, such as the number of faculty members, and subjective factors that could not be measured, such as the reputation of the faculty.[‡]

The *Brown* case came to the Supreme Court with similar desegregation cases from South Carolina, Virginia, Delaware, and Washington, D.C. Thurgood Marshall, who was in charge of legal strategy for the NAACP and would later become the first African American to serve on the Supreme Court, argued the *Brown* case. He readily admitted that the schools in Linda Brown's case were roughly equal in objective characteristics but argued that segregation in and of itself denied black students the equal protection of the laws by creating a feeling of inferiority among them.

The Supreme Court's preliminary vote following the arguments showed a majority favoring striking segregation, with two or three dissenters. Chief Justice Earl Warren, however, thought that a decision that was bound to be met with resistance in the South should be unanimous if at all possible. Following several months of bargaining and persuasion, he eventually got every member of the Court to agree that the Court should strike down school segregation.

1. Can separate schools ever be equal?
2. Why were the courts more likely to be responsive to the problems of segregation than the legislature would be?

[*] *Missouri ex rel. Gaines v. Canada,* 305 U.S. 337 (1938).

[†] *McLaurin v. Oklahoma,* 339 U.S. 637 (1950).

[‡] *Sweatt v. Painter,* 339 U.S. 629 (1950).

federalized the Arkansas National Guard and sent in the 101st Airborne to protect the black students seeking to integrate Central High School, while the Supreme Court, declaring that it had the final say on what the Constitution means, rejected the threat of violence as a justification for delaying integration (see Chapter 11, The Presidency, and Chapter 13, The Judiciary, for more on the Little Rock case).[43]

To desegregate universities, President John F. Kennedy (1961–63) sent twenty-five thousand federal troops to ensure the enrollment of one black man, James Meredith, at the University of Mississippi in 1962. The following year, segregationist Governor George Wallace of Alabama famously "stood at the schoolhouse door" to prevent two black students from registering at the University of Alabama. He stepped aside only when Kennedy again sent troops to enforce integration.

Nevertheless, with few blacks able to vote, there was little need for southern politicians or school board officials to be responsive to their concerns, especially given massive opposition to desegregation by those who could vote. Only when the federal government took action did states respond. After Congress cut off federal aid to segregated schools in 1964, many districts began to integrate.[44] The rate of integration increased further in the late 1960s when the Supreme Court ended the "all deliberate speed" era and required an immediate end to segregated schools, thus pushing open the gateways to greater equality.[45]

Outside of schools, civil rights activists fought segregation in public facilities. The first grassroots action to receive nationwide attention was a bus boycott in Montgomery, Alabama. On December 1, 1955, police arrested Rosa Parks, a 42-year-old black seamstress and an active member of the NAACP, for refusing to give her seat to a white person. In response, the black community, led by a 26-year-old Baptist minister, Martin Luther King Jr., launched a boycott of city buses. Blacks walked, bicycled, and shared rides to avoid using the Montgomery bus system. Although the city arrested boycotters, and violent segregationist terrorists firebombed King's home, the boycotters held firm for more than a year. The Supreme Court then declared Montgomery's segregated bus system unconstitutional.[46] A new ordinance allowing blacks to sit anywhere on any bus ended the boycott. King became one of the national leaders of the emerging civil rights movement and Rosa Parks its first heroine.

With the *Brown* precedent in hand, the Supreme Court struck down state-mandated segregation not only in public transportation but also in other public facilities, such as beaches and city auditoriums. Given the massive opposition to the *Brown* decision, however, the Court refused to hear the appeal by a black woman sentenced to prison for the crime of marrying a white man.[47] As one justice reportedly said when the Court rejected another interracial marriage case, "One bombshell at a time is enough."[48] Not until 1967 in *Loving v. Virginia* did the Court strike down miscegenation, finding no compelling interest in a law that prohibited interracial marriage.[49]

→ KEY QUESTIONS:
What are terrorists? Were the people who bombed King's house terrorists?

→ KEY QUESTIONS:
What is more important, equality or freedom of association?

BETTMANN/CORBIS

Childhood sweethearts Mildred and Richard Loving married in Washington, D.C., because they could not marry in Virginia, where they lived. One month later, police burst into their bedroom and arrested them for violating Virginia's Racial Integrity Act. The couple eventually sued Virginia with legal assistance from the American Civil Liberties Union. In 1967, the Supreme Court struck down Virginia's law.

Dismantling Private Discrimination Based on Race

The decisions of businesses about whether to serve customers or hire workers on account of their race (or sex) were largely beyond judicial authority because the Fourteenth Amendment's equal protection clause only prevents states from discriminating; it does not bar private discrimination. Thus, if a restaurant chose not to serve blacks or an employer chose not to hire them, there was little a court could do unless Congress passed legislation forbidding such actions. The effort to dismantle private discrimination thus took two tracks: protests to pressure businesses into serving blacks, and lobbying to pressure Congress into passing legislation that would make private discrimination in commercial matters illegal.

The grassroots protests began when four African American freshmen at North Carolina Agricultural and Technical College in Greensboro sat down at the whites-only counter at Woolworth's, asked for coffee, and refused to leave when not served. Within weeks, the sit-ins spread to dozens of other cities. One protest leader, Diane Nash, along with other young participants in the sit-ins, formed the Student Nonviolent Coordinating Committee (SNCC), which along with the Congress of Racial Equality (CORE) served as the more activist "younger brothers" of the NAACP.

In 1961, CORE organized freedom rides, trips on interstate buses into the segregated South, where the integrated buses were legal under federal law even though they violated local segregation rules. Mobs attacked the buses—firebombing one of them—and beat the riders. Under pressure from the federal government, including protection of the riders by federal marshals, the states eventually agreed not to interfere with interstate travelers.[50]

In the spring of 1963, Martin Luther King Jr.'s Southern Christian Leadership Conference (SCLC) led demonstrations in Birmingham, Alabama, to bring about the integration of downtown businesses. The police met demonstrators with fire hoses, police dogs, and cattle prods. Police arrested hundreds of protesters, including King. When white clergymen questioned why King, an outsider, had come to Birmingham, King answered in his famous "Letter from Birmingham Jail": "I am in Birmingham because injustice is here."[51] Rejecting violence, King insisted that peaceful civil disobedience was the only gateway to negotiation. The negotiations took place and ended with Birmingham businesses agreeing to integrate lunch counters and hire more blacks. Nevertheless, or perhaps because of this, members of the KKK exploded a bomb at a local black church on a Sunday morning, murdering four young girls.

> **→ KEY QUESTIONS:**
> If a law is immoral, are you right or wrong to disobey it? What is the remedy?

Earlier that summer, King had led two hundred thousand protesters at the March on Washington. It was there that King delivered his historic "I Have a Dream" speech, in which he declared:

> **→ KEY QUESTIONS:**
> Which branch of government has been most powerful in ensuring equality? Why?

> *I have a dream that one day this nation will rise up and live out the true meaning of its creed: "We hold these truths to be self-evident: that all men are created equal." I have a dream that one day on the red hills of Georgia the sons of former slaves and the sons of former slave owners will be able to sit down together at the table of brotherhood. I have a dream that one day even the state of Mississippi, a state sweltering with the heat of injustice, sweltering with the heat of oppression, will be transformed into an oasis of freedom and justice. I have a dream that my four little children will one day live in a nation where they will not be judged by the color of their skin but by the content of their character.[52]*

President Kennedy proposed a civil rights bill that would have banned discrimination in public accommodations, such as restaurants and hotels. Five days after Kennedy's assassination in November 1963, President Lyndon Baines Johnson (1963–69) told Congress that nothing could better honor Kennedy than passage of this bill. The next year, Congress passed the **Civil Rights Act**, which significantly strengthened Kennedy's original bill by also prohibiting employment discrimination on account of "race, color, religion, sex, or national origin."

Because the Fourteenth Amendment's equal protection clause applies only to state-sponsored discrimination, the Supreme Court upheld Congress's authority to ban private discrimination under the interstate commerce clause. Given the Court's broad interpretation of interstate commerce (see Chapter 3, Federalism), the Court ruled that even small inns and restaurants had to abide by the act.[53]

Civil Rights Act: *Prohibits discrimination in employment, education, and places of public accommodation (1964).*

Dismantling Voting Barriers Based on Race

As noted previously, the end of Reconstruction left black men in the South with a constitutional right to vote but a hostile social and legal environment that made it extremely difficult for them to do so. The Supreme Court pushed things along, striking down grandfather clauses (1915) and white primaries (1944), the latter in a suit filed by the NAACP.[54] Congress and the states pushed things along further, outlawing poll taxes with the Twenty-Fourth Amendment (1964). Martin Luther King Jr. identified four gates that kept blacks from voting: white terrorist control of local governments and sheriffs' departments; arrests on trumped-up charges of those seeking to vote; the discretion given to registrars, where "the latitude for discrimination is almost endless"; and the arbitrary nature of literacy tests.[55]

During the summer of 1964, voting rights supporters from around the country, many of them college students, moved south to help with voter registration drives. Klansmen murdered three of the volunteers in Philadelphia, Mississippi, that June. In March 1965, King organized a voting rights march from Selma to Montgomery, Alabama. With national news media on hand, Alabama police, under the authority of Governor George Wallace, beat the marchers with whips, nightsticks, and cattle prods. Selma natives murdered two more voting rights activists.

A week later, President Johnson addressed a joint session of Congress, calling for passage of the strictest possible voting rights legislation. Congress responded by passing the **Voting Rights Act (VRA)** in August 1965. The act limited literacy, interpretation, and other such tests for voting. It required states with low voter registration levels, essentially seven southern states plus Alaska, to receive preclearance from the Justice Department for any changes to its voting laws. It also established new criminal penalties for those who sought to keep people from voting on account of race. The law was an enormous success. By 2008, blacks and whites voted at essentially the same rate nationwide[56] and at slightly higher rates in some southern states.[57] In 2012, blacks had a higher turnout rate than whites.[58] In 2013, however, the Supreme Court voted 5-4 in *Shelby County v. Holder* to strike down the 1965 formula that established which jurisdictions needed to obtain preclearance.[59] Until Congress passes a new formula, no jurisdictions need to obtain preclearance.

Voting Rights Act: *Gives the federal government the power to prevent discrimination in voting rights (1965).*

→ KEY QUESTIONS:
How has expansion of the right to vote affected citizen participation? How has it affected public policy?

This decision may depress future black turnout as states like Texas move to pass Voter ID laws that were previously blocked under the VRA by the Justice Department[60] (see Figure 5.3).

Dismantling Public Discrimination Based on Ethnicity

Similar to African Americans, Latinos began the struggle for civil rights in the court system through interest groups such as the American G.I. Forum, LULAC, and later the Mexican American Legal Defense and Education Fund (MALDEF). One of the first steps Latinos took toward securing civil rights was to be recognized as a protected class of people under the Fourteenth Amendment. As we have seen, the attorneys in *Hernandez v. Texas* argued that Hispanics were a class of individuals entitled to the same due process guarantees as were African Americans and other racial groups.[61] The court agreed and also ruled that Mexican Americans could not be systematically excluded from juries, a key form of citizenship.

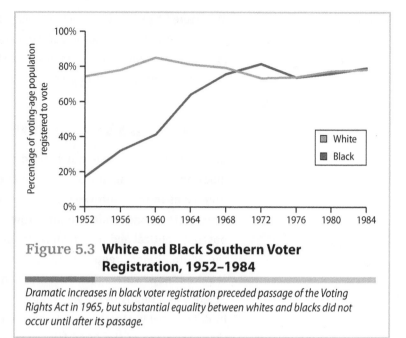

Figure 5.3 White and Black Southern Voter Registration, 1952–1984

Dramatic increases in black voter registration preceded passage of the Voting Rights Act in 1965, but substantial equality between whites and blacks did not occur until after its passage.

Source: Data from Harold W. Stanley, *Voter Mobilization and the Politics of Race* (New York: Praeger, 1987), Appendix A.

In 1970, the Supreme Court extended the *Brown* ruling to apply to Latinos and other minority groups in *Cisneros v. Corpus Christi Independent School District.*[62] Because Mexican Americans were considered white, the Corpus Christi Independent School District created two sets of schools: one set for African American and Latino children and the other for "All-White" (non-Latino) children. In that way, they circumvented the desegregation ruling of *Brown*. Attorney James de Anda, supported by the MALDEF, argued that the separate schools system was unconstitutional because Mexican Americans were a separate and distinct group from whites. The Supreme Court recognized Latinos as a distinct ethnic minority group that had been subject to discriminatory practices.[63] Latino American school children were no longer subject to separate but equal educational facilities. In *Plyler v. Doe* (1982), described in Chapter 1, Gateways to American Democracy, the court expanded protections further, deciding that the children of undocumented workers were entitled to free public education in Texas.[64]

Public education is a major gateway to participation in civic life. Its denial constitutes a gate that prevents equality. Yet other gates in lesser, yet important areas, also existed. The use of public swimming pools, buses, and water fountains, for example, were segregated. In the early 1950s, sometimes there was no "equal" facility available to Latinos. Latino elected officials helped lead the effort to break down these and other types of barriers to citizenship. Prominent among them is Henry B. Gonzalez, the first Mexican American to be elected to the San Antonio City Council. One of his first victories was opening public facilities such as swimming pools to all residents. When he served in the Texas Senate, he filibustered a series of bills aimed at circumventing the *Brown* case. He held the floor for a record twenty-two hours and defeated all but two of the bills. He later served as Congressman from the 20th District in Texas, now occupied by Joaquín Castro (see the opening vignette in Chapter 10, Congress).[65]

Dismantling Voting Barriers Based on Ethnicity

Just as segregation was not limited to African Americans, voting laws created gates blocking Latinos' ability to exercise the right to vote. Poll taxes influenced Mexican Americans in the Southwest, for whom the cost to vote was a greater burden than for white voters. And while the Jim Crow version of literacy tests often involved tests of obscure political and historical facts for first-time voters, such as African Americans in the South, literacy requirements influenced Latinos differently. New York, for example, required "new" voters (i.e., Puerto Ricans) to provide evidence of English language proficiency as a requisite for voter registration. In 1966, however, the Supreme Court ruled in *Katzenbach v. Morgan* (see Supreme Court Cases, Chapter 11) and *Cardona v. Power* that provisions of the 1966 VRA prevented New York from imposing English language requirements for voting.[66] In 1970, the VRA was amended to eliminate all literacy tests, and, in 1975, Congress further amended the VRA to protect language minorities. As a result of those and subsequent amendments to the VRA, states and other political units such as counties or cities, must provide voting information, assistance, and ballots in the minority language if more than 5 percent of the citizens of voting age in the jurisdiction are of a language minority or their number exceeds ten thousand.[67]

DOUGLAS GRAHAM/CO-ROLL CALL GROUP/CONGRESSIONAL QUARTERLY/GETTY IMAGES

Former Congressman Henry B. Gonzalez, the first Latino elected to Congress from Texas, rose to become the Chair of the House Committee on Banking, Finance, and Urban Affairs.

Language requirements were only one type of gate. Other, less obvious gates to participation blocked Latino voters. The manner by which elections are structured may also create gates to meaningful participation. In Dallas County and Bexar County in Texas, for example, elections had been conducted on an at-large basis, meaning that candidates ran in multi-member districts. Ethnic minorities could not corral a high enough percent of the vote to elect Latino or other representatives who embodied their interests. This form of election is still common in many jurisdictions and is not necessarily a violation of voting rights.

In 1973, however, the Supreme Court ruled in *White v. Regester* that the VRA prohibited electoral plans that may effectively dilute the voting strength of minorities, in this case, Latinos.[68] The multi-member district elections in those jurisdictions were being used a means to minimize the voting strength of Hispanic (in San Antonio) and African American (in Dallas) citizens. Such plans limited the effective participation of those groups to elect candidates of their choice. The Supreme Court mandated that single-member districts be used. As a result of this decision, groups such as MALDEF, Communities Organized for Public Service (COPS) and Southwest Voter Registration and Education Project (SWVREP) and their leaders organized to change the way many local elections were structured (see below). Evidence shows the impact of election practices was dramatic. After the switch to single-member districts in 1977, the San Antonio city elected five Mexican Americans to the city council as well as one African American candidate. For the first time in the city's history, a majority of the city council was composed of minorities.[69]

It was MALDEF that brought *White v. Regester* and many other cases forward. In the 1970s, MALDEF undertook ninety-three federal and state cases in Texas alone: 76 percent of the cases involved desegregation, and 14 percent were cases about voting and other political rights.[70] That is one reason why MALDEF has come to be known as the "law firm of the Latino community." See Chapter 9 for a discussion of the impact of the VRA and Supreme Court decisions on Latino voter turnout.

Dismantling Private Discrimination Based on Ethnicity

Like women, Latinos have faced an uphill battle in the workplace. Deprived of their lands following Texas' break with Mexico, deported during the Great Depression and other periods, Latinos have long filled the demand for the need for unskilled labor, particularly in the field of agriculture. As a result, perhaps the most well known of civil rights efforts among Latinos is in the agriculture industry. Cesar Chavez and Dolores Huerta organized the United Farm Workers (UFW) union to secure safe working conditions and increased wages for laborers. Formed in 1962, the UFW continues to work to improve conditions for agriculture workers. When the UFW began, farm workers earned less than one dollar per hour. The first task of Chavez and Huerta was to organize the workers so that they could bargain collectively with growers. Once formed, they called for boycotts of fruit and vegetables as well as strikes against growers in order to gain the right to bargain collectively. The UFW counts among its successes bargaining agreements that required growers to provide rest periods for workers, toilets in fields, clean drinking water, and protections against dangerous pesticides.[71] The UFW increased the collective voice of Latinos in the agriculture industry and fought for basic human and civil rights.

The UFW also registered Latinos to vote and encouraged them to become active politically. The success of the UFW and other Latino organizations to end segregation and discrimination continues as it does for other groups. For Latinos, efforts continue to expand educational opportunities to DREAMers, and prevent the efforts by some to limit political participation (see the discussion of Voter ID laws in Chapter 9).[72] As with any social movement, leadership and organization

Young undocumented immigrants protesting outside the Federal Building in Detroit, Michigan.

→ KEY QUESTIONS:
Why, in U.S. history, do women's rights movements follow, rather than precede, movements to remove racial barriers?

★ **Equal Pay Act:**
Prohibits different pay for males and females for the same work (1963).

→ KEY QUESTIONS:
Should there be an Equal Rights Amendment to the U.S. Constitution?

is vital to the success of groups seeking equal protection and due process. As noted at the beginning of this section, much of the impetus for change begins with pressure from groups. As Cesar Chavez said, "Those who attack our union often say, 'It's not really a union. It's something else: A social movement. A civil rights movement. It's something dangerous. . . .' [T]he UFW has always been something more than a union—although it's never been dangerous if you believe in the Bill of Rights."[73] As Latinos continue to be the fastest growing ethnic group in the United States, it is clear that many gates to political participation have been placed before them. Latinos are slowly becoming a political force in the United States (see Chapter 9). Emerging generations of Latinos such as Erika Andiola, leader of the Arizona DREAM Coalition, are poised to continue working to secure those rights.

Dismantling Discrimination Based on Gender

The success of the civil rights movement inspired other groups, most notably women, to put pressure on the political system to obtain equal rights under the law. Women active in the civil rights movement easily shifted the movement's strategies to promoting rights for women, particularly after the publication of Betty Friedan's *The Feminine Mystique* (1963), a book considered by many to have launched the modern American feminist movement. Based on a survey Friedan sent to her Smith College classmates in advance of their fifteenth reunion, the book broadcast the dissatisfaction that many American women felt in their roles as wives and mothers. About the same time, the Kennedy administration's President's Commission on the Status of Women, charged with making recommendations for overcoming sex discrimination, urged passage of the **Equal Pay Act**. Passed by Congress in 1963, the act prohibits employers from paying different wages for the same job on account of sex. Although the act did not prohibit discrimination in the hiring of male and female workers, that prohibition came with the Civil Rights Act of 1964. See Public Policy and Civil Rights: Workplace Equality.

Following passage of the Civil Rights Act, Friedan helped found the National Organization for Women (NOW), which advocated for women's rights through education and litigation. NOW protested airline policies that forced stewardesses to retire at marriage or age 32 and help-wanted ads that listed jobs by gender, as well as protective legislation. NOW also supported abortion rights and a proposed Equal Rights Amendment (ERA), which would have prohibited the federal government and the states from discriminating on account of sex.

In 1972, the American Civil Liberties Union (ACLU) established the Women's Rights Project, which worked to eliminate discriminatory laws. The first project director, future Supreme Court Justice Ruth Bader Ginsburg, developed a litigation strategy for ending gender-based discrimination. Prior to Ginsburg's work, the Court had rejected equal protection claims for women. Ginsburg first persuaded the Court to strike laws based on the rational-basis

BETTMANN/CORBIS

In 1960, when Columbia law student Ruth Bader Ginsburg applied for a Supreme Court clerkship, Justice Felix Frankfurter chose not to interview her. Ginsburg went on to a distinguished career as a professor of law and chief litigator for the American Civil Liberties Union, eventually arguing cases before the Court, which she joined in 1993 as the second female associate justice. She is pictured here in 1977.

standard and then got the Court to approve a heightened-scrutiny standard. This is a step below the strict scrutiny used in cases discriminating on account of race, but the standard is tough enough that the Court usually strikes laws that discriminate according to sex.

Meanwhile, the Equal Rights Amendment (ERA), passed by Congress and sent to the states for ratification in 1972, began to falter. An anti-ERA movement led by political activist Phyllis Schlafly reversed the momentum by arguing that the amendment would remove special privileges women enjoyed with regard to protective legislation, Society Security benefits, and exemption from the draft. Ironically, another argument against the ERA was that it was unnecessary because the Supreme Court was striking down most laws that discriminated on account of sex. Despite an extension of the deadline to 1982, the ERA ultimately fell three states short of the three-quarters majority needed to pass an amendment (see Figure 5.4).

Checkpoint

CAN YOU:

- Explain why the *Brown* decision by itself had only a minimal effect on school desegregation
- Identify the grassroots protests that opened the gateways to ending private discrimination
- Describe how Congress and the courts have pushed along voting rights
- Draw parallels between the civil rights movement for African Americans and the women's rights movement

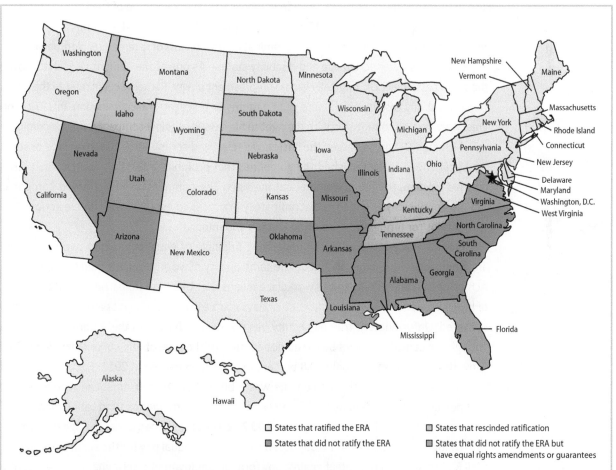

☐ States that ratified the ERA
■ States that did not ratify the ERA
■ States that rescinded ratification
■ States that did not ratify the ERA but have equal rights amendments or guarantees

Figure 5.4 States Approving the Equal Rights Amendment

Passed by Congress in 1972 and sent to the states for ratification, the Equal Rights Amendment got a quick start and then faltered as opposition materialized and grew. In 1979, Congress extended the deadline for ratification to 1982, but in 1982, the amendment expired. Thirty-five states (of the thirty-eight needed) had voted to ratify it, and five states had voted to rescind ratification.

Source: © Cengage Learning®; data from http://www.equalrightsamendment.org.

Public Policy and Civil Rights:
Workplace Equality

Although national legislation and constitutional amendments define civil rights policy, and the Supreme Court interprets such laws—deciding whether they are constitutional and, if so, what they mean—the day-to-day protection of civil rights now falls to two separate executive branch agencies. One is the Civil Rights Division of the Department of Justice, with sections on educational opportunity, employment, housing, voting, and disability rights. The other is the Equal Employment Opportunity Commission (EEOC), which protects against sexual harassment in the workplace and promotes gender equity.

The EEOC is an independent agency with commissioners selected for five-year fixed terms. Unlike the heads of government departments, EEOC commissioners cannot be removed by the president. They are thus thought to be shielded from political pressures, but fixed terms also limit responsiveness to the president, who is the chief executive of the United States.

Congress established the EEOC as part of the Civil Rights Act of 1964. The original EEOC could receive and investigate complaints of discrimination on the basis of race, sex, religion, and national origin (Congress later added age and disability status). As one of the compromises that allowed the act to pass, the EEOC originally had no enforcement power. Rather, it could refer to the Justice Department any case in which there were patterns or practices of discrimination. In 1972, Congress provided the commission with the right to file lawsuits against companies that discriminate.

Although Congress passed the basic law declaring discrimination based on race or sex to be illegal, the EEOC established the guidelines that prohibited discrimination against hiring married women, pregnant women, and mothers. The commission also allowed companies that had previously engaged in discriminatory practices to establish affirmative action plans with quotas for hiring and promoting women and minorities.

From a policy standpoint, the underlying principle of equal pay is that two people who are employed in the same job and do the same quality of work should be paid the same wage. Achieving gender equality in the workplace means that there are no barriers to advancement or hiring based on gender and that gender plays no role in how employees are treated and compensated. Unfortunately, true pay equity has not been achieved in the American workplace. Though the census statistics below do not control for the type of job worked, data from 2012 show that women earned only 80.8 percent of what men earned in 2012. For African American and Latino women, this percentage was a bit higher: African American women earned 90.1 percent and Latinas earned 88.0 percent of what African American and Latino men made.[74] Additionally, the gap falls to slightly above 90.2 percent for women under the age of 35.[75]

Though the Equal Pay Act is supposed to guarantee equal pay for the same work, and the Civil Rights Act aims to protect against any form of employment discrimination on account of sex, the judicial branch has also played a pivotal role. A recent set of Supreme Court decisions has prompted changes in the laws governing discrimination, harassment, and pay equity in the workplace. In one case, the Supreme Court ruled in favor of a woman who was suspended without pay for more than a month and was reassigned to a less desirable position after she claimed sex discrimination in the workplace. The Court decided that an indefinite suspension without pay is retaliation that would reasonably deter any employee from making a discrimination complaint, and, therefore, it was illegal.[76]

But the Court's 2007 ruling in *Ledbetter v. Goodyear Tire and Rubber Co.* had the greatest impact on public policy.[77] In 1998, Lilly Ledbetter filed a complaint with the EEOC that she had consistently received poor job performance evaluations because of her gender and that over the nineteen years she had worked at the Goodyear Tire plant, she had fallen well below her male colleagues who did the same type of job. Her employer countered that, even if that had been true in the past, she did not file her complaint within the 180 days required by the Civil Rights Act. The Court ruled in favor of Goodyear, stating that Ledbetter's claims alleging sex discrimination were time-barred because the discriminatory decisions relating to pay had been made more than 180 days prior to the day she filed the charge with the EEOC. In her dissent, Justice Ruth Bader Ginsburg wrote that the effect of this ruling would allow "any annual pay decision not contested immediately (within 180 days) . . . [to become] grandfathered, a fait accompli beyond the province of Title VII ever to repair."[78] Basically, a company could pay a woman less on the basis of gender, and as long as she did not contest the discriminatory wage within 180 days, the discriminatory wage could not be challenged in federal court.

In 2009, Congress reversed the Court's ruling by passing the Lilly Ledbetter Fair Pay Act, which was the first Act that President Obama signed into law. The act restarts the clock each time an employee receives a paycheck that has been compromised by discriminatory practices.[79] Many equal pay advocates think that this new law will be helpful but not nearly helpful enough to close the salary gap between men and women. Indeed, early reports suggest that some individual women have been able to sue who would not have been able to do so before the act but that these individual suits have done little to close the gender pay gap.[80]

In 2014, President Obama moved to increase equality through the Paycheck Fairness Act, which would revise remedies for paycheck inequality, increase enforcement activity against unequal pay, and limit exceptions to rules against sex discrimination in wages.[81] With every Republican voting against it, the Senate failed to obtain the sixty votes needed to cut off debate.[82] With this legislative stalemate, President Obama issued two executive orders to accomplish what he could on his own. First, federal contractors could not punish workers for discussing their wages among one another. He also required federal contractors to file data with the federal government showing how they pay employees by race and by sex.[83]

Construct Your Own Policy

1. Design a system of evaluation in the private sector workplace to ensure that decisions on pay raises and promotions are not made on the basis of race, sex, or sexual orientation.

2. Develop a plan for state and local government enforcement of workplace equality, replacing federal government oversight.

COMPARE WITH YOUR PEERS

MindTap for American Government

Access the Civil Rights Forum: Polling Activity—Civil Rights Protection.

5.5 Frontiers in Civil Rights

> Describe the new battles for civil rights

Many of the civil rights battles against legal discrimination have been won: Governments cannot discriminate on account of race or sex, and businesses cannot discriminate in hiring employees or serving customers. But the expanded notion of equality promoted by the civil rights and women's rights movements inspired other groups, such as homosexuals and the disabled, to demand full access to equality. At the same time, as the fight over the ERA made clear, the extension of rights for some may involve a loss of privileges for others, and sometimes rights clash. Congress and the courts have sought to define the meaning and limits of rights as new areas of conflict emerge over such issues as racial and religious profiling, the voting rights of felons, and the civil rights of undocumented immigrants. Whatever the new issues, however, the trend in the United States has been for a broader meaning of equality and greater support for civil rights.

> **KEY QUESTIONS:**
> Is the era of civil rights over? Have all the battles been fought and won?

Sexual Orientation and Same-Sex Marriage

The movement to protect the rights of homosexuals first received widespread public attention in 1969 when a police raid on the Stonewall Inn, a gay bar in New York City, turned into a riot by the bar's patrons and gay rights supporters living in the area. The **Stonewall riots** became the signature event of a growing gay rights movement. Activists soon formed the Gay Liberation Front, which established branch organizations around the world. By the 1990s, the movement had expanded into a broader LGBT movement that sought to protect the rights of lesbians, gays, bisexuals, and transgendered persons.

★ **Stonewall riots:**
Street protest in 1969 by gay patrons against a police raid of a gay bar in New York; the protest is credited with launching the gay rights movement.

> **KEY QUESTIONS:**
> Do court decisions follow public opinion? Do they lead public opinion? What should be the relationship?

At the time of the Stonewall riots, all states banned sodomy, which would include virtually all sexual activity between same-sex couples.[84] In the following years, several states decriminalized homosexual activity, but as noted in Chapter 4, the Supreme Court ruled in 1986 that homosexual activity was not a fundamental right, so states could still keep homosexuality illegal if they so chose. Colorado went further, passing an amendment to its state constitution that prohibited the state, or any city or town in the state, from passing laws that granted civil rights protections on account of sexual orientation. The Supreme Court struck this law in 1996, claiming that it was born of dislike toward gays.[85] Then, in *Lawrence v. Texas* (2003), the Supreme Court reversed the 1986 decision and declared that states could not prohibit sexual activity between people of the same sex[86] (see Supreme Court Cases for Chapter 6, Public Opinion and the Media).

> **KEY QUESTIONS:**
> What government (state or federal) or branch of government (executive, legislative, or judicial) should have the power to decide whether same-sex marriage is legal?

Thousands of citizens in same-sex partnerships want to be married but are not eligible for that legally recognized status, which brings advantages with regard to the right to make health care decisions for a spouse, inheritance rights, and tax benefits. The issue of same-sex marriage is highly controversial. State laws typically govern family matters, including marriage, divorce, child custody, and wills, and, in most states, marriage is limited to one man and one woman. While each state can set its own rules, the full faith and credit clause of the Constitution generally requires each state to accept the status granted by other states. Thus, opposite-sex couples who get married in Las Vegas under Nevada law are recognized as married throughout the United States.

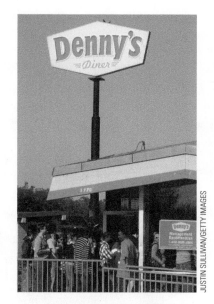

LIBRARY OF CONGRESS PRINTS AND PHOTOGRAPHIC-USF33-20513-M2]

JUSTIN SULLIVAN/GETTY IMAGES

Has discrimination ended? While restaurants are no longer segregated as was the Farmers Cafe Quick Lunch in Durham, North Carolina, in 1940, Denny's restaurant chain was sued for racial bias in the early 1990s. Plaintiffs reported that black customers had been refused service, required to pay cover charges, subjected to derogatory remarks, and forcibly removed, primarily from restaurants in California. In a settlement, Denny's agreed to end the practices in question and train employees to treat all customers equally.

When the Hawaii Supreme Court ruled in 1993 that, under the state constitution, Hawaii would have to show a compelling interest in its prohibition of same-sex marriages, opponents feared that same-sex marriages performed in Hawaii would have legal recognition throughout the United States. In 1996, Congress passed and President Clinton signed the Defense of Marriage Act (DOMA), which defines marriage, for the purpose of federal law, as between a man and a woman. The Act did not prohibit same-sex marriage, but it declared that neither the individual states nor the United States have to recognize same-sex marriages legally performed in other states. Later that year, the Hawaii Supreme Court ruled that the state did not have a compelling interest in prohibiting same-sex marriages, but voters then approved a state constitutional amendment allowing the state legislature to ban same-sex marriage. Since that time, courts, legislatures, and citizen initiatives have battled over same-sex marriage, with judicial protection sometimes overridden by popular opposition, as in California (2008) and Maine (2009) (see Figure 5.5). In 2012, a federal appeals court ruled that the California initiative banning same-sex marriage violated the equal protection clause.[87] This decision was appealed to the Supreme Court. When California refused to defend the law, however, the Supreme Court ruled that proponents of the law did not have standing to bring the case before the court. By dismissing the case in this way, the Supreme Court effectively allowed for the continuation of same-sex marriage in California.

Meanwhile, a new suit challenged DOMA. When Thea Spyer passed away in 2009, she left her wife, Edith Windsor, a substantial estate. If Spyer and Windsor were an opposite-sexed couple, Windsor would not have owed a single penny in estate tax, as husbands and wives can leave each other unlimited amounts of money under federal law. But since they were both female, DOMA required that the United States not recognize Spyer and Windsor as having been married. Windsor filed suit to recover the $363,000 in estate taxes she had paid. On the same day as the California case, the Supreme Court ruled in *United States*

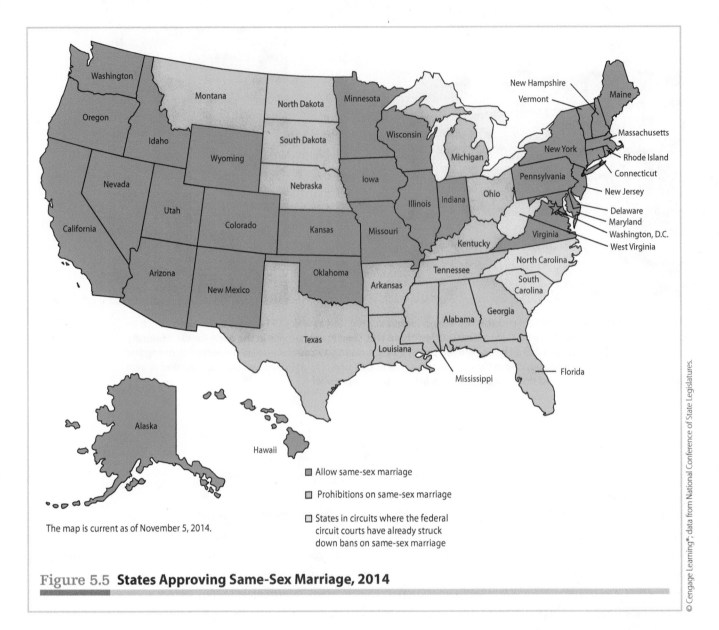

The map is current as of November 5, 2014.

■ Allow same-sex marriage

■ Prohibitions on same-sex marriage

□ States in circuits where the federal circuit courts have already struck down bans on same-sex marriage

Figure 5.5 States Approving Same-Sex Marriage, 2014

v. Windsor that the section of DOMA that limited spousal recognition under federal law to a man and a woman was unconstitutional.[88] By November 5, 2014, the Supreme Court let stand Court of Appeals decisions from various lower court circuits upholding the right to same sex marriages in Wisconsin, Indiana, Virginia, Oklahoma, Utah, Idaho, Nevada, Colorado, Wyoming, Kansas, and Missouri. Those circuits also cover North Carolina, South Carolina, and West Virginia, so it is likely that those states will soon have legal same-sex marriages too.

National public opinion remains mixed on the matter of same-sex marriage (see Figure 5.6). While a substantial majority of Americans favor allowing same-sex marriage,[89] only thirty-four states and the District of Columbia have legally recognized same-sex marriage. The major political parties are divided on the issue: Democrats are typically more supportive of same-sex marriage than Republicans are. Because support for same-sex marriage is much greater among younger Americans than among older Americans, legal recognition of same-sex marriage will almost certainly increase over time. In November 2014, the Sixth Circuit upheld Michigan's ban on same-sex marriage, creating a conflict between circuits that will likely lead to review by the Supreme Court.

Disability Rights

Advocates for the rights of the disabled, encouraged by the civil rights, women's rights, and other movements, successfully lobbied for the Rehabilitation Act of 1973, which prohibits discrimination against disabled individuals by any federal agency or by any private program or activity that receives federal funds. The landmark Americans with Disabilities Act (ADA) passed in 1990 goes further, requiring public and private employers to make "reasonable accommodations" to known physical and mental limitations of employees with disabilities and, if possible, to modify performance standards to accommodate an employee's disability.

To comply with the act, public transportation authorities have made buses and trains accessible to people in wheelchairs. Public accommodations, such as restaurants, hotels, movie theaters, and doctors' offices, must also meet ADA accessibility standards, within reason, removing barriers from existing structures. Related legislation, the Individuals with Disabilities Education Act (IDEA; 1990, updated 2004) requires states to provide free public education to all children with disabilities in the least-restrictive environment appropriate to their particular needs.

Congress does not provide a full list of disabilities covered under the ADA, but rather covers any disability that "substantially limits a major life activity." Thus, a trucking company need not make accommodations for a driver who can see clearly out of only one eye because the disability does not substantially limit a major life activity. On the other hand, the ADA does protect people who have HIV or AIDS. It even protects people with severe drug and alcohol problems, provided the drug use in question is not illegal.[90]

Many organized interests support the rights of the disabled. While prejudice against people of different races, religions, sexual orientation, and country of origin might lead responsive representatives to oppose the rights of minorities, there are few if any votes to be had by lobbying against the rights of the disabled. Nevertheless, when at the end of 2011 the Department of Labor proposed new rules that would push employers toward a goal of having 7 percent of their employees be people with disabilities, business groups opposed the rules, claiming they would be costly to implement.[91]

Undocumented Immigrants

The Fourteenth Amendment's equal protection clause prohibits states from denying to any person—in other words, not just citizens—equal protection under the law. Thus even undocumented immigrants

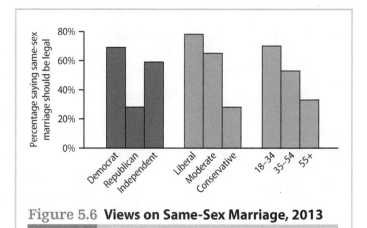

Figure 5.6 Views on Same-Sex Marriage, 2013

Source: Jeffrey M. Jones, "Same-Sex Marriage Support Solidifies above 50% in the U.S.: Support Has been 50% or Above in Three Separate Readings in Last Year," *Gallup*, May 13, 2013, accessed April 14, 2014, http://www.gallup.com/poll/162398/sex-marriage-support-solidifies-above.aspx.

→ KEY QUESTIONS:
Should children of undocumented persons who are born on American soil be U.S. citizens?

AP IMAGES/GERALD HERBERT

Beverly Jones, a plaintiff in a Tennessee case challenging the lack of access for people in wheelchairs to the upper floors of Tennessee courthouses. The U.S. Supreme Court upheld her challenge under the Americans with Disabilities Act.

→ KEY QUESTIONS:

Why do women still earn less than men do for performing the same job? Do women warrant equality of opportunity or equality of outcome?

Checkpoint

CAN YOU:

- Explain why support for same-sex marriage is likely to increase over time

- State the rationale for affirmative action and survey the resistance to it

- Recall why legislatures have been so responsive to people with disabilities

- State why the U.S.-born children of undocumented immigrants are automatically U.S. citizens

receive some degree of legal protection in the United States, as in *Plyler v. Doe* (see Supreme Court Cases, Chapter 1). The level of that protection is deeply controversial, especially as the number of undocumented immigrants, estimated to be about 11.7 million, has leveled off after having peaked at about 12.2 million in 2007, with the recession the most likely cause for the drop-off (see Chapter 14, Public Policy, for further discussion of immigration policy).[92]

Congress has been considering a number of actions, including creating easier paths to citizenship for illegal immigrants or, alternatively, denying natural-born citizenship to U.S.-born children of undocumented immigrants. Only 32 percent of Americans believe that children born in the United States under such circumstances should automatically be granted citizenship.[93] The constitutionality of a law that would deny them citizenship, given the Fourteenth Amendment's citizenship clause, remains unclear.[94]

While the Court reviews laws that discriminate against legal immigrants under its strictest level of scrutiny, it reviews laws that discriminate against undocumented immigrants under the easier rational-basis standard. Yet, the Court has held that states may not deny public education to undocumented immigrants,[95] and federal law requires hospitals to provide emergency care to undocumented immigrants through Medicaid, the federal program that supports health care to poor people. The growth of civil rights to cover undocumented immigrants is surely one of the most controversial of the frontiers we have examined.

Civil Rights and Democracy

The core demand of civil rights is equal opportunity under the law. When laws discriminate or allow discrimination, people are effectively excluded from civic life. The demands for equal opportunity are often made to government, which alone has the authority to prohibit discrimination.

While a democratic system of government works to be responsive to its citizens, responsiveness to minorities is harder to obtain when majorities seek to limit minority rights. Out of all the activities by groups seeking equal rights, voting might be a key gateway. With the vote, declared Martin Luther King Jr. in 1965, comes accountability. Blacks could "vote out of office public officials who bar the doorway to decent housing, public safety, jobs, and decent integrated education. It is now obvious that the basic elements so vital to Negro advancement can only be achieved by seeking redress from government. . . . To do this, the vote is essential."[96] While voting rights provide accountability by allowing citizens to "throw the bums out," they also provide responsiveness. A minority group's elected opponents are not as forceful once a group has the right to vote.

More generally, the voting patterns of southern House and Senate members on issues related to civil rights have moderated over the past forty years, proving that King was certainly correct about the value of the ballot.[97] While members of Congress representing southern states once voted in lockstep opposition to civil rights issues, their votes on such issues now differ only slightly from those of representatives of other states.[98]

These changes are part of a larger evolution in the idea of equality that has proceeded over the course of the nation's more than two centuries. Americans once believed that slaveholding was not inconsistent with demands for equality; today African Americans, women, and others once discriminated against have achieved full participation in the nation's civic life. But the frontiers of civil rights will continue to evolve. Some Americans believe that equal opportunity is not enough, that the government must take stronger measures to ensure greater equality of outcome. Because there is no constitutional right to equal results, the battle over this meaning of equality will be fought not in the courts, but in democratically elected legislatures.

Dr. Martin Luther King Jr. once declared that the "arc of the moral universe is long, but it bends toward justice." Two examples in 2014 from the world of sports show how far we have come. When Donald Sterling, the owner of the San Diego Clippers basketball team, scolded his girlfriend for bringing African American superstar Magic Johnson to Clipper games, he was roundly condemned by nearly everyone, north and south, Republican and Democrat. When Miami Dolphins safety Don Jones tweeted "OMG" and "horrible" after Michael Sam kissed his boyfriend after becoming the first openly homosexual player to be drafted by the National Football League, the Dolphins fined and suspended Jones. Considering that segregation in public facilities were legal in much of the United States until 1965, and that until the *Lawrence v. Texas* (2003) case, states were free to make homosexual relations illegal, the arc of the moral universe appears to be opening more gateways for Americans than ever before.

Master the Concept
of Civil Rights with the MindTap™ for American Government

 REVIEW MindTap™ **for American Government**
Access Key Term Flashcards for Chapter 5.

 TEST YOURSELF MindTap™ **for American Government**
Take the Wrap It Up Quiz for Chapter 5.

 STAY CURRENT MindTap™ **for American Government**
Access the KnowNow blog and customized RSS for updates on current events.

 STAY FOCUSED MindTap™ **for American Government**
Complete the Focus Activities for Civil Rights.

Key Concepts

Brown v. Board of Education (p. 134). What was the reasoning behind the *Brown* decision?

citizenship (p. 123). What are the different paths to citizenship?

civil rights (p. 120). What is the government's role with regards to civil rights?

Civil Rights Act (p. 138). What did the Civil Rights Act prohibit?

Dred Scott v. Sandford (p. 122). What seems wrong about the *Dred Scott* decision?

equality of opportunity (p. 121). How would you measure equality of opportunity?

equality of outcome (p. 121). How would you measure equality of outcome?

Equal Pay Act (p. 142). How effective has the Equal Pay Act been?

equal protection clause (p. 126). What does the equal protection clause command?

Jim Crow laws (p. 127). What were Jim Crow laws?

poll taxes (p. 127). What were the various types of poll taxes?

private discrimination (p. 120). What constitutes private discrimination?

public discrimination (p. 120). What constitutes public discrimination?

Reconstruction (p. 126). What happened when Reconstruction ended?

separate-but-equal doctrine (p. 127). Can separate schools ever be equal?

state action (p. 133). What makes state action so important to government efforts to protect civil rights?

Stonewall riots (p. 146). What movement did the Stonewall riots spark?

Voting Rights Act (p. 138). What did the Voting Rights Act prohibit?

women's suffrage movement (p. 129). What gateways did the women's suffrage movement use to gain the right to vote?

Learning Outcomes: What You Need . . .

To Know	To Test Yourself	To Participate
Define civil rights		
Civil rights relate to the duties of citizenship and opportunities for civic participation that the government is obliged to protect. They are based on the expectation of equality under the law. The most important is the right to vote.	• Compare civil rights to civil liberties. • Track changes in civil rights from the Constitution as originally ratified to today.	• Know your civil rights. • Understand the debt you owe to the actions of citizens for the civil rights you enjoy today.
Explain how the federal and state governments suppressed civil rights		
With regard to civil rights, the government can engage in state-sponsored or public discrimination; treat people equally but permit private discrimination; or try, as it has since the 1960s, both to treat people equally and to prevent individuals or businesses from discriminating. It falls to government to protect individuals against unequal treatment and to citizens to ensure that government does not discriminate against individuals or groups. During the nation's first century, and even thereafter, state laws and the national government actively discriminated against people on the basis of race, gender, and ethnic background.	• Describe the role of the Supreme Court in the expansion of slavery. • Enumerate ways that racial discrimination persisted after emancipation. • Track the steps in the achievement of women's suffrage. • Survey the laws that discriminated against women. • Identify the groups that have been denied rights to U.S. citizenship. • Discuss restraints on civil rights during wartime.	• Read excerpts from the *Dred Scott* decision (http://web.utk.edu/~scheb/decisions/dredscott.htm) and from the Mississippi black code established after the Civil War (https://chnm.gmu.edu/courses/122/recon/code.html) and comment on them. • Consider how disenfranchisement of women affected U.S. politics before 1920. • Speculate on why the United States limited citizenship. • Evaluate what these mean for living in a time of prolonged terrorism.

To Know	To Test Yourself	To Participate

 Assess how equal protection has expanded

During the nation's second century, discrimination was state-sponsored in the South; elsewhere private discrimination was practiced without challenge.	• Track the changing meaning of equality. • Explain why "state action" is so important to the equal protection clause. • Demonstrate that the judicial branch might be a better protector of civil rights than the legislative branch.	• Decide whether we are all equal now. • Weigh your respect for the legislative branch versus the judicial branch.

 Identify the groups at the forefront of the civil rights movement

Today public discrimination has been ended by constitutional amendments and the courts, largely through the Fourteenth Amendment's equal protection clause. Beginning in the 1950s, litigation and grassroots protests led the federal government to end segregation and secure voting rights for African Americans and to end limits to women's full participation in public life.	• Explain why the *Brown* decision by itself had only a minimal effect on school desegregation. • Identify the grassroots protests that opened the gateways to ending private discrimination. • Describe how Congress and the courts have pushed along voting rights. • Draw parallels between the civil rights movement for African Americans, Latinos, and women.	• Weigh the impact on social policy of the legislative branch against that of the judicial branch. • Appreciate the impact active citizens can have on government. • Appreciate the impact law can have on politics and society.

 Describe the new battles for civil rights

The expanded notion of equality promoted by the civil rights and women's rights movements inspired other groups, such as homosexuals and the disabled, to demand full access to equality. The extension of rights for some may involve a loss of privileges for others, and sometimes rights clash. Congress and the courts seek to define the meaning and limits of rights in new areas of contention. The trend has always been for a broader meaning of equality and greater support for civil rights.	• Explain why support for same-sex marriage is likely to increase over time. • Recall why legislatures have been so responsive to people with disabilities. • State why the U.S.-born children of illegal immigrants are automatically U.S. citizens.	• Determine whether you think all of the civil rights battles have been won. • Find disability rights organizations in your community. • Find instances of profiling in the news or in your community. • Analyze the racial and ethnic composition of the prison population, and determine if prohibiting voting rights for felons is discriminatory. • Debate whether the Constitution should be amended with regard to citizenship.

"… you have one thing that may save you, and that is your youth. This is your great strength. It is also why I hate and fear you."

STEPHEN COLBERT
Northwestern University

154

6

Public Opinion and the Media

Stephen Colbert has literally laughed his way to influence in our political system. *The Colbert Report* is a popular satirical news show that seeks to use humor to discuss pressing issues of the day. Colbert's gateway to influence underscores the many changes in public opinion and the media over the past twenty-five years. It used to be that "the media" were dominated by a handful of outlets (e.g., *The New York Times*, *CBS News*) that sought to lay out descriptively the day's events. The media have multiplied and decentralized, seeking often to interpret the news, aid citizens in the formation of their political ideas, and entertain us along the way.

The expression of the public will is the bedrock of democracy. For politicians, knowing which way the public leans or what citizens think is one of their gateways to power. For citizens, being able to express an opinion and know it is being heard is a gateway for their influence. But reading public opinion correctly is not easy. Polls are a great help, but they can be flawed. Even if well measured, public opinion does not always point toward the best path for the country. Making the right choices requires an informed citizenry. However, the days of striving for serious, unbiased media coverage are long gone.

It is a new game in many ways. Just consider Colbert's influence. In 2011, he drew attention to the rise of so called "Super PACs" by forming his own Colbert Super PAC. His goal was to raise awareness about the new election laws that allowed these PACs to form. He was worried that these PACs would inject too much money into the political process. In an e-mail to supporters in October of 2011, he wrote, "As you know, when we began Colbert Super PAC, we had a simple dream: to use the Supreme Court's *Citizens United* ruling to fashion a massive money cannon that would make all those who seek the

White House quake with fear and beg our allegiance . . . in strict accordance with federal election law."[1] By poking fun at *Citizens' United*, Colbert helped inform the public about these new PACs and their possible role in the 2012 campaign.

More recently, during a March 2014 show, Colbert discussed Vladimir Putin and Russia's controversial annexation of the Crimea. He did so through sarcastic commentary about Putin's motives. Colbert has talked about global warming with Al Gore and discussed Jeb Bush's statement

Need to Know

6.1 Decide why public opinion is powerful

6.2 Describe how well polls measure public opinion

6.3 Discover how ideology and partisanship shape public opinion

6.4 Describe how demographic characteristics influence public opinion

6.5 Determine why the media are important in a democracy

6.6 Analyze how the law protects the press

6.7 Explain how changes in the mass media have changed the information environment

6.8 Assess how the news media affect public opinion

6.9 Evaluate the news media

 WATCH & LEARN MindTap° for American Government
Watch a brief "What Do You Know?" video summarizing Public Opinion and Political Socialization.

155

in 2014 that crossing the U.S. border is not a felony, but "an act of love" for those individuals who cross as they seek to support their families. Colbert's goal was to poke fun at those who were adamantly opposed to undocumented immigration. Some may not like his politics, but Colbert shines a bright light on the workings of American politics.

This show carries a good deal of weight with younger Americans. According to a survey by the Pew Research Center, about 5 percent of Americans watch the show regularly. But the audience tends to be young, liberal, and educated. So, for example, 10 percent of Millennials claim to watch the show regularly and just 2 percent of those over 65 years old—a five-fold difference. Liberals are also five times more likely to watch the show than conservatives. Those with a high school degree are three times less likely to watch the show than those who have advanced graduate degrees.[2] But Colbert's influence extends beyond those who tune in on particular nights. His skits are picked up by other outlets and become part of the broader national conversation, increasing his gateway to influence.

Few would have thought that Stephen Colbert was on a path that would lead to such political influence. He grew up in South Carolina, the youngest of eleven children. His father was a physician and died when Colbert was just 10 years old.[3] Colbert first attended Hampden-Sydney College in Virginia—a small private liberal arts college for men. This college has a deep history, striving to instill in its students a desire to "behave as gentleman at all times and in all places."[4] In retrospect, that may not have been a good fit for Colbert, and he did in fact end up transferring to Northwestern University. In 1986, he graduated with a degree in theatre.[5]

His time at Northwestern was transformative. He began doing improv on campus and around Chicago. He had a knack for being good on stage and for being funny. *Second City* gave him a big break, where he served as understudy to Steve Carell. In 1995, he began his career at Comedy Central, joining *The Daily Show* two years later as a correspondent where he developed his now-famous Colbert persona.[6] *The Colbert Report* started as a spin-off from *The Daily Show* in 2005. Early

on, he introduced "Truthiness"[7] to the political discourse. He basically used the concept to lob satirical bombs at the personalities and issues of the day. The term caught on so much that it became the "Word of the Year" in 2006.[8] Even if Colbert gave a guest a hard time on a show, they relished the chance to be on the show. Why? The Colbert Bump. There is evidence that guests got a boost in popularity from being on the show.[9] So what celebrity or politician could resist?

While Colbert is first and foremost an entertainer, he does care about issues and takes his gateway to influence seriously. So, for example, he testified before the House Judiciary Committee's Subcommittee on Immigration, Citizenship, and Border Security in 2010.[10] He did so because he likes "talking about people who don't have any power." He goes on to say that migrant workers "come and do our work, but don't have any rights . . . yet we still invite them to come here and at the same time ask them to leave . . . that's an interesting contradiction."[11]

Colbert's influence speaks volumes about the many changes in the media in just the past decade. In 2015, he took over David Letterman's late night show on CBS. The announcement drew strong reactions from some. Conservative talk show host Rush Limbaugh contended that "CBS has just declared war on the heartland of America."[12] Such partisan reactions are part and parcel of the media today. We can continue to expect such partisan reactions.

The popularity of Stephen Colbert's humor-infused partisanship is a near perfect symbol of the many changes in public opinion and the media, and we will use this chapter to map out and to assess these changes. We do so with a keen understanding of the critical role that the expression of public opinion and the media play in a democracy. In this chapter, we investigate how public opinion is formed, expressed, and measured, and its impact in our democracy. To discuss "the media," we analyze the functions and impact of the press, survey its history, and describe and evaluate these new forms of communication in the twenty-first century. By so doing, we can better understand whether and how the media and a freely expressed public opinion promote democracy.

LISTEN & LEARN
MindTap™ **for American Government**

Access Read Speaker to listen to Chapter 6.

6.1 The Power of Public Opinion

> Decide why public opinion is powerful

"Our government rests on public opinion," claimed Abraham Lincoln. "Public sentiment is everything. With public sentiment, nothing can fail. Without it, nothing can succeed."[13] The nation's sixteenth president (1861–65) was, of course, the great champion of "government of the people, by the people, and for the people," as he expressed it in his Gettysburg Address. He understood that democratic government must be responsive to the will of the people. The hope in a democracy is that each citizen has an equal voice and that those voices, collectively, will be heard by government officials and will guide their actions. Knowing what the public is thinking and having public support are a powerful combination. Writing more than 100 years ago, James Bryce, a famous observer of U.S. politics, contended that public opinion is "the greatest source of power" in the United States, more important than the power of presidents, Congress, and political parties.[14]

What Is Public Opinion?

Public opinion is recognized for its power, but it is ever changing, hard to measure, harder to predict, and nearly impossible to control. **Public opinion** is the aggregate of individual attitudes or beliefs about certain issues or officials, and it is the foundation of any democracy.

> **public opinion:** *Aggregate of individual attitudes or beliefs about certain issues or officials.*

Of course, the electorate expresses its opinion primarily through voting, and elections are the most visible means by which citizens hold elected officials accountable. But a democratic system should not rely just on elections to ensure that politicians are doing the people's will. Elections are not held very often, and they give signals but not directions. For example, the electoral success of the Republicans in the 2014 midterm elections was hailed as a sign that the public was unhappy with the Obama administration's handling of the economy, heath care, the Ebola scare, and conflicts in the Middle East. But what does "unhappiness" say about specific policies? Did the people want big spending cuts? Or did they want additional government efforts to stimulate the economy? Did they want Obamacare reformed or just want it to work better? Election results do not send clear signals on such specific questions. Voters can indicate only whether they like one candidate more than the other; they cannot convey the reasons for their vote. So legislators and elected executives who want to stay in power expend considerable energy trying to find out what the public wants and to respond accordingly. Because public opinion plays such an important role in forging responsiveness, it is central to understanding U.S. politics.

Today, public opinion polls are the most reliable indicators of what Americans are thinking, and a whole industry and science have grown up around measuring opinion on everything from presidents to toothpaste. Polls are not the only sources of public opinion. Other sources of public opinion are the size of rallies and protests, the tone of letters sent to elected officials or newspapers, the amount of money given to particular causes or candidates, the content of newspaper editorials, information gleaned from day-to-day conversations with average Americans, and shifts in public opinion can also be detected in Supreme Court decisions (see Supreme Court Cases: *Bowers v. Hardwick* and *United States v. Windsor in this chapter*).

The Public's Support of Government

The health and stability of a democracy rest with the public. Just as government must respond to what the people want, so citizens must view the system as legitimate and want to be part of it. If the public withdraws its support, the government collapses. For these reasons, political scientists have sought to measure the public's faith in the political system. Two of the most common efforts involve assessing whether the people trust their government and whether they believe their participation in government matters. Political scientists call the latter **efficacy**—the extent to which people believe their actions affect the course of government. **Political trust** is the extent to which people believe the government acts in their best

> **efficacy:** *Extent to which people believe their actions can affect public affairs and the actions of government.*

> **political trust:** *Extent to which people believe the government acts in their best interests.*

Bowers v. Hardwick (1986)
United States v. Windsor (2013)

QUESTION: *Bowers:* May states prosecute consensual sexual activity by members of the same sex?

WINDSOR: May the United States discriminate against legal same-sex marriages?

ORAL ARGUMENT: *Bowers:* March 31, 1986 (listen at http://www.oyez.org/cases/1980-1989/1985/1985_85_140)

WINDSOR: March 27, 2013 (listen at **http://www.oyez.org/cases/2010-2019/2012/2012_12_307**)

DECISION: *Bowers:* June 30, 1986 (read at http://caselaw.lp.findlaw.com/scripts/getcase.pl?court=US&vol=478&invol=186).

WINDSOR: March 27, 2013 (read at http://caselaw.lp.findlaw.com/scripts/getcase.pl?court=US&vol=000&invol=12-307).

OUTCOME: *Bowers:* There is no right to homosexual sodomy (5–4) (1986).

WINDSOR: The United States may not discriminate against legally married same-sex couples (5-4) (2013).

When the police came to Michael Hardwick's home looking for him, his roommate let them in. When the police got to Hardwick's room, they observed him engaged in sexual behavior with another male. They arrested him under Georgia's antisodomy statute, which prohibits "any sexual contact involving the genitals of one person and the mouth or anus of another." Hardwick argued that the statute violated the right to privacy that the Court established in the *Griswold* birth control case (1965), which the Court later held to protect rights that were "deeply rooted in this Nation's history and tradition."* Noting that prohibitions on sodomy had "ancient roots," the Court voted 5–4 against the claim, calling the argument that homosexual sodomy is among those traditions "facetious." Chief Justice Warren Burger concurred, approvingly citing medieval English sources that declared sodomy as an offense of "deeper malignity" than rape. At the time, only about 32 percent of the American public agreed with the opinion that homosexual relations should be legal."

The Supreme Court reversed that decision nearly twenty years later in *Lawrence v. Texas* (2003). With seven new members on the Court, the justices voted 6–3 that the Texas law prohibiting sodomy was unconstitutional, with the majority opinion resting the decision on the liberty protected by the due process clause of the Fourteenth Amendment.

In the *Windsor* case (2013), the Supreme Court struck down the part of the Defense of Marriage Act (DOMA) that prohibited the federal government from granting marriage benefits to same-sex couples. Under federal law, one spouse can leave unlimited amounts of money to a surviving spouse, but DOMA (1996) had declared that the federal government would only recognize marriages as being between one man and one woman. When Edith Windsor's lawful wife died, the federal government claimed that Windsor owed $363,053 in inheritance taxes, an amount Windsor would not have had to pay had she been married to a male. The Supreme Court ruled that the federal government could not discriminate against Windsor's legal same-sex marriage.

In fewer than thirty years, the Supreme Court had gone from holding that states could criminalize homosexual activity to determining that the federal government must recognize same-sex marriages that are lawfully performed in other states. These changes coincide with a near doubling of support for marriage equality in the United States during that time. Whether this new result was directly due to the change in public opinion or due to new justices from a different generation who reflected that changed opinion, the Court's decision aligned with changes in public opinion.§

1. Should the justices of the Supreme Court be influenced by public opinion?
2. How should the Court decide which rights, among those not specifically listed in the Constitution, should be protected as fundamental rights?

Griswold v. Connecticut, 381 U.S. 479 (1965); *Washington v. Glucksberg*, 521 U.S. 702, 721 (1997).
§ Homosexual relationships should be legal: http://www.gallup.com/poll/1651/Gay-Lesbian-Rights.aspx. Support for same-sex marriage: http://www.gallup.com/poll/162398/sex-marriage-support-solidifies-above.aspx. Both accessed April 14, 2014.

interests. It has generally declined over the past fifty years, with steeper declines following the beginning of the Iraq War in 2003 and the financial collapse that began in 2008. One estimate in January 2014 suggested that just 15 percent of the public trusted "the government in Washington to do what is right."[15]

Efficacy has also declined. It stood at more than 70 percent in 1960; by 1994, it had fallen by half. In other words, only one-third of Americans felt that their opinions mattered to government. The figure rebounded to 60 percent by 2002 but then declined again during the Iraq War and financial crisis. It has fallen well below 40 percent in the current environment.[16] There is little doubt, as President Obama said in his first inaugural address, that there has been a "sapping of confidence across our land."

Public trust and efficacy react to changes in government and whether the nation is experiencing good or bad times. Yet, through it all, Americans' commitment to the country and its core institutions has remained strong. Patriotism, for example, shows little decline. In 2014, 5 percent of Americans viewed themselves as unpatriotic.[17] Almost no one in the country favors overthrowing the government.[18]

→ KEY QUESTIONS:
What does a decline in efficacy and public trust mean for American democracy?

> **Checkpoint**
>
> **CAN YOU:**
> - Define public opinion
> - State the reasons public opinion has a powerful impact on the presidency
> - Track efficacy and public trust in government

6.2 Public Opinion Polls

> Decide how well polls measure public opinion

Polls make it possible to gauge the public's thinking on a variety of issues or officials, but they have been scientifically conducted only since the 1930s. Even today, a poorly designed or executed poll can produce misleading results. Moreover, so much information is available from surveys that it is important to know which findings warrant attention and which warrant caution. Poll results can be biased, contradictory, and confusing.

Scientific Polling and the Growth of Survey Research

In the 1800s, newspapers and other organizations polled the people to assess public opinion, but these polls were of limited help because who was being surveyed was unclear. So-called straw polls, for example, sought to predict the outcome of elections. During the presidential campaign of 1824, the *Harrisburg Pennsylvanian* canvassed the opinion of newspaper readers and concluded that Andrew Jackson would get 63 percent of the vote and win easily.[19] As it turned out, Jackson received only about 40 percent of the popular vote.

Though straw polls were often inaccurate, newspapers and magazines continued to poll readers' opinions well into the twentieth century. During the 1936 presidential campaign, the *Literary Digest* conducted a poll that predicted Republican Alf Landon would win the election by 57 percent over President Franklin Roosevelt. The reverse happened: Roosevelt won with a landslide 61 percent of the vote. Why did the *Literary Digest* get it so wrong? It had sent out 10 million ballots. But it had sent them to names drawn from automobile registration lists and telephone books and asked recipients to mail the ballots back. The sample, as a result, was biased. First, in 1936 those who owned automobiles and had telephones were wealthier than average Americans and were more likely to be Republicans. Less wealthy Americans, responding favorably to Roosevelt's actions to end the Great Depression, were increasingly aligning themselves with the Democrats. Second, the poll asked respondents to mail in their ballots, introducing additional bias. Those who would take the time to do so would likely be better off, further increasing the Republican bias of the sample. Even though 2 million ballots were returned, the poll did not offer a very sound basis on which to make a prediction.

George Gallup, who had founded the American Institute of Public Opinion in 1935, correctly predicted the outcome of the 1936 election by using a **random sample** to generate a way to select people to participate in surveys. He made his sample representative of the American public by giving, in effect, every American an equal chance to be part of it. The end product was a sample of five thousand, which was far smaller than the *Literary Digest*'s sample but far more representative of average Americans. As a result of his innovative approach, Gallup is often considered the father of modern polling, and the best-known name in polling today remains the Gallup Poll. His scientific polling and survey research techniques have been refined over the years.

The advent of scientific polling made it possible to assess the opinions of the public with some degree of ease and accuracy. Scientific polling also permitted greater equality in assessing public opinion because the polls had the ability to tap the opinions of all Americans. George Gallup understood this aspect of polling—that scientific polls democratized the measurement of public opinion.[20]

Today, Americans are regularly surveyed on a wide range of things other than politics. Polls ask about sexual practices, television viewing preferences, car purchases, and how often people go bowling. Extensive polling has revealed what proportion of the nation believes in UFOs, what kind of soap people buy, and at what age children stop believing in Santa Claus. In March 2013, for example, *60 Minutes* and *Vanity Fair* asked the following survey question of Americans: Which one of the following celebrities would you least want to sit next to on a long airplane flight? Charlie Sheen, Kim Kardashian, Chris Brown, Richard Simmons, Joan Rivers, or Mel Gibson? Just for the record, Kim Kardashian "won" this survey.[21]

Types of Polls

In a nation of more than 200 million adults, gathering opinions from everyone is not practical. Even the U.S. census, a count of the population required by the Constitution every ten years, has trouble reaching every adult.[22] So polls draw a sample from a larger population. But first the population must be defined. It might be all adults over age 18, or only voters, or only citizens who contributed to Republican candidates in 2014.

The typical size of a sample survey is one thousand people, though it can vary between five hundred and about fifteen hundred. Size does not matter as much as whether the sample is representative of the population being assessed. Having a representative sample means, in effect, that everyone in that population has an equal chance of being asked to participate in the poll. If a random one thousand people are asked to be part of the survey, they should be representative of the population generally—in, say, wealth, ethnicity, or educational attainment. The key to a representative sample is the randomness. It should be much like drawing numbered balls for a lottery: Each ball has the same chance of being chosen.

W. EUGENE SMITH/THE LIFE PICTURE/GETTY IMAGES

In the 1930s, George Gallup developed a scientific approach to polling, greatly increasing its accuracy and authority.

random sample:
Method of selection that gives everyone who might be selected to participate in a poll an equal chance to be included.

→ KEY QUESTIONS:
Are polls the best way to find out what the public thinks?

There are various ways to collect the information being sought. For in-person interviews, survey researchers send interviewers into neighborhoods and communities to ask questions in person. This was long the favored method, but it became increasingly expensive. With the near universal presence of telephones by the 1970s, calling people became a more viable and much less expensive option. Telephone polls have dominated survey research over the past thirty years and continue to be used much of the time. Automated telephone polls, the so-called robo-poll, is on the rise. They are cheaper but tend not to be very accurate.[23]

The latest platform for polling is the Internet. Internet polls have much potential, but the fact that older and poorer Americans may lack access to computers introduces bias. As with telephones in the past century, however, more and more people are using computers and the web, so in the future, Internet polling will likely become the dominant platform for survey research.

Call-in polls or write-in polls are other means of securing a sample. For the former, a telephone number is posted on the television screen, for example, and people are asked to call to register their views. In the latter, a newspaper publishes an appeal for subscribers to write letters offering their opinions. Such approaches can yield a large number of participants, but the size of the sample can be misleading, for those who are willing to call or write are different from those who are not. The samples yielded in these polls are not representative and, thus, are highly suspect.

Presidential elections are awash in polls. In the heat of the fall campaign, nightly polls gauge changes in voters' preferences for the major contenders. These surveys are called **tracking polls**. Another type of survey involving elections is the **exit poll**, conducted as voters leave the polling booth. The goal here is to learn about the reasoning behind the votes citizens just cast but, more important, to predict the outcome of the election before all the ballots are formally counted.

The most famous and consequential exit poll took place in Florida during the 2000 presidential elections, fueling one of the most controversial electoral struggles of all time. The major networks used an exit poll to predict that the Sunshine State would go to Vice President Albert Gore Jr. (1993–2001). Florida's electoral votes would put Gore over the 270 needed, making him the apparent winner of the presidency. These predictions started to roll in at 8 P.M. on election night. The campaign of Republican George W. Bush protested, saying it was too early to call the state and that the race was still too close to know who won. By 10 P.M., the earlier forecast was withdrawn, and the outcome of the presidential election was again unclear. By 2 A.M. the next morning, *Fox News* called the election for Bush, with the other major networks soon following. Just two hours later, however, the call was retracted. There followed a thirty-six-day legal battle over which candidate actually won in Florida. It was not settled until the U.S. Supreme Court halted the Florida recount in mid-December, giving Bush the presidency.

Many have wanted to blame exit polls for the confusion that election night, but the polls were not as big a problem as the news media's use of them. The networks feel real pressure to make early calls, and that pressure sometimes leads them to go beyond what the data support. So while CBS was making that first call around 8 P.M., its polling experts behind the scene were urging caution.[24] Twelve years later, the tables were turned. It was Karl Rove, the well-known Republican consultant from the 2000 campaign, who questioned *Fox News*

tracking polls: *Polls that seek to gauge changes of opinion of the same sample size over a period of time, common during the closing months of presidential elections.*

exit polls: *Polls that survey a sample of voters immediately after exiting the voting booth to predict the outcome of the election before the ballots are officially counted.*

→ KEY QUESTIONS:
Have you ever looked at a poll and questioned its validity? How might you gauge a poll's validity?

→ KEY QUESTIONS:
Do polls make sure the people's voices are heard?

President Harry Truman holding up a newspaper proclaiming that he lost the 1948 presidential election to Thomas Dewey. But Tribune's polls were wrong, and Truman had actually won that election.

push polls: *Polls that are designed to manipulate the opinions of those being polled.*

confidence interval: *Statistical range, with a given probability, that takes random error into account.*

COMPARE WITH YOUR PEERS

MindTap for American Government

Access the Public Opinion and Political Socialization Forum: Polling Activity– New York Times Instant Polls.

→ KEY QUESTIONS:
Should public officials be influenced by polls?

when it called Ohio for President Obama. He did so on live TV, and Megyn Kelly, the *Fox News* anchor on the air at the time, challenged Rove by going directly to the experts who made the prediction. The exit polls proved Rove wrong—Romney did in fact lose that crucial state.

A final kind of election poll is actually a campaign strategy. **Push polls** are conducted by interest groups or candidates who try to affect the opinions of respondents by priming them with biased information. During the 2000 presidential primary in South Carolina, for example, Senator John McCain (R-Ariz.) claimed that George W. Bush ran a push poll against him. Interviewers had called people to ask if they knew that McCain was a "cheat" and a "liar." The question was not designed to get information but to turn people against McCain.[25] Such polls seek to shift public opinion, not to measure it.

Error in Polls

Pollsters do everything they can to ensure that their samples are representative. Even if the sample is drawn properly, however, there is still a chance of error. To capture this uncertainty, all poll numbers come with a **confidence interval** that captures the likely range 95 percent of the time. The poll produces a single estimate of the public's thinking, but the best way to think of that estimate is as a range of possible estimates. For a sample of six hundred respondents, the sampling error is ±4 percent. That 4 percent generates the confidence interval. Assume, for example, that 65 percent of those sampled support the efforts of Congress to reform the campaign finance laws. With a sampling error of 4 percent, the best way to think of the proportion is that, with 95 percent certainty, the actual amount of public support is somewhere between 61 percent and 69 percent. This range is the confidence interval. Note, however, that there is still a one in twenty chance (5 percent) that the true proportion is above or below that eight-point confidence interval. Hence, caution is always required when interpreting poll data.

In addition to sampling error, the wording of the question can introduce bias. The controversial issue of abortion offers a vivid example. What the public thinks about this issue depends a great deal on the way the question is asked. An NBC News/*Wall Street Journal* poll asked a representative sample of Americans the following question: "Which of the following best represents your views about abortion—the choice on abortion should be left up to the woman and her doctor, abortion should be legal only in cases which pregnancy results from rape or incest or when the life of the woman is at risk, or abortion should be illegal in all circumstances?"

The answers show that 53 percent of the public felt that abortion was a decision best left to the woman and her doctor. Only 15 percent of Americans felt it should be illegal in all circumstances, with 29 percent wanting to have exceptions. In short, a majority of the public appeared to support abortion rights for women. That is an important finding.

But is it true? Consider the following question asked at about the same time by Fox News/Opinion Dynamics: "Once a woman is pregnant, do you believe the unborn baby or fetus should have all the same rights as a newborn baby?" The answers tell a different story.

Nearly 60 percent of the public said yes, the unborn fetus should have the same rights as a newborn baby. Only 26 percent said no. According to this poll, a strong majority wants to protect the rights of the unborn and, therefore, to limit abortion rights for women.[26]

So what is American public opinion on abortion? Clearly, the answer depends on the wording of the question, specifically on whether respondents are asked to focus on the rights of women or the rights of the unborn. This same dynamic applies to other controversial issues, such as attitudes toward homosexuality and race. Because of America's long and tortured history of race relations, people often try to give socially acceptable responses so as to suggest they are tolerant and not bigoted or racist. Although interviewers are trained to be neutral in their questioning, respondents sometimes try to give responses that they think the questioner wants to hear.

Another source of error in polls involves what political scientists call **nonattitudes**.[27] When asked, many people feel compelled to answer, even if they do not have opinions or know much about the question. They do not want to seem uninformed, but their responses create error in the survey.

Today polling is in transition. Representative sampling in telephone surveys is increasingly affected by the growing number of cell phones, as many pollsters do not have access to cell phone exchanges, and many cell phone users, especially young people, do not have landlines, which are used in telephone polls. At this point, there is not a lot of evidence to suggest that people without landlines vote differently from those with them, but the shift from landlines to cell phones continues.[28] The widespread use of caller ID and answering machines is also important because it allows more and more Americans to screen their calls and refuse to participate in surveys. In fact, there is a general "polling fatigue" among the public. People are asked to participate not only in political polls but also in surveys for insurance companies, health care providers, and an endless array of commercial products. The result is that fewer people are willing to participate in telephone surveys. The declining response rate is lessening the ability of pollsters to capture public opinion accurately. In the 1990s, the rate of response was nearly 40 percent, and now it is about 15 percent.[29]

Pollsters are finding ways to adjust, but Internet polls represent the future for measuring public opinion. Through the Internet, polls can be done quickly and cheaply, but respondents may not be representative of the population. Once statisticians develop reliable ways to correct for bias, the web will become an even more powerful tool than it is now to measure the public's thinking. As more people gain access to the web, the amount of bias will decline.

nonattitudes:
Sources of error in public opinion polls in which individuals feel obliged to give opinions when they are unaware of the issue or have no opinions about it.

→ KEY QUESTIONS:
Do all Americans have an equal chance of being included in polls?

Checkpoint

CAN YOU:
- Define scientific polling
- Identify three types of polls
- Explain potential errors in polls
- State why the Internet is important to the future of polling

6.3 The Shape of Public Opinion

❯ Discover how ideology and partisanship shape public opinion

To understand public opinion, it is essential to appreciate the ways it is shaped by partisanship and ideology. These two variables can, to a large extent, explain the opinions of citizens. Although not everyone is partisan or ideological, these forces provide useful frameworks for understanding the public's thinking on issues. With a firm understanding of partisanship and

→ KEY QUESTIONS:
Does party loyalty shape
public opinion?

party identification:
*Psychological attachment
to a political party; partisanship.*

political ideology:
*Set of coherent political
beliefs that offers a philosophy
for thinking about the scope of
government.*

liberals: *Individuals
who have faith in
government to improve people's
lives, believing that private
efforts are insufficient. In the
social sphere, liberals usually
support diverse lifestyles and
tend to oppose any government
action that seeks to shape
personal choices.*

conservatives:
*Individuals who distrust
government, believing that
private efforts are more likely to
improve people's lives. In the
social sphere, conservatives
usually support traditional
lifestyles and tend to believe that
government can play a valuable
role in shaping personal choices.*

ideology in place, we can address two major questions about public opinion: How informed is the public? And is the public polarized?

Partisanship

Party identification, or partisanship, is central to understanding how people think politically. Party identification represents an individual's allegiance to a political party. This psychological attachment usually forms when an individual is young. The attachment, through what is called the perceptual lens, shapes the way partisans view the political world and process information. The perceptual lenses of partisans act like prisms that bend light. Democrats have prisms that bend light in one direction; Republicans' prisms bend it in another direction. The result, for example, is that a Republican would be less sympathetic to Barack Obama's reform of health care than would a Democrat.[30]

By knowing party identification, political scientists can predict—with considerable accuracy—attitudes on a range of issues. Republicans, for example, are less likely than Democrats to support government spending to help the poor and elderly. Republicans are not opposed to helping such people, but they want to do so through private charities and individual initiative. More generally, Republicans are less supportive of an activist federal government, while Democrats are more open to giving government an active role in the lives of citizens.

Because party identification is central to understanding public opinion, pollsters have been asking about partisanship since the 1940s. The American National Elections Studies, a premier academic survey organization, has been asking the same question since 1952: "Generally speaking, do you usually think of yourself as a Republican, a Democrat, an Independent, or what?"[31] This question asks respondents how they think about themselves in order to capture political identification and the general tendency, or the perceptual lens, of their thinking. The theoretical underpinnings are psychological. Partisanship can also be likened to loyalty, like the loyalty to sports teams or to friends that lasts through ups and downs.

Partisanship can change over a person's life, but it tends to be stable, especially when compared to other political attitudes.

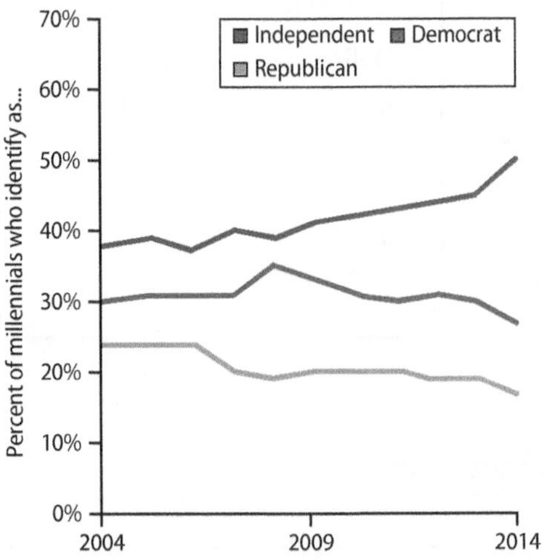

In the past few years, there has been much discussion in the press about Independents, with claims that they are the "largest group in the electorate."[32] With the rise of the Tea Party movement, their numbers are increasing. The view that Americans are mostly Independents has largely been viewed as a myth. Most citizens who claim to be Independents actually behave like partisans. That is, most Independents lean toward one party or the other.[33] This pattern may be changing, however. Consider Figure 6.1 and the sharp growth among Millennials claiming to be independents. This shift might be signifying real unhappiness with the parties among the youth, which could have real, long-term consequences. It is not at all clear yet, so one must be cautious, especially since partisanship has been so central to understanding political behavior in the United States.

Ideology

Political ideology has a complex relationship with partisanship. **Liberals** tend to be Democrats, and **conservatives** tend to be

Figure 6.1 A Recent Rise in Independents

In the last few years, there has been an increase in the share of Americans who claim to be independents.

Source: http://www.pewsocialtrends.org/2014/03/07/
millennials-in-adulthood/sdt-next-america-03-07-2014-1-01/

Republicans, but ideology speaks to both political and social values. Conservatives view a good society as one that allows individuals to pursue their economic interests in an unfettered fashion. Liberals worry that, without some governmental regulation to curb abuse and moderate economic cycles, the rich will get very rich, and the poor will get very poor. This concern leads liberals to believe that government can improve people's lives and prevent inequalities that harm society and the economy as a whole. Conservatives are much more leery of government and view it as a problem in and of itself. They contend that less government interference will give the poor the opportunity to improve their lives by themselves. On social issues, the tables are turned. That is, liberals tend to believe that people should be able to make personal choices free from government interference. Conservatives, by contrast, value more traditional lifestyles and want government, at times, to enforce such choices.

Not all citizens think of themselves as liberals or conservatives. Depending on the wording of the question, 40 percent of Americans in March 2014 viewed themselves as ideological **moderates**, 18 percent as liberals, and 38 percent as conservatives.[34] But there is also a debate among political scientists about whether citizens think ideologically at all. That is, do people have coherent views about politics? One famous effort to measure the ideological foundations, or **levels of conceptualization**, of the public's thinking found little evidence of such organized opinions. Data from the 1950s indicated that only about 12 percent of the public viewed the political parties in ideological terms, whereas more than 40 percent judged the parties by the groups (such as social classes or racial and ethnic groups) they were thought to represent rather than the policies they pursued.[35] This general pattern has remained much the same over the ensuing sixty years.

It is hard to argue that a majority of the public has a coherent, ideologically driven view of politics. Nevertheless, it is still worth looking at the public's overall policy mood. Is the public, collectively, becoming more liberal or more conservative? Such changes should aid understanding of the general direction of the country. Figure 6.2 maps changes in the public's ideological mood between 1952 and 2012.

Is the Public Informed?

A democracy depends on having an engaged and well-informed electorate. Otherwise, how can the public make good choices? If the power is to rest with the people, the people need to be knowledgeable about the issues of the day and the candidates who compete for public office.

The Framers were definitely concerned about the public's capacity to be informed and make good choices, especially because only 10 percent of Americans at the time were literate.[36] These concerns were one of the driving forces behind the gates and gateways in the Constitution, a document that sought to represent the public's views but also to establish institutions that would, according to James Madison, "refine and enlarge" them (see *Federalist* 10 in the Appendix). By that, Madison meant that elected officials would react

→ KEY QUESTIONS:
How does party identification relate to ideology?

moderates:
Individuals who are in the middle of the ideological spectrum and do not hold consistently strong views about whether government should be involved in people's lives.

levels of conceptualization:
Measure of how ideologically coherent individuals are in their political evaluations.

→ KEY QUESTIONS:
Is the public becoming more liberal or more conservative? How can you tell?

→ KEY QUESTIONS:
Is public opinion worth listening to? Should elected official care about public opinion?

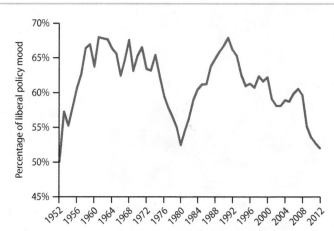

Figure 6.2 Liberal Policy Mood of Americans, 1952–2012

The policy mood of Americans is rarely fixed, moving toward liberalism following George W. Bush's election in 2000 and then toward conservatism following Barack Obama's election in 2008.

Source: Adapted from James Stimson, "Policy Mood," accessed January 17, 2014, http://www.unc.edu/~jstimson/Welcome.html.

to public sentiment but not be a slave to it. Instead, they would debate it in a way that would improve it and allow for better government. Over time, the amount of input by citizens has increased; now senators are voted into office by direct election, not by state legislatures. Literacy in 2014 stands at about 99 percent,[37] suggesting that citizens are better able today than in the eighteenth century to meet the demands of being "informed."

But are they? Political scientists went in search of the "informed voter," and they learned that citizens do not know many details about politics. Only 10 percent of the public knows the name of the Speaker of the House. Only about a third can name one U.S. Supreme Court justice. Only about half of Americans know which party controls Congress, and fewer than half know the name of their own congressional representative.[38] These facts suggest that average citizens do not possess the detailed information necessary to hold their government accountable.

Should these data be taken as evidence that the public is not able to meet its democratic responsibilities? Let us consider some findings that give reason for optimism. First, the public, collectively, seems to make reasonable choices. For example, when the economy is doing poorly, the party in power suffers. Voters hold presidents and legislators accountable; failures are punished, and successes are rewarded. Further, Americans do not favor costly wars, and they tend to reward candidates who pursue peace.[39]

Second, although individuals do not know all the details about candidates' views on all the issues, they do tend to know candidates' views on the issues that are salient to them. Hunters know candidates' views on gun control; college students know candidates' views on student loans. One study estimates that when an issue is salient to an individual, that individual knows candidates' views on that issue correctly more than 90 percent of the time.[40]

Third, the public can learn quickly if an issue is salient enough to them and receives attention in the news media. The public quickly learned about AIDS when it started to become a public health crisis in the 1980s. Following 9/11, the public understood the need to consider some curtailment of civil liberties to ensure security (see Public Policy and Public Opinion).

Fourth, public opinion is more stable than is suggested by the shifting answers people give to the same question just a few months apart. The instability reflected in polls does not speak to a fickle or poorly informed public. Instead, it appears that polls themselves may be at fault.[41] That is, survey questions and the normal error associated with these questions make people's attitudes appear more unstable than they really are.

Finally, personal decision making is not always based on complete information, so why should political decision making be expected to conform to rational models that scholars use? Individuals often rely on cues and instincts to make decisions, rather than on analyses of detailed information. Scholars have termed such thinking low information rationality.[42] There are two famous examples from presidential campaigns. In 1976, President Gerald R. Ford (1974–77), campaigning in Texas, bit into a tamale with the husk still on, a gaffe suggesting that he knew little about the foods and habits of the people he hoped would vote for him. In 1992, President George H. W. Bush (1989–93) asked what milk cost in grocery stores. His admission that he did not know suggested that he was out of touch with

→ KEY QUESTIONS:
How much information does the public need to possess to make self-government possible?

GERALD R. FORD LIBRARY

Campaigning in 1976, President Gerald Ford visited Texas and, as politicians almost always do, sampled the local food. When he bit into a tamale with the husk still on, it was more than a humorous incident. Many interpreted the gaffe as indicating that Ford did not understand the people he claimed, as president, to represent.

ordinary Americans, who do their own shopping. His competitor, William Jefferson (Bill) Clinton (1993–2001), knew the price of milk and other items, such as jeans. Simple things like not knowing how to eat a tamale or what groceries cost turned some voters against Ford and Bush. These individuals concluded that the candidates were not like them and were not likely to understand their problems.

It is easy to make any member of the public—even a president—look uninformed, and of course it would be better if the public knew more about politics. But individuals do appear to learn about the issues that matter to them. Gaining information is a gateway to influence because, individually, people learn what they need to know to advance their interests, and collectively voters do hold government officials accountable.

→ KEY QUESTIONS:
Does polarization prevent good policy making?

Is the Public Polarized?

The engaged and informed citizens of a democracy cannot be expected to agree on everything. They will naturally have different views on issues. When the differences become stark, however, the danger is that **polarization** will fuel controversy and personal attacks to the point that compromise and consensus become impossible. Congress has clearly become more polarized over the past thirty years. Figure 6.3 tries to capture the idea of polarization on a simple left–right continuum. In the 1970s, the parties adopted positions that were closer to the middle; forty years later, their positions are more at the extremes. In fact, Democrats and Republicans disagree on more issues now than at any time since the end of the Civil War.[43]

In the 1970s, there were numerous liberal Republicans and conservative Democrats. By 2008, these two groups were nearly extinct. In 2009, for example, Pennsylvania Senator Arlen Specter, one of the few moderate Republicans in Congress at the time, bolted from the Republican Party and became a Democrat. He switched parties because of what he saw as a swing to the right by the Republicans. The differences between the parties have continued to grow,[49] evidenced by victories by candidates from the Tea Party movement in the 2010 congressional elections.[50] There is little doubt that the parties have polarized since the 1970s, along the lines described in Figure 6.3.

polarization:
Condition in which differences between parties and/or the public are so stark that disagreement breaks out, fueling attacks and controversy.

→ KEY QUESTIONS:
Do political parties influence public opinion, or is it the other way around?

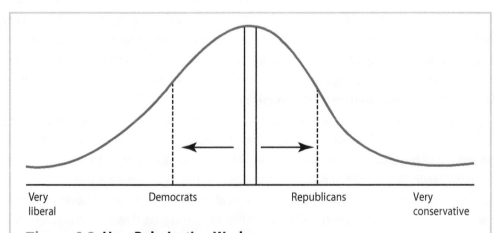

Very liberal | Democrats | Republicans | Very conservative

Figure 6.3 **How Polarization Works**

When the parties are polarized, they move toward the tail of these distributions. When parties are depolarized, they adopt positions near each other. Currently the parties are polarized, but that was not the case in the 1970s.

Source: John G. Geer, © Cengage Learning®.

Public Policy and Public Opinion:
Antiterrorism

To see how public opinion affects the policies pursued by government, we examine foreign policy. In particular, we focus on antiterrorism. With continuing terrorist attacks around the world, it is important to consider the public's support for policies that advance our security and how public opinion impacts policy making in this area.

The September 11th, 2001, terrorist attacks prompted a huge increase in the government's efforts to secure U.S. citizens at home and abroad. In general, public opinion was highly supportive of the steps that President George W. Bush took to fight terrorism. These steps were taken with advice from Defense Department agencies, the Federal Bureau of Investigation, and the Department of Justice. The Bush administration authorized the detention of suspects, whether U.S. citizens or not, without charges or trials, and wiretapping (eavesdropping) without a warrant. With the onset of the 2003 war in Iraq, the measures employed in the name of antiterror security increased. Then, in 2004, CBS News and the *New Yorker* magazine broke the story about the Abu Ghraib facility in Iraq, where Iraqi prisoners were subject to activities that violated international norms of treatment and might be considered torture.[44] Subsequently, it was revealed that the U.S. interrogators used waterboarding, a near-drowning technique, as a means of getting information from prisoners about potential terrorist plots. The international community considers waterboarding to be torture, and many Americans were shocked by the news and demanded an end to the practice. The Bush administration also argued that suspected terrorists detained at the Guantánamo Bay facility located in Cuba, outside the United States, were not entitled to protections guaranteed to all prisoners of war by the Geneva Convention. In the 2006 *Hamdan v. Rumsfeld* case, the Supreme Court ruled that the detainees were protected by Article 3 of the Geneva Convention. Yet allegations of torture continued. The issue of treatment of detainees became a major issue in the 2008 presidential campaign. After he took office, President Obama declared that the United States would no longer engage in any practice that violated international norms. The president also announced that the Guantánamo Bay facility would be closed. Despite an early consensus in the White House to close this controversial facility, deciding what to do with existing detainees and how best to handle others who may be engaged in terrorism has proven difficult.[45]

One of the reasons that these policies are hard to pursue is that Americans remain conflicted about the type of force necessary to preserve national security. In 2013, an AP poll reported that 51 percent of respondents supported the use of harsh interrogation techniques on suspected terrorists, while 38 percent opposed these techniques.[46] The core dilemma is that antiterrorism policies must remain secret to be effective, and the only opportunity the public has to register an opinion about government action is after that action has been taken. If harsh interrogation techniques save American lives by uncovering and then preventing a terrorist attack, the public will support the use of these techniques. But how can we be sure that such efforts are really effective? Does the government go too far sometimes? These are tough questions.

Public uncertainty can also be seen in regards to the public's reaction to Edward Snowden's release of intelligence information. In January 2014, 46 percent of Americans thought what

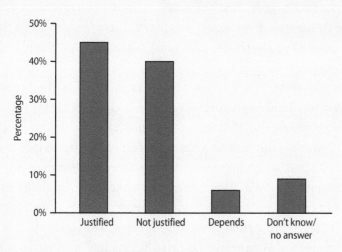

Figure 6.4 Support for Harsh Interrogation Techniques

A majority of the public supports the use of harsh interrogation techniques on terrorism suspects.

Source: Conducted by CBS News, November 6 – November 10, 2011, and based on 1,182 telephone interviews.

he had done was "bad for the country," and 40 percent thought it was good.[47] These are not easy issues, and the public's thinking reflects this kind of division. The public wants society to be open but yet realizes that security demands some secrecy. It is easy to see, therefore, why people can have different opinions about how to approach such a tough topic. Whether you agree or not with what Snowden did, he did remind Americans of an important debate that has been part of the country since its inception (see Figure 6.4).

The debate over secrecy is now taking place in a very different context than just a decade ago. The public is generally less inclined these days to get involved in international affairs. More than 50 percent of the public in 2013 wants the United States to "mind its own business," which represents an all-time high over the past fifty years. Following the 9-11 terrorist attacks in 2001, for example, the proportion of citizens who held such views stood just at 30 percent.[48] This broader context has important implications for U.S foreign policy and how we approach antiterrorism measures.

Construct Your Own Policy

1. Using modern technology, devise a way of accurately measuring public opinion so that the president and Congress consider it before deciding how best to fight terrorism.

2. Design a comprehensive antiterrorist policy that can effectively protect the United States from attack and safeguard individual liberty at the same time.

What is less clear is whether the public is also polarized. Some scholars have argued that the public has polarized along with parties, but there is also evidence that the public is more moderate, even though the choices the parties offer them are not.[51] For example, according to a series of surveys conducted by the Pew Research Center between 1987 and 2007, "the average difference between Republican and Democratic identifiers on forty political and social issues increased from 10 to 14 percent, a surprisingly small difference."[52] These data suggest that the public is more moderate than the choices that are laid before them in elections would suggest. But scholars disagree about the extent of differences among the electorate, with some suggesting that the political center has collapsed.[53]

Even some who think that the public is not as polarized as the parties are worried that polarization will yield more personal attacks and greater incivility. Others offer a more optimistic view, arguing that increasing polarization will activate people's interest in elections, which in turn will spur more interest in politics. In fact, the share of the public that cares about which party wins the presidential election has increased since 1988. Interest in elections, generally, also seems to be on the rise. In 1988, 44 percent of the public paid "a lot" of attention to the presidential campaign. In 2000, the proportion stood at 53 percent, a notable gain.[54] In 2012, around 70 percent of Americans indicated substantial interest in the presidential election.[55]

Having a clear choice engages people and gives them a stake in an election outcome. If the system became depolarized, as in the 1950s, the public would lack a choice. It would no longer matter whether Democrats or Republicans won because they would do the same thing once in office. For these reasons, many scholars in the 1950s called for parties that would offer the public a real choice (see Chapter 8, Political Parties). Citizens, under such conditions, can more effectively hold officials accountable for misdeeds and reward successes.

→ KEY QUESTIONS:
How would you explain the fact that political trust has declined in recent decades, yet interest in elections has increased?

Checkpoint

CAN YOU:

- Explain how partisanship relates to public opinion
- Explain the importance of political ideology
- Assess how well informed the American public is and whether it matters
- Describe polarization and its effects

6.4 Group Differences

> Describe how demographic characteristics influence public opinion

Public opinion is shaped by partisanship and ideology. Social scientists find that demographics also matter—that is, the tendency for certain groups within the American population to hold similar views. In this section, we look at the ways socioeconomic status, religion, gender, race and ethnicity, and education tend to organize public opinion.

Socioeconomic Status

Socioeconomic status is a combined measure of occupation, education, income, wealth, and relative social standing or lifestyle. It influences where one lives, what kind of work one does, whom one knows, the kinds of schools one attends, and the kind of opportunities one can take advantage of. These matters inevitably mold political attitudes. Working-class people are more likely than wealthier people to favor more government programs to help the poor and provide child care, more funding for public education, and more protection for Social Security. Around 70 percent of Americans earning between $15,000 and $35,000 support increased spending by government on such social services. Among those earning between $75,000 and $105,000, the proportion drops to about 55 percent.[56]

Age

Age also influences opinions on issues because the stage of one's life affects how one thinks about issues. For instance, 70 percent of people under 30 years of age favor increased spending on student loans. That drops to 42 percent among those over 55. This gap makes sense because younger people are more likely to need student loans. Younger people are much more likely to favor making marijuana legal than are older people. As of 2014, around 60 percent of those Americans 18–29 years old favor making marijuana legal. For those 65 and older, the percentage drops by nearly half to about 33 percent.[57] In general, older citizens are more socially conservative than are younger citizens,[58] and there is evidence that people tend to become more conservative as they age.

→ KEY QUESTIONS:
Does being a member of a demographic group shape opinion?

Religion

Religious affiliation is another indicator of opinion. Overall, for example, Protestants are more conservative than Catholics or Jews. Only 12 percent of Jews describe themselves as conservative, compared to 36 percent of Protestants. On some issues, Muslims have been found to be more liberal than the general population and significantly more liberal than Protestants and Catholics. For example, 70 percent of Muslims favor an activist government, whereas just 43 percent of the public as a whole subscribes to that view. On social issues, however, Muslims show a much more conservative tendency. When asked "Which comes closer to your view? Homosexuality is a way of life that should be accepted by society, or homosexuality is a way of life that should be discouraged by society," 61 percent of Muslims said that homosexual lifestyles should be discouraged. Only 38 percent of all Americans gave that response.[59]

**CONNECT
WITH YOUR CLASSMATES**
MindTap· for American Government

Access the Public Opinion and Political Socialization Forum: Discussion– How Religion Shapes Public Opinion.

Gender

Starting in 1980, a **gender gap** emerged in U.S. politics. Before 1980, the differences in political attitudes among men and women were not large and did not draw much attention. However, in elections since Ronald Reagan's 1980 victory over Jimmy Carter (1977–81), women have been generally more supportive of Democrats than of Republicans. In 1980, the gap was 8 percentage points: 54 percent of men backed Reagan, and only 46 percent of women backed him. The gap has varied from 4 percent in 1992 to 11 percent in 1996. In 2008, Barack Obama secured 56 percent of the female vote and just 49 percent of the male vote. In April 2012, among women, Obama held a substantial lead in the polls over then-presumptive Republican nominee Mitt Romney—as much as 20 percentage points.[60] Such differences remind us that if only women were allowed to vote, the Democrats might have won every presidential election since 1980 save for Reagan's landslide against Walter Mondale in 1984.[61]

gender gap:
Differences in the political attitudes and behavior of men and women.

In general, women are more liberal than men, and gender gaps are also evident on specific issues. Women tend to favor more spending on social programs than men. In 2013, more men favored cutting Medicare to reduce the deficit than did women.[62] Men are much more likely to support the death penalty than are women (62 percent versus 38 percent). This gap disappears when it comes to abortion. In 2013, around 20 percent of women and men thought abortion should be illegal in all circumstances.[63]

Race and Ethnicity

Another divide in public opinion involves race and ethnicity. The issue of slavery tore the nation apart, and more than one hundred years after the Civil War, Americans remained divided about issues involving race. In 1964, African Americans overwhelmingly endorsed desegregation, whereas white Americans were split on the issue. In 1974, only 23 percent of white Americans felt "government should help blacks," whereas 69 percent of African Americans believed that government should take that role.[64] Similar gaps exist today in regard to support for affirmative action policies that grant preferences to people (not only African Americans but also women) who have suffered discrimination in the past in job hiring, school admissions, and contracting. In 2012, only 14 percent of whites favored "preferences for hiring blacks." Three times as many African Americans favored affirmative action.[65]

The term *Latino* is used to describe a broad array of groups that do not necessarily share common experiences, so opinion among Latinos tends to be divided. Some Latino families have lived in the Southwest for centuries, since before the area became part of the United States in 1848. Others came to the United States within the past few years from homelands throughout Central and South America. Cuban immigrants, who left their homeland following the rise of Fidel Castro and the Communists in the late 1950s, tend to be much more conservative than Puerto Ricans and Mexican Americans. According to one study, about 60 percent of Cuban Americans are Republican identifiers, compared to only about 15 percent of Mexican Americans (see Global Gateways).[66] Latinos are divided in other ways as well. According to one group of prominent scholars:

→ KEY QUESTIONS:
Is your political opinion shaped by your social class, age, religion, gender, race and ethnicity, and/or education level?

> *On many key domestic issues, significant majorities of each [Latino] group take the liberal position. On other issues, there is no consensus and, depending on the issue, Mexicans may be on the right, while Cubans and many Puerto Ricans are on the left of the nation's current political spectrum. Thus, labels such as liberal or conservative do not adequately describe the complexity of any one group's political views.*[67]

Thus, both parties compete for the support of the Latino community. In 2004, Latino support for President George W. Bush helped him defeat John Kerry. In 2008, however, Barack Obama gained two-thirds of the Latino vote, a shift partly owing to actions by Republicans in Congress to block immigration reform. The importance of this group will only grow, as suggested by Figure 6.5. As Latinos comprise more and more of the electorate, issues salient to them will also become increasingly important. Latinos

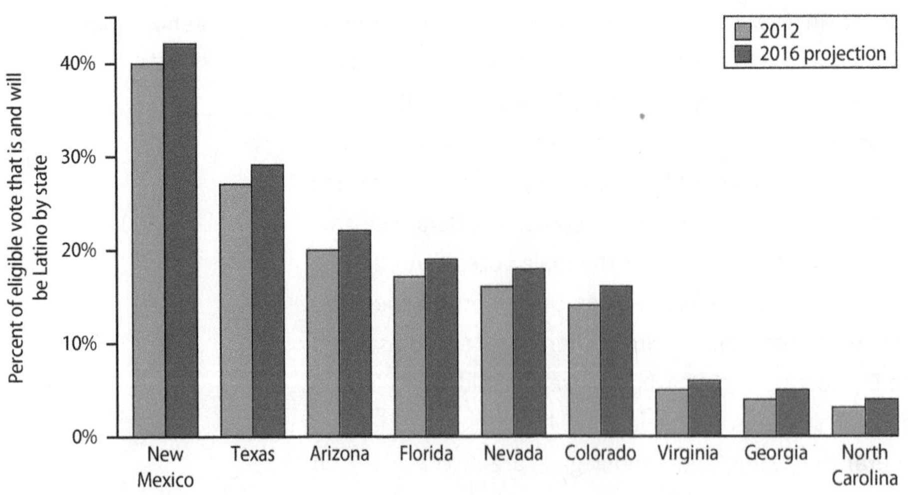

Figure 6.5 Latino Electorate Projected to Grow in Key States

Both parties need to find ways to reach out to Latino voters if they want to win elections in the coming years.

Source: Adapted from http://www.washingtonpost.com/blogs/plum-line/wp/2014/03/10/why-republicans-should-embrace-immigration-reform-in-one-chart/?hpid=z2.

IDENTITY

Amid all the discussion about immigration reform legislation, the DREAM Act, and the efforts of the two major political parties to attract Latino voters (see Figure 6.5 on page 172 to see the projected growth of this segment of the electorate), pundits and politicians use the terms Hispanic and Latino to refer to this emerging and potentially powerful set of voters (the terms are used interchangeably here). But to whom do the terms apply? Why are there two labels for this group, more if one includes Chicano, Mexican American, and so on? More importantly, what difference does it make to those groups, and does their group identity lead to noticeable differences in their political views compared to other demographic groups?

The use of Hispanic and Latino labels began more than forty years ago when Congress added "Americans of Spanish origin" to the types of social statistics that would be collected by the federal government. When asked about their identity, however, most Hispanics prefer to use their family's country of origin rather than terms like Latino or Hispanic. Moreover, large majorities of Hispanics (69 percent) see differences within those catchall labels. That is, Mexican Americans do not believe they share a common identity with, say Cuban Americans.

PARTY IDENTIFICATION

These distinctions may be more than semantics. They may indicate differences in Latinos' political values, in particular their partisan identification. Through socialization, individuals' environment influences their political attitudes. For some Americans, that environment is their or their parents' or even their grandparents' country of origin. In fact, surveys in 2012 revealed overwhelming identification with the Democratic Party among Hispanics, 70 percent among registered Hispanic voters[68] (see Table 6.1).

However, unpacking these data to see how Hispanics of different national origin view the parties reveals a slightly different story. While most groups of Hispanics identify with the Democratic Party, Cuban Americans more closely identify with the Republican Party. That pattern holds when we include leaners.

Of the generational groupings we identified in this chapter, members of the Hispanic baby boomer and silent generations are most likely to identify with the Democratic Party (70 percent) while the Millennial generation shows the lowest, though still strong, level of attachment (61 percent). Ten percent of this youngest generation of Hispanic voters chooses neither party, perhaps providing a glimmer of hope to Republican Party efforts to woo them into their camp.[69] Dampening that glimmer, possibly, is the trend that as noncitizen Hispanics move toward citizenship, roughly half identify or lean toward the Democrats.

Table 6.1 Political Party Affiliation Among Hispanics, 2012

% who...

	Identify with One of the Major Parties			Don't Identify but Lean More Toward One			Don't Identify with/Lean Toward Either
	NET	Dem.	Rep.	NET	Dem.	Rep.	
All Hispanics	58	49	10	25	18	8	16
Hispanic registered voters	71	57	14	21	13	8	9

Source: Pew Research Center July 22, 2013. "Are Unauthorized Immigrants Overwhelmingly Democrats?" http://www.pewresearch.org/fact-tank/2013/07/22/are-unauthorized-immigrants-overwhelmingly-democrats/.

1. What shapes the identity of most Hispanics?
2. What do the trends in Latino partisan identification suggest for politics in future elections?

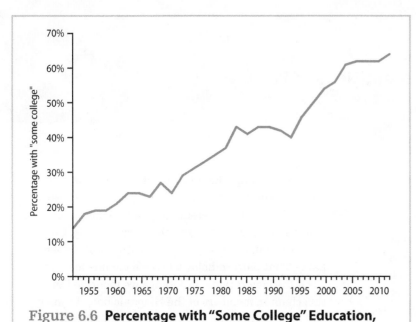

Figure 6.6 Percentage with "Some College" Education, 1948–2012

Since the end of World War II, education levels have steadily increased. Level of education is a factor affecting public opinion on a range of specific issues.

Source: American National Election Study.

support, for example, bilingual education and policies that favor immigration more than do Anglos.[70]

Asian American public opinion has not drawn the same level of attention as that of other groups. Asian Americans are, however, a growing segment of the population and constitute a sizable part of the population of some states, especially California. Like Latinos, the Asian American population is diverse, including people from Korea, Vietnam, Japan, and China. In general, however, Asian Americans are a bit more liberal than white Americans. In 2012, for example, about 73 percent of Asian Americans supported President Obama, whereas only 39 percent of white Americans did so. This support of Democrats by Asian Americans is on the rise as well.[71]

Education

→ KEY QUESTIONS:
Think again: Does being a member of a demographic group shape opinion?

One important change in the American population is the increasing level of education. Figure 6.6 charts the share of Americans who had attended college for at least a year over the past sixty years. The pattern is striking. In 1948, about one in seven Americans had gone to college for at least one year. By 2014, more than one in two Americans had attended college. The upward trend has been continuous since the end of World War II in 1945 for two key reasons. The first is that more young people have access to a college education. The second is what is called "generational replacement"; that is, older, less-educated citizens have passed on, and the average level of education of the American public has thus increased.

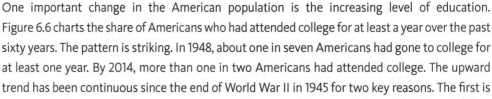

Checkpoint

CAN YOU:

- State the relationship between socioeconomic status, on the one hand, and partisanship and ideology on the other
- Describe how age affects political thinking
- Distinguish the differences in public opinion between different religious affiliations
- Characterize the impact of the gender gap
- Survey the impact of race and ethnicity on political thinking
- Track the effect of increasing educational levels on political views

It matters that people in the United States are more educated. In broad strokes, there is a long-standing belief that a democracy is best able to endure when its citizens are engaged and informed. With more education, the public should be more aware of politics and better able to find ways to ensure that government responds to them. In the language of this book, a better-educated public should be in better position to travel through the gateways of influence and find ways around the many gates in the American political system.

Education level is also connected to public opinion. Views on the controversial issue of immigration reform offer an instructive example. Among college graduates, three quarters favored making it possible for those here illegally to become citizens (providing they pass background checks, pay relevant fines, and have jobs). Among those with a high school education or less, the proportion falls to just over half.[72] The 20-percentage-point gap is significant. Individuals with a higher level of education generally take a more liberal position on a variety of social and economic issues, ranging from government spending to defense policy to gay marriage.[73]

6.5 The Political News

> Determine why the media are important in a democracy

In a democracy such as the United States, citizens and their opinions are supposed to be the ultimate source of power. The decisions made by the public shape the course of government. The public, therefore, needs information about politics to make good choices. Most people cannot directly observe political events, so they rely on the mass media for information about politics and government.

What Are the Mass Media?

The **mass media** represent the vast array of sources of information that are available to the public, including newspapers, television, radio, blogs, online sources, cell phones, and social media such as Facebook or Twitter. The **news media** (also called the press) are a subset of the mass media that have traditionally provided the news of the day, gathered and reported by journalists. With all the new technologies of the twenty-first century, however, the news media are changing; now the average citizen is able to participate in politics through blogs such as *Daily Kos* and websites such as YouTube or Reddit. These "new" media have recast journalism by providing a proliferation of news outlets without a monolithic entity that shapes and defines political reporting. In this chapter, we use the term *mass media* to describe the many ways citizens learn about government and politics.

Access to information is important because an enduring and effective democracy demands a knowledgeable public.[74] For the people to be informed, the press needs to be able to do its job free from government interference, and journalists must feel free to be critical of the government. This **watchdog** role of the press lies at the very heart of a democracy. In 1787, Thomas Jefferson observed, "Were it left to me to decide whether we should have a government without newspapers, or newspapers without a government, I should not hesitate a moment to prefer the latter."[75] What Jefferson meant is that only a well-informed public is capable of self-governing. Freedom of the press is intertwined with the very idea of democratic government, and the First Amendment to the Constitution protects it.

The Functions of the News

The mass media help ensure government accountability and responsiveness by performing three important tasks: informing, investigating, and interpreting the news.

Informing. Journalists, simply put, inform. Coverage of the struggle between Ukraine and Russia that erupted in 2014, for example, might include stories about casualties or about intense fighting in various locales. Coverage of a political campaign might include information about candidates' previous experience, their personal temperaments, or their views on important issues. If there is a crisis in the economy, journalists provide information about the problem, explain the solutions being proposed, and indicate what can be expected in the future. In August 2008—just a month before a financial crisis rocked the nation—about 5 percent of news stories dealt with the economy. In September, that proportion soared to nearly 30 percent.[76] More recently, journalists covered extensively the deadly tornadoes that ravaged the Midwest.[77] A quick scan of any newspaper or network news website can inform readers about a wide range of topics.

mass media: *News sources, including newspapers, television, radio, and the Internet, whose purpose is to provide a large audience with information about the nation and the world.*

news media: *Subset of the mass media that provides the news of the day, gathered and reported by journalists.*

→ KEY QUESTIONS:
How do you get your news?

watchdog: *Role of the press in monitoring government actions.*

Washington Post **reporters Bob Woodward and Carl Bernstein became legends for their work in following up on a news story about what seemed to be a routine break-in. But it was the Democratic campaign headquarters that was broken into on June 17, 1972, and the trail they picked up led to the White House. Certain to be impeached, President Richard M. Nixon resigned on August 9, 1974.**

→ KEY QUESTIONS:
Why is the relationship between the press and politicians adversarial?

Investigating.   The media can also make news by researching and revealing information about events. The Watergate scandal, uncovered by two reporters from the *Washington Post*, revealed questionable activities in the Richard M. Nixon administration (1969–74) (see also Chapter 11, The Presidency). Bob Woodward and Carl Bernstein played the ultimate role of watchdog, creating a news story that gripped the country for more than a year. The episode ended with Nixon's resignation on August 9, 1974, the only time a U.S. president has resigned. This scandal would never have been uncovered without the tireless efforts of the *Post's* investigative reporters.[78] Their work was surely the high point of investigative journalism.

Politicians often court the press, but they want favorable coverage. They want journalists to advertise their accomplishments to voters. Yet journalists and politicians are usually in an adversarial relationship because journalists want to report new stories on topics of interest to the public. So reporters love to unearth scandals—something that politicians want to avoid. Scandals are fresh and exciting, and uncovering them gives journalists real influence. The investigative function not only allows the press to fulfill its role as the watchdog of democracy, but it also makes reporters' jobs exciting and important. Also, scandals sell newspapers, and the profit motive is a central part of the process.

Interpreting.   When the media inform, they also interpret the news. Just giving front-page coverage to one story and relegating another story to an inside page involves interpreting what is more and less important. The role of interpretation has taken on even greater significance in the past few decades. In 1960, for example, journalists covered presidential campaigns in a very descriptive fashion. About 90 percent of campaign stories focused on describing what happened in the campaign that day. But in the following decades, journalists started to interpret events more frequently, assessing why something happened.[79] Today, cable news, for example, delivers far more commentary than hard news. In 2012, 85 percent of the news on MSNBC was commentary and opinion, dwarfing Fox News (55 percent) and CNN (46 percent).[80]

Checkpoint

CAN YOU:

■ Describe the role of the press as watchdog

■ State the functions of the news media

6.6 The Law and the Free Press

❯ Analyze how the law protects the press

As we saw in Chapter 4, very few laws constrain the print media, such as newspapers and magazines. The electronic media, however, are more heavily regulated by the government. As early as the 1920s, Congress sought to regulate radio to ensure it would serve the public interest. It was a new medium, and Congress wanted to guard against it being used in a way that might undermine equality and fairness. In 1934, Congress created the Federal Communications Commission (FCC), now a powerful agency that regulates all forms of electronic media, including radio, broadcast television, cable television, cell phones, and even wireless networks. Anyone can start a newspaper, but starting a radio station requires a license from the FCC.

The FCC monitors media ownership as well. For a long time, the FCC worked to ensure that ownership of the news media was not concentrated in just a few hands, concerned that a monopoly would undermine the ability of the media to be fair and able to perform its watchdog function. The Telecommunications Act of 1996 eased the rules concerning multiple ownership, and the FCC has started to relax this standard. As a result, there has been a trend toward greater concentration of media ownership in the past decade. In 1995, major companies generally owned around ten television stations each; ten years later, each owned nearly forty. The ownership of radio has also changed. Clear Channel Communications owned 520 radio stations in 1999. By 2014, the number stood at 840.[81]

→ KEY QUESTIONS:
What are the newspapers in your city or town? Who owns them?

This recent concentration of media ownership is not unique. Without genuine competition, the press, some fear, will become lapdogs, not watchdogs. But even the changes of the past few years have not eliminated competition. It is true that newspapers are now dominated by seven major chains; Gannett alone controls more than eighty newspapers. But that is still only about a circulation of 7 million (or about 15 percent of newspapers nationally).[82] Of course, newspaper readership is down over the past few decades, making this number even less consequential.[83] With so many outlets for news in the twenty-first century, one person or company will not likely be able to control them all.

Any effort to monopolize the press or curtail its freedom is met by strong protests from people fearing a trend toward authoritarian rule. A government that limits press freedom seeks to insulate itself from criticism, thereby decreasing the chance for the public to hold leaders accountable. The absence of a robust press means that government will no longer be responsive, but that it will instead pursue policies that advance the interests of the few rather than the many. In this situation, greater inequality arises between those in power and those out of power. It is for all these reasons that an evaluation of how democratic a nation is rests on how much freedom its press enjoys.

Checkpoint

CAN YOU:

■ Name the laws and government agencies that regulate press freedom

6.7 The Mass Media in the Twenty-First Century

> Explain how changes in the mass media have changed the information environment

The media have always been a dynamic institution, but the speed of changes in the past few decades is truly staggering. The impact of television, for example, changed further with the rise of cable television from the 1970s to the 1990s. It was now possible to bring news to the public any time of day, reshaping the American news environment. Recent advances in technology have opened up additional avenues of communication—nearly all at the same time. The pace and the depth of these changes make the information environment of the twenty-first century different from those that preceded it.

The Changing Media Environment

The options open to Americans for gathering information about politics have constantly expanded. Figure 6.7 displays the changing media environment and suggests two main lessons. First, Americans adopt new media quickly. In the early 1920s, there were only five radio stations, and few households owned radios. By 1927, there were seven hundred stations, and ownership was rapidly increasing.[84] By the end of the 1930s, almost everyone in the United States had access to a radio. Television caught on even more quickly. Only 10 percent of Americans had TV sets in their homes in the early 1950s; by 1960, the figure was 90 percent. Today, nearly all American households have not one TV but often two or three. Internet access also shows a steep upward trend, from few households in the mid-1990s to about 87 percent of Americans in 2014.[85] The speed by which these new media have entered the marketplace itself increases. It took television thirteen years to reach 50 million users. In just three years on the market, more than 50 million iPods were sold, and when the iPad was released in 2010, about 3 million were sold in eighty days.[86] Twitter has tripled its number of users from about 4 percent in 2010 to now 12 percent in 2014.[87] Of course, among the younger generation, Twitter is a much more common feature of daily lives. Estimates are that about one-third of Millennials use Twitter.[88]

Second, there are more options for gathering news than ever before. In the 1930s, newspapers and radio were the main sources. In the 1950s, television was a new option, but there were only three networks, and they broadcast the news only in the evening. Now cable TV, satellite TV, and the Internet make news available night and day.

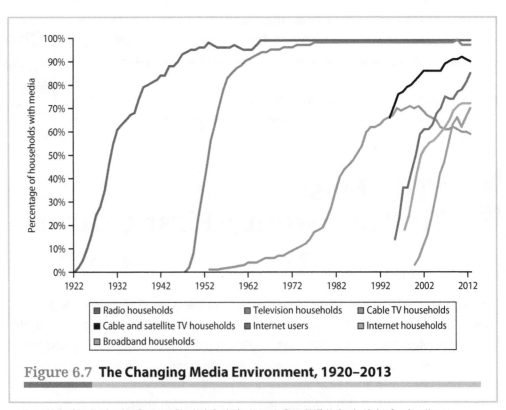

Figure 6.7 The Changing Media Environment, 1920–2013

Source: Markus Prior, *Post Broadcast Democracy* (New York: Cambridge University Press, 2007). Updated with data from http://www.freedomhouse.org/report-types/freedom-press#.UtrnyIPbna2w, accessed May 13, 2014.

The Decline of Newspapers

Traditional printed newspapers are in decline. The number of daily papers has been dropping since 1990.[89] Newspaper readership is also declining. Figure 6.8 shows the drop in readership in the past decade. This pattern is part of an even longer-term trend. In 1977, about 70 percent of the public read newspapers. By 2014, less than 25 percent of the Millennial generation were newspaper readers as compared to nearly 60 percent of those over 65 years of age.[90]

The decline of newspapers and newspaper readership raises concerns because newspapers tend to contain more **hard news**—fact-based stories, as opposed to interpretive narratives—than is reported on TV. Alex Jones, one of the leading observers of the press, indicated that 85 percent of hard news comes from newspapers rather than from TV.[91] Will the decline of newspapers deprive Americans of hard news and the facts they need to hold government accountable?

Some observers counter that readers are simply migrating from printed newspapers to online versions. In January 2004, online newspapers had about 41 million visitors; within the next decade, the number had jumped to well over 100 million.[92] Although the move from the printed to online versions may offer some hope about the continued significance of the newspaper industry, it has not solved the industry's financial difficulties. With revenue plummeting, newspapers survive only by cutting staff. The *Boston Globe* once sent journalists overseas to report on international events. That is no longer true.[93] The *Los Angeles Times* has seen its newsroom decline from 1,200 to 850 reporters.[94] Over the past decade, there has been a loss of 18,000 jobs in newsrooms from 56,000 in 2003 to 38,000 in 2012.[95] Fewer reporters,

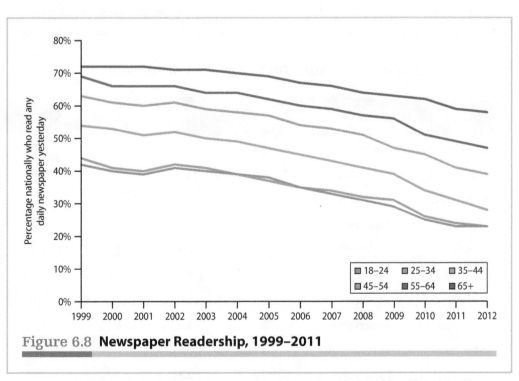

Figure 6.8 **Newspaper Readership, 1999–2011**

Source: Adapted from Scarborough Research survey data, 1999–2011 Scarborough Report, Release 1, Pew Research Center's Project for Excellence in Journalism, *The State of the News Media 2012*. Copyright © 2011 by Pew Research Center. Reproduced by permission. Television households data: http://www.nytimes.com/2011/05/03/business/media/03television.html?_r=0 and http://tvbythenumbers.zap2it.com/2007/08/28/us-television-households-by-season/273/;cable TV households data: http://www.tvb.org/media_comparisons/4729/72512, http://www.nielsen.com/content/dam/corporate/us/en/newswire/uploads/2009/07/tva_2008_071709.pdf, and http://www.tvhistory.tv/Cable_Households_77-99.JPG; Internet users: http://www.pewinternet.org/Static-Pages/Trend-Data-%28Adults%29/Internet-Adoption.aspx; Internet households: http://www.census.gov/hhes/computer/publications/2011.html); broadband households: http://pewinternet.org/Reports/2013/Broadband/Findings.aspx.

→ KEY QUESTIONS:
Are the newspapers in your town struggling? How can you tell?

editors, and other journalists mean that newspapers have less ability to inform and investigate. If the press cannot perform its watchdog role, the people stand to lose the means by which they hold government accountable.[96]

Despite these serious concerns, Americans want the news and continue to seek it out, so newspaper owners have an incentive to develop new ways to make a profit.[97] In addition, today's leading newspapers, such as the *New York Times*, have been powerful for only about 70 years, whereas American democracy has survived for 230 years.

The Durability of Radio

In many ways, radio is underappreciated as a medium of communication; current debates center on newspapers, television, and the Internet. But radio remains important, especially considering how often Americans listen to the radio in their cars. The percentage of Americans who listen to the radio has remained unchanged in the past decade. In 1998, 95 percent of the American public tuned into an AM or FM station at least once a week; thirteen years later, 93 percent had listened to the radio in the previous seven days. Radio is expanding its reach by means of satellite radio and streaming audio on desktop and laptop computers. In fact, it is possible that "radio" is becoming "audio," reflecting advances in digital technology.[98]

Political talk radio, a medium dominated largely by conservatives, is increasingly popular.[99] In 2012, around 50 million Americans listened to talk radio,[100] most to conservative programs. In fact, as Table 6.2 shows, conservatives dominate the airwaves of talk radio. No "liberal" shows are even close to the popularity of the top-rated conservative commentators. Rush Limbaugh is by far the best known and the most controversial. Liberals at one time tried to make inroads into talk radio with the now-defunct Air America radio network but had no

Table 6.2 Top Talk Radio Hosts, 2012 (in millions of listeners)

Host	Political Leaning/ General Topic	2009	2010	2011	2012
Rush Limbaugh	Conservative	15	15	15	14.75
Sean Hannity	Conservative	14	14	14	14
Michael Savage	Conservative	9	8.5	9	8.75
Glen Beck	Conservative	9	9	8.5	8.25
Mark Levin	Conservative	8.5	8.5	8.5	8.25
Dave Ramsey	Financial Advice	8	8	8.5	8.25
Neal Boortz	Libertarian	6	6	6	5.75
Laura Ingraham	Conservative	6	6	6	5.75
Jim Bohannon	Ind./Moderate	3.75	3.75	3.75	3.75
Jerry Doyle	Conservative	3.5	3.75	3.75	3.75

Source: Adapted from *Talker Magazine*, cited in Pew Research Center's Project for Excellence in Journalism's report, *The State of the News Media 2011.* Also, http://stateofthemedia.org/2013/audio-digital-drives-listener-experience/19-limbaugh-audience-dips-slightly-but-still-tops-talk-radio/, Pew Research Center's Project for Excellence in Journalism, *The State of the News Media 2013.*
© CENGAGE LEARNING®

success. The reasons for this lack of success are unclear. Perhaps it is because there are more conservatives than liberals in the United States. In addition, conservatives tend to live in the suburbs and rural areas and therefore spend more time driving their cars than do city dwellers. Their greater opportunities for listening may be another reason for the dominance of conservative programming.[101]

The Transformation of TV News

Newspapers are not the only news outlets facing a decline in customers. The audience for the TV network evening news is also shrinking (see Figure 6.9). Nearly 25 percent of Americans watched the evening news in 1980; by 2013, that figure was around 10 percent.[102] The downward trend is likely to continue because older Americans make up the current audience for TV news. Young people, who represent the future audience, are not big consumers of network news. Their habits are not likely to change, painting a bleak picture for the industry in the coming years.

This decline, like that of newspapers, generates concern about how well informed the public is about politics. But these concerns are counterbalanced by the rise of cable news, which has become increasingly available since 1980. Households are now watching two or three hours a week of cable news, a rate of viewership higher than that for network news in the 1980s. Of the cable networks, Fox has the largest audience, more than CNN and MSNBC combined.

Cable news is not like the evening news shows of the 1970s, which were thirty-minute broadcasts around dinnertime. Cable news is available twenty-four hours a day. Events are covered live, transforming the news cycle. No longer do politicians time public appearances to appear on the evening news. News now comes at viewers at a rapid-fire rate, and cable news networks include interpretation in their constant programming. MSNBC's *Hardball with Chris Matthews* and *The Rachel Maddow Show* and Fox's *The Huckabee Show* are examples. Cable news has taken the interpretive function of the news media to a whole new level in response to the demands of 24-7 news programming.

The web offers yet another platform for gathering and distributing the news, one that seems to be on the rise. Figure 6.9 shows the downward trend for all news outlets save "online," which is on the rise over the past eight years and shows no sign of decreasing. We examine the impact of these developments later in the chapter.

Infotainment

Television viewers also get political news through talk shows, such as *The Ellen DeGeneres Show*, *The Daily Show with Jon Stewart*, and *Jimmy Kimmel Live*. We already know about Stephen Colbert. These sources offer "infotainment" or **soft news**, which is news with fewer hard facts of the kind newspapers generally report and more emphasis on personal stories that engage (or shock) the public and often appeal to the emotions rather than the intellect.

For example, nearly 2.5 million people, mostly young adults, watch *The Daily Show*, which delivers the news with humor and satire four days a week. With Stewart's tough

> → KEY QUESTIONS:
> Which cable news station do you watch? Do you think the presentation of the news is fair?

> → KEY QUESTIONS:
> Would you describe the news you seek as hard or soft?

soft news: *News stories focused less on facts and policies than on sensationalizing secondary issues or on less serious subjects of the entertainment world.*

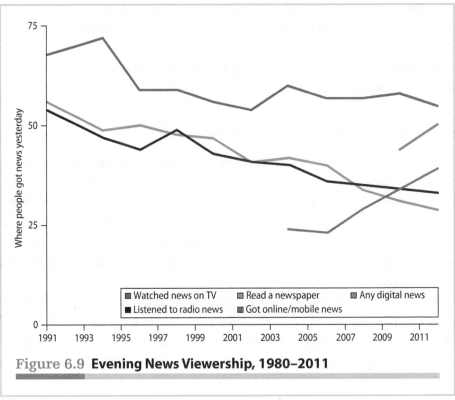

Figure 6.9 Evening News Viewership, 1980–2011

Legend:
- Watched news on TV
- Listened to radio news
- Read a newspaper
- Got online/mobile news
- Any digital news

© CENGAGE LEARNING®

questions and hard-hitting reporting, it would be misleading to suggest that the news the show provides is "soft." The guests who appear on *The Daily Show* cover the full ideological spectrum, and Stewart subjects those in power—regardless of party—to his rapier wit. Though considered by many to be liberal, he aims for on-air balance.[103] Before Stephen Colbert left *The Colbert Report*, it was also an exceptionally popular comedy/news show with 1.9 million Americans tuning in every night.[104]

Blogs

Blogs provide a forum for bottom-up commentary, descriptions of events, video postings, and general conversation. Through blogs, average citizens are able to express their opinions to a wider audience, and blogs offer a gateway for people to influence politics. In fact, blogs have given rise to a new category of journalists—citizen-journalists—who, although not professional journalists, circulate opinions and interpretations that clearly influence political debates. There are all kinds of blogs, with political blogs representing a subset. Of the fifteen most popular blogs in 2014, two are political: the *Huffington Post* (number 1) and the *Daily Beast* (number 8).[105] A blog tailored to the interests and preferences

Jon Stewart's and Stephen Colbert's Rally to Restore Sanity and/or Fear, on the National Mall on October 30, 2010, was star-studded and entertaining, but it also had a serious purpose—to promote reason in political discourse. Concluding the event, Stewart took the media to task: "The country's 24-hour political pundit perpetual panic conflictinator did not cause our problems, but it makes solving them that much harder." He went on to caution, "If we amplify everything, we hear nothing."

of the Millennials, *PolicyMic*, encourages this generation to weigh in on the pressing issues of the day.

In many ways, blogging symbolizes the modern transformation of the mass media. Blogs capture the interest of people of all ages, and some observers hope that they will provide a forum for more participation and deliberation. While there is some evidence that blogs do foster participation, they do not seem to foster deliberation. Liberals read liberal blogs, and conservatives read conservative blogs—in fact, 94 percent of people read blogs that share their ideological viewpoint. These data suggest that blogs reinforce existing preferences and do not provide opportunities to hear the other side.[106] In addition, blogs usually have clear ideological leanings. Conservative blogs include those of Matt Drudge and Rush Limbaugh.[107] *Daily Kos* and *Huffington Post* are liberal blogs.

Blogs have the potential to spread false information. Because no one checks the accuracy of a posting, individuals—some call them trolls—can say outrageous things merely to get attention without penalty.[108] In contrast, the traditional press has a well-established set of norms for vetting the accuracy of information; when false statements do get through, the journalists are likely to pay a heavy penalty. Trolls, on the other hand, often gain notoriety for lying.

Nevertheless, the importance of blogs continues to increase. Bloggers write about business news, iTechnology, political news, trends in Hollywood, and so on. News that is not picked up in the mainstream media often gets play in the blogosphere and can force the mainstream media to cover the story. Politicians understand the powerful effects blogs can have on the news. In the 2012 presidential campaign, both candidates established blogs on their websites with commentary on topics ranging from the cost of student loans to the role of stay-at-home moms.

Social Networking

The Internet has also enabled new social networks for sharing information. Just as personal conversations are important sources of information, social networking websites are increasingly important ways to spread political news. Facebook is, of course, the leading platform for social networking. Its website announces that its mission is "to give people the power to share and make the world more open and connected."[109]

Mark Zuckerberg started the site from his Harvard dorm room in February 2004 as a social networking service limited to the Harvard campus. By the end of March, the service was extended to Stanford, Columbia, and Yale universities. By the end of the year, the network had more than 1 million users, and it reached 5.5 million by the end of 2005 when it was extended to all universities and high schools in the United States and Canada. Facebook stands in 2014 at more than 1.2 billion users, which would make it the world's third largest country, following China and India and well ahead of the United States.[110] Facebook is a worldwide phenomenon with launches in more than fifteen different languages. However, all these platforms are dynamic and undergoing constant change. Consider that now more than 75 percent of all college students use Snapchat.[111]

Just as politicians are using blogs to communicate with the public, they are also using social networks. In 2012, all of the major presidential candidates made use of Facebook.[112] Facebook also teamed up with NBC News and the *Manchester Union Leader* in New Hampshire to sponsor the Republican presidential debates on January 8, 2012. After the debates,

> → KEY QUESTIONS:
> How could you be a citizen-journalist?

> → KEY QUESTIONS:
> Have you ever written a blog? What inspired you?

> → KEY QUESTIONS:
> Is Facebook a source of political news or action for you?

Vice President Joe Biden and President Barack Obama look at an app on an iPhone in the Outer Oval Office, July 16, 2011. President Obama relied on his BlackBerry when campaigning for president and has continued to use it in office despite concerns about security breaches.

users could go to the website and discuss the issues and positions of the candidates. According to Facebook vice president Dan Rose, the goal of these kinds of partnerships was "to extend the debate from being a one-hour session that happens on television to a dialogue that can take place before, after, and now during the debate between voters."[113] Twitter is another platform that is being widely used by political candidates of all stripes, even in local elections such as judge or city council.[114]

Social media is an invaluable means whereby candidates reach out to a younger generation of voters, both to convey their messages and to raise money. Candidates on Facebook, for example, can list biographical details, post advertisements and other Internet feeds, provide links for donations, and create discussion groups. Candidates can use Twitter to communicate with the public, posting new and relevant information. Private individuals—even college professors—have also used Facebook and Twitter to campaign for candidates on their own. These are new gateways for volunteering that are less costly and offer a chance for greater influence in the political process.

Cell phones have made possible text messaging, which is replacing e-mail for many people, especially young people. Cell phone usage is nearly universal now, and text messaging is so common that most people have "unlimited" texting as part of their payment plan. Politicians and political parties use this medium to communicate with supporters. Text messaging is yet another gateway, and the increasing popularity of iPhones and other advanced cellular devices promises new means of communicating and sharing information in the future.

The News Media and Latino Voters

Latinos, as the fastest growing ethnic group in the United States, are also prompting change in the media environment. One recent trend in the dissemination and consumption of news is the increase in viewership for the two major Spanish language networks, Univision and Telemundo.[115] As of 2013, the two networks were reaching more than 5 million Spanish-speaking viewers in more than forty markets in the United States. To compete, other outlets are reaching out to Latino audiences. The growth in Spanish-language television now includes, for example, MundoFox, CNN Latino, and Fusion, a 24-hour cable news channel that broadcasts content in English that is directed at English-speaking Latino Millennials.

Fusion, a joint venture between ABC News and Noticias Univision, reflects an interesting news consumption pattern of Latinos, half of whom rely on both English and Spanish sources of news (see Figure 6.10). Public Broadcasting also has responded to the growing number of Latino viewers who consume news in English and Spanish. In Arizona, for example, PBS produces the public affairs program *Horizonte,* an English-language public affairs program about political issues of interest to Latinos.

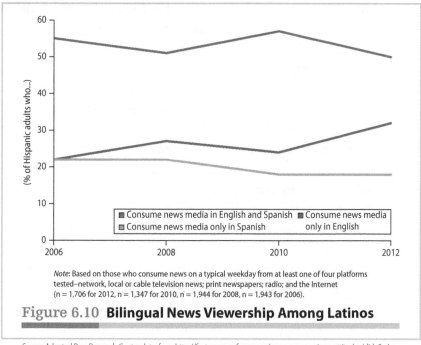

Figure 6.10 **Bilingual News Viewership Among Latinos**

Note: Based on those who consume news on a typical weekday from at least one of four platforms tested–network, local or cable television news; print newspapers; radio; and the Internet (n = 1,706 for 2012, n = 1,347 for 2010, n = 1,944 for 2008, n = 1,943 for 2006).

Source: Adapted Pew Research Center data, from http://features.pewforum.org/same-sex-marriage-attitudes/slide2.php

Of course, the news media's attention to politics is heightened during presidential campaigns. When the presidential debate commission did not include a moderator from their network for any of the four debates in 2012, Univision opted to produce a separate program for their audience of Latino voters. Univision organized a "Meet the Candidate" forum to fill what the network viewed as a void in the campaign coverage. President Obama and Governor Romney appeared on the program and answered questions about their positions on issues of importance to Latino voters. Univision also produces and airs the weekly program, *Voz y Voto* (*Voice and Vote*), focusing on political issues of importance to Latinos.

These trends in increased television news coverage aimed at Latino audiences are paralleled by the increase in their usage of social network outlets. More than half of Latinos report using Internet sources for news.[116] Moreover, of those Internet users, over 80 percent of Millennials are social network users. News platforms are expanding in the evolving media environment and fast becoming bilingual as media markets reflect demographic and political shifts, opening a gateway for Latinos.

The News and the Millennials

The changes in the media environment do not affect all citizens equally, as suggested by Figure 6.11. The Millennial generation, for example, is more than three times more likely to get its news from *The Daily Show* than from a daily newspaper. In addition, when younger Americans read a newspaper or listen to a radio program, they do so for a much shorter period of time than do those who are older than 50. The youth seem to do more channel surfing, while older Americans are more likely to

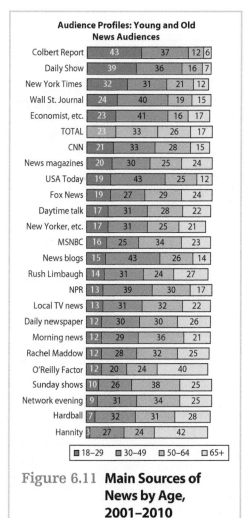

Figure 6.11 **Main Sources of News by Age, 2001–2010**

© Cengage Learning®

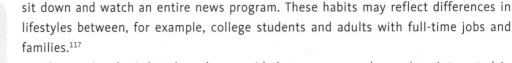

→ KEY QUESTIONS:
Which do you trust more—
bottom-up or top-down
journalism?

→ KEY QUESTIONS:
What is the future of political
communication?

sit down and watch an entire news program. These habits may reflect differences in lifestyles between, for example, college students and adults with full-time jobs and families.[117]

Conventional wisdom has always said that young people are less interested in politics than older Americans are. But Millennials appear to be more interested in politics at this point in their lives than were previous generations. This interest is not gauged by whether they watch the evening news or read newspapers, but by the ways they use new media to share information and learn about and express interest in politics.[118] Young adults tend to reject the top-down approach to learning about politics in which the news is filtered by professional journalists and trusted news anchors such as Cronkite. Instead, they seem much more interested in the bottom-up approach made possible by the wide-open availability of new media for citizen participation.

These changes are going to become more important over time as more Millennials become eligible to vote and older generations pass on. Technological change continues to spread, making the Internet and all of its information increasingly available to more Americans. The United States is in the midst of a major transformation in the media environment, and observers are only beginning to understand the changes in how Americans transmit and consume the news.

Checkpoint

CAN YOU:

■ Describe the changing media environment

■ Survey the impact of radio, TV news, infotainment, blogs, social networking, and the changing media environment.

6.8 The Impact of the News Media on the Public

> Assess how the news media affect public opinion

The press provides information, investigation, and interpretation of the news. The news media, both old and new, make decisions about what to cover, what not to cover, and how to cover it. How does the public respond to this information? This section looks at several models ranging between two extremes: that the mass media have no effect on the public and that the mass media dominate the public's thinking.

The Propaganda Model

Few people believe that the media have no influence on citizens. To hold such a view, one must either believe that the public ignores the media or that citizens learn about politics by observing the events themselves. Neither is true. We can confidently label this the "naïve model" and dismiss it.

propaganda model:
Extreme view of the media's role in society, arguing that the press serves the interest of the government only, driving what the public thinks about important issues.

The polar opposite has been called the **propaganda model**. This approach is exemplified by the Nazi dictatorship in Germany in the 1930s and 1940s. The Nazi Party controlled the content of newspapers and radio. It dictated the information available to citizens, affecting the direction and shape of public opinion. Through controlled programming, the German people often heard about the greatness of Adolf Hitler and the dangers of racial impurity. By holding a monopoly on information, the government could easily marshal public support. This is a dangerous model, and it is also inconsistent with how the press works in open societies. In the United States, media sources control programming, and they compete for audience share; the government does not control the flow of information.

The Minimal Effects Model

Toward the end of World War II, having seen the powerful effects of propaganda in Nazi Germany, scholars in the United States began to study public opinion and the influence of the media on it. Paul Lazarsfeld and others examined the media's influence on voting in the 1940 presidential election. The results were surprising: The researchers discovered that people had made up their minds before the campaign, and new information altered only a handful of people's choices.[119] Lazarsfeld's study gave rise to what has been called the **minimal effects model**. Lazarsfeld and his colleagues contended that the news media had only marginal influence on the public's thinking about politics. The public did not have much information about politics, and attitudes were shaped by long-standing forces such as partisanship or the neighborhood in which people lived.

According to this model, in a process described as **selective exposure**, people secured information from sources that agreed with them, leading to the reinforcement of beliefs, not to a change of beliefs. The minimal effects model was also based on a complementary process called **selective perception**—a concept developed in a study of the American voter published by Angus Campbell and three coauthors in 1960.[120] Selective perception describes partisans as interpreting the same information differently. In other words, partisanship involves a perceptual lens that shapes how outside events are viewed. So, for example, in May 2014, 79 percent of Democrats supported President Obama's health care reform legislation, passed in 2010, whereas only 8 percent of Republicans did.[121]

The Not-So-Minimal Effects Model

In the 1970s, scholars started to gather better data that could more effectively test for the impact of the news media. This next generation of research produced the **not-so-minimal effects model**. While not overstating the power of the news media, the model acknowledges that the coverage of politics by the press matters in subtle and important ways. In particular, there are three kinds of media effects: agenda setting, priming, and framing.

Agenda Setting. By stressing certain issues, the media influence what the American public views as the most pressing concerns. This effect is called **agenda setting**. Given that on any particular day there are literally hundreds of stories that could be reported, journalists' decisions about which stories to cover (and which story to lead with, and which to bury inside the paper or at the end of a newscast) matter considerably. Politicians and their advisers make a huge effort to convince the media to cover some stories and ignore others. Should the news lead with a story about casualties in the war in Afghanistan or about growing problems in the nation's public education system? As one scholar explains, the media "may not be successful most of the time telling people what to think, but it is stunningly successful in telling its readers what to think about."[122]

minimal effects model: *View of the media's impact as marginal because most people seek news reports to reinforce beliefs already held rather than to develop new ones.*

selective exposure: *Process whereby people secure information from sources that agree with them, thus reinforcing their beliefs.*

selective perception: *Process whereby partisans interpret the same information differently.*

→ KEY QUESTIONS:
What are your sources for the news? Do you select sources that agree with your views or that challenge your views?

not-so-minimal effects model: *View of the media's impact as substantial, occurring by agenda setting, framing, and priming.*

→ KEY QUESTIONS:
Have the news media changed your mind about a political issue or figure?

agenda setting: *Ability of the media to affect the way people view issues, people, or events by controlling which stories are shown and which are not.*

© Randy Glasbergen
www.glasbergen.com

GLASBERGEN –

RANDY GLASBERGEN

"Today in school we learned about the three main branches of government: lobbyists, fund-raisers and media."

The evidence is compelling. If the media talk about crime, the public starts to care about it. If the press starts paying additional attention to the federal budget deficit, the issue becomes more salient to citizens. Since only about 1 percent of news coverage is dedicated to the topic of education, it is not surprising that education policy rarely rises to the top of politicians' agendas.[123]

Priming. An extension of agenda setting is **priming**. Emphasis by the media can alter the criteria that citizens use when evaluating political leaders. Following 9/11, for instance, the news media's coverage of terrorism was the most powerful force shaping President Bush's popularity.[124] The public gave Bush credit for dealing effectively with these tragic events. So when terrorism was the focus of the media, Bush's approval rating was high. But late in Bush's second term when the primary topic covered by the media shifted to the economy, the public was less supportive of the president.

Priming can also affect how people vote. In the 2012 campaign, Republican candidate Mitt Romney hoped the public would perceive the economy as struggling and vote for him on that basis. The Obama reelection team wanted the public to perceive the economy as better than it was when Obama started his first term in 2009. Both sides recognized that the way the news media primed the public to think about the economy would have an impact on the election. With Obama's victory, it appears his message was more effective than Romney's.

→ KEY QUESTIONS:
What issues are the media putting on the political agenda right now?

★ **priming:** *Process whereby the media influence the criteria the public uses to make decisions.*

★ **framing:** *Ability of the media to influence public perception of issues by constructing the issue or discussion of a subject in a certain way.*

Framing. **Framing** is the ability of the media to alter the public's view on an issue by presenting it in a particular way. If the battles waged in Afghanistan are framed as an issue of fighting terrorism, the public thinks about the war in a much more favorable light than if these conflicts are framed by the casualties incurred. Framing can have a very powerful effect, actually changing public opinion on an issue.

Perhaps the most famous example of framing comes from the work of Amos Tversky and Daniel Kahneman.[125] In an experiment, they told research subjects that the United States was preparing for the outbreak of an unusual disease, which was expected to kill six hundred people, and asked which program should be implemented to deal with the disease. If program A were adopted, two hundred people would be saved; if program B were adopted, there was a one-third probability that six hundred people would be saved, and a two-thirds probability that no one would be saved. Of those surveyed, 72 percent favored program A, and 28 percent favored program B. Such a strong result suggests that the government should adopt program A. But another group of subjects was also given a choice between two different programs. The options were described as follows: If program C were adopted, four hundred people would die. If program D were adopted, there was a one-third probability that nobody would die, and a two-thirds probability that six hundred people would die. Here, 22 percent of subjects favored program C, and 78 percent favored program D.

There is a 50-percentage point difference in the number of people willing to support program A versus program C, yet the programs yield the exact same policy outcome: Two hundred people live, and four hundred people die. The only difference is that the description of program A stressed saving people, while the description of program C stressed the deaths of people. This experiment underscores the power of framing—that the public reacts to a news event or a policy depending on how it is presented.

Checkpoint

CAN YOU:

■ Define the propaganda model

■ Distinguish selective exposure from selective perception

■ State three ways media coverage of the news affects politics

6.9 Evaluating the News Media

> Evaluate the news media

"The American Press is in crisis," wrote Lance Bennett and his colleagues in their book *When the Press Fails.*[126] Concerns about the modern news media are widespread.[127]

Worries about the news media often center on two general concerns. One is that the media are biased and do not present objective information. The second, which is related, focuses on the general quality of information available to the public. The emphasis on soft news, for example, worries observers who do not think the public has enough exposure to more substantive hard news. Without enough hard news, these observers fear, the public will not be well enough informed to hold elected officials accountable.

Whether these concerns are valid or not (we examine them later), it is clear that the public's faith in the press has declined (see Figure 6.12). In 1973, 15 percent of the public had "hardly any" confidence in the press and 23 percent had "a great deal." Thirty-five years later, those numbers had flipped. Less than 10 percent of the public had "a great deal" of confidence and 45 percent had "hardly any."[128]

Is there reason to worry about the media? Are the mass media of the twenty-first century less able to fulfill their watchdog role? This section looks at media bias, the quality of information, and the implications of the Internet and media choice.

→ KEY QUESTIONS:
Do you trust the news media? What source, if any, gets it right?

Are the Media Biased?

The press claims to be objective, and professional journalists subscribe to an ethic of neutrality. Yet, given that even the selection of stories covered influences public opinion, bias may be inevitable. Nevertheless, it need not be evil or ideological. David Broder, one of the leading journalists of his time, attributed bias to the speed with which journalists have to act. "The process of selecting what the reader reads involves not just objective facts but subjective

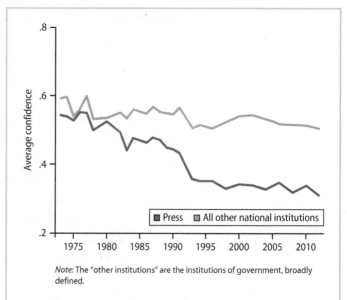

Note: The "other institutions" are the institutions of government, broadly defined.

Figure 6.12 Public Confidence in the Press, 1973–2013

Source: Jonathan M. Ladd, *Why Americans Hate the Media and Why It Matters.* Princeton University Press, 2012. Reprinted by permission of Princeton University Press; updated data provided by Jonathan M. Ladd.

judgments, personal values, and, yes, prejudices," he confesses. Broder points out that "the newspaper that drops on your doorstep is a partial, hasty, incomplete, inevitably somewhat flawed and inaccurate rendering of some of the things we have heard about in the past 24 hours—distorted, despite our best efforts to eliminate bias, by the very process of compression that makes it possible for you to lift it from the doorstep and read it in about an hour."[129]

With the rise of the 24-7 news cycle, bias in selecting what to cover becomes even more evident. For example, during the 2008 presidential campaign, three candidates—John McCain, already the Republican nominee, and Barack Obama and Hillary Clinton, still contending for the Democratic nomination—were scheduled to give speeches on the evening of June 2. McCain spoke first, and all of the major cable networks covered his speech. During the middle of the speech, however, Obama secured the few extra delegates that officially gave him the presidential nomination. Liberal MSNBC broke away from McCain's speech to announce this important development. Conservative Fox News did not. It flashed the information on the lower part of the screen but continued to cover McCain's speech. Both networks were informing the public, but they were making different choices about what was most newsworthy and what was not. Insofar as MSNBC's choice seemed to support a liberal outlook and Fox's choice a conservative outlook, they might be described as biased.

A broader point is that, for many years, conservative commentators have claimed that the news media are liberal. Accuracy in Media, a conservative watchdog organization, contends that more than 80 percent of mainstream journalists support the Democratic Party. Such partisan loyalties, according to critics, drive the liberal bias.[130] Yet the people who own the most major media outlets—such as Rupert Murdoch, whose media properties include the *Wall Street Journal* and Fox News—are conservative. Should one assume that because most news outlets are owned by conservatives, the media are really conservative? It is far from clear whether the media are liberal or conservative.

Yet, complaints about a liberal press seem to resonate with the public. Gallup Poll data measuring the public's belief about ideological bias in the news media indicate that about half the public believes the news media have a liberal bias and perceive a liberal tilt to the press's coverage of politics. The proportion has been quite stable. In 2013, for example, 46 percent of the public thought the press was too liberal while only 11 percent viewed the press as too conservative.[131]

The debate over whether the news media are too liberal or too conservative misses the central point about the news today. With so many sources of information, it is easy to find news with a liberal spin and news with a conservative spin. In fact, in the second decade of the twenty-first century, much news reporting is partisan, more like the party-dominated press of the nineteenth century than the objective and neutral press of the twentieth century. Media choice and multiple outlets mean that a Democrat can find a Democratic-leaning source for news and a Republican can find a Republican-leaning source (see Figure 6.13). It is fair to conclude that individual news outlets are biased, but collectively, the media provide a full range of ideological viewpoints.

Quality of Information

The idea that people are getting news from Stephen Colbert rather than from Walter Cronkite is disconcerting to political observers. The general worry is that people are getting less hard news and instead are relying on what we earlier called soft news—feature stores that are

→ KEY QUESTIONS:
Do you think the news media are too liberal?

→ KEY QUESTIONS:
Does the potential bias of a news source affect the chances of you listening or viewing it? How can you evaluate it?

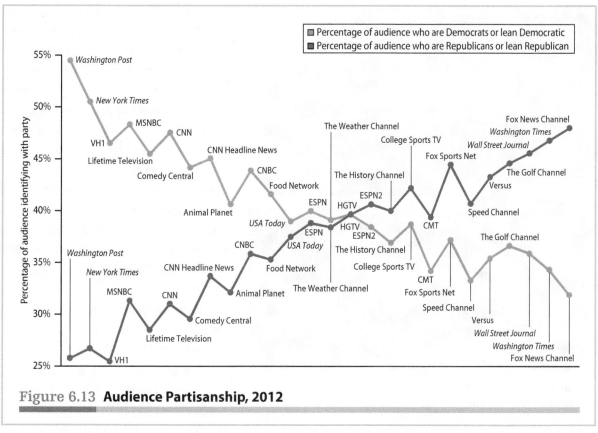

Figure 6.13 **Audience Partisanship, 2012**

Source: Adapted from Thomas B. Edsall, "Let the Nanotargeting Begin," April 15, 2012, *New York Times*, 2012, http://campaignstops.blogs.nytimes.com/2012/04/15 /let-the-nanotargeting-begin/.

more personal and less policy focused, more sensationalized and less objective, than the political facts of hard news.[132] News about crime or natural disasters can fit the soft news category when the focus is about the drama surrounding the event (such as loss of life or homes) rather than a discussion of public policy that could reduce crime or perhaps provide quicker government response to disasters.[133]

Part of this underlying concern is the emphasis on image as opposed to substance. The assumption here is that visuals (television and Internet news, in contrast to print news) appeal to the emotions more than to the intellect, so visual news formats are in themselves less "hard" and more superficial. It is true that visual images convey impressions that go beyond the facts, but that does not mean that such information is not valuable. All media of communication shape how information is shared and digested. Radio, for example, puts a premium on the quality of people's voices. Consider politics before the invention of the microphone. Who were the most effective politicians? Perhaps it was individuals with deep voices that could project to a large audience. A soft-spoken politician would have been at a real disadvantage.

It is also important to realize that images did not begin with the advent of television. Although it may be easier to engage in "image" politics in an era of video, politicians have always wanted to convey a favorable image and have done so using the media of their time. Abraham Lincoln sought to project himself as the self-made man that he was, so his 1860 campaign distributed pictures depicting him working with his hands as a rail-splitter.[137] Andrew

During the presidential campaign of 1860, Republican candidate Abraham Lincoln sought to portray himself as a common man with a humble background who understood the needs of the people. To develop this image, Lincoln's campaign stressed that as a young man he split rails to build a fence around his home. The image became part of campaign lore.

THE GRANGER COLLECTION, NYC

Jackson (1829–37) built a successful run to the White House in part on his reputation as a tough military leader. Image has always been important to politicians.

In the same way, so-called sound bites—very brief snippets of information—did not begin with the advent of television. Many observers fear that by stressing short catchy statements rather than more detailed substantive statements, sound bites undermine the quality of information. Campaigns, however, have always made effective use of simple slogans. In 1900, for example, President William McKinley (1897–1901) sought reelection with the slogan "A full dinner pail," reminding voters about the economic prosperity enjoyed during his first term.[135]

The purpose of this discussion is to urge caution in making hasty judgments about differences in the kinds of information available via the news media over the past two centuries. Soft news may be more informative than hard news because people find it easier to understand and more enjoyable. It is important, therefore, not to let the definition of what counts as news shape judgment of the press. That news reporting is no longer filtered by Walter Cronkite but instead by Megyn Kelly does not mean the news media are no longer doing their job. They are just doing it differently.

Despite recent changes in the mass media, evidence suggests that Americans have as much information about politics as they did before the arrival of the Internet and the 24-7 news cycle. According the Pew Research Center for the People & the Press, "the coaxial and digital revolutions and attendant changes in the news audience behaviors have had *little* impact on how much Americans know about national and international affairs."[136] Americans do not appear less informed; they simply secure information in new ways.

→ KEY QUESTIONS:
Are the people smarter than the news media think they are?

Implications of the Internet

There is evidence that the arrival of the Internet and social media have not changed the overall amount of information the public possesses, but it is important to acknowledge that new media are not equally available to all Americans. In 2014, only about 47 percent of Americans making less than $30,000 a year had access to a smartphone while 81 percent of those making $75,000 or more had access to such a device.[137] Older Americans show an even bigger divide. For those over 65 years, only 19 percent had a smartphone. The Millennials stood at 83 percent. But these patterns are changing as access to things such as smartphones spreads, which will help to bridge the digital divide.[138]

→ KEY QUESTIONS:
What kinds of news do you seek? What should the American people seek?

These data suggest a further inequality—that those with Internet access may be much better informed than the public generally just twenty years ago, whereas those without access may be even less informed. Variations among groups buried in discussions of the public as a whole are significant. These variations will likely decrease as more people secure access to the Internet. Figure 6.7 on page 179, which shows the many options people have for information, suggests that Americans will move toward universal access. There will always be a gap between the well informed and the poorly informed, but in time, the Internet will give older and less wealthy Americans a better chance to become more informed about politics than they currently are.

The Era of Media Choice

Perhaps the best word to describe today's media environment is *choice*.[139] The spread of cable television, the Internet, and satellite radio means that people have many possible sources for political information, as well as a huge array of entertainment programming that may lead them to opt out of political news altogether. In the mid-twentieth century, when the network evening news was the source of information, viewers had fewer choices and less opportunity to opt out. They might change channels at dinnertime, but they would get similar news from a different network. The evening news was the only show available during the dinner hour. The lack of choice may have given people more exposure to politics than they wanted.[140]

→ KEY QUESTIONS:
What are the consequences of media choice?

The TV network news standardized the information that many Americans had access to. With the wide array of choices now available, information is more polarized today. Viewers who choose a conservative TV network such as Fox and listen to Rush Limbaugh on the radio will have different information from those who watch MSNBC and tune in to National Public Radio. Those who lack interest in politics can avoid political news altogether. In other words, media choice cuts two ways: polarizing the type of information available, and making it possible to receive no political information at all.

The consequences of media choice are complex and are only beginning to be understood. New technologies in the future could further fragment what Americans as a people know. Efforts to make political news more interesting may mean a further "softening" of the news. The main point is that Americans have access to a vast amount of information, but the availability of more information does not necessarily mean that the public as a whole is better informed. Moreover, people follow news outlets that conform to their existing ideological preferences. This self-selection can fuel further polarization, because many people are not getting information from the other side.

Checkpoint

CAN YOU:

- State the concerns over media bias
- Track changes in the quality of news and information over time
- Survey the implications of the Internet
- Connect media choice to polarization

Public Opinion, the Media, and Democracy

For a country to be considered democratic, the views of the public must affect the course of government. For this reason, the public must be sufficiently well informed to be able to make good decisions and to ensure that politicians act in a way that is consistent with public preferences. Average Americans do not know a lot of details about politics, but the nation's many successes indicate that the public is equal to the task of self-government.

Elections are one means by which the public expresses its will, but on a year-to-year, even day-to-day, basis, public officials can stay in touch with what the public thinks through public opinion polls. Scientific polling permits researchers to measure people's thinking with considerable accuracy and gives average Americans a chance to speak out on policy and contribute to policy making.

Although it is clear that public officials are generally responsive to public opinion,[141] there are legitimate questions about how responsive American government actually is. Some observers suggest that the connection between opinion and policy is weak. Others point out that the public has mixed feelings on many issues and does not have concrete opinions about some of the toughest questions and can thus offer little guidance. The ability to anticipate public opinion is an invaluable skill, but it is also imperfect in that there are both gates and gateways that shape how the public directs the course of government. The public relies on the media to convey this information.

The news media, as watchdogs, are a central player in democratic politics. In the twenty-first century, the mass media are far more open than they were just a few decades ago, providing additional chances to forge accountability, responsiveness, and equality. But these are only chances because the media are in the midst of a transformation whose repercussions are not yet known.

The more open and more democratic new media thus have the potential to let citizens know more about the politicians who lead them; they also give people more opportunities to express opinions for politicians to consider as they develop and enact laws. Thus blogs and other new media may help forge responsiveness. But these gateways have potential costs: The opinions may come from people who are not representative of the American mainstream. Information offered as fact in these settings has not been checked and is potentially filled with errors.

The many changes in the news media have also led to a decline in the number of professional journalists who are covering politics. With fewer professional journalists, the press may be less able to investigate stories that might unearth corruption or provide a more complete account of some politicians' backgrounds.

The decline in investigative reporting could, in short, undermine accountability. But there is some reason for optimism. For example, Paul Steiger, former editor of the *Wall Street Journal*, has formed a nonprofit organization called ProPublica that pursues investigations, offering the findings to newspapers and magazines. By taking advantage of funding from private sources, the organization offers a way to compensate for the decline of investigative journalism.[142]

Concern about the media's ability to advance democratic government comes mostly from people who favor a top-down approach for providing political information. For those who see the merit and appeal in a bottom-up approach, the changes seem far less worrisome. The Millennial generation sees the potential that the Internet and other media have for promoting equality and for providing more chances to be part of the process.

Master the Concept
of Public Opinion and Political Socialization with the MindTap™ for American Government

 REVIEW MindTap™ **for American Government**
Access Key Term Flashcards for Chapter 6.

 TEST YOURSELF MindTap™ **for American Government**
Take the Wrap It Up Quiz for Chapter 6.

 STAY CURRENT MindTap™ **for American Government**
Access the KnowNow blog and customized RSS for updates on current events.

 STAY FOCUSED MindTap™ **for American Government**
Complete the Focus Activities for Public Opinion and Political Socialization.

 # Key Concepts

agenda setting (p. 187). How can the news media influence political agendas?

confidence interval (p. 162). Why did you need to know the confidence interval for any poll?

conservatives (p. 164). What party do conservatives usually support?

efficacy (p. 157). Why is the efficacy of citizens important in a democracy?

exit polls (p. 161). Describe problems with exit polls.

framing (p. 188). Describe the health care debate as an example of framing.

gender gap (p. 171). Which party do women tend to support?

hard news (p. 179). What is a good source of hard news today?

levels of conceptualization (p. 165). How sophisticated is the public's ideological thinking?

liberals (p. 164). Why did the ideological direction of public mood move away from liberalism following Barack Obama's inauguration as president in 2008?

mass media (p. 175). How are the mass media different than the news media?

minimal effects model (p. 187). Why did scholars think the media only had "minimal effects"?

moderates (p. 165). Are most Americans moderates?

news media (p. 175). What is the role of the news media in a democracy?

nonattitudes (p. 163). Give an example of a nonattitude that might arise from a poll.

not-so-minimal effects model (p. 187). What do scholars mean when they contend the media's effects are "not so minimal"?

party identification (p. 164). What is the main way people develop a party identification?

polarization (p. 167). Describe trends in party polarization over the past twenty years.

political ideology (p. 164). What is the relationship between ideology and partisanship?

political trust (p. 157). What are the trends in public trust in recent years?

priming (p. 188). How do the news media prime the American public to hold certain opinions?

propaganda model (p. 186). Could the propaganda model ever be applicable to the United States?

public opinion (p. 157). Why is public opinion so important to a democracy?

push polls (p. 162). Why are push polls less accurate than random telephone surveys?

random sample (p. 160). Why is it important to have a random sample?

selective exposure (p. 187). Why does selective exposure lead to reinforcement of beliefs?

selective perception (p. 187). How did selective perception help support the minimal effects model?

soft news (p. 181). What are sources for soft news today?

tracking polls (p. 161). How do tracking polls work?

watchdog (p. 175). How do the news media serve as watchdogs in the twenty-first century?

Learning Outcomes: What You Need . . .

To Know	To Test Yourself	To Participate

 Decide why public opinion is powerful.

To Know	To Test Yourself	To Participate
Public opinion—the aggregate of citizen attitudes—is essential to the workings of a democracy.	• State the reasons public opinion has a powerful impact on the presidency. • Define public opinion. • Track efficacy and public trust in government.	• Express your opinion of the presidency. • Grasp the connection between public opinion and democracy. • Evaluate why public trust in government is low.

 Describe how well polls measure public opinion.

To Know	To Test Yourself	To Participate
Scientific polling enables public officials to gauge public opinion with some degree of confidence, although polls can be in error.	• Define scientific polling. • Identify three types of polls. • Explain potential errors in polls. • State why the Internet is important to the future of polling.	• Evaluate whether polling is more or less accurate. • Participate in a political poll. • Improve your reading of polls. • Evaluate Internet polling.

 Discover how ideology and partisanship shape public opinion.

To Know	To Test Yourself	To Participate
Party identification can help predict individual attitudes, and liberal or conservative leanings shape views on political and social issues. People generally know what advances their interests and hold government accountable. Although parties have grown more polarized in recent years, the electorate is more moderate than party choices allow. In recent years, efficacy and public trust in government have fallen.	• Explain how partisanship relates to public opinion. • Explain the importance of political ideology. • Assess how well informed the American public is and whether it matters. • Describe polarization and its effects.	• Examine your partisanship in the context of public opinion. • Examine your political ideology in the context of public opinion. • Determine whether the American public is worth listening to. • Evaluate the impact of partisanship on democracy.

 Describe how demographic characteristics influence public opinion.

To Know	To Test Yourself	To Participate
Socioeconomic status, age, religion, gender, race, ethnicity, and educational background can all impact political values, ideology, and partisanship. Even within an ethnic group, such as Hispanic, the country of origin of parents or grandparents shapes an individual's political values.	• State the relationship between socioeconomic status, on the one hand, and partisanship and ideology on the other. • Describe how age affects political thinking. • Characterize the impact of the gender gap. • Distinguish the differences in public opinion between different religious affiliations. • Survey the impact of race and ethnicity on political thinking. • Track the effect of increasing educational levels on political views.	• Examine your socioeconomic status in light of your partisanship and political ideology. • Speculate whether your position on issues will change as you age. • Evaluate the effect of religion on politics. • Evaluate the effect of race and ethnicity on politics. • Speculate whether your college education and experience will change your political views.

To Know	To Test Yourself	To Participate

 Determine why the media are important in a democracy.

In a democracy, the people rely on the mass media for the information they need to hold government accountable and make it responsive. The press plays the role of watchdog, and the First Amendment protects the freedom of the press. The mass media perform three important tasks: informing, investigating, and interpreting the news.	• Describe the role of the press as watchdog. • State the functions of the news media.	• Evaluate whether the media are fulfilling this role today.

 Analyze how the law protects the press.

When the government attempts to constrain the press, the Supreme Court generally sides with the press, believing that it is better to protect press freedoms than to permit government censorship.	• Name the laws, government agencies, and court rulings that regulate press freedom.	• Consider whether the government should protect or regulate the news media.

 Explain how changes in the mass media have changed the information environment.

In the twenty-first century, technological advances are changing the media environment once again. The rise of cable TV, satellite TV, and the Internet make news available day and night. Soft news, with personal stories and emotional content, is replacing hard news. Blogs are evidence of a new bottom-up journalism by citizens. The decline of newspapers is a real concern. The decreasing number of journalists means that newspapers have less ability to inform and investigate. If the press cannot perform its watchdog role, the public loses a means by which it holds government accountable.	• Describe the changing media environment • Survey the impact of radio, TV news, infotainment, blogs, social networking, and the changing media environment.	• Assess the twenty-first-century mass media as democratic and in service to democracy. • Speculate on how the role of the news media will continue to change as the Millennial generation matures.

 Assess how the news media affect public opinion.

Political scientists describe the impact of the news media on the public as agenda setting, priming, and framing.	• Define the propaganda model. • Distinguish selective exposure from selective perception. • State three ways media coverage of the news affects politics.	• Understand how your partisanship shapes your understanding of political news. • Understand how the mass media can alter your political views.

 Evaluate the news media.

Although the public has lost faith in the media and generally think the media are too liberal, media choice and multiple outlets ensure a full range of ideological viewpoints. The sources of information are changing, but the public has as much information about politics as ever.	• State the concerns over media bias. • Track changes in the quality of news and information over time. • Survey the implications of the Internet. • Connect media choice to polarization.	• Assess media bias. • Decide which source for news you trust. • Debate whether the Internet increases citizen equality or impedes it. • Assess the connections between media choice and polarization.

"Regardless of whether we swing an election or not, we are working with the next generation of leaders on the Democratic and Republican side to learn how to work together and to problem solve jointly."

SAM GILMAN
Cofounder, Common Sense Action

7

Interest Groups

On forty campuses across the United States, college chapters of Common Sense Action (CSA) are attempting to take back politics for the Millennial generation. What began as an idea tossed around by Brown University undergrads Sam Gilman, Andrew Kaplan, and Heath Mayo, has turned into one of the most innovative student-run interest groups trying to change politics. Their mission is to expand "opportunities for Millennials by bringing our generation to the policy-making table and building a movement of Millennial voters committed to advancing generational fairness, investing in Millennial mobility, and repairing politics."

After working as an intern at the Bipartisan Policy Center in Washington D.C., Gilman realized the importance of workforce development. The Millennial generation had twice the unemployment rate of the national average, and yet members of Congress were not discussing this issue, mostly because it would not win elections. No community present in Washington D.C. was pushing for the interests of young people, so Gilman convinced Kaplan and Mayo to form their own bipartisan organization.

A key moment for Gilman occurred on September 11th, 2012, at 1:30 P.M., when his closest friend went to vote in the primary election on campus thirty steps from the campus center and told him that he was only the seventeenth voter that day. "And that really hit me. And when I voted in the general election two days before we officially launched CSA, I was the 130th voter at 10:15 A.M. The critical moment was realizing what happens if we can mobilize Millennials in and around primary elections for issues that impact our generation, in a world in which so few people vote in primary elections, and they are increasingly becoming the most important elections in our country, particularly as districts are becoming more polarized."

Through dorm meetings, Gilman, Kaplan, and Mayo were able to get a sense of the issues their generation cared about. At the subsequent CSA National Summit, the group established a core principle—respecting where people come from—so that liberals and conservatives alike can come together and find common ground on issues that affect their generation the most. Their bipartisan Agenda for Generational Equality seeks to advance generational fairness via a national entitlement solution, encourage Millennial mobility by making college more affordable, invest in the employment of Millennials, and repair politics through increased Millennial political participation.

Need to Know

7.1 Outline how interest groups have developed over time

7.2 Identify the types of interest groups that have evolved

7.3 Describe activities interest groups engage in

7.4 Analyze what balances out power among interest groups

7.5 Assess what makes an interest group successful

WATCH & LEARN MindTap™ **for American Government**
Watch a brief "What Do You Know?" video summarizing Interest Groups.

Their bipartisan approach has paid off. With their chapter model and grassroots organizing, CSA is active in community education, campus organizing, candidate education, voter empowerment, and bringing about change via primary elections in a bipartisan and inclusive manner.

CSA is tapping into the Millennial generation through its campus challenge, which seeks to empower students through education and network building. For CSA, finding strong leaders in the Millennial generation is key to not only running the group but also making real bipartisan changes in politics. The group's dedication to issues particular to their generation does not restrict the group. CSA recognizes the importance of intergenerational discussions, which have taken place through conversations with local senior facilities as well as with CSA's senior advisors: former U.S. Senators Pete Domenici (R-NM) and Byron Dorgan (D-ND). The grassroots origins and activities of CSA are current examples of students engaging in collective action to generate change and using university and political resources to raise awareness and support for issues relevant to the Millennial generation.[1]

Small or large, student-run or long-established national organizations, interest groups are a mechanism of representation in a democracy because they help translate individual opinions and interests into outcomes in the political system. Interest groups form for many reasons: to advance economic status, express an ideological viewpoint, influence public policy, or promote activism in international affairs. In a democracy, the most crucial role of interest groups is their attempt to influence public policy, which is one of the express interests of the student-run CSA. In this chapter, we examine the history of interest groups, why they form, what they do, and their impact on democratic processes. We also identify how and why some groups are more influential than others. Throughout the chapter, we focus on interest groups as gateways to citizen participation and, at the same time, point out how they can erect gates when they pursue narrow policy interests.

→ KEY QUESTIONS:
Why do you think Americans like to join organizations? How does this tendency relate to American political culture?

interest groups:
Groups of citizens who share a common interest—a political opinion, religious or ideological belief, a social goal, or an economic characteristic—and try to influence public policy to benefit themselves.

7.1 Interest Groups and Politics

❯ Outline how interest groups have developed over time

In 1831, the French political theorist Alexis de Tocqueville came to the United States to observe American social and political behavior. He stayed for more than nine months and later published his study as *Democracy in America*, a classic of political literature. He wrote, "The most natural right of man, after that of acting on his own, is that of combining his efforts with those of his fellows and acting together. Therefore the right of association seems to me by nature almost as inalienable as individual liberty."[2] Tocqueville noticed that Americans in particular liked to form groups and join associations as a way of participating in community and political life. To Tocqueville, the formation of group life was an important element of the success of the American democracy.

What Are Interest Groups?

Tocqueville used the term *association* to describe the groups he observed throughout his travels in America; today we call them interest groups. An **interest group** is a group of citizens who share a common interest—whether a political opinion, religious affiliation, ideological belief, social goal, or economic objective—and try to influence public policy to benefit its members. Other types of groups form for purely social or community reasons, but this chapter focuses on the groups that form to exert political influence.

Most interest groups arise from conditions in public life. A proactive group arises when an enterprising individual sees an opening or opportunity to create the group for social, political, or economic purposes. A reactive group forms to protect the interests of members in response to a perceived threat from another group, or to fight a government policy that the members believe will adversely affect them, or to respond to an unexpected external event.

Groups whose members share a number of common characteristics are described as homogeneous, whereas groups whose members come from varied backgrounds are described as heterogeneous. All interest groups are based on the idea that members joining together in a group can secure a shared benefit that would not be available to them if they acted alone.

Citizens most often join groups to advance their personal economic well-being, to get their voices heard as part of a larger group's efforts on an issue, or to meet like-minded citizens who share their views. There is no legal restriction on the number of groups that people can join, and citizens are frequently members of a number of organizations. On the large scale, citizens join groups as a gateway toward participating in democratic society.

The Right to Assemble and to Petition

The First Amendment states that Congress cannot prohibit "the right of the people peaceably to assemble, and to petition the Government for a redress of grievances." This right to assemble is the **right of association**. The Framers believed that the opportunity to form groups was a fundamental right that government may not legitimately take away. At the same time, however, they were fearful that such groups, which Madison called **factions**, might divide the young nation. Although Madison recognized that such groups could not be suppressed without abolishing liberty, he also argued in *Federalist* 51 that, in a large and diverse republic, narrow interests would balance out each other and be checked by majority rule. (See *Federalist* 10 and *Federalist* 51 in the Appendix.) Madison feared that factions could have the same divisive or polarizing effect in a democracy. Nevertheless, the Bill of Rights contains protections for the rights of association and petition because these rights are essential for citizens to be able to hold their government accountable, ensure the responsiveness of elected officials, and participate equally in self-government.

The **right of petition** gives individuals with a claim against the government the right to ask for compensation, and it also includes the right to petition to ask for a policy change or to express opposition to a policy. It was the earliest and most basic gateway for citizens seeking to make government respond to them, and it has been used from the beginning of government under the Constitution. For example, in the First Congress, cotton growers asked the government for direct payment of subsidies to allow them to keep their farms in years with low crop yields. Owners of shipping companies petitioned Congress to limit the amount of goods that foreign ships could deliver to the United States so they could maximize their share of the carrying trade. Even the makers of molasses got together to ask the government to impose higher taxes on imported molasses so they would face less competition.[3] In the nineteenth century, petitions were used for broader and more sweeping issues, such as appeals to end slavery, to ban alcoholic beverages, and to secure the right to vote for women. In the twenty-first century, groups such as change.org use the Internet to make it possible for individuals to directly "ask" Congress for a benefit via e-mail or to sign

THE GRANGER COLLECTION, NYC

Citizens have been using their right to petition to influence government since the earliest days of the democracy. Here female lobbyists in the late nineteenth century are trying to persuade members of Congress in the Marble Room of the U.S. Capitol. Although women did not yet have the right to vote, they still went to Washington to make their voices heard on issues that were important to them.

right of association: *Right to freely associate with others and form groups, as protected by the First Amendment.*

faction: *Defined by Madison as any group that places its own interests above the aggregate interests of society.*

→ KEY QUESTIONS:
Do you think interest groups are divisive and polarizing? Or do they bring citizens together? Can you give examples to support your opinion?

right of petition: *Right to ask the government for assistance with a problem or to express opposition to a government policy, as protected by the First Amendment.*

lobbying: *Act of trying to persuade elected officials to adopt a specific policy change or maintain the status quo.*

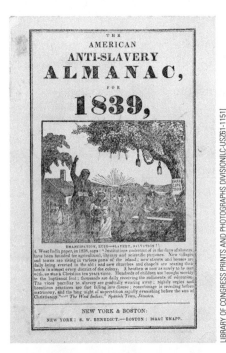

LIBRARY OF CONGRESS PRINTS AND PHOTOGRAPHS DIVISION/LC-USZ61-1151

Abolitionists used stark imagery and words to rally citizens against slavery. In 1843, Lydia Maria Child compiled *The American Anti-Slavery Almanac*. Its cover alone makes the case for abolition. Child was a writer and editor who was also active in the women's suffrage movement.

a "virtual" petition that can be presented to Congress. Interest groups also use their high membership numbers as a proxy for the direct expression of support that once came from petitioners' personal visits to lawmakers.

Today the rights of association and petition most often take the form of **lobbying**, or trying to persuade elected officials to adopt or reject a specific policy change. Lobbying is a legitimate form of petitioning, and interest groups of all sizes and purposes engage in it, from CSA, to big corporations such as Microsoft and Google, to large-scale grassroots groups such as the Sierra Club. The term *lobbying* was coined more than three hundred years ago when individuals seeking favors from the British government would pace the halls, or lobbies, of the Parliament building, waiting for a chance to speak with members. The practice was immediately adopted in the new United States.

Interest groups lobby the legislative, executive, and even judicial branches of government at the state and federal levels. For example, when groups lobby Congress or state legislatures, they typically meet with members' staff aides to make the case for their policy goals. Lobbyists may also try to influence the executive branch by meeting personally with key bureaucrats and policy makers. Lobbying of the judicial branch takes the form of lawsuits against government policies that interest groups see as fundamentally unconstitutional or that go against the original intent of the law. Such lawsuits can be high profile and are initiated by groups of all political ideologies. For example, cases orchestrated by the National Association for the Advancement of Colored People (NAACP) and other liberal interest groups ended school segregation (see Chapter 5, Civil Rights). For other cases, interest groups can also submit *amicus curiae* briefs ("friend of the court") that record their opinions even if they are not the primary legal participants in a case. Interest groups also lobby for and against judicial nominees, especially Supreme Court appointments. Lobbying strategies and tactics differ according to the branch of government at the state and federal levels, but no government entity is outside the scope of lobbyists' efforts.[4]

The History of Interest Groups

As the nation expanded its geographic borders, its population, and its economic base, government took on more responsibilities that affected individual lives. Issues that were once considered local became nationally important, and improvements in travel and communications enabled citizens with a national concern to band together. Slavery was the most divisive of these national issues, and citizens who opposed slavery formed the American Anti-Slavery Society in 1833. Soon many other groups were urging the abolition of slavery, creating the abolitionist movement. Abolitionists held rallies, distributed pamphlets, and collected signatures on petitions to persuade Americans, specifically members of Congress, to abolish slavery.

Advocates for women's suffrage (the right to vote) paid close attention to antislavery efforts, seeing in them an example of the power of organization. In 1848, the women's suffrage movement was officially launched at Seneca Falls, New York.[5] To the members of this group, the refusal to allow women to vote was a gate that stood in the way of true political equality among all citizens. The abolitionist and the women's movements paralleled each other in relying on the principle of equality as a rationale for supporting their policy goals.

Later in the nineteenth century, as America industrialized, the business community began to strengthen its efforts to influence policy. Large trade associations formed, both regional and national, with members that included sugar manufacturers, mining companies, and railroad owners. These businesses combined to form interest groups based on their common economic interests, and these groups gave wealthy owners of corporations a disproportionate influence over public policy.

To counteract the power of wealthy business corporations, workers organized **unions** to protect their interests,

Prohibition was enacted by the Eighteenth Amendment to the Constitution in 1919. Here a restaurant owner in New York City makes it clear that no alcohol is sold on the premises. Prohibition was hard to enforce and was ultimately repealed by the Twenty-First Amendment to the Constitution in 1933.

which were different from the interests of the people who owned industries but at the same time were interconnected with them. The International Ladies' Garment Workers' Union (ILGWU) is an instructive example. It was formed in 1900 by workers (mostly women) who assembled women's clothing. By 1910, workers in this industry had staged several strikes against employers to secure better working conditions. The turning point for the union came in 1911, when 141 workers died in a fire at the Triangle Shirtwaist Factory in New York City because they were trapped on the factory's upper floors. The fire escapes were inadequate, and the elevator was broken. Most of the victims were young, immigrant women who needed this kind of work because it did not require English reading or writing skills.[6] Leaders of the union saw a chance to turn tragedy into accomplishment by expanding its membership and lobbying the government to force manufacturers to improve worker safety. In part due to their efforts, the Department of Labor was created as a separate cabinet-level department in 1913. It enforces mandatory standards for worker safety and oversees bargaining agreements between management and labor unions.[7] In 1935, unions were successful at getting more protections for workers through the National Labor Relations Act, which allowed unions to engage in collective bargaining. The act also provides that only one union can be selected to represent workers in a specific location, so that after a union successfully organizes a work location, those workers have to abide by that union's decisions.[8]

Today business and trade associations, unions, citizens' organizations, and **grassroots movements** are a familiar part of the landscape of interest group politics. With the growth in the economy and in the size and scope of government in the American democracy, citizens have responded by forming more groups. The Chamber of Commerce, the National Rifle Association (NRA), AARP (formerly known as the American Association of Retired Persons), League of United Latin American Citizens (LULAC), and the Sierra Club have existed for more than fifty years. Each claims to have millions of members, and each has

unions: *Interest groups of individuals who share a common type of employment and seek better wages and working conditions through collective bargaining with employers.*

grassroots movement: *Group that forms in response to an economic or political event but does not focus on only one issue.*

Checkpoint

CAN YOU:

- Describe what an interest group is
- Explain why Madison and the Framers feared factions
- Track the history of interest groups

different policy goals. However, not all modern interest groups are national in scope, and some are newly formed, so it is difficult to know how many groups are in existence at any one time. One study by political scientists estimated that there are approximately seven thousand groups operating in the American political system.[9] Their methods of communication and persuasion may differ from those of the very first petitioners of Congress, but they share the common role of serving as a gateway through which the opinions of ordinary citizens are expressed to their elected officials.

7.2 Types of Interest Groups

> Identify the types of interest groups that have evolved

Because the universe of interest groups is so large and diverse, it can be helpful to categorize groups by their core organizing purposes and the arenas in which they seek to influence public policy. In this section, we survey three types of interest groups—economic, ideological, and foreign policy–focused—to illustrate and explain differences in interest group policy goals and strategies.

Economic Interest Groups

economic interest group: *Group formed to advance the economic status of its members.*

Economic interest groups form to advance the economic status of their members and are defined by a specific set of financial or business concerns. Their membership bases tend to be exclusive because their purpose is to secure tangible economic benefits for themselves; if they grow too large or too inclusive, members' benefits are necessarily diluted. However, if the underlying industries represented by these groups disappear or merge with others, the groups have to adapt in order to attract new members.

→ KEY QUESTIONS:
What are the professional associations in the career field you are thinking of now? Are they worth joining?

Trade and Professional Associations. Trade associations focus on particular businesses or industries and make up a subcategory of economic interest groups. Examples include the National Association of Manufacturers, the Chamber of Commerce, the National Retail Federation, and the Semiconductor Industry Association. Trade associations form because business owners believe that they will have more influence on the policy process collectively than they would individually.

Professional associations are formed by individuals who share similar jobs. Examples include the American Bar Association (lawyers), the American Medical Association (doctors), and the American International Automobile Dealers Association (car dealers). These associations are frequently responsible for setting guidelines for professional conduct—from business practices to personal ethics—and for collectively representing the members in the policy process.

Corporations. Large corporations are a type of economic interest group in that they try to influence policy on their own as well as by joining trade associations comprising businesses with similar goals. Corporations such as Walmart, Comcast, and Boeing have thousands of employees, and that fact alone encourages politicians to listen to their concerns. Recently, corporations have aggressively contributed to political campaigns to influence policy, as will be discussed in detail later in this chapter. (For more on campaigns, see Chapter 9, Elections, Campaigns, and Voting.)

Unions. Unions are a type of economic interest group that aims to protect workers through safer working conditions and better wages. They are traditionally organized as local chapters that are part of a national organization representing workers in specific fields and industries. For example, autoworkers might join the United Auto Workers (UAW), truck drivers might join the International Brotherhood of Teamsters, health care workers might join the Service Employees International Union, and high school teachers might join the National Educational Association.

In 2011, the issue of collective bargaining rights for public employees became highly controversial, with several states passing laws that limited or eliminated these rights. Here members of unions in Cleveland, Ohio, rally against a state law that limited collective bargaining rights. An off-year election was held in November 2011, and more than 3 million votes were cast; the law was repealed.

Unions' strength comes from their ability to call or threaten strikes and to bargain collectively with employers over wages and working conditions. In 2012, the 26,500 members of the Chicago Teachers Union called a strike that lasted seven days in order to protest tying teacher salaries to student performance in the classroom. The strike ended when the city of Chicago agreed to a collective bargaining agreement that limited the relationship between teacher pay and student performance and that also preserved significant raises over a four-year time period.[10]

In recent years, however, collective bargaining by public sector unions, such as the Chicago Teachers Union, has come under attack by advocates for smaller government. In Indiana, Wisconsin, and Ohio, Republican governors and state legislators have severely curtailed the collective bargaining rights of state workers. Unions have fought back, however. In November 2011, Ohio voters repealed a law they viewed as too restrictive on the rights of union workers.[11] And in Wisconsin, Governor Scott Walker faced a recall election in June 2012 that was instigated primarily by supporters of collective bargaining rights, but he defeated the Democratic challenger 53 to 46 percent.[12]

The biggest threat to unions, however, is the loss of jobs in the industries they represent. When industries lose jobs, union membership shrinks, and the smaller the union, the less power it can exert on both manufacturers and elected officials. Following the Triangle fire, the ILGWU grew very powerful, but as the manufacture of women's clothing shifted overseas, thousands of jobs disappeared. By 1976, the union existed in name only and merged with the Amalgamated Clothing and Textile Workers Union (ACTWU), but even that merger could not save it. By 1996, the ILGWU was officially extinct.

Overall, private sector union membership has been declining (see Figure 7.1). Part of the reason for this decline is that government regulations now require the protections that unions long sought in terms of safe working conditions, overtime compensation, and

> → KEY QUESTIONS:
> Do you know any union members? Are you a union member, or would you join a union?

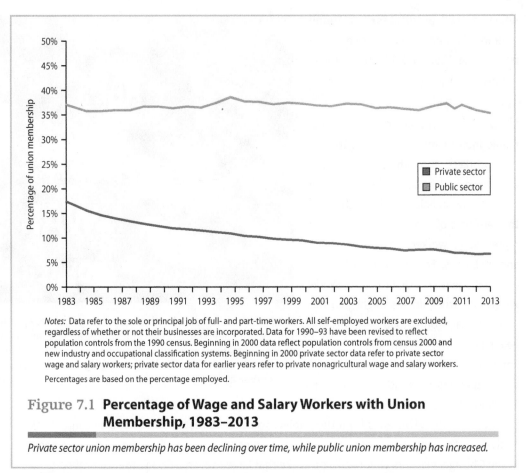

Notes: Data refer to the sole or principal job of full- and part-time workers. All self-employed workers are excluded, regardless of whether or not their businesses are incorporated. Data for 1990–93 have been revised to reflect population controls from the 1990 census. Beginning in 2000 data reflect population controls from census 2000 and new industry and occupational classification systems. Beginning in 2000 private sector data refer to private sector wage and salary workers; private sector data for earlier years refer to private nonagricultural wage and salary workers.

Percentages are based on the percentage employed.

Figure 7.1 **Percentage of Wage and Salary Workers with Union Membership, 1983–2013**

Private sector union membership has been declining over time, while public union membership has increased.

nondiscrimination. In a sense, unions have been victims of their success in pushing for government regulations, and workers do not have to join a union to receive these protections. Thus, the incentive for union membership has decreased.

Additionally, as of 2014, more than one-third of states have right-to-work laws that allow individuals to choose not to join a union even if their workplace has a designated union in place.[13] Unions have responded to this downturn in membership by seeking to represent workers in a wider range of industries. For example, the UAW now represents cafeteria and janitorial staffs on college campuses all over the nation. Despite the downturn in membership in large industrial and manufacturing unions, unions representing teachers, health service workers, communications workers, and government employees have all made large gains over the past two decades. Table 7.1 lists the top six unions in the country, which together have nearly 11 million members. Today unions represent 11.3 percent of the overall workforce in the United States.[14]

American unions are both economically and politically powerful because they can mobilize their members to vote for candidates they see as favorable on issues such as higher minimum wages, standards for overtime pay, better access to health care insurance, worker safety, and international trade agreements. In recent years, public employee unions have come under increasing challenge over issues related to wages and pensions with efforts to reduce their bargaining power with state and local governments. Unions have countered these challenges with a combination of legal challenges and grassroots mobilization.

Table 7.1 Unions with the Largest Membership, 2014

Union	Number of Members (in millions)
National Education Association (NEA)	3.0
Service Employees International Union (SEIU)	2.1
American Federation of State, County and Municipal Employees (AFSCME)	1.6
American Federation of Teachers (AFT)	1.5
International Brotherhood of Teamsters (IBT)	1.4
United Food and Commercial Works International Union (UFCW)	1.3

Source: National Education Association, http://www.nea.org/home/2580.htm; Service Employees International Union, http://www.seiu.org/a/ourunion/fast-facts.php; American Federation of State, County and Municipal Employees, http://www.afscme.org/union; American Federation of Teachers, http://www.aft.org/about/; International Brotherhood of Teamsters, http://www.opensecrets.org/orgs/summary.php?id=D000000066; United Food and Commercial Workers International Union, http://www.ufcw.org/about_ufcw/.

Ideological and Issue-Oriented Groups

Ideological interest groups form among citizens with the same beliefs about specific issues. We describe these groups as ideological rather than economic because economic benefits are not the primary basis for their existence. This category can include **citizens' groups** (Common Cause, Public Citizen), **single-issue groups** (National Rifle Association, Right to Life), and grassroots movement groups (MoveOn.org, National Organization for Women). Citizens' groups, sometimes called public interest groups, are typically formed to draw attention to public issues that affect all citizens equally, such as environmental protection, transparency in government, consumer product safety, ethics reform, and campaign finance reform. Single-issue groups form to present one view about a highly salient issue that is intensely important to its members, such as the national debt and the federal deficit to members of CSA. In contrast, broader organizations typically emerge in response to an economic or political event but do not focus solely on one issue. For example, MoveOn.org was founded by two wealthy men who were angry that President William Jefferson (Bill) Clinton (1993–2001) was impeached even though most people opposed the proceedings. MoveOn.org called for an end to the Iraq War during the George W. Bush administration (2001–2009). More recently, during the Obama administration, the group has worked hard to promote the health care exchanges and Medicaid expansion set forth under the Affordable Care Act.[15]

Ideological groups provide a way for individual members to express their opinions on issues more forcefully than would be possible for any one person alone. Members of ideological groups benefit from knowing that others share their views and from feeling empowered. In this way, ideological groups can encourage political participation in a democratic society. At the same time, these groups contribute to the polarization of the American public. Because a group of this type gets its power from agreement within its ranks on a highly salient issue, it discourages debate and disagreement within the group and any type of compromise on that issue.

For example, NARAL (formerly known as the National Abortion Rights Action League) takes the position that a woman has the right to terminate a pregnancy without

ideological interest groups: *Groups that form among citizens with the same beliefs about a specific issue.*

citizens' groups: *Groups that form to draw attention to purely public issues that affect all citizens equally.*

single-issue groups: *Groups that form to present one view on a highly salient issue that is intensely important to members, such as gun control or abortion.*

→ KEY QUESTIONS:
How do ideological interest groups contribute to polarization?

limitations, whereas the Right to Life organization holds that all abortions should be forbidden except when the life of the mother is endangered by the continuation of the pregnancy. Individual members in each group may hold more moderate views, but the leadership believes that any public compromise will alienate core members and diminish the group's status on the issue within the media and government. In this case, ideological groups not only balance out each other but also block the way forward. The intensity with which each side holds its position discourages cross-group dialogue and makes it harder for elected officials to achieve a reasonable and widely acceptable resolution of the issue. Because an interest group seeks a favorable government response on a narrowly defined issue important to that group, the group can also create imbalances that verge on inequalities.

Foreign Policy and International Groups

Some interest groups address cross-border concerns. Foreign policy groups form to generate support for favorable U.S. policies toward one or several foreign countries. International aid groups encourage citizens to provide voluntary assistance to people in need all over the world. International groups concerned with human rights work to call attention to violations in the hopes of ending oppression.

nongovernmental organizations (NGOs): *Organizations independent of governments that monitor and improve political, economic, and social conditions throughout the world.*

Groups That Influence Foreign Policy.   One of the best-known organizations that seek to influence foreign policy is the American Israel Public Affairs Committee (AIPAC). This group aims to ensure a strongly pro-Israel American foreign policy and uses public advocacy, member mobilization, and campaign contributions to influence members of Congress to support its goals. AIPAC first formed in the early 1950s, and it claims credit for getting the first aid package to Israel—$65 million to help relocate Holocaust refugees—passed by Congress in 1951.[16] Today, AIPAC has more than one hundred thousand active members and is widely considered to be one of the most influential groups of its kind in Washington.

→ KEY QUESTIONS:
Should governments seek to solve hunger, disease, and other worldwide social problems? Or should private charities play this role?

Groups That Advocate International Aid and Support for Human Rights. Religious organizations often encourage members to provide international assistance. For example, Catholic Relief Services sponsors the Global Solidarity Network, which allows college students to communicate with people living in small villages or towns in developing countries. The National Council of the Churches of Christ in the USA provides funding and coordinates religious and humanitarian missions to foreign countries.[17] Since September 11, 2001, Muslim organizations have been hampered by restrictions on fundraising and distribution of funds to Muslims in other nations, especially in the Arab world.[18]

Other interest groups focus attention on human rights violations or starvation in certain areas of the world. Many are **nongovernmental organizations** (NGOs), which are not affiliated with any government and work hard to preserve their neutrality so that they can operate in as many parts of the world as possible. They illustrate the power of interest groups to draw attention to a situation occurring in a foreign land and to solicit a powerful response from both average citizens and elected officials (see Global Gateways: Amnesty International and Human Rights Watch).

Checkpoint

CAN YOU:

- Describe the different types of economic interest groups
- Explain how ideological and issue-oriented groups can lead to polarization
- Compare and contrast the missions of foreign policy and international interest groups

globalgateways

Amnesty International and Human Rights Watch

Amnesty International and Human Rights Watch are two of the most prominent human rights organizations in the world today and two of the most effective in bringing human rights issues to the attention of citizens and onto the desks of politicians.

Amnesty International was started in 1961 by Peter Benenson, an English lawyer, and today has more than 3 million supporters and volunteers worldwide. Its mission is to uphold the United Nations Universal Declaration of Human Rights to guarantee human rights to all citizens around the world. By informing the public through demonstrations and by lobbying members of political bodies throughout the world on the issue of human rights, Amnesty International has become one of the most widely recognized interest groups in the world. Most recently, it has been active in protesting human rights abuses committed by the Syrian government, including the use of chemical weapons to murder civilians, in attempting to put down a popular uprising. Additionally, it has taken a very active role in opposing the use of drone strikes by the United States in foreign lands.

Just over 30 years old, Human Rights Watch is also known worldwide for serving as a gateway to human rights by drawing public attention to injustices that occur on a daily basis in a wide range of countries. Similar to the watchdog role of the media, Human Rights Watch investigates human rights violations, including torture, and exposes those who have committed those violations.

The members of these groups are not necessarily fighting for benefits for themselves. Rather, they are working on behalf of individuals who live in countries where there are no protections against government abuses.

LLUIS GENE/AP/GETTY IMAGES

In 2009, Amnesty International organized a protest in Barcelona, Spain, on behalf of human rights workers in Colombia who were killed, sent out of the country, or are missing. Each of the three hundred cutouts represents one of these individuals. International interest groups draw attention to problems in one country by planning protests such as this in as many places as they can.

1. How are Human Rights Watch and Amnesty International different from interest groups such as unions or trade associations?

2. Do you think Human Rights Watch and Amnesty International should receive direct support from the U.S. government for their efforts on behalf of human rights all over the world?

Sources: Information about Amnesty International was compiled from http://www.amnestyusa.org and a specific report on Syria by Amnesty International Staff, "Eyes on Syria," http://www.eyesonsyria.org/. Information about Human Rights Watch was compiled from Human Rights Watch, "About Us," http://www.hrw.org/about.

What Interest Groups Do

> ❯ Describe activities interest groups engage in

Interest groups perform a number of functions in the political process. They collect information about the implications of policy changes and convey that information to lawmakers and other policy makers. Their lobbying efforts aim to construct policies in ways that will most benefit their members. This section examines the tactics of lobbying, from providing information, to contributing to campaigns, to orchestrating grassroots movements that increase political participation on an issue. Lobbying is one of the fundamental gateways for expressing views and securing a favorable response from government officials.

Inform

All interest groups provide information about the issues they care about to their members, the media, government officials, and the general public. The type of interest group dictates the kind of information it disseminates. Before the Internet, groups provided members with information about government policies and new developments in their issue areas through newsletters and sessions at annual conventions. Today they disseminate such information on their websites and try to limit access by requiring members to register and sign in to the websites. Social media, such as Facebook and Twitter, also enable groups to keep members informed and to rally them to take action on the group's behalf.

Interest groups do more than merely report on current policy developments; they also provide members with interpretations of how the developments will affect their mission and goals. For example, in the area of environmental and energy policy, interest groups are very active in keeping their members up to date on policy developments. For example, in June 2014, when the EPA issued regulations to reduce carbon emissions from power plants by 30 percent, which was considered a strong stance against climate change, the Sierra Club posted a notice on its website informing its members and urging them to express their support.[19] (For more on the climate change issue, see Chapter 14, Economic, Domestic, and Foreign Policy.)

Interest groups also work hard to inform government officials about the impact of specific public policies. Most of the time, lobbyists have pro or con positions on a policy proposal, and their goal is to persuade government officials to agree with their perspective. Legislators and government officials are generally knowledgeable in their areas of expertise, but the vast size of the federal and state governments makes it hard to know the impact of policies on every citizen. Economic and ideological groups constantly monitor policies that might affect their members in a positive or negative way and strive to make legislators and government officials aware of the impact of policy proposals (see Public Policy and Interest Groups: Fracking).

> **→ KEY QUESTIONS:**
> When interest groups gather and disseminate information, are they performing a public service? Or do they do it just to advance their own causes? If so, is there anything wrong with that?

Lobby

Almost every kind of group with every kind of economic interest or political opinion—including business firms, trade and professional organizations, citizens' groups, labor unions, and universities and colleges—engages in one form of lobbying or another.[20] State, county, and city government officials maintain lobbying offices in Washington, D.C., both separately and as part of larger national groups such as the National Governors Association or the

United States Conference of Mayors. Lobbyists for these government entities frequently visit with the state's congressional delegation to keep the representatives informed about how federal programs are operating back home and to ask for legislation that will benefit their states. Mayors and county executives do the same thing, trying to influence their state legislators and governor by keeping them informed about how policies affect their constituents.

The Lobbyists. Groups can use their own employees as lobbyists or contract with firms that specialize in lobbying. According to the Center for Responsive Politics, in 2013, there were 12,279 individuals registered as active lobbyists in Washington, D.C. That amounts to nearly 23 lobbyists for each member of the

Here we see a hallway outside the state capitol in California where lobbyists gathered at the end of a legislative session to see how their proposals fared.

House and Senate.[21] The offices of many of these lobbyists are concentrated in an area of northwest Washington known as the K Street corridor; when people say they work on K Street, it is safe to assume that they are lobbyists.

Although lobbyists are frequently stereotyped as representing only the narrow interests of their clients, they are typically individuals who have held public service jobs at some point in their careers. There are three common pathways to becoming a Washington lobbyist: working on Capitol Hill, working in the executive branch, or working on a political campaign. Lobbyists may start out on a political campaign for a congressional candidate, work in a congressional office, and then leave to join a corporation, lobbying firm, or a law firm with a branch that lobbies on specific legal matters. Or lobbyists may start out as practicing attorneys, then go to work in Congress or the executive branch, and subsequently join a company or lobbying firm.

In 2013, interest groups and lobbying firms spent nearly $3.2 billion on a wide range of expenses associated with lobbying, including salaries for in-house lobbyists, consulting fees charged by lobbying firms, overhead for office space, and travel costs of staff [22] (see Table 7.2 on page 214). In the past, the costs of lobbying also included paid trips for members of Congress and their staffs (known as junkets), as well as expensive meals. Lobbyists justified these expenses as a way of getting to know members of Congress in a smaller and more relaxed setting, which they claimed would enable them to enhance their or their client's influence in the policy process. In 2007, congressional ethics reforms prohibited paid trips and meals for members and staff.[23] Still, lobbyists can use money to maintain their influence in other ways. For example, their salaries typically include allocations to make strategic campaign contributions to members of Congress who preside over issues that are important to their companies or clients.[24]

During a typical day, lobbyists phone, e-mail, or meet with congressional staffers, their clients, and possibly members of the media to gather information about relevant issues for their clients or to promote their clients' policy positions. Lobbyists also attend congressional

> → KEY QUESTIONS:
> Why is the public perception of lobbyists so negative?

Public Policy and Interest Groups:
Fracking

The struggle for power over policy decisions is ongoing, and interest groups are always moving forward to accomplish their agendas within the larger policy-making arena. The issues within the energy and environmental arena are vast, and in this section, we focus on the interest group activity surrounding the use of hydraulic fracturing, otherwise known as fracking, which is a technique that extracts oil and natural gas. Since 1997, the use of fracking has expanded greatly, bringing with it increases in jobs and overall production of oil and gas nationwide, which has contributed to economic growth in some areas.[25] At the same time, there have been serious allegations that fracking poses a threat to the environment, particularly safe drinking water. In response to concerns expressed by residents in areas with fracking, in 2010 Congress requested that the Environmental Protection Agency conduct a study of the effects of fracking on drinking water. The EPA then launched a study and focused on locations in four states: North Dakota, Pennsylvania, Texas, and Colorado where fracking had already been occurring for some time.[26] As such, the issue of fracking presents a clear case study of the trade-offs between jobs, energy production, and environmental protection and how interest groups try to influence public policy in these areas.

Both America's Natural Gas Alliance (ANGA), a group that promotes the use of natural gas, and the Natural Resource Defense Council (NRDC), an environmental advocacy group that opposes fracking, have responded to this investigation in ways that advance their own perspective. ANGA is an example of a corporate interest group designed to advance the policies preferred by its industry members. NRDC is typical of a public interest nonprofit group that addresses issues of public policy which affect a wide group of citizens.

Each group is committed to representing the views of its members; for ANGA that consists of oil and gas companies, and for NRDC, that consists of

MARK OVASKA/REDUX

Fracking is becoming more widespread across previously undeveloped lands. Here a fracking site known as the Marcellus Shale Well sits among farmland in Pennsylvania.

individual and group donors, as well as foundations that support NRDC's environmental protection stances.[27]

In response to the EPA study, ANGA issued an extensive report on the question of water pollution and its ties to fracking in February 2013. The report focused on one community—Washington County, Pennsylvania—an area that engaged in coal mining before turning to fracking. In this report, which was shared with other major oil and gas interest groups, ANGA argued that any existing water contamination could be a result of a number of industrial activities, not solely tied to fracking and that if this were true for Washington County, it could be true for other such affected areas.[28]

In contrast, the NRDC has created the Community Fracking Defense Campaign, which raises money and awareness of the issue and focuses on the impacts on residents of Pennsylvania as well as other states, including New York, Ohio, California, Illinois, and Texas.[29] The organization posts a group of videos on its website that documents statements from residents of areas with fracking as to the degraded quality of the water and air in their communities. These videos are human interest stories designed to gain sympathy for these residents and persuade viewers to support NRDC's efforts to oppose fracking.[30]

Each group's strategy reflects its core organization. As an industry-based organization, ANGA issued a comprehensive study that relies heavily on technical evidence designed to be used to oppose restrictions on fracking by the EPA. As a public issue group, the NRDC works to build grassroots support for its position, which the group hopes in turn will influence regulators and lawmakers. It remains to be seen how the issue of fracking will be resolved. Overall, the struggle to sway public opinion on the issue of fracking is just one illustration of how interest groups try to influence public policy on key issues.

Construct Your Own Policy

1. Develop policy criteria for deciding whether to grant permits for fracking in local communities.
2. Evaluate which set of interest groups should weigh more heavily in this decision from a public policy perspective and explain why.

Table 7.2 Top Spenders on Lobbying, 2013

Lobbying Client	Issues	Dollars Spent
U.S. Chamber of Commerce	Product liability, finance, copyright, patent and trademark	$74,470,000
National Association of Realtors	Taxes, finance, housing	$38,584,580
Blue Cross/Blue Shield	Health issues, taxes, Medicare and Medicaid	$22,618,980
Northrop Grumman	Defense manufacturing, contracts, weapons procurement	$20,590,000
National Cable & Telecommunications Association	Telecommunications, labor, antitrust and workplace, radio and TV broadcasting	$19,870,000
American Hospital Association	Health issues, Medicare and Medicaid, federal budget and appropriations	$19,743,813
Comcast Corporation	Radio and TV broadcasting, telecommunications, copyright, patent and trademark	$18,810,000
American Medical Association	Health issues, Medicare and Medicaid, federal budget and appropriations	$18,250,000
Pharmaceutical Research and Manufacturers of America	Health issues, Medicare and Medicaid, pharmacy	$17,882,500

Source: Adapted from Center for Responsive Politics, "Lobbying: Top Spenders, 2013," accessed August 20, 2014. http://www.opensecrets.org.

hearings, executive branch briefings, and even committee markups in which members of Congress write legislation. Interest groups, businesses, and industries do not survive by lobbying only, but lobbying is a natural outgrowth of their purpose because members expect their leaders to advocate for them when necessary.

Lobbying Strategies. Lobbying frequently involves a multipronged strategy. Groups usually try an inside lobbying strategy first, in which they deal directly with legislators and their staff to ask for a specific policy benefit or to try to stop a policy that they oppose. These insider meetings require access to policy makers, which typically comes about as a result of longtime interactions that build mutual trust. The key aspect of the **inside strategy** is to keep the policy request narrowly tailored to the group's needs because the broader the policy request, the more likely other groups will become involved in the negotiations, and complications can ensue. Either the policy request has to expand, so that each group gets a high level of benefits, or each group has to be satisfied with less, and few groups are ever satisfied with less. Nevertheless, if several groups share the same policy goals, they may form a temporary coalition, working together to improve their chances of success.

When an inside strategy does not work, groups adopt a more public or outside lobbying strategy by getting the press and their members more directly involved. A group may go straight to the press to provide details about the adverse effects of the proposal, hoping that the journalists will inform the general public. In this way, interest groups try to make use of the press's watchdog role over the government. For example, a nonprofit group called Citizens for Responsibility and Ethics in Washington consistently tries to get the press to focus on whether government officials are obeying ethics and campaign finance laws.[31] They monitor the use of campaign funds by

inside strategy:
A strategy employed by interest groups to pursue a narrow policy change and influence legislators directly rather than using a wider grassroots approach.

members of Congress and frequently call for investigations into what they see as misuse of funds. They also post an updated list of members of Congress who are under ethics investigations either by Congress itself, the Federal Election Commission, or the Department of Justice.

Through publicity and coordinated activities, groups also try to promote grassroots lobbying by encouraging action by their own members and the larger public. Energizing constituents in congressional districts used to be the work of regional offices. Today interest groups can generate citizen involvement through the Internet, asking that a message be sent by e-mail, text messaging, or cell phone, or show their members

Peaceful protests are frequently an effective way of voicing opinion on an issue. This gathering was organized to show opposition to fracking.

how to start their own Internet petitions. MoveOn.org, for example, gets grassroots support by asking members to e-mail, call, or send letters to their local legislator as well as to others who might be sympathetic to their cause. In addition, marches and rallies show strength in numbers to elected officials and also generate publicity that can attract new people to join advocacy efforts. In these ways, groups directly give their membership a stronger voice in the policy-making process.

The core organizational purpose also helps shape a group's lobbying strategy. For example, economic groups typically adopt an insider lobbying strategy and limit their activity to key actors in Congress and the executive branch. In contrast, citizens' groups typically adopt the outsider strategy to take advantage of the strength that comes from their large memberships. If they can mobilize their members to communicate to elected officials and simultaneously use the media to spread their message, they believe they will be successful.

Campaign Activities

Interest groups also promote their views by engaging in campaign activities, although federal law regulates their participation through the Federal Election Commission (FEC). Candidates and their campaign organizations must comply with reporting and disclosure requirements, which are monitored by the FEC. Groups with tax-exempt status are prohibited from engaging in any activity on behalf of a candidate or party in an election campaign. These groups, commonly referred to as **501(c)(3) organizations** after the section of the Internal Revenue Code that governs their activities, are likely to be charities, religious organizations, public service organizations, employee benefit groups, and fraternal societies, which are exempt from paying federal tax. Although they cannot engage in lobbying in any significant way, they can produce voter education guides or other nonpartisan educational materials that explain issues brought up during a political campaign and keep the public informed.[32]

There are also groups that fall under the 501(c)(4) category, which are nonprofit and are supposed to be focused on public policy issues, not politics. These groups are not required to reveal their contributors. Such groups include the Sierra Club, the National Rifle Association, and more recently, chapters of the Tea Party movement. Their status as

501(c)(3) organizations: *Tax-exempt groups that are prohibited from lobbying or campaigning for a party or candidate.*

"apolitical" nonprofit groups came under close scrutiny by the Internal Revenue Association in 2012 and 2013, leading some to allege that the Democratic Obama administration was targeting conservative groups. However, the Administration claimed that all groups who were seeking this status were subject to intense investigation and responded by proposing new regulations in 2014 that more closely restricted what kinds of activities these groups could engage in so that it would be clear they could not be overtly political.[33]

Groups that fall outside the tax-exempt category are free to engage in lobbying and campaign activities. But to set boundaries between the group's core mission and politics, they generally create parallel organizations that make campaign contributions to legislators. These **political action committees (PACs)** and their larger versions, Super PACs, raise funds to support electoral candidates and are subject to campaign finance laws (see Chapter 9). In one sense, PACs serve as gateways for expanding interest groups' political influence through financial involvement in campaigns.

PACs began growing in number and force after the Supreme Court's landmark decision *Buckley v. Valeo* (1976) upheld limits on donations to congressional campaigns.[34] As the costs of campaign spending rose over time, groups realized that creating or expanding an affiliated PAC to make campaign contributions could increase their influence over elected officials. Unaffiliated PACs, groups that make campaign contributions but are not associated with specific interest groups, also grew in size as a means of coordinating campaign contributions from individual citizens who wanted to express their campaign support as part of a larger group. All PACs make campaign contributions to the candidates they believe will be supportive of their policy goals (see Table 7.3). Thus PACs expand the reach of interest groups well beyond lobbying to include active engagement in the electoral arena.

Given the amount of money that PACs spend on campaign support, many observers have expressed concern that PACs exert a disproportionate influence over legislators, which creates an imbalance in government responsiveness toward some groups. In 2013, much was made of the influence of Club for Growth, a PAC devoted to lowering taxes because of its influence on Republican members who were advocating for lower government spending. The Club for Growth, originally founded by Stephen Moore in 1999, is a PAC that collects funds and makes campaign contributions to members who supports its platform. It is currently headed by Chris Chocola, a former Republican congressman. In October 2013, the federal government shut down for 16 days at an estimated cost of $2 billion because a group of these congressmen refused to vote to fund it and refused to raise the borrowing limit for the federal government (the debt ceiling). The Club for Growth was widely credited with supporting these congressmen.

More generally, however, scholars have had difficulty establishing exactly what PACs are getting for their money. Although campaign contributions can make it easier for groups to get access to legislators, they generally do not buy results in terms of policy outcomes. Interest groups tend to lobby and contribute to members of Congress who are leaning in their direction, so it is difficult to prove the impact of a campaign contribution.[35]

More generally, campaign finance laws impose limits on what interest groups can do in terms of issue advocacy, the practice of running advertisements or distributing literature on a policy issue rather than for a specific candidate. In general, the Supreme Court ruled that campaign spending is a form of speech and that, as with other forms of speech, Congress must show a compelling interest before it can pass laws to regulate it. The McCain-Feingold Bipartisan Campaign Reform Act (2002) restricted corporations and unions from using television and radio ads for

→ KEY QUESTIONS:
Should there be limits on how much money interest groups can contribute to campaigns? Why or why not?

Table 7.3 Top 20 PAC Contributors to Candidates, 2013-2014

PAC Name	Total Amount	Dem Pct	Repub Pct
National Assn of Realtors	$2,353,925	47%	52%
National Beer Wholesalers Assn	$2,307,500	42%	57%
AT&T Inc	$2,127,200	38%	62%
Credit Union National Assn	$2,107,500	48%	52%
Northrop Grumman	$1,996,250	42%	58%
Lockheed Martin	$1,996,000	40%	60%
Intl Brotherhood of Electrical Workers	$1,926,664	97%	3%
Every Republican Is Crucial PAC	$1,890,000	0%	100%
American Fedn of St/Cnty/Munic Employees	$1,868,200	100%	0%
Honeywell International	$1,860,745	42%	58%
American Bankers Assn	$1,824,000	25%	75%
Blue Cross/Blue Shield	$1,788,550	40%	60%
Operating Engineers Union	$1,788,499	78%	22%
National Auto Dealers Assn	$1,732,700	30%	70%
American Assn for Justice	$1,721,000	95%	5%
National Rural Electric Cooperative Assn	$1,711,272	29%	71%
American Federation of Teachers	$1,684,000	100%	0%
American Crystal Sugar	$1,674,499	58%	42%
Carpenters & Joiners Union	$1,647,750	74%	26%
Boeing Co	$1,562,000	41%	59%

Source: Center for Responsive Politics, www.opensecrets.org, adapted from data released by the Federal Election Commission, Accessed August 20, 2014

"electioneering communications"—commercials that refer to a candidate by name—within thirty days of a primary and sixty days of a general election. Since 2002, many groups have run ads that could be interpreted as issue advocacy or as outright campaigning. In 2007, in *Federal Election Commission v. Wisconsin Right to Life, Inc.*, the Supreme Court ruled that if a campaign advertisement could be reasonably viewed as issue-based, it was protected under the guarantee of free speech and could not be prohibited under the McCain-Feingold Act.[36]

Running issue ads has become a regular feature of interest group activity, even in nonelection years. Before 2010, interest groups could run issue ads on specific issues within a certain time frame prior to an election according to federal election laws; many interest groups used these ads to generate support or opposition to President Obama's health care plan before it became law. Although they served the purposes of interest groups, they also encouraged elected officials to be more responsive to constituents' needs because they focused attention on issues of importance to constituents. In 2010, the Supreme Court removed virtually all limits on issue ads, and individuals, corporations, and unions can spend as much money as they want on

→ KEY QUESTIONS:
Are issue ads fair or unfair? Are they informative or "disinformative"?

Checkpoint

CAN YOU:

- Explain how interest groups keep members informed
- Describe how interest groups lobby
- Define political action committee

supreme court cases

Citizens United v. Federal Election Commission (2010)

QUESTION: Can the government limit campaign spending by corporations and unions without violating First Amendment rights?

ORAL ARGUMENT: March 24, 2009, reargued September 9, 2009 (listen at http://www.oyez.org/cases/2000-2009/2008/2008_08_205)

DECISION: January 21, 2010 (read at http://caselaw.lp.findlaw.com/scripts/getcase.pl?court=US&vol=000&invol=08-205)

OUTCOME: No, governmental restrictions on corporate speech violate First Amendment rights (5–4).

In an attempt to equalize finances in political campaigns, Congress passed the Bipartisan Campaign Reform Act of 2002, also called the McCain-Feingold Act after its two leading sponsors. In 1976, the Supreme Court upheld limits on contributions to congressional campaigns but struck down limits on what independent groups unaffiliated with the campaign could spend. In response, McCain-Feingold restricted corporations and unions from using television or radio ads for "electioneering communications"—commercials that refer to a candidate by name—within thirty days of a primary or sixty days of a general election.

While corporations are often for-profit operations, such as General Motors or Microsoft, nonprofit and political entities such as the NAACP also organize as corporations under the tax code. One such political organization is Citizens United, a conservative interest group "dedicated to restoring our government to citizen control." During the 2008 Democratic primary campaign, it released a documentary called *Hillary: The Movie,* which was severely critical of Senator Clinton (D-N.Y.). Citizens United planned to show the documentary

on pay-per-view television and to market it in advertisements on broadcast television. Concerned about violating McCain-Feingold, Citizens United sued the FEC, seeking an injunction prohibiting enforcement of the act as a violation of the First Amendment rights of corporations.

In a break with past decisions, the Supreme Court declared that corporations and unions had the same First Amendment rights as U.S. citizens. Using the compelling interest test (see Chapter 4, Civil Liberties), the Court ruled that Congress cannot disfavor certain subjects or different speakers. While recognizing that corporations may have more money to spend than individual citizens do, the Court ruled that First Amendment protections do not depend on the speaker's "financial ability to engage in public discussion." Such limitations violate the marketplace of ideas that the First Amendment is designed to protect. The ruling left open the question of whether Congress could limit the speech rights of foreign corporations operating within the United States.

The dissenters claimed that money is not equivalent to speech and that the law was a reasonable attempt to level the playing field in campaigns.

1. Why is campaign spending a form of speech?
2. Should corporations receive the same free speech protections as ordinary citizens?

issue ads. (See this chapter's Supreme Court Cases: *Citizens United v. Federal Election Commission*, as well as the discussion of issue ads in Chapter 9.) In 2014, the Supreme Court went even further in their ruling in *McCutcheon et al. v. Federal Election Commission*, by removing the overall limits on the amount of money one individual could contribute to all federal elections; there are still limits on how much money can be given to one candidate, but an individual can now contribute to every single candidate running for federal office, as well as political parties.[37]

7.4 The Impact of Interest Groups on Democratic Processes

> ❯ Analyze what balances out power among interest groups

"I have often admired the extreme skill," wrote Tocqueville, "with which the inhabitants of the United States succeed in proposing a common object to the exertions of a great many men, and in inducing them voluntarily to pursue it."[38] Both Tocqueville and James Madison assumed that voluntary association or the forming of factions was a natural process of citizens interacting in a free society. Scholars have been interested in the same process, examining why interest groups form and what effects they have in a democratic society. In this section, we survey various perspectives on interest groups that relate to government responsiveness and citizen equality.

→ KEY QUESTIONS:
Do you think interest groups form from the bottom up or from the top down?

Natural Balance or Disproportionate Power

Over the past sixty years, scholarly debate has centered on the process of interest group formation and its consequences. In the 1950s, David Truman agreed with Tocqueville and Madison, describing interest group formation as natural. He observed that when individuals have interests in common, they naturally gravitate toward each other and form a group. As long as those individuals share a characteristic, opinion, or interest, the group continues to exist, but if the commonality disappears, the group disappears.[39]

Writing in the mid-1960s, however, Mancur Olson argued that merely having something in common with other people was not enough to give a group life and keep it going as an effective organization.[40] Olson focused on the costs of organizing and maintaining a group, noting that costs increase as a group grows in size and reach. The people who pay membership dues expect benefits in return. Since the governmental decisions that interest groups obtain are "public goods" that apply whether one has joined the group or not, Olson argues that the cost-benefit structure that underlies group formation contradicts Truman's claim that all groups naturally form and sustain themselves.

The debate between Truman and Olson raises the fundamental issue of whether interest groups are natural and can compete on an equal basis or artificial because they distort public policy in favor of some citizens over others. Other scholars have addressed this question in different ways. Robert Dahl argued that in a **pluralist** society, the battles over public policy by the varied interest groups that emerge to represent their members will produce a consensus that serves the public's common interest.[41] Scholars such as C. Wright Mills worried that a power elite controlled power in the American democracy.[42] His concerns were echoed by Theodore Lowi, who argued that in a democracy, some voices are louder than others and that government is more responsive to louder voices and will consistently

pluralist: *View of democratic society in which interest groups compete over policy goals, and elected officials are mediators of group conflict.*

→ KEY QUESTIONS:
Do interest groups bring people into the democratic process, or do they strengthen some voices at the expense of others?

→ KEY QUESTIONS:
What distinguishes a legitimate interest from an illegitimate interest?

→ KEY QUESTIONS:
Do interest groups balance out each other the way that Madison thought they would?

special interests:
Set of groups seeking a particular benefit for themselves in the policy process.

→ KEY QUESTIONS:
Name two or three interest groups that you think have a lot of power in American politics. Do you agree or disagree with their positions?

serve such groups at the expense of those who cannot make their voices heard. According to Lowi, this kind of policy making is elitist and fundamentally antidemocratic.[43]

Traditionally, the narrow focus of interest groups has engendered a sense of illegitimacy. Interest groups form and survive by appealing to a particular segment of society (economic, ideological, or social), so they are inherently exclusive. Exclusive groups act only in the best interests of their members, even if nonmembers thereby lose out. E. E. Schattschneider described this aspect of interest groups as an actual threat to democracy. He argued that if interest groups are given legitimacy because they claim to represent citizens' interests, but in fact they seek narrow benefits for their members at the expense of nonmembers, there is an inherent unfairness to them. Moreover, citizens will be lulled into a false sense of security about living in an "interest group society" because they believe that every interest group has an equal opportunity to be influential.[44]

There is a middle ground between these contrasting views. Given the approximately seven thousand registered groups in America today, it is clear that group formation is a natural outgrowth of the freedom to associate and of community life in which human beings share social, economic, and political goals. But if Olson is right, and successful cost-benefit strategies determine whether a group can survive or grow, groups led by individuals with sufficient time and money stand a greater chance of winning a policy fight than do groups without such resources. In this view, interests become **special interests**, a term with negative connotations that is more frequently used during campaign season to suggest that some groups exert a disproportionate amount of power in the American democracy. To the extent that a well-funded interest group can more easily pressure the government to produce policies that are beneficial to its members, government responds unequally across all citizens. In this view, financial advantage creates an artificial imbalance of influence that acts as a gate against equality.

Take the example of MoveOn.org, which describes itself as a grassroots interest group but, as noted earlier, was founded by two very wealthy Internet entrepreneurs. As illustrated in the screen shot of the MoveOn.org website, the group advocates for a liberal position on a wide range of issues. MoveOn.org is a nonprofit, progressive, but nonpartisan organization that organizes a wide range of activities designed to inform average citizens and motivate them to participate in the governing process. Its goals and mission sound very democratic, and joining the group requires little more than a click of a button on the Internet. For those who debate the merit of interest groups, the question is whether the public service mission of a group outweighs the fact that it is founded and run by a small, elite set of citizens.

Self-Service or Public Service

In assessing the relative power of interest groups in a democratic political system, it is essential to remember that interest groups do not pass or implement laws; they try to influence state and federal governments to enact their policy goals. To do so, they constantly interact with

As their webpage indicates, MoveOn.org is a non profit grassroots organization that is geared towards increasing political participation on a wide range of issues.

Source: http://front.moveon.org/

political parties, members of Congress, executive branch bureaucrats, and even the judicial system. The question of legitimacy of an interest group's activities comes when a victory for one group means a loss for another, or more broadly a loss for the general public.

For example, during most of the 1990s and 2000s, car manufacturers—acting alone and as part of their larger trade association, the American Association of Automobile Manufacturers—successfully lobbied to block efforts by environmental groups to secure an increase in government-mandated fuel efficiency standards. These standards, known by the general term *corporate average fuel economy* (CAFE), are designed to ensure that automobiles use as little fuel as possible to run efficiently. The government has an interest in requiring such efficiency in order to promote energy conservation more generally. However, automobile manufacturers argued that increased fuel efficiency is more expensive to produce and that CAFE standards would cut into their profits and might even decrease sales. In other words, the auto manufacturers would pay the price for accomplishing the public goal of promoting energy conservation. On this issue, the self-interest of the auto manufacturers conflicted with that of the general public.

But by 2007, with high increases in fuel prices and a general increased awareness of global warming, President George W. Bush agreed to a modest increase in fuel efficiency standards to 33.6 miles per gallon by 2012. When President Obama took office in 2009, he reiterated support for those standards. At the same time, an economic crisis hit the American automobile industry, undermining its financial and organizational ability to fight the increases. As the economic health of the domestic automobile industry slowly improved, the Obama administration felt freer to speed up the timetable for implementing those standards. As a result, the EPA issued regulations, first in 2010 and again in 2012, that require automobile manufacturers to produce vehicles that get 54.5 miles per gallon by 2025[45] (see Figure 7.2). The regulatory process is one gateway for interest groups to offer comments directly to the federal government on public policy proposal. The case of CAFE standards is one example of how time and circumstances almost always shift the playing field and the balance of power in the interest group arena.

The frustrating aspect of the role that interest groups play in a democracy is that groups contesting a single issue frequently talk over each other, not with each other. It is often left to members of Congress and the executive branch to balance their own responses to interest group requests and still maintain responsiveness to constituents and the nation at large. Over time, most interest groups experience wins and losses in the policy system; the necessary condition for a democracy is that every group has a chance to make its case.

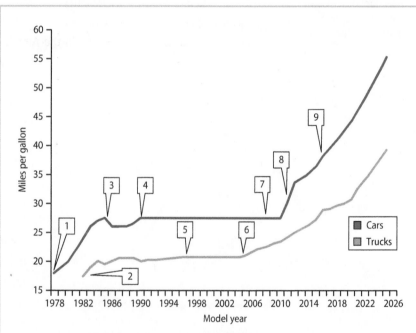

Figure 7.2 Fuel Economy Standards

Over time, the government has steadily increased the standards for fuel economy for cars and trucks. The numbered boxes indicate times when the federal government has taken action to regulate fuel economy.

Open or Closed Routes of Influence

→ KEY QUESTIONS:
Is government responsive to interest groups? Are interest groups responsive to the people?

Although interests may ultimately balance each other, and changing conditions may ultimately level the playing field, the fact that a tightly knit group of specialists often controls policy areas raises concern about fairness both inside and outside interest group organizations. For example, lobbyists work to build good relationships with legislators and officials in the bureaucracy. Given their knowledge of particular policy areas, many of them move in and out of government. Are lobbyists always thinking of their groups' members when they engage in their activities, or are they thinking about their next jobs? Do they constitute an insider group that is ultimately self-serving rather than serving the public?

⭐ **iron triangle:** *Insular and closed relationship among interest groups, members of Congress, and federal agencies.*

Scholars have long used the phrase **iron triangle** to describe the relationship among interest groups, members of Congress, and federal agencies. In essence, an iron triangle is a network forged by members in three categories that works to seal off access to public policy making. Lobbyists and interest groups want to maximize their benefits from federal programs; members of Congress want to maximize their power to shape the programs; and federal bureaucrats want to maximize their longevity as administrators of these programs.

→ KEY QUESTIONS:
Do you think the military-industrial complex exists today?

Critics of the influence of interest groups in a democracy often describe iron triangles as unbreakable and argue that they contribute to the inefficiency of the federal government because they sustain programs that should be eliminated or enlarge programs beyond what is necessary to meet their intended purposes. The criticism is not limited to scholars. In his farewell address in 1961, President Dwight D. Eisenhower (1953–61) warned of what he called the military-industrial complex, a self-serving interconnection among branches of the U.S. military, the defense manufacturing industry, and federal agencies overseeing scientific research. Eisenhower was greatly concerned that the defense industry had undue influence that would be used to unnecessarily increase spending on defense programs. "This conjunction of an immense military establishment and a large arms industry is new in the American experience," he said. "The total influence—

→ KEY QUESTIONS:
How does government prevent corruption among government officials?

economic, political, even spiritual—is felt in every city, every State house, every office of the Federal government. We recognize the imperative need for this development. Yet we must not fail to comprehend its grave implications. Our toil, resources, and livelihood are all involved; so is the very structure of our society."[46] President Eisenhower's stature as a decorated general who commanded U.S. and Allied forces in World War II gave him credibility on the issue of defense spending, and his depiction of the military-industrial complex as a type of iron triangle drew a great deal of notice. Even today, efforts by the Secretary of Defense to reduce the size of the armed forces and eliminate military equipment are met with stiff resistance by the members of the iron triangle that Eisenhower identified more than fifty years ago.[47] Moreover, today the term *iron triangle* is applied to a wide range of issue areas, including health care and prescription drugs (see Figure 7.3).

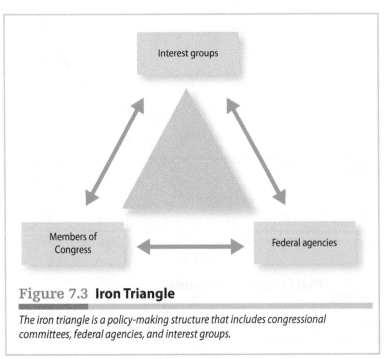

Figure 7.3 Iron Triangle

The iron triangle is a policy-making structure that includes congressional committees, federal agencies, and interest groups.

© CENGAGE LEARNING®

Yet the well-known interest group scholar Hugh Heclo claims that the interconnection of interest groups and the government is more benign, suggesting that the term **issue networks** is better than *iron triangle* to describe the relationship.[48] Heclo argues that interest groups, members of Congress, and bureaucrats all share information constantly, and that their interactions are open and transparent, not closed. Heclo wrote thirty years ago, before the advent of the 24-7 news cycle, Twitter messaging, and other telecommunications innovations, so it stands to reason that it is harder than ever for self-serving interconnections to go unnoticed. In addition, citizens' watchdog groups, such as Common Cause, and policy institutes, such as the Center for Responsive Politics, monitor interest group influence on government activities and policies. When these groups find evidence of wrongdoing in government, they loudly blow a whistle by issuing reports and holding press conferences to inform the media and the general public.

What remains true is that lobbyists, members of Congress and their staffs, and members of the executive branch do pass through what scholars describe as a revolving door of paid positions in one another's organizations, with knowledge and experience on a specific issue as the valued commodity. The term **revolving door** has a negative connotation, suggesting that an iron triangle of influence consists of the same set of people moving from one branch of government to another and then to the private sector. The image of a revolving door also suggests that the system does not stop to include outsiders with new perspectives; in other words, it can act as a gate against wider political participation.

Take, for example, Senator James DeMint, who was a Republican from South Carolina when he resigned abruptly in January 2013, early in his second term as a U.S. Senator, to become head of the Heritage Foundation, a conservative think tank. DeMint had been a leader among the conservative Republicans in the Senate, especially those affiliated with the Tea Party, and political observers were surprised to see him leave that position of power in the Senate. However, DeMint is highly compensated in his new position, with a salary close to $1 million per year, as compared to his previous salary of $174,000. As important, former Senator DeMint has used his position at the Heritage Foundation to more actively promote conservative policies on two fronts. First, he has focused the efforts of the Heritage Foundation on opposing the Affordable Care Act. Second, he has increased the role of the political arm, known as Heritage Action by fundraising for it and using it to support political candidates who oppose the Act.[49] Senator DeMint represents a new version of the revolving door where elected officials who are closely tied to ideological agendas leave their office to head up organizations that seek to influence public policy at the grassroots level as well as inside the beltway—and earn a much higher salary in the process.

It is also essential to remember that not all relationships among lobbyists, members of Congress, and federal officials are tainted or suspicious. Congress and the federal bureaucracy each have elaborate rules governing their behavior with respect to interest groups and lobbyists, and most members and bureaucrats follow them closely.

MICHAEL REYNOLDS/EPA /LANDOV

In a prime example of the revolving door, Senator Jim DeMint (R-SC) who was a conservative leader in the Senate, left office during his term to lead the Heritage Foundation, a conservative think tank, reportedly for a much higher salary.

issue network: *View of the relationship among interest groups, members of Congress, and federal agencies as more fluid, open, and transparent than that described by the term iron triangle.*

revolving door: *Movement of members of Congress, lobbyists, and executive branch employees into paid positions in each other's organizations.*

COMPARE WITH YOUR PEERS
MindTap™ for American Government

Access the Interest Groups Forum: Polling Activity—Regulating Interest Groups.

Checkpoint

CAN YOU:

- Compare the pluralist and elitist views of democratic society
- Explain why interest groups may be detrimental to the general public
- Recall the routes of influence that interest groups can use

7.5 Characteristics of Successful Interest Groups

> ❭ Assess what makes an interest group successful

The measure of a successful interest group is how well it accomplishes its goals. Some groups want to stay in existence forever, but other groups form temporarily for a specific purpose and disband after they accomplish their goal. For the groups that want to establish an enduring voice in a democracy, success can be measured in four ways: leadership accountability, membership outreach, financial stability, and public influence.

Leadership Accountability

As anyone who has tried to get a group of students together to perform a task, lodge a protest, or plan an event knows, coordination can be difficult. It typically takes an individual who acts as an interest group entrepreneur to organize citizens into a formal group that agrees on a united purpose. In return for organizing the group, the interest group entrepreneur typically takes a leadership role in directing the group's activities. For example, Grover Norquist founded the group Americans for Tax Reform in 1985, a group dedicated to lowering taxes, and he has remained its leader and public voice ever since.[50]

Benefits that come from being a group leader range from salary as a paid staff member to prestige and influence over the group's goals and strategies. The interest group scholar Robert Salisbury calls the trade-off between the work and the benefits of being a leader the "exchange theory of interest groups," and he argues that no one would rationally expend the energy and time to start a group if he or she could not take a prominent role in directing it.[51] Members are willing to pay their group leaders and give them power in the group in return for accomplishing the group's collective goals.

Transparency about the group's political and financial activities in pursuit of its goals is an important democratic element of an interest group; without it, there is a risk that the leaders could act in ways that do not properly serve the members. However, leaders do sometimes act in their own self-interest, by misusing group finances, for example, or they may take the group in an ideological direction that does not mirror the majority opinion in the group. More than a hundred years ago, Robert Michels coined the phrase **iron law of oligarchy** to describe this behavior. When leaders take such actions at the expense of rank-and-file members, the internal governance of the interest group breaks down. Flaws in interest group management can be a major problem for a democracy if citizens join a group with the expectation that the group will accurately represent their opinions and interests, and it does not.

Membership Stability

Whether a group is small or large, attracting members and keeping them over time are essential to its survival. People join groups because they share similar interests or political viewpoints or because they want to protect their economic livelihoods. For the leaders of groups, the challenge is to find the right balance between membership size and the organization's purpose. Too many members may create internal disagreements about policy goals, but too few may weaken the group's ability to exert influence in the policy system.

→ KEY QUESTIONS:
Identify two interest groups with an enduring voice in American democracy.

iron law of oligarchy: *Theory that leaders in any organization eventually behave in their own self-interest, even at the expense of rank-and-file members; the larger the organization, the greater the likelihood that the leader will behave this way.*

→ KEY QUESTIONS:
How do groups perpetuate themselves at the expense of their mission? Can you give an example?

Selective Benefits.

One way to attract and keep members is to provide **selective benefits** exclusive to members.[52] These can include material benefits, such as direct monetary benefits from policies that the group advocates, discounts on travel or prescriptions, and even monthly magazines. Solidary benefits are less tangible. They range from the simple pleasure of being surrounded by people with similar interests and perspectives to the networking benefits of interacting with people who share professional or personal concerns. Expressive benefits are the least tangible in that they consist of having a specific opinion expressed in the larger social or political sphere. When individuals join a group, they know that their viewpoint is being actively represented in the policy system, and that knowledge can be gratifying all by itself.

The Free Rider Problem.

Many of the benefits that large interest groups seek on behalf of their members—clean air by the Sierra Club or gun rights by the National Rifle Association—are **public goods**. That is, they are available to all people, whether they have contributed toward the provision of that good or not. Public goods are typically the spillover effects of public policies that affect all citizens. If a group lobbies for public goods or collective benefits that are so widespread that members and nonmembers alike receive them, incentives to join the group disappear. Olson addressed this collective action dilemma, calling it the **free rider problem**.[53] Why pay to join a group if one can get the benefits for free? Why join if the group is so large that it does not actually need an additional member?

The Economic and Political Change Problem.

Changes in the economy and the political environment can also have a negative impact on a group's membership stability. The decline and disappearance of the ILGWU is an example of what can happen to union membership when an entire industry disappears. From a political standpoint, groups can "succeed" their way out of existence. The NAACP is an example: In the course of its hundred-year history, it successfully fought discrimination and secured civil rights, and today it seems less urgently needed than it was in the past. In recent years, the group experienced leadership turmoil and membership decline, and it has reformulated its core mission to focus on multiracial human rights.[54]

Concern for survival in an increasingly crowded interest group society can sometimes bring an interest group into conflict with its core principles. Groups can try to counteract declining membership by creating new issues to rally members around or

selective benefits: *Benefits offered exclusively to members of an interest group.*

public goods: *Goods or benefits provided by government from which everyone benefits and from which no one can be excluded.*

free rider problem: *Problem faced by interest groups when a collective benefit they provide is so widespread and diffuse that members and nonmembers alike receive it, reducing the incentive for joining the group.*

CONNECT WITH YOUR CLASSMATES
MindTap™ for American Government

Access the Interest Groups Forum: Discussion—Participation in Interest Groups.

Spring Membership Drive!

Add your voice to the hundreds of thousands of Americans committed to leaving our children a living legacy — clean air, water, and natural grandeur. From Yosemite National Park to the Grand Canyon, since 1892 the Sierra Club has been instrumental in preserving nature's most splendid wild places.

Your membership counts! As a member, you'll have opportunities to get involved with local chapters, as well as be part of the largest national network of environmental advocates. Become a Member of Sierra Club, America's most effective advocate for the environment, today!

Hurry! This special $15 offer is only for a limited time . . . *join now!*

When you join online during our Spring Membership Drive, get a *free* Field Messenger Bag as well as these exciting Members-only benefits:

- Free Sierra Club Field Messenger Bag (*limited time!*)
- One-year subscription to *Sierra* magazine
- Worldwide Members-only outdoor trips
- Automatic membership in your local Chapter
- Discounts on Sierra Club calendars, books, and other merchandise

Interest groups offer tangible benefits to individuals to encourage them to join. Messenger bags and totes with the names of the organization also provide free advertising.

by portraying serious threats to the issues most important to members, although such actions can be criticized as "disinformation campaigns."

Financial Stability

→ KEY QUESTIONS:
Imagine an AAYP, an American Association for Young People. What would it lobby for? What benefits would it offer?

Together with keeping a membership base, a group must also maintain financial stability. Groups of all types require money to sustain their organizations' staffing, lobbying, and information distribution. The Internet has made fundraising easier because it allows groups to solicit money without incurring costs for printed advertising, mailers, and postage. Most organizations also rely on dues. Grassroots groups that seek to attract as many members as possible keep their dues relatively modest. For example, the dues for the National Rifle Association are between $35 and $125 a year.

Interest groups also achieve financial stability by creating not-for-profit businesses within the organization. AARP is a classic example of a large interest group that wears two hats: a politically powerful lobby on policies that affect senior citizens and a multimillion-dollar business that provides health insurance, life insurance, and discounts on movies, travel, and prescriptions to members, who must be at least 50 years old to join. A basic AARP membership costs only $16 a year, and it provides the opportunity to purchase the other services at discounted rates. In turn, AARP receives payments from businesses that it contracts with to provide services to its members. AARP is among the most successful large-scale interest groups in American history. In 2013, the year for which the most recent data are available, it claimed a membership of 37 million.[55]

The financial challenge for many groups is to keep their operating costs in line with their expected income. For the very largest interest groups, such as AARP, a single year's operating budget can be more than $1 billion; in 2013, the group took in $1.44 billion and spent $1.40 billion.[56] For most other groups, the operating budget ranges from thousands to millions of dollars per year.[57] Groups can experience financial difficulty as a result of financial mismanagement by group leaders, or, in some cases, they may simply outlive their usefulness and members cease paying dues. In such cases, they may be forced to scale back their activities and close local chapter offices.

Influence in the Public Sphere

The extent to which an interest group appears to influence public debate is a sign of its success. One indicator of influence is being quoted in the press. For example, Grover Norquist and Americans for Tax Reform (ATR), mentioned earlier in this chapter, were heavily featured in the press because they persuaded 236 U.S. House members and 41 U.S. senators in the 112th Congress to sign the Taxpayer Protection Pledge—a promise not to vote for any tax increases. The mainstream media has portrayed Norquist and ATR as strongly influential in the debate over how to contain the federal deficit and reduce the national debt. ATR has vocally opposed any tax increase whatsoever and has publicized its intention to inform voters in the districts and states of members who break the pledge. Other, less dramatic, indicators of influence include being asked to testify in Congress or being cited by an elected official when discussing a key issue of concern. Each such instance signals to the group's membership, as well as to the public at large, that it has a significant role in policy formation on the issues about which it is most concerned.

Checkpoint

CAN YOU:

- Explain the importance of leadership accountability in interest group success
- Describe issues in membership stability
- Name sources of financial stability
- Identify indicators of interest group influence

Interest Groups and Democracy

Interest groups are a powerful instrument of democracy because they crystallize the opinions and interests of average citizens and present those views to elected officials during the policy-making process. It was precisely this power to influence policy that Madison feared so much and why he hoped that in a large republic, competition among interest groups would prevent any one of them from gaining too much influence. Interest groups contribute to a democracy by holding the government accountable for its actions, pressuring elected officials to be responsive to their constituents, and serving as a vehicle to equalize the influence of different groups of citizens in the policy process.

A group can channel the power of separate individuals into a single collective voice that is more likely to be heard throughout the policy system. In addition, the very existence of an interest group can keep citizens informed about the direct impact of policy on their lives; with that information, constituents can better hold their elected officials accountable for those policies.

Interest groups engage in several methods to influence economic, social, and foreign policy, including direct lobbying, media campaigns, legal challenges, and grassroots organizing. When interests clash, as in the case of education reform or energy policy, elected officials, bureaucrats, and even the judiciary often act as intermediaries. In Congress, political parties adopt positions that are favored or opposed by specific interest groups and thus create alliances between parties and interest groups. Although there are more interest groups today than ever before, political parties serve as a counterweight to the influence of interest groups. As partisanship has grown stronger in the House, the Senate, and even the White House, members who are asked to choose between an interest group and a political party choose the party. However, given that political parties tend to align very closely with supportive interest groups, members do not have to make that choice very often. To the extent that interest groups can influence politicians to address narrow or exclusive interests to the detriment of what is best for all citizens, they can be viewed as a negative aspect of the U.S. democracy.

Yet interest groups also represent a positive aspect of democracy when they serve to express wide-ranging viewpoints, and they continue to be an effective way of giving voice to citizens' needs and concerns. Interest groups continuously win and lose within the American policy-making system, and they reinvent their lobbying strategies in response to changing political and economic conditions. However, sole reliance on interest groups as a means of citizen participation is dangerous because some groups have more resources—time, money, and membership—than others and consequently win more often. In this way, interest groups can be both gateways and gates to citizen equality and the securing of policy benefits. Ultimately, citizens must hold both their interest group leaders and their elected officials accountable for public policy outcomes.

Master the Concept
of Interest Groups with the MindTap™ for American Government

 REVIEW MindTap™ for American Government
Access Key Term Flashcards for Chapter 7.

 TEST YOURSELF MindTap™ for American Government
Take the Wrap It Up Quiz for Chapter 7.

 STAY CURRENT MindTap™ for American Government
Access the KnowNow blog and customized RSS for updates on current events.

 STAY FOCUSED MindTap™ for American Government
Complete the Focus Activities for Interest Groups.

Key Concepts

citizens' groups (p. 207). How are citizens' groups different from single-interest groups?

economic interest groups (p. 204). What are the concerns of economic interest groups?

faction (p. 201). When is an interest group the same as a faction, and when is it different?

501(c)(3) organizations (p. 215). Why are 501(c)(3) organizations prohibited from lobbying?

free rider problem (p. 225). Why are free riders a problem for interest groups?

grassroots movement (p. 203). How is a grassroots movement different from an interest group?

ideological interest groups (p. 207). How do ideological interest groups differ from economic interest groups?

inside strategy (p. 214). How do interest groups lobby staff and members of Congress to advance their policy goals through direct contact?

interest groups (p. 200). How are interest groups a gateway to democracy?

iron law of oligarchy (p. 224). How is the iron law of oligarchy a problem for democracy?

iron triangle (p. 222). Describe the iron triangle as a gate against democracy.

issue network (p. 223). How is an issue network different from an iron triangle?

lobbying (p. 202). How is lobbying a form of an individual's rights of association and petition?

nongovernmental organizations (NGOs) (p. 208). What role do NGOs play in shaping U.S. foreign policy?

pluralist (p. 219). What is the role of interest groups in a pluralist society?

political action committees (PACs) (p. 216). How are PACs gateways for expanding interest groups' political influence?

public goods (p. 225). How should a public good be defined in a democracy?

revolving door (p. 223). What steps should Congress take to dismantle the revolving door?

right of association (p. 201). Why is the right of association a constitutional guarantee?

right of petition (p. 201). Why is the right of petition a constitutional guarantee?

selective benefits (p. 225). How do selective benefits attract and keep interest group members?

single-issue groups (p. 207). What is the impact of single-issue groups on campaigns and elections?

special interests (p. 220). What is a negative aspect of special interests?

unions (p. 203). What techniques do unions use to gain better wages and working conditions?

Learning Outcomes: What You Need . . .

To Know	To Test Yourself	To Participate

▶ Outline how interest groups have developed over time

Interest groups are groups of citizens who share a common interest—political opinions, religious affiliations, ideological beliefs, social goals, or economic objectives—that try to influence public policy to benefit their members. The constitutional basis for interest groups lies in the First Amendment, which guarantees both the right to assemble and the right to petition the government for redress of grievances. Individuals and interest groups have lobbied legislators from the nation's earliest days, and their numbers have vastly increased. Today groups also lobby executive branch officials and attempt to influence judicial appointments and the courts through lawsuits and *amicus curiae* briefs.	• Describe what an interest group is. • Explain why Madison and the Framers feared factions. • Track the history of interest groups.	• Explain how you think interest groups influence the economic and social policies that affect your life.

To Know	To Test Yourself	To Participate
▶ Identify the types of interest groups that have evolved		
Interest groups can be categorized as economic, ideological, and foreign policy and international, and each has different policy goals and strategies.	• Describe the different types of economic interest groups. • Explain how ideological and issue-oriented groups can lead to polarization. • Compare and contrast the missions of foreign policy and international interest groups.	• Create a set of interest groups that would represent different characteristics of voters such as gender, income, age, race, ethnicity, and ideology.
▶ Describe activities interest groups engage in		
Generally, interest groups gather and disseminate information in their issue areas, lobby using various strategies such as meeting with staff and legislators as well as workers in the executive branch, and contribute to political campaigns and advertising to the extent that federal law allows.	• Explain how interest groups keep members informed. • Describe how interest groups lobby. • Define *political action committee*.	• Take the position as head of an interest group, and describe your policy goal and what strategy you would use to influence legislators, voters, and other groups to support your policy goals.
▶ Analyze what balances out power among interest groups		
Scholars who study why interest groups form and their effects in a democratic society debate whether the wealthy have disproportionate power to use interest groups to their advantage, and so to the disadvantage of others. Scholars also debate whether interest groups balance out each other. Lobbyists, federal regulators, and members of Congress form networks that some describe as "iron" and closed to citizen influence and some describe as transparent and open to citizen influence. In today's democracy, elected officials, bureaucrats, and even the judiciary often act as intermediaries in interest group conflict.	• Compare the pluralist and elitist views of democratic society. • Explain why interest groups may be detrimental to the general public. • Recall the routes of influence that interest groups can use.	• Propose ways of balancing power across interest groups to make sure that government is equally responsive to as many people as possible on a given issue.
▶ Assess what makes an interest group successful		
The success of interest groups can be measured in four ways: leadership accountability, membership stability, financial stability, and public influence. The longer an interest group exists, the more powerful it is. When a policy is debated, some interest groups will win by maintaining the status quo, and others might win by changing current policy.	• Explain the importance of leadership accountability in interest group success. • Describe issues in membership stability. • Name sources of financial stability. • Identify indicators of interest group influence.	• Consider how internally democratic interest groups really are. • Evaluate whether the free rider is a problem for democracy. • Debate whether an interest group can be too powerful.

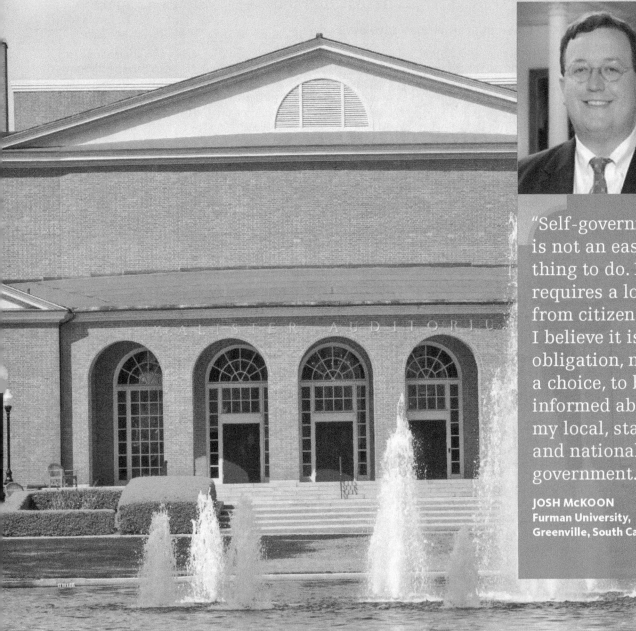

COURTESY OF JOSH MCKOON

"Self-government is not an easy thing to do. It requires a lot from citizens.... I believe it is my obligation, not a choice, to be informed about my local, state, and national government."

JOSH McKOON
Furman University,
Greenville, South Carolina

PATTI MCCONVILLE/ALAMY

8

Political Parties

Josh McKoon, who was first elected to the Georgia senate in 2010, credits his experience at Furman University in Greenville, South Carolina, for launching "his lifetime commitment to conservative politics." As a political science and communications major, he volunteered on Republican Bob Dole's 1996 presidential campaign and worked for both a state representative running for Congress and a U.S. congressman running for the Senate. His wealth of campaign experience was one reason he was elected president of the College Republicans chapter at Furman. McKoon maintains that his time at Furman allowed him to become plugged into the Republican network. "I learned very early," he said in a phone interview, "that it is 90 percent about who you know, and making those contacts with the right individuals."

In 1999, McKoon met George W. Bush, the governor of Texas who was running for president. By making contacts with Bush's campaign team, McKoon landed a job as a director of field operations on Bush's primary campaign in South Carolina. As a field director, he coordinated campaign activities with Bush supporters at Clemson and Furman universities and built volunteer networks that facilitated Bush's get-out-the-vote efforts. After completing law school, McKoon headed back to Columbus, the Georgia city where he was born, reconnected with the Muscogee County Republican Party, and started a Young Republicans chapter, which he eventually chaired.

As party chair, McKoon sought to get more Republicans involved in state and local government using a three-pronged approach. First, he worked to expand grassroots campaign operations throughout Muscogee County to give Republican challengers the capacity to wage better campaigns. Second, he tried to recruit more viable Republican candidates with the talent and qualifications to challenge incumbent Democrats in the Georgia statehouse. Third, he used his fundraising skills to fill the party coffers to support local races. As it turned out, McKoon became one of the Republican candidates himself, running to represent the 29th district in the state senate; in 2014, he won reelection to his third term in office. McKoon got his start with the help of a lot of volunteer support from college students. One of them, Theresa Garcia, was quoted in a local newspaper as saying that she got involved "because of Josh's concerns about issues folks my age are concerned about. . . . Josh is concerned about jobs—and jobs are on everybody's minds. Will there be jobs when

Need to Know

8.1 Outline how political parties evolved in American politics

8.2 Identify which issues divided the first political parties

8.3 Explain why two parties dominate the U.S. political system

8.4 Define partisan affiliation and ideology

WATCH & LEARN MindTap™ for American Government
Watch a brief "What Do You Know?" video summarizing Political Parties.

we graduate? . . . We want to see Josh in the state senate because he is not far removed from us."

McKoon calls the Republican Party his "gateway." "In Columbus as a high school student and as an attorney," he says, "in Tuscaloosa as a law student, and in Greenville as a college student, the Republican Party offered me an access point to candidates, campaigns, and political experiences." Since joining the state senate, McKoon has introduced bills relating to health care, education, and criminal justice, and he is currently the chair of the Georgia Senate Judiciary Committee. His political career shows how young people can themselves run for elective office and generate support among young people who want to elect someone who can relate to and respond to their needs.[1]

Political parties offer every citizen in America the opportunity to participate in politics and even to run for elected office. In this chapter, we look at the role of political parties in the American constitutional system by examining what they do, how they formed and evolved over time, and what role they play in shaping electoral choices for candidates and voters alike.

8.1 The Role of Political Parties in American Democracy

> Outline how political parties evolved in American politics

A democratic government must be responsive to its citizens, and for government to be equally responsive, every citizen must have an equal opportunity to influence it. But mobilizing the more than 318 million people in the United States to take an active role in monitoring their government is a truly momentous challenge. In the United States, political parties fill an essential need by shaping the choices that voters face in elections, which serve as the key mechanism by which voters hold their government accountable. With so many public offices to fill, voters need some sort of road map to compare candidates and make the choices that will serve their best interests. The potential danger of relying on parties to shape these choices is that parties become interested only in winning office, not in serving the interests of the people. It takes action and vigilance on the part of voters to ensure that parties do not go in this direction.

In this section, we look at the role that parties play in the American democratic system, specifically at the way they organize the electorate, shape the elections that determine whether their candidates win office, and guide the actions of elected officials.

→ KEY QUESTIONS:
In what ways are parties gateways for citizen participation? As you read this chapter, look for evidence.

What Are Political Parties?

political parties:
Broad coalitions of interests organized to win elections in order to enact a commonly supported set of public policies.

A **political party** is a group of individuals who join together to choose candidates for elected office—whether by informal group voting or a formal nominating process. These candidates agree to abide by the **party platform**, a document that lays out the party's core beliefs and policy proposals. Parties operate through national, state, and county committees; members include party activists, citizen volunteers, and elected officials. A party's main purpose is to win elections in order to control governmental power and implement its policies; this fundamental goal distinguishes parties from interest groups, who also seek to influence electoral outcomes, but do not formally run candidates for office.

party platform:
Document that lays out a party's core beliefs and policy proposals for each presidential election.

At the national level, the party issues its platform during presidential election years. In their 2012 platforms, for example, the Republican Party (www.gop.org) and the Democratic Party (www.dnc.org) stated their positions on national security, health care, energy policy, the environment, and taxes. These platforms not only define the positions of the presidential and vice presidential candidates but also serve as a general guide to the policy positions of all the candidates running under the party label. From time to time, individual candidates may disagree with elements of the party's platform, but, in general, candidates who choose to run under a party label are defined by it. Using party labels as a shortcut for the party platform, voters can hold the elected officials accountable for their policy successes and blame them for policy failures.

Citizens tend to vote for one party over the other in somewhat predictable patterns. Classic political scientists, such as V. O. Key, use the term *party in the electorate* to describe the general patterns of voters' party identification and their behavior on election day. A main goal of any political party is to maximize party affiliation among voters so that it translates into a solid majority of the party in the electorate, which can in turn translate to a solid majority of the *party in government.* To accomplish this goal, the *party as an organization* is created, with internal structures that guide how the party functions.[2] The modern American political party is multilevel, with committees at the federal, state, and local levels.

What Political Parties Do

In this section, we move from theoretical ideas about political parties to what they actually do in the American political system.

→ KEY QUESTIONS:
Which political party, if any, do you identify with?

Parties in the Electorate.　Parties offer several layers of opportunity for political participation. Most simply, a person can claim to be a member of a party by stating that he or she identifies with it, for example, by saying "I am a Republican." That statement is an acknowledgment of party identification—an attachment or allegiance to a political party. Voters identify with parties for several reasons. The simplest is the belief that the policies put forth by one party will serve their interests better than the policies proposed by other parties in the political arena.

Another reason to join a party stems from family or social environment, in which being a member of a party is similar to other personal characteristics. As Chapter 6, Public Opinion and the Media, explains, many young people adopt the party identification of their parents. Although parties always ask for contributions, there are no membership fees. For this reason, parties provide the broadest and most open gateway to participation in American politics.

A more formal step of party identification is stating party affiliation when registering to vote. Voter registration rules vary by state, but they typically require a citizen to show proof of identity and address to an

AP IMAGES/JACQUELYN MARTIN

Local party organizations provide crucial support to candidates running on a party label in terms of coordinating volunteers and get-out-the-vote (GOTV) efforts. Here in Virginia, workers for the Fairfax County Republican Committee use phone banks to call potential supporters on behalf of Republican presidential candidate Mitt Romney.

→ KEY QUESTIONS:
Have you formally affiliated
with a political party? What
are the advantages and the
disadvantages of doing so?

official government office. In some places, voters can register by mail or when they get their driver's licenses, but in others, they must fill out the forms in person at a local board of elections.

At the next level of participation, voters can become active in the party at the town, county, state, and federal level. Parties encourage people to volunteer on campaigns at every level—making phone calls to prospective voters, passing out bumper stickers, or maintaining e-mail contact through the campaign website. Of course, political parties expect their members to vote on election day and to bring their friends, coworkers, and family members to the polls with them. Parties also rely on supporters to build up the organization and candidates by making financial contributions.

Political parties also serve as a gateway to elected office. Josh McKoon, for example, got his start in politics through volunteer work with a local party on a campaign, and then he ran for the Georgia senate. Many candidates who seek public office start out by affiliating with a party in college and rise through the ranks of party organizations, as McKoon did. Parties also actively recruit individuals in their county, district, or state to run for elected office. Candidate recruitment involves party leaders at all levels trying to identify people who will make good candidates for elected office because they are well known in the community, have personal wealth, or have a professional record that speaks to current issues and would appeal to voters.

Parties in Government.

party caucus: *Group of party members in a legislature.*

Parties also serve to organize members of Congress and state legislatures into cohesive groups, known as **party caucuses**, which consistently vote, year after year, for the policies that the parties promise in their platforms. The party in government is made up of the elected officials who share the same party affiliation and work together to accomplish the party's electoral and policy goals. Elected officials often hold positions in party organizations as well. For example, Terry McAuliffe, who served as the chair of the national Democratic Party from 2001 to 2005, was elected governor of Virginia in 2013. Even the president, whose primary responsibility is to govern, is expected to serve as leader of his political party by setting the agenda according to party policy goals. The president is also increasingly expected to engage in political support for party candidates, from campaign appearances to party fundraisers.

Party Organization.

national committee: *Top level of national political parties; coordinates national presidential campaigns.*

The modern political party is structured as a multilevel organization with units at the federal, state, and local levels. **National committees** are at the top of the party organization, and their members are chosen by each state party organization (see Figure 8.1). A new president can select the national committee chair; in the case of the presidential "out" party, the national committee itself elects the party chair. The national committee is responsible for running the party's presidential nominating convention every four years. Key to that effort is overseeing the states' primary delegate selection process and officially recognizing a state's delegation at the convention.

The main job of the national committee is to do everything possible to elect the party's presidential nominee every four years, which requires strengthening all party organizations from the national down to the local levels. The national committee runs training workshops on party-centered activities, such as candidate recruitment and fundraising. It has to raise money; for example, in the 2012 presidential campaign, the Democratic National Committee raised $316 million, and the Republican National Committee raised $409 million.[3] The national party can spend its money on coordinated expenditures, that is, in cooperation with the presidential campaign, and it can make independent expenditures, which are funds spent separately on general efforts to increase voter turnout for the party's nominee.

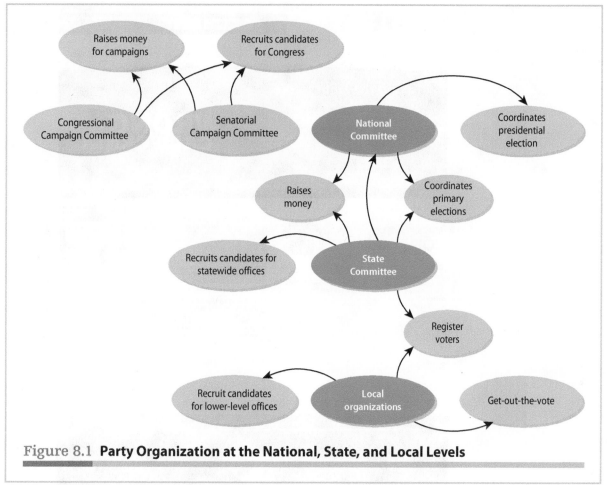

Figure 8.1 **Party Organization at the National, State, and Local Levels**

Each major political party has a committee dedicated to raising money for incumbent House and Senate members. For the Democrats, it is the Democratic Congressional Campaign Committee and the Democratic Senatorial Campaign Committee; for the Republicans, it is the National Republican Congressional Committee and the National Republican Senatorial Committee. These congressional party committees are also responsible for recruiting qualified challengers to run for seats held by the opposing party and helping to fund their campaigns. Through November 5, 2014, the four congressional party organizations raised approximately $558 million in the 2013–14 cycle.[4]

State political parties are the next level of party organization, and they are regulated by state law, so their responsibilities can vary by state. Typically a political party has a state central committee that tries to elect candidates to statewide office and also works with local organizations to recruit new voters and raise money. As you can see from the websites of the California Republican and Democratic parties on page 236, each state party organization displays the structure of the state party organization, provides information about how to become involved with the party, and provides information about the key issues. Each state party organization has its own website, which displays the structure of the state party organization and provides information about how to become involved with the party.

Local party organizations exist at the county, town, and precinct or ward levels. The Muscogee County Republican Party, which Josh McKoon chaired, is an example of a local party organization. The essential functions of local party organizations are to recruit candidates for

Taking the Fight to the GOP

From protecting millionaires and billionaires while voting to end Medicare, to siding with Speaker Boehner and the most extreme elements of the GOP, these incumbent Republican House members are Wrong for California.

LEARN MORE

THE LATEST »

DEM2012
Find out what more than 1,300 Democrats do every month that's making a huge difference, and see how you can join them!

Check out the CADEM Store!
Show your support for the CDP and help keep California blue!

NEWS FEED »

RT @GranholmTWR: .@Astro_Jose says his dad put him on the path to success by saying, With hard work & an education, you can reach i ...
JUN 27 @05:24 PM · FROM TWITTER

RT @OversightDems: BREAKING: Issa acknowledges Holder didn't authorize #FastAndFurious http://t.co/ESBamNgf
JUN 27 @04:43 PM · FROM TWITTER

The threat to the Affordable Health Care Act reveals what House Republicans have in store for all of us. Their prescription is harmful to all Americans. Wall PhotosWe put together this graphic to expl...
JUN 27 @02:42 PM · FROM FACEBOOK

CONNECT

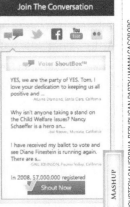

State political parties can be powerful in shaping state politics. They help recruit candidates for the state legislatures; after the primaries, they work hard to elect their party's nominees to statewide office. Here the websites of the California Democratic Party and the California Republican Party announce news, activities, and opinions on issues. California is so large that its statewide elections are considered indicative of national trends.

lower-level elected offices, register voters, and, most important, ensure that voters get to the polls on election day.[5]

The Party Nomination Process

One of the most important functions of parties is to nominate candidates for office and then elect them, a process accomplished in two stages. In elections with more than one candidate seeking the party's nomination, states hold **primary elections**, in which voters determine the party's choice to run in the next stage—the **general election**.

Primaries. Primary elections are a very important way that each voter can have an equal voice in nominating his or her party's candidates for elected office. Although most states rely heavily on the primary, some states authorize nominating conventions and primaries, with the primaries taking place only if the challenger to the party nominee receives a certain percentage of votes at the convention or a certain number of citizen petition signatures.[6]

As noted, state laws regarding elections vary, and there are several types of primaries. A closed primary is one in which voters must affiliate with a party before casting a vote (either by registering before the election or on primary election day). A semiclosed primary is one in which party-affiliated voters cast votes in their party's primary, and nonaffiliated voters can choose which party's primary to vote in. In an open primary, voters do not have to affiliate with a party before voting. Instead, they are given **ballots** with each party's list of candidates, and they can choose which ballot to use but are restricted to voting for only one party's nominees. In a blanket primary, voters are given the ballots from all parties and allowed to cast votes for any party's candidates as long as they cast only one vote per elective office, but, in 2000, the Supreme Court ruled that blanket primaries were unconstitutional (see Supreme Court Cases: *California Democratic Party v. Jones*). Currently some states use a modified version of a blanket primary, known as the nonpartisan blanket primary, in which all the candidates, from all parties, who are running for office are listed without identifying their party affiliation, and if no majority winner emerges, the top two vote-getters face each other in a runoff election.

Primary elections are a fact of political life, but insofar as they create competition within a political party and encourage candidates to reveal negative aspects of each other's professional or personal lives, they can weaken the party's eventual nominee when he or she faces opponents in the general election. Because party organizations want the candidate who is most likely to win the election nominated under the party banner, they try to exert control over the primary election process in several ways. First, state laws govern party ballot access—literally, who can actually get on the primary election ballot. The relationship between elite state party members and state legislators is very close, so the party controls the gate by determining how open or restrictive ballot access is for candidates seeking to run for office on the party label. Second, although party organizations remain technically neutral during the primary election season, they can steer donors toward their preferred candidates and away from candidates who do not agree with their goals. As a consequence, individuals who are perceived as weak or as not loyal to the party may run into major roadblocks set up by the party organization. Later in this chapter, we discuss an example of intraparty conflict as it applies to the Republican Party and the Tea Party movement, which acts as a type of conservative faction within it.

The Presidential Nomination. The process by which each party nominates its presidential candidate has evolved from one that was concentrated in the hands of a small group of elites

★ **primary election:** *Election in which voters select the candidates who will run on the party label in the general election; also called direct primary.*

★ **general election:** *Election in which voters choose their elected officials.*

→ KEY QUESTIONS:
Have you voted in a primary election? What kind of primary was it? Did you have to identify your party affiliation?

★ **ballot:** *List of candidates who are running for elected office; used by voters to make their choice.*

→ KEY QUESTIONS:
Do you think that the presidential nomination process in 2012 was fair?

supreme court cases

California Democratic Party v. Jones (2000)

QUESTION: Do blanket primaries, in which voters can vote for any party's candidate regardless of their own party affiliation, violate the right of association of political parties that want to limit their primaries to those who belong to the party?

ORAL ARGUMENT: April 24, 2000 (listen at http://www .oyez.org/cases/1990-1999/1999/1999_99_401)

DECISION: June 26, 2000 (read at http://caselaw .lp.findlaw.com/cgi-bin/getcase.pl?court=US&navby= case&vol=000&invol=99-401)

OUTCOME: Yes, the right of association means that states cannot force parties to open their primaries to voters who are not party members (7–2).

In 1996, voters in California approved Proposition 198 (see Chapter 3, Federalism, on citizen initiatives), which established a blanket primary in which each voter can vote in any primary election, regardless of party affiliation. In 2000, to prevent Republicans from voting in its primary, the California Democratic Party went to court, claiming that California's blanket primary law violated the state Democratic Party's right to freedom of association as guaranteed by the First Amendment.

Ultimately, the case reached the Supreme Court, where Justice Antonin Scalia wrote the majority opinion in favor of the California Democratic

Party. The Court ruled blanket primaries to be unconstitutional because they violated the First Amendment. The majority argued that a blanket primary violated a political party's right to associate exclusively with its members, which can be extended to mean that political parties have the right to allow only registered party members to choose their party's nominees in a primary. Scalia wrote that "Proposition 198 forces political parties to associate with—to have their nominees, and hence their positions, determined by—those who, at best, have refused to affiliate with the party, and, at worst, have expressly affiliated with a rival."

1. Should a political party be forced to give voters who are not members the same privileges that party members have?

2. Why might a political party want to be responsive to voters who are not members?

to the modern process that allows millions of voters to participate directly in choosing the party's presidential nominee (see Figure 8.2).

In a presidential primary, voters cast a vote for a particular candidate, but what they are really doing is choosing delegates who will support that nominee at the party's national nominating convention. In a presidential **caucus**, which serves the same nominating purpose, the process is less formal and more personal in that party members meet together in town halls, schools, and even private homes to choose a nominee. Each state is awarded a number of delegates to the convention by the national party organization based largely on the number of Electoral College votes the state has but also on the size of party support in that state. The candidate who wins a majority of the delegates from the primary and caucus elections is selected at the national convention as the party's nominee for president.

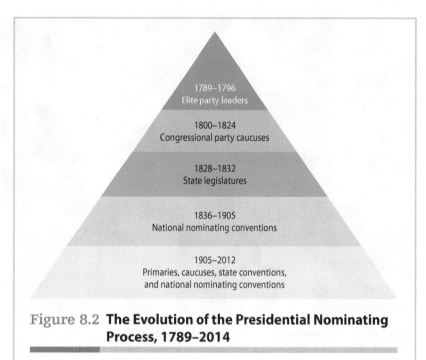

Figure 8.2 The Evolution of the Presidential Nominating Process, 1789–2014

© CENGAGE LEARNING®

The Democratic Party and Republican Party allocate their delegates within the primaries and caucuses differently. The Democratic Party has had a more tumultuous nominating process due in large part to some key rule changes in the 1970s and 1980s. In the 1960s, members of underrepresented groups, such as women and African Americans, began calling for a change in the presidential nominating procedures for the Democratic Party. Specifically, they objected to the use of the unit rule, or **winner-take-all system**, which meant that whoever won the majority of primary or state nominating convention votes would win the entire state's delegates. Activists believed that the unit rule allowed conservative white men to dominate the nominating process. In response to this grassroots movement, the Democrats formed the McGovern-Fraser Commission, which recommended changes in the way that delegates were chosen and awarded to candidates during the primary season. In 1972, the Democratic Party instituted requirements that states' delegations accurately reflect the distribution of preferences for presidential candidates in the state. For the 1976 election, the Democrats formally instituted **proportional representation**; that is, the number of delegates that a candidate receives is based on the percentage of the vote received in the primary or caucus, either at the state level or in each congressional district. In most states, delegates are committed to a candidate before the primary election takes place.

To further address the activists' concern that the nominating process was dominated by white men, the 1972 reforms required a certain percentage of each state's delegates to be women, African Americans, and other underrepresented groups based on their proportion in each state's population. If states did not comply with this requirement, the national party reserved the right not to "seat" or count their delegates in the final nominating vote held at the party's national convention. Although the party stated the goal of increasing delegates from underrepresented groups, it did not really increase African American convention participation until 1984, when Jesse Jackson, an African American, ran for the Democratic

caucus: *Meeting of party members in town halls, schools, and private homes to select a presidential nominee.*

winner-take-all system: *Electoral system in which whoever wins the most votes in an election wins the election.*

proportional representation: *An electoral system that assigns party delegates according to vote share in a presidential primary election or that assigns seats in the legislature according to vote share in a general election.*

→ KEY QUESTIONS:
How does proportional representation affect the dynamics of primaries?

KEVORK DJANSEZIAN/GETTY IMAGES

In the presidential nomination process, primaries provide a crucial vehicle for party members to learn about the candidates and to actively participate in choosing their party's nominee. As part of the process to select the 2012 Republican Party nominee, candidates participated in a number of debates before the primaries began; here, Newt Gingrich, Michele Bachmann, and Mitt Romney are shown discussing their policy positions in a debate held in California in September 2011. Mitt Romney ultimately won the party's nomination.

presidential nomination. Although the nomination went to former Vice President Walter Mondale, Jackson was successful enough to insist that more people of color be delegates to the convention. The cumulative effect of these reforms created a gateway for members of underrepresented groups to exert influence in determining the Democratic Party presidential nominee.

In 1981, the Democratic Party made several other changes, including requiring that each state's delegation comprise an equal number of men and women, and creating a category of delegates known as superdelegates. The superdelegates are not chosen through the primary voting process but rather are active members of the party who will be instrumental in turning out party voters in the general election. Most superdelegates are elected officials in the party, such as governors and members of Congress from each state, as well as state party committee chairs and key activists in interest groups that are loyal to the Democrats. They are uncommitted and free to choose whomever they wish to support at the convention.[7]

In contrast to the Democratic Party, the Republican Party had rarely faced an internal demand for more diverse representation, so it had not significantly changed its nominating system. But in 2010, the Republican Party adopted proportional representation in its nominating system in the hopes of generating more competition and a lengthier campaign season, both of which would increase turnout and enthusiasm among Republican voters.[8] States that did not abide by this system, including Florida and Arizona, were penalized by losing some of their delegates to the national convention. Republicans have no requirements as to the racial or gender composition of a state's delegates, and they have no superdelegates. However, they did add a category of bonus delegates to the 2012 nominating process, awarding these to states based on the percentage of votes cast for the Republican presidential candidate in past elections; in general, bonus delegates are often elected officials and loyal party activists.

However, the 2012 GOP nomination process proved to be too drawn out and conflictual, and turnout among Republicans did not increase appreciably in the general election. Throughout fall 2011 and early 2012, momentum shifted across a number of contenders, including Newt Gingrich and Rick Santorum, before Mitt Romney, former governor of Massachusetts, secured the necessary number of delegates (1,144) in June 2012. There is no question that proportional representation, combined with the role of Super PACs, allowed candidates who did not have a strong majority to stay in the nomination contest and collect delegates longer than under a winner-take-all system (see Chapter 9, Elections, Campaigns, and Voting for a discussion of Super PACs).

→ KEY QUESTIONS:
How do primaries allow voters to register their opinions with party leaders about candidates and about party policy positions?

In response, in 2014, the Republican Party once again changed the nominating process by putting the New Hampshire and South Carolina primaries, and the Iowa and Nevada caucuses, all in February and barring any other state from holding their nominating contests earlier than those four states. Those states that hold their contests between March 1st and March 15th would award their delegates by proportional representation; states holding contests after that can choose either way to award their delegates. States that do not abide by this system will be severely penalized by losing nearly all of their delegates to the national convention.[9]

Checkpoint

CAN YOU:

▪ Define political party

▪ Identify the three arenas in which parties operate

▪ Track the party nomination process

8.2 The Dynamics of Early Party Development

> Identify which issues divided the first political parties

Political parties in 2014 seem very well organized, as if they have existed as long as the nation itself. But parties were not intended to be part of the original fabric of the political system. They emerged from disagreements among the Framers. Today, two large parties include a broad swath of the electorate and must make internal compromises to stay unified. In this section, we trace the background to these developments.

Political Factions: Federalist versus Antifederalist

James Madison, writing in *Federalist Papers* 10 and 51 (see the Appendix), predicted the rise of factions, groups of individuals who share a common political goal and ally with each other on a temporary basis to accomplish that goal. Although factions were not considered the same thing as political parties of the kind that had emerged in Britain, the Framers feared that both factions and parties might encourage divisions in the young democracy that could threaten its existence.

Yet factions emerged even before the Constitution was adopted. In the debate over ratification (see Chapter 2, The Constitution), those who argued for the Constitution called themselves Federalists. They believed that a stable federal government that could collect tax revenue, raise and maintain an army and navy, regulate foreign and domestic trade, and stabilize currency would make the American democratic experiment a success. Opponents of a strong national government, however, viewed the future of the United States in terms of loosely affiliated but sovereign states that governed themselves, managing their own tax policies and internal security. These were the Antifederalists. In their view, the United States had just fought a war to overturn a strong monarch, and they did not want to put themselves under the rule of an oppressive new centralized government that would govern from the top down (see Table 8.1).

Ultimately, the Federalist viewpoint triumphed, and the Constitution was ratified. But the debate did not end there. The nation's first president, George Washington (1789–97), formed a government that included proponents of a strong national government (led by Alexander Hamilton and John Adams) and strong state governments (led by Thomas Jefferson). Washington worried that opposing views could lead to organized political parties that would

> **KEY QUESTIONS:**
> Given the Framers' views on factions and political parties, do you think the development of parties has been good or bad for American democracy?

> **KEY QUESTIONS:**
> Try to relate the modern Democratic and Republican Parties to the viewpoints of the Federalists and the Antifederalists. Which party comes closest to which viewpoint?

Table 8.1 Federalist and Antifederalist Policies

Federalist	Antifederalist
Ratify the Constitution	Oppose ratification of the Constitution
Establish central bank	Oppose central bank
Protect commercial interests	Support agricultural interests
Assert federal supremacy	Preserve state power
See no need for Bill of Rights	Pass Bill of Rights

Source: Adapted from John H. Aldrich and Ruth Grant, "The Antifederalists, the First Congress, and the First Parties," *Journal of Politics* 55 (1993): 295–326.

cause conflict in the new nation.[10] Tensions between the factions accelerated after John Adams's (1797–1801) election as president, especially following passage of the Sedition Act, which severely restricted freedom of the press and freedom of speech critical of the government, in 1798 (see Chapter 4, Civil Liberties). Jefferson opposed this law and in 1800 mounted a campaign against Adams for the presidency, arguing that Adams's use of federal power was too heavy-handed.

THE GRANGER COLLECTION, NYC

Andrew Jackson originated the modern political party by encouraging grassroots participation by voters and party organizations in his election campaigns and by building the Democratic Party while he served as president from 1829 to 1837.

Thomas Jefferson, Andrew Jackson, and the Emergence of the Democratic Party

After winning the election of 1800, Thomas Jefferson used his victory to transform his fledgling political party into a viable long-term organization known as the Democratic-Republicans (most candidates shortened the name to Republican), while the supporters of Adams and Hamilton united around the Federalist Party.[11] The Democratic-Republicans occupied the White House for the next twenty-eight years with the terms of Jefferson (1801–09), James Madison (1809–17), James Monroe (1817–25), and John Quincy Adams (1825–29). The Federalist Party slowly faded away as a force in politics.

The Democratic-Republicans soon split over the nomination process for president. Specifically Andrew Jackson, an ambitious politician, wanted to take the party to a new level of inclusiveness and use that wider reach to become president. Jackson, from Tennessee, had served in both the House and the Senate, but he made his national reputation during the War of 1812, especially as the hero of the Battle of New Orleans. After his military service ended, Jackson returned to Congress and attempted to win the presidential nomination of the Democratic-Republicans in 1824.[12] At that time, presidential nominations were decided by party caucuses in Congress. Fewer than a third of the members of the party showed up to cast their votes, and no one won a majority. The outcome then had to be determined by the House of Representatives, which selected John Quincy Adams, the son of President John Adams.

By 1828, the nomination process had begun to change, with nominations by parties located at the state level, in legislatures and state conventions, rather than the national Congress. By locating the nomination process in the states instead of in Congress, parties enlarged the number of people involved in making the decision about who could run for president. In 1828, using a grassroots state-level strategy to attract both the support of state legislators and the voters themselves, Jackson worked closely with Martin Van Buren, a powerful New York politician, to again challenge Adams for the nomination of the Democratic-Republicans; this time, Jackson won the nomination and the presidential election. Then, as now, it is rare for a challenger to defeat the incumbent president in American politics.

By 1832, the end of Jackson's first term in office, politics had changed in fundamental ways because of the nation's rapid geographic and population growth.[13] The Jackson-led Democrats emerged as a large grassroots majority political party, and Jackson used all the powers of the presidency to strengthen his political party around the country. In the meantime, the anti-Jackson wing of the old Democratic-Republicans had taken the name National Republicans. In the presidential election of 1832, the National Republicans nominated Henry Clay, a U.S. senator from Kentucky, to run against Jackson.

Although Henry Clay lost that election to Jackson, he returned to the Senate and started laying the groundwork for a new political party that would oppose Jackson's policies. He encouraged members of the National Republicans to join forces with others who opposed Jackson and to form the Whig Party, which objected to what they viewed as Jackson's abuse of presidential power for partisan gains. From 1832 to 1856, the Democrats and the Whigs dominated American politics and presidential elections. However, the issue of slavery soon emerged to shake up the party balance.

→ KEY QUESTIONS:
How did Jackson open gateways to citizen participation?

The Antislavery Movement and the Formation of the Republican Party

The Democratic Party's general strategy for opening a larger gateway for citizen participation in politics inadvertently encouraged alternate groups and political parties to emerge on the political scene. In 1833, William Lloyd Garrison, a white journalist, formed the American Anti-Slavery Society to press for the abolition of slavery. Former slave Frederick Douglass and other African Americans in the North also led efforts to end slavery, and the abolitionist movement grew large and vocal enough to pressure the Democrats and Whigs to take a formal position on slavery, especially the extension of slavery into western territories.

Northern and southern Democrats were united against the abolitionist movement, but for different reasons. Northern Democrats recognized that if the slavery question came to the forefront of politics, the nationally dominant Democratic Party would be split between the North and the South. Southern Democrats opposed abolishing slavery outright or limiting its expansion because the plantation economy of the South was heavily dependent on slave labor. The Whig Party was also divided along northern and southern lines for the same reasons.

Further complicating party politics were smaller **third parties** that arose in the North, some explicitly antislavery. Third parties are minor political parties that present an alternative to the two dominant political parties in the American political system. They have been a part of the political system since the early nineteenth century. Typically, third parties focus

third parties: *Minor political parties that present a third alternative to the two dominant political parties in the American political system.*

on a single issue; the Liberty Party, for example, was explicitly antislavery, while the Green Party, active today, focuses on environmental protection (we discuss third parties in greater depth later in this chapter). As frequently happens in American politics, however, third parties are absorbed into larger parties; the Liberty Party was absorbed into a larger coalition of groups, led by the Free Soilers, which opposed the expansion of slavery in the territories. Meeting in Ripon, Wisconsin, in 1854, these groups were also joined by some antislavery northern Democrats, and the modern Republican Party was born. In the words of one activist, Alvan E. Bovay, "We went into the little meeting held in a schoolhouse Whigs, Free Soilers, and Democrats. We came out of it Republicans."[14] Six years later, the Republican Party had consolidated its support and elected Abraham Lincoln (1861–65) to the presidency.

Shortly after Lincoln's election, seven southern states seceded from the union, and the Civil War erupted. The Confederacy dissolved after the war ended in 1865, but southerners resented northerners and the Republican Party because of both the South's physical and economic losses and the continued occupation of the South by northern troops. Since that time, the Democrats and the Republicans have been the nation's two major political parties.

Party Loyalty and Patronage

★ **patronage system:**
Political system in which government programs and benefits are awarded based on political loyalty to a party or politician.

Andrew Jackson set an example of how to build a political party organization using government resources. Just as Jackson worked to expand the electorate, he sought to expand the size of the federal government in order to increase the number of federally funded jobs his party could control. The Jacksonian era provided many opportunities to bring the federal government into the state and local arena by establishing programs to build forts, post roads (for mail delivery), customhouses, and lighthouses. Whoever controlled the jobs associated with these federal programs could also demand political allegiance from those who filled them. By the late nineteenth century, a system emerged whereby the politician became the "patron" of the businessmen and workers who were on the payrolls of the federal or the state governments. Jobs built party loyalty, and those hired often had to declare their political allegiance to the politician who arranged for the job and promise to vote for him. Such a system is commonly referred to as a **patronage system**.

"THAT'S WHAT'S THE MATTER."
Boss Tweed. "As long as I count the Votes, what are you going to do about it? say?"

PROVIDED COURTESY HARPWEEK

William Marcy "Boss" Tweed was the head of the Democratic Party machine in New York City in the 1850s and 1860s. He was notorious for using political office to hand out favors and benefits to loyal party members and to accumulate personal wealth. The editorial cartoons of Thomas Nast helped expose the graft and corruption of the "Tweed Ring."

As the government expanded, so did the party organization. At each level—federal, state, and local—there were parallel party committees. Parties became the top-down organizations they are today, with a national committee, state committees, and local chapters at the county, ward, town, or precinct level. At each level, leaders who had power within the party acted as party bosses, controlling the distribution of public funds and making sure to reward supporters and withhold funds from opponents. The key element in this system was the loyalty of supporters who voted for the boss's preferred set of candidates on election day. Voter support in this kind of system was so reliable and predictable that it became known as machine politics; it ran like a well-oiled machine.

The expansion of party machines was fueled by a huge influx of new immigrants in the late nineteenth century who mostly settled in large cities of the North and Midwest. Democratic bosses in these cities recognized that immigrants, once naturalized, would be a major source of new voters and courted their loyalty through patronage. In turn, parties served as a type of gateway for immigrants to become integrated into American political life. As city populations increased at a much faster rate than rural populations, Democrats gained political power in cities, while Republican power in the North and Midwest tended to be concentrated in rural areas.

→ KEY QUESTIONS:
Do you see the patronage system still at work today in American politics? Explain.

Reform and the Erosion of Party Control

A critical factor in the success of machine politics was party control of voting. In contrast to today's system—in which states manage most aspects of elections, including ballot design and ballot counting—local parties in the late nineteenth century printed their own ballots, called party strip ballots, which listed only their candidates, and gave them to voters on their way into the polling places. In many places, party officials counted the votes as well, further manipulating the voting process to their advantage.

However, three developments eroded party organizations' control over government jobs and elections: the creation of a merit-based system of government employment, the introduction of ballot reforms, and a change in the way nominees for elected office were selected. All three reforms were led by Progressives, coalitions of Democrats and Republicans who believed that government had been captured by corrupt elites who were using government resources to enrich themselves rather than to serve citizens.

Since Andrew Jackson's day, bosses in the old patronage system had taken for granted the right to distribute government jobs to their supporters. But in 1883, the Pendleton Act reformed the civil service by requiring that government jobs be filled based on merit, not on political connections (see Chapter 12, The Bureaucracy, for more on the civil service). This was the first of several laws that slowly transformed the federal bureaucracy from a corrupt insider organization to a neutral, policy-based organization.[15]

★ **Australian ballot:**
Voting system in which state governments run elections and provide voters the option of choosing candidates from multiple parties; also called the secret ballot.

Voting procedures were also reformed between 1888 and 1911 as states adopted the so-called **Australian ballot** system, which originated in Australia in 1858, to replace the party strip ballots[16] (see Figure 8.3). When parties had printed the ballots and had given them to voters, who then put them in the ballot box, there was no privacy, and party officials monitored citizens' votes. The Australian ballot system introduced the secret ballot; each ballot listed all of the candidates from all of the parties who were running for office, and voters marked their choices in private. In addition, poll watchers and ballot counters were expected to perform their tasks without favoring a specific party and without intimidating voters. This reform greatly reduced party boss control over election outcomes.[17]

Lastly, Progressives launched grassroots campaigns for direct primaries run by the state for nominating party candidates. These primaries aimed to replace the nomination of candidates in local and state party conventions, which were typically dominated by party bosses. Although states were relatively slow to adopt direct primaries, eventually this system became the dominant means of choosing party candidates. The effect of direct primaries was to greatly reduce the control that party bosses and machines had over the choices offered in elections.

Checkpoint

CAN YOU:

- Explain the differences between the Federalists and the Antifederalists
- Describe the events that opened up the presidential nomination process
- Explain how the Republican Party formed
- Connect patronage and party power
- Describe reforms that reduced party power

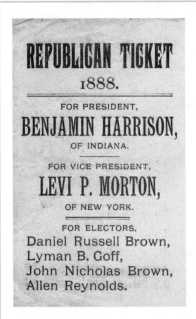
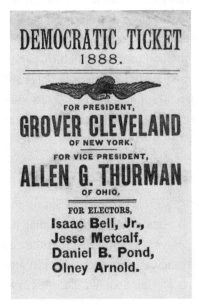
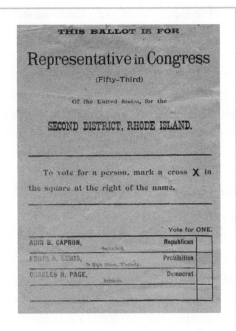

Figure 8.3 **Ballot Reform**

On the left are examples of party strip ballots used in Rhode Island in 1888. These types of ballots were printed by political parties and handed to voters on election day. They gave a voter no opportunity to split the vote among different parties. On the right is an example of the so-called Australian ballot. Like this ballot used in Rhode Island in 1892, Australian ballots were printed by state governments rather than by political parties. They listed all candidates for elected office, not just candidates from a single party, and therefore allowed a voter to split the vote among different parties.

SOURCE: RUSSELL J. DESIMONE AND DANIEL C. SCHOFIELD, "RHODE ISLAND ELECTION TICKETS: A SURVEY," TECHNICAL SERVICES DEPARTMENT FACULTY PUBLICATIONS (KINGSTON: UNIVERSITY OF RHODE ISLAND, 2007), PRIVATE COLLECTION, RUSSELL J. DESIMONE AND DANIEL C. SCHOFIELD.

 # 8.3 The Effects of a Two-Party System

> Explain why two parties dominate the U.S. political system

Following the Civil War, party divisions ran largely along geographic lines, with Republicans dominant in the Northeast and West, and Democrats dominant in the South and increasingly in the nation's largest cities. Today, the Democratic and Republican Parties have reversed their geographic strongholds, but the two-party system remains intact. In this section, we examine the effects of a two-party system not only on citizens' choices but also on the ways that government can respond. We also examine the reasons why the United States, even before the Civil War, never had more than two major parties, and we explore the role of the third parties that have occasionally arisen to challenge two-party dominance.

Limited Political Choice

Surely, there are more than two views on how to solve important policy problems. If a group of students has a conversation about a political issue, whether it is war, civil liberties, education, crime, or same-sex marriage, there will likely be more than two opinions expressed. It might seem logical, therefore, that a large democracy such as the United States should have many parties that vie with each other to capture political offices. But the United States has only two major parties.

In 1957, the scholar Anthony Downs argued that voters whose views fall between the two parties were actually represented in a two-party system. His **median voter theorem** proposed that, in a two-party race, if voters select candidates on the basis of ideology and everyone participates equally, the party closer to the middle will win. As candidates from each party seek to attract a majority of votes, and because most voters fall in the middle of the ideological spectrum, both parties move toward a compromise, or middle position. In this way, moderates have a great deal of potential political influence in a two-party system.[18]

Nevertheless, the impact of ideologically extreme campaign activists and interest groups that align with a party can pressure parties and candidates to move away from the center.[19] In today's highly partisan atmosphere, it seems as though the political center has almost entirely disappeared. Each party appears to be so dominated by its more extreme wing that there is little opportunity within each to make moderate views known or to compromise. The current two-party system increasingly appears to contradict Downs's expectations about convergence to the middle. In regions where one party is very dominant, elected officials may not be responsive to voters from the other party.

The Structural Limits

The two-party system is built into the American electoral system, as the political scientist Maurice Duverger explains: The American electoral system is a **single-member plurality system**, in which one legislative seat (on a city council, in a state assembly, in the House of Representatives) represents citizens who live in a geographically defined district.[20] To win that seat, a candidate usually needs only a **plurality of votes**, not a pure **majority**, that is, more votes than any other candidate, but not necessarily 50 percent plus 1. Because there is only one seat to be won in a district, only the party or parties with the strongest support have a chance to win a seat. In the United States, many districts are noncompetitive, that is, one of the two major parties dominates. Other districts are competitive; the two major parties vie for electoral support. As a result, voters have become accustomed to choosing between candidates from the two major parties.

Other electoral systems work differently. Many democracies assign the number of seats a party wins according to proportional representation, based on the percentage of votes it receives in a particular election. This type of electoral system encourages smaller parties to form around specific issues and to field candidates for office. Voters are likewise encouraged to support smaller parties. With so many parties fielding candidates, no single party is likely to receive a majority, and parties govern by forming coalitions (see Global Gateways: Proportional Representation Electoral Systems).

In the United States, however, the single-member plurality system encourages a two-party system, and the two-party system in turn encourages political debates that ask Americans to take a "for" or an "against" position on an issue. During an election, there is little effort to arrive at the middle ground, although there is often debate within a party as to what its position will be. In fact, the two-party system works to transfer the battleground from between parties to within parties. Each party—rather than government itself—is a coalition.

The Role of Third Parties

Scholars have debated whether this two-party system adequately reflects the range of views among citizens. In one sense, a two-party system stands as a gate that blocks the emergence of alternative viewpoints and reduces the choices available to voters in terms of perspectives on

median voter theorem: *Theory that, in a two-party race, if voters select candidates on the basis of ideology and everyone participates equally, the party closer to the middle will win.*

→ KEY QUESTIONS:
Do you think the major political parties reflect the views of citizens? If not, what can be done to change that?

single-member plurality system: *Electoral system that assigns one seat in a legislative body to represent citizens who live in a defined area (a district) based on which candidate wins the most votes.*

plurality vote: *Vote in which the winner needs to win more votes than any other candidate.*

majority vote: *Vote in which the winner needs to win 50 percent plus 1 of the votes cast.*

→ KEY QUESTIONS:
Do the political parties provide citizens with opportunities for debate on the issues? Do the political parties reflect citizens' views?

globalgateways

Proportional Representation Electoral Systems

In contrast to the U.S. single-member plurality system, many nations in Europe and in Central and Latin America have proportional representation electoral systems. This system assigns multiple seats to a geographic district according to the proportion of votes a political party receives in an election. In this system, there are rewards for forming more than two parties because parties that receive even a small percentage of the vote—for example, 10 percent—are likely to be awarded seats in the legislature. The legislatures typically have coalition majorities, where members from different parties agree on policies and form a working majority. In this way, proportional representation grants multiple parties the power to make policy and deliver benefits to voters.

There are trade-offs in terms of participation, responsiveness, and accountability in each type of electoral system. Single-member plurality electoral systems tend to produce fewer political parties, which reduces the number of opinions that can be actively represented in a political system. Two-party systems also encourage strict partisanship among officeholders and discourage bipartisanship. On the other hand, this stark contrast allows voters to more easily hold their elected officials accountable.

Proportional representation systems produce multiple parties and greater diversity of representation. However, this system tends to produce coalition government because no party can gain a straight majority. Coalitions encourage compromise among parties, but it is also true that the parties that make up the coalition can withdraw at any time, and so the ruling government is potentially unstable.* In addition, voters cannot easily identify which party in the coalition should be rewarded or blamed for government policies, so accountability is more difficult than in single-member plurality systems.

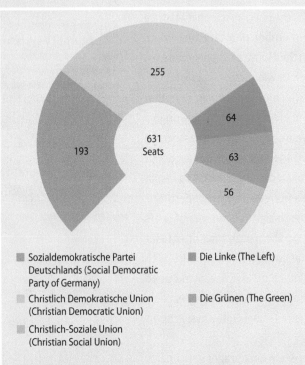

Sozialdemokratische Partei Deutschlands (Social Democratic Party of Germany)

Christlich Demokratische Union (Christian Democratic Union)

Christlich-Soziale Union (Christian Social Union)

Die Linke (The Left)

Die Grünen (The Green)

SEATS ALLOCATED BY PARTY IN THE GERMAN BUNDESTAG, 2014.

The German Bundestag, which is equivalent to the U.S. House of Representatives, awards a percentage of seats to each party depending on its vote share in the election (each citizen votes for a district representative and for a party). Following an election in 2013, the Christian Democratic Union and their Bavarian ally, the Christian Social Union, formed a coalition government with the Social Democrats.

© CENGAGE LEARNING®

1. How does a proportional representation electoral system translate votes into legislative power in the government?

2. Why are governments established under proportional representation systems inherently unstable?

*Ko Maeda and Misa Nishikawa, "Duration of Party Control in Parliamentary and Presidential Governments," *Comparative Political Studies* 39 (2006): 352–74.

how to govern. On the other hand, when the two parties together do not offer policy proposals that a significant number of voters want to see enacted, third parties form. These third parties can mount challenges so significant that the major parties are compelled to act, often by incorporating the third party's policy proposal into their platforms.

Theodore "Teddy" Roosevelt ran for president as the Progressive Party candidate. Roosevelt, a Republican, had served as president from 1901 to 1909. He decided to run for president again in 1912 to mobilize voters around a host of progressive reforms that would weaken party machines, most notably the idea of popular elections for U.S. senators. At that time, U.S. senators were elected in state legislatures rather than directly by the voters. Although Roosevelt lost, the Progressives were successful in getting Congress to pass and the states to ratify the Seventeenth Amendment on April 8, 1913, which allowed for the direct election of U.S. senators.

Since Teddy Roosevelt's run, five contenders representing significant third parties have entered presidential elections, but none has been able to build a sustained organization over time. Two of these candidates, Strom Thurmond (Dixiecrats) and George Wallace (American Independent Party), ran on segregationist platforms of parties that were splinter groups of the Democratic Party. John Anderson (National Unity Party) and Ross Perot (United We Stand) each ran on a platform that favored moderate social policy and strict fiscal discipline. Ross

Here we see members of Operation American Spring, a Tea Party affiliated group, marching in Washington to protest against the Obama Administration in 2014.

Perot was given credit for using his United We Stand Party to force the two major party candidates in 1992, President George H. W. Bush (1989–93) and William Jefferson (Bill) Clinton (1993–2001), to address the federal deficit, the amount by which annual government spending exceeds incoming revenue. Ralph Nader ran for president on the Green Party ticket in 2000, 2004, and 2008 promoting a platform that called for stronger environmental and consumer protections. Although Nader did not win, his messages of change and open government were clearly echoed by the mainstream Democratic candidate, Barack Obama, in his successful first campaign for president. For a compact list of significant parties in American politics, see Figure 8.4.

Though third parties have not fared well in national electoral contests, they sometimes find success in lower level elections. The Libertarian Party, for example, currently claims more than 140 elected officials.[21] Most are members of school boards and town councils, with mayors holding the highest offices. Another example of a third party that found success in local elections was the La Raza Unida Party (LRUP) in the 1970s.[22] The LRUP organized in 1970 in the south Texas counties of Zavala, Dimmitt, and La Salle, all near the U.S.-Mexico border. Its founders' goals were to advance the economic, social, and political interests of Mexican Americans. Their mobilizing efforts led to electoral victories in Crystal City, Cotulla, and Carrizo Springs school boards and town councils, all areas heavily populated by Latinos yet whose local offices Anglos had historically held. The La Raza Unida

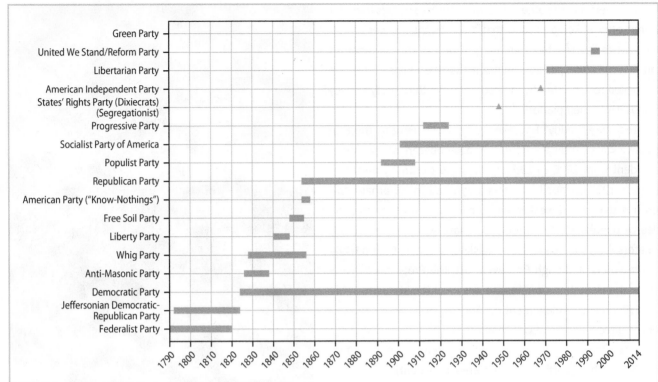

Figure 8.4 **American Political Parties, 1789–2014**

Note that the Democratic Party is the nation's oldest political party. The graph shows it beginning under President Andrew Jackson, but some argue that it actually began with President Thomas Jefferson's Democratic-Republicans.

→ KEY QUESTIONS:
What are the benefits and the risks of voting for a third-party candidate?

COMPARE WITH YOUR PEERS
MindTap® for American Government

Access the Political Parties Forum: Polling Activity—Hurricane Sandy and Politics.

Party spread throughout the Southwest into rural and urban areas from Texas to California, electing members to various local offices. Part of its legacy is the activation of Latinos into the political process and providing a gateway for Latinas; one notable veteran of the party is Rosie Castro, former Bexar County LRUP Chairwoman and mother of Secretary of Housing and Urban Development Julián Castro and his twin brother, Congressman Joaquín Castro (TX-20) (who is featured in Chapter 10, Congress).

The Tea Party

Third parties do not have to stand by themselves to have an impact on party politics; they can also be an influential force within one or more parties. For example, in 2010 and 2012, the Tea Party movement was very effective at supporting challengers to incumbents in primary elections in the Republican Party or supporting a third candidate in the general election. By one count, 129 candidates running for the House of Representatives and 9 candidates running for the U.S. Senate Congress in the 2010 elections affiliated themselves with the Tea Party.[23] Its message was fiscal responsibility, lower taxes, and paying down the national debt, and the Tea Party was successful in electing members of Congress, such as Senator Rand Paul (R-Ky.), who share its concern that the federal budget ought to be at the top of the American political agenda.[24]

More recently, the established wing of the Republican Party started to fight back against efforts to undermine incumbent Republicans or candidates that did not subscribe entirely to the Tea Party's agenda. In March 2014, Senator Mitch McConnell (R-KY), who was facing a Tea

Party challenger in his primary, was quoted as saying, "I think we will crush them everywhere." The first test of that came in Texas where a Tea Party challenger, Representative Steve Stockman, was in fact overwhelmingly defeated by the incumbent Republican candidate, John Cornyn, in the Senate primary. In the face of the enormous resources of the mainstream Republican Party, the Tea Party had more difficulty in 2014 recruiting and funding strong challengers to Republican incumbents in the House and Senate.[25]

The Tea Party movement, although not officially a political party, illustrates how third parties can force the two major political parties to be more responsive; in this case, the Tea Party has given voice to more conservative voters. When they are large enough, these groups have the potential to move the party platforms in new directions and, in turn, to change federal laws.[26] The Tea Party movement's success in defeating incumbent Republicans in primaries and in electing Republicans who espoused more conservative views has created a more polarized and less effective governing environment in Congress (see Chapter 6, Figure 6.4, and Chapter 10).

Senator Rand Paul (R-KY) is a favorite of the Tea Party and an example of a candidate who was supported by a faction of the party who went on to win a Senate seat. In Kentucky, Rand Paul defeated a candidate for the U.S. Senate who was supported by the more established wing of the Republican Party and went on to win the general election. Since then, he has championed Tea Party issues such as smaller federal government, reduced spending, and freedom from government surveillance.

Obstacles to Third Parties and Independents

Because third-party candidates can act as spoilers, the two major parties do everything they can to discourage them, from challenging signatures for ballot access in court to preventing them from participating in presidential debates. The Democrats and Republicans have controlled state legislatures and Congress for so long that they have successfully established gates within state electoral laws that favor a two-party system over a multiple-party system. In addition, without the backing of a major party to get out the vote, collect campaign contributions, and arrange for media coverage, most third-party and Independent candidates do not stand much chance of being elected. Consequently, voters who consider themselves Independents do not have the opportunity to vote for candidates who might be closest to them in terms of policy preferences.

Candidates who are elected from third parties have little influence in legislatures because parties shape the internal power structure there. The party that wins the majority of seats in the legislature becomes the majority party and consequently controls the legislative process. After the legislative session begins, members are asked to express their opinions in subcommittees, committees, and on the floor by voting with or against their party's proposed legislation, and it is rare that an alternative to the major party proposal is considered (see Chapter 10). Those who are elected as Independents, such as Senator Bernie Sanders (I-VT), have no party organization to join in the legislature. Independents must pledge to support one of the two major parties in order to sit on committees and perform their other responsibilities as

→ KEY QUESTIONS:
Should laws that discourage third parties be changed? What would be the effects in terms of government responsiveness?

→ KEY QUESTIONS:
What are the advantages and disadvantages of being an Independent?

→ KEY QUESTIONS:
How do interest groups encourage citizen participation in political parties? How do they limit it?

Public Policy and Political Parties:
Assault Weapons Ban

In Chapter 4, we explained how the Supreme Court has interpreted the provisions of the Second Amendment to allow individuals to own firearms. As we noted, gun control is a highly contested public policy area, especially between the Democrats and the Republicans. However, tragic events such as the shooting of former Congresswoman Gabby Giffords and six other people in Arizona; the Aurora, Colorado movie theatre shootings; and the Newtown school shootings have precipitated a national discussion surrounding the specific issue of banning assault weapons.

Although not all party members agree, the majority of self-identified Democrats favor stricter gun possession laws, and the majority of self-identified Republicans oppose restrictions on gun possession. In an October 2013 Gallup Poll, 77 percent of Democrats said they favored stricter gun control while 23 percent of Republicans agreed.[27] On the question of an assault weapons ban, however, the margin is closer, with 68 percent of Democrats in support compared to 39 percent of Republicans.[28]

During the 2012 presidential election, the Democratic Party made gun control part of its party platform, stating that "We can focus on effective enforcement of existing laws, especially strengthening our background check system, and we can work together to enact commonsense improvements—like reinstating the assault weapons ban and closing the gun show loophole—so that guns do not fall into the hands of those irresponsible, law-breaking few."[29] The Republican Party had a contrasting statement in their platform about the assault weapon ban, stating that "We oppose legislation that is intended to restrict our Second Amendment rights by limiting the capacity of clips or magazines or otherwise restoring the ill-considered Clinton gun ban."[30] By including these statements in their party's platforms during a presidential candidate, each party was staking out a distinct policy position designed to attract support from their base.

In Congress, these party differences are also strongly visible. For example, in the 113th Congress, Senator Feinstein (D-CA) introduced a bill to reinstate the assault weapons ban that would outlaw a number of types of firearms capable of holding large amounts of ammunition. Her bill, the Assault Weapons Ban of 2013, had twenty-four Senate cosponsors, all of whom are Democrats. In the House of Representatives, Representative Carolyn McCarthy (D-NY) introduced a bill with the same language, and there were eighty-one House cosponsors, all of whom are Democrats. However, because the House of Representatives was controlled by the Republicans, and Republicans in the Senate could filibuster the legislation, there was little to no chance that it would have passed. Despite the odds against passage, the assault weapons ban was an important focal point for Democrats to mobilize supporters of gun control.

Interest groups influence gun policy as well. The National Rifle Association (NRA), which is a large grassroots group and one of the most effective in the nation, figures prominently in the national discussion on a ban on assault weapons. Like many interest groups, the NRA has formed a PAC to contribute to campaigns. Most PACs contribute to incumbents, current members of Congress who are much more likely to win than challengers. Most PACs support incumbents from both parties. Unlike many groups, however, the NRA's PAC contributes overwhelmingly to candidates from one party: the Republican Party. In the 2011–2012 congressional election cycle, the NRA's affiliated PAC contributed a total of $984,037 to congressional campaigns, with 87 percent going to Republicans and 13 percent going to Democrats. Safari Club International, a group that promotes wildlife conservation and protects the rights of hunters, also throws its support primarily behind Republican candidates. Its Arizona-based PAC contributed $381,563 with 92 percent going to Republicans and 8 percent going to Democrats. There was only one group, the Brady Campaign to prevent gun violence, that overwhelmingly supported Democrats, contributing a total of $4,018 to pro-gun-control Democrats, and no funds to Republicans.[31] Campaign contributions are important and so is the potential to bring voters out the door to vote for candidates who support their policy positions. Political parties depend on interest groups who agree with their policy stances to help mobilize voters; without them, that job becomes much more difficult.

The issue of thwarting gun violence through gun control, with specific measures such as the assault weapon ban, will likely remain a strong source of division in parties at the top levels of the organizations, among party identifiers, and among members of Congress.

Construct Your Own Policy

1. Write a version of an assault weapons ban that you believe might attract more support from Republicans who are currently opposed to it.
2. Construct a strategy of cooperation between parties on the issue of gun violence that does not involve any new restrictions on gun ownership.

legislators. When he was elected to the Senate in 2006 and reelected in 2012, Sanders chose to caucus with the Democrats. When Angus King was elected to the Senate from Maine in 2012 as an Independent, he chose to subsequently caucus with the Democrats as well.

Challenges to Party Power from Interest Groups

In addition to challenges from third parties, the two major parties face challenges from established interest groups and from broader social groups formed at the grassroots of American politics (see Chapter 7, Interest Groups). These groups and movements draw attention to each party's failings in specific issue areas and engage in activities from staging protest rallies to nominating alternative candidates to run in primaries in order to get parties to move closer to the policy positions the group or movement advocates.

Over the past two decades, interest and social movement groups have become more tightly aligned with specific political parties, and that alignment has undermined their capacity to serve as independent checks on—or competitors with—political parties. For example, unions such as the Service Employees International Union (SEIU) and environmental groups such as the Sierra Club are generally supportive of the Democratic Party, whereas business groups such as the Chamber of Commerce and the National Rifle Association are supportive of the Republican Party. For interest groups, the risk in continuously supporting one party is that the party will take their support for granted. In fact, parties are most responsive to interest groups when they threaten to withdraw their support or start their own party organizations. Consequently, interest groups maintain their influence with political parties by constantly expressing their preferences on policies to party leaders and providing support only when the party is responsive to their concerns.

For example, on the issue of gun control, interest groups on both sides of the issue have been very active in lobbying elected officials and trying to persuade the public to support their preferred policy position.

Checkpoint

CAN YOU:

- Explain the median voter theorem
- Describe how a single-member plurality system encourages two parties
- Summarize the role third parties have played in American politics
- Survey the obstacles to third parties and Independent candidates
- Explain how interest groups and political parties have become more closely aligned

8.4 Party Alignment and Ideology

> Define partisan affiliation and ideology

Throughout U.S. history, there have been long stretches of time during which the party affiliations of voters remained stable, but there have also been key elections in which parties lost or gained significant blocs of voters. Scholars have tried to identify the factors that explain why voters make large, permanent shifts from one party to another. Shifts in party allegiance can occur when there is an external shock to the nation, such as an economic depression or a foreign military attack. Shifts can also occur when public attitudes change considerably, and one party appears to respond more quickly to those changes than another.

The Parties after the Civil War

Following the Civil War, as we have seen, the Republicans were dominant in the Northeast and West, and the Democrats were dominant in the South and increasingly in large cities with big immigrant populations. This **party alignment**—voters identifying with a party in repeated elections—was relatively stable until 1896, when a number of smaller parties challenged the Republican and Democratic Parties. The Republican Party emerged from that election with a victory, and the smaller parties faded from the national political scene.

From 1896 to 1932, the basic geographic pattern of party alignment stayed the same, but the combination of the stock market crash of October 24, 1929, a global depression that followed, and a drop in worldwide agricultural prices brought political trouble to the Republican Party. By 1932, voters in every part of the country were ready for a change, not only in political leadership but also in the entire approach to government.

The New Deal and the Role of Ideology in Party Politics

During the election of 1932, voters were exposed to a new political ideology, or set of consistent political views, about the way that the federal government could work. Today's voters might describe themselves as liberal or conservative, but voters before 1932 typically identified themselves with a political party. In that election year, Franklin Delano Roosevelt (1933–45), governor of New York State, ran for president on a platform designed to reverse the effects of the Great Depression. The idea that the federal government would help individuals to help themselves was transformative in American politics. The Democratic Party platform resonated with voters, and Roosevelt won the election.

After he took office, Roosevelt championed a vast array of new government programs that are commonly referred to as the New Deal. These programs were designed to help individuals

→ KEY QUESTIONS:
Should the federal government help individuals to help themselves?

who were jobless, homeless, or otherwise in financial need. Essentially the New Deal was a promise by the federal government to provide a safety net for workers and their families who fell on hard times. Following his electoral victory in 1932, Roosevelt built a coalition of white southerners, working-class ethnic northerners, advocates for liberal social policies, and northern African Americans who had previously been Republicans. This was a radical shift for African Americans, who since the Civil War had followed the party of Abraham Lincoln and shunned the Democrats, whom they associated with racism and slavery. This electoral coalition was large but fragile, and Roosevelt engaged in a great deal of political balancing and a wide distribution of government benefits to maintain it.

In his campaign for president in 1932, Franklin Delano Roosevelt introduced an innovative campaign platform. "I pledge you," he said, "I pledge myself, to a new deal for the American people." The term "New Deal" came to describe federal programs that took an active role in helping individual citizens find jobs, save for retirement, and benefit from fair working conditions.

In supporting the New Deal, voters came to accept the ideological viewpoint that government involvement in the economic aspects of individuals' lives was legitimate and, on balance, a good thing. As we noted in Chapter 1, Gateways to American Democracy, this perspective on government serves as a foundation for the modern definition of a liberal. Today the liberal viewpoint builds on the New Deal perspective by favoring government redistribution of income through higher taxes on the wealthy to provide social benefits, such as health care, unemployment insurance, and welfare payments to the poor. Those who opposed the New Deal are the forefathers of the modern conservatives, who believe in lower taxes and less government involvement in economic life.

In response to Roosevelt's big government approach, the Republicans seized what they saw as the main weakness of the New Deal, which was the high cost of all these newly created programs. To pay for them, the federal and state governments would have to raise taxes on businesses and workers alike. The Republicans recognized that they had an opportunity to reshape their party platform to exploit the Democrats' weakness.

In the aftermath of 1932, the two parties transformed; it was almost as if they had switched places. The Democrats changed from a party that believed in states' rights, low taxes, and little government intervention in individuals' lives to the party that created a large social safety net that relied on the federal government to ensure personal economic stability. The Republicans changed from a party that believed in a strong central federal government and in intervention in the economy when necessary to the party of a strictly limited federal government and fiscal responsibility.

Voters responded to these partisan and ideological changes by changing their own party allegiances over time, essentially producing a **realignment** of the electorate. In the broadest sense, today's Democrats generally support expanding the size of government to accomplish specific policy goals, even if it means raising taxes, and support liberal social values. In contrast, Republicans generally support limiting the size of government by keeping taxation and regulation of the economy to a minimum and support preserving conservative social values.

Civil Rights, the Great Society, and Nixon's Southern Strategy

The Democratic and Republican Parties remained divided mainly along this economic dimension until the early 1960s, when the Democratic Party established itself as the party of civil rights for African Americans. During the presidency of Lyndon Baines Johnson (1963–69), the Civil Rights Act of 1964, the Voting Rights Act of 1965, the Department of Housing and Urban Development Act of 1965, and the Fair Housing Act of 1966 were all signed into law. These acts gave the federal government strong enforcement powers to guarantee African Americans the fullest extent of the civil rights afforded to every American and served as a key gateway for full political participation by African Americans. Johnson's policies brought a second dimension to liberal ideology: Now the federal government was granted the power not only to help individuals in need economically but also to take affirmative steps to overrule state and local governments to prevent discrimination on all levels. As noted in Chapter 5, Civil Rights, the government's role evolved from preventing unequal treatment under the law to ensuring equality in all walks of life, from education to employment to housing.

By putting the stamp of the Democratic Party on the pledge to preserve civil rights, Johnson appealed to those who opposed segregation. Today African Americans remain the most loyal of any demographic constituency in the Democratic Party. In 2004, 88 percent of

→ KEY QUESTIONS:
How does the realignment that followed the election of 1932 echo the divisions between the Federalists and the Antifederalists? Or is the political ideology of the modern era entirely different?

→ KEY QUESTIONS:
Which perspective comes closest to your own views— liberal or conservative?

realignment:
Long-term shift in voter allegiance from one party to another.

African American voters chose the Democratic candidate, John Kerry, over President George W. Bush.[32] In 2008, 95 percent of African American voters chose the Democratic candidate, Barack Obama, who was elected as the nation's first African American president.[33] In 2010, a nonpresidential election year, 89 percent of African American voters cast their ballots for Democratic candidates for Congress.[34] In 2012, 93 percent of African American voters cast their ballot for the Democratic incumbent, President Obama.[35]

The Johnson administration also expanded federal programs that granted aid to individuals and to state and local governments in the areas of health care, education, housing, job training, and welfare to families with children (see Chapter 11, The Presidency, for an extensive discussion of Johnson's programs). This set of policies was called the Great Society and was founded on the idea that federal expansion would strengthen American society by helping all citizens reach their potential. By expanding the reach of the federal government this way, Johnson reinforced the liberal ideological underpinnings of the Democratic Party.

→ KEY QUESTIONS:
What would the Federalists think of the federal government today? What would the Antifederalists think?

As this shift in Democratic policies occurred, Republicans saw a new opportunity to attract support from voters who opposed the expansion of the federal government into race relations or the regulation of the economy. Beginning with the campaign of Barry Goldwater in 1964 and continuing with the campaigns of Richard M. Nixon (1969–74) in 1968 and, to a more limited extent, of Ronald Reagan (1981–89) in 1980, the Republicans employed a so-called southern strategy, presenting themselves to southern white voters as holding views on civil rights and race that were opposite those of the Democrats.

Although Republicans did not sanction racism and discrimination, they made it clear that they would not take the same strong steps as the Democrats to impose federal law on states to remedy these problems. Republicans extended their philosophy of limited government intervention by asserting that each state was responsible for enforcing civil rights and that the federal government was overstepping its bounds by interfering at the state and local levels. At the same time, Republicans opposed the Great Society policies as too expensive, and they were philosophically opposed to the federal government giving so much aid directly to individuals without asking for something in return. In this way, the Republican Party continued to move toward a more conservative ideology that sought to limit the powers and programs of the federal government.

The Reagan Revolution and Conservative Party Politics

In 1980, Ronald Reagan, former Republican governor of California, defeated the incumbent President Jimmy Carter (1977–81), a Democrat, partly by appealing to those who opposed the Supreme Court's legalization of abortion in *Roe v. Wade* (1973). Following the ruling, the national stance of the parties diverged, with the Democratic Party publicly supporting the decision and the Republican Party split on the issue. When Reagan won the Republican Party's presidential nomination, he moved the Republicans more firmly into the anti-abortion camp. In the general election, Reagan's campaign offered a consistent conservative ideology that focused on limiting the size of the federal government, opposing abortion, and allowing religious prayer in public schools, which had been prohibited by the Supreme Court ruling in *Engel v. Vitale* in 1962 (see Chapter 4 for further discussion of prayer in school).[36] Reagan's campaign strategy was designed to attract conservative Democrats who were alienated by their party's official position on abortion and to attract the growing numbers of active evangelical Christian voters, especially in the South.

Reagan also took advantage of the instability in foreign relations that marked Jimmy Carter's four years in office. Although Carter had increased defense spending for the military while in office, he focused on protecting human rights. For Reagan, protecting individual political freedom was a moral obligation for the United States. Reagan campaigned on a strong defense and tough foreign policy that actively promoted freedom, and he made it clear that, under his administration, the United States would work to undermine the Communist political and economic system that was dominant in the Soviet Union, eastern Europe, and Cuba.

The combination of these issues brought Reagan the support of many working-class, ethnic, northern voters and southern white voters. These voters were subsequently referred to as Reagan Democrats, and it was in large part due to them that Ronald Reagan won the presidential election of 1980.

Although the Republicans held the presidency for the next twelve years, many of the voters who supported Republicans at the national level stayed loyal to the Democrats in congressional, state, and local elections, especially in the South. This split-ticket voting made it hard for parties to sustain complete voter allegiance at all levels of elected office.

→ KEY QUESTIONS:
What are the advantages and disadvantages of split-ticket voting? Is it best to be an Independent?

The Modern Partisan Landscape

Bill Clinton was governor of Arkansas when he successfully ran for president in 1992. As had Reagan, Clinton changed his party's direction with a campaign platform that advocated dropping opposition to the death penalty, facilitating free trade, and promising a middle-class tax cut. These policies moved the Democrats away from liberal policies, but Clinton still ran under the established Democratic Party label. Clinton thus appealed to a wider range of voters, and he was able to recapture some electoral territory the Democrats had lost in the southern states.

→ KEY QUESTIONS:
Is realignment a generational change of the social contract?

In office, however, Clinton lost popularity by veering away from core issues such as the middle-class tax cut and economic growth to address socially liberal policies on abortion and gays in the military, which he had given far less emphasis to on the campaign trail. This political misstep set the stage for a Republican Party resurgence.

Presidential nominees typically make an acceptance speech at their party's convention when they are nominated to run. Here we see Bill Clinton, then governor of Arkansas, greeting convention delegates in New York City in 1992 when he was nominated to run for president for the first time.

In the 1994 midterm congressional elections, Republicans took control of both the House and the Senate for the first time since 1954. Led by Newt Gingrich, a Republican House member from Georgia, the Republicans put forth a party platform called the Contract with America, which promised ten major policy initiatives, such as a balanced federal budget and less federal regulation. Every Republican candidate for the House signed it, and by coordinating candidates this way, the Republican Party presented a single national message to voters about what it would do if it won control of Congress. In addition, Gingrich strategically targeted seats in the South that were held by conservative Democrats, trying to appeal to the same set of southern voters who elected Ronald Reagan. Republican efforts were successful, finally overcoming the split-ticket voting of southern voters who had previously voted Democratic in congressional elections.[37]

At the presidential level, George W. Bush, the son of former President George H. W. Bush and a conservative Republican governor of Texas, built on the momentum of the Republicans to launch a successful bid for the presidency in 1999. Josh McKoon's first paid job on a presidential campaign was working for Bush in South Carolina to get out the college-age vote.

In 2006, the Democrats began to regain electoral momentum with voters who self-identified as Democrats but had not been voting that way in recent elections, as well as with Independent voters. That year, there were powerful short-term forces, such as corruption scandals and the Iraq War, which put voters in a particularly sour mood toward incumbent Republicans.

The results of the 2008 elections, however, were a sign that the party landscape was shifting again[38] (see Figure 8.5). Clearly the election of an African American president is a significant turning point in race relations; Barack Obama received 43 percent of the white vote in 2008, 2 percentage points higher than John Kerry, a white Democrat, received in 2004.

→ KEY QUESTIONS:
Do political parties help voters hold government responsible? Why?

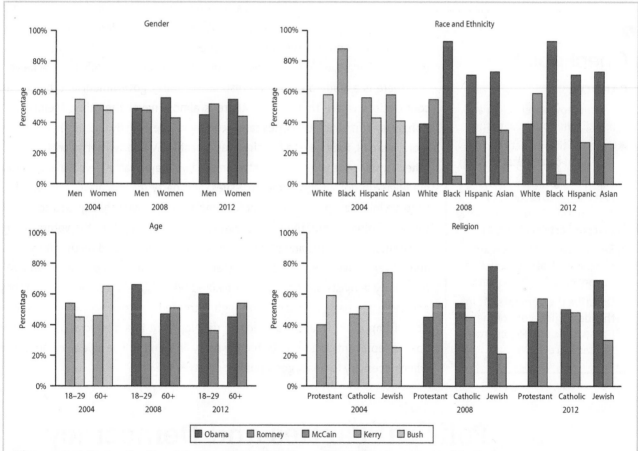

Figure 8.5 Votes for President in 2004, 2008, and 2012 by Demographic Group

Patterns of support among voters can change from one election to the next, depending on the candidate the party chooses as its nominee.

NEW YORK TIMES, HTTP://ELECTIONS.NYTIMES.COM.

responsible parties: *Parties that take responsibility for offering the electorate a distinct range of policies and programs, thus providing a clear choice.*

→ KEY QUESTIONS:

What are the advantages and disadvantages of responsible parties?

→ KEY QUESTIONS:

Do you think partisanship is taking precedence over policy making? What can be done about that?

→ KEY QUESTIONS:

Are consensus and compromise good or bad for American democracy? Give examples.

Checkpoint

CAN YOU:

▪ Explain how voters align and realign with political parties

▪ Describe the impact of the New Deal on political ideology

▪ Explain how the Democratic Party came to be seen by African Americans as the party that supported civil rights

▪ Recall how Ronald Reagan's campaign strategy appealed to conservative Democrats

▪ Describe the general shift in the ideological core of the Democratic and Republican Parties since 1994

Obama won five states that had been considered solidly Republican in previous presidential elections: Florida, Indiana, North Carolina, Ohio, and Virginia.

However, when voters give one party majority party control of the White House and Congress, they have high expectations for a strong governing track record. In one way, that is what political scientists mean by **responsible parties**; if the parties offer voters clear choices, voters can hold the party in charge responsible for policy outcomes. When President Obama and the Democrats took charge of government in 2009, they faced some of the greatest economic challenges since the Great Depression, as well as ongoing wars in Iraq and Afghanistan. Additionally, Obama and the Democrats in Congress set out to build on the Great Society legacy of government social policy by passing the Affordable Care Act to make health insurance available to all Americans. The 2010 congressional midterm elections were the first opportunity that voters had to register their satisfaction or dissatisfaction with the president and his party, and they did so by giving Republicans control of the House of Representatives and electing more Republicans to the Senate. The Democratic losses and Republican gains showed the responsible party system in action, because voters held the incumbent majority party accountable for its performance on the economy, health care, and the ongoing wars.

However, in 2012, Barack Obama won reelection by a margin of 51 to 47 percent and a margin of 5 million votes, although his share of the white vote declined to 39 percent.[39] From the president's perspective, winning reelection as an incumbent was a reaffirmation of his—and by extension—the Democratic Party's policy agenda. At the same time, Republicans held on to their majority control of the House of Representatives, and the Democrats held on to the U.S. Senate, which made responsible party government difficult to achieve.

There is a trade-off between responsible party government and bipartisan cooperation; where there is one, there is almost never the other. Members of Congress from opposite parties rarely communicate directly with each other anymore; instead, they take to the airwaves on cable TV and Twitter to criticize each other. Despite the wide divide between the two major parties, within each party, members do not always agree on issues, and party leaders are not always able to forge internal cooperation. Elected officials are constantly exposed to a wide range of opinions, and they face pressures to respond both to the voters and to party elites. Politicians and party activists can communicate directly with voters, and citizens have many ways to register their opinions on most issues. In addition, party activists are able to track elected officials and monitor how well they adhere to the party's policies. Although increased participation in the deliberation of important issues is a welcome development in a democracy, it makes it hard to represent constituents, toe the party line, and still be able to compromise when necessary to enact good public policy.

Political Parties and Democracy

Political parties, which emerged in the nation's first decade, now play a major role in American democracy. The Democrats and the Republicans together claim the allegiance of more than 90 percent of voters when one includes strong identifiers and voters who consistently lean toward one party.[40] Political parties determine the choices voters have at the polls by crafting the laws that allow candidates to be on the ballot and overseeing the primaries that allow voters to choose candidates. Parties also recruit candidates for elected office, raise funds for campaigns, register voters, and organize get-out-the-vote drives. In sum, parties shape the selection of candidates who seek, run for, and win elected office.

Do political parties make it easier for voters to hold elected officials accountable? Party platforms tell voters what candidates intend to do if elected, and voters can compare their actions against their campaign pledges. If pledges and policies match up, voters typically reelect the officials; if they do not, voters can vote for the opponents in the next election. One advantage of clear dividing lines between the parties is that it makes the job of monitoring the government easier for the average voter. However, such clear divisions also bring the disadvantages of conflict and stalemate that make bipartisan policy making difficult.

Parties do a mixed job of promoting equal political participation among all citizens. On the one hand, they are a gateway to participation because membership in a political party is free, and citizens can work a little or a lot on behalf of the party. Primaries and caucuses give every party member a say in determining who will represent the party in elected office, and they force candidates who seek the party's endorsement to shape their campaign platforms according to party voters' preferences. Because voters are free to join and leave political parties as frequently as they wish, parties are always seeking to represent their members' viewpoints.

On the other hand, parties can discourage political participation by putting obstacles in the way of third-party formation. The U.S. party system is structured around two major parties, and even though third parties have arisen at various times, they are quickly subsumed or defeated by one of the two major parties. The two-party system reduces major policy issues to two-sided questions, when, in fact, the complexity of these issues warrants multiple perspectives. The problem for democracy is that there is no formal venue for presenting multiple perspectives in elections or in the governing institutions.

The larger question is whether the twenty-first-century U.S. party system fulfills the role of enabling widespread participation in the governing process. In terms of responding to changes in public opinion, political parties fall short of meeting their responsibilities as agents of democratic government. They are large, entrenched organizations with multiple layers—federal, state, and local—that can differ in their viewpoints on specific issues. The breadth of the national parties makes it difficult to reach internal consensus on issues at every level of government.

The combination of intraparty divisions with interparty polarization and conflict has produced a party-dominated democracy that is not consistently responsive to voters' interests and opinions. However, in a democracy, power rests on winning elections, and for that, parties will always depend on voters like you, who hold the power to change them by staying loyal or switching your allegiance.

CONNECT WITH YOUR CLASSMATES
MindTap for American Government

Access the Political Parties Forum: Discussion—Working Together After Elections.

Master the Concept
of Political Parties with the MindTap™ for American Government

 REVIEW MindTap™ **for American Government**
Access Key Term Flashcards for Chapter 8.

 STAY CURRENT MindTap™ **for American Government**
Access the KnowNow blog and customized RSS for updates on current events.

 TEST YOURSELF MindTap™ **for American Government**
Take the Wrap It Up Quiz for Chapter 8.

 STAY FOCUSED MindTap™ **for American Government**
Complete the Focus Activities for Political Parties.

 # Key Concepts

Australian ballot (p. 245). How did the Australian ballot reduce the party boss's control over election outcomes?

ballot (p. 237). What types of ballots were used before electronic voting?

caucus (p. 239). How is a caucus different from a primary?

general election (p. 237). What is the role of parties in general elections?

majority vote (p. 247). What is the difference between plurality and majority vote?

median voter theorem (p. 247). Why does the median voter theorem contribute to limited political choice?

national committees (p. 234). What are the responsibilities of the national committees?

party alignment (p. 255). Is party alignment stable today?

party caucus (p. 234). Which form of the party—party in the electorate, party in government, party as an organization—are party caucuses affiliated with and why?

party platform (p. 232). What role do party platforms play in electoral politics?

patronage system (p. 244). How did the patronage system strengthen political parties?

plurality vote (p. 247). How does plurality voting encourage third parties?

political parties (p. 232). How are political parties a gateway to democracy?

primary election (p. 237). When did primaries first emerge in U.S. politics?

proportional representation (p. 239). How does proportional representation work?

realignment (p. 256). What precipitates a realignment?

responsible parties (p. 260). How does a responsible party system produce accountability?

single-member plurality system (p. 247). Why does a single-member plurality system promote a two-party system?

third parties (p. 243). Are third parties viable options in the United States?

winner-take-all system (p. 239). What are the advantages and disadvantages of a winner-take-all system?

Learning Outcomes: What You Need . . .

To Know	To Test Yourself	To Participate

▶ Outline how political parties evolved in American politics

They have one primary purpose: to win elections in order to control government power and implement their policies. Parties organize the electorate by giving them choices of policies and candidates, and they also organize Congress and state legislatures into cohesive groups that consistently vote for the policies that they promise in their platforms. Parties nominate candidates for office in primary elections, which are open to all voters, although in some states voters must affiliate with a party before voting.

- Define political party.
- Identify the three arenas in which parties operate.
- Track the party nomination process.

- Design a system that allows the greatest number of voters to participate in choosing the party nominee.

▶ Identify which issues divided the first political parties

The basic division between the Federalists and the Antifederalists over the ratification of the Constitution survived into the Washington administration to become factions; by the time of Jefferson's election in 1800, the factions had become political parties. Between 1800 and the Civil War, various parties rose and fell, but since the end of the war, the two major parties—the Democratic Party and the Republican Party— have dominated the American political system.

- Explain the differences between the Federalists and the Antifederalists.
- Describe the events that opened up the presidential nomination process.
- Explain how the Republican Party formed.
- Connect patronage and party power.
- Describe reforms that reduced party power.

- Design your own political party, identify which issues to focus on, and explain how you would attract members; explain why your party would be more accountable than the existing two other major parties.

▶ Explain why two parties dominate the U.S. political system

The effects of the two-party system are to limit voter choices to "for" and "against" and to discourage third parties, although the issues third parties arise to address are frequently adopted by one of the major political parties.

- Explain the median voter theorem.
- Describe how a single-member plurality system encourages two parties.
- Summarize the role third parties have played in American politics.
- Survey the obstacles to third parties and independent candidates.
- Explain how interest groups and political parties have become more closely aligned.

- Imagine yourself as head of the Tea Party, and devise a strategy that would enable this third party to win the presidency.

▶ Define partisan affiliation and ideology

Voter realignments occur when the parties readjust the focus of their policies, typically as a result of a major event such as an economic depression or a military conflict. Since Franklin D. Roosevelt's New Deal of the 1930s, liberals have generally aligned with the Democratic Party and conservatives with the Republican Party. The modern political landscape is marked by a partisan divide, with the parties taking on starker opposing positions and ramping up the rhetoric to the point that voters sometimes wonder if partisanship is taking precedence over policy making.

- Explain how voters align and realign with political parties.
- Describe the impact of the New Deal on political ideology.
- Explain how the Democratic Party came to be seen by African Americans as the party that supported civil rights.
- Recall how Ronald Reagan's campaign strategy appealed to conservative Democrats.
- Describe the general shift in the ideological core of the Democratic and Republican Parties since 1994.

- Identify three issues that you believe cut across ideological dividing lines. How would you encourage lawmakers to use these issues as examples of how to work together?

BRIGHAM YOU

THE WORLD IS OUR C

"It's my hope I'll be reelected to serve this community. . . . There's a lot of work we still have to do to fight for the middle class and make sure every Arizonan has a shot at the American dream."

KYRSTEN SINEMA
Brigham Young University

Elections, Campaigns, and Voting

Congresswoman Kyrsten Sinema (D-AZ) is unconventional. Just consider her educational background. She graduated high school at the age of 16 in Arizona as valedictorian and graduated Brigham Young University (BYU) in 1995 at the age of 18. She earned a master's degree in social work in 1999, a JD in 2004, and her PhD in Justice Studies in 2012—all from Arizona State University. Sinema also has a strong bipartisan streak—again something unusual these days. She first ran for state legislature in 2002 as an independent, but after losing the race, ran as a Democrat in 2004 and won. In the Arizona State Legislature, she worked closely with Republicans on legislation tied to human trafficking. In her race for Congress in 2012, the *Arizona Republic*, the local Phoenix newspaper, endorsed her for her nonpartisan style, arguing that for "Sinema, it's always about the issue, not the personalities."[1] Finally, Sinema's personal choices make her unique: Although raised in a conservative Mormon family, she is the first openly bisexual person elected to Congress. In an era when the country has become quite use to openly gay politicians, her sexuality drew quite a bit of attention. She was not fond of the attention either, explaining that "I'm not a pioneer. I'm just a regular person who works hard."[2]

Yet Sinema is a pioneer. She uses the political process as a gateway to make a difference for the better. During her childhood, she faced some hard times as a child, living for a time in an abandoned gas station without electricity or running water.[3] Those early experiences shaped her life and convinced her to get involved and make the lives of people better. She supported the DREAM Act as a member of the Arizona State Legislature. She also fought to rein in

Maricopa County Sheriff Joe Arpaio's hard-line immigration stances, which often drew attention across the entire country.[4] She hired undocumented DREAM activist Erika Andiola (featured in Chapter 5, Civil Rights) on her staff—a strong signal about her position on that issue. Since being in the U.S. Congress, she has focused a good deal of attention on issues tied to veterans. She argues that "our country has a

Need to Know

9.1 Describe the ideas that molded the Framers' thinking about elections.

9.2 Outline the steps in presidential campaigns.

9.3 Identify the issues that shape presidential campaigns.

9.4 Determine which issues shape congressional campaigns.

9.5 Explain why there are battles over ballot access.

9.6 Outline how the right to vote has expanded.

9.7 Identify who tends to turn out in American elections.

9.8 Articulate the main theoretical approaches that explain voting.

9.9 Evaluate how low turnout is in American elections.

9.10 Analyze how changes in voting laws have affected participation rates.

 WATCH & LEARN MindTap™ for American Government
Watch a brief "What Do You Know?" video summarizing Elections and Campaigning for Office.

moral responsibility to do right by the men and woman who serve in our military."[5]

In 2012, she won an open seat for a new district that arose from the redistricting following the 2010 Census. In this fairly competitive district, she won the election with about 49 percent of the vote. Her Republican opponent, Vernon Parker, garnered 45 percent, and a Libertarian candidate secured about 6 percent of the vote. As a first-term member of Congress from a competitive district, she faced a tough battle for reelection. And having tackled the tough issues in Congress and being openly bisexual, she faced harsh attacks. But Simena knew from the moment she won in 2012 that 2014 would not be easy. Knowing that, she has raised a good deal of money to not only respond to any attacks but also to send signals to potential challengers that she is more than capable of competing for votes. Even in a Republican year, Sinema won 54 percent of the vote. Interestingly, her campaign only ran positive ads. She wanted to advance her reputation as an atypical politician. Sinema also benefited from that fact that her opponent, Wendy Rogers, would not even debate her. Sinema's ability to raise money

was a huge advantage. She's a very successful fundraiser—a fact that should help her in future re-election efforts.

Elections, campaigns, and voting, as the experience of Kyrsten Sinema demonstrates, offer a gateway into the American political system. They provide many opportunities for participation, not only running for office but also volunteering and working at the polls. During campaigns, candidates offer competing visions of the role of government and promise to enact specific policies. The people decide to support a candidate and a campaign program when they go to the polls. Elections provide the most common (and easiest) gateway for the people to express their opinions and to hold elected officials accountable. In combination, elections, campaigns, and voting offer the public a chance to shape the course of government. In this chapter, we examine how elections, campaigns, and voting work, asking whether, and how, these institutions promote government responsiveness and equality for citizens. The chapter also addresses other forms of participation that help hold government accountable. Finally, we look at recent and future public policy concerning participation and voting.

9.1 The Constitutional Requirements for Elections

> Describe the ideas that molded the Framers' thinking about elections

→ KEY QUESTIONS:
Why did the Framers set up gates against popular participation in elections?

LISTEN & LEARN
MindTap for American Government

Access Read Speaker to listen to Chapter 9.

Given the importance of elections to the democratic process, it is surprising that the Constitution says so little about them. The requirements that the Constitution lays out for elections indicate that the Framers wanted to set up barriers against direct democracy. Only the House of Representatives was to be elected directly by the people. In elections for the president and for the Senate, the public's role was indirect and complex. Today, senators are elected directly by the people. Presidential elections also give citizens more say in the process, but these contests continue to be shaped by constitutional requirements that serve as a gate between the people and the presidency. In this section, we explain the constitutional requirements for American elections as background for understanding the ways in which presidential and congressional campaigns are run.

Presidential Elections

→ KEY QUESTIONS:
Why did the Framers give so much authority over presidential elections to the states?

The constitutional rules governing the selection of the president reflect three fundamental themes that guided the Framers' thinking. First, the states were given broad discretion on key matters regarding presidential elections to ensure their importance and to counterbalance the power of the national government. Second, the Framers designed the presidency with George Washington in mind and did not spell out all aspects in great detail, including elections. Over time, the details were filled in. Third, the presidency was intended to stand above party politics, doing what was right for the nation rather than supporting one faction over another. That assumption went awry early on, and parties formed almost from the start.

The Electoral College.   The means by which the president of the United States is elected was born of compromise between the interests of the states and the interests of the people, yielding a system that even today is indirect and confusing. Like the Connecticut Compromise that produced a legislature with an upper chamber to represent the states and a lower chamber to represent the people, the system for electing the president was intended to be similarly balanced. The formal selection of the president is in the hands of electors, who collectively constitute the **Electoral College**.

The Constitution gave state legislatures the responsibility of deciding how best to choose electors. Because state legislators were, for the most part, elected by the people, this arrangement gave the public an indirect say in the choice. The idea was that the state legislatures would serve as gatekeepers against rash or ignorant voters. There was little support among the Framers for letting the people choose the president directly. In fact, during the debates at the Constitutional Convention, George Mason said that allowing the people to select the president would be like referring "a trial of colors to a blind man."[6] Today the people of each state, not the members of state legislatures, choose the electors in an arrangement that has given citizens a new gateway for influence (see Figure 9.1).

The electors, however, remain the formal decision makers for choosing the president. They are selected in a variety of ways in the fifty states. Before the election, each party lines up electors for its candidate. In the 2012 presidential elections, when Barack Obama won the most votes in the state of California, his electors were chosen to serve in the Electoral College. Republican candidate Mitt Romney had different electors ready to serve if he had won. Both Romney and Obama chose people they could trust to be loyal to them. This is important because many states allow electors to vote their conscience; they are not bound by the results of the election in their state. However, electors who deviate from the candidate to whom they are pledged are rare.

Each state receives a number of electoral votes equal to its number of senators and members of the House of Representatives. The minimum is three, because every state has at least one House member and two senators. In 2012, seven states (Alaska, Delaware, Montana, North Dakota, South Dakota, Vermont, and Wyoming) and the District of Columbia had only three votes each in the Electoral College. With fifty-five electoral votes, California had the most. In all but two states, all the state's electoral votes are allocated to the candidate who finishes first in the voting. This winner-take-all system means that if a candidate wins California by just a single vote, that candidate gets all fifty-five of the state's electoral votes. The two exceptions are Nebraska and Maine, which allocate votes by congressional district and so can split their electoral votes. In 2008, Barack Obama won one congressional district in Nebraska, securing one of Nebraska's five electoral votes. This was the only time either state split its votes.

To win the presidency, a candidate needs to win a majority (270) of the 538 electoral votes (538 is the total of 435 representatives and 100 senators plus 3 votes from the District of Columbia, whose residents can vote for president but do not have representation in

Electoral College:
The presidential electors, selected every four years to represent the votes of their respective states, who meet to cast the electoral votes for president and vice president.

→ KEY QUESTIONS:
Is the winner-take-all system fair?

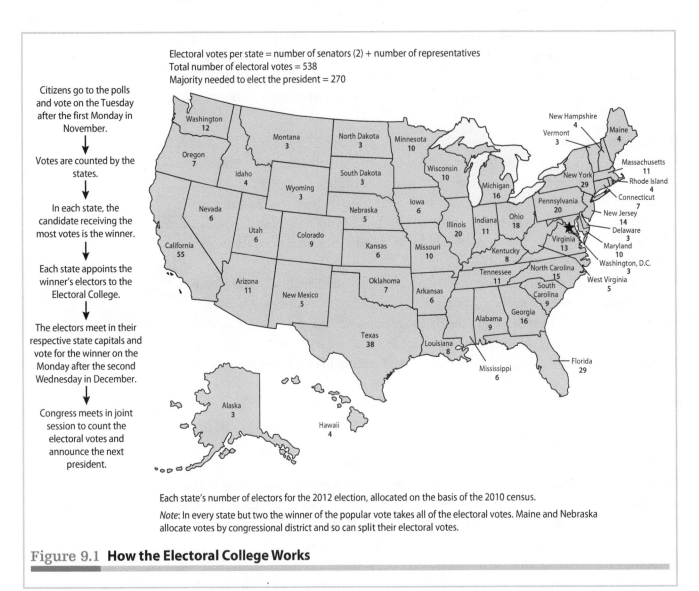

Electoral votes per state = number of senators (2) + number of representatives
Total number of electoral votes = 538
Majority needed to elect the president = 270

Citizens go to the polls and vote on the Tuesday after the first Monday in November.

↓

Votes are counted by the states.

↓

In each state, the candidate receiving the most votes is the winner.

↓

Each state appoints the winner's electors to the Electoral College.

↓

The electors meet in their respective state capitals and vote for the winner on the Monday after the second Wednesday in December.

↓

Congress meets in joint session to count the electoral votes and announce the next president.

Each state's number of electors for the 2012 election, allocated on the basis of the 2010 census.

Note: In every state but two the winner of the popular vote takes all of the electoral votes. Maine and Nebraska allocate votes by congressional district and so can split their electoral votes.

Figure 9.1 How the Electoral College Works

© CENGAGE LEARNING®

Congress). If no one wins a majority of electoral votes, the election is thrown into the House of Representatives. At this point, each state delegation gets a single vote, and the candidate who wins a majority of the states becomes the next president. That last happened in 1824.

Problems with the Electoral College. The Electoral College has never worked as the Framers envisioned, as an institution that would allow a group of independent decision makers to get together in the many states and deliberate over whom would make the best president. The Framers viewed the presidency as a contest between individuals, not between political parties, and in the first four presidential elections (1789, 1792, 1796, and 1800), electors cast ballots for their top two choices; the winner became president, and the second-place finisher became vice president. The process ignored the parties of the candidates; the goal was to select the most qualified person. In 1796, the process yielded John Adams (1797–1801) as president and his chief rival, Thomas Jefferson, as vice president. Just imagine Mitt Romney becoming Barack Obama's vice president!

Problems increased in 1800, when political parties had fully emerged. Thomas Jefferson and Aaron Burr, both running as Democratic-Republicans, received the same number of Electoral

College votes, even though everyone knew that Jefferson was seeking the presidency and Burr the vice presidency. Adams, who was also running again as a Federalist, finished third. Because there was no outright majority in the Electoral College, and Burr would not concede, a lengthy battle in the House ensued, lasting thirty-seven ballots before Thomas Jefferson (1801–1809) won the presidency. The Twelfth Amendment, adopted in 1804, fixed this problem by combining the vote for president and vice president into one ballot, with the person running for each office named.

→ KEY QUESTIONS:
How did the emergence of political parties change the way the Framers hoped elections would work?

Electoral College Reform.   The biggest problem with the Electoral College occurs when winning the nation's popular vote does not automatically translate into a win in the Electoral College, meaning that the individual who received fewer votes could become the president. This happened in the 1824, 1876, 1888, and 2000 presidential elections. Such outcomes raise questions about equality. If a democracy rests on the idea of majority rule—that is, the candidate with the most support in the public wins the election—then four or five presidential elections (about 10 percent) have been undemocratic.

Some may wonder why the country does not just change the rules to select the president through the popular vote. This method would appear more democratic because all votes would be treated equally. But the current system has some advantages. For example, the Electoral College system encourages candidates to secure support in all corners of the country, not just in areas with dense populations. A system of popular votes would privilege Los Angeles over New Hampshire. In America's federal system, the states do matter. Eliminating the Electoral College would decrease the role of the states, dampening the significance of state interests. There are also practical problems. Doing away with the Electoral College through a constitutional amendment would be difficult because it is unlikely that three-quarters of the states, needed to ratify an amendment, would support such a reform. Small states see merit in the system.

→ KEY QUESTIONS:
Should the Electoral College be eliminated? What would be the consequences?

The 2000 Presidential Election.   Because elections are a centerpiece of democracy, it is important for them to be viewed as fair. The events surrounding the 2000 presidential election tested the credibility of the American electoral process. The margin between Vice President Albert Gore Jr. and George W. Bush (2001–2009) was razor thin. In the popular vote, Gore received nearly 600,000 more votes than Bush—just a 0.5 percentage point difference (48.4 percent to 47.9 percent). The number of electoral votes did not identify a winner on election night because the state of Florida was too close to call, and without that state's electoral votes, neither candidate had the necessary 270 votes. Bush led in Florida by 537 votes out of 5.8 million votes cast—a 0.0001 percent difference. Demands for a recount ensued, and the Florida recount revealed how difficult it is to produce an accurate vote count. A series of court cases resulted in a Supreme Court decision that determined the outcome of the election (in *Bush v. Gore* [2000]).

Many votes had not been counted in Florida, and some had been counted for the wrong candidate. Citizens across the country lost faith in American elections. Since that time, the public's confidence has been restored. By 2008, only one in twenty Americans had doubts about whether his or her vote had been counted. By 2012, such questions were not even asked by pollsters. In short, the controversy surrounding the Gore-Bush contest raised distrust in the short run but did little lasting damage to the nation's electoral institutions. The overall credibility of American elections becomes even clearer when contrasted to that of other countries. Russia, for example, holds elections, but there is little evidence to believe they advance democracy (see Global Gateways: Elections in Russia).

globalgateways
Elections in Russia

On March 6, 2012, Vladimir Putin was elected president of Russia by a margin of 65 percent of the votes cast.* He had already served two terms as president (2000–2008) but was barred from running for a third consecutive term, so he stepped down in 2008 and assumed the post of prime minister. But in 2012, he was allowed to run again for the presidency. Before the presidential contest, in parliamentary (Duma) elections held at the end of 2011, Putin's party had lost seats but retained control of the legislature with a small majority.

Vocal protests against Putin and his party began with the Duma elections and continued after the presidential elections. Protesters claimed that the elections were unfair and marred by voter fraud as well as by issues concerning the separation of government and party and infringement on freedom of speech.† These protests further undermined Russia's standing in the world by calling into question the legitimacy of those elected.

Free and fair elections are a key component of a democratic society. In a measure of the quality of a democracy, the Economist Intelligence Unit of *The Economist* ranks 167 independent states and 2 territories in the following five categories in Masy 2014: electoral process and pluralism, civil liberties, functioning of government, political

participation, and political culture. The United States, which is considered a full democracy, is ranked 19th and gets high marks for its electoral process and pluralism, with a value of 8.11 on a 10.0 scale. In stark contrast, Russia ranks 125nd with a 3.59 score. It is categorized as an authoritarian regime due to its "deeply flawed parliamentary elections" and low scores for electoral process and pluralism, functioning of government, and political culture.[7‡]

Elections in a democracy require a free and fair media that is able to cover all candidates and parties equally. In this way, candidates can compete for votes on an equal basis and citizens are able to make real choices. Although the structure for democratic elections is formally present in Russia, the control of power by a few individuals and the silencing of important forms of communication make the Russian elections a gate against democracy.

* Timothy Heritage and Guy Faulconbridge, "Tearful Putin Wins Back Russian Presidency," Reuters, March 4, 2012, http://www.reuters.com/article/2012/03/04/us-russia-election-idUSTRE8220SP20120304.

† Office for Democratic Institutions and Human Rights, *Russian Federation, Elections to the State Duma: OSCA/ODIHR Election Observation Mission Report*, December 4, 2011, January 12, 2012, 23–24, accessed June 4, 2012, http://www.osce.org/odihr/86959.

‡ Economist Intelligence Unit, *Democracy Index 2011: Democracy under Stress*, December 2011, Table 2, pp. 1, 4, and 7, https://www.eiu.com/public/topical_report.aspx?campaignid=DemocracyIndex2011.

The opposition movement activists take part in an anti-Putin rally in the Central Arabat area in Moscow on March 10, 2012. The poster featuring Russia's prime minister, Vladimir Putin (left) reads: "Thank you, no!" Putin retained power, but his selection remains highly controversial.

YURI KADOBNOV/STAFF/AFP/GETTY IMAGES

1. In what ways do the media ensure free and fair elections in the United States?

2. How important are elections as a gateway to democracy compared to other processes or institutions?

TITLE IMAGE: © KLETR/SHUTTERSTOCK.COM

Congressional Elections

The constitutional guidelines for congressional elections also reflect the compromise between the interests of the states and the interests of the people. The Framers intended that the Senate would bring state interests to bear on the legislative process, while they intended that the House would represent the people. Each state, regardless of size, has two senators, while representatives are elected from congressional districts within states whose boundaries are adjusted to accommodate changes in population. Senators serve staggered six-year terms, while House members serve two-year terms.

→ KEY QUESTIONS:
How do differences in term lengths and constituencies affect how senators and House members behave?

Senate Elections.   The Constitution originally gave the choice of senators to state legislatures. Again the Framers inserted a gate between the people and those who were to serve their interests in the Senate. In the late nineteenth century, however, Progressive reformers called for elimination of this gate, arguing that the people ought to have a direct say in the election of senators. This reform became a reality with the adoption of the Seventeenth Amendment in 1913. Even with this change, however, there are barriers against overwhelming change in the composition of the Senate because Senate elections are staggered; only one-third of senators are up for election at a time. This arrangement ensures that the Senate is insulated from large shifts in public sentiment.

House Elections and Redistricting.   In contrast to the Senate, the entire House of Representatives is up for election every two years. Also in contrast to the Senate, House members have always been elected directly by the people.[8]

The Constitution requires that representatives be apportioned, within each state, according to population, which is counted every ten years in a census. Originally each member was to represent no more than thirty thousand people. As the population grew, the House of Representatives grew as well, from 65 members in 1789 to 237 members in 1857. The House continued to grow until 1911, and in 1929, the number was capped at 435. A member now represents, on average, more than seven hundred thousand people, as set by the 2010 census. Every ten years, new district lines are drawn following a census. Depending on patterns of population growth or decline, states win or lose congressional seats with each new census. Currently seven states have populations so small that they qualify for only one member of the House of Representatives (Alaska, Delaware, Montana, North Dakota, South Dakota, Vermont, and Wyoming). These states do not need to worry about drawing new congressional districts.

State legislatures are responsible for drawing the district lines in a process known as **redistricting.** While the official aim of redistricting is to try to keep districts equal in terms of population, the majority party in the state legislature tries to construct each district in such a way as to make it easier for its candidates to win congressional seats. Although citizens are not required to disclose party affiliation in the census, past voting patterns give parties a strong indication of where they have the advantage. A main limitation of this redistricting process is that the boundaries of the district must be contiguous (uninterrupted).

redistricting: *Process whereby state legislatures redraw the boundaries of congressional districts in the state to make them equal in population size.*

Redistricting has also been used as a tool to achieve greater minority representation in the House of Representatives. Following passage of the Voting Rights Act (VRA) in 1965, some states sought to dilute the effect of minority voters by drawing district lines so as to split their voting strength. In 1982, amendments to the VRA forbade this

→ KEY QUESTIONS:
Do majority-minority districts help advance equality or introduce inequalities?

practice, and in response, state legislatures created majority-minority districts, in which African Americans or Hispanics would constitute a majority of the voters in the district, thereby increasing the possibility of their electing African American or Hispanic candidates. In 2012, for example, Joaquin Castro won election to the House from the Twentieth Congressional District in Texas, which is a Latino majority-minority district (see Chapter 10, Congress). In the past decade, however, the federal courts have ruled that state legislatures overemphasized the racial composition of these districts to the point that the districts made no geographic sense. As a result, current guidelines on redistricting call for the consideration of race in drawing district lines, but not to the extreme that it has been employed in the past.[9]

gerrymandering: *Redistricting that blatantly benefits one political party over the other or concentrates (or dilutes) the voting impact of racial and ethnic groups.*

Any change to the size and shape of a district can have political implications because shifts in its partisan makeup alter which party might be able to capture the seat. For these reasons, there are major battles over the composition of districts. The politicization of drawing districts is called **gerrymandering**. Chapter 10 provides more details about this process and explains how different compositions of districts can alter the kind of gateway congressional elections offer.

For example, the Supreme Court in *Thornburg v. Gingles* unanimously struck down a North Carolina redistricting plan that had a discriminatory effect (a discriminatory intent is not necessary for a violation of the VRA, just a discriminatory effect) of diluting the ability of African Americans to choose state representatives of their choice by splitting "politically cohesive groups of black voters" into districts where blocs of white voters would consistently defeat the black candidates.[10] Twenty years later, the Supreme Court in *LULAC v. Perry* upheld a partisan gerrymander by the Texas legislature but struck down one of the districts where a Latino majority had been diluted by moving a bloc of Latinos into a different district.[11]

Checkpoint

CAN YOU:

- Summarize the constitutional requirements for presidential elections
- Summarize the constitutional requirements for congressional elections

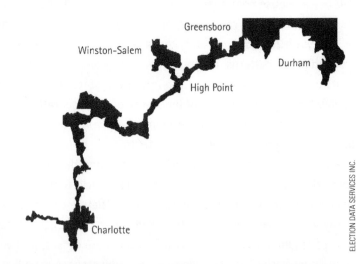

The term *gerrymander* comes from the salamander-shaped district in Massachusetts (above left), which Governor Elbridge Gerry approved following the census of 1810. Political rivals denounced the blatant seeking of political advantage that had produced such an oddly shaped congressional district, and the taunt stuck, passing into common usage in politics. Nevertheless, gerrymandered districts remain. In 1991, a North Carolina redistricting was designed to create a district with African Americans in the majority (above right). Federal courts later ruled that North Carolina had to revise these district lines so that the congressional district was more compact.

The Presidential Campaign

❯ Outline the steps in presidential campaigns

Presidential campaigns capture the interest of the vast majority of Americans. In September 2012, two months before the presidential election, 83 percent of the electorate paid at least some attention to the contest between Mitt Romney and Barack Obama.[12] Every move a presidential candidate makes is watched and assessed. This focus on the presidency would have surprised the Framers, who expected the legislative branch to be the center of attention. But as the executive branch has gained power, so has the importance of the contest to fill the office of president.

The course of the modern presidential campaign is long and difficult. From the decision to run to the final victory and concession speeches, the road to the White House is shaped by constitutional requirements, interparty struggles, and strategies for attracting votes that highlight the many gates and gateways along the way.

Evolution of the Modern Campaign

As in so many matters of custom and protocol, George Washington shaped the way future presidential aspirants would campaign for president. Like others at the Constitutional Convention, he worried that a chief executive could morph into a monarch, so he deliberately avoided doing anything to advance his candidacy. Washington's conduct continued to influence presidential campaigns until the start of the twentieth century. Candidates allowed their political parties to campaign on their behalf but avoided looking too ambitious.

Although candidates in the early nineteenth century sought to appear aloof and above the fray, their supporters took every opportunity to advance their candidacies. Buttons and slogans promoted favorites, and parades and barbeques sought to convince the undecided. Participation had much more of a social component than it does now. Many observers argue that the high rate of voting in the late nineteenth century reflected the fact that campaigns were often fun.[13]

By the early twentieth century, presidential contenders began to campaign actively, too, and campaigning started earlier and earlier. Starting the day after the 2012 election, speculation began about who might run in 2016. A number of candidates have been testing the waters for 2016, including Senator Ted Cruz (R-Tex.), Senator Rand Paul (R-Ky.), Governor Chris Christie (R-N.J.), and former Governor Jeb Bush (R-Fla.) It is no wonder that many observers have expressed concern over what has been called the **permanent campaign**,[14] a worry that politicians, especially presidents, spend too much time working toward reelection and not enough time governing. Some argue that if politicians spent more time governing and less time running for elections, the nation would be better off. Nevertheless politicians must win elections to be able to govern, and constant campaigning may be an indication of responsiveness.

permanent campaign: *Charge that presidents and members of Congress focus more on winning the next election than on governing.*

After a candidate decides to run for president, he or she enters what is called the **invisible primary**. No votes are cast, but candidates are jockeying for position so they can be ready to do well in the initial primaries and caucuses. They must line up party support, financial backing, and credibility with journalists in the news media. Candidates who can get attention from the news media can raise more money and secure more endorsements from party leaders. Running for election is a game that relies heavily on momentum.

invisible primary: *Period just before the primaries begin during which candidates attempt to capture party support and media coverage.*

Republicans meet to discuss who should be their party's nominee for president. A caucus allows people to talk about their views, which is one of its advantages.

The Caucuses and Primaries

To win a party's nomination, a candidate must secure a majority of delegates to the national party convention. The national party allocates delegates to each of the fifty states (plus the District of Columbia, Guam, and Puerto Rico) and sets guidelines on how the states may choose their delegates. (See Chapter 8 for more details about the delegate distribution process.)

About 70 percent of the states use some form of primary election in which citizens go to the polling booths and vote for their favorite party candidates. The other 30 percent use caucuses, which are something like town meetings. During the Iowa caucus, the nation's first and most famous caucus, each party requires people to attend a meeting of about two hours in which they indicate their preferences and then try to convince those who are undecided to join a particular candidate's group. Because caucuses demand more time from voters, participation is usually low.

Caucuses and primaries take place over six months, from January through June of the election year. The first states to hold these events wield tremendous influence; in most election years, the early primaries quickly build momentum for a front-runner and yield a likely nominee. Iowa is the first state to hold a caucus. New Hampshire holds the first primary.

→ KEY QUESTIONS:
What inequalities are imposed by the primary system?

CONNECT WITH YOUR CLASSMATES
MindTap™ for American Government

Access the Elections Forum:
Discussion—Bringing the Party
Together After Primaries.

The National Convention

Following the primary season, each party meets in a national convention. Before the 1960s, conventions were often exciting because it was far from clear who would be the nominee. In 1924, for example, it took the Democrats 124 ballots to decide on their nominee. But by the 1960s, conventions began to be televised, so the parties wanted to ensure that they were orderly. To avoid projecting an image that would cost votes in the upcoming election, party leaders instituted rule changes designed to increase the odds that the likely nominee would be known well in advance of the convention. Convention planners could then stage the event to emphasize party unity, rather than discord, to impress television viewers.

Today party conventions usually last for four days and provide a chance for activists and party leaders to get together to discuss strategy and policy behind the scenes. The highlight of these four days is the acceptance speech, in which the party's nominee has a chance to speak directly to the nation, laying out a vision for the country. Also in front of the cameras, the party platform is formally adopted, laying out its plan for government. There is much excitement surrounding these events. Because one party dominates the news for these four days, the convention is both an advertisement for the party and its candidate and an important springboard for the fall campaign.

Checkpoint

CAN YOU:

- Compare and contrast nineteenth-century and twenty-first-century presidential campaigns

- State the importance of the invisible primary to candidate momentum

- Explain how caucuses and primaries work

- Describe what happens at the national conventions

9.3 Issues in Presidential Campaigns

> Identify the issues that shape presidential campaigns

Citizen participation in American politics peaks during presidential campaigns. Supporters and people who are undecided have the chance to attend rallies, hear speeches, read commentary, and watch the never-ending advertisements on television. There seems to be almost no way for the public not to be involved. Because the campaigns are important gateways for public participation, we look in particular at fundraising and campaign strategies that make public engagement possible but may also introduce inequalities.

Fundraising and Money

Of course, no one could run for president without funding. How candidates raise money, how much money they raise, and the influence of money in presidential elections have been concerns of Congress and voters for decades, especially as the amount of spending on campaigns has risen sharply. Some believe these huge sums inject inequalities into presidential campaigns, as it seems candidates who lack personal fortunes and established fundraising operations are less likely to be able to compete.

In 1971, Congress tried to put candidates on an equal financial footing and make them less beholden to special interests by passing the Federal Election Campaign Act (FECA). This law transformed the way campaigns are conducted and monitored, as it requires candidates and political parties to disclose their campaign financial records. In 1974, Congress amended the law to set strict limits on how much money could be contributed by individuals and parties to campaigns, and more important, created the Federal Election Commission as an independent agency to monitor campaign finance.[15] Under the rules, candidates seeking their party's nomination are given public funds for the campaign in the form of matching funds: a dollar amount equal to the amount the candidates raise from private contributors, with a limit per individual contributor and an overall cap. In 2014, the limit per contributor was $2,600 in the primary and $2,600 in the general campaign.[16] After the Supreme Court's ruling in *McCutcheon, et al. v. FEC*, individuals have no limit on the number of campaigns to which they may contribute.[17]

> **→ KEY QUESTIONS:**
> What are the pros and cons of laws that regulate campaign finance?

The rules for the public financing of presidential nomination campaigns are complicated, as they are designed to ensure that candidates are serious contenders before receiving matching funds. First, candidates must raise at least $5,000 in twenty states from donations that are less than $500 each. Then they must get at least 10 percent of the vote in two consecutive primaries or they lose eligibility; to reestablish it, they must get 20 percent of the vote in a subsequent primary. These standards are hard to meet when the field of candidates is crowded, and they discourage third-party candidates from running. Even if candidates remain eligible, matching funds pose constraints in addition to the cap, as a candidate can spend only a certain amount of money per state. This constraint produces odd behavior. For example, because the New Hampshire primary is the first and perhaps the most important primary, candidates want to invest heavily in it. Yet under matching funds, they face a spending limit in the state, so they might spend the night in a hotel in an adjoining state, Vermont or Maine, to avoid having to charge that expense against the New Hampshire limit.

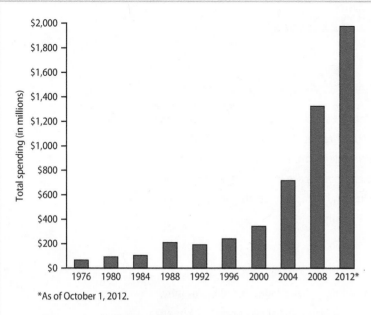

$2,000

$1,800

$1,600

$1,400

$1,200

$1,000

$800

$600

$400

$200

$0

Total spending (in millions)

1976 1980 1984 1988 1992 1996 2000 2004 2008 2012*

*As of October 1, 2012.

Figure 9.2 Total Spending by Presidential Candidates, 1976–2012

Spending in presidential campaigns has shown a steady increase over the past four decades, with big increases in the last two elections. By election day 2012, spending by presidential candidates had risen to about $1.8 billion.

Source: From "Presidential Fundraising and Spending 1976-2008," Center for Responsive Politics, 2008.

Since the 1970s, candidates and their contributors—including interest groups and corporations—have sought ways to fund campaigns within the FEC regulations and by finding loopholes they can exploit. Some contributors have amplified their impact by bundling—that is, by amassing individual contributions. Others have formed political action committees (PACs) with the express purpose of donating money to candidates who agree with their political agenda, although these amounts are also limited—in some cases $5,000 per candidate (see Chapter 7, Interest Groups).[18]

But the FEC rules matter far less now. Since 2000, presidential candidates have started to forego matching funds in their quest for the nomination. One reason is to be able to spend money in states important to the contest without regard to FEC limits. But primarily they believe they can raise (and spend) more money if they do not accept federal matching funds. In the 2008 general election, John McCain used public funds, receiving about $80 million from the government, but Barack Obama opted out of general election funding for the first time since the system began in 1976. By so doing, he had access to far more money than did McCain. Over the course of the yearlong campaign, he spent $730 million, breaking all previous fundraising records. McCain spent $333 million dollars during that same period, a huge amount by historical standards, but dwarfed by Obama's spending (see Figure 9.2 for total spending). Obama's record fundraising changed how presidential campaigns are funded. In the 2012 presidential election, no serious candidates used federal funds in the primaries, raising and spending their own money instead.

During the 2012 election cycle, the 2010 Supreme Court's ruling in *Citizens United v. Federal Election Commission* (2010) (see Supreme Court Cases in Chapter 8) also increased campaign fundraising amounts and spending, as it undid many of the restrictions formerly placed on corporations and unions. One consequence was the rise of **Super PACs**, which—unlike PACs—can raise funds from corporations, unions, interest groups, and individuals without legal limits.[19] These organizations are not allowed to coordinate directly with the candidates they support, but often those who run a Super PAC are friends and former aides to the candidates, making the distinction questionable.

Super PACs:
Independent groups that can raise unlimited amounts of money from individuals, labor unions, and corporations and can spend it to support or oppose political candidates but cannot coordinate directly with candidates or political parties.

In the 2012 Republican presidential primary alone, Romney's Super PACs spent more than $46 million, and many observers credit this money for helping him secure the Republican nomination.[20] During the entire presidential campaign, 1,301 Super PACs raised $828 million, spending a staggering $609 million in an effort to determine the next president.[21]

→ KEY QUESTIONS:
Are presidential campaigns too expensive?

Many observers worry about the influence of money on the election process and believe that these huge amounts raise questions about fairness and equality, as people who have money will have more gateways than those who do not. But even with bundling, the $5,000 total limit does offer some important constraints. It is impossible to "buy" a candidate with $5,000. In addition, the money is being spent on getting candidates' messages out to the public and building organizations to get out the vote. It can be argued that putting money into the system informs people and activates them to participate.[22] Campaign spending stimulates interest in the election, and that is also a public benefit. Last, some of the Super PACs allowed candidates such as Newt Gingrich and Rick Santorum to stay in the 2012 primary contests a little longer than they might have otherwise. That outcome may end up ensuring more competition, not less competition.[23]

Finally, the rise of Internet fundraising has made it worthwhile for candidates to pursue small contributions—as small as $15—rather than large contributions only. The Internet has made small donations cost-effective, encouraging candidates to broaden their base of contributors. By setting up websites that permit online donations, candidates do not need to pay people to call potential voters or knock on doors. They just need to maintain the websites and ensure that lots of people know about them. The Internet has given more people a gateway to be part of the electoral process by offering them a way to contribute small amounts of money.

→ KEY QUESTIONS:
Are presidential campaigns fair?

The real problem with Super PACs and the issue ads they sponsor is that voters do not always know where the money is coming from. Under the new campaign rules, there is less transparency. Thus it is possible for one or two wealthy donors to fund a Super PAC, and to the extent that the Super PAC's issue ads impact an election outcome, some observers contend that these results distort the electoral process. Of course, the changes may give a boost to party fundraising and candidates as well. We will need to watch what happens in the coming elections.

Swing States

Although partisanship is extremely high, **swing voters** still exist—people who do not fall into either the Republican or Democratic camp—and so do **swing states** that might vote either Democratic or Republican in an election. Parties avidly pursue swing voters during a presidential election, as they can swing the results one way or the other. In the past, swing voters have constituted about 20 percent of the electorate, but that share has been falling. Six months before the November 2012 election, only about 10 percent of the electorate was undecided, and the share fell to about 5 percent during the fall campaign.[24] The same can be said about the 2014 midterm elections. One estimate suggested that less than 10 percent of the electorate were potential swing voters in these recent contests.[25]

More important for campaign strategy are the swing states, which can mean the difference between victory and defeat. Because of the Electoral College's winner-take-all system, presidential candidates invest time and effort only in states that they can win. In 2012, for example, it made no sense for Mitt Romney to campaign in New York, a reliably Democratic state that he could not win. But both Romney and Barack Obama campaigned hard in Ohio—a **battleground state** that each thought he had a chance to win.

Citizens in these states got lots of attention. Nearly 90 percent of campaign visits by presidential candidates are to battleground states.[26] TV viewers were deluged with campaign ads, and party-based get-out-the-vote organizations were active in even the smallest towns. This flurry of activity filtered down to the public. Citizens in these states were well informed and increasingly interested in the campaign. But the strategy of pursuing votes in swing states yields an important inequality, for citizens in nonswing states do not get such attention, and interest in the campaign lags, especially among the poor. In 2012, there were nine states considered to be truly battleground states: Colorado, Florida, Iowa,

swing voters: *Voters who are neither reliably Republican nor reliably Democratic and who are pursued by each party during an election, as they can determine which candidate wins.*

swing states: *States that are not clearly pro-Republican or pro-Democrat and therefore are of vital interest to presidential candidates, as they can determine election outcomes.*

→ KEY QUESTIONS:
Do you live in a swing or a battleground state? What is the impact on you?

battleground state: *State in which the outcome of the presidential election is uncertain and in which both candidates invest much time and money, especially if its votes are vital for a victory in the Electoral College.*

→ KEY QUESTIONS:
What is your microtargeting profile? Can the category predict how you will vote?

Ohio, Nevada, New Hampshire, North Carolina, Virginia, and Wisconsin. Only 21 percent of the nation's population resides in these states.[27] It is a problem that voters in different states are getting treated differently by the campaigns. Theoretically, all voters should receive equal treatment, yet one in five Americans is the focus of attention of presidential candidates.

Microtargeting

★ **microtargeting:**
Gathering detailed information on cross sections of the electorate to track potential supporters and tailor political messages for them; also called narrowcasting.

Since the 1960s, when consumer behavior became a popular field of study, direct marketers have refined the practice of gathering detailed information about different cross sections of consumers to sell their products.[28] Today, the technique of **microtargeting** has become a boon to political parties and electoral campaigns. By identifying and tracking potential supporters, campaign strategists can design specific political messages tailored for each of the voting profiles developed from the data. In 1996, for example, President Bill Clinton's reelection campaign sought to reach so-called soccer moms—"busy suburban women devoted to their jobs and kids, who had real concerns about real presidential politics."[29] Polls and other information suggested that these voters could be moved into the Clinton camp, although men, for the most part, seemed to have already made up their minds. In 2004, the focus was on "NASCAR dads"—working-class white males who lived mostly in the South. Many thought the Democrats had to win this group to capture the presidency. In the 2012 campaign, both Mitt Romney and Barack Obama microtargeted Latino voters, believing that this growing block of voters was critical to the election outcome.[30] As we approach the 2016 campaign, Latino voters remain important "targets," as are single women and Millennials.[31]

As a campaign strategy, microtargeting has begun to replace traditional polling techniques and precinct-by-precinct get-out-the-vote drives (see Chapter 6, Public Opinion and the Media). By combining information from polling surveys with political participation and consumer information obtained from data-gathering companies such as Acxiom and InfoUSA, political parties and campaigns can establish profiles of the many different types of voters and the issues they support. The resulting database can then be "mapped" to get a geographic depiction of the trends in voting habits and political interests of different voters. Each party builds its own database that it can share with candidates: The Democratic National Committee's database is called VoteBuilder, and the Republican National Committee's is called GOP Data Center.[32]

→ KEY QUESTIONS:
What should shape a presidential campaign— issues or character?

Rather than a general political message sent through a specific medium, campaigns are now able to send dozens of versions of the message using various methods— mail, phone calls, e-mail, text messages, home visits—to reach targeted audiences. This strategy takes a person-by-person view of the electorate rather than a view of the electorate en masse. So, instead of targeting a broad category such as women, campaigns can now focus on narrow subgroups such as undecided iPhone owners in their 30s who follow the news and hence are open to a message from a campaign.

JOHN GRESS/GETTY IMAGES

Senator Marco Rubio (R-FL) has drawn a lot of national attention being both young and Latino.

Campaign Issues

Campaigns are very much shaped by issues. Many observers think that the personalities of the candidates dictate the race, but that view is not consistent with the evidence. Between 1960 and 2000, for example, 56 percent of the content of advertising in presidential campaigns involved policy, with 26 percent concerning the personal traits of the candidates, and the remaining 18 percent focusing on general values such as freedom, hard work, and patriotism.[33] In 2008, the economy dominated the discussion between John McCain and Barack Obama. According to one estimate, more than 50 percent of the appeals made by these contenders dealt with the economy alone.[34] The economy was the main issue in 2012 as well.

To understand how issues influence campaigns, political scientists have drawn a distinction between **valence issues** and **position issues**.[35] A valence issue is a vague claim to a goal, such as "a strong economy," "improved education," or "greater national security." These are goals all candidates talk about and voters seek: No candidate has ever opposed a strong economy or called for less national security. Valence issues provide limited insight into the policies a candidate might pursue once in office. A position issue is different. Here candidates adopt views that allow voters to understand specific plans for government. Two examples from the 2012 campaign are Barack Obama's support for increasing taxes on the wealthy and Mitt Romney's opposition to the Affordable Care Act. Because views on position issues may drive some votes away, presidential candidates rely more heavily on valence issues than on position issues. According to one study, about three-quarters of their TV ads highlight valence issues.[36]

Because campaigns are competitive struggles for votes, candidates look for ways to secure extra votes while maintaining existing support. This dynamic is especially true for candidates who trail because they need to find some way to break up the support for the candidate in the lead. One strategy is to use a **wedge issue** that has the potential to break up the opposition's coalition.[37] Wedges usually involve controversial policy concerns, such as affirmative action, that divide people rather than build consensus. In 2012 and 2014, the Democrats also sought to use various gender issues as wedges against the Republicans, including debates over contraception and equal pay.[38]

Negativity

Candidates are very good at telling voters why they should vote for them, but they are also good at telling the public why they should not vote for their opponents. These reasons often involve issues. A candidate might, for example, remind voters that his or her opponent raised taxes. But other times, a campaign releases an array of information about a candidate that raises doubts and concerns about fitness for office. Because the public does need to know both the good and the bad, **negativity** plays an important, and usually underappreciated, role in campaigns.

One of the most famous negative ads was the "Daisy spot," aired only once by President Lyndon B. Johnson in his 1964 campaign against the Republican nominee, Arizona Senator Barry

AP IMAGES/DEMOCRATIC NATIONAL COMMITTEE

The "Daisy spot" is perhaps the most famous negative ad in American history. It was aired only once by President Lyndon Johnson in the 1964 campaign, and it never explicitly mentioned his opponent, Senator Barry Goldwater. But Goldwater had made statements about the possible use of nuclear weapons, and those statements made the meaning of this ad clear and emotionally resonant.

valence issues: *Noncontroversial or widely supported campaign issues that are unlikely to differentiate the candidates.*

position issues: *Political issues that offer specific policy choices and often differentiate candidates' views and plans of action.*

→ KEY QUESTIONS:
Identify three wedge issues that are important to you. Do they determine your vote?

wedge issue: *Divisive issue focused on a particular group of the electorate that candidates use to gain more support by taking votes away from their opponents.*

negativity: *Campaign strategy of telling voters why they should not vote for the opponent and of highlighting information that raises doubts about the opponent.*

→ KEY QUESTIONS:
What is your response to negative ads?

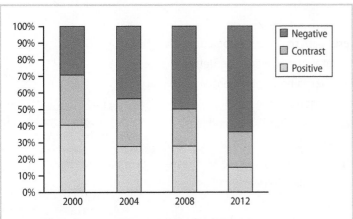

Note: Data from 2000, 2004 and 2008 come from the Wisconsin Advertising Project. Data from 2012 come from the Wesleyan Media Project.

Figure 9.3 **Share of Positive, Contrast, and Negative Ads in Presidential Campaigns, 2000–2012**

Negativity in presidential campaigns is clearly on the rise. From 2000 to 2004, the proportion of the messages in presidential campaign ads jumped from 30 percent to 40 percent of all ads and continued to increase to 50 percent in 2008. In the 2012 campaign, the figure reached over 60 percent, leaving less than 20 percent of the ads in the presidential campaign sending positive messages.

Erika Franklin Fowler and Travis N. Ridout, "Negative, Angry, and Ubiquitous: Political Advertising in 2012," DOI 10.1515/forum-2013-0004, *The Forum 2012*, 10(4): 51–61.

Source: John Geer, © Cengage Learning®.

Checkpoint

CAN YOU:

■ Track trends in fundraising for presidential campaigns

■ Describe the impact of the Electoral College on presidential campaigns

■ Explain microtargeting as a campaign strategy

■ Compare and contrast valence issues and position issues

■ Describe the role of negativity in campaign strategies

Goldwater. The implication was that if Goldwater were elected president, he would start a nuclear war. It was a very hard-hitting claim that many thought unfair.[39] But was it? Goldwater had called for the tactical use of nuclear weapons and made some loose statements about attacking the Soviet Union with nuclear weapons. This issue was among the most important facing the nation—much like terrorism is now. The public needed to know Goldwater's views, and this negative ad helped generate a debate.

In recent years, the amount of negativity has been on the rise (see Figure 9.3). In the 2008 campaign, less than 30 percent of campaign ads were positive—another 20 percent were a mix of negative and positive appeals (so called "contrast" ads). That means half the ads were negative. Over 60 percent of the ads in the 2012 presidential campaign were negative, with just 14 percent of spots being purely positive.[40] Many observers worry about this trend, viewing attacks on the opposition as weakening the fabric of democracy, especially since about 80 percent of the public says they dislike negative ads.[41]

But negative ads serve a purpose. To ensure accountability, candidates need to be able to critique the other side. So, in 2012, Mitt Romney reminded the public of the slow economic growth endured during the Obama administration. At the same time, Barack Obama questioned whether Romney really cared about average Americans. But despite the negative tone of these ads, they contain information about the candidates that voters need to know. After hearing each side attack the other during a campaign, voters are better able to make informed decisions. Most important, negativity promotes accountability—and accountability is essential to the proper functioning of a democracy.

 9.4 **Issues in Congressional Campaigns**

❯ Determine which issues shape congressional campaigns

Congressional elections do not draw as much attention as presidential elections, but they involve many of the same issues. Money and fundraising are concerns, and again the FEC sets limits. Political parties attempt to work within—or get around—these limits to help their candidates. Voters almost always reelect House and Senate members, so whether congressional elections actually serve to hold Congress accountable is a question for American democracy.

Voters know less about these candidates than about the candidates in presidential elections, suggesting perhaps that there is not much accountability. Nevertheless, the composition of Congress changes in response to conditions in the country. If times are good, voters reward the party that controls the presidency. In general, the pattern of Republican and Democratic gains and losses indicates that voters hold members of Congress accountable and that Congress is, therefore, a responsive institution.

Fundraising and Money

A key element in launching and running a congressional campaign is fundraising. Every campaign needs an office, staff members, computers, posters and pamphlets, a website, and money for television and radio ads. Senate campaigns generally cost more than House campaigns because they seek to reach voters across an entire state rather than just a district.

Federal campaign finance laws set the same limits on congressional elections as on presidential elections: An individual could contribute up to $2,500 to a candidate for the primary election in 2012, and the same amount for the general election for as many campaigns as she or he wishes. Candidates also raise money from PACs, which are limited to donating $5,000 for a primary election, and $5,000 for a general election, to a single candidate.[42] In the 2014 midterm elections, the cost of running for office continued to climb. Consider that Mitch McConnell (R-KY) and Alison Lundergan Grimes (D) spent $45 million in the Kentucky Senate race. Major candidates in the 8th District of Ohio spent about $17 million. In the 2002 midterm elections, total spending in congressional races was about $2 billion. Just twelve years later the amount spent by candidates had more than doubled.[43]

The Role of Political Parties

Of the other sources of financial support available to candidates, the most important is the political party. Parties are forbidden by campaign finance laws from actively coordinating a specific individual's congressional or senatorial campaign, but local parties can engage in general activities, such as voter registration drives, partisan rallies, and get-out-the-vote efforts on election day that help party-endorsed candidates at every level.

Incumbency Advantage

Incumbents almost always win,[44] and in the past two decades, more than 70 percent of House incumbents won by 60 percent or more of the vote[45] (see Figure 9.4). Since the 1960s, the number of competitive races has been in decline, a trend called **vanishing marginals**. Fewer and fewer congressional elections are competitive. Noncompetitive districts are often referred to as **safe seats**. The high rates of incumbent reelection may indicate that incumbents are doing a good job, especially with constituent services that build support with voters (see also Chapter 10).

Concerns about incumbency advantage have led some observers to fear a lack of accountability and to call for

vanishing marginals: *Trend marking the decline of competitive congressional elections.*

safe seat: *Seat in Congress considered to be reliably held by one party or the other.*

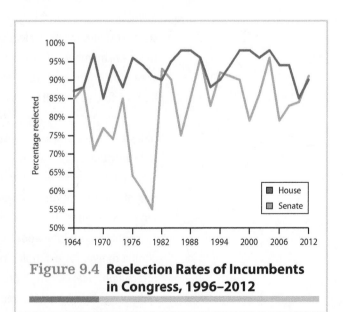

Figure 9.4 Reelection Rates of Incumbents in Congress, 1996–2012

Source: https://www.opensecrets.org/bigpicture/reelect.php.

term limits: *Rule restricting the number of terms an elected official can serve in a given office.*

Are term limits for Congress a good idea? What are the pros and the cons?

term limits, which would force members to retire after serving a maximum number of terms. Presidents, for example, can serve only two terms, and most governors are similarly constrained. But chief executives have more concentrated power than do legislators, so ensuring turnover in the executive branch does keep gateways to responsive government open.

Further, more turnover actually occurs in the House than the 90 percent reelection rate suggests. Members often engage in strategic retirement, deciding not to run for reelection when the outcome is likely to be unfavorable. It is also unclear what reelection rates exactly mean. For example, the lower reelection rates of senators do not imply that the Senate is more responsive than the House. Instead, the gap may be a function of differences between the two chambers. A seat in the Senate, the upper house, is a more coveted position than a seat in the House, and Senate races generally attract higher-quality challengers than do House races. Better challengers yield more competitive elections and more defeats for incumbents. The ability of challengers to do better in Senate races than in House races is also related to the additional media attention these races receive; quite simply, voters learn more about the challengers. Finally, the difference in terms—six years as opposed to two—may indicate that House members stay in closer touch with constituents than do senators, and their constituents reelect them.[46]

Incumbents also win reelection at high rates because they are known commodities to their constituents. Name recognition for House and Senate incumbents is often higher than 80 percent. Senate challengers do better than House challengers, but still about a quarter of the electorate does not recognize their names.[47] Compare these percentages to those of the 2012 presidential election, in which only 1 percent of the public claimed not to know the name of Mitt Romney, who was challenging President Obama.[48]

Additional explanations have been advanced to explain incumbency advantage. For example, with the bureaucracy growing in size and reach, people expect more from their government. As a result, citizens need a mediator to handle issues that arise with the bureaucracy. Members of Congress serve as a conduit to help connect people with government services. Thus a citizen who fails to receive a Social Security check or has trouble with a passport calls his or her member of Congress for help. The result is constituent loyalty and an increased willingness to support that official's reelection. Other scholars have offered a more sinister interpretation. In this view, members of Congress design bureaucratic agencies and programs in ways that assure their inability to carry out the tasks that constituents demand. In a sense, the bureaucracy is built to fail, so constituents have to contact their representative or senator to make it work; when help arrives, loyalty to the incumbent is built.[49] There is also a simple explanation for why reelection rates of incumbents are so high: Candidates who win once obviously have the skills to be elected, and these serve them well in reelection campaigns.[50]

In addition, recent evidence suggests that members of Congress may be the beneficiaries of the migration of Americans. That is, incumbency advantage appears to be increasing because districts are becoming "deep red" (Republican) and "deep blue" (Democrat) due to people's decisions about where to live. The assumption is that a Republican who has a choice to live, for example, in San Francisco or Dallas, will tend to choose Dallas because it offers a political culture more in line with his or her preferences. In this sense, because of the redrawing of district lines and the desire of individuals to live near people with similar values and political leanings, congressional districts are becoming heavily Democratic or heavily

Republican. The result is that fewer races are competitive and incumbents are more successful.[51]

Much has been written on the exact mechanisms that drive voters and congressional elections. While there is disagreement over the specifics, it is clear that the composition of Congress changes in response to economic conditions. In good times, the president's party benefits, whereas in bad times, the president's party suffers. It is also true that big issues can matter. In 2014, the controversy of the Affordable Care Act certainly shaped a lot of congressional campaigns and outcomes in those elections as well.

Checkpoint

CAN YOU:

■ Explain how fundraising needs restrain candidates

■ Describe the role of political parties in congressional campaigns

■ Give reasons for incumbency advantage

9.5 The Practice and Theory of Voting

> Explain why there are battles over ballot access

Americans enjoy near universal opportunities to vote. Even so, no one should assume that such opportunities have always existed or that they are permanent. Despite the widespread belief in the importance of elections for democratic institutions, some Americans have argued that voting rights should not be universal. Who votes shapes the outcome of elections and the conduct of government. Voting, in short, is a central gateway to power, so there are always battles over who gets access to the ballot.

The Constitution and Voting

The Constitution is nearly silent on the rules about voting in elections, leaving such choices to the states. As Article I, Section 4, of the Constitution states, "The Times, Places and Manner of holding Elections for Senators and Representatives, shall be prescribed in each State by the Legislature thereof." The Constitution does spell out in some detail the workings of the Electoral College, which chooses the president. But state legislatures were given nearly complete latitude about how to select their members for the College. Similarly, the Constitution makes the states the prime players in setting voting requirements.

→ KEY QUESTIONS:
Why does the Constitution say so little about voting?

The consequence of this delegation of authority is a system of voting that is very complicated because state rules vary considerably. The differing rules also lead to inequalities among the states. It is, for example, easier to vote in some states than in others. We explore some of these issues in the following section.

Competing Views of Participation

Debates about voting and the removal of obstacles to voting have often centered on whether potential voters would be qualified to cast ballots. For example, in the nineteenth century, many lawmakers did not think women would make wise political choices and were therefore reluctant to consider granting them **suffrage**.[52] Others worried that too much participation yields too many demands on government, making government less able to respond. It seems that those opposed to removing obstacles to voting feared that too much democracy could be bad for democracy.[53]

suffrage: Right to vote; also called *franchise.*

→ KEY QUESTIONS:
Can you think of any reason why a citizen should not be allowed to vote?

We label these ideas the Hamiltonian model of participation. Alexander Hamilton represents a perspective that sees risks in greater participation and, thus, favors a larger role

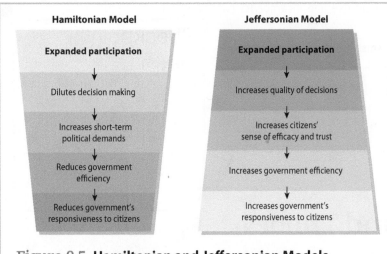

Figure 9.5 Hamiltonian and Jeffersonian Models of Participation

Checkpoint

CAN YOU:

■ Explain why it matters that the Constitution delegated authority over voting to the states

■ Compare and contrast the Hamiltonian and Jeffersonian models of participation

for elites. In this model, not only would the quality of the decision be diluted by more participation, but government would be less able to advance the national interest because it would be responding to uninformed voters. The Hamiltonian model stands in stark contrast to the Jeffersonian model, which holds that more participation yields a more involved and engaged public and that, in turn, produces better outcomes.[54] In other words, democracy thrives with more democracy. Thomas Jefferson had more faith than Hamilton did in the people's ability and worried that excessive reliance on elites would make government less responsive to its citizens.

Figure 9.5 offers a summary of these competing views. Proponents of the Hamiltonian model do seek accountability, but they place much more faith in the ability of elites than in the ability of the general public to make the right decisions. The people, they contend, are often uninformed and cannot make the best choices. In contrast, proponents of the Jeffersonian model want to see more participation, believing that the people can be trusted and that getting more people involved will push government to be more responsive to the people's interests. They contend that if certain groups of people are disenfranchised, government will be less responsive. People may not be well informed about politics, but if they have a chance to be involved, they will become better informed. An informed citizenry that actively participates in politics will ensure that government is both accountable and responsive.

Obviously the Jeffersonian model holds equality as an important political value, whereas the Hamiltonian model places more emphasis on efficient and effective outcomes. These competing visions of citizen involvement have played out in nearly all debates about expanding the opportunity for more citizens to cast ballots. In the course of the nation's history, proponents and opponents of expanding the right to vote have each achieved victories. Although the overall trend has been constant expansion, the contest has been fraught with conflict—not only debate in Congress and the courts but also violence in the streets.

9.6 The History of Voting in America

> Outline how the right to vote has expanded

The history of voting in America falls into three general eras.[55] First, from the 1790s to 1870, voting rights expanded, and by 1860 universal white male suffrage had been achieved. After the Civil War, voting rights were extended to African American males by means of the Fifteenth Amendment. But states, localities, and political parties sought by various means

Figure 9.6 Constitutional Amendments That Pertain to the Right to Vote

Fifteenth	1870	Prohibits states from denying the right to vote on account of race
Seventeenth	1913	Gives the people (instead of state legislatures) the right to choose U.S. senators
Nineteenth	1920	Guarantees women the right to vote
Twenty-Third	1961	Grants residents of the District of Columbia votes in the Electoral College
Twenty-Fourth	1964	Prohibits poll taxes
Twenty-Sixth	1971	Guarantees 18-year-olds the right to vote

© CENGAGE LEARNING®

to block African Americans, Asian immigrants, and others from voting. From the 1870s until 1920, the barriers to voting often increased. Reforms were under way as well, and beginning with the Nineteenth Amendment in 1920, which granted women the right to vote, voting rights began to expand again. The civil rights movement of the 1950s and 1960s culminated in the passage of laws protecting voting rights for African Americans, Latinos, and others, and a Constitutional amendment in 1971 extended the right to vote to 18-year-olds. In 1961, citizens of the District of Columbia were given the opportunity to vote in presidential elections (see Figure 9.6). Thus, in the twentieth century, there was a second wave of expansion of voting rights. These three eras suggest that voting and the electorate have expanded in the long run, although not consistently and with contractions that have violated civil rights (see Chapter 5, Civil Rights).

COMPARE WITH YOUR PEERS
MindTap™ for American Government

Access the Elections Forum: Polling Activity—Presidential Election Process.

In 1975, Congress extended the Voting Rights Act to include "Language Assistance Amendments." Those laws ensured that in areas in which more than 5 percent of the citizens of voting age are members of a single language minority and have limited English proficiency, governments must provide election materials and assistance in their native language (as well as in English).[56] This change opened a significant gateway for Latinos and other non-English speakers to participate in elections. In comments before the Senate Judiciary Committee, Senator Orrin (R-UT) explained his support for the provisions this way:

> The right to vote is one of the fundamental human rights. Unless government assures access to the ballot box, citizenship is just an empty promise. Section 203 of the Voting Rights Act, containing bilingual election requirements, is an integral part of our government's assurance that Americans do have such access.[57]

Considering the many gates facing Latino voters, their socialization into the electoral arena has been stilted. Gates such as Jim Crow laws, Mexican Repatriation, and language requirements, for example, discouraged Latinos from voting and inevitably passed this uneven and constrained sense of citizenship to succeeding generations. Even so, the Voting Rights Act proved a boon to the participation of Latinos. Together with voter mobilization, Latinos are overcoming these early gates and now voting in much larger numbers. Although it seems that there are now more gateways to participation, new efforts in the form of voter identification laws have been enacted by some states, constructing new gates that will hinder many Latinos (and others) from exercising the right to vote (See Public Policy, Voting, and Participation: Voter ID Laws.)

supreme court cases

Katzenbach v. Morgan (1966)

QUESTION: May Congress prohibit states from enforcing English language literacy tests?

ORAL ARGUMENT: April 18, 1966 (listen at http://www.oyez.org/cases/1960-1969/1965/1965_847)

DECISION: June 13, 1966 (read at http://laws.findlaw.com/us/384/641.html)

OUTCOME: Yes, Congress has the authority (7-2).

Section 4 (e) of the Voting Rights Act of 1965 prevented states from establishing English language literacy tests for voting if the resident had finished the sixth grade in an accredited school in the U.S. Commonwealth of Puerto Rico in which the language of instruction was "other than English" (this almost always meant Spanish). Although voting qualifications were traditionally left to states, the Fourteenth Amendment, which, among other things, prohibited states from denying to any person the equal protection of the laws, also gave Congress the authority to enforce its provisions through "appropriate legislation." As many people of Puerto Rican heritage had been denied the right to vote in New York due to an inability to read and write English, Congress added the above-noted protection.

Morgan and other registered voters in New York City brought the lawsuit to challenge Congress's authority to prohibit English language voting requirements. A special three-judge district court struck down the Congressional requirement. U.S. Attorney General Nicholas Katzenbach appealed that decision directly to the Supreme Court, as the Voting Rights Act allows.

The Supreme Court ruled that the enforcement provision of the Fourteenth Amendment gave Congress the same broad powers to enact legislation to protect voting rights that the Necessary and Proper clause did for the enumerated powers in the Constitution (see Supreme Court Cases, *McCulloch v. Maryland* in Chapter 3, Federalism). The Court declared that legislation prohibiting discrimination in voting on account of language fell within the constitutional authority of Congress.

1. What reasons, valid and invalid, might New York have had for restricting the right to vote to those who can read or write in English?

2. Why might the Voting Rights Act have protected Americans educated in Spanish in Puerto Rico but not Americans educated in Spanish in Mexico?

Figure 9.7 provides some clear data on Latino voting by comparing the rates of participation to other relevant groups. As the figure shows, Latino voting in presidential elections continues to lag behind the rates of both white and African American voters. Over the past four election cycles, whites have voted at rates between 60 percent and 70 percent, while African American turnout has increased from 52 percent to an historic 66 percent in the 2012 election. In the same time period, voting rates for Latinos have hovered in the range of 45–51 percent. The gap between black and Latino turnout has increased in recent years, surely reflecting the mobilization of the African American community with the Obama candidacy.

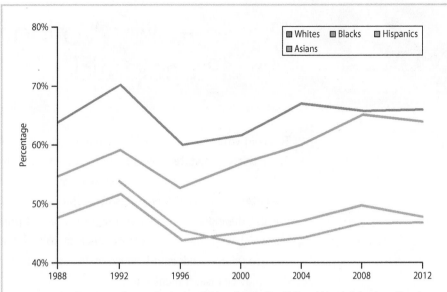

Figure 9.7 **Voter Turnout Rates in Presidential Elections by Race and Ethnicity, 1988–2012**

Note: Hispanics are of any race. For the years 1988 through 2008, whites, blacks, and Asians include only non-Hispanics. For 2012, blacks and Asians include Hispanics. Data for non-Hispanic Asians were not available in 1988.

Source: Pew Resource Center, http://www.pewresearch.org/fact-tank/2013/05/08/six-take-aways-from-the-census-bureaus-voting -report/

This lower turnout masks, however, the fact that Latinos comprise an ever growing segment of the total voting population. While turnout rates have been pretty flat, the number of eligible Latino voters has grown from 13.2 million to 23.7 million since the year 2000. While the 2000 Latino turnout rate of 45 percent brought around 6 million people to the polls, the 2012 turnout rate of 48 percent resulted in around 11 million Latino voters. Latinos now constitute about 10 percent of the electorate,[58] and the percentage will only grow in the coming years.[59]

Checkpoint

CAN YOU:

- Survey the expansion of suffrage between 1790 and 1860
- Describe how minorities and immigrants have at times been prohibited from voting

9.7 Who Votes?

> Identify who tends to turn out in American elections

Voting is an important gateway to influence, but not everyone has the inclination or the desire to participate. Failure to vote has real implications for the political process; it affects which representatives govern and make laws, and who governs has policy consequences that affect everyone in the United States. Low turnout raises questions about government's responsiveness, and unequal turnout by various demographic groups suggests that government's response is unequal, too. Low turnout among young people, for example, in contrast to older Americans, means that elected officials may give more attention to issues affecting senior voters, such as Social Security, than to issues affecting

Public Policy, Voting, and Participation: Voter ID Laws

To avoid voter fraud, many states have instituted voter identification requirements. As of 2014, thirty-one states have identification laws in force.[60] Of these, eight states require voters to show a photo ID, and three states require a nonphoto ID, such as a bank statement with the voter's address. Other states ask voters to show ID with or without a photo but do not prevent the individuals from voting if they do not present a ballot ID at the polling stations. Voter ID laws, however, are controversial as some argue that it creates a gate to participation. The poor and less educated, for example, may find it harder to meet these new standards and, if so, may be disenfranchised.

Opponents of Indiana's 2005 photo identification law sought to block its implementation through a lawsuit. The fundamental issue in this case was whether state laws that were intending to prevent voter fraud had the result of preventing citizens who were legally entitled to vote from doing so. Indiana argued that the requirement of a photo ID was not unduly burdensome because the state provided voter identification cards to citizens who had no other photo IDs. But opponents argued that the process of getting such a card was too complicated and that the overall effect of the law would be to disenfranchise thousands of citizens. In 2008, the Supreme Court upheld the Indiana law by a 6–3 vote. Justice John Paul Stevens wrote on behalf of the majority, "The state interests identified as justifications for [the law] are both neutral and sufficiently strong to require us to reject" the lawsuit. However, Justice David Souter wrote in dissent that the law "threatens to impose nontrivial burdens on the voting right of tens of thousands of the state's citizens."[61]

Today, the issue is still not settled. In 2012, the American Civil Liberties Union filed suit against Pennsylvania's new strict voter ID law, and the State Supreme Court struck down the law.[62] In addition to not "[assuring] fair and free elections," as the Pennsylvania judge wrote, these laws may have a disproportionate effect on some groups of voters.

For example, elderly, poorer citizens, and even women whose surnames may change as they marry, divorce, or simply maintain their maiden names[63] may not have acceptable forms of photo identification. Latinos may also be less likely than other voters to have valid photo identification. In Wisconsin, for example, scholars showed that not only were Latinos less likely to have such IDs, but they were also less likely to have the documents necessary to obtain them (see Figure 9.8).[64] In a federal court case brought by the League of United Latin American Citizens (LULAC), the courts used such evidence to strike down a Wisconsin law requiring citizens to present photo identification to vote. At issue was whether the Wisconsin law violated Section 2 of the Voting Rights Act that prohibits voting practices or procedures that discriminate on the basis of race, color, or membership in one of the language groups identified in the VRA.[65]

These are all complicated issues and as such must be thoughtfully assessed, especially as they affect differentially the ability of certain groups to influence the political process.

Political considerations also come into play. The two political parties may see their electoral fortunes tied to either increased or decreased voter participation and thus have different incentives to cooperate with each other on voting requirements.

With the Hamiltonian and Jeffersonian views of voting in mind, it is important to decide what standards should be imposed for citizens to vote. Clearly, the federal government has taken steps to make the voting process easier and more convenient. But ultimately states and localities administer and oversee elections, and states have responded inconsistently to the federal efforts. Some appear to have made it easier to vote, but others, such as Indiana, have made it harder by requiring photo identification at the polling place. It would seem that, in a democracy, all citizens should have an equal opportunity to cast their votes because voting is the fundamental mechanism by which we hold government accountable. As states introduce more laws regarding identification, disparities in the opportunity to vote may be growing.

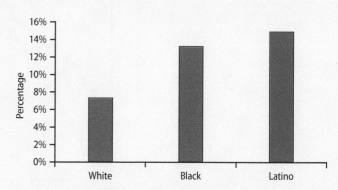

Figure 9.8 **Percent of Eligible Voters Who Lack Photo ID by Race and Ethnicity**

Source: Matt A. Barreto, and Gabriel R. Sanchez, "Rates of Possession of Accepted Photo Identification, Among Different Subgroups in the Eligible Voter Population, Milwaukee County, Wisconsin," Expert Report Submitted on Behalf of Plaintiffs in *Frank v. Walker,* Civil Action No. 2:11-cv-01128(LA), April 23, 2012, https://www.aclu.org/files/assets/062-10-exhibitjexpertreport.pdf.

Construct Your Own Policy

1. Write a set of requirements that you think citizens should meet to in order vote and that balances concerns for voter fraud with easing access to voting.

2. Construct a strategy for cooperation regarding voting requirements that addresses voter fraud concerns mostly voiced by Republicans as well as easy access for voters that Democrats embrace.

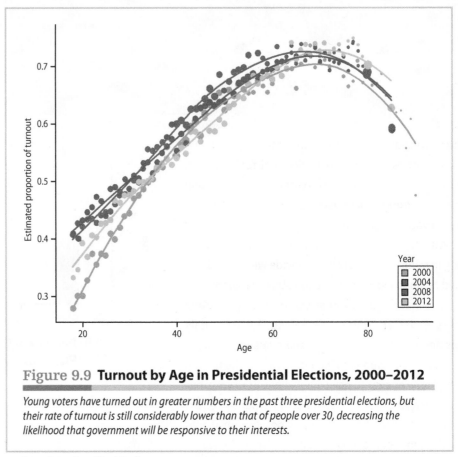

Figure 9.9 Turnout by Age in Presidential Elections, 2000–2012

Young voters have turned out in greater numbers in the past three presidential elections, but their rate of turnout is still considerably lower than that of people over 30, decreasing the likelihood that government will be responsive to their interests.

Source: Census Current Population Surveys.

younger voters, such as the costs of education. Figure 9.9 documents that the youngest voters have the lowest turnout and that voters turn out more often as they age. In this section, we examine turnout rates generally and then look at turnout rates by various demographic groups.

Turnout

Even with widespread opportunity to cast ballots and shape the course of government, Americans often choose not to vote. In 1996, fewer than half of eligible voters (about 48 percent) took the time to vote in the presidential contest between William Jefferson (Bill) Clinton (1993–2001) and Senator Robert Dole (R-Kans.). In 2012, the rate of participation improved to about 58 percent.[66] While that proportion was higher than in 1996, it was less than in 2008. Presidential elections are high-stimulus events that generate more interest and voting than any other American election. In midterm congressional elections, which are low-stimulus elections, turnout is usually less than 40 percent. For primary elections during presidential nominations, turnout is even lower. In 2012, in the all-important New Hampshire presidential primary, turnout was less than 31 percent, and it was lower still in other states. Illinois had a turnout of just 11 percent, and Florida had only 13 percent.[67] For local school board elections, the electorate is even smaller: Often fewer than 10 percent of eligible citizens vote in such contests. A general assessment of turnout in the United States is offered later in the chapter. Here, we turn to the demographics of turnout.

→ KEY QUESTIONS:
When some groups vote less frequently than other groups, what is the effect on government?

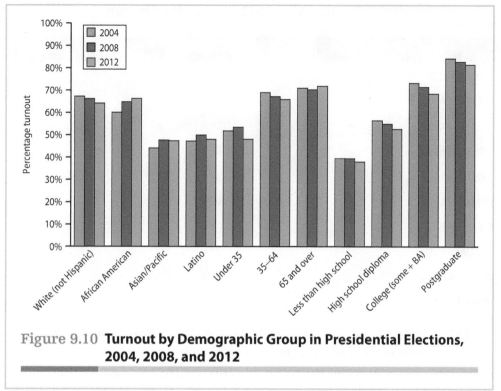

Figure 9.10 Turnout by Demographic Group in Presidential Elections, 2004, 2008, and 2012

Source: Census Current Population Surveys.

The Demographics of Turnout

Given the important power that voting brings in a democracy, the following becomes a central question: Who votes? Do various demographic groups vote in equal proportions? If not, what are the consequences for government responsiveness?

The data suggest that people who are most likely to vote tend to be better educated, better paid, and older than those who are unlikely to vote (see Figure 9.10). There are some modest race, ethnicity, and gender differences, but when scholars control for differences in education and income, differences in race pretty much disappear.[68] The key lesson is that the driving force of participation is the development in young people of the kinds of skills and habits that prepare an individual for active citizenship.

Sex. Women turn out at a slightly higher rate than men, by perhaps 3 to 5 percentage points. According to one estimate, 59 percent of women reported voting in 2012 compared to 54 percent of men.[69] The gender gap is important in American politics, but it relates to the tendency of women to support Democrats over Republicans, not to the difference in turnout between women and men.

Age. Age affects rates of participation. Turnout peaks once voters are about 60 years old (see Figure 9.9 on page 290). Even when differences in education and income are controlled for, participation remains higher for older Americans. In 2012, around 70 percent of citizens older than 65 claimed to have voted. The proportion is just 41 percent for those 24 and younger, and it is even lower for those 21 and younger.[70] Such findings are tied to the fact that younger citizens are often more mobile and less integrated into the community than are older citizens.[71]

It is worth noting that participation by the very youngest voting-age citizens (18–24) climbed to more than 49 percent in 2008, from 36 percent in 2000. Much of this gain was

→ KEY QUESTIONS:
Why do better-educated, better paid, and older people vote at higher rates than less-educated, more poorly paid, and younger people? What is the effect on government?

→ KEY QUESTIONS:
What can you do to get young people in your community to vote? Why is it important?

Table 9.1 Turnout by Income in the 2012 Presidential Election

	Percent Turnout
Less than <$15	48%
$15,000–19,999	52%
$20,000–29,999	56%
$30,000–39,999	58%
$40,000–49,999	62%
$50,000–74,999	66%
$75,000–99,999	70%
$100,000–150,000	74%
Over $150,000	76%

© CENGAGE LEARNING®

among young blacks, whose rate of participation jumped in response to Obama's candidacy. But the excitement of the youth faded four years later with 41 percent turnout in 2012.[72,73] One has to be cautious in making too much of these changes, but it does suggest that younger people can, under some conditions, become more active in politics. The general shift from the mid-1990s, where turnout was about 35 percent, to now being over 40 percent is in line with some of the early patterns of greater participation that have been found among the Millennials—the youngest cohort of voting-age citizens.

Income. The higher one's income, the more likely one is to vote. More income generally means that people believe they have more at stake and thus more reason to vote. Individuals with higher incomes are also likely to be in environments in which politics is frequently discussed and that provide greater opportunities for learning about the political process. Political knowledge is strongly correlated with the propensity to vote. Further, individuals with higher incomes are more likely to be able to arrange to vote than are those with low-paying jobs, who may be less able to take time off from work to go to the polls.

Data from the U.S. Census Bureau in Table 9.1 strongly confirm this relationship. In 2012, about 75 percent of people with total family incomes between $100,000 and $150,000 reported that they went to the polls. For people whose incomes fell in the range that represents the annual median family income in America—$40,000 to $50,000—turnout was 62 percent. For the least-well-off (those earning less than $15,000), the proportion who claimed to have voted was 48 percent.

Education. Although race and ethnicity, sex, age, and income have some effects on the propensity of people to vote, the number of years of formal education seems to be the most important influence. Social science research has documented the connection between education and voting.[74] The youngest voting-eligible citizens (18- to 24-year-olds) who have college degrees have turnout rates 13 percentage points higher than the rates of older citizens (65–75) who do not have a high school education.[75] Table 9.2 shows the propensity to vote by educational level from 1988 to 2012. The gap between people with the least education

Table 9.2 Turnout by Education in Presidential Elections, 1988–2012

Years of Education	1988	1992	1996	2000	2004	2008	2012
				Turnout			
8 years or fewer	37%	35%	30%	27%	24%	23%	22%
Less than high school	41%	41%	34%	34%	34%	27%	32%
High school	55%	58%	49%	49%	50%	50%	49%
Less than college	65%	69%	61%	60%	66%	65%	61%
College or more	78%	81%	73%	72%	74%	73%	72%

Source: Harold Stanley and Richard Niemi, *Vital Statistics on American Politics* (Washington, D.C.: CQ Press, 2013).

and those with the most was 50 percentage points in 2012—a huge difference. Nearly three-fourths of college-educated people vote, whereas less than a quarter of those with just a grade school education do so.

The relationship between education and voting may not be as simple as these data suggest, however. New evidence indicates that going to college does not matter as much as childhood socialization, which imbues the values of citizenship and similarly affects the decision to attend college. It is not, therefore, spending four years in college that makes college graduates more likely to vote; rather, it is having been raised in an environment that stresses the importance of education that shapes willingness to vote.[76]

The gap in turnout between people who are more educated and those with little education has increased over the past forty or so years. The increase can be explained by expanded access to education. Individuals who lack a high school education are at a much larger disadvantage than in the past. These patterns suggest that inequalities may result as government responds more effectively to those who vote than to those who do not.

Checkpoint

CAN YOU:

- Generalize about turnout in the United States
- Identify the characteristics of individuals who are more likely to vote

9.8 Why Citizens Vote

> Articulate the main theoretical approaches that explain voting

With the right to vote guaranteed and widely available, why do some people choose not to vote? Perhaps we can start to answer that question by reversing it, that is, by looking at why people *do* vote. Political scientists have developed three approaches to explain why eligible voters choose to cast ballots. One model draws from the field of economics, the second draws from psychology, and the third focuses on the rules and context of the election. In this section, we present these explanations as well as some new ideas about the relationship of genetics and voting.

→ KEY QUESTIONS:
Did you vote in the 2014 midterm elections? Why or why not?

An Economic Model of Voting

The economic model of voting starts with the assumption that all choices involve calculations about self-interest that balance costs and benefits. In choosing a college, students consider the price of tuition, the location of the school and its reputation, the quality of the education, and the potential social life. The decision to vote is no different. According to the economic model, citizens consider the costs and benefits of voting; when the benefits exceed the costs, they turn out to vote. So, according to this model, if voting becomes less costly to all citizens, there should be an increase in participation. If it becomes more costly, fewer people will turn out. Under this model, voters act in a rational, self-interested fashion.

However, economic voting is not straightforward. In *An Economic Theory of Democracy* (1957), Anthony Downs describes **rational voting** as a puzzle. He points out that there are some costs tied to voting, such as the time it takes to become informed, to register to vote, and to go to the polls.[77] Costs could also involve lost work time and the cost of gas to drive to the local polling place. These costs are not huge, but they are real.

The conclusion of the economic model is that voting is not in one's self-interest and in fact is irrational. If the decision to vote is driven by a self-interested assessment of costs and benefits, people should not take the time to vote. That is a troubling conclusion for the workings of democratic government. Obviously, if citizens do not bother to vote, government cannot be responsive, and public officials will not be held accountable.

Downs understood the troubling implications of his model and claimed that people voted because they knew that the system would collapse if no one voted. To save the system from collapse, it was rational to vote. This observation has appeal at first glance, but the logic is flawed: One vote will not save the system from collapsing. So even if the system is about to crumble, it remains rational to abstain from voting.

The prediction from Downs's model has drawn much attention from scholars. William Riker and Peter Ordeshook sought to save the model by introducing the idea of civic duty as a benefit of voting. The notion of civic duty is important, but the argument describes a psychological attitude voters might have.[78] Thus Riker and Ordeshook's argument does not solve the problem in Downs's model.[79] Narrow self-interest does not explain why people vote. As a consequence, political scientists tend to view voting as more of a psychological process than as a narrow economic or self-interested process.

A Psychological Model of Voting

The psychological model views participation in elections as a product of citizens' attitudes about the political system. These attitudes are often a product of socialization and early political experiences. People who are raised in households in which voting is important are likely to think that participation matters. Those who have a strong sense of trust in government or believe that their votes matter are more likely to participate. The focus here is on what we called civic interest in Chapter 1, Gateways to American Democracy.

Riker and Ordeshook's concept of civic duty fits well in this psychological model of voting. Many people who vote recognize that being a citizen in a democracy carries the obligation to vote. In 2012, for example, 90 percent of the public believed that "it's my duty to always vote."[80] The act of voting makes citizens feel good and feel that they are part of the political system. Surveys have found a strong correlation between civic-mindedness and the propensity to vote. In fact, there is often guilt associated with not voting, so much so that people tend to over-report the frequency with which they go to the polls.[81]

rational voting:
Economic model of voting wherein citizens weigh the benefits of voting against the costs in order to take the most personally beneficial course of action.

→ KEY QUESTIONS:
Should the government adopt laws that advance the Jeffersonian or Hamiltonian approach to participation?

→ KEY QUESTIONS:
Do you feel like you have a civic duty to vote? If so, where did you get that sense of duty?

Another psychological component tied to the act of voting is partisanship. Citizens who align themselves with the Democratic Party or the Republican Party are more likely to vote. Being a partisan implies an engagement in politics, and partisans see importance in the outcomes of elections. Partisanship increases the prospects that an individual will vote.

Both civic duty and partisanship are attitudes formed in childhood. One survey found that a person's attitude about citizenship expressed in 1965 was a powerful predictor of his or her voting in the 1980 presidential election.[82] The relationship between socialization and voting holds even after education and other important variables that drive participation are taken into account. In addition, parents' electoral activism in 1965 also explains their children's willingness to vote in 1980. Much has changed since 1980, but socialization continues to have a long and powerful reach.

It is also clear that citizens who express greater trust in government are more willing to participate. In addition, people who think they have a voice in government are more likely to vote. Political scientists call this attitude **efficacy**—the belief that one's involvement influences the course of government.

efficacy: *Extent to which people believe their actions can affect public affairs and the actions of government.*

An Institutional Model of Voting

A third explanation of voting looks at political context. In the **institutional model**, voting is understood to be shaped by the rules of the system, by political party behavior, by the ways candidates run their campaigns, and by the context of the election.[83] This model does not ignore individuals' personal resources or psychological attitudes; it simply points out that the political environment is a factor that shapes participation.

institutional model: *Model of voting that focuses on the context of the election, including whether it is close and whether the rules encourage or discourage participation.*

It is clear, for example, that the popularity and appeal of the candidates affect turnout.[84] Contenders who are viewed as unexciting, even boring, offer voters few reasons to participate. But both very popular and very unpopular candidates might spur turnout. A highly controversial candidate might lead people who are strongly opposed to show up in great numbers on election day. A highly popular candidate likewise brings out supporters.

The competitiveness of an election also influences motivation. Elections that look to be close draw voters' interest and attention, especially if they think their votes might influence the outcome. A close race is exciting, and people like to be part of it. But elections often are not competitive, lessening citizens' incentive to make time to cast their ballots.

Because voting takes time, the efforts by parties, interest groups, and civic organizations to bring people to the polls can make a difference. Get-out-the-vote drives seem to pay big dividends, especially at the local level.

Musician Kid Rock performs during a campaign rally for Mitt Romney at the Royal Oak Music Theatre in Royal Oak, Michigan, on February 27, 2012. Campaigns try many ways to encourage younger citizens to participate.

JUSTIN SULLIVAN/GETTY IMAGES

For example, direct personal contact, such as going door to door, may increase the rate of voting by 7 to 10 percentage points in local elections.[85] Even text messaging seems to increase turnout by about 3 percentage points, according to a recent study.[86] The size of these effects is not likely to apply to presidential elections because many people are already inclined to vote in these high-stimulus elections. Parties, too, can increase turnout by mobilizing their base to participate.[87] Canvassing by telephone or in person not only may lower information costs but also may activate citizens' sense of civic duty. In some cases, parties or other organizations pick up people and bring them to the polls, lowering the costs of voting.

Is Voting in Your Genes?

It makes sense that voting is a product of psychological forces or perhaps of the costs and benefit of participating. But might the choice to be active in politics have a deeper cause? Might it be in your genes? More than two thousand years ago, Aristotle contended that "man is by nature a political animal." Political scientists have tended to believe that citizens are "blank slates," nurtured by socialization, education, and environment. Recent evidence, however, has suggested a genetic component to participation. James Fowler and his colleagues found a strong relationship between genes and turnout.[88] Another study reported "that two extensively studied genes are significant predictors of voter turnout."[89] These new data are important because they suggest that scholars may need to move beyond looking at the nurture side of the equation and start to consider the role nature plays in shaping individuals politically.

Checkpoint

CAN YOU:

■ Describe the economic model of voting

■ Describe the psychological model of voting

■ Describe the institutional model of voting

■ Address the genetic model of voting

9.9 Assessing Turnout

❯ Evaluate how low turnout is in American elections

As this chapter has established, most Americans do not vote in most elections. Even in presidential elections, for which turnout is highest, only slightly more than half of eligible voters go to the polls. In this section, we assess turnout in the United States. Is it too low for responsive and responsible government? Even more important, does turnout increase the prospects of governmental action that ensures equality?

Is Turnout Low?

There is a widespread belief among political scientists, political observers, and journalists that turnout in American elections is low. Consider the titles of the following books on the topic of voting in the United States: *Why Americans Still Don't Vote, Where Have All the Voters Gone?*, and *The Vanishing Voter.*[90] When just 37 percent of the American public took the time to vote in the 2014 congressional elections, the concern about low turnout expressed in these books seems justified. Even with all the attention and interest surrounding the 2012 presidential elections, turnout of the voting-age population was about 58 percent.[91] Such data strike many as disappointing. But further investigation of turnout can offer a different way to interpret the situation.

The United States Compared to Other Democracies.

Compared to other democracies, turnout in the United States is low. Between 1948 and 2012, the average rate of turnout in U.S. presidential elections was about 57 percent,[92] while in other democracies it was 90 percent or more.[93] These numbers compel an assessment of why U.S. turnout is so low.

One reason has to do with the rules for voting. Australia has **compulsory voting**—citizens are required by law to vote. Those who do not vote must pay a $20 fine, and the fine increases to $50 if the nonvoter does not answer the Australian Election Commission's inquiry about why he or she did not vote. New Zealand requires all citizens to register to vote. In most of the countries of Western Europe, the government is responsible for registering citizens to vote. In the United States, by contrast, both voting and registering are voluntary, and only about 70 percent of the public is registered. That means that nearly one-third of potentially eligible voters cannot cast votes on election day even if they want to do so.

Another reason has to do with the convenience of voting. Most European countries lessen the costs of voting by allowing it to take place on Sunday. In the United States, voting takes place on Tuesday, a workday for most people. Federal law stipulates that the first Tuesday after the first Monday in November is the day on which voting for president and members of Congress will take place, and most states have also selected Tuesdays as the day for voting in primaries and in state and local elections. The costs of voting are increased because people may be at work and may have difficulty finding the time to vote.

According to one estimate, turnout in the United States would be 27 percentage points higher (or more than 80 percent) if the nation had laws and rules that foster voting.[94] At the least, this figure suggests that comparisons of turnout in various democracies require a careful accounting of the rules and institutions that shape the willingness of citizens to go to the polls.

Trends in Turnout.

A second problem is noted regarding turnout trends in the last fifty years. One of the lines in Figure 9.11 (see page 299) represents the percentage of turnout in presidential elections measured against the **voting-age population (VAP)**, an estimate of those old enough to vote. In the United States, all citizens 18 or older constitute the VAP. The graph shows a lot of change—a decline in the 1970s, a surge in 2004 and 2008, a drop off in 2012. This pattern is much the same for midterm elections. In 1962, turnout for congressional elections was 48 percent. It fell to a low of 38 percent in 1986, with a slight rebound to about 41 percent in 2010. But regardless of how you want to interpret these shifts, one thing is clear: Turnout today is less than it was fifty years ago.

This pattern becomes more worrisome in light of rising levels of education since 1960, as education is one of the strongest predictors of turnout. Even though education levels have increased over the past fifty years (see Table 9.2 on page 293), the rate of participation in elections has not increased.

compulsory voting:
Practice that requires citizens to vote in elections or face punitive measures such as community service, fines, or imprisonment.

→ KEY QUESTIONS:
Should the United States adopt compulsory voting?

→ KEY QUESTIONS:
Should the United States vote on Saturday or Sunday instead of a weekday?

voting-age population (VAP):
Used to calculate the rate of participation by dividing the number of voters by the number of people in the country who are 18 and over.

generational replacement: *Cycle whereby younger generations replace older generations in the electorate.*

These kinds of data have led political scientists to study why fewer Americans seem to be voting.[95] Explanations have varied. One explanation looks at the difference between those who enter the electorate and those who leave. The concept of **generational replacement** describes a trend in which older voters who pass away are replaced in the electorate by less reliable young voters.[96] It is very difficult, however, to sort out generational differences from changes in self-interest. That is, do older voters turn out to vote because of the generation they were part of, because they are older and have more experience in dealing with politics, or because they want to protect their interests or expand the benefits that directly affect them, such as Medicare and low payments for prescription drugs?

A second explanation has been the decline of party organizations.[97] Local parties have been less able to turn out the vote on election day than they were in the late nineteenth and early twentieth centuries, and therefore the voting rate has declined. Some scholars have estimated that half of the decline in turnout can be attributed to the drop in mobilization efforts.[98] This explanation has appeal, but parties in many ways are stronger today than they were in the past, although the days of big city bosses and urban political machines are gone. Obama and the Democratic Party were successful in turning out the vote in 2012, especially in key states such as Ohio, and citizens are voting along party lines more than any time since scientific surveys began in the 1950s. So a decline in party strength (perceived or real) is not an adequate explanation for low turnout.

→ KEY QUESTIONS:
What effect do negative ads have on you?

A third explanation for declining turnout is the increasingly harsh tone of political campaigns. Some argue that negative campaigns have fueled voter apathy. It is clear that negative advertising on TV often fosters voters' disgust with politics. About 80 percent of people say they do not like these campaign tactics.[99] Initial studies suggested that negative campaigns could decrease turnout by about 5 percentage points.[100] In addition, there is clear evidence that negativity in campaigns has been on the rise since the 1960s, so there has been an apparent correlation between the two trends.[101] Scholars and pundits rushed to endorse this hypothesis. But subsequent studies have called the hypothesis into question.[102] A harsh campaign is likely to be competitive, and competitive campaigns draw interest and therefore increase turnout. Further, negative attacks can activate partisanship, which also increases turnout. People often choose to affiliate with a party in part because they do not like members of the opposite party. An attack ad by the Republicans can remind their supporters why they oppose the Democrats, giving them more reason to participate. A recent comprehensive study of all research on this topic shows clearly that negativity is not responsible for lowering turnout.[103]

A New Way to Measure Voting. There is another explanation that actually contends that turnout has *not* declined over the past forty years: The VAP measure has been in error because it does not take into account increases in the number of immigrants and convicted felons who are ineligible to vote. Over the few decades, there has been a steep increase in the number of undocumented immigrants. With the sagging economy of the past few years, the numbers have declined, but even so, in 2011 the number of illegal immigrants was estimated to be nearly 12 million (or about 4 percent of the population).[104] Over the past twenty years, there has also been nearly a threefold increase in the

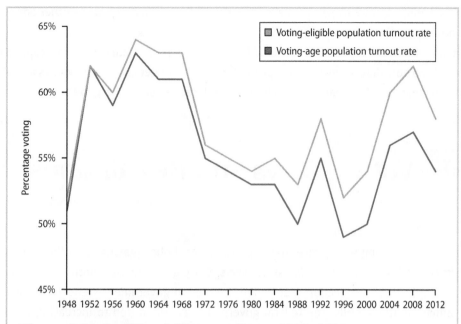

Figure 9.11 Presidential Turnout Rates, 1948–2012

The VAP measure is the traditional approach to assessing turnout, dividing the number of voters by the voting-age population. The VEP seeks to correct for overcounting in the voting-age population by removing noncitizens and people in jail who are not eligible to vote. Until 1972, this correction made only a modest difference. But given the surge of immigration and the growth in the number of convicted felons since then, the VEP measure is more accurate. Turnout in the 2004 and 2008 elections is actually comparable to turnout in the 1950s and 1960s, but dropped in 2012.

Source: "Presidential Turnout Rates, 1948–2012," United States Elections Project, accessed January 28, 2014, http://elections.gmu.edu /voter_turnout.htm. Copyright © 2012 by Michael McDonald. Reproduced by permission.

number of people in prison (from 585,000 to 1.6 million), reflecting tougher sentencing in American courts of law.[105]

A new measure called the **voting-eligible population (VEP)** corrects for these trends. The top line in Figure 9.11 presents the VEP estimates for turnout. It indicates that aggregate turnout in the 2008 presidential election was actually about 62 percent. By this measure, turnout has not declined over the past thirty years. In fact, turnout is now a full 10 percentage points higher than in the presidential election of 1948, when it was 52 percent. These revised estimates put a new spin on what has been perceived as a problem with U.S. elections, suggesting that Americans are not less willing to vote than in the past or than citizens in other democracies.[106]

 voting-eligible population (VEP): *Used to calculate the rate of participation by dividing the number of voters by the number of people in the country who are eligible to vote rather than just of voting age.*

→ KEY QUESTIONS:
Do Americans have equality in voting? Explain.

Do Turnout Rates Create Inequality?

Voting is a hallmark of democratic politics and is certainly a cherished American value. The idea is simple. Each person has one vote, and each vote should be equal. The fact that those who are better educated or better off participate at a greater rate is a potential source of concern (see Table 9.1 on page 292 and Table 9.2 on page 293). That the wealthy are more likely to vote than the poor is an especially troubling trend because the income gap between the rich and the poor is increasing.[107] As the rich become richer, they become better able to

Checkpoint

CAN YOU:

- Explain why turnout is lower in the United States than in some other democracies
- Address the issue of turnout and inequality

contribute more money to parties and candidates.[108] Such donations only further advance their potential influence.

It makes sense that politicians respond to people who participate and do not respond to those who do not. That is why it is so important for people to get involved in politics and also why the increasing rate of participation in the past decade or so is such good news.

 # 9.10 Voting Laws and Regulations

> Analyze how changes in voting laws have affected rates of participation

The rules surrounding voting alter participation rates. Policy making regarding voting is undertaken at both the federal and state levels. State governments continue to manage most voting laws and procedures, although the federal government steps in to prevent discrimination at the polls. The federal government is committed to increasing participation by making voting as easy as possible. At the same time, both state and federal governments work to prevent voter fraud, as we saw when we examined voter ID laws. Thus, policy making regarding voting has the effect of both expanding and potentially contracting turnout. This section reviews policies that have altered the way voting works in the United States.

Reforms to Voting Laws in the 1890s

Rules matter, as the institutional model of voting suggests. Any change in the laws governing voting (or any process related to voting) will alter how that process works. A classic example of the power of rules can be found in the late nineteenth century, when the Progressives called for a series of reforms to the voting process to end corrupt practices. The reforms affected who was eligible to vote and the way people actually voted. In other words, they altered who participated in elections.

Corrupt voting practices needed to end. Big-city political machines routinely "stuffed" the ballot box,[109] and party members manipulated the results to ensure victory. Turnout in some cities exceeded 100 percent, meaning that not only were some people voting who should not have been but also that some were voting multiple times. Party members often rounded up people and brought them, in sequence, to various polling precincts around the city, making sure they voted in each one. Someone who had died would remain on the rolls, and the party machine would "allow" that person to vote. This corrupt practice has been referred to as **graveyard voting**.[110]

In response to these excesses, Progressives called for voter registration.[111] The idea was that voters would have to preregister with a government official to be placed on an official list of voters. The list would be updated when someone died, and it would be used at the polls on election day to ensure that a potential voter had the right to vote and had not already voted. This reform spread rapidly. Today, all states except North Dakota require voter registration. The specific rules of registration vary a great deal among the states. For example, only in Idaho, Iowa, Maine, Minnesota, Montana, North Carolina, New Hampshire, Wisconsin, and

graveyard voting:
Corrupt practice of using a dead person's name to cast a ballot in an election.

→ KEY QUESTIONS:
If you are a registered voter, what was your experience with registration? Was it a gate or a gateway?

Wyoming can a person register and vote on election day.[112] All other states require registration before the actual voting.

The National Voter Registration Act

In 1993, Congress sought to streamline voter registration procedures so that more Americans would exercise their right to vote, at least in federal elections. The National Voter Registration Act, commonly known as the "Motor Voter" law, requires states to allow citizens to register to vote at the same time they apply for or renew their driver's licenses. This law also requires states to inform citizens who are removed from the approved voter rolls and limits removal to a change of address, conviction for a felony, and, of course, death. These requirements were in response to charges that local governments, controlled by political parties, improperly removed voters from the voter rolls without their knowledge; under the guise of updating voter registration lists, officials of one party were disqualifying voters who would tend to vote for the other party's candidates. The 1993 law imposes criminal penalties on anyone who tries to coerce or intimidate voters on their way to the polling place or tries to prevent registered voters from casting their ballots.[113]

New Forms of Voting

As indicated earlier, some states are experimenting with laws that make voting easier. Some have instituted early voting, allowing voters to cast ballots before the Tuesday on which a general election is held. This flexibility helps working people, who might find it hard to find time to vote on a Tuesday. It also provides more than a single day for voting, so that schedule conflicts (such as a dental appointment or a sick child) do not interfere. In Texas, for example, citizens can vote any time between seventeen and four days before election day, so "you don't have to stand in long lines on election day."[114] Other states, such as Oregon, have started to make use of a **vote-by-mail (VBM) system**. Voters get ballots in the mail two weeks before the election, giving them a chance to research the candidates and cast their ballots. They can make their choices at home and avoid the often long lines at the polling booth. This innovation, proponents argue, lowers the cost of voting, and there is some evidence it has increased participation. Oregon has had a very high rate of voting, although it did drop from about 70 percent in 2008 to about 64 percent in 2012.[115] California has had less success with voting by mail. Some now worry that, under the rules of VBM systems, less-educated people are less likely to vote.[116]

Over the past three decades, nearly two-thirds of states passed "early voting" provisions that allow citizens to cast ballots prior to election day (see Figure 9.12).[117] The idea was that limiting participation to a single day kept many people from participating. The idea seemed sensible, and a lot of states followed suit. Although there is little evidence that early voting increases turnout, the provisions clearly lower the costs of voting.[118] Recently, however, some states have begun to reverse those laws and reduce the availability of early voting, eliminated same-day voter registration, and enacted new strict photo identification requirements.[119] These new laws increase the cost of voting, making it more

COMPARE WITH YOUR PEERS
MindTap for American Government

Access the Voting Forum: Polling Activity—Voter Registration.

→ KEY QUESTIONS:
Should the government take steps to increase voting? Why?

vote-by-mail (VBM) system: *Method of voting in an election whereby ballots are distributed to voters by mail, and voters complete and return the ballots by mail.*

CONNECT WITH YOUR CLASSMATES
MindTap for American Government

Access the Voting Forum: Discussion—Election Day.

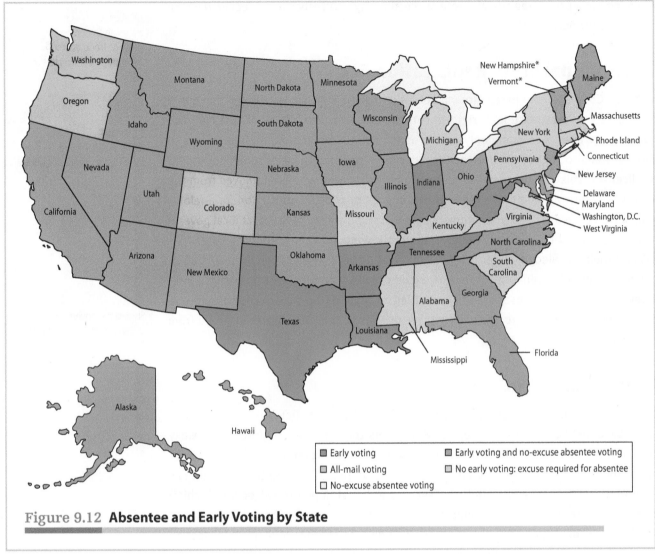

Figure 9.12 **Absentee and Early Voting by State**

Legend:
- Early voting
- All-mail voting
- No-excuse absentee voting
- Early voting and no-excuse absentee voting
- No early voting: excuse required for absentee

Source: http://www.ncsl.org/research/elections-and-campaigns/absentee-and-early-voting.aspx

→ KEY QUESTIONS:
What are the risks and benefits of early voting? Of voting by mail?

→ KEY QUESTIONS:
Aside from voting, how have you participated in politics and civic life?

difficult for some citizens to vote. Others say the laws are necessary to protect the integrity of the ballot box.

Nevertheless, new technologies, including the Internet, Twitter, and cell phones, may be used in the future, and they could make it easier for some people to vote—elderly and disabled, for example—thus increasing turnout. However, opponents of using these technologies argue that they would be too susceptible to voter fraud for two reasons: First, there would be no way to identify the person who is casting the vote, unless citizens are given individual pin codes or use their Social Security numbers. Given the number of Internet security breaches, opponents argue that such a system would not guard personal privacy. Second, votes at polling places are counted by election officials, but Internet and cell phone voting data would likely be collected and counted by computer servers, which are vulnerable to hacking and other security breaches.

In considering the effects of voting by new technologies, the beneficial effects on community and civic life of having everyone vote on a single day should also be considered.

The act of standing in line and talking with fellow voters, or discussing the act of voting with friends and family at the end of the day, can reinforce the sense of political efficacy and provide a foundation for the democratic process. Voting by mail, cell phone, or via twitter may detract from this shared experience, and that cost must be weighed against the added benefits of increased voter participation.

Elections, Campaigns, Voting, and Democracy

American elections and the campaigns that precede them are the means by which citizens participate in selecting those who will govern them. It is inevitable that they are at the center of concerns about American democracy. Many observers worry that campaigns are too long, that candidates spend too much money, and that the voters are not very well informed. These concerns often focus on the fairness of the process and of the outcome. In the long term, the process has worked reasonably well. In the short term, it is those who lose who see the process as unfair.

In any assessment of the American political system, your own partisanship needs to be set aside. The general lesson is that elections and campaigns, although imperfect, provide a real chance to ensure government responsiveness and have done so over many years and decades. The public digests information and chooses a candidate. People's votes are a blunt instrument, but they help to forge accountability. It is through this competitive struggle that American democracy works. Critics worry that the public does not know many of the details of candidates and their platforms, and that is clearly true. But the American public should not be underestimated. The fact that the public collectively seems to act in reasonably coherent ways is testimony to political scientist V. O. Key's classic observation that "voters are not fools."[120]

Moreover, the U.S. government has lasted more than two centuries. This longevity is not an accident and is attributable, in large part, to the fact that Americans have, collectively, taken the time to participate. There have been many barriers, from limited suffrage to rules that discourage voting, but the long-term trend has been increased participation, which speaks to the health of American democracy. Now suffrage—the right to vote—is available to all citizens except those convicted of a felony (see Chapter 5).[121] The rate of voting in the United States is not as low as many observers tend to assert. Further, looking at participation more broadly, Americans do more than just vote in elections. They are engaged in political campaigns and in making their communities better at the local level.

There is a danger to a democracy from a distortion in turnout; the rich participate more than the poor, and this gap seems to be growing. With nonvoters being poorer and less educated, their failure to participate may help explain why government is not as responsive to their needs. Put another way, the government may be overly responsive to the needs of the well-off. This disparity in responsiveness threatens the underpinnings of a democratic and egalitarian society. If the political system responds to one segment of the population and systematically ignores other segments, general support for democracy, based on principles of fairness, could drop significantly.

With the Internet's growing influence, there may be other dangers to democracy. Wealthier citizens have more access to the information and resources on the Internet and therefore become even more informed and better able to make government responsive to their needs. The rich have always had advantages, but their advantages may be growing. At the same time, the Internet might be used to extend participation. As recent presidential campaigns have demonstrated, this technology can be used to expand the number of contributors to include people who have only a few dollars to contribute or who might want to show up at a local meeting to learn about an issue of relevance to them.

Let us now return to Figure 9.5 (page 284), which offered two models of participation. The Hamiltonian model argued that more participation is not always a good thing and that government works best with limited involvement from the public. The Jeffersonian model contended that greater participation improves both the quality of the input and the lives of citizens. Within our book's gateway approach, the participatory model of voting has more appeal than the elite model. Democracy becomes more responsive, more accountable, and more equal if more people participate. The cycle is reinforcing. Citizens themselves need to do all they can to encourage participation; doing so is in their self-interest and their civic interest. Democracy rests on the active and healthy participation of the citizenry. In other words, as the number of gateways increase, so does the quality of American civic life.

Master the Concept
of Elections and Campaigning for Office with MindTap™ for American Government

 REVIEW MindTap™ **for American Government**
Access Key Term Flashcards for Chapter 9.

 TEST YOURSELF MindTap™ **for American Government**
Take the Wrap It Up Quiz for Chapter 9.

 STAY CURRENT MindTap™ **for American Government**
Access the KnowNow blog and customized RSS for updates on current events.

 STAY FOCUSED MindTap™ **for American Government**
Complete the Focus Activities for Elections and Campaigning for Office.

Key Concepts

battleground state (p. 277). Why do presidential candidates focus on battleground states?

compulsory voting (p. 297). Should the United States make voting compulsory?

efficacy (p. 295). How should democracy increase people's sense of efficacy?

Electoral College (p. 267). Is the Electoral College a gate or a gateway to democracy?

generational replacement (p. 298). What changes in turnout can be expected as young people become eligible to vote and older citizens no longer can?

gerrymandering (p. 272). Does gerrymandering weaken responsiveness?

graveyard voting (p. 300). How was graveyard voting curtailed?

institutional model (p. 295). What are the weaknesses of the institutional model of participation?

invisible primary (p. 273). What is the importance of the invisible primary?

microtargeting (p. 278). Why do politicians engage in microtargeting?

negativity (p. 279). What are the benefits of negativity for voters?

permanent campaign (p. 273). Why is the permanent campaign a problem for Congress?

position issues (p. 279). Why are position issues uncommon in campaigns?

rational voting (p. 294). Why might rational voting be bad for democracy?

redistricting (p. 271). What is the difference between redistricting and gerrymandering?

safe seat (p. 281). Are safe seats a sign of government responsiveness or unresponsiveness?

swing states (p. 277). Is your state a swing state?

swing voters (p. 277). Why are swing voters less common today?

suffrage (p. 283). When were women first extended the right of suffrage?

Super PACs (p. 276). What was the effect of Super PACs on the 2012 presidential election?

term limits (p. 282). What are the advantages and disadvantages of term limits?

valence issues (p. 279). Why are valence issues common in campaigns?

vanishing marginal (p. 281). Why do vanishing marginals mean elections are less competitive?

vote-by-mail (VBM) system (p. 301). Why might VBM increase turnout?

voting-age population (VAP) (p. 297). How is VAP different from VEP?

voting-eligible population (VEP) (p. 299). Explain the merits of this measure.

wedge issue (p. 279). Why do politicians like to use wedge issues?

Learning Outcomes: What You Need . . .

To Know	To Test Yourself	To Participate

 Describe the ideas that molded the Framers' thinking about elections.

To Know	To Test Yourself	To Participate
The constitutional requirements for elections set up gates against direct democracy by allowing only the House of Representatives to be elected by the people. State legislatures chose both senators and the electors who would elect the president. Today senators are elected directly by the people. The Electoral College enhances the influence of small states over states with large populations and affects the strategy of presidential campaigns. Because of the structure of the Electoral College, the candidate with the highest number of popular votes sometimes does not win the presidency.	• Summarize the constitutional requirements for presidential elections. • Summarize the constitutional requirements for congressional elections.	• Argue that the constitutional requirements for elections create citizen inequality. • Vote in a local or state election this year.

To Know	To Test Yourself	To Participate

▶ **Outline the steps in presidential campaigns.**

Presidential campaigns are demanding on the candidates and are shaped by constitutional requirements, interparty struggles, and strategies for attracting votes.	• Compare and contrast nineteenth-century and twenty-first-century presidential campaigns. • State the importance of the invisible primary to candidate momentum. • Explain how caucuses and primaries work. • Tell what happens at national conventions.	• Debate whether the permanent campaign increases government responsiveness or impairs government performance. • Attend a caucus or vote in a primary.

▶ **Identify the issues that shape presidential campaigns.**

Campaigns make public engagement possible but are very expensive. Strategies for winning states crucial to winning the electoral vote introduce inequalities, as does the shaping of appeals to voters.	• Track trends in fundraising for presidential campaigns. • Describe the impact of the Electoral College on presidential campaigns. • Explain microtargeting as a campaign strategy. • Compare and contrast valence issues and position issues. • Describe the role of negativity in campaign strategies.	• Evaluate the role of money in presidential elections. • Assess whether the Electoral College creates citizen inequality. • Evaluate the pros and cons of negative advertising.

▶ **Determine which issues shape congressional campaigns.**

Campaign promises, including those in party platforms, are the measure against which citizens can evaluate the performance of the president and Congress. The presidency and the composition of Congress change in response to economic conditions and foreign relations, and the pattern of party gains and losses indicates that voters use elections to hold officials accountable and that the presidency and Congress are responsive institutions.	• Explain how fundraising needs restrain candidates. • Describe the role of political parties in congressional campaigns. • Give reasons for incumbency advantage.	• Decide if campaigns are too expensive. • Decide if incumbents are too entrenched.

▶ **Explain why there are battles over ballot access.**

Participation is essential to the functioning of democracy, and voting is the most common means by which people get involved. The Constitution gives states authority over the "Times, Places and Manner of holding Elections." State rules vary, introducing some inequalities in access. Because voting shapes the outcome of elections and the conduct of government, there have always been debates over who gets access to the ballot. The Hamiltonian model of participation sees risks in the extension of the franchise to groups that may be uninformed and favors a larger role for elites. The Jeffersonian model of participation maintains that greater participation produces better outcomes and encourages citizens to get more involved in self-government.	• Explain why it matters that the Constitution delegated authority over voting to the states. • Compare and contrast the Hamiltonian and Jeffersonian models of participation.	• Debate the relationship between citizen voting and democratic government.

▶ **Outline how the right to vote has expanded.**

Today Americans enjoy almost universal opportunities to vote, but in the past, the vote was denied to African Americans, women, Native Americans, and immigrant groups denied citizenship.	• Survey the expansion of suffrage between 1790 and today. • Describe how minorities and immigrants have at times been prohibited from voting.	• Appreciate your right to vote. • Investigate the status and causes of disfranchisement today.

To Know	To Test Yourself	To Participate

 Identify who tends to turn out in American elections.

Unequal turnout by various demographic groups suggests that government's response is unequal. Most troubling for democracy is the tendency for people with higher incomes to vote at higher rates than the poor. Older people and those with more education also tend to vote at higher rates than younger people and those with less education.

- Generalize about turnout in the United States.
- Identify the characteristics of individuals who are more likely to vote.

- Critique citizen equality in light of turnout.

 Articulate the main theoretical approaches that explain voting.

Political scientists explain why people vote (and choose not to vote) using theoretical models. The economic model examines the costs and benefits of voting. The psychological model examines attitudes, including the idea of civic duty and the influence of partisanship. The institutional model examines the rules and regulations surrounding voting, including political party behavior, campaign strategy, and the context of the election. Genetic factors are a new consideration.

- Describe the economic model of voting.
- Describe the psychological model of voting.
- Describe the institutional model of voting.
- Address the genetic model of voting.

- Analyze your own reasons for voting.
- Assess the impact of civic duty, partisanship, and the competitiveness of elections in turning out the vote.

 Evaluate how low turnout is in American elections.

Turnout in the United States is lower than in many other democracies, but it can be explained by the institutional model.

- Explain why turnout is lower in the United States than in some other democracies.
- Address the issue of turnout and inequality.

- Evaluate whether low turnout invalidates the idea of self-government.
- Assess whether higher turnout among the wealthy than among the poor has an impact on public policy.

 Analyze how changes in voting laws have affected rates of participation.

From the 1790s to the 1870s, voting rights expanded. From the 1870s to the 1920, barriers to voting, especially for African Americans, increased. After 1920, voting rights expanded again and were increasingly protected by the federal government. The overall trend has been toward constant expansion of the right to vote. Voter registration helps prevent fraud in elections but also poses a gate that decreases turnout.

- Identify the goals of the Progressive voting reforms.
- Assess how the Motor Voter law, vote-by-mail, and early voting have impacted affected voter turnout.

- Propose ways to increase turnout in the United States.

ZUMA PRESS, INC./ALAMY

"Just as there are streets and highways that help us get to where we want to go on the road, there is an infrastructure of opportunity in America that allows us to get to where we want to go in life."

JOAQUÍN CASTRO
Stanford University

©DJ40/SHUTTERSTOCK.COM

10 Congress

Very few people can claim that their sibling is the Secretary of Housing and Urban Development, but even fewer can say this while they are already a sitting member of the U.S. House of Representatives. Joaquín Castro (TX-D) from Texas's 20th district was born in 1974 to a community activist mother and a schoolteacher father. As a second generation Mexican American, Representative Castro and his identical twin brother Julián were well aware of the sacrifices their grandparents had to make to give their children a better life in America. His family history has deeply affected how he serves his congressional district.

Public service did not come naturally for one of the Castro brothers: Joaquín Castro was uninterested in politics and public service despite growing up in a political household. Only after they left Texas and went to school at Stanford did both the Castro brothers recognize the importance of public service. After earning law degrees from Harvard Law School, the Castro brothers went back home and joined a private law firm. Representative Castro fulfilled his interest in public service by running for the state legislature in District 125, while Julián Castro entered into city politics, running for the city council seat his mother lost three decades before. During his five terms in the state legislature, Joaquín Castro took a deep interest in education and health care, and he served as the vice chairman of the Higher Education Committee.

During his 2012 campaign for the U.S. House, Representative Castro promised to pursue his "Infrastructure of Opportunity," a program that Castro believes "allows each of us to pursue our American dreams." Castro wants to see the United States build an infrastructure of exemplary public schools and universities, a strong health care system, and an economy that pays people well so they can support their families.

As Representative Castro passionately declared from the House floor after he won his seat with nearly 64 percent of the vote, the infrastructure of opportunity is just as important for the future of America as is a sound transportation infrastructure. Representative Castro has put his support behind bills that will help improve the infrastructure of opportunity, such as his sponsorship of the Student Aid Expansion Act of 2013 and the Paycheck Fairness Act. He even spends a large portion of his free time improving education opportunities in his home district, which includes parts of San Antonio. He has helped to raise money for underprivileged youths to go to college through the Trailblazers College Tour, and he created SA READS, which has provided more than 200,000 books to more than 150 schools and shelters in San Antonio.

Need to Know

10.1 Describe how Congress has developed

10.2 Define the powers of Congress

10.3 Outline how Congress is structured

10.4 Explain how a law is made in Congress

10.5 Assess what a member of Congress does

 WATCH & LEARN MindTap™ **for American Government**
Watch a brief "What Do You Know?" video summarizing The Congress.

Beyond education and health care, Representative Castro also cares deeply about the nation's defense and military needs. Through his assignments on the House Armed Services Committee and the House Foreign Affairs Committee, Representative Castro was able to visit Afghanistan as they were holding elections in March 2014. During his visit, Castro was able to personally thank Texas service members and present them with a Texas flag. Castro's service on the House Armed Services Committee is particularly important for his constituents, as the city of San Antonio has three military bases, and the state of Texas has more than 120,000 active military personnel and 1.7 million veterans. Representative Castro's committee service as well as his prior service in the state legislature have uniquely positioned him as a trusted leader willing to give voice to the needs of his constituents and act as an advocate for the many servicemen and women whom he represents.[1]

In this chapter, we explain how members of Congress navigate the gates and gateways embedded in the legislative branch to best serve the interests of their constituents. The fact that members of Congress must repeatedly return home to ask the voters to reelect them helps keep them responsive to their constituents, who hold them accountable for the policies they enact into law. But the process of congressional representation—that is, of putting good ideas into practice as law—is difficult and complex. Structural gates are embedded in a separation of powers system of government and in a democratic legislative process that encourages competition among groups with conflicting interests. Navigating this terrain is not easy, but Joaquín Castro's efforts to represent his district show how an individual member of Congress seeks to be an advocate as well as a legislator.

10.1 Congress as the Legislative Branch

> Describe how Congress has developed

→ KEY QUESTIONS:
Is Congress a gateway to democracy, or a gate?

LISTEN & LEARN
MindTap® for American Government

Access Read Speaker to listen to Chapter 10.

In Chapter 2, The Constitution, we discussed the ideas of representation that shaped the Framers' thinking. They believed that a democratic government had to be responsive and accountable to the people. In such a government, leaders would not inherit power; rather, they would be chosen by the people at regular intervals, and these elections would be the key way that voters would hold government officials accountable for their actions. The Framers of the Constitution designed Congress to be the legislative branch of the federal government, and they gave it broad powers to enact laws. At the same time, they wanted the process of lawmaking to be complex and deliberative so that members of Congress would not succumb to impulsive actions that might harm constituents or violate fundamental constitutional rights. Over time, Congress has increased the scope and range of its powers, but the new responsibilities have added a layer of complexity that makes it harder than ever to pass laws.

Representation and Bicameralism

Essential to understanding how Congress facilitates representation in the American democracy is to recognize that it is bicameral; that is, it is divided into two separate chambers: the House of Representatives and the Senate. This structure reflects the Framers' fear that the power of the legislative branch might grow to the point where it could not be controlled by the other two branches. Because the legislative branch is closest to the people—its members represent specific population groups, by region, and can be removed by election—the Framers believed that Congress would have a democratic legitimacy that neither the executive nor the judicial branches would possess.

→ KEY QUESTIONS:
What did the Framers do to control Congress's power?

The solution, according to James Madison, was to divide the legislature into two parts that would check each other. In *Federalist* 51 he explained that this would "render them . . . as little connected with each other, as the nature of their common functions, and their common dependence on the society, will admit." The House of Representatives would be a large body that reflected population size within states and was directly elected at frequent intervals (every two years). The Senate would be an elite chamber, with two senators for every state regardless of population size elected by state legislatures for six-year terms. In that way, both the popular opinions of average voters and the elite opinions of the well educated and the wealthy would be represented in Congress. This arrangement also guaranteed that large states could not overwhelm smaller states in determining the content of laws. The specific differences between the two parts of Congress are discussed in the next section.

Constitutional Differences between the House and Senate

To accomplish Madison's goal, the Constitution establishes four key differences between the two chambers of Congress: qualifications for office, mode of election, terms of office, and constituencies (see Table 10.1).

Qualifications for Office.   To serve as a member of the House of Representatives, an individual must be at least 25 years old, reside in the state that he or she represents, and have been a U.S. citizen for seven years before running for office. The qualifications for the Senate are that an individual must be at least 30 years old, reside in the state he or she represents, and have been a U.S. citizen for nine years before running for office. Senators are expected to be older and to have lived in the United States for a longer period of time than House members because the Framers believed those characteristics would make the Senate the more stable partner in the legislative process.

The Framers created the House of Representatives and the Senate as separate chambers of Congress, but both are located in the U.S. Capitol. In this view from the National Mall, the Senate chamber is on the left, and the House chamber is on the right. There are six office buildings for members of Congress and their staff members, three on each side of the Capitol.

Table 10.1 Comparison of House and Senate Service

	House	Senate
Minimum age	25 years old	30 years old
Citizenship	7 years	9 years
Term of office	2 years	6 years
Geographic constituency	District	State
Redistricting	Every 10 years	—
Mode of election until 1914	Direct	Indirect through state legislatures
Mode of election after 1914	Direct	Direct

© CENGAGE LEARNING®

Although the members of the First Congress (1789–91) were all white men, no provision in the Constitution delineates a specific race, gender, income level, or religion as a prerequisite for serving in Congress. Twenty-first-century Congresses have been much more diverse, with female, African American, Hispanic, Pacific Islander, and Native American members in the House (see Figure 10.1). Nevertheless, note that women held only 18 percent of the seats in the 113th Congress (House and Senate combined), although they constituted 51 percent of the nation's population. African Americans hold forty House seats and two Senate seats, while Latinos hold thirty-one House seats and four Senate seats. Despite the advancements made by underrepresented groups in electing members to Congress, it is still predominantly white and male.[2] The average House and Senate member is older than 57. House members tend to serve an average of five terms (ten years) and Senators an average of two terms (twelve years).[3] The twenty-first-century House has included members from the Protestant, Catholic, Jewish, Greek Orthodox, Mormon, Buddhist, Quaker, and—for the first time— Muslim faiths. The religious background of senators has been slightly less varied but has also included members from the Protestant, Roman Catholic, Mormon, and Jewish faiths.[4]

House members have more varied prior experience than their Senate colleagues. A majority of House members served in their state legislatures before coming to Congress; others were mayors, law enforcement officers, teachers, doctors, ministers, radio talk show hosts, accountants, business owners, and even three airline pilots. Just as House members use state legislatures as stepping-stones, senators use the House of Representatives to launch their bids for the Senate. In the 113th Congress, fifty-one senators had previously served in the House of Representatives, and others had been mayors, governors, and attorneys general or had held executive branch positions.

Mode of Election. House members are elected directly by citizens. Senators are elected directly as well, but that is a more recent development. From 1789 to 1914, the mode of election for the Senate was indirect: Citizens voted for members of their state legislatures, who then selected the U.S. senators. The mode of election for the House and Senate was different on purpose. The House was supposed to be more immediately responsive to the opinions of the people, but the Framers designed the Senate to insulate senators from the direct voice of the people, in other words, to make them less directly responsive to the people.

The mode of election for the Senate was changed from indirect to direct with the ratification of the Seventeenth Amendment in 1913. At the end of the nineteenth century, in

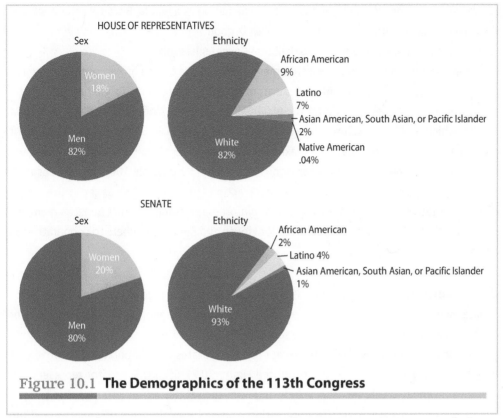

HOUSE OF REPRESENTATIVES

Sex

Women 18%

Men 82%

Ethnicity

African American 9%

Latino 7%

Asian American, South Asian, or Pacific Islander 2%

Native American .04%

White 82%

SENATE

Sex

Women 20%

Men 80%

Ethnicity

African American 2%

Latino 4%

Asian American, South Asian, or Pacific Islander 1%

White 93%

Figure 10.1 The Demographics of the 113th Congress

Source: Jennifer E. Manning, *Membership of the 113th Congress: A Profile*, CRS Report for Congress, R42964 (Washington, D.C.: Congressional Research Service, March 14, 2014).

response to charges of deadlock and corruption during the election of U.S. senators in state legislatures, Progressives led a movement to allow voters to directly elect their senators.[5] The amendment opened up a much more direct gateway of influence for constituents over their U.S. senators.

Terms of Office.   A term of office is the length of time that an elected official serves before facing the voters again in an election. The term of office for House members is two years, and the term of office for U.S. senators is six years. The difference in term of office leads to key differences in how each chamber operates. House members have a shorter amount of time to demonstrate their effectiveness before they face reelection, so the House of Representatives as a whole is usually in a greater hurry to pass legislation than is the Senate. Senators know they have six years before they have to face their voters, so they have a bit more flexibility in working out disagreements among their constituents and balancing

Barbara Mikulski (D-Md.) is the longest serving woman in Congress. She served in the House of Representatives from 1977 to 1986, when she was elected to the Senate. Throughout her career, she has championed women's health and labor issues. She has also been a strong advocate for her home state of Maryland.

constituents' interests against the interests of the nation as a whole. Because senators know they have a longer time in which to establish a good reputation among their home state voters, the Senate takes more time to deliberate over legislation.

In any given election year, the entire membership of the House of Representatives must face the voters, but only one-third of senators stand for reelection. To guarantee that the whole Senate would never stand for reelection all at once, the Constitution divided the first Senate, which met in 1789, into three classes of senators who would be elected at different six-year intervals.[6] To this day, the maximum number of senators who stand for regularly scheduled reelection in the same year is thirty-four (out of a possible 100), thereby ensuring that a majority of the Senate is never up for reelection at the same time as the entire House of Representatives.[7] This electoral condition reinforces the stability of the Senate's membership; it also limits the electoral incentives for House and Senate members to cooperate with one another to pass legislation.

Constituencies.   A constituency is the set of people that officially elects the House or Senate member; in the United States, constituency is defined geographically. Each member of the House of Representatives represents a congressional district with established geographic boundaries within the state (except for seven states with populations so small that they have just one congressional district; see Figure 10.2). Each U.S. senator represents an entire state, and two U.S. senators are elected from each state.

→ KEY QUESTIONS:
Which congressional district do you live in? Which congressional district is your college in?

In 1789, the average size of a congressional district was about 30,000 people, and the average size of a state was about 300,000 people; in 2014, a congressional district had about 711,000 people, and the nation's largest state, California, had approximately 38 million residents.[8] Because the Framers knew that the country's population would change, they required a count, or census, of the population every ten years. Following the census, the number of congressional districts in each state would be adjusted to reflect population changes. The House started with 65 members and, when capped by Congress at 435 in 1929, had increased by 670 percent.[9] Congress was concerned that if the House grew any larger it would not be possible to conduct legislative business.[10] Today, because there is an absolute limit on the total number of House members, population growth or decline has a direct bearing on a state's representation, increasing or decreasing the state's number of representatives and thus its relative influence in the House.

Redistricting.   Only the House of Representatives is subject to redistricting, which is the redrawing of the boundaries of congressional districts in a state to make them approximately equal in population size. Because the size of the House is limited to 435, the overall number of congressional seats per state must be adjusted following a census if there have been population changes. Based on the state's allocation of congressional districts, the state legislature redraws the districts, and the only real limitation on redistricting is that the boundaries of the district must be contiguous (uninterrupted). During redistricting, the majority party in the state legislature tries to influence the process to construct each district in such a way that a majority of voters favors its party, thereby making it easier for its candidates to win, in a process known as gerrymandering. Sometimes the majority party will combine two existing districts that have House members from the other party, forcing them to run against each other.

→ KEY QUESTIONS:
With each state having the same number of senators, what are the consequences for citizen equality across small and large states?

Figure 10.2 States by Population, 2013

The U.S. Senate has two senators for every state, regardless of population. This arrangement makes states equal in Senate votes: Wyoming has the same number of votes as California. But it also means that the 582,658 citizens of Wyoming have the same voice in the Senate as the 38,332,521 citizens of California. Equal representation in the Senate did not seem as imbalanced when states had more similar population sizes, but today, with such huge differences, some observers think representation in the Senate is inherently unfair.

Source: © Cengage Learning®; data from U.S. Census Bureau, "Population Estimates," http://www.census.gov/popest/data/state/totals/2013/index.html, accessed May 12, 2014.

Redistricting has also been used as a tool to achieve greater minority representation in the House of Representatives following the theory of descriptive representation, whereby an individual represents a constituency not just in terms of geography but also in terms of race or ethnicity. The Voting Rights Act of 1965 prohibits states and political subdivisions from denying or limiting "the right of any citizen of the United States to vote on account of race or color"; it was later amended to protect the voting rights of non-English-speaking minorities—referring to Latinos—as well. This act is discussed in detail in Chapters 5, Civil Rights and 9 Elections, Campaigns, and Voting; here we focus on the fact that many states initially responded to the law by redrawing congressional districts to group minority voters in a way that would deny them the voting strength to elect a minority member of Congress. In 1982, Congress amended the Voting Rights Act to prevent this kind of manipulation. In response, some state legislatures

→ KEY QUESTIONS:
How do majority-minority districts provide a gateway for better representation of minority interests?

created so-called majority-minority districts in which African Americans or Latinos would constitute a majority of the voters and would have enough votes to elect an African American or Latino candidate.[11] The Texas district that Congressman Castro represents is considered a majority-minority district, with 70 percent of the population there identifying as Latino.[12] Since then, the federal courts have ruled that state legislatures overemphasized the racial composition of these districts to the point that the districts made no geographic sense. Current guidelines on redistricting call for the consideration of race in drawing district lines but not to the extent that it was employed in the past.[13]

Checkpoint

CAN YOU:

- Explain the reasons for and consequences of bicameralism
- Explain the constitutional differences between the House and Senate

Because representation in the Senate is related to state boundaries, not to population size, some scholars have argued that the Senate is less responsive than the House. It is true that there are vast differences in population size among the states[14] (see Figure 10.2). As we explore later in this chapter, the rules of the Senate amplify this imbalance of influence by granting each senator equal power to delay, or block, legislation. As a result, a senator who represents a state such as Wyoming, with fewer than six hundred thousand people, can delay, or in the final day of a session, actually prevent, the passage of a policy that might benefit a state such as California, with 38 million people.

10.2 The Powers of Congress

› Define the powers of Congress

As Chapter 2 describes, the Framers granted Congress powers that were necessary to construct a coherent and forceful federal government. Some of these, such as the power to tax and to regulate commerce among the states, had been denied to Congress under the Articles of Confederation, and their absence had weakened the new republic. At the same time, the Framers worried that the legislative branch would grow too powerful. So they limited the powers of Congress to a list in Article I, Section 8, of the Constitution, together with a few stated responsibilities in other sections. The following discussion highlights the most important powers of Congress. It also examines the ways that Congress has used its constitutional powers to expand its role in the policy-making system and ways that Congress is balanced and checked by the executive and judicial branches.

→ KEY QUESTIONS:
How have the powers of Congress increased? Why did they increase?

Taxation and Appropriation

Congress has the power "To lay and Collect Taxes." In a division of this important power, the Constitution states that all bills for raising revenue should originate in the House of Representatives, but the Senate "may propose or concur with Amendments, as on other Bills." Initially, the Framers thought that tax revenue would come primarily from levies placed on imported goods. As the industrial economy grew, so did the need for government services and programs that cost money. With the Sixteenth Amendment, ratified in 1913, Congress gained the power "to lay and collect taxes on incomes," whatever the source. This amendment overturned prohibitions on certain types of income taxes.

Paralleling the power to tax, Congress also has the power to spend—"to pay the Debts and to provide for the common Defence and general Welfare." The general welfare clause has proven to be a major means by which Congress's power has expanded. Congress **appropriates** (or allocates) federal monies on programs it **authorizes** (or creates) through its lawmaking power. This "power of the purse" has been instrumental in the expansion of Congress's relative strength among the branches of government.[15] The Constitution also gives Congress the authority to borrow money, to coin money, and to regulate its value, and it requires a regular accounting of revenue and expenditures of public money.

War Powers

The Constitution gives Congress authority to "provide for the common Defence." In reality, the war powers are shared with the president. For example, Congress has the sole power to declare war, but this power is typically used only after the president has requested a declaration of war. In many cases, the president may ask Congress for specific authorization to take military action; under its power of taxation and appropriation, Congress has the authority to fund or refuse to fund military operations. Generally, Congress also has the power "to raise and support Armies," "to provide and maintain a Navy," "to provide for calling forth the Militia," and to make rules and regulations regarding the armed forces and their organizations. Relations between Congress and the president over war powers have sometimes been harmonious, but in recent decades, they have become contentious. The struggle between the president and Congress over the war powers is examined in detail in Chapter 11, The Presidency.

Regulation of Commerce

The Constitution gave Congress an important power that it did not have under the Articles of Confederation: the power "to regulate Commerce with foreign Nations, and among the several States, and with the Indian Tribes." Using the power in this commerce clause, Congress established a national set of laws regulating commerce that are applicable to all states equally.[16] In time, the authority to regulate interstate commerce has allowed Congress to expand its power to the point that almost no economic activity is beyond its reach. In 2012, the Court ruled that Congress's requirement, set forth in the Patient Protection and Affordable Care Act, that individuals purchase health insurance went beyond Congress's commerce clause authority but upheld most of the act as within Congress's taxing authority (see Supreme Court Cases: *National Federation of Independent Business et al. v. Sebelius*).

Appointments and Treaties

In recognition of the Senate's perceived wisdom and stability, the Framers gave the Senate, and not the House, the power of advice and consent. In the appointment of high-level executive branch appointees, such as cabinet secretaries and ambassadors, this power allows the Senate to evaluate the qualifications of a presidential nominee and, by majority vote, to approve

→ KEY QUESTIONS:
Why do you think the Framers gave the House, rather than the Senate, the authority to originate revenue bills?

appropriate: *Congress's power to allocate a set amount of federal dollars for a specific program or agency.*

authorize: *Congress's power to create a federal program or agency and set levels of federal funds to support that program or agency.*

→ KEY QUESTIONS:
What is meant by the term "general welfare" with respect to Congressional power? How would you define it today?

COMPARE WITH YOUR PEERS
MindTap for American Government

Access The Congress Forum: Polling Activity—The Power to Declare War.

supreme court cases

National Federation of Independent Business et al. v. Sebelius (2012)

QUESTION: May Congress impose a mandate to purchase health insurance on those who do not wish to carry it? Did Congress exceed its spending authority with the Medicaid expansions?

ORAL ARGUMENT: March 26–28, 2012 (listen at http://www.oyez.org/cases/2010-2019/2011/2011_11_400)

DECISION: June 28, 2012 (read at http://www.oyez.org/cases/2010-2019/2011/2011_11_400)

OUTCOME: Yes, the authority is within Congress's taxing power (5–4). Yes, Congress exceeded its spending authority (7-2). Overall, however, the law is constitutional.

The Obama administration argued that because the decisions of individuals not to purchase health insurance have a substantial effect on hospitals and insurance companies involved in interstate commerce, Congress has the right to mandate the purchase of such insurance. Those opposed to the act argued that if Congress could make people purchase health insurance because of the substantial effect it has on interstate commerce, why couldn't it, under the same reasoning, make people buy broccoli? As a fallback, the administration argued that even if the act was not itself a regulation of commerce, it was necessary and proper to the regulation of commerce (see Supreme Court Cases: *McCulloch v. Maryland* in Chapter 3, Federalism). As a second fallback, the administration argued that the mandate was a valid exercise of Congress's authority to tax to provide for the general welfare. Opponents pointed out that when Congress was debating the bill, the Obama administration insisted that the payments for not purchasing health insurance were a penalty and not a tax, so that members of Congress could not be accused of passing unpopular tax increases. Additionally, opponents claimed that the threat states faced of losing all Medicaid funding if they did not voluntarily expand their Medicaid coverage was coercive, in violation of the Tenth Amendment (see Chapter 3).

In a complicated decision, Chief Justice John Roberts, joined by the Court's four more conservative

justices (Samuel Alito, Anthony Kennedy, Antonin Scalia, and Clarence Thomas), declared that Congress did not have the authority under the commerce clause or the necessary and proper clause to mandate that individuals enter the insurance market. This part of the opinion weakens Congress's commerce clause powers. Crucially, however, Chief Justice Roberts, joined by the Court's four more liberal justices (Stephen Breyer, Ruth Bader Ginsburg, Elena Kagan, and Sonia Sotomayor), ruled that the penalty for not purchasing insurance could be considered a tax, and that as a tax, it was well within Congress's authority.

Finally, by a 7–2 vote, all justices except Ginsburg and Sotomayor, argued that Congress cannot rescind previously committed funds to states that refuse to accept the new Medicaid requirements, imposing the first limits on Congress's spending power in seventy-five years. But by a 5–4 vote, with Roberts joining the liberal bloc, the Court upheld the withholding of new funds from states that did not accept the new Medicaid expansion, as well as the rest of the law. In November 2014, the Supreme Court agreed to review the section of the Affordable Care Act that provides insurance subsidies only to the states that have established insurance exchanges (16) and not to the residents of the 34 states that chose not to establish exchanges. Without the subsidies, the law may be unworkable.

1. Why does it matter whether the payment for not having health insurance is a "penalty" or a "tax"?
2. What was unusual about the Court's decision involving Congress's spending authority?

or reject the nominee. Similarly, the appointment of all federal judges, from district courts to the Supreme Court, is subject to the approval of the Senate (see Chapter 13, The Judiciary, for more details on this process). Additionally, the Senate acts as a check on the president's power to make treaties with foreign nations: Treaties must be approved by a two-thirds vote, or they fail to take effect (see Chapter 11 for more on treaty negotiation and ratification). The advice and consent role of the Senate acts as a gateway for citizen influence over presidential appointments and treaties because senators are more likely to block appointments and treaties that they believe are unpopular with their constituents.

The Senate exercises its advice and consent powers when it holds hearings on presidential nominees and then votes to approve or reject them. In the summer of 2009, senators questioned President Barack Obama's first Supreme Court nominee Sonia Sotomayor, an appeals court judge from New York. She was confirmed on August 6, 2009, by a vote of 68 to 31, and she is the first Latina Supreme Court justice.

Impeachment and Removal from Office

Congress's ultimate check on the executive and judicial branches is its power to remove officials and judges from office by impeachment. The president, vice president, and high-level officials are subject to impeachment for "Treason, Bribery, or other high Crimes and Misdemeanors." This power is rarely used. In Chapter 11, we examine the two cases in which presidents have been impeached, but not removed from office. In the case of President Richard Nixon (1969–74), the threat of impeachment was credible enough that he resigned from office.

The process of impeachment and removal from office takes place in two steps. First, a majority of the House of Representatives votes to bring formal charges against the president or other federal official, an action called impeachment. Then the Senate conducts the trial, with the chief justice of the United States presiding in the case of the president's impeachment, and votes to convict or acquit. If two-thirds of the senators present vote to convict, the president or the federal official will be removed from office.

→ KEY QUESTIONS:
Why did the Framers give the Senate the power of advice and consent?

Lawmaking

Congress, as the legislative branch, is responsible for lawmaking. Unlike the enumerated powers listed at the beginning of Article I, Section 8, and explained previously, the final paragraph of Section 8 gives Congress broad authority "to make all Laws which shall be necessary and proper for carrying into Execution the foregoing Powers." In combination with the general welfare clause and the commerce clause, this necessary and proper clause allows Congress a great deal of leeway to carry out its responsibilities under the assumption that additional powers are implied in these clauses, although not explicitly stated in the Constitution. Over time, Congress has made full use of this flexibility to expand its authority in a wide range of areas, such as regulating interstate railroads, establishing civil rights protections, funding school lunch programs, limiting greenhouse gases, and providing student loans. Essentially, if an argument can be made that a service or program is reasonably tied to an enumerated power, Congress has used its powers to create that service or program.

Authorization of Courts

In Article I, the Constitution also gives Congress the power to "constitute Tribunals inferior to the Supreme Court." Article III, the section on the judiciary, reiterates congressional control by saying that Congress may "ordain and establish" courts at levels lower than the Supreme Court. In 1789, Congress used this power to pass the Judiciary Act, which established federal district courts and circuit courts of appeal. Today, there are ninety-four district courts and thirteen appellate circuits.[17]

The federal judicial branch asserted more authority over the other two branches in the Supreme Court case of *Marbury v. Madison* (see Chapter 2). This case established judicial review, which is the federal judiciary's power to declare laws passed by Congress as unconstitutional. The *Marbury* decision gave the courts the power to interpret the Constitution and determine how congressional laws (and even executive branch actions) conform to its explicit language and its intent (see Chapter 13 for further explanation of this decision).

In recent years the Senate has tried to reassert its influence over the federal courts through the nomination process.[18] As we discuss later in the chapter, individual senators can try to defeat presidential nominees for federal judgeships with whom they disagree on key constitutional questions.

Oversight

After a bill becomes a law, the executive branch, headed by the president, is supposed to carry out the law according to Congress's wishes. But the executive branch is a bureaucracy with many departments and agencies that have authority to implement laws. The sheer size and complexity of the federal bureaucracy make it difficult for Congress to determine whether laws are being administered according to the intent behind them (see Chapter 12, The Bureaucracy, for more details). Over time, Congress has asserted its oversight authority to monitor the ways in which the executive branch implements law. This authority stems from Congress's responsibility to appropriate money to provide for the general welfare of the nation. Congress constantly exercises this authority, but less so under unified government, when the same party controls Congress and the White House, than under **divided government**, when the party that controls Congress is not the party of the president. Under unified government, members of Congress assume that because they share the same partisan affiliation as the president, his administration is more likely to implement laws according to congressional intent.

In contrast, legislatures in countries that have parliamentary systems typically choose their executives from among the members of the majority party so that the executive and legislative branches always share the same policy goals. Consequently, legislative oversight is not a fundamental element of those political systems (see Global Gateways: The Parliamentary System of the United Kingdom).

divided government: *Situation in which one party controls the executive branch, and the other party controls the legislative branch.*

→ KEY QUESTIONS: Think about the power to investigate. Which branch should have this power?

globalgateways

The Parliamentary System of the United Kingdom

All democracies have a legislature and an executive, but their relationship to each other produces differences in the way people are represented. The United States has separate legislative and executive branches. In the United Kingdom, the executive and the legislative branches are intertwined. The United Kingdom is a limited monarchy democracy, with a queen as the head of state and a parliament for its legislature. The British Parliament is bicameral; the House of Commons has 650 members, and elections are held in single-member districts, as they are in the United States. The party that wins the most seats wins control of the chamber. The House of Lords has 779 members; some members inherit their seats, and others are appointed by the queen. The approval of both branches of the legislature, in the same year, is necessary to pass legislation.

In the British system, the prime minister, who is the chief executive of the government, is an elected member of the House of Commons chosen by the majority party and officially recognized by the queen. He appoints ministers and advisers to his cabinet without the formal approval of the legislature. Because the prime minister comes from the majority party in the legislature, the executive and the legislature typically agree on the legislation that needs to be passed to accomplish the party's goals. As party leader, the prime minister is responsive to the party's voting base. There are no regularly scheduled parliamentary elections, but elections must be held at least once every five years, and the campaigns last for less than three weeks. The prime minister calls for elections either when the majority party is very popular, so that it can retain power, or when it is so unpopular that the public calls for a change.

In 2010, Prime Minister Gordon Brown, a member of the Labour Party, had lost popularity, and in the May 6 election the Conservatives, led by David Cameron, won more seats than the Labour Party did but fell short of a working majority. As a result, the Conservatives joined with members of a third party, the Liberal Democrats, to form a working majority party in Parliament, producing a complete change in the coalition of parties that constitute the majority.

Source: UK House of Commons, http://www.parliament.uk/mps-lords-and-offices/mps/current-state-of-the-parties/ and UK House of Lords, http://www.parliament.uk/mps-lords-and-offices/lords/composition-of-the-lords/ accessed April 16, 2014.

1. How does the British parliamentary system differ from the U.S. separation of powers system?
2. Compare citizen control in elections that are regularly scheduled and in elections that are scheduled by the majority party in power.

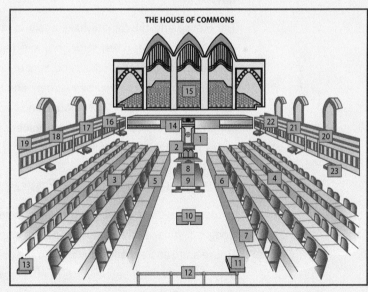

THE HOUSE OF COMMONS

1. Speaker	7. Leader of Second Largest Party in Opposition	13. Interpreters	19. Members' Gallery
2. Pages	8. Clerk and Table Officers	14. Press Gallery	20. Members' Gallery
3. Government Members	9. Mace	15. Public Gallery	21. Speaker's Gallery
4. Opposition Members	10. Hansard Reporters	16. Official Gallery	22. Senate Gallery
5. Prime Minister	11. Sergeant-at-Arms	17. Leader of the Opposition's Gallery	23. T.V. Cameras
6. Leader of the Official Opposition	12. The Bar	18. Members' Gallery	

In the House of Commons, members of the two major parties sit on opposite sides, as in the U.S. Congress, but they are identified as "government" and "opposition."

Checkpoint

CAN YOU:

- State what the general welfare clause allows Congress to do

- Recall why war powers are shared with the president

- Define the commerce clause and explain its power

- Explain the power of advice and consent

- Describe the process of impeachment

- Compare and contrast the enumerated and implied powers

- Explain Congress's role in the authorization of courts

- Characterize how Congress uses its powers of oversight on the other two branches

Members of Congress engage in oversight activities in several ways. They hold hearings with cabinet officials and bureaucrats to analyze how well programs are working, and they frequently invite members of the public to describe how federal programs operate in their communities. Members of Congress regularly write letters to executive branch agency heads to inquire about specific programs, and they keep careful track of the responses they receive. In cases of oversight hearings, special investigations, or suspected wrongdoing by members of the executive branch, Congress can legally require members of the administration to testify. For example, the House Oversight and Government Reform Committee and the Senate Judiciary Committee both asked Attorney General Eric Holder to testify in person about a federal law enforcement operation, named Fast and Furious, which allowed U.S. government-owned weapons to fall into the hands of suspected drug lords, who were later suspected of killing a federal border patrol agent. In some instances, Congress convenes special committees, such as the Iran-Contra Committee (see Chapter 11 for more details), to investigate actions involving members of the president's staff or even the president himself. In these ways, members of Congress provide a gateway for the people to constantly monitor and hold the federal government accountable for how it implements the law.

The Organization of Congress

> Outline how Congress is structured

The House and the Senate have evolved into very different institutions by virtue of their differences in size, rules, structure, and responsibilities. The Constitution establishes few guidelines for how the House and Senate should operate, so it was left to the members to determine how to choose their leaders and how much power to give them. Some aspects of leadership are shared by the House and Senate, but there are important differences in the amount of power each grants to its leaders. Notably, the power of political parties to shape policy is vastly different in each chamber.

The Role of Political Parties

In today's political world, political parties seem natural and intrinsic to the organization of Congress. Indeed members of Congress align more closely with their political parties in the House and Senate than in any time in the past 100 years (see Chapter 6, Figure 6.4). But this degree of difference between the political parties did not always exist in Congress. The House did not organize itself along strict partisan lines until well into the nineteenth century. As scholars Sarah Binder and Eric Schickler each show, not until after the Civil War did the House change its internal rules to give the majority party the ability to get its preferred policies passed over the objections of the minority party.[19] Since then, party affiliation and party loyalty have become the defining features of how policy is made in the House of Representatives.

Although the Senate also became more party-oriented at the end of the nineteenth century, its members never changed the rules of the chamber to give the majority party complete

→ KEY QUESTIONS:
Why is the Speaker of the House so powerful? Why is the person who holds this position third in line in presidential succession, after the vice president?

dominance. Because the number of senators has remained small, it is still possible to conduct legislative business in a personal manner, and each senator exerts individual influence over policy outcomes. Senators also have the chance to make individual impressions on voters over a longer time (six years) and from a more visible vantage point, as they represent entire states rather than just one district. In this age of increased polarization, voters weigh a senator's ideology and party affiliation more heavily than they used to, but it is still not as important as in House elections. Consequently, senators have had fewer incentives to hand over their individual powers to a single party leader to accomplish party goals.

As a result, members of the minority party in the Senate have far more power in the policy-making process than do their counterparts in the House.[20] In essence, getting any legislation passed in the Senate usually requires compromise and cooperation among all senators—majority and minority party members—in one way or another.

→ KEY QUESTIONS:
What evidence of compromise and cooperation do you see in the Senate today?

The House of Representatives

As is the case with any large organization, success requires leadership. To maximize party cohesion, members of the House meet in a party caucus ("to caucus" literally means "to gather") of the members of their political party. Each party's caucus chooses its party leaders: For the majority party, the top party leader is the Speaker of the House, and for the minority party, it is the minority leader.

The Speaker of the House.   Speaker of the House is the only formal leadership position written into the Constitution. Article I, Section 2, states that "the House of Representatives shall chuse their Speaker and other Officers," but there the official description ends. The Speaker is elected by a majority of House members every two years, on the first day of the first session of each new Congress. The position first became organizationally powerful under the tenure of Thomas Brackett Reed (R-Maine), who served as Speaker from 1889 to 1891 and again from 1895 to 1899.[21] Reed was elected to the House in 1876, and by the early 1880s he was already displaying political ambition.

As Speaker, Reed implemented a set of procedural changes known as Reed's Rules that strengthened the power of the majority party over the minority party. Because the House ran on majority rule, the party that had the most votes could pass a bill outright. Reed's party granted him the power to appoint all committee chairmen, approve all members' committee assignments, refer bills to committee, bring bills that reflect the majority party's ideas to the House floor, and refuse to allow the minority party to delay legislation.[22] Both former Speaker of the House Nancy Pelosi (D-Calif.) and current Speaker John Boehner (R-Ohio) used many of the same powers to run the House, although they each presided over a more complex decision-making environment than did Reed.

In the century following Reed, the leadership styles of Speakers varied according to how much power the rank-and-file party members wanted to give to their leaders. The scholar David Rohde and others argue that the variation in leadership style can be explained by the underlying coherence of the majority party during these years. When the rank-and-file membership of the majority party is unified in its policy goals, it hands power to party leaders, especially the Speaker, to accomplish those goals under what Rohde called conditional party government.[23] The leadership of Speaker Newt Gingrich (1995–98) represents this model of party leadership because he came to power with a large class of newly elected Republicans on a party platform called the Contract with America. They captured control of the House from Democrats after forty years in the minority and produced a cohesive ideological party that

Speaker of the House: *Constitutional and political leader of the House.*

KEVIN DIETSCH/UPI/LANDOV

Nancy Pelosi (D-CA) was elected the first female Speaker of the House of Representatives in 2007. She was generally considered a strong Speaker because she exerted control over committee chairs and the conditions under which bills were considered on the House floor.

was willing to give Gingrich strong powers to accomplish policy goals. However, just three years later, Gingrich resigned the Speakership after the 1998 midterm elections; the Republicans lost seats as a result of an unpopular attempt to impeach President Clinton (see Chapter 11).

After Gingrich, the Republicans chose a less powerful Speaker, Dennis Hastert (R-Ill.), and moved from a conditional party government system to what scholars call a party cartel system. According to Gary Cox and Mathew McCubbins, in this system, the power of party leaders rests on their ability to set the legislative agenda and provide services, such as campaign finance funds, and organizational positions, such as committee positions, to party members in exchange for their loyalty.[24] This type of cartel system worked better for the Republicans after 2001, when a Republican was elected to the White House and set the policy agenda for members of the party. Typically under unified government, members of the majority party in the House use the president's agenda as a starting point. As a result, the Speaker can lose independence in setting the policy direction for the House. A case in point is the Hastert Rule, named after former Speaker Dennis Hastert. The Hastert Rule states that when the Republicans are in majority control of the House, they will not bring a bill to the House floor without a majority of Republicans (i.e., a majority of the majority) agreeing to do so. In adopting that rule, the House Republican Party as a whole was ensuring that the Speaker would only bring bills to the House floor that followed their preferences.

After the Democrats won control of the House in the 2006 elections, Nancy Pelosi was elected the first female Speaker of the House. She lost that post after the Republicans gained a House majority in 2010 and elected John Boehner as Speaker. The ability of the Speaker to make the most of party power depends a great deal on how unified the party is on any given issue, or a whole range of issues, and on whether he or she represents the same party as the president. In the 112th and 113th Congresses, Speaker Boehner, with an opposite party president, had the most difficulty holding his majority party together on votes related to federal spending and deficit reduction. On these issues, he faced both an internal party division and a small wing of the Republican majority, led by Tea Party affiliated members, that did not want to cooperate with President Barack Obama under any circumstances. In fact, cooperation broke down so severely over the federal budget and national debt in late 2013 that the government shut down for sixteen days (see Chapter 14, Public Policy, for a full discussion). To resolve this impasse, Speaker Boehner had to violate the Hastert Rule in order to make sure the government was funded, and the debt ceiling was increased.

Whether he or she works with a same- or an opposite-party president, the Speaker's most important responsibility is to maintain power in the House for the majority party, and that means getting the members of the majority party reelected. To do so, the Speaker supports a set of policies that he or she believes are popular with voters, and he or she tries to get those policies enacted into law. For example, during the consideration of health care reform in the House, the Democrats shared the goal of passing a health care reform bill, so they allowed the Speaker to use all the tools at her disposal to get the bill passed. The Democrats suffered big losses in the 2010 elections in part due to voter backlash on this issue. For Speaker Boehner, the 2012 elections represented his first test of holding onto power in the House, and he focused his efforts on bringing bills to the House floor on issues such as federal aviation, transportation, and insider trading in Congress, all of which he knew had support within Congress and were popular with voters. By the time the 2014 elections came around, Boehner and the Republicans were more secure in holding the majority. Still, Pelosi and Boehner share the dubious distinction of presiding over Congresses with some of the lowest approval ratings ever recorded; in early 2014, only 12 percent of Americans approved of the job that Congress was doing.[25]

House Party Leaders.   The **House majority leader**, as second in command, works with the Speaker to decide which issues the party will consider. He or she also coordinates with committee leaders on holding hearings and reporting bills to the House floor for a vote. The House majority leader must strike a compromise among many competing forces, including committee chairs and external interest groups. He or she is also expected to raise a significant amount of campaign contributions for party members, and that role produces more pressure to appease as many interest groups as possible. The majority leader also has nine majority whips to help "whip up" support for the party's preferred policies and keep lines of communication open between the party leadership and the rank-and-file membership. The majority leader and whips work hard to track members' intended votes—in a process called the whip count—because they want to bring to the floor only those bills that will pass; any defeat on the floor could weaken voter confidence in the majority party.[26]

John Boehner (R-OH) replaced Pelosi as Speaker in 2011 after the Republicans won control of the House in the 2010 elections. Boehner has faced more internal party division than Pelosi did, but the Republicans still managed to hold on to the House in the 2012 and 2014 elections.

MARK WILSON/GETTY IMAGES

The minority party in the House is the party that has the largest number of House members who are not in the majority party. The highest-ranking member of the minority party is the **House minority leader**, and his or her main responsibility is crafting the minority party's position on an issue and serving as the public spokesperson for the party. If the minority party is the same as the president's party, the House minority leader is also expected to garner support for the president's policies among minority party members. The House minority leader works with minority whips who are responsible for keeping all the minority members in line with the party's public positions.

The challenge for the minority party in the House of Representatives is that it has very little institutional power; the majority party uses its numerical advantage to control committee and floor actions. Because of its institutional disadvantages, the minority party in the modern House of Representatives rarely has the power to stop majority party proposals from passing. Minority party members can vote no, but their real power lies in making speeches, issuing press releases, and stirring up grassroots opposition to majority party proposals.

⭐ **House majority leader:** *Leader of the majority party in the House and second in command to the Speaker.*

⭐ **House minority leader:** *Leader of the minority party in the House.*

→ KEY QUESTIONS:
Does the institutional structure of the House promote party dominance? Responsible lawmaking? What can be done about the structure of Congress?

The Senate

The Senate has always been a smaller chamber than the House because it is based on the number of states in the union and does not adjust according to population growth. Since 1959, when Hawaii and Alaska joined the union, the Senate has had 100 members, and the magic number to secure majority control in the Senate has been fifty-one senators. Not until the 1910s did senators formally appoint individual senators to speak for them as majority and minority party leaders. However, the Senate majority leader has fewer formal powers to advance the party's agenda compared to the Speaker of the House. Because the Senate never grew to be as large and unwieldy as the House, the individual members have rarely seen the benefit of giving up power to party leaders to make the Senate run efficiently or enact the party's agenda.

President Pro Tempore. Article I, Section 3, of the Constitution states that the vice president shall be the president of the Senate, but that in his absence the Senate may appoint a president pro tempore (temporary president) to preside over the Senate. For most of the Senate's history, the vice president presided over the Senate, and his main functions were to recognize individual senators who wished to speak and to rule on which procedural motions were in order on the Senate floor. The vice president can also break a tie vote in the Senate, a power that can give the president's party control of the outcome on the floor. But in the 1950s, the vice president became more active in executive branch business and less active in the Senate. Subsequently, the Senate began appointing the oldest serving member from the majority party as the president pro tempore to serve as the temporary presiding officer. The president pro tempore is closely advised by the Senate parliamentarian, who is responsible for administering the rules of the Senate.

Senate majority leader: *Leader of the majority party in the Senate.*

→ KEY QUESTIONS:
Does the institutional structure of the Senate promote party dominance? Responsible lawmaking? Individual careers? What can be done about the structure of Congress?

Senate minority leader: *Leader of the minority party in the Senate.*

Senate Party Leaders. The majority party elects the **Senate majority leader**, but unlike the Speaker of the House, this position is not written into the Constitution. The job of the Senate majority leader is to make sure the Senate functions well enough to pass legislation. To accomplish that goal, the Senate majority leader tries to craft legislation as close to the preferred policies of his or her party as possible, necessitating a great deal of compromise and the "power of persuasion."[27]

Still, the Senate majority leader does have several formal powers. For instance, he or she is the official scheduler of Senate business and is always recognized first to speak on the Senate floor. Every senator has the right to speak on the Senate floor, but senators must speak one at a time. Being recognized first, before any other senator, gives the majority leader the power to control the floor and prevent any other senator from speaking. But because the Senate majority leader relies on the senators' voluntary cooperation to conduct the business of the Senate, there are limits on how tough he or she can be on Senate colleagues. If a Senate majority leader tries to bully senators, they might retaliate by constantly using their individual floor powers to try to delay or block key legislation.

The **Senate minority leader** is the leader of the minority party in the Senate and is expected to represent minority party senators in negotiations with the majority leader on which bills are brought to the Senate floor and under what circumstances. Similar to the House counterpart, the Senate minority leader's job is to organize minority party senators into a coherent group that can present viable alternatives to the majority party's proposals.

The extended leadership structure of the Senate looks similar to that of the House (see Figure 10.3). It consists of an assistant majority leader, majority and minority whips, and conference chairs, all of whom are responsible for uniting the senators in their respective parties and crafting legislative proposals that can garner enough support to pass the Senate.

The Committee System

Almost all legislation that passes the House or Senate goes through a committee. The House and Senate are organized into separate committees to deal with the different issues, such as agriculture, energy, and education. The party that has the majority in the entire House or Senate also has the majority of seats on each committee, and the committee chair is chosen from the majority party, with the approval of the party caucus. Typically, each House member or senator gives the party leadership a list of desired committee assignments, and the leadership assigns committee seats according to seniority and the availability of seats on specific committees.

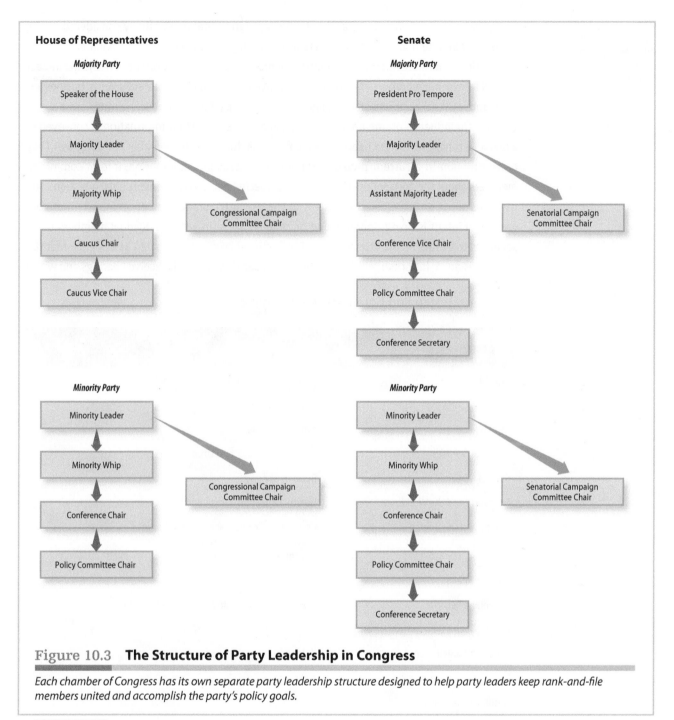

House of Representatives

Majority Party

Speaker of the House → Majority Leader → Majority Whip → Caucus Chair → Caucus Vice Chair

Majority Leader → Congressional Campaign Committee Chair

Minority Party

Minority Leader → Minority Whip → Conference Chair → Policy Committee Chair

Minority Leader → Congressional Campaign Committee Chair

Senate

Majority Party

President Pro Tempore → Majority Leader → Assistant Majority Leader → Conference Vice Chair → Policy Committee Chair → Conference Secretary

Majority Leader → Senatorial Campaign Committee Chair

Minority Party

Minority Leader → Minority Whip → Conference Chair → Policy Committee Chair → Conference Secretary

Minority Leader → Senatorial Campaign Committee Chair

Figure 10.3   The Structure of Party Leadership in Congress

Each chamber of Congress has its own separate party leadership structure designed to help party leaders keep rank-and-file members united and accomplish the party's policy goals.

The House and Senate each have several types of committees. A standing committee is a permanent committee with the power to write legislation and report it to the full chamber. Select committees, joint committees, and special committees are usually focused on a more narrow set of issues, such as aging or tax policy, but none has the same legislative clout and authority as a standing committee. In the House, there are twenty standing committees, and the average House committee has forty-three members. In the Senate, there are sixteen standing committees, and the average Senate committee has twenty members. The committee system is the central hub of legislative activity in Congress.[28] Committees hold hearings to consider members' bills, to conduct oversight of the executive branch, or to draw attention to a pressing issue. Committees also write the legislation that is eventually considered on the House and Senate floors. Table 10.2 lists the standing committees in each chamber.

During committee hearings, committee members hear testimony on the content and impact of a bill from other members of Congress, executive branch officials, interest groups, businesses, state and local government officials, and citizens' groups. For the public, hearings are a direct gateway for influence on members of Congress because important information is conveyed in a public setting. Committee hearings serve five basic functions for members of Congress: They draw attention to a current problem or issue that needs public attention, inform committee members about the consequences of passing a specific bill, convey constituents' questions and concerns about an issue, exert oversight of the executive branch to determine whether congressional intent is being honored, and provide an arena in which individual members make speeches to attract media attention that is often used later in a campaign as evidence that the member is doing his or her job. Committee chairs decide which bills receive hearings and which

Table 10.2 Standing Committees in Congress

House of Representatives (20 committees)	Senate (16 committees)
Agriculture	Agriculture, Nutrition, and Forestry
Appropriations	Appropriations
Armed Services	Armed Services
Financial Services	Banking, Housing, and Urban Affairs
Budget	Budget
Education and the Workforce	Health, Education, Labor, and Pensions
Energy and Commerce	Commerce, Science, and Transportation Energy and Natural Resources Environment and Public Works
Foreign Affairs	Foreign Relations
Homeland Security	Homeland Security and Governmental Affairs
Oversight and Government Reform	
House Administration	Rules and Administration
Judiciary	Judiciary
Natural Resources	
Transportation and Infrastructure	
Rules	
Science, Space, and Technology	
Small Business	Small Business and Entrepreneurship
Ethics	
Veterans' Affairs	Veterans' Affairs
Ways and Means	Finance

Source: U.S. House of Representatives, http://www.house.gov/committees/; and U.S. Senate, http://www.senate.gov/pagelayout/committees /d_three_sections_with_teasers/committees_home.htm. See the committee membership lists.

go on to **markup**, a meeting in which committee members write the version of the bill that they may send to the entire chamber for a vote. In both the hearing and markup process, the committee chair gives preference to the views of the majority party members of the committee.

Committee chairs have powerful roles. The chair is typically the majority party member who has the most seniority (longest time) on the committee. However, the Speaker or the Senate majority leader reserves the right to suggest a less senior member as chair if he or she believes that person will better serve the party's interests. In 2010, the Republicans selected Fred Upton (R-Mich.) as chair of the same committee, passing over Joe Barton (R-Tex.), who had served as **ranking member**—the member of the committee from the minority party with the greatest seniority—since 2006. The party leadership believed that Congressman Barton's views were out of sync with the party majority, especially after his public apology to the BP oil company for the federal government's demand for a monetary settlement to pay for the cleanup of the Gulf oil spill in 2010. This case illustrates the steps that party leaders will take to maintain control over committee agendas through the selection of committee chairs. Additionally the Republicans have a three-term limit on committee chairmanships; the Democrats do not. Term limits on chairmanships sustain the party's power to make a change in leadership of committees on a regular basis.

In general, when a bill is referred to a committee, it is assigned to a subcommittee, a smaller group of committee members who focus on a specific subset of the committee's issues. Subcommittees can consider legislation, but only the full committee can report a bill to the chamber floor for consideration.

Advocacy Caucuses

In addition to committees in the House and Senate, there are also advocacy caucuses, groups whose members have a common interest and work together to promote it. Members might have similar industries located in their districts and states, such as coal mining; or share a background, such as the Congressional Black Caucus or the Hispanic Caucus; or hold similar opinions on issues, such as abortion or land conservation. Members join an advocacy caucus because it gives them an opportunity to work closely with colleagues to represent specific interests and to draw attention to issues of concern to them and to their constituents. Many advocacy caucuses are bipartisan, that is, both Democrats and Republicans join as members. Advocacy caucuses are important to the interactions of Congress because they bring together members from different parties and regions that might not otherwise work closely with each other.[29]

Nearly three hundred advocacy caucuses are registered with the Committee on House Administration. In contrast, the Senate has only one official caucus, on International Narcotics Control. However, the Senate has a number of informal caucuses, such as the Senate Air Force Caucus and the Senate Steel Caucus, with members from both parties.

Advocacy caucuses have no formal legislative power, but they can be influential on a bill, especially in the House, because they represent a bloc of members who could vote together in support or opposition. As an alternative to joining a caucus, senators can join together in a temporary coalition and call a press conference to draw attention to the group, industry, or issue that unites them. Senators can also join a congressional caucus even though it is lodged in the House. When he was a senator from Illinois (2005–2008), Barack Obama joined the Congressional Black Caucus.

markup: *Process by which bills are literally marked up, or written, by the members of the committee.*

ranking member: *Leader of the minority party members of a committee.*

→ KEY QUESTIONS:
How do advocacy caucuses counteract the role of parties in Congress? How can they be a gateway for citizen influence?

Checkpoint

CAN YOU:

- Describe the role parties play in Congress
- Explain the role of party leaders in the House of Representatives
- Compare and contrast the functioning of the Senate and House
- State how the committee system works
- Identify the role of advocacy caucuses in Congress

10.4 The Lawmaking Process

> Explain how a law is made in Congress

In this section, we examine the lawmaking process. The process by which a policy proposal becomes a bill and then a law is long and winding, and the Framers designed it deliberately to ensure that laws were reasonable and well thought out. The gates against passage are almost too successful. In the 112th Congress (2011–2012), members introduced 7,837 bills in the House of Representatives and 4,461 bills in the Senate. Of the total 12,298 bills, Congress enacted only 283—or 2.3 percent—into law.[30] It requires compromise and cooperation for a bill to become a law. For an overview of the process, see Figure 10.4.

The Procedural Rules of the House and Senate

→ KEY QUESTIONS:
Do the procedural rules of the House and Senate serve as gates or gateways to legislation? Why would there be gates that prevent Congress from fulfilling its fundamental responsibility to pass laws?

rule: *Guidelines issued by the House Rules Committee that determine how many amendments may be considered for each bill.*

Just as the roles of political parties and leaders differ in the House and Senate, so do the internal rules of these chambers. Over time, House and Senate members have adopted different procedures for considering legislation, and these procedures can make compromise between the two chambers more difficult.

The House Committee on Rules.   To proceed from committee to the House floor, all bills must pass through the House Rules Committee. Because the House is so large, bills cannot proceed to the floor from committee unprotected; otherwise, the number of legislative amendments that could be offered by the 435 members of the House would overwhelm lawmaking.

The Rules Committee maintains control before the bill goes to the floor by issuing a **rule** dictating how many amendments may be considered. A closed rule means that no amendments may be offered; a modified closed rule allows a few amendments; and an open rule, as its name suggests, allows any number of amendments. The most typical rule is a modified closed rule, which allows the minority party to offer at least one alternative to the bill supported by the majority party. The rule is voted on by all members of the House; if it is approved, debate on the bill begins. If the rule is defeated, the bill is returned to the House Rules Committee or the originating committee for further consideration.

The majority party has learned over time how to use the Rules Committee to maintain policy advantages over the minority party. The majority party uses its numerical advantage on the Rules Committee (9–4 in the 113th Congress) to structure floor debate to limit the minority party's opportunity to amend or change a bill. The Speaker appoints all the majority party members to the Rules Committee, and they are expected to use their powers to advance the party's preferred version of a bill.

AP IMAGES/SENATE TELEVISION

All senators have the right to speak on the Senate floor, and sometimes they use this power to delay or block legislation, or draw attention to an issue they see as important. Here we see Senator Rand Paul (R-KY) using his power to speak indefinitely on the Senate floor.

Agenda-Setting Tools in the Senate.

The Senate does not have a gatekeeper committee like the Committee on Rules in the

When the president signs the bill or allows it to become law without his signature, or if Congress overrides a presidential veto, the bill becomes law.

The House and Senate bills are reconciled to produce one bill, which is sent to the president.

House of Representatives

Senate

12. House votes to pass or defeat the bill.

11. If the House accepts the rule, the bill is debated, and amendments may be offered.

10. Members of the House vote to adopt or reject the rule.

9. Rules Committee writes the rule on the bill, which determines what amendments, if any, can be offered when the bill is considered on the House floor.

8. Committee votes to recommend the bill to the full House, and the bill is sent to the House Rules Committee (the gatekeeper).

7. Full committee marks up the bill.

6. Full committee may hold hearings on the bill.

5. Subcommittee reports the bill to the full committee.

4. Subcommittee holds a markup session on the bill.

3. Subcommittee holds hearings on the bill.

2. Bill is referred by the Speaker of the House to a committee and subcommittee.

1. Bill is introduced by a House member on the House floor.

11. Senate votes to pass or defeat the bill.

10. Senators may offer amendments to the bill and debate the bill.

9. Majority leader crafts a unanimous consent agreement outlining which amendments will be offered and how long debate will continue; if unanimous consent is not achieved, there is unlimited debate on the bill unless cloture is invoked.

8. Majority leader brings up the bill on the Senate floor.

7. Bill is placed on the Senate legislative calendar.

6. Full committee holds a markup session and recommends the bill to the Senate.

5. Full committee may hold hearings on the bill.

4. Subcommittee may hold hearings on the bill; depending on the committee, the subcommittee may or may not mark up the bill.

3. Committee may refer the bill to a subcommittee.

2. Bill is referred to a committee by the Senate parliamentarian.

1. Bill is introduced by a senator on the Senate floor.

Figure 10.4 **How a Bill Becomes a Law**

House, and all senators have the power to try to amend legislation on the floor. The tool that they use is Rule XIX of the Standing Rules of the Senate, which grants senators the right to speak on the Senate floor. Over time, senators have used this right to make speeches, offer amendments to bills, object to consideration of a bill on the floor, or engage in **filibusters**, extended debates that members start with the purpose of delaying or even preventing the passage of bills.[31] All senators in the majority and the minority parties can use the filibuster.

filibuster: *Tactic of extended speech designed to delay or block passage of a bill in the Senate.*

Throughout Senate history, a wide range of bills, from civil rights legislation to product liability legislation, have been delayed or defeated by filibusters.[32]

cloture: *Vote that can stop a filibuster and bring debate on a bill to end.*

The only way to stop a filibuster is by invoking **cloture**, a motion to end debate that requires a supermajority of sixty votes to pass. In November 2013, the Democratic majority, led by Senator Harry Reid (D-Nev.), changed the threshold for cloture on presidential nominations and judicial nominations for district and appeals court judges to fifty-one rather than sixty. This made it easier for President Obama to get his nominees confirmed because the Democrats had a working majority of fifty-five members, which meant that approval for these nominees was virtually guaranteed and could not be blocked by the Republicans. This was an historic change; the Senate had not changed the cloture threshold since 1975 when it lowered it from two-thirds of the Senate (67) to three-fifths (60).

However, this cloture change was not without significant controversy. Typically major rules changes in the Senate require two-thirds of Senators to agree but in this case, the majority party used procedural tools to get around this requirement. When the Republicans blocked an Obama judicial nominee for the Court of Appeals, the majority leader, Senator Harry Reid (D-Nev.) made a motion to reduce the threshold for cloture for judicial nominations other than for the Supreme Court to fifty-one votes, rather than sixty votes. The presiding officer of the Senate, who chairs the proceedings, ruled that Senator Reid's motion was out of order. Reid in turn asked for a roll call vote; it takes only a majority of the Senate to accept or reject the ruling of the chair. The Democrats had fifty-five votes, and fifty-two of them voted to reject the ruling of the chair, which allowed Senator Reid's motion to replace existing rules, and effectively eliminated the filibuster on presidential executive branch nominees and federal judges (except for the Supreme Court).[33] However, it is important to note that the Democrats did not seek to eliminate the sixty-vote threshold for filibustering legislation. Given that the majority control of the Senate and the White House can change hands, it was deemed too risky to shut off the option just in case the Democrats became the minority party in the Senate, and lost the White House in 2016. It is clear from the action by the Democrats that a simple majority of the Senate has the authority to eliminate the filibuster at any point that it desires. After cloture has been invoked on a bill, no more than thirty additional hours of debate are permitted. All amendments must be germane to the bill's issues, and a time for a final vote is set. Figure 10.5 illustrates the variation in the number of cloture motions in the Senate over time.

In addition, Senate rules no longer require those seeking to block a bill to speak continuously

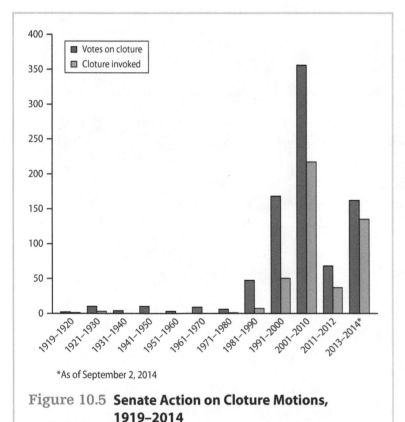

*As of September 2, 2014

Figure 10.5 Senate Action on Cloture Motions, 1919–2014

In November 2013, the number of votes required to invoke cloture on executive nominations and federal judicial nominations lower than the Supreme Court was lowered from sixty votes to fifty-one votes.

Source: United States Senate, http://www.senate.gov/pagelayout/reference/cloture_motions/clotureCounts.htm.

on the floor. Senators who oppose a bill can merely state their intention to filibuster, and that will be sufficient to block the bill from consideration on the floor. Senators also use the threat of a filibuster to block the president's judicial nominations, a practice that has come under increasing scrutiny. Filibusters of this type are an expression of partisanship or ideology, and they can disrupt the operation of the federal courts.[34] To counteract the filibuster in recent years, the Senate has resorted to a two-track system in which a bill that is being filibustered can be set aside to allow the Senate to proceed to other bills. But even with this two-track system, the filibuster has imposed substantial costs on the Senate, both in terms of the legislation that has failed to pass and the legislation that could not be brought to the floor.

→ KEY QUESTIONS:
Is the filibuster a legitimate means of protecting minority rights?

Some scholars have argued that the filibuster has been used too frequently as a way of blocking action on important public policies and is not a legitimate democratic instrument of power. Others argue that filibustering is a responsive and effective means of representation in Congress; if there is intense opposition to a bill in a senator's state, or from a minority of voters nationwide, the senator may consider it a responsibility to block the bill's passage.[35]

Without a gatekeeper like the House Committee on Rules and with the constant threat of a filibuster, there are few restrictions on a bill when it comes to the Senate floor. When the Senate majority leader wishes to bring a bill up for consideration, he or she must ask unanimous consent. Consequently, the Senate typically operates under **unanimous consent agreements** to establish guidelines for debating a bill. Senators strike a deal about how a bill will be debated on the Senate floor, how and when amendments will be offered, how much time will be allocated to debate and vote on amendments, and at what time on what date the final vote on the complete bill will take place. Senators have accepted this form of limitation on their rights to amend or block a bill because it requires their consent and enables the Senate to move forward and pass key legislation.

 unanimous consent agreement: *Agreement among all 100 senators on how a bill or presidential nomination will be debated, changed, and voted on in the Senate.*

Nevertheless, a senator can object to a unanimous consent request to bring a bill to the Senate floor in a practice known as a **hold**. A hold is a less drastic measure than a filibuster, but it can be used by any senator to delay a bill for a minimum of twenty-four hours. The majority leader can circumvent a hold by requesting a vote on cloture; if sixty senators agree, the Senate proceeds to consider the bill. Typically, senators hold up bills to extract concessions from Senate leaders or from the administration on the legislation being considered. They also use the hold to draw increased attention to a bill in the hope that public opposition will develop.

hold: *Power available to a senator to prevent the unanimous consent that allows a bill or presidential nomination to come to the Senate floor, which can be broken by invoking cloture (sixty votes).*

Legislative Proposals

The lawmaking process starts with an idea. Ideas for legislation can come from a number of sources, including constituents, interest groups, local or national newspaper stories, state or local governments, staff members, and the members' own personal interests.[36] When an idea is agreed on, the House or Senate member's staff consults with the Office of Legislative Counsel, which turns the general outlines of a bill into the technical language that will alter the U.S. Code, the set of federal laws that governs the United States. After approving the final legal language of a bill, the member introduces the bill into the respective chamber (House or Senate), an action known as bill sponsorship. After a bill is introduced, other members can sign on to be cosponsors (sponsorship of legislation is discussed in more detail later in this chapter). In reality, many freestanding bills that are introduced separately are later incorporated into larger omnibus bills that are passed by Congress. Combining bills into omnibus

→ KEY QUESTIONS:
How can you as a citizen influence legislation in Congress?

→ KEY QUESTIONS:
How do omnibus bills make accountability more difficult?

legislation can be useful, especially in periods of divided government. These big bills allow Congress to pass numerous provisions that might not pass if each were presented separately.[37]

Committee Action

After a member introduces a bill, it is referred to one or more committees or subcommittees that have jurisdiction over its subject matter. The first step in getting the bill enacted into law is to secure a hearing on a bill in subcommittee or full committee. In general, a committee tends to act first on bills that are sponsored by the chair of the committee, then on those sponsored by the subcommittee chairs, and last on bills sponsored by regular members of the committee. If the sponsor is not on the committee to which the bill is assigned, it is much harder to get action on the bill. This arrangement also makes sense because committee members are more likely to have expertise on the issues covered by the committee than are other legislators, so their bills are taken more seriously by their fellow committee members.[38] In rare cases, however, as a result of intense interest group lobbying or media pressure, a committee might hold a hearing on a bill sponsored by someone who is not a committee member, but the committee typically drafts its own bill to address the same issue.

After the hearings, the committee may move to the markup. At this point, the stakes intensify in terms of what the bill will ultimately look like, so the stakeholders in the policy process try to exert influence. In this era of increased partisanship and party leadership control, committees have less freedom to craft legislation that differs from the leadership's goals. After the full committee approves a bill, it and an accompanying committee report are sent to the full House or Senate for consideration by all members.

Floor Action and the Vote

→ KEY QUESTIONS:
What is the purpose of floor debate? Does it change minds and votes?

When a bill is sent to the full House or Senate—commonly known as "going to the floor"—all the members of the chamber gather to debate and vote on it. Debate takes different forms in each chamber. In the House, it is heavily structured, and most members are allowed no more than five minutes to speak on a measure, leaving almost no time for actual deliberation among members. In contrast, the Senate has few limits on the time allowed for members to speak on an issue on the floor. If the Senate is operating under a unanimous consent agreement or cloture, time is limited; otherwise, senators can make speeches and even engage in active debate on an issue for much longer than their House counterparts. Unfortunately for the current political system, real debate rarely occurs on the floor; instead, representatives and senators use their opportunity to speak to make partisan speeches or to direct their remarks to their constituents back home, knowing that the proceedings are televised by C-Span, and C-Span2.

During a roll call vote, the clerks of the House or Senate call the name of each member, who registers his or her vote electronically. Members cast up or down votes on legislation (to pass or reject), to table (set aside) legislation, or to approve a motion to recommit (send it back to committee with instructions to rewrite it). In addition to individually recorded votes, general voice votes can be taken when a consensus exists and there is no perceived need to record each member's vote.

→ KEY QUESTIONS:
Who are your representatives and senators? Do you want them to be trustees or delegates?

A roll call vote is the most fundamental way that a member of Congress represents constituents. When members of Congress cast their votes, they can act as trustees who exercise independent judgment about what they believe is best for the people or as delegates who do exactly as the people wish. Over time, congressional representation has evolved into a hybrid of both types of representation; thus, members of Congress act as both trustees and delegates. Roll call voting is therefore a key gateway for citizen influence in the legislative process.

Scholars have long characterized roll call voting by partisan dimension and by ideological or spatial dimension because in the past both the Democratic and Republican parties contained both liberals and conservatives.[39] Currently, the vast majority of Democratic members are liberal, and the vast majority of Republican members are conservative. Consequently, scholars now can examine roll call voting through both the partisan and ideological lens simultaneously. They confirm that most members of the House and Senate vote along party lines; in the 112th Congress, in the House, 90.5 percent of Republicans and 87 percent of Democrats voted with their party; in the Senate, 83 percent of Republicans and 92 percent of Democrats voted with their party. Overall, 73 percent of all votes taken in the House and 60 percent of all votes in the Senate divided along party lines.[40] Party leaders in Congress frame the content of bills and the choices for roll call votes along the lines of party platforms and ideology. Essentially, they are engaging in what is called message politics, designing legislation to push members into casting votes that may later be used in campaigns against them.[41] This framework reflects a responsible parties system (see Chapter 8) in which voters can clearly distinguish Democratic and Republican legislative policy goals. Although the increased emphasis on partisanship makes it easier for citizens to more clearly hold Congress accountable, it decreases the likelihood of bipartisan cooperation and makes passing legislation more difficult.

Conference Committee

For a bill to become law, the House and Senate have to pass an identically worded version of it to send to the president for signature. The last stage in the congressional legislative process takes place when the House and Senate meet in conference committee to resolve any differences in the versions that passed each chamber. The Speaker of the House and the Senate majority leader typically appoint the chairs and ranking members from the committees that originated the bills, plus other members who have been active on the bill. If the bill is very important to the party leaders, they also have the power to appoint themselves to the committee. If the conferees can reach agreement, the conference committee issues a conference report that must be voted on by the entire House and Senate. Because the conference report represents the end of the negotiation process between the two chambers, members cannot offer amendments to change it. However, if a majority of members of the House or Senate are displeased with the final results of the conference, they can defeat the report outright or vote to instruct the conference committee to revise the agreement.

In the past twenty years, Congress has decreased its use of conference committees. Instead, party leaders take on the responsibility of producing a final bill themselves. In choosing this path, they concentrate power in the hands of fewer members of Congress than in the traditional conference committee system.[42] Although this alternative provides a more streamlined way of legislating, it also acts as a gate against input from committee members who wish to represent their constituents' views on the final version of the bill.

The Budget Process and Reconciliation

Although the federal government tries to spend about as much money as it takes in from revenues, it does not typically succeed. Instead, it usually runs a **federal budget deficit**, which

federal budget deficit: *Difference between the amount of money the federal government spends in outlays and the amount of money it receives from revenues.*

national debt: *Sum of loans and interest that the federal government has accrued over time to pay for the federal deficit.*

requires it to borrow money to meet all its obligations (see Chapter 14 for more detail on current deficits and national debt). Although the process is complex, essentially this means that the federal government pays interest on outstanding loans, and the loans and interest that accumulate over time constitute the **national debt**.

The modern Congress operates under a budget process created in the Congressional Budget and Impoundment Control Act of 1974, which was enacted to give Congress more power over the federal budget.[43] It was passed at a time of relatively low deficits, but many new government programs were being implemented, and government financial obligations were steadily rising. The act created the House and Senate Budget Committees and the Congressional Budget Office so that Congress could construct its own budget blueprint as an alternative to the president's annual budget.

concurrent budget resolution: *Congressional blueprint outlining general amounts of funds that can be spent on federal programs.*

The federal government's fiscal year begins on October 1 and ends on September 30, and the key aspect of the budget process is that the congressional budget, known as the **concurrent budget resolution**, is supposed to be approved by both chambers by April 15. Because the budget resolution does not have the force of law, it is not sent to the president for his signature; rather, it serves as general instructions to congressional committees about how much money can be allocated for federal programs in the fiscal year. The authorizing committees take this blueprint into account when they reauthorize existing programs or create new ones, and the appropriations committees in the House and Senate use it to allocate funds in twelve separate bills. They typically begin their work in May in the hope of enacting all appropriations bills by September 30. If Congress and the president fail to agree on any one of the twelve appropriations bills, Congress enacts a **continuing resolution** that funds the government temporarily while disagreements about spending are worked out.

→ KEY QUESTIONS:
Does the congressional budget process help or hurt deficit reduction efforts?

From 2009 to 2012, the House of Representatives passed a budget resolution, but the Senate did not. This failure to produce a concurrent budget resolution left the appropriations process less structured. As a result, Congress relies more heavily on continuing resolutions than on passing separate appropriations bills. Congress's failure to produce a budget resolution makes it harder for voters to hold it accountable for federal budget policy. In December 2013, Congress broke the trend and passed a concurrent budget resolution, which allowed them to subsequently pass an omnibus appropriations bill that would last until October 1, 2014. For more details on the conflicts surrounding these bills, see Chapter 14.

continuing resolution: *Measure passed to fund federal programs when the appropriations process has not been completed by September 30, the end of the fiscal year.*

The 1974 Budget Act also created a parallel budget bill, known as **reconciliation**, which does require the president's signature. Reconciliation was specifically designed as umbrella legislation to bring all bills that contain changes in the tax code or entitlement programs in line with the congressional budget. Entitlement programs, such as Social Security, Medicare, and Medicaid, are considered mandatory because they pay out benefits to individuals based on a specified set of eligibility criteria. When Congress wants to make a change to one of these programs, it must pass a reconciliation bill. The reconciliation bill has special procedural protections in the Senate: It cannot be filibustered, and it can be debated for no more than twenty hours. A bill that cannot be filibustered was a tempting target for those who wanted to add nonbudget-related provisions. Consequently, in 1985, the budget process was modified to include the Byrd rule, which required that reconciliation be used only to reduce the federal deficit, which at the time was $212.3 billion.[44] In subsequent years, the Byrd rule has been interpreted to mean that all provisions of reconciliation must be directly related to the budget.[45]

reconciliation: *A measure used to bring all bills that contain changes in the tax code or entitlement programs in line with the congressional budget.*

→ KEY QUESTIONS:
Why did the Framers give Congress the final say in whether a bill should become a law?

Despite the Byrd rule, Congress has found ways to use the reconciliation process to pass controversial legislation. In 2010, the Democratic majority in Congress used it to pass part of its comprehensive health care reform, commonly known as Obamacare. Both Democrats and Republicans have used the reconciliation process to go beyond changes in the tax code, or to balance the budget, on issues ranging from welfare reform to children's health insurance.[46]

Presidential Signature or Veto, and the Veto Override

In the last step in the legislative process, the bill is sent to the president for his approval or rejection. A president can actively reject, or veto, a bill. If Congress will be going out of session within ten days, the president can wait for the session to end and simply not sign the bill, a practice known as a pocket veto. If Congress remains in session, and the president neither vetoes the bill nor signs it, the bill becomes law.

The veto is a powerful balancing tool for the president against the overreach of Congress; however, the Framers also gave Congress the **override**, which is the power to overturn a presidential veto with a two-thirds vote in each chamber. When the president vetoes a bill, it is returned to the chamber from which it originated; if two-thirds of the members of that chamber vote to override the veto, it is sent to the other chamber for a vote. A two-thirds vote by each chamber, rather than just a majority vote, is required for an override because the Framers wanted to enable the president to block a bill passed by Congress if he does not believe that it is in the best interest of the nation as a whole. The president can use the veto either to prevent a bill from becoming law or to pressure Congress into making changes that are closer to his policies.[47]

override: *Congress's power to overturn a presidential veto with a two-thirds vote in each chamber.*

Checkpoint

CAN YOU:

■ Compare the procedural rules in the House and Senate

■ State how a bill is proposed

■ Describe what happens to a bill in committee

■ Characterize floor action and voting

■ Explain what happens in conference committees

■ Identify the key components of the congressional budget process

■ Define the president's role in the lawmaking process

10.5 The Member of Congress at Work

> Assess what a member of Congress does

The cardinal rule of succeeding in the House or Senate is simple: Never forget where you came from. Representative Joaquín Castro has shown how a member tries to balance the competing demands of legislating with the core responsibility of serving constituents. The following sections describe exactly what the job of a House or Senate member entails.

Offices and Staff

For all newly elected members in the House and Senate, the first steps are to set up an office and hire staff members. In the House, each representative receives about the same amount of money for office operations. In the Senate, the office budget is determined by the population size of the senator's home state, based on the reasoning that senators from larger states have more constituents and more issues to deal with than their smaller-state colleagues. Most members bring some of their campaign workers to Washington to work on their staffs

Public Policy and Congress:
Unemployment Insurance

In times of economic difficulty, Congress is often asked to act quickly to help individuals in need of income support. During the Great Depression, President Franklin Delano Roosevelt (1933–45) proposed a number of programs that would try to help workers get back on their feet, and provide a safety net for their retirement years. The Social Security Act of 1935 set out to accomplish a number of these goals, and we discuss it in depth in Chapter 14. As part of the Social Security Act, Congress enacted a program designed to provide temporary cash payments to unemployed workers who have lost their jobs, due to downsizing or layoffs, known as Unemployment Insurance. Workers who quit their jobs or are fired from their jobs are not eligible for Unemployment Insurance. In nearly all states, Unemployment Insurance is funded by a tax on employers, which is collected by the federal government and placed in the Unemployment Trust Fund, but the program is administered by state governments. Although the federal government gives states the power to run the program, it sets basic rules for its administration.

Since its creation, the Unemployment Insurance program has grown from covering businesses that employ eight or more workers to any business that employs one or more workers, essentially covering the entire workforce. Typically, unemployment benefits are available for twenty-six weeks before an individual exhausts his or her benefits. However, during economic crisis periods, Congress has agreed to extend unemployment insurance for longer periods of time and provide federal funding to states to pay for the extra weeks of benefits for unemployed workers.

Such was the case in 2008 when the housing and stock market declines left a lot of people without work. President George W. Bush worked with a Democratic-controlled House and Senate to pass a federally funded extension program, called Emergency Unemployment Compensation (EUC), which allowed workers to collect UI for up to seventy-three weeks on top of the twenty-six weeks normally allowed, for a total of ninety-nine weeks of eligible benefits. In February 2009, shortly after President Obama took office, unemployment stood at 8.3 percent, and he requested that Congress extend EUC as part of the American Recovery and Reinvestment Act of 2009, otherwise known as the stimulus package.[48] The Democratic-controlled Congress passed that bill, and the extended time frame for benefits lasted until June 1, 2010. However, the unemployment rate had increased in the intervening year and after several short-term renewals, in December 2010, President Obama worked with Congress to renew EUC through June 2012.

After the House Republicans took control of the House of Representatives in 2011, it was unclear whether future renewals of extended unemployment would be possible because of their general opposition to longer term government relief programs. Proponents of extended unemployment benefits argue that by giving cash benefits to individuals who are out of work, the government is helping to keep the economy afloat. By some estimates every dollar paid out in unemployment benefits generates $1.60 in return.[49] However, opponents argue that extending unemployment benefits beyond twenty-six weeks discourages individuals from taking jobs that might pay less than the value of their unemployment benefits. In turn, individuals who stay out of the workforce for longer periods of time have a more difficult time finding jobs, thereby creating an entrenched cycle of long-term unemployment.

Despite these objections, the Republicans in the House did agree to renew EUC through January 2, 2013, because unemployment continued to be very high, but they insisted on reducing the total number of weeks a recipient could receive benefits.[50] As it was set to expire at the end of 2012, Congress and President Obama agreed to renew the program for one more year as part of a larger bill that also extended tax cuts that were enacted in the Bush administration.

However, in December 2013, as EUC was again set to expire, the unemployment rate stood at 6.7 percent, and Republicans in the House and Senate argued that it was no longer necessary to extend unemployment benefits past the traditional twenty-six weeks. Because the Republicans controlled the House of Representatives, it was not possible to renew the program without their support. In the months that followed in 2014, President Obama negotiated with the U.S. Senate, which was controlled by the Democrats, and asked for bipartisan support from Republican Senators to put pressure on the House Republicans to support a limited extension of EUC. The Senate did pass a temporary UI extension in April 2014, but the House did not take up the measure; with unemployment rates falling steadily through September 2014, the Congress adjourned without passing the UI extension.

> ## Construct Your Own Policy

1. Construct an unemployment safety net that would help those who lose their jobs but not discourage people from seeking employment.

2. Create a government work program that would employ individuals who have no other job and who have run out of unemployment benefits. How long could people stay employed by such a program?

and try to hire people from their districts or states. New members of Congress also seek out individuals with prior Capitol Hill experience to help orient them to their new surroundings and provide specific issue expertise.

Generally, a member of Congress's Washington office has a chief of staff who oversees the entire office, a scheduler who makes the member's appointments, a press secretary who handles all interactions with the media, and a legislative director who supervises the member's legislative work. In addition, legislative assistants handle specific issues, and legislative correspondents are responsible for answering constituent mail.

House and Senate members aim to be responsive to constituents, and that means providing prompt and extensive constituent services. To do so, they establish district offices in the congressional district for representatives and around the state for senators. These offices help constituents navigate federal agencies if they have difficulty—for example, getting a Social Security check or a passport—and advise constituents on how to win federal contracts. Specific requests for help are assigned to caseworkers. These local offices serve as direct and important links between voters and members of Congress and affect both accountability and responsiveness.[51]

→ KEY QUESTIONS:
Have you ever contacted your representative or senators? If so, was it to express an opinion or to ask for help?

Legislative Responsibilities

A successful legislator typically fulfills four responsibilities: securing desired committee assignments and performing committee work, sponsoring and cosponsoring bills, casting votes, and obtaining federal funds for the district or state.

Committee Work.   Just before the start of each new Congress, members are asked which committees they would like to join, and party leaders try to accommodate their wishes, although freshman members rarely get their most favored committees immediately. Freshman members choose committee assignments based on the needs of their district or state, their professional background, their personal experience, and their desire to increase chances for reelection. A House member from Oregon might seek a seat on the House Natural Resources Committee because that committee oversees logging and other land use issues that are important to constituents. A senator from Iowa might seek membership on the Senate Agriculture, Nutrition, and Forestry Committee because farming is a key economic interest in that state. However, a new senator has to accommodate his or her committee assignment wish list to the reality of the existing committee assignments of the senior senator from the state. All members of the House and Senate try to put themselves in the best possible institutional position to address issues that matter to their constituents.

Committee work consists of attending hearings and participating in markups as well as initiating ideas for legislation for consideration by the committee. Committee members also meet with interest groups, businesses, and citizens' groups that are specifically concerned about bills to be considered in the committee. The extent to which members participate actively in committee business varies according to the local concerns of their constituents, their personal interests, and whether the committee might provide an opportunity for political advancement.[52]

Committees themselves provide different gateways for members to serve their constituents and advance their careers. For example, the Appropriations Committee and the Environment and Public Works Committee distribute federal funds for a wide range of programs and projects, and thereby provide an opportunity for members to influence how these funds are spent. Serving on other committees, such as the Armed Services Committee, can provide members with credentials in the area of defense policy, which can be useful if they represent areas with high military employment or envision themselves running for president one day.

Bill Sponsorship.   Members can sponsor a bill by themselves, or they can ask colleagues to cosponsor bills with them; the higher the number of cosponsors, the greater the show of support for the bill. Members sponsor and cosponsor bills for three important reasons: First, bill sponsorship is an effective tool for giving voters in a district or state a voice in the federal policy-making system. Second, it is a means of staking out specific territory that members can claim as their area of expertise and can be a means of fulfilling campaign promises.[53] Third, it attracts the attention of the media, relevant interest groups, and the press, and thereby can help House and Senate members build their reputations as legislators.

Roll Call Votes.   Each representative and senator is expected to cast a roll call vote on the bills and amendments that reach the floor of the House and Senate. In the House alone, members cast 1,083 roll call votes during the 112th Congress, and Senators cast 484 roll call votes.[54] Given the large number of roll call votes, voters have difficulty identifying how their members of Congress voted on bills that affect them directly. Because most members of Congress vote the party line, party identification can be helpful in holding members accountable for their roll call votes. If members do not vote the party line, they risk losing the support of party voters in their district or state. However, most members will not vote for a measure that goes against their constituents' opinions or interests. For this reason, majority party leaders try to construct bills that will benefit the constituents of the members of their party.

Federal Funds.   Most members of Congress try to secure federal funds for their districts and states. The effort to carve out some piece of the federal financial pie is typically referred to as "bringing home the bacon" or pork barrel spending, and it can work through funding formulas for federal programs or **earmarks**, which are narrowly defined federally funded projects.[55] Federal funds can be used to rebuild a highway, build a fairground, fund a local orchestra, construct a research center on the effects of pig odor, and even support a water taxi service in Connecticut. One of the most controversial earmarks was the so-called bridge to nowhere in Alaska championed by the late Senator Theodore (Ted) Stevens (R-Alaska). A bipartisan group of members of Congress, as well as public watchdog groups, raised media awareness about the enormous cost of this bridge. In response, the House and Senate directed the state of Alaska to spend the money allocated for the bridge on more necessary transportation projects.[56] Over the past decade, spending on earmarks has increased; in fiscal year 2010, $16.5 billion was authorized to fund 9,129 earmarks.[57] When the Republicans won control of the House of Representatives, they proposed a total ban on earmarks

→ KEY QUESTIONS:
Federal funds for local projects are often denounced as "pork." How does pork figure in your decision to vote for or against an incumbent?

★ **earmark:** *Federal dollars devoted specifically to a local project in a congressional district or state.*

All members of Congress try to build a good reputation among their constituents. Part of that effort includes going back to the district and meeting with voters to hear their concerns. Here Joaquín Castro is shown meeting with residents of his district.

beginning in 2011, which the Senate also adopted. It is not clear that this ban actually eliminates the kind of localized spending that earmarks directed toward constituents because now legislators find ways to hide their efforts to direct federal dollars back home. For this reason, it may be that the ban on earmarks actually makes it harder to hold Congress accountable for federal spending.

Despite the conflict over the earmark and federal funding process generally, one could argue that obtaining federal dollars for the district is a form of responsiveness to the local needs of voters. Voters are taxpayers, and members of Congress are simply seeking to bring some of that tax money back home in a directed fashion. On the other hand, many of the projects are not necessary to most voters, and they create waste and inefficiency that can make the federal government less effective.

Communication with Constituents

Congressional representation depends on good communication between constituents and their representatives and senators. It is important to remember that members of Congress have two distinct places of work: Washington, D.C., and their home district or state.

In Washington, members take advantage of technological innovations, such as e-mail and the Internet, to stay in touch with their constituents. Before e-mail and the rise of social media, members used the franking privilege, which is free mail service, to respond to constituent letters and to send quarterly newsletters as updates on their activities. Today the vast majority of members of Congress use social media such as Twitter and Facebook to transmit information about their activities to constituents, in addition to hard copy mailings. To help members stay in touch with their constituents, the federal government pays for House and Senate members to return home to their districts or states approximately thirty-three times a year. These trips home are crucial for building bonds with voters, and members make sure to meet with individuals, speak to local interest groups, attend local parades and business openings, and attract local media coverage.

Cultivating direct links with constituents and making a good impression on them is what the political scientist Richard Fenno calls **home style**, or the way members portray themselves to constituents.[58] Members can choose to emphasize their local work for constituents, or they can emphasize their influence on national policy; some try to do both. Members can be very good at giving charismatic speeches, or they can be quiet, unassuming workers; successful members adapt their home style to the expectations and customs of constituents.

→ KEY QUESTIONS:
What communications have you received from your representative and senators? Have they arrived in the mail or via the Internet?

home style: *The way in which incumbents portray themselves to constituents.*

The Next Election

As political scientist David Mayhew explains, members of Congress are always looking ahead to the next election.[59] Elections are the means by which constituents express approval or disapproval of the job members of Congress are doing, and they are the fundamental tool that voters use to hold their members accountable for individual legislative work and the collective performance of their party in office. House members have only two years to show that they can manage to gain influence in the House and be responsive to local concerns at the same time. Senators have six years, but a senator has to share the job with another senator from the same state and compete for voter support, media attention, committee assignments, and the chance to be the "go-to" senator on key issues affecting the state. Because Senate elections are staggered, voters in a state elect each senator separately, at different times. A newly elected senator almost always finds that the senior colleague is established on key committees and well positioned on issues that are important to the state. Junior senators, therefore, are left to scramble for the leftovers and to establish good reputations among constituents in the shadows of their senior colleagues.[60]

Despite the fact that congressional job approval has fallen, constituents typically like their own Representative or House member. In 2012, 90 percent of House incumbents and 91 percent of Senate incumbents won reelection, and control of the House and Senate remained divided between the Republicans and Democrats, respectively.[61] In 2014, Republican incumbents held onto their seats at a consistently high rate, while a number of Democratic incumbents lost their seats and had a lower reelection rate than in previous years.

Congressional campaigns are typically divided into two categories: those with an incumbent seeking reelection, and those with open seats, where no incumbent is seeking reelection. In elections in which an incumbent is running, the contest becomes an evaluation of the job he or she has done in office compared to what the challenger promises to do if elected. Incumbents have major advantages because they have already won at least one election in the district, they are likely to have moderate name recognition, and they have the power to use their congressional offices to provide services to constituents. However, incumbents can also suffer if the reputation of Congress suffers (see Figure 10.6), and so they work to stake out individual reputations that contrast to the institution as a whole.

→ KEY QUESTIONS:
If an election were held today, would you vote for the incumbent in the House? In the Senate? What would you base your decision on?

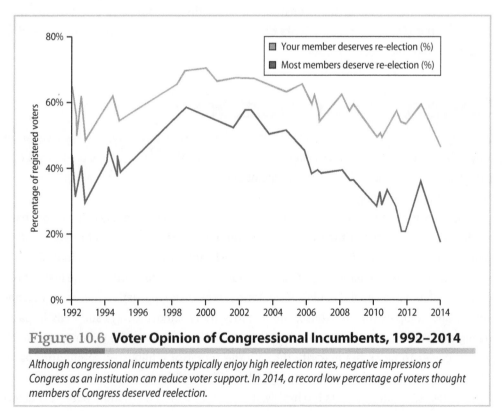

Figure 10.6 **Voter Opinion of Congressional Incumbents, 1992–2014**

Although congressional incumbents typically enjoy high reelection rates, negative impressions of Congress as an institution can reduce voter support. In 2014, a record low percentage of voters thought members of Congress deserved reelection.

Source: Gallup poll, http://www.gallup.com/poll/167024/record-low-say-own-representative-deserves-election.aspx.

Consequently, reelection is far from automatic. Part of the incumbent advantage rests on incumbents' efforts to use all their resources to serve their constituents responsively; successful incumbents have a strong motivation to perform well so that they will be reelected. Many members come from areas in which they grew up or have lived a long time, so they have a genuine desire to help constituents, who could be their neighbors or former schoolmates. Incumbents also have an electoral incentive to work on behalf of constituents to earn high approval ratings. In addition, if incumbents have any ambition to run for another political office in their state, such as governor, they want to make sure constituents have a good impression of them.

Members' concern for their local districts or states can be one of the biggest gates standing in the way of a productive Congress, and frequently the party works to overcome division among its members. Parties provide a collective set of policy goals that will benefit or appeal to party members at the local level. For a member of Congress, however, tying electoral fortunes to the political party can be risky if the majority party falls out of favor with voters who hold it accountable for policy outcomes. Holding a high-ranking party position will require a lot of time away from the district and cause the member to lose touch with his reelection base. Former House Majority Leader Eric Cantor (R-Va.) served in that role from 2011 to July 2014 but resigned after he was unexpectedly defeated in a primary by a little-known college professor who ran a campaign saying that Cantor was out of step with the views of the district. Because Cantor knew he could not run in the general election as a Republican, he resigned his leadership in the party and his seat in the House a short time later. Although these types of primary election upsets are infrequent, they are powerful reminders that incumbents must constantly balance the needs of their constituents with the ideas and requirements of their party and stay responsive, or risk losing their bids for reelection.

Checkpoint

CAN YOU:

- Explain the importance of constituent services
- Recall the four legislative responsibilities of congressional members
- Describe the key ways in which members of Congress communicate with constituents
- State how elections shape the work of members of Congress

Congress and Democracy

CONNECT WITH YOUR CLASSMATES
MindTap™ for American Government

Access The Congress Forum: Discussion—Representation in Congress.

The composition of Congress has changed considerably over the nation's history. The lawmaking body is five times larger and now includes men and women from a wide range of ethnic, racial, and religious backgrounds. From the standpoint of equality of opportunity in a democracy, the increased diversity in Congress is a positive step.

Is Congress a responsive decision-making body? Individual members clearly work hard to address the concerns of their constituents, both at home in the district or state and in their Washington offices. But Congress as a whole is not always capable of addressing the immediate needs of the nation in a timely fashion. The bicameral nature of the institution, with each chamber's separate rules of operation, makes the legislative process time-consuming and complex. In the House, the majority party almost always succeeds in passing legislation that reflects the party's policy goals. In the Senate, the minority has much greater power to block the majority through the threat of a filibuster, so minority party views are typically incorporated into legislation. These differences offer advantages and disadvantages; if Congress acts too hastily, it can pass harmful legislation, but if it acts too slowly, it can fail to meet its fundamental responsibilities to address issues that citizens care about.

Are individual members of Congress accountable for the collective output of Congress as a whole? Not always. The fundamental difficulty with the representative structure of Congress is that each member is elected separately, so that voters may reelect their own representative or senator but still be unhappy with Congress as a whole. It is too easy for one member of Congress to say to constituents, "I am working hard to help you; it is all those other men and women who are not doing their jobs." Only in the rarest of election years do voters actually hold all the members of the Congress accountable for their collective performance. This lack of collective accountability can be a significant obstacle or gate to Congress's productivity and responsiveness to important policy needs.

Is Congress equal in its treatment of each citizen relative to all others? Because each state has the same number of senators regardless of population size, are the citizens of small states more powerful in the Senate than citizens who live in large states? Are the laws that Congress passes fair and balanced, or do they benefit one group more consistently than another? There are no simple answers to these questions. Some voices in society are louder and more prominent than others, and members of Congress tend to respond to citizens whom they perceive to be supportive, who donate more money, and who vote regularly. In some issue areas, the more prominent members of society win out over citizens who are less active and less visible. It is not clear that Congress sets out to give some people greater advantages than others, but the process of balancing the different individual and regional interests in national policy making produces winners and losers. The fundamental challenge to Congress is to make sure that there are no permanent winners or losers, and the challenge to all citizens is to monitor their members of Congress to be sure they are performing their legislative responsibilities.

Master the Concept
of The Congress with MindTap™ for American Government

 REVIEW MindTap™ for American Government
Access Key Term Flashcards for Chapter 10.

 STAY CURRENT MindTap™ for American Government
Access the KnowNow blog and customized RSS for updates on current events.

 TEST YOURSELF MindTap™ for American Government
Take the Wrap It Up Quiz for Chapter 10.

 STAY FOCUSED MindTap™ for American Government
Complete the Focus Activities for The Congress.

 ## Key Concepts

appropriate (p. 317). What is the difference between appropriation and authorization?

authorize (p. 317). How is authorization a part of Congress's "power of the purse"?

cloture (p. 332). How is cloture invoked?

concurrent budget resolution (p. 336). How is a concurrent budget resolution used by congressional committees?

continuing resolution (p. 336). When is a continuing resolution used?

divided government (p. 320). How does divided government make it harder to compromise?

earmark (p. 341). Why did Congress ban earmarks?

federal budget deficit (p. 335). What causes the federal government to run a budget deficit?

filibuster (p. 331). How does the filibuster give power to individual senators?

hold (p. 333). How is a hold used in relation to unanimous consent agreements?

home style (p. 342). How does a member of Congress use home style to help get reelected?

House majority leader (p. 325). What is the House majority leader's role within the House?

House minority leader (p. 325). What is the role of the House minority leader in policy making when he or she shares the president's party?

markup (p. 329). What is the committee chair's role in relation to markup?

national debt (p. 336). How is the national debt related to the federal budget deficit?

override (p. 337). How does the override strengthen Congress's power over the president?

ranking member (p. 329). Who gets to serve as ranking member on a committee?

reconciliation (p. 336). Why was the reconciliation process created?

rule (p. 330). What are the different types of rules and their implications?

Senate majority leader (p. 326). What is the primary means through which the Senate majority leader wields power?

Senate minority leader (p. 326). How does the Senate minority leader represent his or her party members?

Speaker of the House (p. 323). How did Thomas Brackett Reed increase the power of the Speaker of the House and the majority party in the House of Representatives?

unanimous consent agreement (p. 333). What does a unanimous consent agreement do?

Learning Outcomes: What You Need . . .

To Know	To Test Yourself	To Participate
▶ Describe how Congress has developed		
The Framers designed Congress as a bicameral legislature so that the House of Representatives and the Senate—with different qualifications for office, modes of election, terms of office, and constituencies—would check and balance each other. Although its enumerated powers are limited, Congress has built on its implied powers to become the powerful legislative branch it is today. Differences in size, rules, structure, and responsibility have molded the House and the Senate into very different institutions.	• Explain the reasons for and consequences of bicameralism. • Explain the constitutional differences between the House and Senate.	• Weigh the gridlock caused by bicameralism against the checks and balances it provides.

To Know	To Test Yourself	To Participate

▶ Define the powers of Congress

The Framers structured Congress to give it the powers necessary to govern the newly formed union, especially the powers to tax and spend and declare war. Over time, the powers of Congress have evolved under the separation of powers system. In some ways, congressional powers have expanded, especially in the area of advice and consent, but at the same time congressional productivity has declined.	• State what the general welfare clause allows Congress to do. • Recall why war powers are shared with the president. • Define the commerce clause and explain its power. • Explain the power of advice and consent. • Describe the process of impeachment. • Compare and contrast the enumerated and implied powers. • Explain Congress's role in the authorization of courts. • Characterize how Congress uses its powers of oversight on the other two branches.	• Debate whether Congress's power over interstate commerce should be limited but its power over going to war should be strengthened. • Consider whether Congress's power over the executive and judicial branches should be expanded, and, if so, how.

▶ Outline how Congress is structured

Political parties play a stronger role in the organization and operation of the House than of the Senate. In the Senate, each member has relatively equal power, and passing legislation requires compromise and cooperation. In recent years, intense partisanship, including party-line voting and message politics, has decreased the likelihood of bipartisan cooperation and made it more difficult for Congress to pass legislation.	• Describe the role parties play in Congress. • Explain the role of party leaders in the House of Representatives. • Compare and contrast the functioning of the Senate and House. • State how the committee system works. • Identify the role of advocacy caucuses in Congress.	• Is Congress too partisan? If so, how would you change the structure of the House and the Senate to encourage bipartisan cooperation? Would you have to change our electoral structure?

▶ Explain how a law is made in Congress

The procedures through which a bill becomes a law are different in the House and Senate, but each chamber engages in committee work, hearings, floor debate, and voting. Following passage by each chamber individually, a formal conference committee or an informal group of party leaders resolves differences between the two bills to produce a single bill that is presented to the president for signature. If the president vetoes a bill, Congress can override the veto with a two-thirds majority in each house.	• Compare the procedural rules in the House and Senate. • State how a bill is proposed. • Describe what happens to a bill in committee. • Characterize floor action and voting. • Explain what happens in conference committees. • Identify the key components of the congressional budget process. • Define the president's role in the lawmaking process.	• Map out ways you could influence the content of legislation as it is being considered in Congress. • Design a federal budget that does not create a deficit.

▶ Assess what a member of Congress does

Members of Congress try to balance the competing demands of legislation and constituent service, and they are always anticipating the next election. A successful legislator seeks to be responsive to constituents by engaging in committee work, sponsoring and voting on bills, and securing federal funds for his or her district or state.	• Explain the importance of constituent services. • Recall the four legislative responsibilities of congressional members. • Describe the key ways in which members of Congress communicate with constituents. • State how elections shape the work of members of Congress.	• Identify three policies you believe your representative and senators should address, and devise a plan to communicate to them about your interests.

"As a second-generation Greek immigrant, I was raised to be thankful for the gifts that this great nation gave to me and to my parents before me. Throughout my childhood in Hinton, West Virginia, my father, an optometrist and small business owner, and my mother, a teacher, were both engaged in service through our community and church. And so, with this core commitment to service and passion for impact, I am humbled and excited by this next challenge. . . . I look forward to working alongside the remarkable men and women of the Department [of Health and Human Services] to continue to ensure that children, families, and seniors have the building blocks of healthy and productive lives."[1]

SYLVIA MATHEWS BURWELL
Harvard University

11

The Presidency

From a very young age, Sylvia Mathews Burwell showed a keen interest in politics. In elementary school, she helped campaign for a friend's father, and at age 11, she volunteered for Jay Rockefeller's bid for governor. Later Sylvia's mother ran for the mayoral election of her hometown, Hinton, West Virginia, at age 65. She won, without ever having run for public office before. Sylvia graduated from Harvard with a degree in government and became a Rhodes Scholar at Oxford University, which introduced her to the world of professional politics. In 1992, Sylvia worked on the Clinton presidential campaign. She led Clinton's economic transition team, and after he won his election, became a staff director on the National Economic Council (NEC).

Sylvia Mathews Burwell was promoted to the chief of staff for the Treasury Secretary and then served the president as his deputy chief of staff. In 1998, she assumed the position of deputy director in the Office of Management and Budget (OMB). When Republican candidate George W. Bush won the 2000 presidential election, she turned her focus to the world of nonprofit foundations, initially working for the Bill and Melinda Gates Foundation. As president of the Walmart Foundation, she tackled global health issues. Her past experience with the OMB put her on the top of a short list of candidates to head the agency after Democratic President Barack Obama was reelected in 2012. In 2013, Obama nominated her for the position. Burwell's appointment as OMB director was impressively smooth, and she was confirmed by the Senate in a 96-0 vote on April 24, 2013. On April 11, 2014, President Obama nominated Burwell as the next Health and Human Services (HHS) Secretary.

The president put one of his most important policy legacies—the Affordable Care Act (ACA)—in her hands. Although this confirmation process was also relatively smooth, Burwell did have to answer questions about how she would improve the implementation of the ACA. The Senate Finance Committee approved her nomination by a vote of 21-3 on May 21, 2014, and the full Senate confirmed her on June 5, 2014 by a vote of 78-17.

Sylvia Mathews Burwell's career exemplifies the gateways that open when you get involved in politics: the political networks that talented and hardworking volunteers establish on campaigns. Burwell's experience demonstrates how campaign work can be the beginning of a lifetime of

Need to Know

11.1 Outline the requirements to serve as president

11.2 Identify the powers of the president and explain how they are limited

11.3 Describe the growth of executive influence

11.4 Analyze why the president is so powerful during wartime

11.5 Summarize how the White House is organized

11.6 Assess presidential greatness

 WATCH & LEARN MindTap™ for American Government
Watch a brief "What Do You Know?" video summarizing The Presidency.

public service. As Secretary of HHS, Burwell will be carrying out the remainder of the health care law that has yet to be implemented, and Republicans used her nomination to reiterate their criticisms of the law. Burwell's appointment is also the perfect example of how the gates of Congress can get in the way of executive branch policy implementation, even for laws that have already passed through their chambers.[2]

In this chapter, we examine how the president governs and how responsive he can be to the people. We look at his constitutional powers and the way he uses the executive power to achieve his policy goals, from nominating appointees such as Sylvia Mathews Burwell to issuing executive orders to accomplish policy goals. We also look at the limits on presidential power. As presidential scholar Charles Jones has argued, successful presidents work within a separation of powers system and alongside the legislative and judicial branches, compromising, persuading, and overcoming opposition. The most successful presidents are strong leaders with clear policy visions and excellent communication and negotiation skills. In the twenty-first century, the American president has to implement existing law and, equally important, leads the effort to turn his policy goals into law and achieve his visions for the nation.

LISTEN & LEARN
MindTap™ for American Government

Access Read Speaker to listen to Chapter 11.

11.1 Presidential Qualifications

> Outline the requirements to serve as president

The American presidency was invented at the Constitutional Convention in 1787. The Framers had no definitive models to help them determine what sort of person should serve as a democratically elected head of state because nations were still run by monarchs whose power to rule was hereditary. But the Framers had George Washington, the hero of the Revolutionary War, in mind for the office, and he helped shape the idea of what a president should be. Still, they left the qualifications as open as possible, and men with diverse experiences have served as president.

Constitutional Eligibility and Presidential Succession

Article II, Section 1, of the Constitution states that the president must be a natural-born citizen (or a citizen at the time the Constitution was adopted), at least 35 years old, and a resident of the United States for at least fourteen years. The original Constitution did not specify eligibility for the vice presidency, as the person who came in second in the vote for president would be vice president. But in 1800, Thomas Jefferson (1801–1809) and Aaron Burr ended up in a tie in the Electoral College when in fact supporters wanted to elect them as a team, with Jefferson as president and Burr as vice president. The Twelfth Amendment, ratified in 1804, changed the process so that candidates are elected for president and vice president separately. The amendment also directs that the vice president must meet the same eligibility requirements as the president and that electors cannot vote for both a president and a vice president from the elector's home state. This requirement makes it difficult for parties to nominate presidents and vice presidents from the same state.

The Constitution also states that when the president is removed from office by death, resignation, or inability to perform the duties of the office, the vice president becomes president. It stipulates that if neither the president nor the vice president is able to complete the elected term, Congress should designate a successor by law. In 1792, Congress passed the Presidential

Succession Act, which designated the president pro tempore of the Senate as next in line, and then the Speaker of the House. In 1841, John Tyler (1841–45) became the first elected vice president to succeed a president when President William Henry Harrison insisted on giving a two-hour inaugural speech in freezing rain while wearing no hat or coat, and consequently came down with a cold. Besieged by candidates hoping that he would appoint them to public office, he had little time to rest. Only one month after assuming office, the new president died after his cold developed into pneumonia. The order of succession today is illustrated in Table 11.1.

There was no constitutional provision for replacement of the vice president, and in the course of the nation's history, the office has occasionally been vacant. Eventually, the Twenty-Fifth Amendment, ratified in 1967, required the president to nominate a replacement vice president, who must be approved by a majority vote of the House and the Senate. The first vice president to assume office in this manner was Gerald R. Ford, nominated by President Richard M. Nixon (1969–74) in 1973, following the indictment and subsequent resignation of Vice President Spiro T. Agnew on charges of tax fraud.

The amendment also allows for a temporary transfer of power from the president to the vice president in cases of incapacity when invoked by either the president or vice president and a majority of the cabinet. To date, only the president has invoked this clause and then only when he has had to have surgery that would require sedation. For example, in 1985, when President Ronald Reagan (1981–89) had a colonoscopy, Vice President George H. W. Bush was acting president for eight hours.[3] In contrast, no one invoked the clause when President Reagan was shot in a failed assassination attempt in 1981; Vice President Bush stood in for him at official functions and meetings for approximately two weeks but did not serve as the official acting president during this time.

Today another constitutional amendment, the Twenty-Second (1951), limits the president to two elected terms. For a century and a half, presidents followed the precedent established by George Washington (1789–97) when he stepped down after two terms. But in 1940, President Franklin Delano Roosevelt (1933–45) chose to run for a third term and won and also won election to a fourth term in 1944. Though the dangers of World War II were a factor in his staying in office, many Americans, especially Republicans, worried that a long-standing president could expand executive branch power too much, so they sought a way to limit presidential terms of service. In 1946, Republicans captured a majority in the House and Senate, and on the very first day the new Congress met, they proposed a constitutional amendment limiting the president to two full terms in office.[4] For a list of constitutional amendments that pertain to the presidency, see Figure 11.1.

Table 11.1 Presidential Order of Succession

1. Vice president
2. Speaker of the House
3. President Pro Tempore of the Senate

Cabinet Secretaries

4. State
5. Treasury
6. Defense
7. Attorney General
8. Interior
9. Agriculture
10. Commerce
11. Labor
12. Health and Human Services
13. Housing and Urban Development
14. Transportation
15. Energy
16. Education
17. Veterans' Affairs
18. Homeland Security

© CENGAGE LEARNING®

→ KEY QUESTIONS:
How do term limits make the president less responsive to public opinion?

Figure 11.1 Constitutional Amendments Pertaining to the Presidency

Twelfth	1804	Requires that electors cast separate votes for president and vice president and specifies requirements for vice presidential candidates
Twentieth	1933	Declares that presidential term begins on January 20 (instead of March 4)
Twenty-Second	1951	Limits presidents to two terms
Twenty-Fifth	1967	Specifies replacement of the vice president and establishes the position of acting president during a president's disability

© CENGAGE LEARNING®

lame duck: *Term-limited official in his or her last term of office.*

→ KEY QUESTIONS:
Unlike members of Congress, presidents represent all the people of the United States. How can a president represent all the people?

Presidential term limits enforce turnover and open opportunity for new leadership, but they also act as a gate that prevents voters from reelecting a popular president whom they want to keep in office. Because a president in his second term cannot seek reelection, he is commonly referred to as a **lame duck**. Lawmakers know that the president's time in office is limited, so they are less likely to cooperate or compromise with him. On the other hand, a president who wants to chart a policy course that is unpopular may be more likely to do so when he does not have to face the voters. Lame duck status therefore has the advantage of giving the president more political freedom, but the disadvantage of making him less directly responsive to public opinion.

Background and Experience

In keeping with the democratic spirit of the founding of the United States, the Framers did not specify qualifications for the presidency beyond age and citizenship, and in the ensuing two centuries, men of varying backgrounds have served in the office. Presidents have come from all walks of life and from almost all regions of the country. The clearest path to the White House is through the office of the vice president, but most presidents have some combination of service in the military, in a state legislature, or as governor; in the U.S. House of Representatives and Senate; or in a prior presidential administration. For example, James Monroe (1817–25) was a soldier in the Revolutionary War, a U.S. senator, minister to France, secretary of state, and secretary of war. Herbert Hoover (1929–33) was an international food relief worker and secretary of commerce.[5]

There are advantages and disadvantages for presidents, depending on their prior experience. Lyndon Baines Johnson (1963–69) was very successful in passing his domestic policy agenda in large part due to his experience as a House member, U.S. senator, and Senate majority leader. His prior

THE GRANGER COLLECTION, NYC

George Washington was a successful military general who led American troops in the Revolutionary War. He was widely admired and was chosen to be the first president of the United States because it was believed that his experience and personal characteristics would be a model for the future. He took the oath of office on April 30, 1789, on the balcony of Federal Hall in New York City, then the nation's capital.

experience taught him crucial negotiating skills with members of Congress, and he used his skills to their fullest extent. In contrast, Jimmy Carter (1977–81) was generally considered to have failed in getting his domestic policy agenda enacted because of his lack of experience in Washington. He came to the White House from the governor's mansion in Georgia, where he exercised executive power with little challenge from the legislature. When he faced a Congress that did not embrace his agenda, he lacked the negotiating skills to be successful. Of course, no single set of qualifications or experiences can guarantee success as a president. When voters cast their ballots for president, they take a leap of faith that the person who wins will be trustworthy, accountable, and responsive to their needs and will implement the laws equally for every citizen. For a list of the presidents of the United States, see Table 11.2.

Table 11.2 **The Presidents of the United States, 1789–2014**

President	Term Dates	Party	Prior Experience
1 George Washington	1789–97		General
2 John Adams	1797–1801	Federalist	Vice president
3 Thomas Jefferson	1801–1809	Democratic-Republican	Vice president, secretary of state
4 James Madison	1809–17	Democratic-Republican	Secretary of state, U.S. House, state legislator
5 James Monroe	1817–25	Democratic-Republican	Secretary of war, secretary of state, U.S. Senate
6 John Quincy Adams	1825–29	Democratic-Republican	Secretary of state, U.S. Senate
7 Andrew Jackson	1829–37	Democrat	U.S. Senate, general, U.S. House
8 Martin Van Buren	1837–41	Democrat	Vice president, U.S. Senate
9 William Henry Harrison	1841 (died in office)	Whig	U.S. Senate, general, territorial governor
10 John Tyler	1841–45	Whig	Vice president, U.S. Senate, governor, U.S. House
11 James K. Polk	1845–49	Democrat	Governor, U.S. House
12 Zachary Taylor	1849–50 (died in office)	Whig	General
13 Millard Fillmore	1850–53	Whig	Vice president, U.S. House
14 Franklin Pierce	1853–57	Democrat	U.S. Senate, U.S. House, state legislator
15 James Buchanan	1857–61	Democrat	Secretary of state, U.S. Senate, U.S. House
16 Abraham Lincoln	1861–65 (died in office)	Republican; National Union	U.S. House
17 Andrew Johnson	1865–69	Democrat; National Union	Vice president, U.S. Senate, U.S. House
18 Ulysses S. Grant	1869–77	Republican	General
19 Rutherford B. Hayes	1877–81	Republican	Governor, U.S. House, general
20 James A. Garfield	1881 (died in office)	Republican	U.S. Senate, general, U.S. House, state legislator
21 Chester A. Arthur	1881–85	Republican	Vice president, collector of the port of New York
22 Grover Cleveland	1885–89	Democrat	Governor, mayor
23 Benjamin Harrison	1889–93	Republican	U.S. Senate
24 Grover Cleveland	1893–97	Democrat	U.S. President, governor, mayor
25 William McKinley	1897–1901 (died in office)	Republican	Governor, U.S. House

Table 11.2 (Continued)

President	Term Dates	Party	Prior Experience
26 Theodore Roosevelt	1901–1909	Republican	Vice president, governor
27 William Howard Taft	1909–13	Republican	Secretary of war, governor general of the Philippines, federal judge
28 Woodrow Wilson	1913–21	Democrat	Governor, university president
29 Warren G. Harding	1921–23 (died in office)	Republican	U.S. Senate, lieutenant governor, state legislator
30 Calvin Coolidge	1923–29	Republican	Vice president, governor
31 Herbert Hoover	1929–33	Republican	Secretary of commerce
32 Franklin Delano Roosevelt	1933–45 (died in office)	Democrat	Governor, assistant secretary of the navy, state legislator
33 Harry S. Truman	1945–53	Democrat	Vice president, U.S. Senate
34 Dwight D. Eisenhower	1953–61	Republican	University president, general
35 John F. Kennedy	1961–63 (died in office)	Democrat	U.S. Senate, U.S. House
36 Lyndon Baines Johnson	1963–69	Democrat	Vice president, U.S. Senate, U.S. House
37 Richard M. Nixon	1969–74 (resigned)	Republican	Vice president, U.S. Senate, U.S. House
38 Gerald R. Ford	1974–77	Republican	Vice president, U.S. House
39 Jimmy Carter	1977–81	Democrat	Governor, state legislator
40 Ronald Reagan	1981–89	Republican	Governor, actor
41 George H. W. Bush	1989–93	Republican	Vice president, CIA director, U.S. House
42 William J. Clinton	1993–2001	Democrat	Governor, state attorney general
43 George W. Bush	2001–2009	Republican	Governor
44 Barack Obama	2009–	Democrat	U.S. Senate, state legislator

© CENGAGE LEARNING®

The Expansion of the Presidency

President George Washington had the enormous responsibility of setting the standard for how a president should govern in a democracy, and he was very careful not to infuse the office with airs of royalty or privilege. The Framers anticipated that the executive branch would be led by one person whose primary responsibility would be the defense of the United States. As commander of the Continental Army during the Revolutionary War, Washington had military experience, but he was also a cautious and thoughtful statesman who wanted to establish a precedent for how the chief executive should operate.

In the course of the nineteenth century, from the presidencies of Thomas Jefferson, to Andrew Jackson (1829–37), to Abraham Lincoln, and finally to William McKinley (1897–1901), the nation grew in size, population, and economic power. The job of the chief executive grew accordingly, but, though increasingly demanding and complex, it remained essentially focused on national defense and economic growth. In the twentieth century, however, the United States became a leading international military and economic power. Its role in World War II and the subsequent Cold War against the Soviet Union expanded the authority of the presidency. Historian and presidential adviser Arthur Schlesinger Jr. used the term **imperial presidency** to describe

→ KEY QUESTIONS:
What defines an imperial presidency?

⭐ **imperial presidency:** *Power of the president to speak for the nation on the world stage and to set the policy agenda at home.*

the power of the president to speak for the nation on the world stage and to set the policy agenda at home.[6] Schlesinger's view suggests that as long as the United States is engaged in military conflicts all over the world to promote and protect its interests, the president will be considered the most important figure in American politics. However, after two very long wars, public opinion has shifted against intervening in foreign conflicts (see Chapter 6, Public Opinion and the Media), which leaves less support for presidential military action on foreign soil. As the public looks more inward and focuses on domestic policy, Congress and the president stand on more balanced scales.

Checkpoint

CAN YOU:

- State the constitutional qualifications and succession requirements for the presidency
- Summarize the background and experience of U.S. presidents
- Explain what is meant by imperial presidency

11.2 Presidential Power: Constitutional Grants and Limits

> ❭ Identify the powers of the president and explain how they are limited

As we saw in Chapter 10, Congress, the Framers enumerated Congress's powers, both to assert powers that were missing under the Articles of Confederation, such as the powers to collect taxes and to regulate commerce, and to constrain the branch they anticipated would be the most powerful. The Framers expected the executive branch to be smaller and less powerful and did not believe it necessary to enumerate the executive powers as they did the legislative powers (see Table 11.3). Instead, in the very first sentence of Article II, they "vested" the president with a general grant of "executive Power" and then, later in the article, stated certain additional powers and responsibilities. The general grant of executive power has allowed the presidency to become the powerful office it is today. In this section, we look at the constitutional sources of the president's powers, the ways in which presidents have sought to expand their constitutional powers, and the ways in which the other branches, especially Congress, act to check and balance the president.

Commander in Chief

The president is the **commander in chief** of the armed forces of the United States, which includes the Army, Navy, Air Force, Marine Corps, and Coast Guard, plus their Reserve and National Guard units. An elected commander in chief, rather than an appointed military officer, is a distinctly important element of American democracy. The president directs all war efforts and military conflict. Congress, however, has the power to officially declare war and to authorize funding for the war effort. Because the war powers that are divided between the president and Congress are so contentious, we examine them later in the chapter.

commander in chief: *Leader of the armed forces of the United States.*

→ KEY QUESTIONS:
Why is it important that the commander in chief of the U.S. military is a civilian?

Power to Pardon

The president has the power to grant clemency, or mercy, for crimes against the United States, except in the case of impeachment from federal office. Clemency is a broad designation that includes a **pardon**, which is forgiving an offense altogether, and a commutation,

 pardon: *Full forgiveness for a crime.*

Table 11.3 A Comparison of Legislative and Executive Authority under the Constitution

While the Constitution grants specific legislative authority to Congress, it provides a general grant of authority to the president that does not require specific enumerated grants of power, nor is there an executive equivalent of Article I, Section 9, which specifically limits congressional authority.

	Legislative	Executive
Authority	"All legislative Powers herein granted shall be vested in a Congress of the United States"	"The executive Power shall be vested in a President of the United States"
Specific Powers	Article I, Section 8, including: • lay and collect taxes • provide for the common defense • regulate interstate and foreign commerce • authorize courts • set uniform rules for naturalization and bankruptcy • establish post offices • make all laws that are "necessary and proper" for carrying out the listed powers	Article II, Section 2, including: • act as commander in chief of armed forces • grant pardons • make treaties • receive foreign ministers • appoint ambassadors, judges, cabinet-level officials Article II, Section 3: • ensure that the laws are faithfully executed Article I, Section 7: • veto legislation
Limits on Power	Explicit limits on powers: Article I, Section 9, including: • no bills of attainder • no ex post facto laws • no titles of nobility Bill of Rights: • substantive limits of the First through Eighth Amendments Ninth Amendment: • enumeration of rights does not grant general authority Tenth Amendment: • people and states retain reserved powers not granted to Congress	Mostly through checks and balances: • veto override • Senate confirmation on appointments • Senate treaty ratification • removal by impeachment

© CENGAGE LEARNING®

which is shortening a federal prison sentence; in general, pardoning someone is considered a more sweeping act of clemency than commuting a sentence. Election considerations can also come into play because presidents who are in their first term may want to appear tougher on crime than in their second term, when they will not be seeking reelection. For example, in his first term in office, President George W. Bush issued nineteen pardons and commuted two sentences, but in his second term, Bush granted 170 pardons and commuted seven sentences. In comparison, President Barack Obama issued 22 pardons and commuted one sentence in his first term, and by September 2014, he had already issued 52 pardons and commuted ten sentences.[7]

Treaties and Recognition of Foreign Nations

The president or his designated representative has the power to negotiate and sign treaties with foreign nations, but he must do so with the "Advice and Consent of the Senate," as specified by the Constitution. For a treaty to be valid, two-thirds "of the Senators present" must

→ KEY QUESTIONS:
Should the president have the power to pardon? What impact does this power have on citizen equality?

approve. Historically, the Senate has refused to approve some notable treaties, ranging from the Treaty of Versailles ending World War I signed by President Woodrow Wilson (1913–21), to the Kyoto Protocol on climate change signed by Vice President Albert Gore Jr. who was representing President William Jefferson (Bill) Clinton (1993–2001). These examples illustrate how the requirement that the Senate approve treaties serves as a gateway for public input into presidential actions, and how it can be a gate that blocks a president's attempt to reach agreements with foreign nations. Today, with the expansion of globalization, the president's representatives negotiate treaties over a wide range of areas, such as military alliances, human rights accords, environmental regulations, and trade policies (see Global Gateways: The World Trade Organization and Global Trade). The president also enters into executive agreements, which do not require Senate approval and tend to be less expansive in scope than treaties.

The president's authority in foreign affairs includes the power to "receive Ambassadors and other public Ministers," which allows the president to recognize the legitimacy of foreign regimes. Such decisions are frequently based on the internal political system of the foreign nation. For example, revolutionaries overthrew Russia's czarist regime in 1917, but the new Soviet Union, a Communist nation, was not recognized by the United States until 1933, through the action of President Franklin Delano Roosevelt. In contrast, in 2008, when the young democracy of Kosovo declared its independence from Serbia, President George W. Bush immediately recognized it as an independent nation.[8] However, the president also reserves the power not to recognize self-declared independent nations as in the case of Russian separatists who took over control of the Crimean peninsula and eastern parts of Ukraine.

Executive and Judicial Nominations

The president has the power to appoint all federal officers, including cabinet secretaries, heads of independent agencies, and ambassadors. The presidential appointment process has two steps: nomination, and subsequent approval by a majority of the Senate. The appointed officers are typically referred to as political appointees, and they are expected to carry out the president's political and policy agenda (in contrast to civil servants, who are hired through a merit-based system and are politically neutral; see Chapter 12, The Bureaucracy). During Senate recesses, the president can make appointments that will expire when the Senate officially adjourns at the close of a Congress (adjourns *sine die*), unless the appointee is subsequently confirmed. Presidents have sometimes used recess appointments to bypass the Senate, as President Obama did in appointing Richard Cordray director of the Consumer Financial Protection Bureau in 2012. Obama used the recess appointment power to get around strong Republican opposition to Cordray's appointment and the creation of the bureau he was nominated to lead (for more on this bureau, see Chapter 12). In order to prevent the president from making recess appointments when the Senate is on short breaks, the Senate has taken to officially staying in session but not conducting any business. In response, President Obama has acted as if the Senate was in recess and made a set of appointments to several agencies, including the NLRB. In the 2014 case *National Labor Relations Board v. Noel Canning*, the Supreme Court ruled that only the Senate can decide when it is in recess, thus striking down three NLRB appointments.

globalgateways

The World Trade Organization and Global Trade

One of the areas in which the president can exercise his power is through global trade because the executive branch negotiates trade agreements, which are then approved by Congress. For example, in 2014, President Obama spent considerable time and energy negotiating the Trans-Pacific Partnership trade agreement with twelve nations, foremost Japan, but the agreement was not finalized. With globalization, trade has become increasingly important to the U.S. domestic economy in two ways. First, as U.S. companies expand by manufacturing and selling goods overseas, they press the president to forge trade agreements with other countries. Likewise, foreign companies have started to locate in the United States, and this development makes it all the more important for the president to remove trade barriers that might deter investment in the United States.

From 1948 to 1994, world trade was governed by the General Agreement on Tariffs and Trade (GATT), which was the gateway through which nations set up trade agreements, sometimes bilaterally but frequently on a multi-country basis. The first round of GATT involved only 23 nations; in 1994, at the final round, 123 nations participated. That year these nations agreed to form the World Trade Organization (WTO), a neutral body responsible for settling trade disputes among member countries.*

U.S. membership in the WTO presents an opportunity and a challenge to presidential power. On the one hand, it provides a means for resolving trade disputes, but, on the other, it constrains the United States, which must abide by WTO rulings even when they are detrimental to U.S. trade interests.

Another check on the president's power is the requirement that Congress approve global trade agreements. Moreover, because Congress is elected by the people, it serves as a gateway for public opinion to influence global trade. Indeed, Congress has required that trade agreements include environmental protections and meet certain labor standards to ensure that the countries doing business with the United States follow the same rules as U.S.-based companies.

1. Should the president be able to use unilateral action when it comes to trade agreements with foreign nations?
2. Is U.S. involvement in international trade organizations such as the WTO good for American democracy?

Leaders of major industrialized countries meet in various locations in high-level meetings, known as summits, to discuss global trade and other economic issues. Here President Obama is a guest of Prime Minister David Cameron of Great Britain when that country hosted the G-8 summit in 2013.

* Information in this paragraph is from the World Trade Organization, http://www.wto.org. For more on trade politics, see David Karol, "Divided Government and U.S. Trade Policy: Much Ado about Nothing?" International Organization 54, no. 4 (2000): 825–44, and Jeanne J. Grimmett, "Why Certain Trade Agreements Are Approved as Congressional-Executive Agreements Rather Than as Treaties," CRS Report for Congress, 97-896 (Washington, D.C.: Congressional Research Service, November 3, 2011), http://www.fas.org/sgp/crs/misc/97-896.pdf.

The president also nominates judges in the federal judicial system, from the district court level to the Supreme Court, and they too must receive majority approval in the Senate (see Chapter 13, The Judiciary, for more details on the judicial nomination process). In recent years, this process has become more ideological and contentious; rather than considering only qualifications for the job, presidents and members of the Senate also consider a nominee's ideological views on key issues. As we discussed in Chapter 10, the Senate changed its rules in 2013 to make it easier to confirm district and Appeals Court nominees, but did not change the process for Supreme Court nominations. As with the treaty process, the Senate's advice and consent role in appointments and nominations is a gateway for citizen influence.

→ KEY QUESTIONS:
Consider the Senate's power to check the president in making treaties and appointments. What are the costs and benefits of this power sharing in terms of government efficiency and responsiveness?

The president has the power to fire federal officers but not to remove judges, who can be removed only by impeachment. Even though they have the formal power to do so, presidents rarely remove cabinet members because that would entail an admission of error in making the appointment in the first place. Some cabinet secretaries who disagreed with presidents about policies or, worse, committed acts of corruption were subsequently fired or were asked to resign. In an example we discuss later in the chapter, President Andrew Johnson fired his secretary of war, who disagreed with Johnson about the policy of Reconstruction in the South after the Civil War.

Veto and the Veto Override

The president has an important role in the enactment of legislation. He has the power to **veto** bills passed by Congress before they become law by refusing to sign them and sending them back to the chamber in which they originated with his objections. If Congress will be going out of session within ten days, he can simply not sign the bill, a practice known as a **pocket veto**. In cases in which the president refuses to sign the bill and Congress remains in session, the bill is enacted into law.

To counter the power of the veto, the Framers gave Congress the veto override, the power to overturn a presidential veto with a two-thirds vote in each chamber. Because the two-thirds threshold is higher than the majority vote needed to pass a bill in the first place, it is difficult for Congress to overcome presidential opposition to a bill. The high threshold reinforces the power of the president in blocking congressional action and so serves as a gateway for presidential influence in the legislative process. One could also see the veto as a gate that legislation must pass through to become law, which can be unlocked only with a congressional supermajority.

veto: *Authority of the president to block legislation passed by Congress. Congress can override a veto by a two-thirds majority in each chamber.*

pocket veto: *Automatic veto that occurs when Congress goes out of session within ten days of submitting a bill to the president and the president has not signed it.*

The veto is the most direct way that the president checks the power of Congress. Presidents use the veto power either to prevent a bill from becoming law or to pressure Congress into making changes to bring the bill closer to his policies and his view of the national interest[9] (see Table 11.4). For most of the twentieth century, Congress sent the president a large number of single-issue or narrowly drawn bills each year. In recent decades, however, Congress has learned to get around the threat of a presidential veto by passing **omnibus bills** that include provisions affecting a number of issue areas. These bills are costly to veto because they affect a wide range of voters and generate a lot of public support, so they give Congress an advantage in negotiating with the president.[10]

COMPARE WITH YOUR PEERS
MindTap® for American Government

Access The Presidency Forum: Polling Activity—Presidential Veto Power.

omnibus bill: *One very large bill that encompasses many separate bills.*

Table 11.4 Presidential Vetoes, 1945–2014

President	Congresses	Regular Vetoes	Pocket Vetoes	Total Vetoes	Vetoes Overridden
Harry S. Truman	79th–82nd	180	70	250	12
Dwight D. Eisenhower	83rd–86th	73	108	181	2
John F. Kennedy	87th–88th	12	9	21	0
Lyndon Baines Johnson	88th–90th	16	14	30	0
Richard M. Nixon	91st–93rd	26	17	43	7
Gerald R. Ford	93rd–94th	48	18	66	12
Jimmy Carter	95th–96th	13	18	31	2
Ronald Reagan	97th–100th	39	39	78	9
George H. W. Bush	101st–102nd	29	15*	44	1
William Jefferson Clinton	103rd–106th	36	1	37	2
George W. Bush	107th–110th	11	1	12	4
Barack Obama	111th–113th	2	0	2	0
Total		485	310	795	51

* "President George H. W. Bush attempted to pocket veto two bills during intrasession recesses. Congress considered the two bills enacted into law because the president had not returned the legislation. These two disputed vetoes are not included in [this table]."

Source: Kevin R. Kosar, *Regular Vetoes and Pocket Vetoes: An Overview*, CRS Report for Congress, RS22188 (Washington, D.C.: Congressional Research Service, November 18, 2010), 2–4, https://www.hsdl.org/?view&did=740060; source for veto information is John T. Woolley and Gerhard Peters, "Presidential Vetoes: Washington–Obama," The American Presidency Project, accessed October 17, 2014, http://www.presidency.ucsb.edu/data/vetoes.php.

Presidents naturally tend to veto more bills when Congress is controlled by the opposite party, a condition known as divided government. One of the most dramatic veto battles occurred in the fall of 1995 and early winter of 1996 between Democratic President Bill Clinton and the Republican-controlled Congress led by then-Speaker Newt Gingrich (see Chapter 3, Federalism). President Clinton and Congress differed over the size of cuts in **entitlement programs** such as Medicare, the health care program for the elderly (see Chapter 14, Public Policy, for a longer discussion of entitlement programs). Clinton vetoed two omnibus funding bills that Congress sent him, resulting in the shutdown of the entire government both times. The second shutdown lasted several weeks and affected veterans' hospitals, all national parks and monuments, and other government-run services. The public blamed the Republican Congress, not the president, for the impasse, and many of the voters who generally supported the Republicans lived in areas that were hard hit by the shutdown. In January 1996, Congress compromised by agreeing to a funding bill that was closer to President Clinton's position. For the rest of 1996, President Clinton and the Republican majority in Congress worked to produce key legislation on welfare reform, health insurance portability, and the minimum wage. In this case, the president used the threat of more vetoes to get members of Congress to produce legislation closer to his policy positions.[11]

★ **entitlement programs:** *Federal programs, such as Social Security, Medicare, or Medicaid, that pay out benefits to individuals based on a specified set of eligibility criteria.*

→ KEY QUESTIONS:
How does the veto power give the president influence in the legislative process?

Other Powers

The president works within this framework of formal powers and constraints to lead the nation, and in doing so becomes the chief agenda setter for domestic and foreign policy. In a later section of this chapter, we discuss agenda setting in more detail; here it is important to note that, over time, smaller tasks assigned to the president in the Constitution have evolved into powerful tools for influencing legislation. One tool is the **State of the Union address**, which is authorized in Article II, Section 3: The president "shall from time to time give to the Congress Information of the State of the Union, and recommend to their Consideration such Measures as he shall judge necessary and expedient." Nothing in this passage requires the president to inform Congress on a yearly basis or to do so in person. Presidents George Washington and John Adams (1797–1801) delivered the State of the Union address in person, but subsequent presidents began sending a written message instead, a tradition that lasted until 1913, when President Woodrow Wilson went to Congress once again to give the report as an address.[12] Over the past century, presidents have turned this obligation into an opportunity to outline a broad policy agenda for the nation. That same passage also says that the president "may, on extraordinary Occasions convene both Houses, or either of them." Thus the president can call Congress into a special session to consider legislation or to hear him deliver an important speech.[13]

Congress's Ultimate Check on the Executive: Impeachment

Congress has general oversight of the executive branch (a power discussed in Chapters 10 and 12), but its ultimate check on the president is its power to remove him from office. As discussed in Chapter 2 of this book, Article II, Section 4 of the Constitution stipulates that the president, vice president, and all civil officers (including cabinet secretaries and federal judges) are subject to removal for "Treason, Bribery, or other high Crimes and Misdemeanors." Should these officers be removed from office, they may be subject to normal criminal charges and proceedings, where applicable.

The process of removal begins with **impeachment** in the House of Representatives. Typically, the House Judiciary Committee investigates charges and recommends to the full House whether to impeach or not. If the House votes to impeach a federal officer, the Senate holds a trial, and if the president is impeached, the chief justice of the Supreme Court presides. If two-thirds of the senators vote to convict, the official is removed from office.

At the highest level of federal office, two presidents—Andrew Johnson and Bill Clinton—have been impeached, but neither was convicted by the Senate, and both remained in office. Impeachment resolutions have been introduced by individual members of the House of Representatives against other presidents, but they were not acted on. The greatest impact stemming from the power to impeach came in the case of Richard M. Nixon, which shows how the threat of impeachment can be enough to remove a president from office. Knowing he was about to be impeached, Nixon resigned instead. In addition to charges of wrongdoing, partisan disagreements can influence some members of Congress in their votes to move forward with impeachment proceedings.

As the following discussion of Richard Nixon will show, impeachment is a rarely used but powerful instrument that makes it possible for Congress to hold the president accountable for his actions. In a democratic nation guided by the rule of law, all citizens are equally obligated to obey the laws of the land, including the president.

Richard M. Nixon. President Richard M. Nixon was embroiled in a serious scandal known as Watergate, after the name of a complex in Washington where the Democratic National Committee had its headquarters. It was there that the scandal began with a break-in on June 17, 1972. In August, the *Washington Post* reported that the bank account of one of the five men caught in the act and arrested had $25,000 in funds originally given to the Nixon 1972 reelection campaign.[14]

Nixon denied any connection and was reelected in the fall, but all the while he and his aides were working to cover up the fact that his reelection committee had ordered the break-in to install listening devices on Democratic Party phones. Two *Washington Post* reporters, Bob Woodward and Carl Bernstein, continued to investigate the story (see Chapter 6, Public Opinion and the Media). As connections between Nixon and the break-in were revealed, several of his aides were convicted of conspiracy, burglary, and wiretapping, and others resigned. In May 1973, the Senate's newly formed Watergate Committee began televised hearings on the Watergate break-in and cover-up, and the Justice Department appointed Archibald Cox as the special prosecutor in charge of the Watergate investigation.

In the months that followed, a Nixon staffer revealed that the president had tape-recorded all of his White House conversations, and both the Senate Watergate Committee and the House Judiciary Committee formally issued subpoenas demanding that Nixon turn over the recordings. The turning point in what became known as the Watergate scandal came on Saturday, October 20, 1973, when President Nixon asked his attorney general, Elliot Richardson, to fire Archibald Cox and abolish the office of special prosecutor entirely. Richardson refused, as did the deputy attorney general. Both resigned. Solicitor General Robert Bork, next in command, then carried out the president's wishes. What had been a struggle for information became a question of obstruction of justice by the president.

President Nixon turned over a limited number of tapes, but there was an eighteen-and-a-half-minute gap on one tape, and Congress wanted to know what was discussed during that time and why it was erased. The administration claimed that the tape was erased by mistake. During the next months, Nixon released only partial transcripts and said that others were protected by **executive privilege**—the president's right to engage in communications with his advisers that he does not have to reveal. The justification for

→ KEY QUESTIONS:
In a democracy, should the president have executive privilege?

executive privilege: *President's right to engage in confidential communications with his advisers.*

BETTMANN/CORBIS

When Richard Nixon resigned the presidency in August 1974, it was the first time in U.S. history that a president had relinquished his office. President Nixon left office under charges of abuse of power arising from a cover-up of the Watergate scandal, which forever changed the nation's faith in the presidency as a trustworthy institution.

this privilege is that the president must make difficult choices and, without the guarantee of privilege, may not receive or deliver the fullest information in the course of his deliberations.

The Supreme Court created an exception to this privilege in *United States v. Nixon* when on July 24, 1974, it unanimously ruled that executive privilege is not absolute and must give way when the government needs the information for a trial. The tapes showed that Nixon and his aides had conspired to cover up the Watergate break-in. Three days later, the House Judiciary Committee approved three articles of impeachment against Nixon.[15] With the full House of Representatives ready to vote on the articles, President Nixon resigned on August 9, 1974.

In 1975, Nixon's successor, former Vice President Gerald R. Ford (1974–77), pardoned Nixon of all federal offenses he might have committed. The Watergate scandal had a negative impact on the American presidency, raising public mistrust of the office and of the federal government more generally. However, the process leading up to Nixon's resignation also revealed the ways in which members of both parties can work together in Congress to exercise congressional oversight of the executive.

Impeachment is not a power to be used lightly, but it does serve as a gateway for the public, through its elected officials in Congress, to hold the president, cabinet officials, and federal judges accountable for abuses of power.

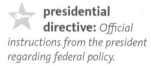

Checkpoint

CAN YOU:

- Characterize the presidential power of commander in chief
- Compare pardon and commutation
- Describe the role of the Senate in the president's power to negotiate and sign treaties
- Recall the steps to presidential appointments
- Survey the power of the veto
- Explain how the State of the Union address has evolved as a tool for the president
- Compare and contrast examples of impeachment (or impending impeachment)

11.3 The Growth of Executive Influence

> Describe the growth of executive influence

→ KEY QUESTIONS:
Should the president be subjected to civil lawsuits while he is in office? State the reasons for your answer.

With all the formal constitutional restrictions on the president, one has to wonder how the modern presidency became so powerful. The answer lies in the general grant of executive power and the constitutional provision that the president "take Care that the Laws be faithfully executed," which he promises to do when he takes the oath of office. Presidents have found ways to unlock the enormous powers inherent in these constitutional provisions to expand their informal powers over policy making and implementation. The president's veto power and Congress's power to override and to impeach the president counteract each other and help ensure that each branch remains responsive to its governing responsibilities. However, Congress has no formal means to balance and check the president's growing executive power, though at times the judicial branch has been able to do so.

→ KEY QUESTIONS:
What should be done about the growth of executive power? Is it a problem for checks and balances among the separate branches?

Presidential Directives and Signing Statements

Presidents use the executive power to issue **presidential directives** that give specific instructions on a federal policy and do not require congressional approval. Recent presidents have used this unilateral power much more frequently than previous presidents, especially under conditions of divided government or interbranch policy conflict.[16] Presidential directives

★ **presidential directive:** *Official instructions from the president regarding federal policy.*

might take the form of executive orders, proclamations, or military orders. They are the primary way that presidents shape policy implementation, and they are the instruments presidents use to act quickly in national emergencies.[17]

executive order:
Presidential directive that usually involves implementing a specific law.

The best-known type of directive is the **executive order**, which can be used for a wide range of purposes. Typically, executive orders instruct federal employees to take a specific action or implement a policy in a particular way. Some scholars argue that executive orders are an important source of "independent authority" that is used solely at the discretion of the president.[18] Even though presidents since Washington have issued executive orders, the orders were not officially numbered until 1862 and not published in the *Federal Register* until 1935.[19] In 1948, President Harry Truman integrated the armed forces with Executive Order 9981, stating "there shall be equality of treatment and opportunity for all persons in the armed forces, without regard to race, color, religion, or national origin."[20] Truman used the power of executive order to bypass congressional and some military opposition to integration of the armed forces because he believed it was the right thing for the country.

Still, a presidential directive is not completely immune from scrutiny or accountability. In 1952, during the Korean War, the United Steelworkers union threatened to stop work at steel mills. In response, President Truman used his executive powers to order the seizure of steel mills and put them under the control of the United States government. Although the steel workers were willing to put off the strike and work in the newly government-controlled mills, the steel mill owners sued to challenge the legality of the seizure. In *Youngstown Sheet and Tube Co. v. Sawyer,* better known as the Steel Seizure case, the Supreme Court ruled against the president, claiming he had no statutory authority from Congress to seize the mills and that his commander in chief status did not allow him to seize domestic property when the United States was at war in a foreign land (see Supreme Court Cases: *Youngstown Sheet and Tube Co. v. Sawyer*).

In foreign and military affairs, presidents can issue presidential directives on national security, which have a similar purpose to executive orders but are not published in the *Federal Register,* which is the official record of government regulations (see Chapter 12). These directives can announce specific sanctions against individuals who are considered enemies of the United States or make larger statements about U.S. policy toward a foreign country. President George W. Bush used this power frequently in what he described as a war on terror and in the conduct of the wars in Afghanistan and Iraq. For example, he issued an order in 2001 to create military tribunals that would try suspected enemy combatants and terrorists, rather than allowing them to be tried in a regular military court. He also created a special subcategory called homeland security presidential directives, which are not as widely publicized as other directives and deal only with homeland security policy.

signing statements:
Written remarks issued by the president when signing a bill into law that often reflect his interpretation of how the law should be implemented.

When a president signs a bill into law, he can issue **signing statements**, written remarks that reflect his interpretation of the law that are not required or authorized by the Constitution. Signing statements can be classified as nonconstitutional and constitutional. Nonconstitutional statements are typically symbolic, celebrating the passage of the law or providing technical instructions for implementing a new law. Constitutional statements are more serious in that the president uses them to indicate a disagreement with Congress on specific provisions in the law. In constitutional signing statements, the president may go so far as to refuse to implement specific provisions of laws. This kind of statement is a challenge to Congress's constitutional authority to legislate.[21] Even when the presidency and the Congress are controlled by the same party, signing statements can be used to shift the implementation of policy toward presidential preferences. President Obama recognized the controversy over signing statements, and he issued a memorandum early in his administration stating that he would use signing statements "to address constitutional concerns only when it is appropriate to do so as a means of discharging my constitutional responsibilities."[22] In issuing this memorandum, President Obama was trying to alleviate concerns about abusing executive power but at the same time preserving the presidential power to interpret legislation that is inherent in signing statements. As of September 2014, President Obama had issued twenty-eight signing statements and 187 executive orders.[23]

→ KEY QUESTIONS:
What limits can Congress, the courts, and/or the American people place on the president?

Presidential directives and signing statements create tension between the president and Congress and between the president and the judiciary because they are an expansion of presidential power. At times they have been deemed illegal.[24] Many presidents, from Lincoln to Franklin Delano Roosevelt to George W. Bush, have taken temporary actions that have violated constitutional rights in the name of national security, from suspending *habeas corpus* to interning Japanese Americans to eavesdropping on U.S. citizens (see Chapter 4, Civil Liberties, and Chapter 5, Civil Rights, for expanded discussions of these actions). Judging the merit of such actions is difficult because citizens have to decide whether the president is acting in good faith on behalf of the country or seeking to expand his own power and agenda.

Power to Persuade

Presidents understand that communicating well with the public is essential to building support for their policies. They also face the challenge of using their personal reputations

bully pulpit:
Nickname for the power of the president to use the attention associated with the office to persuade the media, Congress, and the public to support his policy positions.

and negotiating skills to generate support among members of Congress. President Theodore Roosevelt (1901–1909) described the office of the president as a **bully pulpit**, where presidents could use the attention associated with the office to make a public argument in favor of or against a policy.[25] The key to using the bully pulpit effectively is to explain a policy in simple and accessible terms, to get the public's attention, and to frame an issue in a way that is favorable to the president's policy position. Using the bully pulpit can accomplish the president's goals only if he already has a receptive audience. In today's highly partisan and divided political climate, there is no guarantee that the president's detractors will listen to his message.[26]

A president's relationship with the members of the news media is a crucial factor in successful communication, and it has evolved dramatically over time. Samuel Kernell, a presidential media scholar, argues that over the past seventy years, presidents have increased the extent to which they control their interactions with the press. Press conferences are one important way of sustaining a relationship with the news media, and presidents have tried to use them to their advantage. Some presidents are more comfortable with the

President Theodore Roosevelt was a larger-than-life figure who challenged corporate monopolies, sought to strengthen U.S. international power, and increased federal efforts at land conservation. He was known for using the office of the president as a bully pulpit to persuade the public to support his policies.

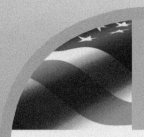

supreme court cases

Youngstown Sheet and Tube Co. v. Sawyer (1952)

QUESTION: Can the president seize steel mills to prevent a strike during wartime?

ORAL ARGUMENT: May 12, 1952

DECISION: June 2, 1952 (read at http://caselaw.lp.findlaw.com/scripts/getcase.pl?court=US&vol=343&invol=579)

OUTCOME: No, the seizure was overturned (6–3).

After North Korea's invasion of South Korea in June 1950, President Harry Truman sought and received a United Nations resolution permitting intervention on behalf of South Korea. In 1952, with the Korean War still raging, the United Steelworkers announced plans for an April strike. President Truman feared that the strike would severely harm America's war effort. One alternative for putting off the strike was to seek a temporary court order prohibiting a strike when national security is at stake, a provision allowed under the Taft-Hartley Labor Act.

Uncomfortable with what was perceived to be an anti-labor policy, Truman instead ordered Secretary of Commerce Charles Sawyer to seize the steel mills and run them under the flag of the United States. Because the steelworkers preferred working at the steel mills under the government to the Taft-Hartley alternatives, they agreed to come back to work after the seizure.

The steel mill owners then brought suit challenging the seizure. Truman claimed the authority to do this under his power to make sure that the laws were faithfully executed and under his power as commander in chief of the armed forces. The Court's decision rejected the president's authority to seize the steel mills, noting that Congress had not passed a law allowing the seizure, so there were no laws involving the seizure to be faithfully executed.

The Court also ruled that the president's authority to rule as commander in chief did not extend to domestic seizures during foreign wars. Without congressional authorization, the president could not seize the steel mills. A separate concurring opinion, since treated as the heart of the case, noted that the president's authority is at its peak when he acts under the express authority of Congress, is in a middle category when Congress has not acted, and is at its lowest when the president acts contrary to congressional will. As Congress had rejected granting the president the authority to seize property in labor disputes, Truman was acting under the lowest level of authority. Without congressional authorization, the president could not seize the steel mills.

The Steel Seizure case still stands as the leading decision on presidential authority. The Supreme Court relied heavily on it in deciding that President George W. Bush did not have the authority to hold enemy combatants from the war in Afghanistan at the U.S. naval base at Guantanamo Bay, Cuba, without a hearing, since Congress had not authorized the action.*

1. Why did the Court block President Truman's seizure of the steel mills?
2. Did the decision place the president above Congress, below Congress, or equal to Congress in terms of making policy?

* *Hamdan v. Rumsfeld*, 548 U.S. 557 (2006).

press than others. Franklin Delano Roosevelt held an average of eighteen solo press conferences per year, Lyndon Baines Johnson held twenty-five, Ronald Reagan held six, Bill Clinton held six, and George W. Bush held five. President Obama averaged five press conferences per year in his first term, he held eight in 2013, and as of September, 2014, held four.[27] Press conferences are somewhat risky because, unlike speeches, presidents do not control the content of the questions that are asked, and they can sometimes make unrehearsed statements that have political consequences. In addition to press conferences and televised speeches, President Obama also used new technologies to bypass the media and speak directly to the people. Recognizing that many voters get their news and political information from sources such as cable TV and Twitter instead of from traditional network television, he created a blog on the White House website, posted videos of his speeches, and sent mass e-mails to citizens who inquired about specific proposals.[28]

In conjunction with public outreach, the president also tries to personally persuade members of Congress and other policy makers to support his policies. Political scientist Richard Neustadt has argued that this personal persuasion is the root of presidential power. Several factors affect a president's power to persuade, notably his professional reputation and his approval ratings.[29] A presidential approval rating is usually expressed as the percentage of the American people who say the president is doing a good job. A president's professional reputation is a combination of his prior experience and the steps he takes throughout his term. When a president comes to the Oval Office with executive experience or a strong reputation as a productive legislator, he is likely to have a reservoir of respect from members of Congress, the public, and the media. That reservoir can become depleted if the president makes missteps and is not successful with his legislative agenda. Lawmakers are more likely to pass a president's policy proposals when his approval rating is high, and they are less cooperative when the president is unpopular. Public approval can be essential to presidential policy success, which is why the president tries to maintain public support throughout his years in the White House.[30]

To be persuasive, a president has to balance his own policy preferences with those of members of Congress and convince the American public that he is leading the country in the right direction.[31] The stakes can be very high for presidents as they navigate the legislative process (see Chapter 10). The president's need to be responsive to public opinion serves as a gateway for influence by the public on his decision making.

Agenda Setting

As the chief executive officer of the entire federal government, the president has an obligation and an opportunity to work with Congress to set the foreign and domestic policy agenda for the nation, from determining how to configure military strength, to overseeing economic growth, to ensuring the health and safety of individual citizens. The president is the sole occupant of his elected office, as compared with 535 members of the House and Senate. Consequently, the president has the power to focus the nation's attention on his ideas and policy proposals.

→ KEY QUESTIONS:
Does the bully pulpit serve as a communication gateway between the president and citizens?

→ KEY QUESTIONS:
How does the current president use the bully pulpit to generate public support for his ideas?

→ KEY QUESTIONS:
Has the increased emphasis on job approval ratings strengthened the power of the public to hold the president accountable?

AP IMAGES

President John F. Kennedy was completely at ease with the press and held sixty-four press conferences during his time in office. They were televised, and not only White House reporters but also the American public looked forward to the lively exchanges between the press and the president, who was known for his sense of humor and ready wit.

head of state: *Title given to the president as national leader.*

In dealing with foreign powers, the president is **head of state** and commander in chief of the military. As head of state, the president oversees a vast organization of employees in the State Department and the office of the U.S. Trade Representative who lay the groundwork for negotiations with foreign leaders on issues ranging from nuclear weapons control to trade policy. Upon their recommendation, the president proposes new treaties or revisions to existing agreements as needed. Ultimately, the president is the public face of and the authority behind U.S. foreign policy decisions. He must establish working relationships with foreign leaders and demonstrate an understanding of how other nations' political systems operate, especially the extent to which the executive power is placed in one person or shared, as it is in parliamentary systems (see Chapter 10).

Because the president is presumed to serve the best interest of the entire nation, the American public frequently supports most of his foreign policies—at least initially. The main congressional counterweights to the president's powers in these areas are the power of the Senate to ratify treaties and the power of Congress to appropriate money for federal programs, including foreign aid and diplomatic programs. These congressional powers come in the form of responses to the president's proposals. Congress can have some influence on the president's foreign policy agenda through hearings and press statements, but if the president is able to persuade the public to support his positions, he is typically able to forge his own path on foreign policy.

→ KEY QUESTIONS:
How effective are the president's agenda-setting tools?

In the area of domestic policy, the president uses the State of the Union address, the federal budget, the power to make executive appointments, the bully pulpit, the executive power to implement laws, and the veto power as his agenda-setting tools. He issues his federal budget in early February, shortly after he delivers the State of the Union address. The budget is a blueprint that indicates his spending priorities for all areas of the federal government. Congress does not have to abide by this budget, and Congress frequently ignores it and constructs its own federal budget (see Chapter 10 for a discussion of the budget). All measures that raise taxes and spend federal money can be vetoed by the president, and, as we have seen, the veto or the threat of a veto gives the president a means of exerting pressure on Congress to follow his budget priorities.

Checkpoint

CAN YOU:

- Recall the different types of presidential directives
- List the tools available to a president as he uses his power to persuade
- Describe how the president can set the public agenda

11.4 The President in Wartime

> Analyze why the president is so powerful during wartime

As executive branch powers have grown, presidents have increasingly come into conflict with the judicial branch and Congress, especially in times of national crisis and war (see also Chapter 4). In this section, we examine the power struggle between the president and Congress over war powers, which the Constitution divides between the two branches, and the power struggle between the president and the judiciary on the scope of presidential powers and civil liberties. It is crucial to understand that the balance of power among the three branches of the federal government is constantly evolving in response to changing internal and external conditions.

→ KEY QUESTIONS:
What powers should the president have during wartime?

Power Struggles between the President and Congress

The Constitution gives Congress the power to declare war, but it has been the practice for presidents to first formally ask Congress for a declaration of war. After Congress declares war, the president as commander in chief has the authority to direct the conflict. Through its constitutional powers in Article I, Section 8, "to raise and support Armies" and "to provide and maintain a Navy," Congress retains the power to cut off the flow of money for the war effort. Generally, the president and Congress have worked together in times of military conflict, but in the late 1960s, opposition to the Vietnam War brought about significant divisions between the executive and legislative branches over war powers.

Vietnam and the War Powers Act.   Vietnam had been a divided nation since 1954, with Communist forces controlling North Vietnam and anti-Communists controlling South Vietnam, and a civil war had erupted between them. President Dwight D. Eisenhower and then Presidents John F. Kennedy and Lyndon Baines Johnson believed that containing Communism and keeping the North Vietnamese Communists from taking over South Vietnam were important, but the U.S. troop buildup was slow at first. In 1964, however, President Johnson presented evidence to Congress that the North Vietnamese were attacking U.S. ships on patrol duty in international waters in the Gulf of Tonkin off the shore of North Vietnam. Johnson asked Congress for the authority to fight back, and Congress responded with the Tonkin Gulf Resolution, stating that "The Congress approves and supports the determination of the President, as Commander in Chief, to take all necessary measures to repel any armed attack against the forces of the United States and to prevent further aggression."[32] Congress passed the resolution with only two dissenting votes, few restrictions, and no time limit on how long the United States would stay involved in the conflict.[33]

By 1968, the United States had more than five hundred thousand troops in Vietnam, and the conflict was commonly referred to as the Vietnam War, although there was never a formal declaration of war by Congress. The conflict had become highly unpopular, and President Johnson was forced to give up his bid for reelection. That year, Richard M. Nixon was elected president and promised to end the Vietnam War; however, he actually broadened the conflict to the neighboring countries of Cambodia and Laos in his efforts to win the war.

By 1971, Congress had repealed the Tonkin Gulf Resolution, and, following the Paris Peace Accords signed in January 1973, U.S. troops were withdrawn from Vietnam. In October 1973, Congress passed a more formal proposal to limit presidential authority to engage in military conflict. This **War Powers Act** states that the president cannot send troops into military conflict for more than a total of ninety days without seeking a formal declaration of war, or authorization for continued military action, from Congress. President Nixon vetoed the act, but Congress overrode the veto.

The War Powers Act was ostensibly a gate that would stand in the way of a president's decision to launch a war without first gauging congressional support. Although the act tried to clarify presidential authority and limits, the scholar Louis Fisher argues that it is flawed because the ninety-day limit does not begin until the president has officially reported the troop engagement to Congress. A president could send troops into a conflict and not report it to Congress, thereby avoiding a trigger of the War Powers Act.[34] In addition, the act did not really give Congress the power to end a military conflict except by denying all funding for it, as

War Powers Act: *The 1973 act which provides that the president cannot send troops into military conflict for more than a total of ninety days without seeking a formal declaration of war, or authorization for continued military action, from Congress.*

→ KEY QUESTIONS:
Think about the conduct of war. Who should be in charge? The president? Congress? The military?

it ultimately did with Vietnam. However, if there is considerable public support for an ongoing military engagement, the president can make the case that it is too dangerous to cut off all funding, and Congress would be reluctant to cut off funding when troops were still in the field and could be harmed. The irony of the War Powers Act is that it gives presidents an incentive to seek a declaration of war or authorization to use military force, after which time Congress loses much of its control of the operation of the conflict.[35] In other words, once Congress gives the president permission to go to war, it is next to impossible for Congress to stop the war.[36]

The Iraq War.   The U.S. has been in major military conflicts in the past decade in Iraq and Afghanistan. The two wars ran parallel to each other, but their origins are quite different. The Iraq War began in 2003, but its origins date back to August 1990, when Iraq, led by Saddam Hussein, invaded Kuwait. This act of aggression prompted multilateral military action known as the Gulf War, which aimed to push Iraq out of Kuwait. The Gulf War was short-lived; as part of the peace settlement, Iraq was prohibited from developing weapons of mass destruction and was required to submit to constant UN monitoring.

→ KEY QUESTIONS:
How much responsibility should Presidents Bush and Obama assume for the Iraq and Afghanistan Wars, respectively? Does Congress have shared responsibility for those conflicts?

By 2002, it had become increasingly difficult for UN inspectors to accurately assess Iraq's capabilities for producing weapons of mass destruction. Although there had been no concrete evidence of such weapons, President George W. Bush argued that a preemptive strike against Iraq was necessary to preserve the security of the United States. In accordance with the War Powers Act, President Bush asked Congress for a resolution authorizing military action. On October 10, 2002, the House of Representatives approved a joint resolution that gave the president the authority to use all military force to "defend the national security of the United States."[37] The Senate approved the resolution the next day by a vote of 77–23.

The Iraq War was launched on March 19, 2003; Saddam Hussein was captured in December 2003 and was tried and hanged for war crimes. Nevertheless, instability in Iraq continued. By 2006, with violence in Iraq at a high level, the Democrats in Congress—many of whom had initially supported the war—withdrew their support and called for the return of all U.S. troops and an end to the war. During the midterm congressional elections that year, Democrats made ending the war a campaign issue, and they won majority control of the House and the Senate. However, in January 2007, President Bush increased the number of troops in Iraq in an effort known as the "surge," which was intended to reduce violence there.

As of January 2009, the three dominant groups in Iraq—the Sunnis, the Shiites, and the Kurds—were operating under a parliamentary system of government, and the U.S. government worked with the Iraqis to end the war and transfer full governmental control to them. On August 31, 2010, President Obama announced the end of the nation's formal combat involvement, and by the end of December 2011, the last official combat personnel departed from Iraq, although some U.S. soldiers are there in an advisory role. Since then, the Iraqi government has struggled to maintain security among the different factions vying for power, which has led to violence and casualties. Iraq today represents a nation forever changed by U.S. involvement; what remains uncertain is whether that change will enable or prevent democratic government there.

The Afghanistan War.   The war in Afghanistan began after the September 11, 2001, terrorist attacks were traced back to al-Qaeda operatives harbored by the Afghan Taliban regime. President George W. Bush addressed Congress on September 20, 2001, indicating that the Taliban would be held responsible for the attacks, and, in October, the United States and its allies launched a military action on Afghanistan designed to find those responsible for the 9/11 attacks and bring down the Taliban regime. However, Bush did not ask for a declaration of war against the nation of Afghanistan. Although the Taliban regime was subsequently toppled and a new leader, Hamid Karzai, was elected and later reelected, the Taliban has mounted a resurgence in Afghanistan. In 2009, President Obama, as commander in chief, responded to resurgent Taliban-sponsored attacks on U.S. troops and civilian Afghans by ordering a surge of thirty thousand additional troops to Afghanistan, bringing the total there to nearly a hundred thousand.[38] In the next two years, as the number of American and Afghan casualties increased, public support for the war decreased, and it was hard for President Obama to maintain U.S. involvement there. The Republicans' takeover of the House of Representatives in the 2010 election complicated his decision making because they publicly resisted efforts to reduce the U.S. presence in Afghanistan until the government could demonstrate it had defeated the Taliban and al-Qaeda.

On May 1, 2011, President Obama announced that Osama bin Laden, who had claimed to be the head of al-Qaeda and the coordinator of the 9/11 attacks, had been killed in a military operation in Pakistan. With the death of bin Laden, public support for the war diminished further. In 2012, President Obama and Secretary of Defense Leon Panetta announced their intention to work with the Afghanistan government to reduce the number of U.S. troops in Afghanistan at a faster rate. As of September 2014, the number of U.S. troops stationed in Afghanistan was approximately 28,970, but the U.S. planned to have fewer than 10,000 troops there by 2015.[39]

Uprisings in Foreign Lands.　Ongoing military conflicts such as those in Iraq and Afghanistan have spillover effects that can limit the president's flexibility in responding to conflicts in other foreign nations. Protests in 2011 known as the Arab Spring that threatened to topple authoritarian regimes offer an example. Seeking UN approval and international cooperation, the United States only became militarily involved in Libya. When in March 2011 President Obama authorized the use of air strikes and drones in Libya, he was acting in conjunction with NATO forces to enforce a UN Security Council resolution that authorized international military action to enforce a no-fly zone to stop the Libyan leader, Muammar al-Qaddafi, from committing violence against his own people. The decision to intervene in Libya was controversial given ongoing involvement in Afghanistan, so Obama gave a national address to explain his decision and inform the American people that U.S. ground troops would not be deployed. Nevertheless, some members of Congress argued that the air strikes violated the War Powers Act because the president had not formally notified Congress of military involvement there. The president moved forward anyway, and by October 2011, the rebel forces had prevailed, and Qaddafi was killed as he resisted capture.[40]

Unlike Libya, President Obama did not propose intervening in the Syrian conflict, although the United States did support a UN resolution condemning the violence committed by President Bashar al-Assad's regime against protesters. That resolution was vetoed by Russia and China, and without multilateral or congressional support for intervention, Obama lacked the same justification for entering that conflict as he had in the case of Libya.[41] However, Obama worked with the United Nations and Russia to broker a deal whereby Syria agreed not to use chemical weapons and to turn over all chemical weapons to the United Nations for safe destruction. Although that turnover has been completed, the civil war rages on in Syria. Meanwhile, the Obama administration has supplied Syrian rebels with light arms and humanitarian aid, while Russia has sold advanced aircraft and missile systems to the Syrian government. In the summer of 2014, with the rise of the ultra violent extremist group ISIL, the U.S. role in Syria expanded.

Public Policy and the President:
Use of Drones

Since the terrorist attacks of 9/11, and subsequent terror attacks in the United States, such as the Boston Marathon bombings, and others around the world, the United States has sent ground forces into Iraq and Afghanistan, and also used alternative means of warfare such as drones—unmanned aircraft guided remotely and able to be used to target individuals who are viewed to be engaged in terrorist activities directly against the United States and its allies. However, these aircraft are not 100 percent accurate and have resulted in the deaths of innocent civilians.

As commander in chief, the president has the authority to order a drone strike. President Obama has starkly increased the number of these attacks in Pakistan, Yemen, and Somalia, where known terrorists groups, such as al-Qaeda, have set up bases of operations. In 2014, President Obama ordered drone strikes against ISIL a newly emergent terrorist group operating in Syria and Iraq. A British organization, known as the Bureau of Investigative Journalism, has reported the number of people killed by drone attacks exceeds three thousand, including civilian men, women, and children.

Drone strikes became controversial as the media began to report on civilian casualties. Then in 2011, a drone strike in Yemen killed two American citizens, Anwar Al-Awlaki, a known leader of al-Qaeda, and his associate named Samir Kahn.[42] That same year, a U.S. drone strike also killed Al-Awlaki's 16-year-old son, also a U.S. citizen, in Yemen.[43] Some people claim that as American citizens, these individuals should have been captured and tried in an American court of law, and these drone attacks deprived them of their rights under the U.S. Constitution. Others argue that by engaging in activities designed to harm U.S. security, they relinquished those rights.

President Obama has defended the use of drones as a more effective way of combating individuals and groups that are intent on killing Americans and that as commander in chief,

Table 11.5 U.S. Drone Strikes and Related Casualties, 2004–2014

Total Obama strikes: 332
Total U.S. strikes since 2004: 383
Total reported killed: 2,296–3,719
Civilians reported killed: 416–957
Children reported killed: 168–202
Total reported injured: 1,089–1,639

Source: Bureau of Investigative Journalism, Monthly Updates on the Covert War, May 1, 2014, http://www.thebureauinvestigates.com/2014/05/01/april-2014-update-us-covert-actions-in-pakistan-yemen-and-somalia/.

his first obligation is to take any and all steps that he believes will protect Americans. After signing a type of presidential directive known as a Presidential Policy Guidance statement on the use of drones in May 2013, the president said this:

> Nevertheless, it is a hard fact that U.S. strikes have resulted in civilian casualties, a risk that exists in every war. . . . But as commander in chief, I must weigh these heartbreaking tragedies against the alternatives. To do nothing in the face of terrorist networks would invite far more civilian casualties—not just in our cities at home and our facilities abroad, but also in the very places like Sana'a and Kabul and Mogadishu where terrorists seek a foothold. Remember that the terrorists we are after target civilians, and the death toll from their acts of terrorism against Muslims dwarfs any estimate of civilian casualties from drone strikes. So doing nothing is not an option.[44]

Presidents weigh the costs of ensuring the safety of American citizens, both in terms of dollars and the lives of American soldiers, against the costs of using tactics that may result in civilian deaths.

The American Civil Liberties Union (ACLU) and the Center for Constitutional Rights has filed lawsuits on behalf of Al-Awlaki both before and after his death in an attempt to block the president and the executive branch from targeting American citizens. However, federal courts have dismissed these suits. Moreover, American public opinion indicates strong bipartisan support for drone strikes, with 69 percent of Republicans and 59 percent of Democrats approving Obama's decision.[45] In such an atmosphere, President Obama is likely to continue to use this advanced technology, which he believes is effective and justified in the interests of national security.

Construct Your Own Policy

1. Devise a more transparent policy on reporting the use of drones and the number of casualties associated with this type of weapon.
2. Create a set of guidelines for the executive branch to follow in determining who will be the subject of a drone attack.

The U.S. led a coalition of nations in air strikes against ISIL, and provided weapons to groups fighting against ISIL.

Tensions with Russia intensified when Ukrainian rebels ousted their pro-Russian president. Ukraine, Russia's neighbor to the West, is home to many individuals of Russian heritage. Subsequently, Russian separatists staged takeovers of Ukrainian government buildings in southern and eastern Ukraine, essentially declaring them part of Russia. The Ukrainian government was not well prepared to stop these takeovers, which Russia actively supported. In response, President Obama and leaders of European nations imposed economic sanctions on Russia in an

Here we see the conflict in Ukraine where separatists waged protests in favor of breaking free of Ukraine and aligning with Russia. In 2014, the conflict escalated from protests to civil war.

GENYA SAVILOV/AFP/GETTY IMAGES

effort to pressure them to withdraw their support of these separatists. In September 2014, the Ukrainian government and the separatists declared a cease fire, but fighting continued, with both military and civilian casualties.

President Obama and Congress understand that the United States is expected to take the lead in responding to this crisis. However, it is also clear to both Obama and Congress that the American public are weary of war and international conflict. Still, Americans view global instability as a threat to their safety. In 2014, it became increasingly clear to both Obama and Congress that public opinion among American people at this time leaned strongly against intervention in foreign conflicts. In contrast, after the 9/11 terrorist attacks in 2001, for example, only 30 percent of Americans said that the U.S. should "mind its own business."[46] This broader context has important implications for U.S. foreign policy because presidents, and members of Congress, recognize the difficulty of waging a military intervention without public support.

These examples demonstrate that tension between the presidency and Congress over war powers compels the president to make the case to Congress that military action is necessary. Moreover, as in the case with Ukraine and Syria, presidents face challenges in persuading a war-weary nation to intervene militarily. In such cases, the Obama administration has sought to actively intervene only with strong international support and with as limited U.S. ground troop involvement as possible.

Power Struggles between the President and the Judiciary

→ KEY QUESTIONS:
What limits should the judiciary impose on presidential actions in wartime? Give examples.

Power struggles between the president and the judiciary in wartime generally focus on civil liberties. In Chapter 4, we examined the Court's rejection of Abraham Lincoln's argument about the suspension of *habeas corpus*, and in Chapter 5, we discussed the Court's acquiescence in President Franklin Delano Roosevelt's executive order on the internment of Japanese Americans. In this chapter, we have already noted the limits on presidential actions imposed by the Steel Seizure case.

The most significant recent clash between the president and the judiciary over wartime powers arose during President George W. Bush's declared war on terror. Following 9/11, President Bush greatly expanded the powers of the executive branch of government. As we have seen in previous chapters, he created separate military tribunals to try captured terrorists, claimed exemption from the Geneva Convention rules on the treatment and detainment of prisoners, and authorized the National Security Agency to monitor conversations of suspected terrorists with residents of the United States without obtaining warrants. President Bush's justification was that, as commander in chief, he had the foremost responsibility to protect American citizens and actions taken for that purpose should not be subject to the approval of Congress or the courts.

A combination of congressional action and Supreme Court decisions following the guidelines of the Steel Seizure case constrained most of these presidential actions. In 2004, the Supreme Court's *Hamdi v. Rumsfeld* decision rejected Bush administration attempts to deny *habeas corpus* protections to an enemy combatant who was a U.S. citizen because federal law prohibits such denial to U.S. citizens.[47] That same day, the Court also rejected the administration's authority to deny *habeas corpus* to an enemy combatant who was not a U.S. citizen.[48] The Bush administration then established special military tribunals to review the detention of enemy combatants at Guantanamo Bay, but the Court rejected the authority of the tribunals because Congress had not authorized them.[49] The Court rejected congressional and presidential efforts to limit the Court's jurisdiction to hear such appeals, claiming that those limits did not apply to cases that had been filed before Congress passed the law. Even when Congress and the president authorized tribunals, the Supreme Court declared that neither Congress nor the president has the authority to suspend the writ of *habeas corpus*, which the Constitution allows only during "Cases of Rebellion or Invasion."[50] Thus, in cases involving terrorism, the Court has put gates in the way of Congress and the president in their efforts to restrict civil liberties in the name of national security. (For a broader discussion of the balance between laws against terrorism and civil liberties, see Chapter 4.)

→ KEY QUESTIONS:
How are acts of terrorism different from or the same as acts of war? How should the president, Congress, and the judiciary respond to terrorist attacks?

Checkpoint

CAN YOU:

■ Track trends in the struggle between the president and Congress over war powers

■ Describe issues in the struggle between the president and the judiciary in wartime

11.5 The Organization of the Modern White House

❯ Summarize how the White House is organized

The way that a president organizes the Executive Office and the cabinet reveals a great deal about his management style as well as his policy preferences. The president relies on his White House advisers for policy recommendations. The modern president has the challenge of encouraging cooperation between political appointees and members of the civil service and making sure that employees in each category are held accountable for their decisions.

→ KEY QUESTIONS:
How does the Executive Office of the President reflect individual management styles?

The Executive Office of the President

The president runs a large organization known as the Executive Office of the President (EOP), a loosely knit unit of several key organizations that report directly to him. These include the White House Office; the Office of Management and Budget (OMB), which Sylvia Mathews

Burwell led until she became Secretary of HHS; the National Security Council (NSC); and the Council of Economic Advisers (CEA). Each office has influence over budgetary, military, and economic policies.

Staff organizations can have a real impact on the success of a presidential administration. For many presidents, the choice of how to organize their staffs rests with their own personalities and operating styles. These personal characteristics can make a president more or less likely to take advice from one adviser, or balance the advice from several advisers and come to a final decision on his own; how much presidents rely on their advisers often depends on how much they trust their own judgment.[51]

In general, a tightly organized White House staff organization yields a productive presidency, and the chief of staff is central to that effort in several ways. He serves as a gatekeeper by controlling the flow of staff and paperwork and focuses the president's attention on key issues. The **chief of staff** also monitors the coherence of presidential policies across cabinet departments and can serve as a referee for disagreements among members of the president's senior staff. Last, he can be important in forming bridges between the president and Congress.

Another important element in presidential productivity is staff continuity, and new presidents often bring former executive branch personnel into their administrations. These staff members bring personal experience to a new president's organization. They also bring policy expertise that will help bolster the president in dealing with members of Congress who specialize in specific policy areas. Some prominent individuals who have served in multiple administrations include Patrick Buchanan, Donald Rumsfeld, Colin Powell, Condoleezza Rice, Bill Daley, and Leon Panetta.

One of the effects of a lame duck presidency is that many members of the president's inner circle start to leave the administration as it enters its final two years. However, presidents can counteract that loss by replacing the departed advisors with staff who have also worked for the administration, just in different positions. President Obama did so when he appointed Jacob Lew Secretary of the Treasury after he served as OMB director and Chief of Staff, and with Sylvia Mathews Burwell when he appointed her Secretary of HHS after she replaced Jacob Lew as OMB director.

The Office of the Vice President

Traditionally, the office of the vice president has not had many important responsibilities. It was not until the twentieth century that vice presidents were chosen by presidential candidates to enhance their electoral prospects, and even then, once they were in office, they were given little more than ceremonial tasks. However, with the increasing complexity and international significance of the presidential role following World War II, President Dwight D. Eisenhower assigned his vice president, Richard M. Nixon, the task of traveling around the world to meet with foreign leaders. Twenty years later, Walter Mondale, President Jimmy Carter's vice president, expanded the role of the office by serving as a close adviser to the president on issues ranging from national security to domestic policy.[52]

Twenty years after the Carter presidency, George W. Bush allowed his vice president, Richard (Dick) Cheney, to play a prominent role in the nation's military and foreign policy. Cheney had been secretary of defense under Bush's father, George H. W. Bush (1989–93),

→ KEY QUESTIONS:
President Harry S. Truman had a sign on his desk that read "The Buck Stops Here." What did it mean?

→ KEY QUESTIONS:
What constitutional responsibilities does the vice president have? What authority should he have?

and oversaw the Gulf War; he was widely perceived to be highly influential on such issues as the Iraq War, antiterrorism policies, and energy development. The fact that George W. Bush relied so heavily on Cheney to make key decisions elevated the power, visibility, and even controversy of the role of the vice president.[53] Joseph Biden, who serves as vice president under President Obama, has also been given considerable responsibility for foreign affairs. Vice presidents can push policies forward even when the president is reluctant to do so. For example, in 2012, Vice President Biden's public support for same-sex marriage pressured President Obama to speed up his announcement of support. Ultimately, however, even if a vice president exerts influence, it is the president who bears responsibilities for the outcomes.

Checkpoint

CAN YOU:

- Track the growth of the executive staff
- Explain how the role of the vice president has evolved over time

11.6 Presidential Greatness

> Assess presidential greatness

President Obama is the forty-fourth president of the United States. The men who came before him served with varying degrees of success as leaders in foreign and domestic policy. Presidential leadership is judged by whether a president is able to get his preferred policies passed by Congress and enacted into law and by how well he oversees the bureaucracy to make the government run effectively and efficiently (for more on the bureaucracy, see Chapter 12).

Scholars typically judge presidential greatness by looking at the clarity of a president's vision for policy, his communication and negotiation skills, and the effectiveness of his use of presidential powers, especially the general grant of executive power. Good presidents do not have to excel in every one of these categories, but they have to compensate for a weakness in one area with greater strength in another. Stephen Skowronek argues that presidents have opportunities to continue the policies of their predecessors or forge new paths, but that a president's success is often determined by external events, such as a terrorist attack or a global economic downturn.[54] The scholar Aaron Wildavsky suggests that there are actually "two presidencies": a foreign policy presidency and a domestic policy presidency.[55] On foreign policy, the president often must work quickly and in private, as negotiations must be conducted discretely. Domestic politics rarely require immediate action and usually entail open debate, with many citizens and interest groups vested in the outcome.[56]

The following discussion focuses on three presidents who are frequently singled out for their impact on domestic and foreign policy: Franklin Delano Roosevelt, a Democrat from a wealthy, elite New York family; Lyndon Baines Johnson, a Democrat from a very poor Texas family; and Ronald Reagan, a Republican from a middle-class family in Illinois.[57] Each had strengths and weaknesses, and each knew how to maximize his greatest asset—intellect, negotiating skills, public communications—to try to accomplish his goals.

→ KEY QUESTIONS:
Who are two presidents you think should be called great?

Franklin Delano Roosevelt (1933–45): The New Deal and World War II

When Franklin Delano Roosevelt (FDR) took office in 1933, the nation was experiencing the Great Depression. Unemployment had reached 25 percent, and Americans, many of them homeless and hungry, were suffering. To combat the effects of the depression, FDR had a

New Deal: *Franklin Delano Roosevelt's program for ending the Great Depression through government intervention in the economy and development of a set of safety-net programs for individuals.*

→ KEY QUESTIONS:
What was one of Franklin Roosevelt's successes and one of his failures?

clear policy vision, which he called the **New Deal**. In the first three years of his presidency, he succeeded in getting Congress to pass legislation that radically altered the size and shape of the federal government. His immediate need was to find a way to get cash into the hands of individual citizens, but he opposed handouts. Instead, he created job programs, including the Conservation Corps, the Works Progress Administration, and the Tennessee Valley Authority, all of which both employed and trained workers.

FDR also expanded the government's role in regulating the economy. The creation of the Securities and Exchange Commission and other laws relating to banking and finance helped restore confidence in banks and the stock market. The National Labor Relations Act established federal oversight of working conditions, labor standards, and labor disputes. This legislation brought the government and the business and labor sectors closer together. The Social Security program, a pension program to which workers contributed through a payroll tax that was also paid by employers, further entwined business and government.

Franklin Roosevelt used the bully pulpit and advanced the use of communication technology in the office of the president. He invented the fireside chat, a radio address to voters explaining the reasoning behind his governing decisions. Because fewer than half of all Americans owned radios at this time, FDR also turned the chats into newsreels that were shown in movie theaters. Ever since, presidents have found direct communications with voters to be an effective governing device.[58] President Roosevelt was also open and available to the Washington press corps, and his very first press conference in 1933 was a success. As a media-savvy president, FDR created the formal position of White House press secretary.[59]

Roosevelt took a personal role in negotiating legislative deals with members of the House and Senate, which were controlled by the Democrats. He allowed his staff to lay out the conditions for a compromise, but Roosevelt would finish the negotiations himself.[60] During his first five years in office, Roosevelt had great success in getting legislation through Congress. But in 1937, he overstepped by proposing to expand the size of the Supreme Court. The Court had struck down several of Roosevelt's favored policies, often by closely divided votes, and his so-called Court-packing plan would have allowed him to appoint additional justices and secure a majority favorable to him. Congress rejected Roosevelt's attempt to circumvent the checks and balances, and after that, his relationship with Congress began to falter.

Franklin Delano Roosevelt faced the worst economic crisis in the nation's history during the Great Depression. He proposed a series of policies known as the New Deal to provide economic opportunity and financial security in old age for America's workers. Here people lined up for food provided for the unemployed by private organizations.

PHOTOQUEST/GETTY IMAGES

On December 7, 1941, Japan attacked the United States at Pearl Harbor in Hawaii, drawing the United States into World War II. From that point on, foreign affairs dominated Roosevelt's presidency, but the New Deal legislation of the previous decade laid the groundwork for the modern structure of domestic programs in the United States. On April 12, 1945, President Roosevelt died in office and was succeeded by Vice President Harry Truman.

Lyndon Baines Johnson (1963–69): The Great Society and Vietnam

President Lyndon B. Johnson (LBJ) focused his mission on improving race relations and ending poverty because he believed they stood in the way of social, political, and economic progress. Most of his programs, which he called the **Great Society**, built on the infrastructure of FDR's New Deal, but they went much further in connecting the individual to the federal government. Johnson believed that as president he had an obligation to try to guarantee civil rights to all Americans.[61] In the area of race relations, he persuaded Congress to pass the Civil Rights Act of 1964, the Voting Rights Act of 1965, and the Fair Housing Act of 1968, which together formed a powerful set of laws protecting the rights of African Americans and subsequently the rights of other minority groups as well (see Chapter 5).

As 2014 marks the fiftieth anniversary of the passage of the Civil Rights Act (see Chapter 5), it also brings renewed attention to President Johnson's legacy, especially on current issues such as income inequality and fair pay. LBJ believed that it was possible for people to work very hard but still remain poor and that poor people were severely disadvantaged in terms of education, access to jobs, and affordable housing. He transformed the relationship between the individual and the federal government into one that included pure need, rather than merit based on work. He created two major federal health insurance programs: Medicaid, a health insurance program for the poor, and Medicare, a health insurance program for the elderly. He was also responsible for creating the Food Stamp Program, the School Lunch Program, Head Start, the Job Corps, and the Elementary and Secondary Education Act.

Johnson was not a skilled communicator or comfortable giving speeches, and he did not come across well on television, which by this time had succeeded radio as the dominant form of political communication. He compensated for his lack of communication skills by relying more heavily on his very strong negotiation skills. From his prior experience as a member of Congress and Senate majority

HULTON ARCHIVE/GETTY IMAGES

Lyndon Baines Johnson proposed sweeping changes to the nation's civil rights laws, as well as domestic health and welfare programs. Here he is seen signing the Civil Rights Act on July 2, 1964; Dr. Martin Luther King is seen standing behind him.

leader, Johnson understood how to convince members of Congress that it was in their best interests to pass legislation. Johnson made sure that his programs would benefit all poor people, white and black, rural and urban. By creating wide eligibility criteria, Johnson almost guaranteed that every congressional district in the country would receive some benefit from the programs. For example, both Medicaid and Medicare legislation included subsidies to rural hospitals and to big inner-city hospitals for services and capital expenditures such as improving facilities and building new ones. School lunch programs benefited schoolchildren as well as farmers, who sold the federal government their meat, milk, cheese, and grains at a guaranteed price, so they always had a market.

Johnson also used his presidential powers to distribute and award federal contracts and federal funds to key members of Congress and key state officials in return for their support of his programs. He understood that if a member of Congress needed to explain his vote in support of a liberal bill, he could do so more easily if he could point to some other federal benefit he had secured, such as a bridge, a Navy or Army base, or a new hospital wing.

Although Johnson's personal relationship with the press and the public started out reasonably well, as U.S. involvement in the Vietnam War escalated, the press began to distrust him, and many journalists believed he was not being candid about the war with them and the American people. By the end of his presidency, Johnson's relationship with the press was downright hostile. In fact, negative reporting on the progress of the Vietnam War, combined with significant health concerns, was among the reasons that Johnson ultimately chose not to seek reelection, a decision he announced on March 31, 1968. Lyndon Johnson died five years later, on January 22, 1973.

Ronald Reagan (1981–89): The Reagan Revolution and the End of the Cold War

President Ronald Reagan's vision of the relationship between the individual and the federal government was different from the views of Roosevelt and Johnson, and it is still invoked to this day by conservative Republicans seeking to limit the size and scope of the federal government. In the 2012 presidential election, a number of Republican candidates referenced Ronald Reagan in an effort to associate themselves with the powerful ideological legacy he left behind. Reagan believed that the New Deal and the Great Society had combined to weaken individual initiative and responsibility. When he took office, he mounted an aggressive campaign to scale back federal programs that provided benefits to individuals without asking for anything in return. He believed that big government and high taxes were crushing personal initiative, creativity, and innovation. "Government is not the solution to the problem. It is the problem," Reagan announced in his first inaugural address.

→ KEY QUESTIONS:
What is one of Ronald Reagan's successes, and what is one of his failures?

Tax cuts were the first thing on Reagan's agenda for two reasons. First, he believed that if taxes went down, the economy would flourish. Second, he knew that if tax revenue went down and spending increased, federal deficits would be created. These deficits would serve as justification for proposing cuts in entitlement programs, such as Social Security, Medicaid, and Aid to Families with Dependent Children (replaced in 1996 by the Temporary Aid to Needy Families program). Entitlement programs put a strain on the federal budget, especially as the number of people living in poverty grew and the elderly lived longer. Reagan managed to make cuts in the programs for the poor and elderly by restricting eligibility for benefits, but he did not succeed in dismantling them.

At the same time Reagan was implementing his domestic policy vision, he was also implementing his foreign policy vision. He took a firm stand against the Soviet Union, which he perceived as a direct threat to the United States and as a major promoter of Communism throughout the world. The defense buildup he ordered set off a military spending race that strained the Soviets' state-controlled economy to the breaking point. By the end of Reagan's second term, it was clear that the Soviet Union was moving toward collapse and could no longer control its satellite nations in Eastern Europe. Reagan's foreign policy was arguably an important factor in the end of Communism and the Cold War.

Ronald Reagan is referred to as the "Great Communicator" because he came across very well on television; as a former actor, he was able to give engaging, persuasive, and even comforting speeches. He won American hearts in 1981 during a failed assassination tempt, when he turned to his wife, Nancy, and quipped, "Honey, I forgot to duck."[62] In January 1986, when the space shuttle *Challenger* blew up shortly after takeoff as millions of Americans watched their TVs in horror, Reagan's words eased the national pain: "The crew of the space shuttle *Challenger* honored us by the manner in which they lived their lives. We will never forget them, nor the last time we saw them, this morning, as they prepared for their journey and waved goodbye and slipped the surly bonds of earth to touch the face of God."[63] The power of speech cannot be overestimated in an analysis of presidential success because it is the most basic way that the president tries to connect with the people.

Ronald Reagan was known for his tough foreign policy and pressuring the Soviet Union to withdraw from nations that it had controlled since World War II. Here he is seen at the Brandenburg Gate at the Berlin Wall which separated free West Germany from communist East Germany. It is at this spot that he uttered the famous words, "Mr. Gorbachev, open this gate; Mr. Gorbachev, tear down this wall."

Reagan did not hesitate to use his formal presidential powers to their fullest. Early in his presidency, when the Federal Air Traffic Controllers Union went on strike in 1981, he ordered the controllers back to work. When they refused, he fired all of them and replaced them with Air Force and civilian (private) air traffic controllers. Eventually, the union relented, and most of the air traffic controllers were hired back, but with fewer benefits and at lower salaries. This action sent a clear signal to members of Congress and to interest groups that Reagan was not afraid to take a potentially unpopular stand to accomplish his goals.

President Reagan delegated much of the actual negotiating over policy to staff members. He also enhanced the power of the director of the Office of Management and Budget to negotiate with Congress on budgetary matters. Reagan and his staff were frequently successful in these negotiations, but on issues on which they were at a public disadvantage, Reagan knew when to compromise. During his last two years in office, he worked with a Democratic-controlled Congress to pass trade legislation, welfare reform, and the first comprehensive AIDS funding and treatment bill.

Reagan's presidency was not without controversy, however. In late 1986, the Iran-contra scandal erupted when it was revealed that members of the National Security Council were selling U.S. weapons to Iran for cash, which was then given to the contra resistance movement in Nicaragua that was fighting the Communist-leaning Sandinista regime.

> → KEY QUESTIONS:
> How would you rate the past two presidents, George W. Bush and Barack Obama?

Congress had passed a law expressly prohibiting aid to the contras and held hearings to investigate the administration's actions. President Reagan himself was never directly implicated, but the scandal raised questions about the accountability of the president for his staff's actions, and it tarnished the last two years of his presidency. Although Reagan enjoyed relatively consistent popularity and was perceived as highly responsive to his base of supporters, his record came under greater scrutiny after he left office because his policies produced higher federal budget deficits and reduced funding for programs for the disadvantaged.

The example of Reagan, in the context of Roosevelt and Johnson, shows how the office of the presidency can shape domestic and foreign policy for future generations. Thirty-five years after Roosevelt died and eleven years after Johnson left office, Reagan ran for president on a campaign platform of scaling back the New Deal and the Great Society. In turn, Reagan left a conservative political legacy about the limited role of the federal government that remains a powerful rallying cry for Republicans today. Ronald Reagan died on June 5, 2004.

Checkpoint

CAN YOU:

- Explain how Franklin Delano Roosevelt had such a large impact on public policy
- Recall the programs of Lyndon B. Johnson's Great Society and how they were passed
- Describe the impact of Ronald Reagan on the economy with his support of tax cuts

CONNECT WITH YOUR CLASSMATES
MindTap° for American Government

Access The Presidency Forum: Discussion—Electing a Female President.

The Presidency and Democracy

From George Washington to Barack Obama, the presidency has evolved from an institution with strictly limited responsibilities to the large and powerful institution it is today. Whoever assumes the presidency in 2017 will face an ever-changing and increasingly complicated policy landscape. Certainly the Framers would be surprised by the growth of the presidency, and they might wonder whether the executive branch is too focused on serving the president individually and not focused enough on the needs of citizens more generally.

Nevertheless, the president operates in a separation of powers system, and laws must be passed with the cooperation of Congress, so the president cannot be rewarded or blamed entirely for the federal government's policies.[64] Moreover, individuals have gateways of influence on the presidency. Voters can render their direct verdict on the president's job performance when they choose whether to reelect him, provided he runs for a second term. Voters also indirectly register their opinions in congressional midterm elections, which focus on members of the House and Senate but are also interpreted as judgments on the president's record. Because high presidential approval ratings help presidents sway Congress, presidents are frequently responsive to public opinion. Because there is no possibility of a third term in office, presidents in their second term are typically freer from public accountability. In cases of very serious wrongdoing, Congress has the power to impeach and convict the president, but the threshold for impeachment is extremely high, and it happens very rarely.

In the course of the nation's history, presidents have grown less accessible to the average voter. However, technological innovations as simple as fast airplane travel and, more recently, e-mail, texting, and social networking websites, provide many more modes of communication between voters and the president or the president's staff. Although the president will not meet most of the people he represents, each town meeting he holds and public speech he gives is an opportunity for an exchange of views. And the job of presidential staff is to keep him as well informed on public opinion as possible.

In the modern age, presidents are considered their political party's leaders, and they want their records to reflect well on other elected officials from their party. All presidents see it as their responsibility to do what they believe to be best for the country, even in the face of opposition from the media, the public, and Congress. At times, this opposition can result in a less effective president than some might want, but the operation of checks and balances on presidential power accords with the Framers' vision of presidential leadership.

Overall, the modern presidency acts as both a gate and a gateway to democracy at the same time. It is a gate in that the president oversees a very large federal government that can be complex and difficult to change in response to public needs. It is a gateway in that any natural-born citizen can run for the most powerful office in the land, and although wealth, education, and connections are extremely helpful in winning, they are not prerequisites for victory. The men who have been elected president have come from a wide range of economic, educational, and professional backgrounds. With the election of an African American president, major entry barriers to the presidency have been broken; one might argue that the path to the White House is more open than ever before.

Master the Concept
of The Presidency with MindTap™ for American Government

REVIEW MindTap™ for American Government
Access Key Term Flashcards for Chapter 11.

STAY CURRENT MindTap™ for American Government
Access the KnowNow blog and customized RSS for updates on current events.

TEST YOURSELF MindTap™ for American Government
Take the Wrap It Up Quiz for Chapter 11.

STAY FOCUSED MindTap™ for American Government
Complete the Focus Activities for The Presidency.

Key Concepts

bully pulpit (p. 365). Give examples of presidents using the bully pulpit.

chief of staff (p. 376). What is the role of the chief of staff?

commander in chief (p. 355). What are the responsibilities of the commander in chief?

entitlement programs (p. 360). Should entitlements be considered rights?

executive order (p. 364). Give an example of when the president used an executive order to exercise his independent authority.

executive privilege (p. 362). What is the basis for executive privilege?

Great Society (p. 379). How did Johnson's Great Society expand the role of government in society?

head of state (p. 368). How does the president function as head of state?

impeachment (p. 361). Is impeachment an effective check on executive power?

imperial presidency (p. 354). What defines an imperial presidency?

lame duck (p. 352). Why are legislators less likely to cooperate with a lame-duck president?

New Deal (p. 378). How did Roosevelt's New Deal expand the role of the government in the economy?

omnibus bill (p. 359). Why are omnibus bills harder to veto?

pardon (p. 355). What does a presidential pardon mean?

pocket veto (p. 359). How is a pocket veto different from a regular veto?

presidential directive (p. 363). What are the forms a presidential directive can take?

signing statements (p. 364). How has the use of signing statements increased the powers of the presidency?

State of the Union address (p. 361). How has the use of the State of the Union address evolved from its creation in the Constitution?

veto (p. 359). How can Congress counteract the president's veto power?

War Powers Act (p. 369). How did the events of the Vietnam War lead to the passage of the War Powers Act?

Learning Outcomes: What You Need . . .

To Know	To Test Yourself	To Participate
Outline the requirements to serve as president		
The American presidency was an innovation in governance. As the nation grew, the presidency grew accordingly. Today the president speaks for the nation on the world stage and sets the policy agenda at home. Presidents have come from a wide range of backgrounds. All have been male so far.	• State the constitutional qualifications and succession requirements for the presidency. • Summarize the background and experience of U.S. presidents. • Explain what is meant by imperial presidency.	• Discuss ways to open the pathways to the presidency.

To Know	To Test Yourself	To Participate

▶ **Identify the powers of the president and explain how they are limited**

Among the president's constitutional powers are those associated with being commander in chief. The president also has the power to pardon, to negotiate and sign treaties and recognize foreign nations, to veto bills passed by Congress, and to appoint federal officers.	• Characterize the presidential power of commander in chief. • Compare pardon and commutation. • Describe the role of the Senate in the president's power to negotiate and sign treaties. • Recall the steps to presidential appointments. • Survey the power of the veto. • Explain how the State of the Union address has evolved as a tool for the president. • Compare and contrast examples of impeachment (or impending impeachment).	• Evaluate the president's power over the military. • Design a way to make appointments and judicial selection less partisan. • Evaluate the role of partisanship in impeachment.

▶ **Describe the growth of executive influence**

The Constitution vests the president with a general grant of executive power and requires that he "take Care that the Laws be faithfully executed." These responsibilities have been used by presidents to vastly increase presidential power. The president uses his executive power to issue presidential directives. He also uses the office to persuade the people and Congress and to set the agenda for domestic and foreign policy.	• Recall the different types of presidential directives. • List the tools available to a president as he uses his power to persuade. • Describe how the president can set the public agenda.	• Determine whether you think the presidency has become too powerful.

▶ **Analyze why the president is so powerful during wartime**

As presidential power has grown, the president has come into increasing conflict with the other two branches of government, particularly during wartime. The War Powers Act has proven to be weak because when Congress authorizes military action, the president has sole powers as commander in chief.	• Track trends in the struggle between the president and Congress over war powers. • Describe issues in the struggle between the president and the judiciary in wartime.	• Design a way to broaden Congress's power to limit intervention in foreign conflicts. • Evaluate the importance of civil liberties in wartime.

▶ **Summarize how the White House is organized**

The Executive Office of the President has great influence over budgetary, military, and economic policies. The roles of vice president and first lady have grown in recent years.	• Track the growth of the executive staff. • Explain how the role of the vice president has evolved over time.	• Evaluate whether the vice president should be given an expanded set of formal powers.

▶ **Assess presidential greatness**

Presidential leadership is generally judged on how successful a president is in getting his preferred policies passed into law and in getting the bureaucracy to be effective and efficient. Americans also judge their presidents on their communication and negotiation skills.	• Explain how Franklin D. Roosevelt had such a large impact on public policy. • Recall the programs of Lyndon B. Johnson's Great Society and how they were passed. • Describe the impact of Ronald Reagan on the economy with his support of tax cuts.	• Develop criteria for judging presidents. • Describe the ideal president for the twenty-first century.

"If front-line, non-intelligence government employees cannot disclose wrongdoing to the public that was never classified and then that information can be stamped years later with a classified TSA marking, the First Amendment is now meaningless."[1]

ROBERT MACLEAN
Air Force

MICHAEL GOULDING/ZUMA PRESS/NEWSCOM

DANNY MOLOSHOK/REUTERS

12

The Bureaucracy

Every day, Americans board domestic and international flights with men and women whose sole job is to protect the passengers, crews, and airlines in the air. Federal Air Marshals (FAMs) carry out their jobs silently, unbeknownst to their fellow airline passengers. After being honorably discharged from the military, Robert MacLean became a federal air marshal; a position that has become increasingly important since the September 11th, 2001 terrorist attacks.

MacLean's career as a FAM changed forever when he became a whistleblower following serious security concerns in 2003. In July 2003, various U.S. security agencies received elevated terrorist threats. The Transportation Security Administration (TSA) was notified of the threats and conducted meetings with air marshals during which they were briefed on the nature of the threats. Despite the elevated danger, the TSA cancelled months of air marshal missions citing budget concerns. They notified the air marshals via unencrypted text messages to their cell phones. This greatly concerned MacLean, and he took his concerns to his direct supervisor and finally to the Inspector General of the Department of Homeland Security, to no avail. Feeling it was his duty to protect the American public in light of these security breaches, MacLean anonymously leaked the text message he received that canceled the air marshal missions to MSNBC. After the leak, many congressional members raised concerns about the canceled missions, and in response to that criticism, the TSA quickly moved to reinstate them.

MacLean did not stop there, though. One year later, he anonymously went on television to discuss his concerns on the air marshal dress code, which he felt made the marshal's conspicuous to potential terrorists. His concerns over the air marshal dress code in tandem with a report by the Government Accountability Office (GAO) resulted in changes to the air marshal dress code to better conceal marshal's identities. After his television appearance, the TSA recognized MacLean, and they were also able to link him to the earlier text message leak in 2003. In 2006, MacLean was fired from his position as a FAM. When MacLean contested his dismissal, he discovered that the text message he had leaked was retroactively classified, which was a large part of the reason he was fired.

Since his dismissal, MacLean has been fighting the TSA to be reinstated, arguing he is a protected whistleblower under the Whistleblower Protection Act of 1989 (WPA). As a federal employee, MacLean argued it was not only legal but expected to disclose any wrongdoing taking place in the agency he was

Need to Know

12.1 Explain what the bureaucracy does

12.2 Outline the essential elements of a bureaucracy

12.3 Describe the growth of the bureaucracy over time

12.4 Assess how the bureaucracy is both accountable and responsive, and how it can fail

 WATCH & LEARN MindTap™ **for American Government**
Watch a brief "What Do You Know?" video summarizing The Bureaucracy.

employed by, especially if his disclosure could save American lives. His removal as a FAM is a violation of this law, which is supposed to protect him from any retaliation.

Two Merit Systems Protection Board (MSPB) chairmen have upheld MacLean's termination, as did an administrative judge in May 2010. MacLean appealed to the Federal Circuit Court of Appeals, and in April 2013, the Court repealed the MSPB ruling and sent the case back to the MSPB to review its termination of Robert. The federal government continues to disagree with the decision, arguing that the TSA has wide discretion to determine which information should not be disclosed and has regulations that restrict the disclosure of "unclassified sensitive security information." The Federal Circuit Court argued that the main reason for MacLean's termination was a regulation and not a statute, which the WPA protects MacLean from. The legal battle is not over, however, as the Department of Justice appealed the decision to the Supreme Court which agreed to take the case and rule on it in 2015.

MacLean's case is unique because it directly questions the difference between a statute created by the legislature and a regulation, which is issued by the bureaucracy. According to the Federal Circuit Court, laws created by Congress trump regulations created by agencies and departments, even if they make those regulations to fill the holes in a statute. Whether or not the Supreme Court takes on MacLean's case, the events surrounding his disclosure of TSA information demonstrate the gates that Congress can put in the way of bureaucratic regulation and the amount of power those regulations can wield when left unchecked by the legislature.[2]

In this chapter, we examine the cabinet-level departments, agencies, and other organizations that constitute the executive branch. We look at their structure, characteristics, rationale, procedures, accountability, and responsiveness to citizens' concerns. A fundamental question for students of American government is whether the sprawling nature of the bureaucracy makes it a gate or a gateway to effectively serving the people.

12.1 The American Bureaucracy

> Explain what the bureaucracy does

→ KEY QUESTIONS:
What federal employees have you come in contact with in the past? What was the most recent experience like?

Just mention the word *bureaucracy,* and most people roll their eyes and utter phrases like "red tape" or "slow as molasses." Of all the components of American government, the bureaucracy is most likely to be perceived as annoying and daunting, as a gate against getting things done. Of all the components of American government, the bureaucracy is also the most likely to have a direct impact on citizens' lives. Most Americans have never met a president or a member of Congress or a federal judge, but every American has likely interacted with an employee of the government. Whether the interaction involves showing identification to a TSA agent in the airport or waiting in line at the post office, the rules and regulations of the federal bureaucracy present numerous opportunities for frustration.

Bureaucracies generally are not afforded much respect because they seem so complicated and impenetrable, and bureaucrats are often portrayed as faceless robots who merely enforce the rules. Yet enforcing the rules is the bureaucracy's job; as an extension of the presidency, bureaucratic implementation is how the president executes the law. Rules must be enforced equally across all citizens. In the most obvious example, a first-class stamp costs the same in every state and will take a letter to any place in the nation, just across town or from Houston to Honolulu.

CHIP EAST/REUTERS/CORBIS

The federal bureaucracy has a direct impact on your life. Most Americans are familiar with waiting in line at the post office, but not everyone is aware that the quality of the grains in breakfast cereal they eat in the morning, the safety of the highways they drive during the day, and the purity of the water they drink are also regulated by government agencies.

Despite the well-known problems associated with bureaucracies, organization is essential to modern government. In the late nineteenth century, the German sociologist Max Weber described bureaucracies as highly rational organizations that enabled large numbers of people to get difficult jobs done efficiently.[3] If the federal bureaucracy does not seem efficient today, that may be because of the enormous responsibilities it bears, not only to implement complex policy and law established by the president and Congress, but also to do so in a way that is orderly, predictable, fair, equal for all citizens, and transparent. The formal aspects of bureaucratic structure promote accountability, while the informal operations—the bureaucratic culture—determine how well the organization carries out its own mission and how well it interacts with other organizations. We discuss these elements in detail to draw a practical road map not only to understanding the federal government but also to actually make it work better for ordinary citizens.

→ KEY QUESTIONS:
What is your impression of the federal bureaucracy? Which branch of government do you think works best? Which works least well?

LISTEN & LEARN
MindTap® for American Government

Access Read Speaker to listen to Chapter 12.

What Is the Bureaucracy?

The **bureaucracy** is the large collection of executive branch departments, agencies, boards, commissions, and other government organizations that carry out the responsibilities of the federal government. At first, the nation did not require many employees to fulfill the government's duties, which were limited to large national issues such as defense, tariffs on imported goods, and settling western lands. As the nation's lands and economy grew, so did the need for a more complex structure at the federal level to oversee government activities. These responsibilities are established by laws passed by Congress and signed by the president; however, for execution, they often entail expertise, so the legislature relies on specialists—the bureaucrats—to write the **regulations** that implement the law.

In 2014, the number of federal employees, including the armed services, totaled almost 4.2 million people.[4] The jobs of federal employees vary widely. A national park ranger is a federal employee, as is a TSA officer, a border patrol officer, a bridge designer with the Army Corps of Engineers, an accountant with the Securities and Exchange Commission (SEC), and a lawyer with the Department of Justice. For every federal job classified as "professional," there are also staff jobs, including clerks, office managers, janitors, mechanics, and delivery personnel, who keep the bureaucracy running. Skills and specialties in almost any type of work can be a gateway to employment in the federal government, which we discuss in more detail later in the chapter.

One simple way to understand the basic structure of the bureaucracy is to imagine a piece of furniture called a cabinet that stores different types of items in different drawers. It is no accident that the term *bureaucracy* has *bureau* at its base, an old-fashioned term for a cabinet. President Thomas Jefferson (1801–1809) had a separate room in the White House that he called his cabinet, and the centerpiece of the room was a long table with drawers on each side that served as his desk, in which he stored all important federal papers according to issue area.[5] President Barack Obama could not fit all the paperwork of the federal bureaucracy in a single desk, but the idea of compartmentalizing federal responsibilities has endured over time. Today, a president builds a **cabinet**—his set of key advisers who are responsible for the areas under their jurisdiction. As noted in Chapter 11, The Presidency, the cabinet is distinct from the president's White House staff, which works directly for the

bureaucracy: *Executive branch departments, agencies, boards, and commissions that carry out the responsibilities of the federal government.*

regulations: *Guidelines issued by federal agencies for administering federal programs and implementing federal law.*

cabinet: *Set of executive departments responsible for carrying out federal policy in specific issue areas.*

president, because cabinet members oversee entire departments constructed to implement federal policy. For example, President Obama appointed Chuck Hagel as secretary of the Department of Defense based on his experience as a decorated soldier in Vietnam, and later as a U.S. senator who handled military issues. Most cabinet members are **cabinet secretaries** and head executive departments, but presidents may select additional advisers for cabinet-rank status. In the Obama administration, these included the vice president, the chief of staff, the heads of the Environmental Protection Agency and of the Office of Management and Budget, the U.S. trade representative, the U.S. ambassador to the United Nations, and the chair of the Council of Economic Advisers.[6]

Constitutional Foundations

→ KEY QUESTIONS:
Why do you think the Constitution provides so little direction for the bureaucracy?

The word *bureaucracy* does not appear in the U.S. Constitution, but the foundations of the federal bureaucracy can be traced to a few key sentences in Article II that relate to the powers of the president.

Appointments. Article II, Section 2, gives the president the power to "nominate, and by and with the Advice and Consent of the Senate, . . . appoint . . . all other Officers of the United States, whose Appointments are not herein otherwise provided for, and which shall be established by Law." This section goes on to state that Congress can "by Law vest the Appointment of such inferior Officers, as they think proper, in the President alone, in the Courts of Law, or in the Heads of Departments." Thus the discussion of the president's appointment power implies the existence of executive departments.

Opinions on Federal Policies. Article II, Section 2, references the executive branch more directly when it authorizes the president to "require the Opinion, in writing, of the principal Officer in each of the executive Departments, upon any subject relating to the Duties of their respective Offices." The Framers envisioned that the president would manage a staff of federal officers who would oversee executive departments managing the operations of government, although it is doubtful that they expected the president's staff to be as large as it is today.

Execution of the Laws. Article II, Section 3, gives the president broad powers to "take Care that the Laws be faithfully executed." At the same time that the Framers wanted to make sure that the president would follow the intent of Congress, they also gave him wide discretion in how he carried out the laws. This broad executive power is the foundation for the growth of the federal bureaucracy as well as for the growth of the presidency, as we saw in Chapter 11.

The Structure of the Bureaucracy

For more than two centuries, the federal bureaucracy has been changing, growing, and developing into today's interlinked set of organizations that implement federal policy. Some organizations are vast, such as the executive departments, and some are small advisory boards and commissions. Coordinating the authority and operations of these different types of organizations is a significant challenge for the executive branch as it carries out its constitutional duties. The structure of the U.S. bureaucracy and the challenges it faces are not unique. Bureaucratic organization is essential for the operation of modern governments and organizations, as a look at the bureaucracy in the United Nations indicates (see Global Gateways: The United Nations Bureaucracy).

global gateways

The United Nations Bureaucracy

As the most important international governmental organization, the United Nations is a gateway for peace by acting as a neutral forum where nations can attempt to resolve conflicts before they lead to violence. Founded at the end of World War II, the United Nations today has 193 member nations, each of which pays dues. It has grown into a large and complex governmental organization with a bureaucratic system that aims to carry out the policies on which the member nations agree.

As the UN bureaucracy has grown in size and complexity, there have been increasing complaints of inefficiency and corruption. Many argue that it has too many overlapping organizations, large budgets

(estimated at more than $5.5 billion in 2014), and a lack of transparency in its operations.[7] Corruption and inefficiency can serve as a gate against effective governance and undermine the legitimacy of the UN as a global organization.

1. Is the lack of transparency in the UN bureaucracy damaging to its mission as a protector of peace and human dignity?

2. Do you think the U.S. bureaucracy has any of the problems that the UN bureaucracy suffers from?

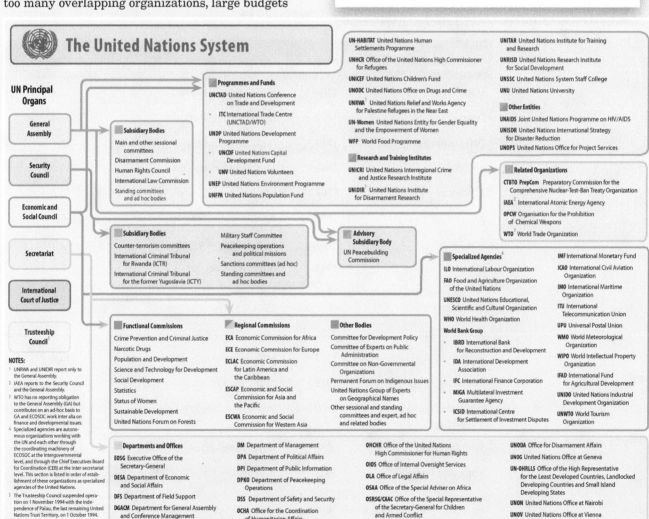

Source: United Nations Department of Public Information, "The United Nations System," United Nations, accessed May 19, 2014.

Executive Departments.   Today there are fifteen executive, or cabinet-level, departments in the federal bureaucracy. A cabinet department is an executive branch organization led by a cabinet secretary appointed by the president. Cabinet departments are responsible for implementing laws and policies in specific areas through the regulatory and enforcement process. Regulations are the guidelines that detail how a law will be carried out, and what has to be done to comply with the law (see Chapter 14, Economic, Domestic, and Foreign Policy, for a full description). Regulations go through several versions, and after a lengthy review process, the final regulations are printed in the **Federal Register**, which is the federal government's official publication for implementation of laws.

The job of the secretary is to oversee implementation, provide advice to the president about the issues under the department's control, and develop an annual budget for the department. Congress has the authority to create a cabinet department, but once it is created, it is under the control and supervision of the president as head of the executive branch. Table 12.1 lists each department, the year it was created, its website, and its number of employees.

Each cabinet department consists of subdivisions arranged in a hierarchical form to divide up its tasks and theoretically maximize efficiency and responsiveness. Figure 12.1 shows how the Department of Health and Human Services (HHS) is organized. This organizational chart

Federal Register:
Official published record of all executive branch rules, regulations, and orders.

Table 12.1 Cabinet Departments, 2014

Department	Year Established	Website	Employees (in thousands)
State	1789	http://www.state.gov	33.3
Treasury	1789	http://www.treasury.gov	101.4
Defense (originally, War)	1789	http://www.dod.gov	755.4
Interior	1849	http://www.interior.gov	69.2
Agriculture	1862	http://www.usda.gov	90.2
Justice	1870	http://www.justice.gov	116.8
Commerce	1903	http://www.commerce.gov	42.6
Labor	1913	http://www.dol.gov	17.2
Housing and Urban Development	1965	http://www.hud.gov	8.7
Transportation	1966	http://www.transportation.gov	55.9
Energy	1977	http://www.energy.gov	15.7
Education	1979	http://www.education.gov	4.1
Health and Human Services	1980	http://www.hhs.gov	72.5
Veterans Affairs	1989	http://www.va.gov	319.2
Homeland Security	2003	http://www.dhs.gov	190.1

Source: The White House, http://www.whitehouse.gov; The White House, Office of Management and Budget, Fiscal Year 2015 *Analytical Perspectives, Budget of the U.S. Government* (Washington, D.C.: U.S. Government Printing Office, 2014), Table 8-2, Federal Civilian Employment in the Executive Branch, p. 80, http://www.whitehouse.gov/sites/default/files/omb/budget/fy2015/assets/spec.pdf. For the history of each department, see the websites listed in the preceding table.

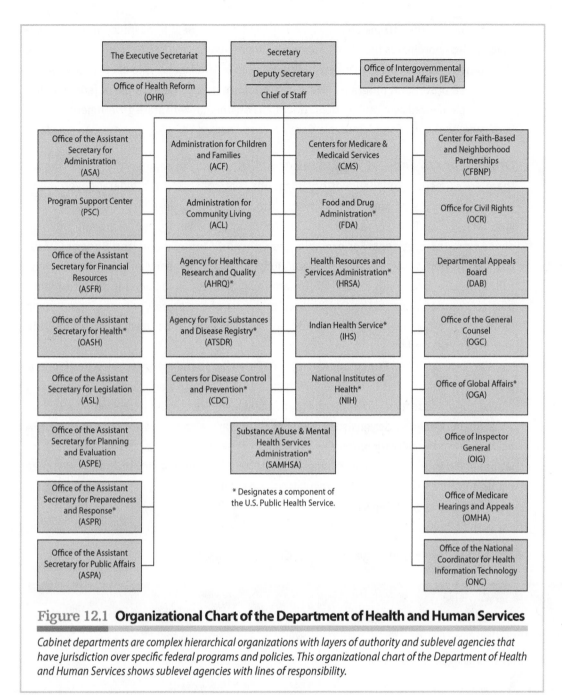

Figure 12.1 Organizational Chart of the Department of Health and Human Services

Cabinet departments are complex hierarchical organizations with layers of authority and sublevel agencies that have jurisdiction over specific federal programs and policies. This organizational chart of the Department of Health and Human Services shows sublevel agencies with lines of responsibility.

Source: U.S. Department of Health and Human Services, Organizational Chart, accessed May 8, 2014, http://www.hhs.gov/about/orgchart/index.html.

makes it clear that each department has many subdivisions, or layers, with each assigned a specific federal policy to implement. HHS oversees three hundred programs, with more than 72,000 employees and a budget of $961.9 billion.[8] This massive and complex organization is necessary to respond to the needs of all the individuals affected by the programs that HHS manages.

The responsibilities of HHS grew even broader when President Obama signed the Patient Protection and Affordable Care Act into law on March 23, 2010. Because HHS administers Medicaid, Medicare, and other federal health-related programs, it bears the bulk of the responsibility to implement the new programs associated with this legislation. For example, HHS tries to remedy deficiencies in the Medicare prescription drug program for senior citizens and inform citizens about expanded eligibility for health insurance through Medicaid. It also coordinates health insurance exchanges, works with states to enhance existing state-based insurance programs, and joins with other federal agencies to encourage wellness and disease-prevention programs.[9] Health care reform is just one example of federal policy that is implemented by a cabinet department, in conjunction with state governments. For an in-depth discussion of the Affordable Care Act, see Chapter 14.

Other Types of Federal Organizations.   In addition to cabinet-level departments, there are numerous independent organizations that constitute the federal government, including agencies, commissions, administrations, boards, corporations, and endowments (see Table 12.2). These organizations vary by structure, mission, and degree of independence from the president. For example, the **Office of Management and Budget (OMB)** has final authority over the entire federal budget, and each agency and department must submit its proposed budget to OMB for approval before it is included in the president's official proposed budget. The OMB's director is part of the president's cabinet, although OMB is not a cabinet department. Additionally, all regulations must go through OMB before they take effect.

The Environmental Protection Agency (EPA) is an **independent agency**, a type of federal organization established by Congress with authority to regulate an aspect of the economy or a sector of the federal government. Independent agencies do not operate within a cabinet department. Congress designs such agencies to operate with their own authority. The EPA bears the responsibility for preserving the quality of the air, water, and land. It can issue regulations and create policy in a wide range of areas, including limiting emissions from coal-fired plants and auto fuel emissions. Its regulations are subject to OMB approval, just like regulations from any cabinet department.

Office of Management and Budget (OMB): *Federal agency that oversees the federal budget and all federal regulations.*

independent agency: *Federal organization that has independent authority and does not operate within a cabinet department.*

Table 12.2 **Selected Independent Agencies and Commissions, 2014**

Department	Year Established	Website	Employees (in thousands)
Environmental Protection Agency (EPA)	1970	http://www.epa.gov	15.6
Equal Employment Opportunity Commission (EEOC)	1965	http://www.eeoc.gov	2.3
General Services Administration (GSA)	1949	http://www.gsa.gov	12.5
National Aeronautics and Space Administration (NASA)	1958	http://www.nasa.gov	17.9
National Labor Relations Board (NLRB)	1935	http://www.nlrb.gov	1.6
National Science Foundation (NSF)	1950	http://www.nsf.gov	1.4
Office of Personnel Management (OPM)	1978	http://www.opm.gov	5.4
Securities and Exchange Commission (SEC)	1935	http://www.sec.gov	4.2
Small Business Administration (SBA)	1953	http://www.sba.gov	3.3
Social Security Administration (SSA)	1935	http://www.socialsecurity.gov	62.2

Source: The White House, http://www.whitehouse.gov; The White House, Office of Management and Budget, FY 2015 *Analytical Perspectives, Budget of the U.S. Government* (Washington, D.C.: U.S. Government Printing Office, 2014), Table 8-2, Federal Civilian Employment in the Executive Branch, accessed May 19, 2014 http://www.whitehouse.gov/sites/default/files/omb/budget/fy2015/assets/spec.pdf.

A **federal regulatory commission** is an agency typically run by a small number of officials, known as commissioners, who are appointed by the president for fixed terms and are responsible for overseeing a sector of the economic or political arena. One example is the Securities and Exchange Commission (SEC), which is responsible for monitoring all business practices involving the stock market. The SEC has five commissioners who serve staggered five-year terms and together manage 4,200 employees.[10] The SEC oversees the work of accountants, stockbrokers, hedge fund managers, financial advisers, and small business owners. It has legal authority to demand information from these professionals, impose fines for bypassing investment rules, and even bring formal charges for serious violations of the law.

A federal administration is responsible for running a federal program or overseeing specific areas of federal responsibility. The Transportation Security Administration (TSA), which Robert MacLean worked for, is a type of federal administration that was created after the attacks of 9/11 and later placed under the Department of Homeland Security (discussed later in this chapter). TSA has approximately 50,000 employees and oversees airport security, both in the terminals and with federal marshals aboard aircrafts.[11]

AP IMAGES/STEVEN DAY

The National Transportation Safety Board investigates the causes of transportation accidents, such as the bird strike that forced US Airways Flight 1549 to land in the Hudson River on January 15, 2009. Not all accidents have such fortunate outcomes, and the NTSB makes recommendations for preventing similar accidents in the future.

A federal board typically has a more narrow scope of authority but can possess the power to require changes in operating procedures and to suggest fines. It usually consists of individuals appointed for a specific term and who, ideally, have expertise in the area of the board's jurisdiction. For example, the National Transportation Safety Board (NTSB) is responsible for investigating transportation-related accidents such as the emergency landing of US Airways flight 1549; dubbed the "Miracle on the Hudson," the jetliner's engines lost power after encountering a flock of geese. There were no fatalities, and only a few injuries, in that water landing. Whenever an accident involves any form of transportation, one of the NTSB's five board members is appointed to oversee an investigation of the event. When the investigation is completed, the agency issues a report that includes findings about the accident's cause and recommendations for avoiding a similar event. Despite its authority in these investigations and its members' knowledge of safe transportation practices, the NTSB does not have the power to issue federal regulations.

A federal corporation is a type of federal organization similar to a private business in that it provides a service or commodity for a price to the public, but it also receives federal funding. For example, the National Railroad Passenger Corporation, better known as Amtrak, is essentially a for-profit railroad, but it receives federal funding and is subject to federal restrictions and controls.

→ KEY QUESTIONS:
Why would the government fund a for-profit railroad?

Checkpoint

CAN YOU:

- Define bureaucracy
- Explain how the Constitution provides a basis for bureaucratic power
- Describe the structure of the federal bureaucracy

A national endowment is also a type of federal organization that uses funds specifically allocated to promote a public good or service. The National Endowment for the Arts, for example, was created to support scholarship and art that would be available to the general public, but it does not have any formal responsibility to monitor private- and public-sector activities in a specific set of issue areas. Because endowments are funded by the federal government, they are expected to serve as gateways for the expression of a wide range of viewpoints and perspectives in the work that they support.

12.2 Core Components of the Bureaucracy

> Outline the essential elements of a bureaucracy

All these bureaucratic organizations share four core components that determine how government implements policy and, more immediately, how government responds to the individual needs of citizens. These components are mission, hierarchical decision-making process, expertise, and bureaucratic culture.

Mission

Each federal agency has a stated mission that defines its role and responsibilities within the federal bureaucracy. For example, the mission of the Department of Health and Human Services is stated on its website:

> *THE DEPARTMENT OF HEALTH AND HUMAN SERVICES (HHS) is the United States government's principal agency for protecting the health of all Americans and providing essential human services, especially for those who are least able to help themselves.*[12]

A mission statement is important as the public face of the department, and it is the measure by which members of Congress and the general public can hold the department accountable for the success or failure of its efforts.

→ KEY QUESTIONS:
How has the Internet made it easier to interact with, and influence, the bureaucracy?

Hierarchical Decision-Making Process

To carry out its mission, every federal organization has a hierarchical decision-making process that structures the way policy is implemented. The hierarchy of authority in a bureaucracy means that an employee's decision on the implementation of policy is reviewed at each higher level in the organization. For example, HHS contains the following levels of authority, in ascending order: bureau chief, assistant secretary, deputy secretary, secretary. Each of these officials puts his or her expert input into policy implementation and then sends the decision up to the next level for approval. Not every department uses these levels of authority in the same way, but each leads up to the secretary, who is responsible for all of the policy decisions that come out of a department, and, ultimately, to the president.

The hierarchical decision-making process has advantages and disadvantages. It ensures that the unit responds consistently and predictably. The process also requires careful

→ KEY QUESTIONS:
How important is a hierarchical decision-making process to government responsiveness and citizen equality?

consideration of a policy before it is implemented. These two structural characteristics, taken together, are designed to ensure that policies are administered equally across citizens. However, this same hierarchical structure can present an obstacle to speedy decision making. Despite efforts to streamline the process, the step-by-step review of decision making inevitably slows down the implementation of federal laws.

Expertise

Fundamental to the core of the federal bureaucracy is the presumption that the people who hold bureaucratic positions have expertise in the issue areas they oversee and implement. This expertise can come from a number of sources. Individuals can enter the bureaucracy at the lowest possible levels and stay in their jobs long enough to acquire knowledge about federal programs. An employee might have worked in a particular industry, such as nuclear energy, and then have brought his or her preexisting knowledge to the bureaucracy—in this case, the Nuclear Regulatory Commission—as a mid-level employee. Other bureaucrats may have studied a federal policy area in academia or at policy think tanks and then may have been offered government positions. Congress, with members who chaired or served on relevant congressional committees, is a major source of cabinet secretary appointments.

Bureaucratic Culture

The fourth core component of a bureaucracy is the bureaucratic culture. As one political scientist explained, "Every organization has a culture, that is, a persistent, patterned way of thinking about the central tasks of and human relationships within an organization. Culture is to an organization what personality is to an individual. Like human culture, it is passed on from one generation to the next."[13]

→ KEY QUESTIONS:
What are the causes of bureaucratic failure?

Fundamental to bureaucratic culture is the constant drive to self-perpetuate; employees in a bureaucratic organization want to preserve their jobs and their influence in the policy-making system. For this reason, bureaucratic culture can act as a gate that prevents efficiency and responsiveness in government because it can create situations in which employees in different organizations duplicate tasks, counterbalance one another's efforts, and ultimately fail to accomplish their agency's or department's mission.

At its worst, bureaucratic failure can result in a terrible loss of life, as in the case of the terrorist attacks of September 11, 2001. Many politicians, members of the media, and citizens blamed the federal agencies that oversee intelligence gathering—the Federal Bureau of Investigation (FBI), the Central Intelligence Agency (CIA), and the National Security Agency (NSA)—for failing to uncover and prevent the attacks. Each agency detected warning signs of such an attack, but the agencies did not work together. The bureaucratic culture of each agency was insular and distrustful, and lack of coordination among them resulted in an intelligence failure.[14]

To remedy the lack of coordination among the nation's national security and disaster relief agencies, Congress created the cabinet-level Department of Homeland Security in 2003. The hope was that a single large federal organization, presumably with one culture and one overarching mission, would be more effective. The new department consolidated several key units that had been operating independently, including the Coast Guard, U.S. Citizenship and Immigration Services, Customs Service, Secret Service, and Federal Emergency Management Agency, and also created new intelligence offices that would try to serve as bridges between the FBI and the CIA.

On April 20, 2010, the Deepwater Horizon oil rig, leased by the BP oil company, exploded in the Gulf of Mexico, killing eleven workers and unleashing millions of gallons of oil into Gulf waters. Controversy surrounded this massive environmental disaster, with the states asking how such an event could have been allowed to occur. Here emergency responders clean pelicans at a Louisiana facility.

Other types of disasters do not involve as large a loss of life but still reflect mismanagement of risk by the government. In 2010, the Deepwater Horizon oil rig exploded in the Gulf of Mexico near Louisiana, killing eleven workers and unleashing approximately 4.9 million barrels of oil into Gulf waters.[15] The oil rig was leased by the British-owned company BP. At first it appeared that the oil spill would be contained, but the rig sank, creating complications in the cleanup effort, and the oil spill grew larger and approached U.S. shores from Florida to Texas. This bureaucratic failure began in the office of the Minerals Management Service, the agency in the Department of the Interior that gave BP permission to drill without first requiring assessments from other federal agencies, specifically the National Oceanic and Atmospheric Administration, about the risks to endangered species in the area, as well as the overall probability of an accident similar to the one that occurred.[16]

This lack of coordination, a clear example of bureaucratic culture getting in the way of good policy implementation, has proved costly to the environment and to the people who live along the shores of the Gulf of Mexico. As a result of the disaster, the chief federal bureaucrat responsible for overseeing offshore drilling resigned, as did the head of the Minerals Managements Service. President Obama responded by issuing an executive order to form a commission to investigate the failure, instituted a temporary ban on all offshore drilling projects, and addressed the nation to explain how the federal government was addressing the crisis. On October 12, 2010, he lifted the ban on offshore drilling but put greater safeguards into permit approval and safety guidelines.[17] In 2012, BP initially agreed to a $7.8 billion settlement with individuals who claimed economic and medical hardship as a result of the spill, but these claims against BP remain as of 2014 unresolved.[18]

Although each of the disasters just discussed was brought about by entirely different circumstances, a common lack of communication and expert direction exposed the inherent dangers of a flawed bureaucratic culture. If such failings are serious enough, the president may ultimately be held accountable for them. Federal agencies may continue to resist change, not wanting to give up any authority. Change in any long-standing organization is difficult to achieve and generally happens only when the people at the top of the chain of command tear down the barriers to cooperation.

One counteracting force to the drawbacks of bureaucratic culture and its tendency to block cooperation among agencies is bureaucratic reputation. Federal agencies want to develop good reputations for their effective implementation of federal policy. Most people take pride in the jobs they do, and bureaucrats are no different.[19]

→ KEY QUESTIONS:
What are the advantages of a government job? What are the disadvantages?

Checkpoint

CAN YOU:

- Explain how the mission of a bureaucracy shapes its goals
- State the advantages and disadvantages of the hierarchical decision-making process
- Characterize bureaucratic expertise
- Describe bureaucratic culture

12.3 The Historical Evolution of the Bureaucracy

> Describe the growth of the bureaucracy over time

The federal bureaucracy is as old as the nation itself, but it has evolved in ways that some of the Framers would barely recognize. Although they understood that the population would increase and the country's borders would expand, they could never have imagined that the federal government would have so many responsibilities and be so integral to citizens' daily lives. Over time, in tandem with economic, social, and technological developments, Congress passed laws creating new executive departments and other bureaucratic organizations. Here we trace the growth of the federal bureaucracy and the development of professional staff positions to implement federal policy.

→ KEY QUESTIONS:
What made the bureaucracy grow? Is it too big?

The Expansion of Executive Branch Departments

The first departments created by Congress in 1789 were State, Treasury, and War. The attorney general also sat on the president's cabinet, though he did not yet head a department. In addition, the Post Office, first created in 1775 by the Continental Congress to serve the vital function of establishing communication routes among the colonies, became a permanent government organization in 1794.[20] Through these organizations, Congress intended to fulfill the constitutional responsibilities set forth in Article I, Section 8—to regulate commerce among the states and with foreign nations, to provide for defense, to collect taxes and borrow money, and to establish post offices and post roads.

→ KEY QUESTIONS:
Why was the Post Office so important in the early days of the United States?

In 1849, Congress created the Department of the Interior to deal with the demands of Western expansion, such as sale of federal lands and the management of Indian affairs. The Department of Agriculture was created in 1862 to mitigate the hardships caused by crop and price fluctuations through crop subsidies that remain in place today. In 1870, the Office of the Attorney General, first set up in 1793, was transformed into the Department of Justice to handle the legal business of the nation.

The next two departments, Commerce and Labor, represented economic concerns. Congress addressed them by creating a single department in 1903, but within a decade, the issues of child safety and workers' standards became so important that Congress divided the department, giving Labor its own cabinet status. This sequence was paralleled later in the twentieth century by the creation of the Department of Health, Education, and Welfare in 1953 and its subsequent division into two departments—the Department of Education, created in 1979, and the Department of Health and Human Services in 1980 to oversee health care and welfare programs. In 1949, the War Department was transformed into the Department of Defense, coordinating the Army, Navy, and Air Force. In 1965, Congress created the Department of Housing and Urban Development to oversee federal programs designed to build more affordable housing for people with low incomes and to help restore inner cities that were losing residents. The Department of Transportation was created in 1966, following a decade of interstate highway building authorized by the Highway Act of 1956. Increases in trucking also put pressure on the federal government to maintain highways and regulate business and labor practices in trucking and the air travel industry. As a direct response to the energy crisis of the early 1970s, the Department of Energy was created in 1977 to promote

→ KEY QUESTIONS:
The expansion of executive departments reflects the growth of the nation. What do you think will be the next executive department created?

fuel conservation as well as the development of alternatives to fossil fuels, including nuclear, ethanol, and solar power.

In 1989, the Department of Veterans Affairs was created with the support of President George H. W. Bush (1989–93). Finally, as noted earlier, Congress created the Department of Homeland Security in 2003 in a direct response to the widely perceived intelligence failures associated with the terrorist attacks of 9/11.

The Growth of Regulatory Agencies and Other Organizations

→ KEY QUESTIONS:
How did the government go from monitoring railroads to funding them? How does this change illustrate the increased role of government in private industry?

In addition to the formal cabinet departments, the executive branch contains numerous regulatory agencies and other organizations that are responsible for administering the details of laws in specific areas, as well as for overseeing the practices of businesses and individuals involved in all facets of economic and political life. These agencies serve as gateways for the federal government to respond to citizens in targeted ways on a localized level, and they are especially important in ensuring safety and economic fairness for citizens in daily life. Among the concerns these agencies address are highway and air travel, food inspection and product labeling, and bank and the stock market practices.

One of the most familiar types of regulatory agency is the Food and Drug Administration (FDA), which monitors food safety and handling practices as well as pharmaceutical drug development and approval procedures. The motto of the FDA summarizes its mission, "Protecting and Promoting *Your* Health." The agency fulfills its mission by issuing guidelines and standards for companies to follow. Well-publicized cases of *E. coli* contamination in ground beef and salmonella in raw tuna, which resulted in illness and even death, illustrate just how difficult it is for the FDA to monitor food safety. Americans consume billions of pounds of ground beef each year, most of it processed by private companies that are subject to FDA inspection but are expected to do most of the food quality and safety monitoring themselves.[21]

→ KEY QUESTIONS:
Is protecting people from food poisoning the government's job? Why?

As the nation's economy has grown, so has the number of industries, products, and services that may warrant government regulation. This growth has expanded the workload of existing agencies and may require the creation of new ones. For example, Congress established the Federal Trade Commission to protect consumers from unfair financial and marketplace practices and the Consumer Product Safety Commission to ensure that basic goods purchased by consumers are safe.[22] In 2010, President Barack Obama and Congress worked together to create a new regulatory agency—the Consumer Financial Protection Bureau—that would help consumers navigate mortgage and other housing loans as well as real estate investments.[23] This new government agency was included in the Dodd-Frank Wall Street Reform and Consumer Protection Act, which overhauled the banking and investment industries.

There are limits to the effectiveness of regulatory agencies. They have government authority to monitor practices, issue fines, and even shut down businesses, but the government must rely on voluntary cooperation by the vast majority of private businesses in following agency guidelines. The distinct separation between the government and private businesses that is the hallmark of the American economy can also stand as a gate against effective government regulation and **oversight**. Nevertheless, regulatory agencies are

oversight: *Powers of Congress to monitor how the executive branch implements the laws.*

gateways through which citizens can ask government to protect them from fraudulent and unsafe products sold in the marketplace.

From Patronage to the Civil Service

For the nation's first forty years, jobs in the executive branch were filled by wealthy elites who had personal political and social connections to members of Congress and the president.[24] But President Andrew Jackson (1829–37) used the executive powers of the president to appoint people from wider social and economic backgrounds to federal positions. He also demanded political loyalty from federal employees; to get a job in the Jackson administration, one had to be an active political supporter of Jackson and the Democratic Party. This arrangement, in which the politician appoints employees who pledge loyalty to him, is generally referred to as the patronage system. Jackson's political enemies called it the spoils system, charging Jackson with awarding jobs to political friends in the manner of the saying, "To the victor belong the spoils."

For most of the nineteenth century, Congress and the president shared the patronage power; the president allowed members of Congress to recommend individuals for government posts. With each election in which a different party assumed office, there was a large turnover in staff. The federal patronage system allowed politicians to manipulate federal programs and positions for political and private gain.[25] For example, the Republican-controlled Congress created programs to provide pensions for Civil War veterans who had fought for the North, which was heavily Republican.

As the nation grew larger and the economy more complex, the federal bureaucracy needed more expertise and stability. The assassination of President James A. Garfield in 1881 by an individual who had sought, but had not received, a federal job caused a public outcry against patronage in government employment. Although the assassin had had

Pendleton Act: *1883 act that established a merit- and performance-based system for federal employment.*

no direct contact with Garfield, he evidently held the president responsible for his failure to secure a federal job. In response, Congress passed the **Pendleton Act**, which was signed into law by President Chester A. Arthur (1881–85) on January 16, 1883. It was the first of the reforms that slowly changed the federal bureaucracy from a corrupt and partisan insider organization to a neutral, policy-based organization.[26]

However, there are examples of federal agencies being accused of overstepping their authority for political purposes. The Internal Revenue Service has been under scrutiny for targeting groups that claim to be non-profit but might also be engaged in political activity; in the past decade,

Nineteenth-century presidents complained of being besieged by office seekers, men who hoped their connections with members of Congress or the president could help them land lucrative or powerful positions in the executive departments. In this engraving, office seekers wait to see Abraham Lincoln.

Public Policy and the Bureaucracy:
Consumer Financial Protection

The federal bureaucracy has grown, in part, because Congress has continually responded to changes in the economy and society that have required government action. However, at times, industries that are regulated by the government create new technologies or businesses practices that become widely adopted so quickly that the government cannot keep up with them in terms of regulation. One example of this kind of innovation is the packaging of risky mortgages (known as sub-prime) into bundles that could be purchased by investors who counted on the high interest from these mortgages to make large profits. The problem with these risky mortgages was that when the economy slowed down, many homeowners could no longer pay the interest or even the basic principal payment: Homeowners lost their homes, and investors lost all their investments. The collapses of both the housing industry and the investments in mortgages are considered to be major causes of the recent recession, and many voters blamed large banks and mortgage companies.

In response, Congress and President Obama passed comprehensive financial reform legislation known as the Dodd-Frank Wall Street Reform and Consumer Protection Act. This legislation made a number of important changes designed to place the banking industry under greater federal supervision and protect against future financial crises. It prohibits banks and other companies from engaging in unethical lending practices, such as offering high-interest mortgages and credit cards to individuals who do not have incomes or assets to afford them. It requires banks to set aside large sums of money to guard against losses from risky or highly unprofitable investments. Additionally, the law requires large banks to organize their investment practices as separate entities apart from their more traditional banking functions, so if investments, such as derivatives and credit-default swaps, go bad, the entire bank will not be put at risk. All these provisions illustrate the way the president and Congress as institutions try to adapt to the invention of new products, services, and economic practices. Opponents of regulation, however, including major banks and financial institutions affected by the legislation, argued that the new law interferes with the free market, and, during a recession, could slow down recovery.

The law also created a new Consumer Financial Protection Bureau, an independent bureau within the Federal Reserve, to ensure that banking and credit-related businesses operate in a way that is transparent and fair to consumers and businesses alike through enforcement and consumer education. However, it took a year for the Consumer Financial Protection Bureau to begin operations. The delay was due to a provision in the law requiring that a director be confirmed before any regulations could be issued. Opponents of the law in the Senate blocked President Obama's first nominee and were delaying action on the second nominee when, in January 2012, the president appointed Richard

Cordray as the bureau's first director as a recess appointment. Some of the most important parts of the law, such as the regulations to ensure that lenders do not give mortgages to people who cannot repay them have been finalized and were put into effect in January 2014.

The regulatory process is never easy, and delays are common, but the implementation of the Dodd-Frank Act has been especially complex because it involves the overhaul and installment of financial regulations and the establishment of a new agency. The act has a wide impact, ranging from protecting homeowners to safeguarding consumers against unfair credit and debit card fees. The regulatory process has been prolonged by another factor as well—the degree of coordination required among the other agencies involved, including the Federal Reserve and the SEC, each of which has time and workload constraints. Finally, the public comment periods and the backlash from financial institutions have made the process even more complicated, with many vigorously opposing the regulations that will force them to adopt new practices to achieve fairness and transparency. As of September 2, 2014, only 280 of the 398 regulations had been finalized, demonstrating that laws which are a gateway for consumer protection may have to work past the gates that the regulatory process, interest group lobbying, and partisan politics might put in their way.[27]

Construct Your Own Policy

1. Design three reforms that would provide consumer protections for credit card use.
2. Develop a system whereby the federal government would lend money directly to individuals wanting to buy their own homes, instead of working through private banks.

the IRS has been accused of giving extra scrutiny to groups ranging from the NAACP to the Tea Party. It could be argued that these actions stem from a deeply ingrained culture at the IRS of auditing individual, businesses, and groups to make sure they comply with tax laws. But to the public, it looked as if the bureaucracy failed to maintain its mission of neutrality in implementing the law.

The Pendleton Act created the **Civil Service Commission** to administer entrance exams for the federal civil service and set job requirements and promotion standards based on a **merit system** and performance, not political affiliation. At first the civil service covered only a small fraction of federal jobs; the rest were controlled primarily by powerful members of Congress who used their influence to direct federal jobs to loyal supporters. But over time, successive presidents wrested more control over the federal bureaucracy from Congress by issuing executive orders to classify a greater percentage of jobs as merit-based and as part of the **civil service**. By 1897, 50 percent of federal jobs were covered by the civil service, and by 1951, 88 percent of federal jobs were civil service jobs.[28] The remaining federal employees are **political appointees** appointed by the president to carry out his political and partisan agenda within the federal policy-making system.

Career Civil Service

Career civil servants are nonpolitical personnel who must pass an exam to secure their jobs and compete on an equal playing field with anyone else who has the same credentials. For the number of executive branch employees, and other members of the federal workforce, see Figure 12.2. The vast majority of executive branch employees are located in the metropolitan Washington, D.C., area.[29] In general, federal civil service employees fall into three categories: blue-collar, white-collar, and senior executive positions. Blue-collar jobs consist of "craft, repair, operator, and laborer jobs," and employees in this category are under the Federal Wage System, which sets pay levels associated with specific jobs. Executive-level management employees are governed by the Senior Executive Service guidelines, which generally follow the General Schedule (GS) pay scale. All federal employees are subject to performance evaluations and may receive gradual raises, promotions up the career ladder, and incentive and merit bonuses for outstanding job performance.[30]

Some departments and agencies are staffed by career employees who are not in the civil service but nonetheless operate under similar structures. For example, the State Department oversees a corps of diplomats known as Foreign Service officers who are sent all over the world to manage U.S. embassies and consulates. To join the Foreign Service, one must meet certain qualifications and pass an entrance exam, similar to the procedure for entering the civil service generally. However, the Foreign Service has its own pay scale and promotion criteria.

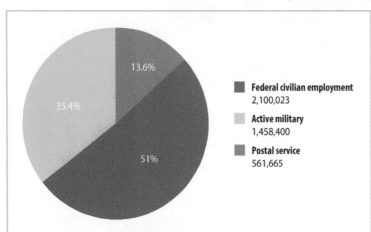

Federal civilian employment
2,100,023

Active military
1,458,400

Postal service
561,665

13.6%

35.4%

51%

Figure 12.2 Distribution of Federal Government Workforce, 2014

Federal employment is divided into several categories: executive branch, active military forces, and the U.S. Postal Service.

Source: The White House, Office of Management and Budget, FY 2015 Analytical Perspectives Budget of the U.S. Government, Table 8-3, "Total Federal Employment," p. 81, http://www.whitehouse.gov /sites/default/files/omb/budget/fy2015/assets/spec.pdf.

Although politics may permeate any workplace, the civil service is designed to protect employees from partisanship, and employees are expected to be objective as they carry out their job responsibilities. Civil servants remain in their positions from one administration to the next, and they cannot be asked to resign for partisan reasons.

Political Appointees

Political appointees, unlike civil servants, get their jobs because they are members of the same party that controls the executive branch, they have connections to politically powerful people, or they have served in a prior presidential administration. Political appointees can occupy a wide range of positions, from cabinet secretary to commissioner to administrator. Although it is uncommon, political appointees can also come from the opposition party, especially when they have particular expertise in a policy area or a president wants continuity in department leadership early in his administration. No matter their personal views, political appointees are expected to carry out the president's policy agenda.[31]

→ KEY QUESTIONS:
What are two gateways to becoming a presidential appointee?

Political appointees can come from a variety of backgrounds. Typically they are members of the president's inner circle or campaign team, served as congressional committee chairs, or served in former presidential administrations. In some cases, they come from the private sector. There are advantages and disadvantages to the president in choosing people from any of these backgrounds. Sometimes a president's trusted campaign advisers are not talented administrators; sometimes members of the private sector find government work too frustrating. Presidents try to make the best choices possible, but occasionally a cabinet secretary is replaced during a presidential term, especially if he or she has become a lightning rod for a broader controversy or an unpopular position. When a president is reelected for a second term, he customarily requests the resignations of his entire cabinet and then chooses which resignations to accept and which to reject. This custom gives presidents the opportunity to change policy direction and bring fresh perspectives into the executive branch at the start of a second term. For example, in President Obama's second term, many cabinet secretaries have left the administration, including the Secretary of State, Defense, Treasury, Commerce, HHS, and Homeland Security. In some cases, members of the cabinet will leave one position to assume another; in 2014, Secretary of Housing and Urban Development Shaun Donovan left that job to become head of the Office of Management and Budget. Donovan was replaced by Julián Castro, former Mayor of San Antonio (see Chapter 10, Congress, for more on Castro and his brother Joaquín who is a Congressman from Texas).

In large part due to the unpopularity of the Iraq War, which he oversaw, Secretary of Defense Donald Rumsfeld announced his resignation on November 8, 2006, after big Republican losses in the congressional midterm election. The announcement took place in the Oval Office.

AP IMAGES/GERALD HERBERT

→ KEY QUESTIONS:
How much authority should the president have over executive branch employees?

Schedule C appointees: *Federal employees appointed by the president to oversee civil service employees.*

Senior Executive Service (SES): *Senior management personnel in the federal government appointed by the president.*

Top-level political appointees require Senate confirmation, a process made slightly easier when the Senate is controlled by the president's party and now by the Senate rules change that reduced the cloture threshold to 51 votes for presidential nominees and judicial appointments lower than the Supreme Court (see Chapter 10 for more details). Under Franklin Delano Roosevelt (1933–45), the number of such employees was 73, but it has risen to 499 under President Obama. But there are hundreds of other jobs that are considered political appointments. For example, President Dwight D. Eisenhower (1953–61) appointed a layer of federal employees, known as **Schedule C appointees**, to oversee civil service employees. By some accounts, in creating this category Eisenhower was able to add approximately one thousand politically appointed positions to the bureaucracy over the course of his administration.[32] Subsequently, Presidents John F. Kennedy (1961–63), Lyndon Baines Johnson (1963–69), and Richard M. Nixon (1969–74) added more political appointees.

In 1978, President Jimmy Carter (1977–81) created the **Senior Executive Service (SES)**, experienced personnel who can be assigned by the president to senior management positions throughout the federal bureaucracy. For SES positions, the president generally chooses career civil service employees who have shown expertise in their jobs, but the president also has the authority to bring in individuals from the private sector. The SES provides a layer of administration over federal programs that is directed by the president, infusing the federal bureaucracy with political perspectives that can clash with the goal of objective implementation of federal policy. Since 1980, the total number of political appointees has averaged about three thousand.[33] Although that may not seem like a high number compared to the total federal workforce, the category of political appointee has been used successfully by many presidents to expand their direct influence within the bureaucracy.

Diversity in the Federal Bureaucracy

Presidents Bill Clinton, George W. Bush, and Barack Obama explicitly aimed to diversify the federal workforce. Figure 12.3 shows the percentage of ethnic, racial, gender, and LGBT groups that comprise the federal bureaucracy. Within these statistics, one can argue that women, at 51 percent of the population, and Latinos at 17 percent of the population, are the least well represented proportionally. In addition to high ranking appointments, the Obama administration is also trying to recruit members of underrepresented groups to lower level federal jobs, both political and in the civil service, to ensure that future administrations will have as diverse a talent pool to hire from as possible.

Building a diverse federal workforce serves as a gateway to the advancement of women and minorities within the public and private sectors, as these employees can later obtain political appointments to the president's cabinet. At this highest level of cabinet appointees, President Obama's administration can lay claim to having the greatest number of women ever. However, he has been criticized by advocates for failing to attract other underrepresented groups such as Latinos and African Americans. The head of the National Council of La Raza, Janet Murguia, pointed out that these groups heavily supported Obama in 2008 and 2012, and should be rewarded with a greater number of prominent appointments in the administration.[34] In Obama's first term, cabinet rank officials consisted of seven women and fifteen men,

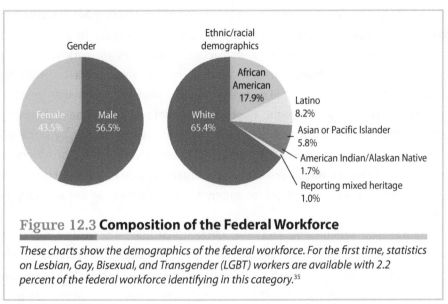

Gender

Female 43.5%
Male 56.5%

Ethnic/racial demographics

White 65.4%
African American 17.9%
Latino 8.2%
Asian or Pacific Islander 5.8%
American Indian/Alaskan Native 1.7%
Reporting mixed heritage 1.0%

Figure 12.3 Composition of the Federal Workforce

These charts show the demographics of the federal workforce. For the first time, statistics on Lesbian, Gay, Bisexual, and Transgender (LGBT) workers are available with 2.2 percent of the federal workforce identifying in this category.[35]

including four African Americans, one Latino, one Asian American, and one Pacific Islander. In 2014, in his second term, his cabinet consisted of six women, and sixteen men, including three African Americans, four Latinos, and one Pacific Islander. When Julián Castro was appointed to be Secretary of HUD, many believed that the administration did so to address the concerns of the Latino community about high-level representation within his cabinet.

Private-Sector Contract Workers

In addition to civil service employees and political appointees, the federal government hires thousands of individuals and companies from the private sector to administer programs and carry out tasks associated with specific policies. These companies can range from non-profit community organizations, to midsize security firms, to large health care conglomerates. They are not under the direct control of the federal bureaucracy, but they carry out crucial tasks for it. President Clinton was the first Democrat since the 1930s to suggest that some of the services provided by the federal government could be more efficiently done by the private sector. In addition, incentive programs were put in place to reward federal civil servants for efficiency, in the same way that employees in the private sector receive bonuses.

The federal bureaucracy often employs private-sector workers and organizations to administer federal programs or help support military operations. Here private security personnel help government officials in Afghanistan. Although there is a need for more personnel to supplement U.S. efforts, controversies can arise in terms of oversight of private workers, as well as the dangers they encounter on the job.

President George W. Bush continued this trend of contracting out the performance of government tasks to private companies. For example, during the Iraq War, the federal government contracted with major construction companies to work with the Army Corps of Engineers to rebuild war-torn areas of Iraq. It also contracted with private security firms to provide additional security for U.S. diplomatic and civilian personnel in both Iraq and Afghanistan. At home, much of the actual administration and provision of benefits under the Medicare and Medicaid programs is carried out by large private health maintenance organizations (HMOs) and other private service providers. When such large programs are run by private-sector organizations, it is sometimes more difficult to conduct proper oversight to prevent cost overruns or unnecessary billing charges.[36]

→ KEY QUESTIONS:
Are there government services that should not be contracted out to the private sector?

There are costs and benefits to the privatization of federal services. One concern is that the federal government does not have close oversight over the quality, experience, or job performance of the employees who work in the private companies. Although company employees have an incentive to do their jobs well, fraud, waste, and abuse can go undetected for years because of the lack of direct federal oversight. Sometimes the federal government ends up paying more for the provision of services through private contractors than it would if federal employees administered the program directly. The benefit of using private firms is that they do not technically count as additional federal employees, so when they are used, the overall size of the federal workforce appears smaller, and costs associated with job-related benefits are reduced. In some cases, it is more efficient to use a private firm that has expertise in an area to provide a service at a lower cost than to use permanent employees and achieve the same outcome. That allows the government to increase or decrease employment for specific projects; it is much more difficult to eliminate federal positions.

Bureaucrats and Politics

The civil service was created to protect federal employees from partisan politics, but by 1939 it had become clear that political influence was still rampant throughout the bureaucracy, not only at the federal level but at state and local levels as well. In response, Congress passed the Hatch Act, which prohibited government employees from working on political campaigns, using their positions to solicit campaign donations, or promoting candidates for elected office. This mandated separation of politics from the bureaucracy was designed to eliminate the last vestiges of patronage. It took pressure off bureaucrats, who could tell campaigning politicians that they were prohibited from engaging in certain political activities. In 1993, the Hatch Act Reform Amendments (HARA) significantly loosened restrictions on political activities by government employees as long as the activities occurred while they were off duty. Now political appointees are explicitly allowed to engage in political activities on behalf of the president so long as the costs for these activities are not paid with tax dollars. However, bans on political activities remain in force for employees in law enforcement and intelligence agencies as well as for employees of the Federal Election Commission, which monitors federal campaign activities.[37]

→ KEY QUESTIONS:
Should there be a gate that blocks government employees from engaging in certain kinds of political activities? Would such a gate compromise citizen equality?

Conflict between civil servants, who take a programmatic approach and aim to make programs work efficiently over the long term, and political appointees, who want to carry out the president's partisan agenda while the president is in office, was addressed by the Civil Service Reform Act of 1978. President Jimmy Carter proposed the act to encourage cooperation between political appointees and civil servants and to make sure that each was held accountable for decision making. The act created the Office of Personnel Management (OPM) to oversee both categories of federal employees. The OPM, under the direct control of the Executive Office of the President, can expand the number of political appointees and reduce the number of career civil servants. With more politically appointed personnel in the bureaucracy, presidents assert greater control over how federal policy is formulated and implemented. To preserve the essential political neutrality of the career civil service, the act also created the Merit Systems Protection Board, which ensures that the protections afforded to career civil servants through the merit system remain in place.

→ KEY QUESTIONS:
Why was the civil service designed so that employees remain in place despite turnover in the presidency and in Congress?

Nevertheless, bureaucrats do face conflicting pressures when Congress is controlled by one political party and the executive branch is controlled by the other political party—a condition known as divided government. Under divided government, federal bureaucrats are frequently caught in the middle because they are pressured by Congress to implement policy one way and by political appointees in their agencies to implement policy in a different way. Objectively, policy is supposed to be implemented in a manner that will produce the most efficient and responsive results, but trying to please two powerful bosses can result in inefficient and ineffective policy. Fortunately, the career nature of the civil service, with its built-in protections against political pressure, helps mitigate the negative consequences of divided government. In addition, because career civil servants frequently outlast presidents and some members of Congress, they have a longer-term perspective on the impact of their decisions.

At the same time, bureaucrats tend to form long-term working relationships with members of Congress and even with interest group lobbyists in the policy areas in which they specialize. In Chapter 7, Interest Groups, we explored the concepts of iron triangles (see Figure 7.3) and issue networks, both of which are used to describe these relationships. Bureaucrats want to maximize their longevity as administrators of federal programs, so they try to be as responsive as possible to the other members of the network, and each member constantly shares information with the others.[38] Critics of iron triangles and issue networks argue that they contribute to the inefficiency of the federal government because they sustain programs that may be duplicative or outdated, and they may encourage corruption within the government. However, given the 24-7 news cycle and the amount of government information available on the Internet, the public, the media, and watchdog groups are able to monitor such relationships, and they are now more transparent than ever before. Nevertheless, iron triangles are another indication that, despite the protections of a merit-based civil service, politics will always influence, to some degree, the bureaucrats who implement federal policy.

Checkpoint

CAN YOU:

- Equate the establishment of cabinet departments with developments in the U.S. economy and society
- Describe what regulatory agencies do
- Explain how and why the civil service evolved
- Survey the types of jobs career civil servants perform
- Recall why political appointees have increased in number over time
- Explain the growth of the use of private-sector contract workers
- Describe how Congress has attempted to protect the bureaucracy from partisan politics

12.4 Accountability and Responsiveness in the Bureaucracy

> ❯ Assess how the bureaucracy is both accountable and responsive, and how it can fail

Typically, the power of the vote in regularly scheduled elections is used to monitor elected officials, but there are no ways for the average voter to register an opinion about the collective job performance of employees of the federal bureaucracy. Because the bureaucracy varies by type of agency, size of agency, and type of employee, it is difficult for citizens to evaluate job performance and hold bureaucrats collectively accountable for their actions. At the individual level, the job performance of civil servants is reviewed by supervisors at regular intervals, and political appointees can be removed by the president if the president is unhappy with their work. But democracy requires that citizens be able to hold their entire government accountable for the policies it implements, and there is no readily available mechanism for the public to hold civil servants accountable for their job performance. There are, however, certain standards and procedures that Congress has put in place to hold the bureaucracy accountable and encourage responsiveness. Legal challenges to regulations are another means by which the bureaucracy can be held accountable.

The Roles of the Legislative and Judicial Branches

Congress contributes to the accountability and responsiveness of the bureaucracy through its oversight of implementation and its so-called "power of the purse." Congressional committees with jurisdiction in a set of issue areas can request that agency and cabinet officials testify before them to explain the way they implement programs under their jurisdiction. A serious issue of bureaucratic failure came to light closer to home in 2014 when the Veterans' Administration was accused of systematically denying or delaying care to veterans at a dozen or more VA hospitals across the country.[39] In Phoenix, Arizona, for example, VA employees allegedly tried to cover up the fact that between 1,400 and 1,600 veterans were on long waiting lists to see doctors, and that at least 40 veterans died waiting to be seen for care.[40] Typically veterans are expected to receive care between fourteen and thirty days after they request an appointment.[41] After the delays in care in Phoenix and other centers around the country were brought to light by the news media, the House and Senate Veterans' Affairs Committees each held hearings where Secretary Shinseki, a decorated veteran in his own right, testified before Congress. Veterans' groups called for bureaucratic accountability at the VA and asked President Obama to seek Secretary Shinseki's resignation. President Obama maintained his support for his cabinet Secretary but as more information came out in public, the pressure grew to the point that he accepted Shinseki's resignation on May 30, 2014; two more high-ranking officials resigned shortly thereafter. When Congress exercises its oversight power, and an agency becomes viewed as incompetent, it risks budget and personnel cuts, being rolled into a larger agency, or being dissolved altogether. Or as in the case of the VA, members of the executive branch can be asked to resign or be impeached if there is sufficient evidence of incompetence or illegal activity.

Another way Congress can hold the bureaucracy accountable is through its powers to authorize and appropriate. Authorization and appropriation hearings give Congress a chance to evaluate federal agencies and to withhold or reduce funds if there are dissatisfactions. Agency heads are fully aware of this congressional power, and it is a key reason that they take congressional opinion into account when they implement federal programs. Congressional influence of this type thus serves as a gateway for the public—which elects members of Congress—to hold the bureaucracy accountable for its actions.

In 2014, the Veterans Administration came under heavy criticism when it was discovered that thousands of veterans were forced to wait months for health care services and that personnel in the VA had falsified records to hide these delays. Here General Eric Shinseki is testifying before the Senate Veterans Affairs Committee about the scandal; he resigned two weeks later.

The judicial branch, too, helps hold the bureaucracy accountable. The courts can serve as effective monitors of implementation because they are a gateway for groups adversely affected by a federal regulation to argue their case against it. Typically, the courts intervene when there is a dispute between Congress and the executive branch on the interpretation of a law, and not when the two branches agree (see Supreme Court Cases: *Chevron U.S.A. v. Natural Resources Defense Council*).

Efficiency and Transparency

One of the biggest challenges a bureaucratic organization faces is carrying out its mission efficiently while maintaining transparency to the American public. A chronic complaint about the bureaucracy is that it is slow. Yet issuing rules and regulations takes so long because the process solicits input from all sectors, including members of Congress, businesses and industries that are being regulated, and average citizens with a stake in the issue. For example, it took President Obama six years into his administration to issue sweeping regulations to reduce emissions from coal-fired power plants by 20 percent as part of his policies on climate change. As stated earlier, though, even after regulations are issued, they are subject to the kind of input described previously and may not even be finalized until the end of his second term. The government can justify the slowness of the decision-making process on the grounds that it considers many points of view in implementing policy. Unfortunately, inclusiveness comes at the expense of efficiency.

In addition, the issues related to food and drug safety, transportation safety, working conditions, and antiterrorism measures can be matters of life and death. Citizens expect the federal government to act in their best interests, but such issues require caution, and caution

supreme court cases

Chevron U.S.A. v. Natural Resources Defense Council (1984)

QUESTION: Can the Environmental Protection Agency (EPA) allow pollution-producing plants to update equipment at some sources of pollution at a plant without requiring that it update all equipment at the plant?

ORAL ARGUMENT: February 29, 1984 (listen at http://www.oyez.org/cases/1980-1989/1983/1983_82_1005)

DECISION: June 25, 1984 (read at http://www.law.cornell.edu/supremecourt/text/467/837)

OUTCOME: Yes, the EPA can adjust regulations because courts recognize a responsibility to defer to agency decisions in the absence of specific congressional instructions to administer the law differently (6–0; three justices did not participate).

Congress establishes agencies to handle both routine administrative chores and highly technical decisions. Because Congress cannot foresee all questions that may arise, it delegates rule-making authority to agencies. These rules are subject to review by the federal judiciary to ensure that they are consistent with the intent of Congress.

Under the Carter administration, the EPA made rules governing the emission of air pollution from sources such as plants and factories. Under those rules, replacing any equipment at a source would mean that all equipment at the source would have to meet the stringent standards of the 1977 amendments to the Clean Air Act. During the Reagan administration, the EPA subsequently loosened the rules so that plants with multiple sources of pollution could update some of the sources at a plant as long as total pollution from the plant did not increase.

The National Resources Defense Council sued Chevron U.S.A., claiming that the EPA's decision to loosen the rules violated congressional intent. The Court of Appeals for the District of Columbia agreed, striking the new EPA rule and restoring the older rule. Chevron appealed the court of appeals decision to the Supreme Court.

The Supreme Court reversed the decision of the court of appeals. Although the decision allowed looser regulations of pollution control, it also stated that federal courts should grant a great deal of deference to the decisions and rules made by federal agencies. Specifically, the Court declared that if Congress has explicitly expressed a preference on an issue, the agency must follow that intent. If, however, as is often the case, Congress has not explicitly expressed a preference on the issue, courts must accept the agency's rule as long as the rule is reasonable. In the *Chevron* suit, the Supreme Court declared that it was reasonable for the EPA to allow plants to replace equipment at some sources without having to replace equipment at all sources. Otherwise, plants might simply put off any improvements in equipment. Reasonableness is a very broad standard, so this decision grants federal agencies a great deal of flexibility in how to implement federal law.

1. Why would the Supreme Court generally want to defer to the judgment of bureaucracies on a rule?
2. How might responsiveness suffer when Congress and the Court delegate authority to the bureaucracy?

can lead to delay. On the other hand, if the government fails to make its practices transparent and does not consider all the implications of its decisions, citizens may lose trust in government.

→ KEY QUESTIONS:
Why is transparency important in a democracy?

These concerns were part of the rationale behind a series of bills designed to open up the workings of the federal bureaucracy to the general public. In 1966, the Freedom of Information Act established a procedure by which ordinary citizens can directly request documents and reports from the federal government by paying a nominal fee, as long as the documents are not classified. Access to a classified document or report is automatically restricted to federal employees who hold security clearances and have a legitimate need to see the document. In times of military conflict, such as during the Vietnam and Iraq Wars, presidents typically restrict access to public documents relating to war efforts. In response to the mistrust of the federal government that grew out of the Vietnam War and the Watergate scandal, in 1976 Congress enacted the Government in the Sunshine Act, which tried to increase transparency by requiring government agencies to hold open forums to allow the public to comment on their decisions, regulations, and performance.

To highlight the tension between efficiency and transparency, let us return to the Food and Drug Administration, discussed earlier in the chapter. One of the agency's most important responsibilities is monitoring pharmaceutical development from the initial testing of drugs to final approval for widespread use. Even before a drug is submitted to the FDA for approval, pharmaceutical companies have conducted three phases of clinical trials, which are experiments and applications on human subjects that measure the efficacy and safety of the drug. If the drug shows promise, the company submits a New Drug Application to the FDA. If agency employees agree that the clinical trial results are reliable, the FDA forms a review panel whose members have different types of expertise about the potential effects of the drug. The panel serves as a gateway for nonemployees of the agency to participate in the drug approval process. Members of the panel consider all the results of the trials and offer opinions as to whether the drug can be approved for sale. Ultimately, the FDA makes the final decision.

This process illustrates the trade-off between efficiency and transparency.[42] When a new drug is effective against disease, the public wants access to that drug as soon as possible. However, every new drug has unforeseen side effects, some of which may not be visible in the short term, so the more information the FDA has, the more likely the drugs it approves for the market will be safe. Forming review committees with members from outside the agency is one way of collecting a wide range of information about the possible impacts of the drug. Yet this process is time-consuming; the more participants, the more slowly it moves. Like many federal agencies, then, the FDA must weigh the cost of efficient decision making against the cost of approving a drug before it has been thoroughly tested. The FDA is constantly updating consumer advisories about a wide range of food and medical products. For example, in 2014, the FDA issued a warning to diabetics using a specific type of glucose test strip because it was found to be inaccurate.[43] In most, if not all, instances when the FDA issues such an advisory to the public, the manufacturer usually withdraws the product from the market.

→ KEY QUESTIONS:
What is more important, transparency or efficiency?

SCIENCE SOURCE

The Food and Drug Administration conducts onsite inspections of food products both domestically produced and imported. Here two FDA field employees are inspecting fish shipments at Los Angeles International airport.

Whistleblowing

Most federal employees are careful, dedicated, and hardworking. However, as in all organizations run by human beings, there can be inefficiency, error, abuse of power, and corruption. Each federal agency has an Office of Inspector General (IG) that monitors the activities of the agency's employees. But unless a wrongdoing is identified and brought to the IG's attention, it frequently goes unpunished.

To encourage more candid disclosure of wrongdoing in federal agencies, Congress passed the Whistleblower Protection Act in 1989 to protect **whistleblowers**, government employees who report mismanagement, corruption, or illegal activity within their agencies.[44] Before the passage of this act, whistleblowers had no real protection against reprisals from their colleagues, especially from those at higher levels of authority. The act established grievance and appeal procedures for employees who believe they have been retaliated against for reporting wrongdoing in their agencies. In 2010, Congress extended protections to employees in the financial services industry who act as whistleblowers, but they did not extend such protection to TSA workers or federal marshals; Robert MacLean (see beginning of chapter) is suing the federal government to get such protection.

→ KEY QUESTIONS:
Are private contractors working for the government likely to be whistleblowers? Why or why not?

whistleblowers: *Employees who report mismanagement, corruption, or illegal activity within their agencies.*

→ KEY QUESTIONS:
What can be done about lack of responsiveness by the bureaucracy?

Bureaucratic Failure

Whether whistleblowers come from inside or outside the federal government, it is up to the federal government to respond to them in an effective fashion. Unfortunately, there are serious cases in which a government agency has failed to respond. What happens when an entire agency fails to accomplish its mission?

One of the realities of federal management and oversight is that a federal agency or a congressional committee needs to be aware of a problem in order to address it. The dual responsibilities of accountability and responsiveness in the federal bureaucracy require the bureaucracy to do its job well enough to protect citizens from physical and financial harm. Unfortunately, the American people are so familiar with the failures of the federal bureaucracy that its successes are overlooked. The fact that 318 million people live in relative peace and security; experience safe and reasonable working conditions; trust that the medications they take are well tested; travel on trains, buses, and planes without incident; drink clean water; and receive their mail every day is a testament to the ways in which the federal bureaucracy meets its obligations. It is up to the voters to hold their elected officials—in Congress as well as the president—accountable for the performance of the federal bureaucracy.

Checkpoint

CAN YOU:

■ Explain ways the legislative and judicial branches can check the bureaucracy

■ Examine how the need for bureaucratic efficiency and transparency can counteract each other

■ Describe what it means to be a whistleblower

■ Relate the consequences of bureaucratic failure

The Bureaucracy and Democracy

The federal government that started with three cabinet departments has grown to include fifteen cabinet departments and many powerful independent agencies. The federal bureaucracy, including the armed services, employs nearly 4.2 million people. Their jobs affect the lives of every citizen, from the quality of the food they eat, to the safety of the highways they drive, to the purity of the water they drink.

In some important ways, the federal bureaucracy has become far more responsive to the needs of average individuals in the course of the nation's history, especially in the areas of social benefits, health care, environmental protection, and civil rights enforcement. The federal bureaucracy has tried to be more transparent in its operations by placing comprehensive information on the Internet for the public to access at any time. However, the responses to the Gulf of Mexico oil spill of 2010 and the VA hospitals example each show that there have been notable and serious failures in the government's action to secure the safety of citizens.

The structure of the bureaucracy includes many gates against speedy implementation of federal policy. The fact that there are so many layers of authority even within one agency, much less an entire cabinet department, adds considerable delay to the process of policy implementation. Multiple agencies can have jurisdiction over the same federal program or share responsibility for responding to natural disasters such as hurricanes. Such overlap can lead to miscommunication and to competition over authority and power. The hierarchy and procedural barriers that come with a large federal bureaucracy can stand in the way of efficient government.

At the same time, the rules and guidelines governing decision making in the bureaucracy are designed to ensure equal implementation of the law, which is a crucial element of a democracy. Americans expect federal laws to be applied in a consistent manner, with openness and vigilant congressional and public oversight. Understanding how laws are implemented, especially the gateways through which federal regulations are issued and enforced, gives citizens the power to hold the government accountable.

Citizens such as Robert MacLean have the opportunity, in a democracy, to pressure the government to be responsible and implement the laws with vigor in all areas. But one might also argue that advocates should not be needed to ensure that the bureaucracy works with efficiency and transparency and that the average citizen should not experience frustration in trying to navigate the gateways of the bureaucracy. Fortunately, it is possible to overcome these gateways with enough persistence.

CONNECT WITH YOUR CLASSMATES
MindTap™ for American Government

Access The Bureaucracy Forum: Discussion—Bureaucracy at Work.

Master the Concept
of The Bureaucracy with MindTap® for American Government

 REVIEW MindTap® **for American Government**
Access Key Term Flashcards for Chapter 12.

 TEST YOURSELF MindTap® **for American Government**
Take the Wrap It Up Quiz for Chapter 12.

 STAY CURRENT MindTap® **for American Government**
Access the KnowNow blog and customized RSS for updates on current events.

 STAY FOCUSED MindTap® **for American Government**
Complete the Focus Activities for The Bureaucracy.

 # Key Concepts

bureaucracy (p. 389). Is the bureaucracy a gate or a gateway to democracy?

cabinet (p. 389). What departments make up the cabinet?

cabinet secretaries (p. 390). What do cabinet secretaries do?

career civil servants (p. 404). How do career civil servants move up the career ladder?

civil service (p. 404). Why is the civil service important to implementing federal law fairly and equitably?

Civil Service Commission (p. 404). What role does the Civil Service Commission play in overseeing federal employment practices?

Federal Register (p. 392). What is the role of the Federal Register in executive implementation of the law?

federal regulatory commission (p. 395). What does a federal regulatory commission do?

independent agency (p. 394). How is an independent agency different from a cabinet department?

merit system (p. 404). Compare the merit system with the patronage system.

Office of Management and Budget (p. 394). What is the OMB's role in the regulatory process?

oversight (p. 400). How does congressional oversight serve as a check on the bureaucracy?

Pendleton Act (p. 401). What is the significance of the Pendleton Act?

political appointees (p. 404). How do political appointees implement the president's policies?

regulations (p. 389). What are regulations, and how do they facilitate implementation of federal law?

Schedule C appointees (p. 406). Explain this category of presidential appointees.

Senior Executive Service (SES) (p. 406). How can the SES be used to expand a president's influence in the bureaucracy?

whistleblowers (p. 414). Does the government provide enough incentives and protections to whistleblowers?

Learning Outcomes: What You Need . . .

To Know	To Test Yourself	To Participate
▶ **Explain what the bureaucracy does**		
The bureaucracy is the collection of executive branch departments, regulatory agencies, and other organizations that carry out the responsibilities of the federal government. Today nearly 4.2 million people, including those in the armed services, work for the federal government. The constitutional foundations for the bureaucracy include the president's power to nominate and appoint officers of executive departments, from whom he may request advice. The bureaucracy is also based in the president's broad grant of executive power.	• Define bureaucracy. • Explain how the Constitution provides a basis for bureaucratic power. • Describe the structure of the federal bureaucracy.	• Recognize how the federal government affects your daily life. • Evaluate how well bureaucrats serve the people. • Consider whether the bureaucracy is too large to be responsive.

To Know	To Test Yourself	To Participate

► Outline the essential elements of a bureaucracy

Each bureaucratic organization has a clear mission, a hierarchical decision-making process, an area of expertise, and a bureaucratic culture. Aside from cabinet departments, there are various types of organizations within the bureaucracy, some designed to be more or less independent of the president.

- Explain how the mission of a bureaucracy shapes its goals.
- State the advantages and disadvantages of the hierarchical decision-making process.
- Characterize bureaucratic expertise.
- Describe bureaucratic culture.

- Evaluate the degree of accountability associated with a bureaucratic mission.
- Design a bureaucracy that is more efficient and responsive.

► Describe the growth of the bureaucracy over time

Since 1789, the bureaucracy has grown from three to fifteen executive departments as government's responsibilities have grown, primarily in the area of the economy. The first regulatory agency was established in 1887 to regulate railroad practices. Federal employment has developed from a corps of wealthy elites with political connections to members of the Congress and the president into a merit- and performance-based civil service designed to be protected from political influence. The president appoints cabinet secretaries and other high-level political appointees who are expected to carry out the president's agenda.

- Equate the establishment of cabinet departments with developments in the U.S. economy and society.
- Describe what regulatory agencies do.
- Explain how and why the civil service evolved.
- Survey the types of jobs career civil servants perform.
- Recall why political appointees have increased in number over time.
- Explain the growth of the use of private-sector contract workers.

- Evaluate the bureaucracy in terms of government responsiveness.
- Assess why merit-based employment is better than patronage in a democracy.
- Consider whether you would like to work for the government.
- Evaluate the accountability of private-sector contract workers.

► Assess how the bureaucracy is both accountable and responsive, and how it can fail

Following a consistent regulatory process, agencies draft regulations, which are open to comment by citizens, members of Congress, interest groups, and relevant businesses and industries before they are finalized. Congress exercises influence over policy through its oversight responsibilities and power to authorize and allocate funds. Lawsuits can involve the judicial branch in the interpretation of public policy. The bureaucracy is subject to criticism for acting slowly, but in a democracy, the need for efficiency is counterbalanced by the need for transparency. Reform efforts have improved transparency by providing protections for whistleblowers. The policy-making process and regulatory process together exemplify government responsiveness and accountability to citizens even as they also reflect the concerns of competing interests.

- Explain ways the legislative and judicial branches can check the bureaucracy.
- Examine how the need for bureaucratic efficiency and transparency can counteract each other.
- Describe what it means to be a whistleblower.
- Relate the consequences of bureaucratic failure.

- Describe how you can influence the bureaucracy.
- Evaluate the importance of offering protection to whistleblowers.

"Theresa, I think this fish has found her pond."

SONIA SOTOMAYOR, TO A PROFESSIONAL FRIEND AFTER OVERCOMING HER FEARS ABOUT BEING A JUDGE
Princeton University

ALLIANCE IMAGES/ALAMY

MARTIN SHIELDS/ALAMY

13

The Judiciary

There were many gates on Sonia Sotomayor's path to the Supreme Court: She was female (no female had served on the Court until Sandra O'Connor in 1981), Puerto Rican (no Latino had ever served on the Court until Sotomayor), had a case of juvenile diabetes (which at the time, substantially lowered life expectancy), and had an alcoholic father who died when she was nine. Sotomayor used her intelligence and diligence to overcome what for others would have been disadvantages. As she noted in her memoir, despite these setbacks, "I did have sources of deep happiness, and these bred in me an optimism that proved stronger than any adversity." That inner strength led her to become high school valedictorian; attend Princeton University where she won the prestigious Pyne Prize, the highest general distinction Princeton confers on an undergraduate; and then attend Yale Law School. She has readily admitted that she probably got admitted to Princeton due to the University's affirmative action program.

In 2014, affirmative action faced its most recent challenge at the Supreme Court. In 2006, the voters of Michigan passed an amendment to their state constitution banning race- and gender-based affirmative action in public education, public employment, and public contracting. The Coalition to Defend Affirmative Action filed suit against the amendment, and, in 2012, a federal district court ruled that the ban was unconstitutional. Michigan's attorney general, Bill Schuette, appealed the ruling, and the U.S. Court of Appeals declared the amendment unconstitutional. Schuette then appealed the Court of Appeals decision to the Supreme Court, which agreed to hear the case. On April 22, 2012, the day that the case came before the U.S. Supreme Court, Sonia Sotomayor found herself sitting in judgment over the constitutionality of efforts to block racial- and gender-based affirmative action.

The 2014 case *Schuette v. Coalition to Defend Affirmative Action* culminated from two prior cases involving the University of Michigan. In 2003, the Supreme Court struck down the affirmative action plan at Michigan's undergraduate college (*Gratz v. Bollinger*) but upheld the constitutionality of the affirmative action plan at the University of Michigan Law School (*Grutter v. Bollinger*). One of the litigants, or parties to the suit, Jennifer Gratz helped organize the initiative for the 2006 statewide constitutional amendment that banned the state of Michigan or any of its public universities from taking race or gender into account in hiring or admissions.

Need to Know

13.1 Describe what the judicial branch does

13.2 Explain how state and lower federal courts operate

13.3 Review the procedures the Supreme Court uses

13.4 Identify factors that influence judicial rulings and the impact those decisions have

13.5 Discuss how federal judges get selected

13.6 Outline how the Supreme Court has expanded and contracted national powers

WATCH & LEARN MindTap™ for American Government
Watch a brief "What Do You Know?" video summarizing The Judiciary.

On April 22, Sonia Sotomayor was in the minority as she argued that the Michigan amendment banning affirmative action was unconstitutional. The Supreme Court upheld that amendment in a 6–2 vote in 2014. Justice Clarence Thomas joined the concurring opinion of Justice Scalia, which cited an earlier opinion of Justice Thomas that disputed whether affirmative action plans *ever* helped minority students (emphasis in original). Justice Sotomayor, on the other hand, read her dissent from the bench, a rare occurrence for any justice and the first time Justice Sotomayor had ever done so. She took issue with Chief Justice Roberts' statement that "the way to stop discriminating on the basis of race is to stop discrimination on the basis of race," declaring it to be "out of touch with reality." Sotomayor insisted that it is the role of the judicial system to protect minorities from the tyranny of the majority. She wrote, "The Court abdicates that role, permitting the majority to use its numerical advantage to change the rules mid-contest and forever stack the deck against racial minorities in Michigan."

For a Puerto Rican girl raised in the poverty-stricken South Bronx, affirmative action was a gateway to an Ivy League education. That gateway eventually led to Sonia Sotomayor being the first Latino to sit on the Supreme Court of the United States.[1]

As the Court's **affirmative action** cases show, the judicial system of the United States, because of its authority to rule on the constitutionality of federal and state laws and policies, has an extraordinary amount of power in the American political system. As the highest court in the land, the Supreme Court not only decides whether affirmative action may be allowed but also decides other issues, such as whether health insurance can be mandated, abortion can be prohibited, or the death penalty inflicted. The justices on the Court make important decisions that affect the lives of individuals and the policies of the nation at large despite the fact that they are not elected by the people and cannot be removed from office if the people disagree with the decisions they make. In this chapter, we investigate the structure and procedures of the judicial system, the factors that influence judicial decisions, how judges are selected, and the role the Supreme Court has played in determining public policy and federal authority. Thus we examine, too, the controversial role and power of the judiciary in a democracy.

affirmative action:
Policies that support greater equality, often by granting racial or gender preferences in hiring, education, or contracting.

LISTEN & LEARN
MindTap for American Government

Access Read Speaker to listen to Chapter 13.

adversary process:
Confrontational legal process under which each party presents its version of events.

> **KEY QUESTIONS:**
> Do courts produce the fairest decision possible? Can you give examples?

13.1 The Role and Powers of the Judiciary

> ❯ Describe what the judicial branch does

The job of courts is to resolve legal disputes. The American legal system is based largely on the English system, which is the system that the colonists were familiar with. The legal system under the Constitution kept many of the same practices but added some innovations.

English Legal Traditions

Resolution of legal disputes follows an **adversary process**. In an adversarial system, each party, usually represented by an attorney, presents its version of events, with virtually all attempts to slant information short of lying under oath deemed acceptable.

Although in some cases a judge decides which side is correct, a group of ordinary citizens usually determines the outcome. The right to trial by jury dates back in England to the Magna Carta (1215), where it replaced trial by ordeal, the practice of subjecting people to drowning or burning to see if they were innocent. Trial by jury is crucial to liberty because it inserts a gate of citizen judgment between the accused person and the government that protects the accused from arbitrary detention and unjust punishment. It also provides a gateway of citizen involvement through juror participation.

Trials involve questions of fact (for example, did the University of Michigan set different standards for white and minority students?) and questions of law (for example, do such differing standards violate the Fourteenth Amendment?). Trial court decisions about questions of fact are presumed to be valid because the trial judge or the jury directly hears the evidence in the case. But because trial courts sometimes make mistakes about questions of law, the American legal system has followed the British practice by allowing **appeals** from trial court rulings. In the U.S. federal system, the **courts of appeals** and the Supreme Court hear appeals, which involve issues of law. These courts do not retry the facts as established by the trial court.

Trials resolve two distinct types of disputes. In a **criminal case**, the government prosecutes an individual for breaking the law. Criminal cases are based almost exclusively on prohibitions on behavior written into statutes (laws) passed by federal, state, or local legislatures. In a **civil suit**, a plaintiff, such as Jennifer Gratz, sues a defendant, such as the University of Michigan, to enforce a right or to win monetary damages.

Criminal law is based on statutory authority, but statutory authority cannot cover all possible civil disputes between individuals. Many disputes involve actions that no legislative authority could have ever imagined. When there are gaps in statutory law, courts rely on judge-made law known as **common law**. Common law requires judges to accept and rely on previous decisions (if each judge makes his or her own decisions on each case, there can be no common law). Thus, British royal judges developed the practice of reaching decisions based on **precedents**, that is, the previous decisions of other royal judges. Deciding cases based on precedents means that similar cases are decided similarly. Precedent is perhaps the most fundamental feature of English and American law. Because similar cases get decided similarly, following precedent promotes greater equality, predictability, and stability in law.

Constitutional Grants of Power

Article III of the Constitution establishes the judicial branch of government. It briefly refers to a Supreme Court of the United States and grants Congress the authority to create lower courts at its discretion. The Constitution grants the federal courts the authority to hear "cases" or "controversies." The Supreme Court has interpreted this provision to require that people who initiate lawsuits have standing. That is, they must establish that they have suffered a harm that the law protects them against. Standing is a gate that limits access to the judicial system.

Because the Constitution says so little about the judicial branch, one of the early acts of the First Congress, the Judiciary Act of 1789, established thirteen **district (trial) courts** and three circuit courts with both trial and appellate authority that serve at an intermediate level between the district courts and the Supreme Court. Today, there are 667 district court judges serving in ninety-four separate district courts and 179 court of appeals judges serving in thirteen intermediate appellate circuits.[2] The thirteen intermediate appellate courts include eleven numbered courts, a court of appeals for the District of Columbia, which handles most litigation involving federal agencies, and the Court of Appeals for the Federal Circuit, which handles customs and patent claims. In addition, Congress established the Foreign Intelligence Surveillance Court in 1978 (see Chapter 4, Civil Liberties)

appeal: *Legal proceeding whereby the decision of a lower court on a question of law can be challenged and reviewed by a higher court.*

courts of appeals: *Intermediate federal courts that are above the district courts and below the Supreme Court.*

criminal case: *Government prosecution of an individual for breaking the law.*

civil suit: *Lawsuit by a person, organization, or government against another person, organization, or government.*

common law: *Judge-made law in England and the United States that results from gaps in statutory law.*

precedent: *Practice of reaching decisions based on the previous decisions of other judges.*

→ KEY QUESTIONS:
If you recognize an injustice but have not been harmed by it, how can you get government to respond?

district courts: *Federal trial courts at the bottom of the federal judicial hierarchy.*

Table 13.1 Article I Courts

Name	Jurisdiction	Location
Bankruptcy Court	All bankruptcy cases	Each federal district
Military Appeals	Appeals of court-martial trials	Washington, D.C.
Veteran Appeals	Appeals of veterans and survivors' benefits	Washington, D.C.*
Federal Claims	Suits against the United States for more than $10,000	Washington, D.C.
Tax Court	Taxpayer lawsuits	Washington, D.C.*
Territorial Courts	U.S. trial courts for Guam, U.S. Virgin Islands, and Northern Mariana Islands	In their respective territories

*Can hear cases outside of Washington, D.C.

Source: http://www.lectlaw.com/def/a148.htm; http://www.uscourts.gov/FederalCourts/Bankruptcy.aspx

and the Court of International Trade in 1980. Separately, Congress has established six so-called Article I or "legislative courts" whose purpose is to help Congress perform its Article I duties. Unlike Article III judges, Article I judges do not serve for life. These courts are listed in Table 13.1.

The lawful authority of a court to hear a case is its **jurisdiction**. In general, jurisdiction for any federal court requires either that the case involves federal law (including the Constitution and treaties); or that the parties include the United States, ambassadors, or other public ministers; or that the parties are residents of different states. The Constitution further divides the Supreme Court's jurisdiction into original jurisdiction, the authority to hear a case directly from a petitioning party (as in a trial), and appellate jurisdiction, authority to hear cases on appeals from lower courts. The Supreme Court has original jurisdiction in "all Cases affecting Ambassadors, other public Ministers and Consuls, and those in which a State shall be Party" (Article III, Section 2). The Constitution then declares that "in all the other Cases" properly before the Court, it would have appellate jurisdiction subject to such exceptions and regulations that Congress shall make.

The Constitution grants the federal courts the authority to hear cases of law and equity. Cases of law and equity can involve (1) the common law when there are gaps in legislative authority; (2) statutory interpretation, where the courts have to determine what Congress meant by a statute (for example, is discrimination on the grounds of pregnancy included in the prohibition on sex discrimination in the Civil Rights Act of 1964?), and (3) constitutional interpretation, where the courts must decide whether a law or practice violates a provision of the Constitution.

Constitutional interpretation brings forth the greatest power of the federal judiciary, **judicial review**. Judicial review, established by *Marbury v. Madison* (1803), is the power of courts to declare actions of Congress, the president, or state officials unconstitutional and therefore void (see Chapter 2, The Constitution). The Supreme Court, for example, has exercised the power of judicial review on laws pertaining to affirmative action (see Public Policy and the Judiciary: Affirmative Action).

 **jurisdiction:** *Lawful authority of a court to hear a case.*

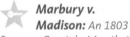 **judicial review:** *Authority of courts to declare laws passed by Congress and acts of the executive branch to be unconstitutional.*

 ***Marbury v. Madison:*** *An 1803 Supreme Court decision that established the Supreme Court's power of judicial review.*

Checkpoint

CAN YOU:

▪ Summarize the U.S. legal traditions derived from English legal traditions

▪ Restate what the Constitution says about the organization and powers of the federal judiciary

13.2 State and Lower Federal Courts

> Explain how state and lower federal courts operate

While the Supreme Court is the highest court in the United States, it hears only a small percentage of the cases filed in federal court. The overwhelming majority of federal cases are resolved in the district courts, which conduct civil and criminal trials. Cases appealed from the district courts go to one of the U.S. Courts of Appeals, in which three-judge panels usually decide cases. From those panels, losing parties can appeal cases to the entire circuit for an ***en banc*** ("by the full court") hearing, or they can appeal directly to the U.S. Supreme Court (see Figure 13.1).

en banc: *Decision by an entire Court of Appeals circuit, typically following an original judgment by a three-judge panel of the circuit.*

State Courts in the Federal Judicial System

Each state has its own judicial system, and unless a case involves federal law or the type of parties that create federal jurisdiction, cases get resolved in state courts, each of which has its own hierarchy of trial and appellate courts. Cases that involve federal issues that begin in one of the fifty separate state court systems can be appealed to the federal court system in one of two ways. First, criminal defendants who have exhausted their state appeals, that

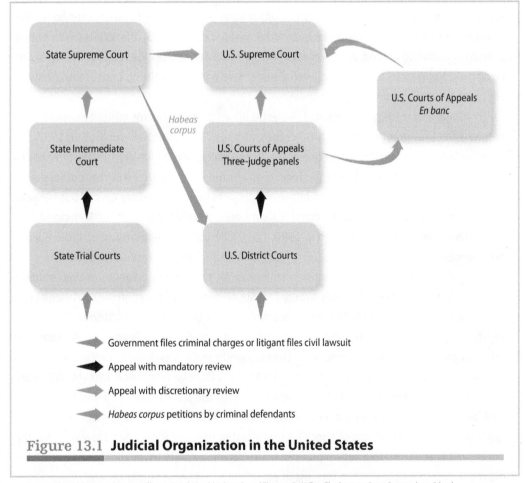

Figure 13.1 Judicial Organization in the United States

Source: Adapted from Lee Epstein, Jeffrey A. Segal, Harold J. Spaeth, and Thomas G. Walker, *The Supreme Court Compendium*, 5th ed. (Washington, D.C.: CQ Press, 2010), Figure 7-3.

Public Policy and the Judiciary:
Affirmative Action

An overly simple view of American politics holds that the legislative branch makes the law, the judicial branch interprets the law, and the executive branch enforces the law. However, in interpreting the law, judges often go beyond mere interpretation and get actively involved in policy making. While Presidents John F. Kennedy and Lyndon Johnson first proposed affirmative action plans, the Supreme Court has interpreted what that means for private business, government contracting, and public education.

With regard to private businesses, the Supreme Court has ruled that businesses and unions can agree to establish voluntary affirmative action programs where there has been a substantial racial imbalance in the workforce. In the famous case of *Steelworkers v. Weber* (1979), white steelworker Brian Weber was turned down for a promotion to craft worker. In a workforce that was 39 percent black, fewer than 2 percent of the skilled craft workers were black. Kaiser Aluminum and the United Steelworkers had agreed that 50 percent of future promotions would go to blacks, even if that bypassed whites with higher seniority. Weber sued, but the Supreme Court upheld the affirmative action plan.[3] On the other hand, the Court ruled that seniority cannot be overridden when it comes to layoffs: Whites with higher seniority cannot be laid off ahead of minorities with lower seniority, even if seniority-based layoffs will harm racial balance and even if minorities had less seniority because original hiring practices discriminated against them.[4]

National and state governments have established preferences for minority-owned businesses when they grant contracts and licenses, although the Court has wobbled. In 1987, the Court upheld a plan, similar to the one in the *Steelworkers* case, which granted preferences to women.[5] A 1980 decision allowed the federal government to require 10 percent of its grants to state and local governments for public works projects to go to minority-owned businesses.[6] Nine years later, however, a more conservative Court prohibited the city of Richmond, Virginia, from doing the same thing.[7] In 1990, the Court upheld the granting of radio license preferences to minority broadcasters; six years later, the Court reversed that decision.[8]

As colleges and universities actively sought racial and gender balances in their student bodies, several controversial cases arose. The Supreme Court first confronted college affirmative action plans in 1978. The medical school at the University of California, Davis, had eighty-four seats in each entering class for which anyone could apply and sixteen seats set aside for minority candidates only. Allan Bakke, a white male, was denied admission although he had a 3.5 grade point average (GPA) and a Medical College Admission Test (MCAT) score in the 90th percentile, whereas the average scores for the sixteen minority seats were a 2.6 GPA and an MCAT score in the 20th percentile. Bakke sued, and a split Court decreed in *Regents v. Bakke* that this sort of quota system violated the Civil Rights Act. Nevertheless, the Court held that affirmative action plans in which race is a "plus" in an applicant's overall file did meet the state's compelling interest in establishing a diverse student body.[9]

In 1996, a Court of Appeals Court in Texas declared affirmative action unconstitutional within the Fourth Circuit.[10] The University of Texas responded by implementing a program that guarantees admission to the University of Texas to anyone who graduates in the top 10 percent of his or her high school class. Because public schools are highly segregated in Texas, the university believed this would be an effective means of obtaining a diverse student body.

In the meantime, the Supreme Court revisited the *Bakke* decision in a pair of 2003 cases (*Gratz* and *Grutter*), discussed in this chapter. Despite surpassing the average qualifications required by the University of Michigan to gain entrance, Jennifer Gratz and Barbara Grutter were both rejected—Gratz from the undergraduate program and Grutter from the law school. With the legal assistance from the Center for Individual Rights, a conservative legal group that actively sought students looking to fight affirmative action, both women sued the university. As we saw earlier, the Supreme Court struck down the undergraduate and upheld the law school admissions policy.

In the case of the law school, Justice Sandra Day O'Connor expressed the belief that the Constitution required affirmative action programs to be temporary solutions only and the hope that by 2028 they would no longer be necessary. Opponents of affirmative action, such as Ward Connerly, chair of the American Civil Rights Institute, hope that such plans will not last that long. Connerly has launched state-level initiatives in Arizona, California, Colorado, Michigan, Nebraska, and Washington to let voters decide whether such programs should be allowed. Voters rejected affirmative action in all those states except Colorado.

California voters passed their amendment in 1996. Since that time, and despite fears that the initiative would reduce the number of underrepresented minorities in colleges and universities, Latino students have become the largest ethnic group at the University of California.[11]

In 2014, the Michigan case reached the Supreme Court, which declared in *Schuette v. Coalition to Defend Affirmative Action* that the people of Michigan had the right to pass a constitutional amendment via initiative that prohibits the state's public universities from using race as a factor in admissions or public employment.[12]

Construct Your Own Policy

1. Construct an employment policy that maintains equal opportunity but does not explicitly consider race, ethnicity, or gender.
2. Revise the judicial nomination and confirmation process to reduce the emphasis on ideology as a legitimate consideration.

is, have gone through their last appeal at the state level, can file a writ of *habeas corpus* with a U.S. District Court, which then allows the court to determine whether one or more of the defendant's federal legal rights have been violated. Second, any parties who have exhausted their state appeals can file a request for review, known as a **petition for a writ of** *certiorari*, directly with the Supreme Court.

The District Courts

The Judiciary Act of 1789 established thirteen district courts for the thirteen states. Today, there are ninety-four districts. Many states have more than one district, but no district covers more than one state. Districts that cover only part of a state receive geographical names, such as the Northern District of Illinois. Altogether there are 667 district judgeships. Many districts have only one judge, but the Southern District of New York has twenty-eight, and the Central District of California has twenty-seven. Nevertheless, with rare exceptions, district judges oversee trials alone, not in panels.

Trials in the district courts are either criminal or civil. In civil suits, plaintiffs (the parties bringing the suit) often request monetary damages to compensate for harm done to them, such as by a broken contract or a defective product. When rights are alleged to have been violated, they may ask that the practice be stopped. Litigants filed more than 278,000 civil suits in the district courts in 2012, and the federal government initiated nearly 71,000 criminal prosecutions.[13]

When Gratz and Grutter sued the University of Michigan over its admissions policies, the first stop for each was the U.S. District Court. Both had standing to sue, as their rejections by the university were real injuries, and because they claimed that their rights to equal protection under the Fourteenth Amendment had been violated, their cases raised a constitutional issue and entered the federal court system. Gratz and Grutter sought not only their own admission to the University of Michigan but also an end to the university's use of race in admissions decisions. The district courts allowed both suits to move forward as **class action lawsuits**, meaning that Gratz and Grutter were suing not only on behalf of themselves but also on behalf of all people denied admission at Michigan on account of their race. Class action lawsuits can open the gateways of access to groups of citizens in the same circumstances, thus broadening the impact over the possible result of an individual lawsuit.

Civil Procedure. The overwhelming majority of lawsuits filed in federal court settle out of court with a negotiated agreement between the plaintiff and the defendant. In 2012, the district courts terminated nearly three thousand civil cases.[14] Litigants settled nearly 99 percent of these cases before going to trial. Of the few cases that went to trial, nearly two-thirds were decided by juries. The other third were bench (nonjury) trials, as the *Gratz and Grutter* cases were.

After a case is assigned to a judge, the next step in a civil suit is discovery. Discovery grants each side access to information relevant to its suit held by the other side. Crucial to the *Gratz* and *Grutter* suits were University of Michigan documents showing differential admission rates for whites and minorities who had similar grades and standardized test scores. During discovery, the attorneys for each side can also question witnesses for the other side in a process known as deposition. Following discovery, litigants file briefs with the court, laying out their arguments.

Outside interests can file *amicus curiae* ("friend of the court") briefs, stating their concerns in a case.[15] The most influential *amicus* briefs are those filed in the name of the United States, as represented by the Office of the **Solicitor General** in the Justice Department.[16] In the *Gratz* and *Grutter* cases, the Clinton administration filed briefs in favor of the University of Michigan, which argued that affirmative action was necessary to obtain a diverse student body. General Motors also filed a brief in favor of the university's affirmative action program, stating that it needed a diverse pool of highly qualified attorneys, managers, and the like. Eventually, Microsoft and nineteen other Fortune 500 companies signed briefs supporting the university.[17]

Trial courts make determinations as to fact and as to law, whereas appellate courts generally make determinations only as to law,

AP IMAGES/SUSAN WALSH

Barbara Grutter was in her 40s when she applied to law school. The mother of two children, she also ran a consulting business. In this photo, Jennifer Gratz listens on the right.

applying the facts as determined by the trial court. That would normally mean that it would be up to the district court to determine factually whether race played a role in admissions at Michigan and how much of a role it played. Then it would decide as a matter of law whether that role was allowable or not. The parties in the *Gratz* and *Grutter* cases made the decision a bit easier for the judges, for the University of Michigan readily admitted—indeed, strongly defended—its use of race in admissions. Therefore, the question for the trial judge was not a question of fact, but a question of law: Does the equal protection clause of the Fourteenth Amendment prohibit the use of race as a factor in university admissions?

While trial judges or juries have nearly complete discretion in deciding questions of fact, they are constrained by the courts above them on questions of law. In affirmative action, the key precedent was the 1978 Supreme Court decision in *Regents of the University of California v. Bakke*.[18] A divided Court ruled in *Bakke* that the University of California's quota system of reserving a certain number of seats for minorities was unconstitutional, but that a system in which race was a "plus" in admissions could be justified due to the benefits that a diverse student body provides all the students.

In December 2000, Judge Duggan ruled in the *Gratz* case that the point system used by the university—in which each applicant could receive up to one hundred fifty points, including twenty for being from an underrepresented minority group—was a valid and necessary means of obtaining a diverse student body. On the other hand, Judge Friedman ruled in March 2001 that the law school's use of race in admissions violated the Constitution, finding that it was an "enormously important factor" in admissions and not the mere plus approved by the Supreme Court in *Bakke*. The University of Michigan appealed Friedman's decision to the Sixth Circuit Court of Appeals, while the Center for Individual Rights backed Gratz's appeal to the same circuit.

★ **amicus curiae:** *Latin term meaning "friend of the court" that is used to describe individuals or interest groups who have an interest in a lawsuit but are not themselves direct parties to the suit.*

★ **solicitor general:** *Official in the Justice Department who represents the president in federal court.*

→ KEY QUESTIONS:
How important is a diverse student body on your campus? How important is a diverse workforce? What is your experience?

→ KEY QUESTIONS:
Should race be a factor in university admissions?

Criminal Procedure.   Beyond civil cases such as the Michigan affirmative action suits, trial courts also conduct criminal trials. A federal criminal prosecution begins with an alleged violation of federal criminal law. In the U.S. federal system, states have primary authority over law enforcement, but the federal government frequently prosecutes drug, weapons, terrorism, and immigration cases, plus other crimes that involve interstate commerce or the instrumentalities of the federal government, such as the post office and government buildings.

The clearance rate for state and federal crimes—that is, the percentage of reported crimes in which someone is arrested, charged, and turned over for prosecution—is highest for violent crimes (47 percent in 2012) but much lower for property crimes such as burglary (19 percent).[19] Under the Constitution, an accused criminal in a federal court has a right to indictment by a grand jury, a specially empanelled jury consisting of between sixteen and twenty-three citizens who determine whether the government has sufficient evidence to charge the suspect with a crime. In the rare occasions in which a grand jury chooses not to indict, the suspect is freed.

Following indictment, the accused is arraigned, or informed of the charges against him or her, and asked to enter an initial plea of guilty or not guilty. About 90 percent of federal criminal cases are resolved through **plea bargains**, in which the accused plead guilty, usually in exchange for reduced charges or lesser sentences.[20] This arrangement greatly enhances the ability of trial courts to deal with large criminal caseloads.

In the small number of cases that proceed to trial, the accused has the right to a trial by jury but is free to request a bench trial, in which the judge decides guilt or innocence. A jury in a federal felony case consists of twelve individuals who must reach a verdict unanimously. (Neither twelve people nor unanimity is required in a state court.) The accused can appeal a guilty verdict, but the double jeopardy clause of the Constitution prohibits the government from appealing a verdict of not guilty. If the accused is found guilty, the judge determines the sentence based on guidelines that depend on the nature of the offense, the number of prior convictions, and other factors as recommended by the U.S. Sentencing Commission. In death penalty cases, the decision on the punishment is left to the jury. That is, following a guilty verdict, the jury hears new testimony by the prosecutor and defense attorney about whether death is the appropriate punishment.

The Courts of Appeals

Sitting hierarchically above the ninety-four district courts are the U.S. Courts of Appeals. Congress has divided the Courts of Appeals into eleven numbered circuits plus a circuit for the District of Columbia and a "federal circuit" that hears appeals from specialized lower courts that deal with patents and customs (see Figure 13.2). Each of the numbered courts of appeals has jurisdiction over several states. Randomly assigned three-judge panels usually hear appeals from the district courts.

The courts have mandatory jurisdiction over cases appealed to them. That is, if a losing party from the district court appeals to the appropriate court of appeals, the court must hear the case. Because the circuit courts are in the middle of the federal judicial hierarchy, cases can be both appealed to the court of appeals and appealed from the court of appeals (refer to Figure 13.1). Appeals from a court of appeals can happen in two ways. First, losing litigants at the court of appeals who believe that the three-judge panel that heard their case did not represent the judgment of the circuit as a whole can request an *en banc* review. Alternatively, losing litigants can request review by the Supreme Court. In both cases, further review is at the discretion of the court that is being petitioned.

plea bargain:
Agreement by a criminal defendant to plead guilty in return for a reduced sentence.

→ KEY QUESTIONS:
Do plea bargains make efficiency more important than justice?

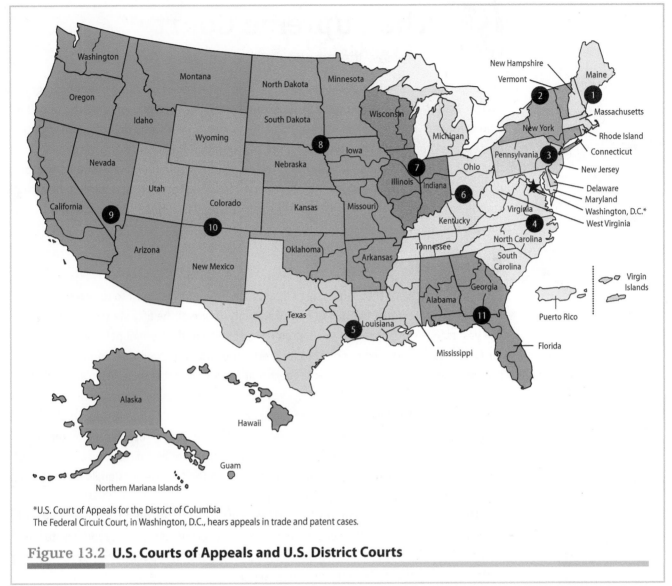

Figure 13.2 **U.S. Courts of Appeals and U.S. District Courts**

*U.S. Court of Appeals for the District of Columbia
The Federal Circuit Court, in Washington, D.C., hears appeals in trade and patent cases.

© Cengage Learning, data from United States Courts, Court Locator, http://www.uscourts.gov/court_locator.aspx.

Given the importance of the *Grutter* and *Gratz* cases, the cases made it through the U.S. Court of Appeals in anything but a normal manner. Rather than a hearing with a three-judge panel, possibly followed by *en banc* and/or Supreme Court review, the Center for Individual Rights, which represented Gratz and Grutter, requested and was granted an immediate *en banc* review. On May 14, 2002, the Sixth Circuit ruled in favor of the university in the law school case by a 5–4 vote. The **majority opinion** argued that the law school's approach resembled the plus system approved by the Supreme Court in the *Bakke* case. Not surprisingly, Barbara Grutter appealed the decision to the Supreme Court.

On October 1, 2002, ten months after oral arguments, the court of appeals still had not issued its ruling in the undergraduate case. In an unusual step, Gratz's attorneys asked the Supreme Court to bypass the court of appeals and rule directly on their appeal. On December 1, the Supreme Court accepted review in both cases.

majority opinion:
Opinion of a court laying out the official position of the court in the case.

Checkpoint

CAN YOU:

- Explain how state court cases can end up in federal court
- Give an overview of the responsibilities and procedures in district courts
- Give an overview of the responsibilities and procedures in courts of appeals

13.3 The Supreme Court

> Review the procedures the Supreme Court uses

The Supreme Court's procedure in handling cases consists of deciding whether to grant review and, if review is granted, of receiving briefs, hearing oral arguments, deciding who wins, and writing the majority opinion. If desired, justices who do not agree with the decision of the Court majority (that is, the decision about who wins the case) can write dissenting opinions. Those who agree with the majority opinion on who should win but differ as to the reasoning can write concurring opinions. The majority opinion, however, stands as the precedent for lower court judges to apply in similar cases dealing with the same issue.

Granting Review

Each year, about eight thousand losing litigants ask the Supreme Court to review their cases. Most have lost in one of the U.S. Courts of Appeals or one of the fifty state supreme courts. The vast majority of appeals to the Supreme Court come in the form of petitions for writs of *certiorari*, often shortened to petitions for "cert." The Supreme Court's decision to grant cert is purely discretionary, but its rules suggest that a grant of cert is more likely when a lower court resolves issues of law differently from the way other lower courts have or issues a decision that conflicts with decisions of the Supreme Court. The Supreme Court is also more likely to grant review when the government of the United States, represented by the solicitor general's office, requests it, either as a petitioning party or as *amicus curiae*. The filing of *amicus* briefs by other parties can also be important to the Court, as it signals that the case involves important questions of public policy.[21]

The large number of petitions for cert prevents the justices from fully reviewing each one. Instead, they rely on their clerks, who are usually recent law school graduates, to write summaries. Most of the justices' chambers have joined the "cert pool," which splits the cert petitions among the clerks of the justices in the pool.

The large number of petitions also prevents the justices from fully discussing each one. Rather, the chief justice passes around a "discuss list," a set of cases he thinks worthy of discussion. Any justice can add any other case to the list if he or she wishes. Cases not on the discuss list are automatically denied cert, leaving the lower court's decision as final. The justices then meet in conference to consider each of the cases on the discuss list. The Court grants cert through a **rule of four**. That is, although five votes constitute a majority, the Court will agree to hear a case if any four justices vote to grant cert. Overall, the Court grants only about 1 percent of cert petitions, leaving the lower court decision as final in the remaining 99 percent of the cases.

rule of four: *Supreme Court rule that grants review to a case if as few as four of the justices support review.*

The justices' votes on petitions for *certiorari* remain secret unless a justice leaves his or her papers to the public, as justices sometimes do after they retire. To date, the justices' votes in the *Gratz* and *Grutter* cases are unavailable, but the importance of the issue plus a split between the Sixth Circuit Court upholding affirmative action and an earlier Fifth Circuit decision striking it down at the University of Texas made a grant highly likely.[22] On December 2, 2002, the Court granted review to both cases.

Oral Arguments

Following a grant of cert, the justices receive written briefs from the litigants explaining why their position should win. Other parties may file *amicus curiae* briefs urging the Court to affirm or reverse the lower court decision. Again, the most influential of these briefs come from the solicitor general's office, which represents the current presidential administration at the Supreme Court. Thus, while the Clinton administration sided with the university at the district court level in the *Gratz* and *Grutter* cases, the George W. Bush administration switched sides and asked the Supreme Court to strike down the law school and undergraduate admissions programs.

Parties normally receive thirty minutes each for oral argument, although the justices frequently interrupt with questions. The quality of oral argument varies enormously, and not surprisingly, can influence which party wins.[23]

The Supreme Court heard oral arguments in the *Gratz* and *Grutter* cases on April 1, 2003, hearing the *Grutter* case first. Grutter's attorney, Kirk Kolbo from the Center for Individual Rights, spoke first, arguing that the Constitution prohibits distinctions based on race. Justice O'Connor immediately interrupted, asking the attorney about Court precedents holding that race could be used if the government had a compelling interest in doing so. Kolbo responded that the school could legally achieve a diverse student body without using racial preferences by using factors that are not explicitly racial, such as economic status. U.S. Solicitor General Theodore Olson spoke next, opposing the University of Michigan's (hereafter just "Michigan") use of affirmative action but, under President Bush's directive, not calling for a complete ban on the use of race.

Kolbo represented Gratz as well as Grutter, arguing in Gratz's case that the use of race as a factor must be extraordinary and rare, and that diversity does not meet that extraordinary standard. Michigan's attorney in the undergraduate case defended the need for a "critical mass" of minority students, so that those students would not feel like tokens.

The Decision

Within a few days of oral argument, the justices meet in conference to vote on the merits of the case, that is, to decide which side wins, and to assign a justice to write the Opinion of the Court in the case. If the chief justice is in the majority, he determines who will write the opinion. If the chief justice is not in the majority, the assignment is made by the most senior justice who is in the majority.

The opinion is the heart of the Court's legal and policy-making power. It explains the Court's justification for its decision and sets guidelines for other courts to follow in subsequent cases. To have this authority, it must become a majority opinion by gaining the assent of a majority of the justices.

Assigning the writing of the Opinion of the Court to a justice does not mean that a majority opinion will result. If a justice writes an opinion siding with one side, and other justices agree with the result (that is, agree on who wins) but not with the reasoning, they can concur in the judgment. That means that they are not joining the Opinion of the Court. Such justices will typically write a **concurring opinion** that explains their reasoning or join the concurring opinion of another justice. Justices who disagree with the result reached by the majority can write a **dissenting opinion** explaining why they believe the Court's decision

→ KEY QUESTIONS:
Should the federal government be allowed to try to influence a court decision?

→ KEY QUESTIONS:
Why did the Office of the Solicitor General switch positions on the Michigan affirmative action cases between 2000 and 2001?

concurring opinion: *Opinion that agrees with the results of the majority opinion (that is, which party wins) but sets out a separate rationale.*

dissenting opinion: *Opinion that disagrees with the majority opinion as to which party wins.*

was in error. If, due to a combination of concurring and dissenting justices, fewer than five justices join the Opinion of the Court, that opinion becomes a plurality judgment rather than a majority opinion. Plurality judgments have less value as precedents than majority opinions.

The vote in the affirmative action cases revealed a split in the justices' preferences: 5–4 in favor of the law school program, but 6–3 against the undergraduate program. As Figure 13.3 shows, four conservative justices thought that both the undergraduate and the law school affirmative programs violated the Fourteenth Amendment and were unconstitutional, whereas the three most liberal justices thought that both programs were acceptable because of the university's compelling interest in creating a diverse student body and the narrow tailoring of the affirmative action programs to meet that interest. Justices Sandra Day O'Connor and Stephen Breyer were the swing justices. They agreed that diversity constituted a compelling interest but did not believe that the undergraduate program, which automatically gave a set number of points to minority applicants, was narrowly tailored to meet that interest. They thus voted with the more conservative justices to strike the undergraduate program. But O'Connor and Breyer voted with the liberals to uphold the law school program, which overall gave strong preferences to underrepresented minorities but was more careful in considering the importance of race in each individual's application.

Because Chief Justice Rehnquist dissented in the law school case, Justice Stevens, the senior justice in the majority, assigned the opinion. Given Justice O'Connor's role as the swing justice in the case, he assigned the opinion to her. O'Connor declared that while racial categorizations could be used only if the state had a compelling interest in doing so, the need

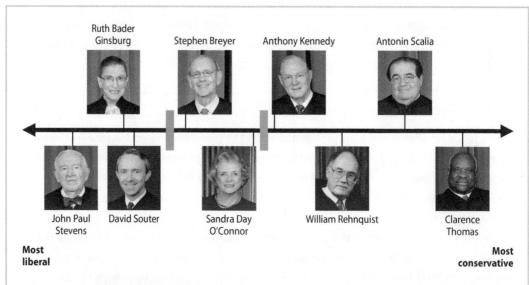

Figure 13.3 **Ideology and Votes of Supreme Court Justices in the *Gratz* and *Grutter* Cases**

The justices are aligned from most liberal to most conservative. The six justices to the right of the blue line voted with Gratz to strike the undergraduate affirmative action program at the University of Michigan. The five justices to the left of the brown line voted with the University of Michigan in upholding the law school's affirmative action program.

Source for Justices' Ideology: Martin-Quinn Scores, http://mqscores.berkeley.edu. Jeffrey A. Segal, © Cengage Learning. Photos: Ginsburg, Breyer, Kennedy, Scalia, Stevens, and Thomas by Steve Petteway, Collection of the Supreme Court of the United States; Souter by Joseph Bailey, National Geographic Society, Courtesy of the Collection of the Supreme Court of the United States; O'Connor by Dane Pennland, Smithsonian Institution, Collection of the Supreme Court of the United States; Rehnquist by Dane Pennland, Smithsonian Institution, Collection of the Supreme Court of the United States.

for diversity was such an interest. She quoted from *amicus* briefs by businesses, which cited the need for a diverse workforce in the global economy, and she cited extensively from the military brief's stated need for a diverse officer corps.

Chief Justice Rehnquist was in the majority in the undergraduate case, and he assigned the majority opinion to himself. His opinion accepted the notion that diversity was a compelling interest—he did not have the votes to declare otherwise—but wrote that the automatic granting of twenty points toward admission to every minority student did not meet the precedent required in *Bakke* of considering each particular applicant as an individual.

Though Gratz won her case, she had by this point graduated from a different Michigan campus, the University of Michigan–Dearborn. The University of Michigan changed its admissions procedures to be more like the law school's procedures: Race would still be used as an admissions factor, but there would be no automatic point total added just because of an applicant's race.

Checkpoint

CAN YOU:

- Explain how cases reach the Supreme Court
- Describe the process of oral argument
- Survey how the Court reaches and issues decisions
- Discuss the impact Court decisions do and do not have

13.4 Judicial Decision Making

> Identify factors that influence judicial rulings and the impact those decisions have

We have now discussed the structure of the court system and the procedures it follows in both civil and criminal cases. In this section, we will examine how judges make decisions about a case and the impact those decisions have on public policy. Because judges are unelected and serve for life, they are not accountable to the people in the same way that presidents and members of Congress are. Nevertheless, they have an extraordinary power—the power of judicial review. Judicial review allows an unelected branch of government to strike the laws and actions of the elected branches of government—Congress and the president. This authority by the judicial branch is questionable in a democracy, where the people are supposed to have the final say. Therefore, along with judicial review comes what law professor Alexander Bickel has labeled the **countermajoritarian difficulty**.[24] We expect the judiciary to enforce limits on governmental power, but when it does so, it acts in a countermajoritarian manner because unelected judges are using this power to strike the actions of democratically elected executives and legislatures.

The Supreme Court first held an act of Congress unconstitutional in 1803, and then did not hold another one unconstitutional until 1857. Since that time, however, the Court has struck down 169 congressional laws, slightly more than one per year, with 7 laws struck down in 1935 during the height of the Court's battle with the New Deal (see Figure 13.4). Since the 1986 term, the Court has struck down more than twice as many state and municipal laws (104) as federal laws (43).[25]

Given the undemocratic nature of judicial review, politicians frequently decry **judicial activism**, judges who go beyond what the law requires and seek to impose their own policy preferences on society through their decisions. These critics insist that judges should act with **judicial restraint**, that is, judges should respect the decisions of other branches or, through the concept of precedent, the decisions of earlier judges.

→ **KEY QUESTIONS:**
Is judicial review a problem for democracy?

countermajoritarian difficulty: *Alexander Bickel's phrase for the tension that exists for representative government when unelected judges have the power to strike laws passed by elected representatives.*

judicial activism: *Decisions that go beyond what the law requires made by judges who seek to impose their own policy preferences on society through their judicial decisions.*

judicial restraint: *Decisions by judges respecting the decisions of other branches or, through the concept of precedent, the decisions of earlier judges.*

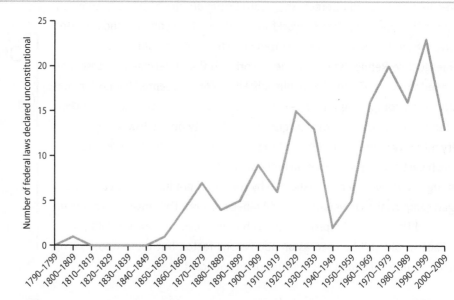

Figure 13.4 Number of Federal Laws Declared Unconstitutional, 1790–2013

The Supreme Court declared one federal law unconstitutional in the 2010 term, one in the 2011 term two in the 2012 term, and one in the 2013 term.

Sources: Harold W. Stanley and Richard G. Niemi, eds., *Vital Statistics on American Politics*, 3rd ed. (Washington, D.C.: CQ Press, 1992); Lawrence Baum, *The Supreme Court*, 8th ed. (Washington, D.C.: CQ Press, 2004), 170, 173; Harold J. Spaeth, Lee Epstein, Andrew D. Martin, Jeffrey A. Segal, and Thomas W. Walker, United States Supreme Court Database, scdb.wustl.edu. Jeffrey A. Segal, © Cengage Learning.

We will explore two broad approaches to understanding judicial policy making: a legal approach, which suggests that courts rely on legally relevant factors, and an extralegal approach, which suggests that courts rely on legally irrelevant factors. We then examine the consequences for a democracy of the reliance on extralegal factors by an unelected judiciary.

→ KEY QUESTIONS:
On what should judges and justices base their decisions?

Judicial Restraint: The Legal Approach

According to the legal approach, justices base their decisions on legally relevant materials, such as prior court precedents, the plain meaning of the text of the law under consideration, and the intent of the framers of the law, rather than on their own preferences. This viewpoint is known as judicial restraint.

As we explained earlier in the chapter, precedent means a reliance on the prior decisions of the Court. In the *Grutter* case, the Court accepted the arguments from the *Bakke* case that the government had a compelling interest in achieving a diverse student body but concluded that systems that establish racial quotas go too far. Reliance on precedent creates stability in law: Decisions change gradually rather than abruptly. Reliance on precedent also generates a degree of equality and fairness. If you slip on your neighbor's walkway, it is not necessarily clear whether your neighbor is at fault for a slippery surface or you are at fault for not being careful. It is hard to say in advance that ruling one way is just and ruling the other way is unjust. But if the judge rules that the owner is not liable and the next week under similar conditions the neighbor slips on your walkway, fairness demands that the judge should again rule that the owner is not liable. That is what ruling based on precedent accomplishes. Lower courts are bound by Supreme Court precedents, but the Supreme Court does not necessarily consider itself strictly bound to its own precedents. Otherwise, there would be no growth in the law, and, for example, the United States might still have the separate-but-equal school systems that were declared unconstitutional in *Brown v. Board of Education*.

Beyond precedent, legal-based approaches consider the plain meaning of the law being interpreted. Justice Antonin Scalia is the Court's foremost proponent of this approach. If there is no right to privacy written in the Constitution, he claims, then the Supreme Court should not be creating privacy rights. According to Scalia, if such rights are to be protected, they should be granted by democratically elected legislatures, not by life-appointed judges. However, while a textual approach makes some issues perfectly clear—for example, that a 34-year-old cannot be president—it does not necessarily answer whether affirmative action plans designed to increase diversity or fair representation in an unequal society violate equal protection of the law.

Similarly, Justice Clarence Thomas often argues for decision making based on the intent of the Framers. This approach places the meaning of the Framers ahead of the literal meaning of the words that they wrote. Thus, while dissenting in a case that upheld federal prohibitions on medicinal marijuana under Congress's authority to regulate interstate commerce, Thomas ignored more than seventy years of precedent that had expanded the scope of the commerce clause. He argued that local activities such as the medical use of homegrown marijuana were not what the Framers meant by commerce.[26] This may well be true, but in many circumstances, it is difficult to know what the Framers meant or what they would have thought if they could have envisioned modern American society. For example, does the Fourth Amendment's protection of one's person, houses, papers, and effects against unreasonable searches and seizures include telephone wires, cell phones, and wireless e-mail?

Judicial Activism: The Extralegal Approach

Legal approaches often fail to provide a good indicator of what the Supreme Court will do. While some precedents, notably the 1978 *Bakke* decision, supported affirmative action, more recent cases prior to *Grutter* had pushed in the opposite direction. The text of the Fourteenth Amendment guarantees equality, but there is no evidence that the Framers of the amendment intended it to prohibit policies that tried to help disadvantaged groups.

Alternatively, we can consider extralegal approaches to Supreme Court decision making. Extralegal factors go beyond the legal factors that courts are supposed to consider. The most important sets of extralegal considerations include the justices' own preferences and strategic considerations based on the preferences of others. Many, if not most, justices may be labeled activists, justices who decide cases based on their own policy preferences.[27]

The Justices' Preferences.   In the affirmative action cases, the four most conservative justices voted to strike both the undergraduate and the law school plans, the three most liberal justices voted to uphold both, and the two justices in the middle voted to uphold the law school program but to strike the undergraduate program. (For the ideology of the justices currently on the Court, see Figure 13.5.)

This sort of relationship between the justices' ideology and their votes is fairly common. But because Supreme Court scholars cannot obtain information from the justices themselves about their ideology, they use indirect measures. As Figure 13.6 shows, there exists a very strong relationship between the justices' ideology and their votes once on the Court.[28] Note,

> → KEY QUESTIONS:
> What role should ideology play in judicial decisions? What role does it play?

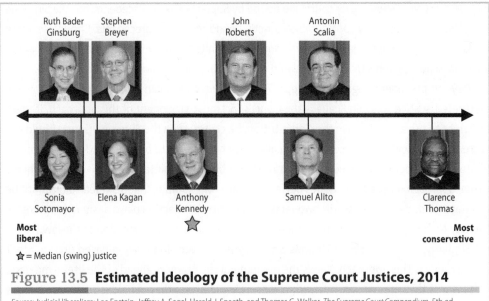

Most liberal

Most conservative

☆ = Median (swing) justice

Figure 13.5 Estimated Ideology of the Supreme Court Justices, 2014

Source: Judicial liberalism: Lee Epstein, Jeffrey A. Segal, Harold J. Spaeth, and Thomas G. Walker, *The Supreme Court Compendium*, 5th ed. (Washington, D.C.: CQ Press, 2010), Table 6-4. Justices' ideology: Martin-Quinn Scores, http://mqscores.wustl.edu/. Jeffrey A. Segal, © Cengage Learning. Photos: Steve Petteway, Collection of the Supreme Court of the United States.

however, that this strong relationship does not necessarily apply to state courts or lower federal courts, both of which must follow precedents established by the Supreme Court, at least on matters of federal law.

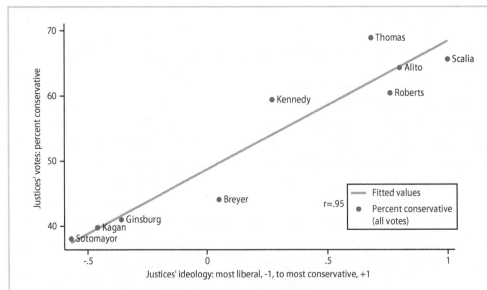

Figure 13.6 Justices' Votes by Their Ideology, 1953–2013

The graph shows that, as justices' ideology (shown from left to right) against the percentage of times justices voted in a conservative direction line up from the left (most liberal) to the right (most conservative), the percentage of the time they vote conservatively increases substantially. Generally speaking, the most liberal justices, those farthest to the left on the graph (Sotomayor, Kagan, and Ginsburg), vote in the liberal direction (toward the bottom of the graph), whereas the most conservative justices (Scalia and Alito) vote conservatively most of the time (toward the top of the graph).

Source: Justices' ideology: Data updated by Jeffrey Segal from Jeffrey Segal and Albert Cover, "Ideological Values and the Votes of Supreme Court Justices," *American Political Science Review* 83 (1989): 557–65. Justices' votes: Harold J. Spaeth, Lee Epstein, Andrew D. Martin, Jeffrey A. Segal, Theodore J. Ruger, and Sara C. Benesh. 2014 Supreme Court Database, Version 2014 Release 01. URL: http://Supremecourtdatabase.org. Jeffrey A. Segal, © Cengage Learning.

Strategic Considerations. Justices cannot behave solely on the basis of their ideological preferences. Justice Rehnquist, while writing the *Gratz* opinion, may have preferred to declare that virtually all affirmative action plans are unconstitutional, but if he had done so, he might have lost the support of Justices O'Connor and Breyer. So he compromised and accepted diversity as a rationale but nevertheless was able to strike down the undergraduate program. Negotiations over the content of the majority opinion are a routine part of Supreme Court decision making.[29]

As the *Gratz* and *Grutter* cases show, the courts have a major role in the American policy-making process, balancing equality of opportunity against affirmative action policies aimed at providing greater equality of outcome. Given the play of extralegal factors in such decisions, are judges, in fact, policy makers?[30] When the Supreme Court decides for the nation that affirmative action programs are allowed as long as they provide individualized assessments of students' records, they are making policy. The fact that this is not merely interpretation of the law is supported by the fact that the justices' ideological preferences overwhelmingly explain their votes on the Court.

Restraint and Activism in Judicial Decision Making

Contemporary research suggests that justices respect the decisions of legislatures and earlier judges when those decisions are consistent with the justices' ideology. Thus, for example, liberal justices such as Ginsburg and Breyer overwhelmingly vote to uphold liberal precedents[31] or federal laws favored by liberals.[32] But when conservative precedents or laws favored by conservatives are under consideration, liberal justices are more than willing to strike them. Similarly, conservative justices such as Scalia and Thomas overwhelmingly vote to uphold conservative precedents or the constitutionality of federal laws favored by conservatives. But when precedents are liberal in direction or when liberals favor the laws under review, conservative justices are more than willing to strike them.

The vast majority of justices are restrained toward laws and precedents that they agree with ideologically but are quite willing to overturn laws and precedents that they are distant from ideologically. Does this bode poorly for a democratic society that expects its judicial system to exhibit impartiality? Perhaps, though as we shall see later, our elected representatives appoint judges and so indirectly the people help choose which judges will make judicial policy in the United States.

> → KEY QUESTIONS:
> How do elections affect judicial decisions? Should they?

The Impact of Court Rulings

Now that we understand how judges make decisions, we will examine what impact those decisions have for our democratic system. The fact that the federal court issues a decision does not necessarily mean that government officials charged with implementing it will comply. The courts have no power of enforcement. The Supreme Court's school desegregation decision in *Brown*, for example, met with massive resistance from supporters of segregation: Elected officials urged disobedience, local boards of education ignored the decision, and lower courts complied with the decision halfheartedly at best. All the while, citizens rallied in the streets in opposition (see Supreme Court Cases: *Cooper v. Aaron*; see also Chapter 11, The Presidency). In part because of these reactions, very few schools desegregated in the ten years following *Brown*.[33] And the fact that a decision might be complied with does not necessarily mean

that it will have the impact that the Court intended. The advances in school desegregation over time have not meant that educational equality has been achieved in the United States.

Additionally, many types of court decisions can be overturned by Congress, state legislatures, or other legislative mechanisms such as state-level referenda. When a court's decision is based on the meaning of a statute (for example, is carbon dioxide considered a pollutant under the Clean Air Act?), Congress can simply overturn the court's decision if it disagrees with the court's conclusion.

In the constitutional realm, if the Court declares that a practice is not unconstitutional, as in the law school affirmative action case, that practice can still be prohibited through the legislature or, if the state allows, through a referendum. So when the Supreme Court rules that affirmative action is not prohibited by the Constitution, that does not mean that the university is required to implement an affirmative action program or that the state is required to allow such a program. As we saw earlier, following the Supreme Court decision in her case, Jennifer Gratz used the gateway provided by Michigan's initiative procedure, organizing a statewide proposal in Michigan that banned the use of race, gender, or ethnicity for admissions or hiring in higher education.

Several bills were introduced for a constitutional amendment to overturn the Supreme Court's rulings protecting flag burning under the First Amendment. None received the required two-thirds vote in each chamber of Congress.

On the other hand, when the Supreme Court declares that the Constitution prohibits an activity, legislatures find that prohibition difficult to overturn. For example, when the Court declared that Congress did not have the authority to set the voting age at 18 for state elections, the only recourse was for Congress and the states to pass a constitutional amendment overturning that decision. Only five of the Supreme Court's constitutional decisions have ever been overturned via amendment (see Table 13.2 on page 440). While relatively more of the Court's statutory decisions get overturned by Congress, such instances are still fairly rare.

Thus, the federal court system and the Supreme Court in particular play an important role in determining public policy. Yet, as we have seen, the people play an indirect role in choosing federal judges. We will now take a closer look at how the selection process occurs.

→ KEY QUESTIONS:
How are court decisions enforced? Would government work better if the courts had the power of enforcement?

→ KEY QUESTIONS:
Did the Michigan ballot initiative undermine justice or help ensure it?

Check**point**

CAN YOU:

- ▨ Distinguish judicial activism and restraint
- ▨ Identify nonideological factors that influence judicial decision making
- ▨ Discuss the impact Court decisions do and do not have

 13.5 # The Appointment Process for Federal Judges and Justices

› Discuss how federal judges get selected

→ KEY QUESTIONS:
Describe the lasting impact of Supreme Court appointments.

The Constitution grants the president the authority to nominate judges, but these nominations are subject to the advice and consent of the Senate. Judges confirmed by the Senate serve during "good behavior," which, short of impeachment, essentially means a life term. The

supreme court cases

Cooper v. Aaron (1958)

QUESTION: Does the threat of violence negate a school district's obligation to desegregate?

ORAL ARGUMENT: September 11, 1958 (listen at http://www.oyez.org/cases/1950-1959/1958/1958_1)

DECISION: September 12, 1958 (read at http://laws.findlaw.com/us/358/1.html)

OUTCOME: No, desegregation is required, even when mobs threaten violence (9–0).

Despite substantial opposition in the South to the 1954 *Brown* desegregation decision, the Little Rock school board approved a plan in May 1955 that would begin to integrate its schools as of September 1957. In response, the state legislature declared that no student could be required to attend an integrated school. Nevertheless, the National Association for the Advancement of Colored People (NAACP), a civil rights interest group, selected John Aaron, his sister Thelma, and seven other exceptional African American students to attempt to integrate Central High School.

As September 1957 approached, Governor Orval Faubus called out the Arkansas National Guard to physically prevent the students from entering the school. For three weeks, the Guard kept the school off limits to the nine students. This action encouraged segregationists, who took to the streets around the school, to protest integration.

On September 20, 1957, a federal district court issued an order prohibiting the Arkansas Guard from interfering with desegregation efforts. In response, Faubus withdrew the Guard, leaving the streets under the control of a dangerous and angry mob.

On September 23, the African American students entered school under police protection, but the police were unable to control the mob and quickly removed the students. Two days later, President Dwight D.

Eisenhower sent the 101st Airborne Division to Little Rock to disperse the mobs and protect the students. Eight of the nine black students remained at the school for the remainder of the school year. Given the unrest, William Cooper and other members of the Arkansas Board of Education filed suit to thwart the board's own desegregation plan. In June 1958, the district court upheld its request. In August, the court of appeals reversed the district court. The Supreme Court granted the board's petition for a writ of *certiorari*.

In an unusual opinion signed the day after oral argument by all nine justices, the Supreme Court refused to allow the board to back out of its desegregation plan due to the threat of violence. The Court declared that the Constitution of the United States and the Supreme Court's interpretation of the Constitution are the supreme law of the land. In response, Governor Faubus closed the school for the year, but it reopened as an integrated school in 1959. The Court's expansion of its authority—adding its interpretation of the Constitution to those items that are the "supreme law of the land"—has drawn criticism of judicial overreaching from people on the right and the left.

1. Why is the judiciary the branch of government best able to make decisions that a majority of citizens strongly oppose?

2. Can the Supreme Court be effective in guaranteeing equality when the majority of citizens actively oppose equality?

Table 13.2 Constitutional Amendments Overturning Supreme Court Decisions

Supreme Court Decision	Amendment
Chisolm v. Georgia (1793) allowed citizens to sue other states in federal court.	Eleventh Amendment (1795) establishes sovereign immunity for states.
Dred Scott v. Sandford (1857) denied citizenship to African Americans.	Fourteenth Amendment (1868) makes all people born in the United States citizens of the United States.
Minor v. Happersett (1874) denied voting rights to women.	Nineteenth Amendment (1920) guarantees women the right to vote.
Pollock v. Farmers' Loan and Trust (1895) limited Congress's authority to tax income.	Sixteenth Amendment (1913) grants Congress the authority to tax income from whatever source derived.
Oregon v. Mitchell (1970) prompted Congress to set the voting age at 18 for all elections. The case struck the law as applied to state elections.	Twenty-Sixth Amendment (1971) sets the voting age at 18 for all elections.

© Cengage Learning

★ **judicial independence:** *Why does the United States need judicial independence?*

House has impeached only one Supreme Court justice, Samuel Chase (1805), in an attempt by the Democratic-Republicans to remove an ardent Federalist from the bench. The Senate rejected every charge against Chase (just three votes short of the required two-thirds majority on one of the counts),[34] establishing a custom crucial to **judicial independence** that judges would not be removed due to partisan disagreements with their decisions.

As procedures have evolved, the president and the Senate accommodate each other on district court appointments, but sometimes clash at the appeals court level. At the Supreme Court level, presidential nominees face intense scrutiny by the Senate, which often reflects concerns by citizens and interest groups.

The District Courts

When a vacancy occurs in a district court, the president consults the senators from the state in which the court is located. If one of them is opposed to the nomination, he or she can invoke the norm of senatorial courtesy and receive the support of other members of the Senate in blocking that nominee. When the two senators are from different parties, the senator from the president's party sometimes offers the other senator a percentage of the appointments, hoping the favor will be returned if the other party wins the presidency.

This norm is enhanced by the chair of the Judiciary Committee sending "blue slips," so-called because of the color of the paper, to the senators of the president's party of a nominee's home state, asking whether they approve of the choice. Without a positive response, the Judiciary Committee generally will not hold a hearing on the nominee; with no hearing, there is no vote. Even with a positive response to the blue slip, the Judiciary chair may choose not to hold a hearing, particularly if he or she is of the opposite party of the president.

UNITED STATES SENATE

COMMITTEE ON THE JUDICIARY

12-Mar-99

Dear Senator Moynihan

You will kindly give me, for the use of the Committee, your opinion and information concerning the nomination of:

Robert A. Katzmann to be United States Circuit Judge for the Second Circuit

Please return this form as soon as possible to the nominations office in Dirksen G-66. No further proceedings on this nominee will be scheduled until both blue slips have been returned by the nominee's home state senators.

Respectfully

Orrin G. Hatch
Chairman

Via courier to: SR-464

REPLY

TO: Senator Hatch, Chairman

_X_ I approve

_____ I oppose

Comments: Superb choice! (ours, that is!)

U.S. Senator

Senator Daniel Patrick Moynihan (D-N.Y.) signed a blue slip approving the appointment of Robert Katzmann to the Second Circuit Court of Appeals. The Xerox copy that Judge Katzmann gave us was white.

COURTESY OF ROBERT A. KATZMANN

Sonia Sotomayor, who would go on to become President Barack Obama's first Supreme Court nominee, received her district court nomination during the presidency of Republican George H. W. Bush (1989–93) due to an appointment-sharing deal between New York's two senators, Republican Alfonse D'Amato and Democrat Daniel Patrick Moynihan. Like the president, senators use a variety of criteria in naming district court judges, including ideology, qualifications, and the rewarding of party loyalty.[35]

Confirmation of district court judges is generally routine, with nearly 90 percent of nominees between the administration of Jimmy Carter (1977–81) and Barack Obama approved.[36] With an increasingly partisan confirmation environment following the 2010 elections, and a Democratic majority in the Senate but not enough votes to end filibusters (but see below on the end of lower court filibusters), the confirmation rate during the Obama administration was closer to 80 percent.[37] Following the nomination, the Senate Judiciary Committee conducts hearings on nominees. At the hearings, the American Bar Association (ABA), an organized interest group representing the nation's attorneys, evaluates the merits of nominees. District court nominees may also be requested to testify. If the Judiciary Committee approves the nomination, it moves to the Senate floor for a vote. Under recent rules changes that prohibit filibusters on lower court nominees, a majority is all that is needed for approval.

→ KEY QUESTIONS:
Is the judicial appointment process fair?

The Courts of Appeals

The formal process of appointment for court of appeals judges is the same as that of district court judges, but the greater authority of court of appeals judges means that the Senate and outside interest groups pay much closer attention to the president's nominees. While court of appeals judges formally represent multiple states, seats are informally considered to belong to particular states. Thus, senatorial courtesy still applies.

→ KEY QUESTIONS:
Should judicial appointments be subject to partisanship?

Senate Democrats twice blocked the nomination of future Chief Justice John Roberts, a conservative Republican, to the U.S. Court of Appeals. Only after a third nomination in 2003, at which point Republicans controlled the Senate (and thus the Judiciary Committee), did Roberts receive a hearing and a vote. Overall, the Senate has failed to confirm more than 20 percent of court of appeals nominees since Clinton's administration (1993–2001), with the overwhelming majority being blocked in the Judiciary Committee.[38] In 2010, Senate Republicans began extensive use of holds, a process by which a single senator can block the unanimous consent agreements by which the Senate operates, to delay votes on many of President Obama's nominees. The Democrats responded in November 2013 by changing Senate rules to prohibit filibusters on all executive or judicial nominations except those for the Supreme Court.

→ KEY QUESTIONS:
Should judges be appointed without regard to race, ethnic background, gender, or religion?

The Supreme Court

Given the Supreme Court's authority, the appointment of a Supreme Court justice is a high-stakes affair with extensive media coverage, interest group mobilization, public opinion polls, and the occasional scandal. As President Nixon correctly noted, "The most important appointments a President makes are those to the Supreme Court of the United States."[39] While Nixon was no doubt referring to the ideological and policy implications of such appointments, presidents also use Supreme Court appointments for electoral advantage.

Presidents also try to choose nominees who are close to them ideologically, hoping to shape the direction of the Court for years to come. Ronald Reagan had this in mind when he nominated the conservatives Robert Bork (whom a Democratic-controlled Senate rejected) and Antonin Scalia (whom a Republican-controlled Senate approved). Considerations of ideology are not new. George Washington named eleven consecutive Federalists to the first Supreme Court, and Franklin Roosevelt appointed only supporters of his New Deal programs, most of whom were Democrats.

Other interest groups mobilize for and against nominees, too. When in 1987 Ronald Reagan nominated Robert Bork, who was outspoken in opposing the constitutional right to privacy, the pro-choice interest group Planned Parenthood released an ad stating: "State controlled pregnancy? It's not as far-fetched as it sounds. Carrying Bork's position to its logical end, states could ban or require any method of birth control, impose family quotas for population purposes, make abortion a crime, or sterilize anyone they choose."[40]

Bork's hearings changed the nature of testimony by nominees before the Senate. An outspoken conservative, Bork answered questions about his legal beliefs directly, openly discussing his opposition to the right to privacy. The result was a 58–42 vote against him by the full Senate. Since the Bork rejection, nominees have dodged questions about their beliefs. Recently, they have stated that it would be improper to answer any questions about any issue that might conceivably come before the Court. With testimony from the nominees carefully scripted, hearings have become less informative and more of a showcase for senators.

Once the nomination is on the floor, senators debate the pros and cons of the nominee until the vote is set. Floor votes can be postponed indefinitely through a filibuster, a tactic used with increasing frequency for court of appeals nominees, but Abe Fortas's chief justice nomination (1968) is the only Supreme Court nomination to be defeated by a filibuster.

The confirmation process has also become a much more partisan process over the years. While Chief Justice John Roberts received unanimous support from Republicans, Senator Barack Obama and seventeen other Democrats opposed him. Similarly, while Sonia Sotomayor, nominated by Democratic President Obama, received unanimous support from Democrats (57 out of 57), only nine out of forty Republicans supported her.

Among opposition party senators, ideology can sometimes be decisive. In the Roberts vote, only 25 percent of liberal Democrats supported him whereas more than 80 percent of more moderate Democrats did so. With Sotomayor, however, support was below 40 percent for both moderate Republicans (33 percent) and more conservative Republicans (10 percent) (see Figure 13.7). Constituent preferences matter too:[41] Only three of the Republicans who voted for Sotomayor came from a state that Obama lost in 2008. Given the highly partisan nature of Supreme Court nominations over hot-button issues such as affirmative action, many Republicans reacted negatively to an earlier statement expressing her hope that "a wise Latina with the richness of her experiences would more often than not reach a better conclusion than a white male who hasn't lived that life."[42]

The nominees' perceived qualifications are no less important than ideology. While the high-quality nominees of recent years—Kagan, Sotomayor, Alito, and Roberts—all received substantial opposition, the Senate confirmed all of them. Lower-qualified nominees have long faced decisive trouble, with G. Harrold Carswell, a little-known federal judge whom Richard Nixon nominated to the Supreme Court in 1970, a case in point.

→ KEY QUESTIONS:
What are the effects of televising congressional Judiciary Committee hearings?

CONNECT
WITH YOUR CLASSMATES
MindTap for American Government

Access The Judiciary Forum: Discussion—Supreme Court Confirmation Process.

→ KEY QUESTIONS:
Should public opinion affect judicial appointments?

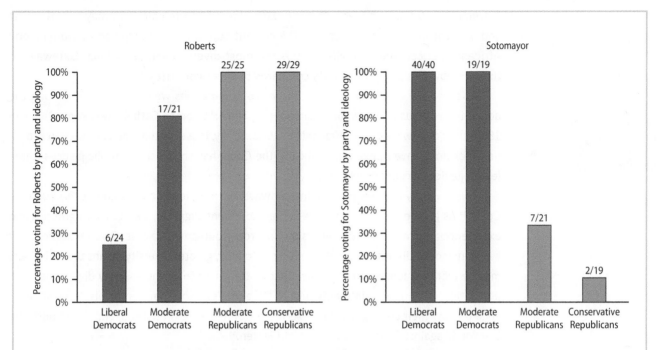

Roberts

Sotomayor

Figure 13.7 **Ideology and Partisanship in the Roberts and Sotomayor Votes**

Every Republican voted to confirm John Roberts for Chief Justice, while moderate Democrats were more likely to support him than liberal Democrats. Similarly, all Democrats voted to confirm Sonia Sotomayor for Associate Justice, while moderate Republicans were more likely to support her than conservative Republicans.

The question of qualifications includes not just ability, but also ethics. The Reagan administration withdrew the nomination of Douglas Ginsburg in 1987 following media reports that he had smoked marijuana while a professor at Harvard Law School. Much larger ethical questions surrounded the nomination of Clarence Thomas in 1991. During the televised hearings for Thomas, Anita Hill, who had worked for him at the Department of Education and later at the Equal Employment Opportunity Commission (EEOC), charged Thomas with sexual harassment. Thomas vociferously denied the charges. Many people watching the hearings were disturbed by the harshness of the attacks on Hill by the all-male Judiciary Committee. The senators acted the way elected officials of both parties normally do in such circumstances: Those who were ideologically close to the nominee—in this case, conservatives—believed him, whereas those who were ideologically distant did not.[43] The end result was that the Senate approved Thomas by a 52–48 vote.

Demographic Diversity on the Court

In a Court long dominated by white males, Clarence Thomas was only the second African American to serve; Thurgood Marshall (1967), a distinguished lawyer for the National Association for the Advancement of Colored People (NAACP) who argued *Brown v. Board of Education* (1954) before the Court, was the first. The Senate has confirmed 112 justices to seats on the Supreme Court. Of those 112, only 4—Sandra Day O'Connor (1981), Ruth Bader Ginsburg (1993), Sonia

In 1991, President George H. W. Bush nominated Clarence Thomas to the Supreme Court to replace the retiring Thurgood Marshall. Thomas was not a supporter of affirmative action, and civil rights and feminist groups objected to his nomination. Then Anita Hill, who had worked for Thomas at the Department of Education and the Equal Employment Opportunity Commission, accused him of sexual harassment. Despite her testimony, the Senate confirmed Thomas by a narrow margin.

Sotomayor (2009), and Elena Kagan (2010)—have been female. Sotomayor is the first and only Latino. By some measures, the current Supreme Court, with three women, one African American, and one Hispanic, is the most diverse ever. See Global Gateways to find out how this gender diversity compares to other countries.

It is also the case that the first thirty-two nominations went to Protestants, long the dominant religious group in American politics. The first Roman Catholic was Roger Taney in 1836; the first Jew was Louis Brandeis in 1916. Today, in a sign that the gateways to prominent positions have opened dramatically, the Court has six Roman Catholic justices, three Jewish justices, and no Protestants.

This diversity matters in a number of ways, both on lower courts and at the Supreme Court.[44] As Justice Sotomayor's "wise Latina" comment suggests, a judges' backgrounds and experiences can influence their views on the proper outcome of a case. Given that the Court has tremendous discretion about which cases to hear, greater diversity means that the Court may be more responsive to the issues that matter most to an increasingly diverse national population. Historic appointments such as O'Connor's or Sotomayor's can also have an influence on how their colleagues vote.[45] As more women serve on the U.S. Supreme Court, the bias found against female attorneys might lessen.[46]

On the other hand, for the first time in history, not one member of the Supreme Court held elective office prior to service on the Court. This lack of experience in electoral politics might play into their decisions striking down campaign finance laws (see *Citizens United v. Federal Election Commission,* in Chapter 7, Interest Groups). The educational background of the current justices also is fairly narrow. Every one of them attended either Harvard or Yale Law School. Professionally, only Sotomayor served as a trial judge, and all the justices except Kagan came to the Supreme Court from federal appeals courts. This narrowness of background has not always been the case. In the past, many Supreme Court nominees graduated from modestly ranked law schools, and the justices often came to the Court from governorships, cabinet positions, the Senate, and private practice. To people who believe that the justices simply make decisions that are commanded by the Constitution, this narrowness does not matter. But to those who believe that experience does matter, the lack of this form of diversity hurts both the Court and the nation.

→ KEY QUESTIONS:
Does diversity on the Court matter? Should the Supreme Court be age diverse?

Checkpoint

CAN YOU:

▪ Explain senatorial courtesy

▪ Describe issues in nominations to courts of appeals

▪ Discuss the ways in which partisanship and ideology influence Supreme Court nominations

13.6 Historical Trends in Supreme Court Rulings

> Outline how the Supreme Court has expanded and contracted national powers

In *Federalist* 78, Alexander Hamilton described the judiciary as "the least dangerous branch" because it has no power over the sword or the purse. But, as we have seen, due to the power of judicial review, the Supreme Court has actually played a major role in policy making: dividing authority between the nation and state, between Congress and the president, and between local and state governments, and the people. Through the Court's history, its interpretations

globalgateways

Female Justices

Compared to the percent of women in Congress (roughly 20 percent), the number of women who serve as lawyers and judges is impressive. Almost half of all first-year law school students in the U.S. are women as are one third of the U.S. Supreme Court justices.

This relatively heavy concentration of women on the U.S. Supreme Court is not unusual worldwide. In central and eastern Europe and central Asia, women make up over 40 percent of high court judges. In Latin America and the Caribbean, they constitute 36 percent. Only in South Asia (India, Pakistan, Bangladesh, and Afghanistan) do women make up less than 10 percent of nations' high court judges.

The number of high court justices in Latin America has risen sharply in recent years. In 1998, six Latin American nations had no female judges on their high courts. Only two countries (Panama and Venezuela) had passed the 20 percent mark. By 2010, only Panama and Uruguay had no female justices.

At the other end of the spectrum, Puerto Rico, a self-governing Commonwealth of the United States, topped the list at 43 percent.

Women face continued legal discrimination (for example, laws that limit inheritance by females) and extralegal challenges (for example, domestic violence) around the globe. The rising percent of women sitting on higher courts serves as a promising gateway to greater gender equality.

1. Why are more women than ever before on national supreme courts?
2. Does equality require 50 percent representation, or can the benefits of female representation be reached with something less than that?

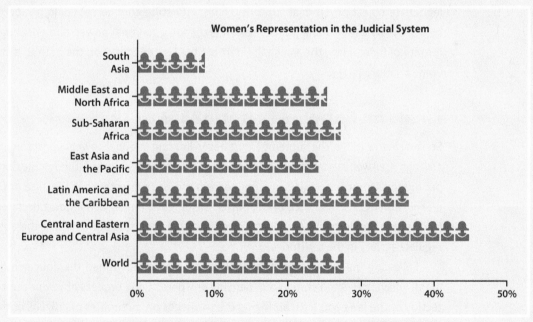

Women's Representation in the Judicial System

Source: http://www.americasquarterly.org/women-in-robes, and http://progress.unwomen.org/pdfs/EN-Report-Progress.pdf.

have expanded, then contracted, and once again expanded national powers. After a long and slow start, it has also moved, fairly consistently, toward greater protections of equality. In this section, we will take a look at the policies issued by this least dangerous but also least democratic branch of American government.

Expansion of National Power under the Marshall Court

During George Washington's administration (1789–97), the Supreme Court had so little power or status that its first chief justice, John Jay, resigned to become governor of New York. Not until the fourth chief justice, John Marshall, did the Court begin to establish itself as a major player in national politics. The Marshall Court (1801–35; Courts are often named after the sitting chief justice) did so not only by affirming its power of judicial review in the *Marbury* case but also by setting forth a broad interpretation to the scope of national power in the cases of *McCulloch v. Maryland* (1819) and *Gibbons v. Ogden* (1824) and by limiting the authority of state judiciaries in a series of decisions culminating in *Cohens v. Virginia* (1821; see Supreme Court Cases: *McCulloch v. Maryland* in Chapter 3, Federalism).[47]

→ KEY QUESTIONS:
In *Marbury*, the Court established its power over laws made by Congress. Why, then, did the Marshall Court also expand Congress's power?

The decision in *McCulloch v. Maryland* expanded national power in two ways: by granting the national government the right to create a bank through the necessary and proper clause, and by limiting state power by denying the states the authority to tax activities of the national government. Similarly, in *Gibbons v. Ogden*, the Court took an expansive view of national power, declaring that the commerce clause, which granted the national government the authority to regulate commerce "among the several States," would be broadly defined to include not just the shipping of goods across state lines but also the economic activities within a state that concern other states. As in *McCulloch*, what the Constitution grants as a legitimate object of national authority (here, interstate commerce) could not be regulated by a state. By establishing judicial review, expanding national power, and ensuring the uniformity of federal law, the Marshall Court set the United States on the path to a strong and unified nation.

Limits on National Power, 1830s to 1930s

Starting in the 1830s, the Supreme Court began limiting national power over slavery and, later, civil rights, as well as governmental efforts to regulate the economy. Although the Constitution permitted slavery, the justices did not address the issue directly until the case of *Dred Scott v. Sandford* (1857).[48] As noted in Chapter 5, Civil Rights, the Supreme Court declared that no black person could be an American citizen and that Congress did not have the authority to regulate slavery in the territories.

Following the war, Congress proposed and the states ratified the Fourteenth Amendment, which prevented states from denying any person due process of law or the equal protection of the laws and from abridging the privileges or immunities of citizens of the United States. The Supreme Court interpreted the Fourteenth Amendment narrowly, thus limiting national power. For example, the *Slaughterhouse Cases* restricted the privileges or immunities clause that states could not abridge to the right of access to the seat of government, the right to pass freely from state to state, and the right to demand the protection of the federal government on the high seas or abroad, but little more.[49] Through precedent, the limited reading of the clause largely remains in effect today.

In *United States v. Cruikshank*, the Supreme Court reversed federal charges against the perpetrators of the Colfax massacre (see Chapter 5), arguing that the right to enforce the Fourteenth Amendment's due process clause gave Congress the authority to act only against states, not against individuals.[50] Similarly, in the *Civil Rights Cases*, the Court refused to grant Congress the authority to prohibit discrimination by private individuals under the equal protection clause, declaring that state-sponsored inequality was all that the amendment prohibited.[51]

The Supreme Court limited national authority in the economy, too. Following the Civil War, as the

CONTINENTS HISTORY/EVERETT COLLECTION

An 1873 battle over voting rights in Colfax, Louisiana left 100 African Americans dead, many of them murdered in cold blood. The Supreme Court reversed federal charges against the private citizen perpetrators, as the Fourteenth Amendment only limits state discrimination.

American economy shifted from agriculture to industry, powerful business and industrial interests sought to limit attempts by Congress and the states to regulate economic activity and labor. The Supreme Court generally backed business and industrial interests by setting up barriers to regulation. It promoted *laissez-faire*, the belief that the government should not intervene in the economy.

Strengthened National Power, 1930s to the Present

Following the onset of the Great Depression in 1929, citizens called on the states and the national government to try to regulate the economy and to assist workers, but the Supreme Court held firm in creating a constitutional gate that declared much of the economic legislation passed in the early years (1933–36) of the Franklin Delano Roosevelt administration (1933–45) unconstitutional. Under pressure from Congress and Roosevelt, the Court eventually reneged, opening a gateway by allowing governments greater leeway in regulating the economy. During this same period, the Court began restricting state government limits on civil rights and liberties, while strengthening national power to protect civil rights.

> → KEY QUESTIONS:
> Do you think justices over the age of 70 should be allowed to stay on the Supreme Court? Is appointment for life a good or a bad idea?

Economic Regulation.   Elected president in 1932 on a platform of economic recovery and reform, Franklin Roosevelt saw several pieces of his New Deal legislation—which aimed to alleviate the nation's economic hardships—struck down by the Court, often by closely divided votes. After his 1936 reelection, Roosevelt struck back at the Court, proposing a so-called Court-packing plan that would have allowed him to appoint a new justice for every justice older than 70 who failed to resign. This scheme would have increased the Court's size to fifteen and guaranteed judicial support for his economic plans.

In the historic "switch in time that saved nine," two of the moderate backers of the Court's *laissez-faire* policies, Owen Roberts and Chief Justice Charles Evans Hughes, proved themselves responsive to the hostile political environment facing the Court. They began to change their votes, providing majorities for both national and state plans to regulate the economy, thereby removing the need for Roosevelt's controversial Court-packing plan. In a series of cases decided in 1937, the Court upheld state-level minimum wage laws. Nationally, the Court recognized the right of unions to organize and bargain collectively as within the powers of Congress to regulate under the commerce clause.

Increased Protections for Civil Liberties and Civil Rights.

With the government's authority over the economy established, cases before the Court dealt increasingly with questions of civil rights and civil liberties, topics discussed more fully in Chapters 4 and 5. The Court incorporated various provisions of the Bill of Rights, making them binding on the states. This selective incorporation doctrine began slowly, with First Amendment rights among the few incorporated before the 1950s. The doctrine expanded during the liberal Warren Court (1953–69), which made most of the criminal procedure guarantees of the Bill of Rights binding on the states.

Outside of incorporation, the Warren Court greatly expanded the interpretation of liberties involving the First Amendment, equal protection, the right to privacy, and criminal procedure. In First Amendment cases, the Court protected the speech rights of those advocating violence against religious and racial minorities, the press rights of newspapers against libel suits by public figures, and the right to publish allegedly obscene materials as long as they had even the slightest amount of redeeming social value. It also limited prayer and Bible readings in the schools.[52] Regarding equal protection, beyond the momentous *Hernandez v. Texas* and *Brown v. Board of Education* decisions, the Court launched a reapportionment revolution, setting forth a "one person, one vote" requirement.[53] The Warren Court also created a right to privacy that is not explicitly in the Constitution.[54] Finally, regarding criminal justice, the Warren Court demanded that evidence obtained by police in violation of the Fourth Amendment's protection against unreasonable searches or seizures should be excluded at trial (the exclusionary rule) and that subjects in custody not be interrogated without being informed of their right to remain silent and have an attorney (the so-called *Miranda* warnings, after the plaintiff in the case).[55]

→ KEY QUESTIONS:
Is there a right to privacy? Where should the line be drawn against government intrusion in private life?

Neither the more conservative Burger (1969–86) nor Rehnquist (1986–2005) Courts undid what the liberal Warren Court had done. For a summary of the Supreme Court's leading decisions, see Table 13.3. The Burger Court allowed children to be bused away from their neighborhood schools to increase integration. The Burger Court also established abortion rights, limited the death penalty, protected women's rights under the equal protection clause of the Fourteenth Amendment, and, in a precursor to the *Gratz* and *Grutter* lawsuits, first allowed affirmative action at colleges and universities.[56] On the other hand, the Burger Court chose not to extend equal protection rights to the unequal funding of school districts and, in the criminal justice area, limited the reach of the exclusionary rule and the *Miranda* warnings.[57]

Although conservative, the Rehnquist Court, over Chief Justice William Rehnquist's dissent, first extended privacy rights to homosexual conduct[58] (see *Lawrence v. Texas,* Chapter 6, Public

Table 13.3 Leading Decisions of the Marshall, Taney, Warren, Burger, Rehnquist, and Roberts Courts

Court	Case (Year)	Description
Marshall (1801–1835)	*Marbury v. Madison* (1803)	Established judicial review
	McCulloch v. Maryland (1819)	Used implied powers to allow Congress to establish a national bank
	Cohens v. Virginia (1821)	Declared that federal courts have final say on meaning of federal law
	Gibbons v. Ogden (1824)	Established expansive interpretation of commerce clause
Taney (1836–1864)	*Dred Scott v. Sandford* (1857)	Stated that "negroes of the African race" cannot be citizens and that Congress cannot prohibit slavery in the territories
Warren (1953–1969)	*Hernandez v. Texas* (1954)	Recognized Latinos as a separate class for equal protection purposes
	Brown v. Board of Education (1954)	Prohibited segregation of public schools
	Wesberry v. Sanders (1964)	Required equality in the size of legislative districts
	New York Times v. Sullivan (1964)	Made it very difficult for public officials to sue newspapers for libel
	Miranda v. Arizona (1966)	Required that criminal defendants be told of their rights
	Griswold v. Connecticut (1965)	Established the right to privacy
Burger (1969–1986)	*Reed v. Reed* (1971)	Granted women rights under the equal protection clause
	New York Times v. United States (1971)	Set extremely high bar for government censorship of newspapers
	Roe v. Wade (1973)	Extended privacy rights to cover abortion rights
	United States v. Nixon (1974)	Required President Richard M. Nixon to hand over incriminating evidence in Watergate case
	Regents v. Bakke (1978)	Allowed universities to use race-based affirmative action admissions
	Plyler v. Doe (1982)	Guaranteed right of undocumented children to attend public schools
Rehnquist (1986–2005)	*Planned Parenthood v. Casey* (1992)	Cut back but did not eliminate abortion rights established in *Roe v. Wade*
	Bush v. Gore (2000)	Ended the Florida presidential recount with George W. Bush holding a small lead, leading to Al Gore's concession
	Lawrence v. Texas (2003)	Extended privacy rights to homosexual conduct
	Gratz/Grutter v. Bollinger (2003)	Upheld race-based affirmative action as long as racial considerations are made on a case-by-case basis
Roberts (2005–present)	*District of Columbia v. Heller* (2008)	Upheld the right to bear arms as an individual right
	Citizens United v. FEC (2010)	Declared that corporations and unions have the same First Amendment rights to contribute to political campaigns as individuals
	National Federation of Independent Business v. Sebelius (2012)	Upheld the constitutionality of the Affordable Care Act
	United States v. Windsor (2013)	Struck down the provision in the Defense of Marriage Act that prohibited the federal government from recognizing same-sex marriages lawfully conducted in other states or countries

© CENGAGE LEARNING

Opinion and the Media). On the other hand, the Rehnquist Court limited, however slightly, the scope of abortion rights and cut back, again only slightly, the scope of congressional authority under the commerce clause and sovereign immunity.[59] And perhaps most important, as noted in Chapter 9, Elections, Campaigns, and Voting, it ended the dispute over the 2000 presidential election with its decision in *Bush v. Gore.*[60]

The Roberts Court has been decidedly pro-business, hearing more such cases than previous courts and ruling on them in a decidedly pro-business direction.[61] It protected Walmart against a large discrimination lawsuit.[62] Even more important, it ruled that corporations

Checkpoint

CAN YOU:

- Describe the ways in which the Marshall Court expanded national power
- Explain how the Supreme Court acted to limit equality between the 1830s and 1930s
- Discuss what might have led the Supreme Court to accept greater national authority starting in 1937

have the same speech rights as citizens, enabling corporations to spend unlimited amounts of money on political campaigns[63] (see Chapters 7 and 9). On the other hand, the Court upheld Obama's health care plan in 2012, in what was not the conservative position in the case.[64] It also struck down the provision of the Defense of Marriage Act that prohibited the federal government from recognizing same-sex marriages.[65] In 2014, it upheld the Michigan initiative that banned affirmative action in that state.[66]

The Judiciary and Democracy

The judicial system of the United States promotes the equal right of participation by allowing a single individual who has been harmed by a law to challenge its constitutionality. People who have financial resources or who can find support from organized interests may fare better than those who have to act on their own. The action may not be successful. Nevertheless, the judiciary provides a separate gateway to the political system, one that is different in kind from the gateway to the legislative or executive branch. By filing a suit through the judiciary, a single individual—such as Oliver Brown (in the *Brown v. Board* school desegregation case) or the anonymous "Jane Roe" (in the *Roe v. Wade* abortion decision)—can have an enormous influence on the American political system.

Representative democracy requires government to be accountable and responsive to the public. Yet the judicial branch is not accountable in any meaningful way: Even if the public is dissatisfied with justices' decisions, Congress has not successfully used the impeachment process to remove justices for those decisions. Yet this does not mean that the Court is not responsive to the public or to the public's representatives. Responsiveness can happen through four different gateways.

The first gateway is through the electoral process.[67] During the 1960s, the Warren Court made a series of decisions on contentious issues such as criminal procedure and religious freedom that were significantly more liberal than many Americans might have preferred. Richard M. Nixon campaigned for president in 1968 with promises to appoint justices who were significantly more pro-police and significantly less pro-defendant. Nixon won the election and, in the course of his first term, appointed four justices, all of whom were considerably more conservative on criminal procedure than the rest of the Court. The result was a conservative shift in Supreme Court decisions in criminal cases that mirrored public preferences as expressed in the 1968 election.

Second, in cases in which the Court is unresponsive to congressional preferences, Congress can threaten the Court's institutional authority. During the Civil War, Congress took away the Court's appellate jurisdiction over *habeas corpus* appeals. In the 1930s, Franklin Roosevelt threatened to dilute the Court by adding six new members. In both cases, the Court backed down and responded favorably to congressional (and thus, presumably, public) preferences.

The third gateway is through current events, which can move public opinion and judges' behavior in the same direction. During the Vietnam War, as events in Southeast Asia led American citizens to oppose the war in greater numbers, those events also led federal judges to impose shorter sentences on draft dodgers.[68] As society became more progressive on women's rights and same-sex marriage, judges, who themselves are members of society, presumably became more progressive on those issues, too. Immediately after the attacks of September 11, 2001, Americans were increasingly willing to allow the government to examine personal mail and Internet activity (see Chapter 6), and judges moved in the same direction.

Fourth, judges might believe that they have an obligation to rule consistently with public opinion, even if they are not subject to electoral sanctions. It is probably no accident that the Supreme Court's split decision in the Michigan affirmative action cases reflected America's ambivalence about whether equality meant treating everybody exactly the same or whether, to promote equality of outcomes, underrepresented groups should be given advantages in admissions. Justice O'Connor, who split the difference over what can be done in the name of equal protection in the *Gratz* and *Grutter* cases, has spoken often about the need of the Supreme Court not to vary too far from public preferences.

That argument cuts both ways. As Justice Robert Jackson declared in a 1943 case striking down mandatory flag salutes, "The very purpose of a Bill of Rights was to withdraw certain subjects from . . . political controversy, to place them beyond the reach of majorities and officials and to establish them as legal principles to be applied by the courts. One's right to life, liberty, and property, to free speech, a free press, freedom of worship and assembly, and other fundamental rights may not be submitted to vote; they depend on the outcome of no elections."[69] If justices are responsive, it is not because the Constitution's framework requires it; it is because they choose to be.

Master the Concept
of The Judiciary with the MindTap™ Logo for American Government

REVIEW MindTap™ **for American Government**
Access Key Term Flashcards for Chapter 13.

TEST YOURSELF MindTap™ **for American Government**
Take the Wrap It Up Quiz for Chapter 13.

STAY CURRENT MindTap™ **for American Government**
Access the KnowNow blog and customized RSS for updates on current events.

STAY FOCUSED MindTap™ **for American Government**
Complete the Focus Activities for The Judiciary.

⭐ Key Concepts

adversary process (p. 420). How does the adversary process seek to discover truth?

affirmative action (p. 420). Why might Justice Sotomayor view affirmative action differently from other justices?

amicus curiae (p. 427). Why might courts care about the position in a case taken by an *amicus curiae*?

appeal (p. 421). What sort of questions can generally be appealed to a higher court?

class action lawsuit (p. 426). How do class action lawsuits promote equality in the legal system?

civil suit (p. 421). Why do civil suits exist?

common law (p. 421). What led to the development of common law?

concurring opinion (p. 431). Why might a justice concur in an opinion rather than dissent?

countermajoritarian difficulty (p. 433). Why is the countermajoritarian difficulty a bigger problem for the federal courts than for most state courts?

courts of appeals (p. 421). What is the role of the U.S. courts of appeals?

criminal case (p. 421). What is the most likely outcome when a criminal case is filed?

dissenting opinion (p. 431). How might dissenting opinions influence the public's view of the Supreme Court?

district courts (p. 421). What is the role of the U.S. district courts?

en banc (p. 423). Why might losing litigants prefer to appeal *en banc* rather than to the Supreme Court?

judicial activism (p. 433). How do judges who are judicial activists behave?

judicial independence (p. 440). Why does the United States need judicial independence?

judicial restraint (p. 433). What is the evidence for the practice of judicial restraint at the Supreme Court level?

judicial review (p. 422). How does judicial review create the countermajoritarian difficulty at the federal level?

jurisdiction (p. 422). What generally happens if a court does not have jurisdiction to hear a case?

majority opinion (p. 429). Why is the majority opinion so important for the Supreme Court?

Marbury v. Madison (p. 422). What doctrine did the *Marbury* case establish?

petition for a writ of certiorari (p. 426). How often are petitions for writs of *certiorari* granted?

plea bargain (p. 428). Why is plea bargaining so prevalent?

precedent (p. 421). Why is a general rule for the following of precedent essential to justice?

rule of four (p. 430). How does the rule of four work?

solicitor general (p. 427). What is the role of the solicitor general?

Learning Outcomes: What You Need . . .

To Know	To Test Yourself	To Participate
Describe what the judicial branch does		
The American legal system is based on the English system, following an adversary process, guaranteeing a right to trial by jury, and depending on common law in the absence of statuary authority. The Constitution established the Supreme Court. Congress has created federal district courts and courts of appeals. The Supreme Court has both original jurisdiction and appellate jurisdiction. Through the power of judicial review established in *Marbury v. Madison*, the Supreme Court has the authority to declare laws and executive actions unconstitutional and thus void.	• Summarize the U.S. legal traditions that derive from English legal traditions. • Restate what the Constitution says about the organization and powers of the federal judiciary. • Explain *Marbury v. Madison* and its importance.	• Assess whether courts are gateways to citizen influence and to justice. • Determine the extent to which judicial review is consistent with democratic government.

To Know	To Test Yourself	To Participate

 Explain how state and lower federal courts operate

State cases that contain issues of federal law or that contain particular types of parties can be appealed from state courts to the federal courts. District courts conduct civil and criminal trials, while courts of appeals hear appeals from district courts. Cases from the courts of appeals can be appealed to the Supreme Court.	• Explain how state court cases can end up in federal court. • Give an overview of the responsibilities and procedures in district courts. • Give an overview of the responsibilities and procedures in courts of appeals.	• Understand what would happen if federal courts could not review state court decisions on questions of federal law. • Evaluate whether average citizens are able to use the gateway of filing lawsuits.

 Review the procedures the Supreme Court uses

Supreme Court decisions are made by a majority, though the justices sometimes write concurring opinions that agree with the majority but give a different rationale. The minority who disagree may write dissents.	• Explain how cases reach the Supreme Court. • Describe the process of oral argument.	• Read and critique a recent majority opinion (http://supreme.lp.findlaw.com).

 Identify factors that influence judicial rulings and the impact those decisions have

Judicial policy making can be explained by both legal and extralegal approaches, with legal approaches having more sway at lower levels and extralegal approaches at higher levels, where judicial activism can be problematic for a democracy. Although the Supreme Court is not directly accountable to the public, it is to some degree responsive to public opinion.	• Survey how the Court reaches and issues decisions. • Discuss the impact Court decisions do and do not have.	• Evaluate why and whether Supreme Court decisions might have limited impacts. • Identify the gateways that create responsiveness of Supreme Court decisions to public opinion.

 Discuss how federal judges get selected

The president appoints federal judges with the advice and consent of the Senate. The higher the court, the more likely the Senate is to scrutinize nominees and refuse consent on the basis of nominees' ideology and/or qualifications. The Supreme Court, which once contained only white male Protestants, has increasingly diversified with respect to religion, race, and gender. This more-equal access to the Supreme Court may also make the Court more responsive to an increasingly diverse nation.	• Explain senatorial courtesy. • Describe issues in nominations to courts of appeals. • Discuss the ways in which partisanship and ideology influence Supreme Court nominations.	• Consider the merits of diversity in the courts.

 Outline how the Supreme Court has expanded and contracted national powers

Through the Court's history, its interpretations have expanded, then contracted, and once again expanded national powers, especially with regard to economic regulation. After a long and slow start, the Court has also moved, fairly consistently, toward greater protections of equality.	• Describe the ways in which the Marshall Court expanded national power. • Explain how the Supreme Court acted to limit equality between the 1830s and 1930s. • Discuss what might have led the Supreme Court to accept greater national authority starting in 1937.	• Understand why it is important for courts to protect minority rights.

"Get involved. You have no idea what you can accomplish until you become unstoppable…. If I had a nickel for every time someone said we would fail, I would never have to work again."

KATE HANNI
College of the Redwoods,
Eureka, California

14

Economic, Domestic, and Foreign Policy

When Kate Hanni was a student at the College of the Redwoods, she was a theater arts major who dreamed of being a rock star—"to be in front of a gazillion people with their lighters on," as she put it. Today she is a different kind of rock star, founder and first president of Flyersrights.org, a coalition group that claimed a major victory when the Department of Transportation ruled that domestic airlines must allow passengers who have been stuck on a stranded plane for more than three hours to get off the plane. Since that rule was passed, it has been extended to international airlines that operate in the United States for delays lasting more than four hours. Flyersrights has become a powerful gateway organization for advocacy on behalf of travelers seeking safe and well-regulated modes of transportation.

Hanni had not planned to be a political activist. For years, she was a successful real estate broker in Napa County, California, who enjoyed spending time with family and friends and still sang on occasion with her rock band, the Toasted Heads. But in 2006, her life took a new direction. With 134 other passengers, she and her family were stranded for nine hours and sixteen minutes in a jet parked at the airport in Austin, Texas. There was little food or water, and the lavatories reeked. "People got so angry they were talking about busting through the emergency exits," Hanni recalled. "I was fuming. It was imprisonment."

When Hanni got home, she drafted an online petition demanding legal rights for airline passengers. The following month, when an ice storm at New York's Kennedy International Airport stranded thousands of passengers in planes for up to eleven hours, her cause took off. She gave up her real estate business, and she and her husband took out a line of credit on their house to build a website. Soon her petition had eighteen thousand signatures, and people in her e-mail network wrote to Congress and the Federal Aviation Administration and posted videos of the stranded flight experience on YouTube. Hanni got media attention, promoting passengers' rights in radio and TV interviews. Her coalition gained support from airline labor unions, air traffic controller unions, and consumer groups. She talked her congressman, Mike Thompson (D-CA), into introducing legislation. The following year, Hanni staged a "strand-in" near the Capitol in Washington D.C., with a tent outfitted to resemble the interior of an airplane and invitations to members of Congress to see what it felt like to be trapped. As the movement's theme song, she got the Toasted Heads to rewrite the Animals' 1965 hit, "We've Gotta Get Out of This Place."

Need to Know

14.1 Outline the steps in the policy-making process

14.2 Identify the key federal programs that comprise domestic policy

14.3 Explain how the federal government intervenes in the economy

14.4 Evaluate the effectiveness of U.S. foreign policy

 WATCH & LEARN MindTap™ **for American Government**
Watch brief "What Do You Know?" videos
summarizing Domestic Policy and Foreign Policy and National Security.

In response, the airlines fought back by claiming that conditions were not as bad as reported. The Air Transport Association argued that deplaning would only cause delays and cancellations and might compromise passenger safety. A version of Congressman Thompson's bill passed the House, but a similar bill introduced by Barbara Boxer (D-CA) did not pass the Senate. New York and California passed airline passenger laws, but a federal court of appeals struck down New York's law on the grounds that only the federal government has the authority to regulate airline service.

In the end, that's exactly what happened. On December 21, 2009, Transportation Secretary Ray LaHood announced new airline regulations. After two hours on the tarmac, airlines must give passengers food and water. After three hours, they must let them off or face stiff fines—$27,500 per passenger. In an e-mail to supporters, an elated Hanni called the regulations "an early Christmas present" but reminded them that "we're not done yet!" Five years later, in 2014, Hanni and the organization she founded is still active; citing fees for checked bags and chronically delayed or canceled flights, she continues to advocate for passengers' rights and push for formal legislation to more strictly oversee airline travel.[1]

The story of Kate Hanni is remarkable because she, as an ordinary citizen, demanded that the federal government live up to its responsibility of ensuring the safe travel of passengers. She took matters into her own hands and used the gateways of citizen influence on policy making to draw attention to the issue. Her activism changed federal policy on transportation.

Through this book, we have looked at examples of activists and how they and the groups they joined have transformed the policies that affect each of our daily lives. We have examined the minimum wage, fracking, the assault weapons ban, the use of drones, the death penalty, voter ID laws, and unemployment laws—just to name a few. In this chapter, we will bring it all together, giving these issues a wider context and providing an in-depth description of the policy-making process in the domestic, economic, and foreign arenas and examples of the process in each of these arenas. We will look at the formal process of policy making, the ways in which the government interacts with the private sector in implementing domestic and economic policy, and the effectiveness of foreign policy in promoting U.S. values and interests around the globe. A fundamental question for students of American government is whether public policy making serves as a gate or a gateway to effectively serving the peoples' interest.

 # 14.1 Public Policy under a Constitutional System

> ❯ Outline the steps in the policy-making process

public policy:
Intentional actions of government designed to achieve a goal.

Public policy can be described as the set of laws and regulations that govern American political and social life to meet a specific need and accomplish a goal. It is in the arena of public policy—in determining who gets what, when, and how, and with what result—that we can see whether the constitutional system created by Madison and the Framers really works. Can the people pursue policies that advance their own interests? Can the people's representatives, while pursuing policies that advance their constituents' interests, produce a nation that looks out for the welfare of all the people?

With a government deliberately designed to represent competing interests, public policy has tended to cycle. One argument gains favor, driving policy in one direction. But new problems arise, calling for a redirection of policy. In the early years of the American republic, for example, Congress raised tariffs (taxes on imports) to help support new manufacturing enterprises, which could then undersell foreign competitors. But when agricultural interests complained about having to pay high prices for foreign goods, Congress lowered tariffs. Banking policies were similarly adjusted, sometimes to favor debtors and other times to favor creditors.

LISTEN & LEARN
MindTap® for American Government

Access Read Speaker to listen to Chapter 14.

The Process of Policy Making

The development of good public policy is always difficult and complex. A policy, for example, of providing tax benefits to homeowners to spur home ownership sounds like a good thing, as would policies that make it easier for people to obtain mortgages. It would help homeowners, support the home construction industry, and create jobs, building more stable communities. But what sounds simple rarely is that simple because there are usually unintended consequences. A policy of tax benefits for homeowners can also encourage sprawl that turns agricultural land into suburbs, thus decreasing crop yields and altering food production, while leaving cities with vacant housing and declining tax bases. Making it easier for people to obtain mortgages means more people default on their loans when the economy goes into a downturn, as happened during the most recent recession (2007–2009). Subsequently, government responds to these new problems by developing additional policies to revitalize agriculture, urban infrastructure, and the banking system.

With so many competing interests and the potential for unintended negative consequences, government seeks to pursue policy making that maximizes benefits and minimizes costs. This is not easy and often does not happen. Political scientists—scholars who study politics and the processes of government—have categorized the steps in policy making to make the process more understandable.

The main stakeholders in the policy process include members of Congress, the president, the executive branch agency that deals with the issue, the courts, political parties, interest groups, and interested citizens. These stakeholders attempt to formulate a policy that will address the problem (see Figure 14.1).

Although presidents and members of Congress formally appear to be in command of the federal policy-making process, they face a complex set of gates standing in the way of implementing policy. In Chapter 3, Federalism, we explained how governmental powers are shared among the federal, state, and local governments. Frequently, policy changes at the federal level require cooperation from these other governmental units, and that can be a complicated task across all fifty states. Encouraging all the states to adopt the same policy is not always possible, at which point, the federal government must step in and implement the policy itself. In this chapter, we discuss economic, domestic, and foreign policy and show how public policy is an outcome of all the actions taken by a wide array of stakeholders at the federal, state, and local levels.

The first step is **problem identification** of the problem. For example, constituents might complain to members of Congress that the cost of college is too high. The second step is for the issue of the cost of higher education to make it to the **policy agenda** of policy makers.[2] Of all the problems that government might be able to solve, only a small fraction can receive attention at any one time. Those that get on the policy agenda get the attention of Congress, the president, the executive branch agency that deals with the issue, the courts, political parties, interest groups, and interested citizens. These stakeholders attempt **policy formulation** that will solve the problem (see Figure 14.1). In the example of the

→ KEY QUESTIONS:
What is the definition of public policy? How does government balance the costs and benefits of a policy?

★ **problem identification:** *The first step in the policy-making process, in which a problem in politics, the economy, or society is recognized as warranting government action.*

★ **policy agenda:** *The second step in the policy-making process, in which a problem that has been identified gets the attention of policy makers.*

★ **policy formulation:** *The third step in the policy-making process, in which those with a stake in the policy area propose and develop solutions to the problem.*

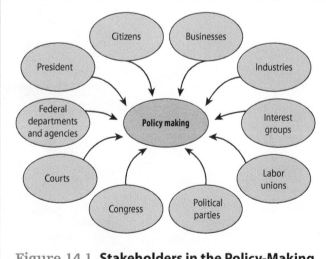

Figure 14.1 Stakeholders in the Policy-Making Process

© CENGAGE LEARNING

policy enactment:
The fourth step in the policy-making process, in which Congress passes a law that authorizes a specific governmental response to the problem.

 policy implementation:
The fifth step in the policy-making process, in which the executive branch develops the rules that will put the policy into action.

 policy evaluation:
The final step in the policy-making process, in which the policy is evaluated for its effectiveness and efficiency; if changes are needed, the issue is placed back on the policy agenda, and the cycle starts again.

 regulatory process:
System of rules that guide how a law is implemented; also called the rule-making process.

 regulations:
Guidelines issued by federal agencies for administering federal programs and implementing federal law.

high cost of college, the stakeholder network considered three proposals: direct federal loans to college students; promoting private loans by paying banks the interest on student loans while the student is in college; and guaranteeing the loans if students are unable to repay them.

In a fourth step, **policy enactment**, the legislative branch passes a law that enacts one or more of those proposals, as Congress did with student loans in 2010. Following passage, the legislature grants the executive branch **policy implementation** authority over the program. In this case, the Department of Education was given the authority to direct the student loan program. After a few years, Congress may engage in **policy evaluation** of the program. Following this policy evaluation, the cycle of policy making might begin again with new legislation to adjust the program to make it work better (see Figure 14.2).

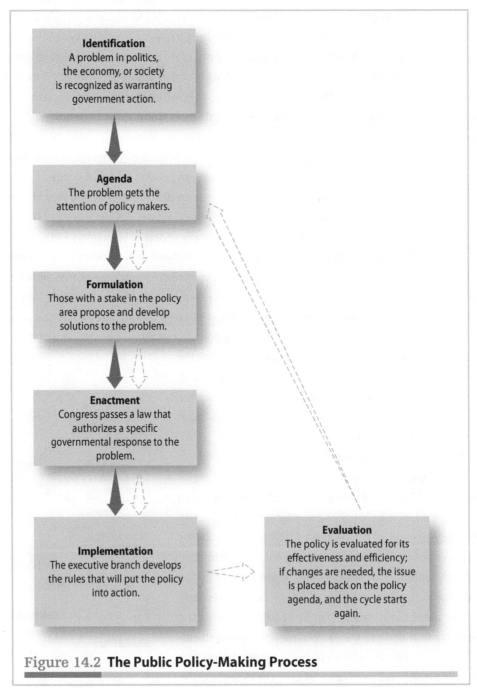

Figure 14.2 The Public Policy-Making Process

© CENGAGE LEARNING

In this chapter, we will focus on domestic, economic, and foreign policies. In each of these domains, the stakeholders mentioned earlier wield influence in different ways, depending on the characteristics of the issue being considered. In most cases, the origins of an implemented policy start with Congress when it passes a law, and the president approves it (discussed in more depth in Chapter 10, Congress). But in other cases, the president can use his executive regulatory power to effect change without a new congressional law, or Congress can decide to change funding allocations for specific programs in order to slow down or prevent their implementation. In the next section, we will examine more closely this second method of policy implementation.

The Regulatory Process

For laws to be implemented, there must be rules to instruct policy makers, government officials, organizations, and businesses. The formal responsibility for policy implementation falls to the bureaucracy in what is commonly called the **regulatory process** (see Figure 14.3). The current framework for the regulatory process has its foundation in the Administrative Procedures Act (APA) that Congress passed in 1946 to provide a consistent blueprint for all federal agencies in the issuing of regulations.

The federal government typically issues regulations when a law is first enacted and when a new circumstance or policy need arises that requires updates to the way the law is implemented. One such circumstance might be a change in the political control of the White House. Frequently, an incoming president of a different party issues new regulations to reverse the previous administration's policies. More commonly, a new president instructs federal agencies and the Office of Management and Budget (OMB), which oversees budgetary and regulatory issues, to revise existing regulations to better reflect his policy preferences. For example, in April 2014, President Obama issued an executive order requiring private contractors doing business with the federal government to pay the men and women they employ equal wages for equal work.

The bureaucracy produces these regulations by working within a process that begins with identifying the agency that has jurisdiction. The agency in charge will then offer preliminary **regulations** during which the political appointees of the agency will determine whether they are in line with the president's policy views. Although the bureaucracy is theoretically supposed to be insulated from direct political pressure, the reality is that the president's policy preferences are considered during this process.

When there is some agreement on the content of the preliminary regulations, they are submitted to the Office of Information and Regulatory Affairs (OIRA) within the OMB for approval to be printed in the *Federal Register*, the official published record of all executive branch rules, regulations, and orders. As noted previously, the OMB must review all regulations before they take effect. When preliminary regulations appear in the *Federal Register*, a period for public comment is defined (typically outlined in the originating legislation) ranging from thirty to ninety days. During this period, ordinary citizens, interest groups, and relevant industries and businesses can submit their opinions to the agency about the regulations. In

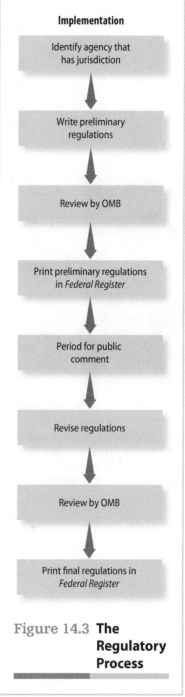

Implementation

Identify agency that has jurisdiction

↓

Write preliminary regulations

↓

Review by OMB

↓

Print preliminary regulations in *Federal Register*

↓

Period for public comment

↓

Revise regulations

↓

Review by OMB

↓

Print final regulations in *Federal Register*

Figure 14.3 **The Regulatory Process**

© CENGAGE LEARNING

Federal Register: *Official published record of all executive branch rules, regulations, and orders.*

→ KEY QUESTIONS:
What role can citizens play in the regulatory process?

addition, the agency or its local affiliate can hold public hearings in locations across the country to solicit opinions on the regulations.

Based on all the responses it receives, the responsible agency revises the preliminary draft regulations and issues final regulations. These are once again sent to the OMB and then are published in the *Federal Register* thirty days in advance of taking formal effect. Once the final regulations are issued, the program is officially ready to be implemented. A current example of this process concerns the disposal of coal ash from coal-burning power plants. After a major coal ash spill into local rivers and streams in Tennessee, environmental groups pushed the EPA to issue new regulations outlining the requirements for safe coal ash disposal. The preliminary regulations were issued in October 2009, but after the public comment period was up, the EPA still had not issued final regulations. In response, environmental groups, led by Earthjustice, sued the EPA, and a judge forced the agency to agree to issue the final regulations by December 19, 2014. Only a few days later, a second major coal ash spill occurred in North Carolina, adding more pressure for the EPA to act in a timely manner.[3] Such extreme delays in issuing final regulations are not typical, but this example shows how the regulatory process itself can act as a gate to effective oversight of industry and environmental protection.

Public comments are a vital part of the regulatory process because they are a gateway by which citizens can communicate their opinions about the impact of policy to regulators. Here residents of communities affected by fracking offer their comments to the Environmental Protection Agency on proposed regulations.

Blocking Implementation

Even after final regulations are issued, groups can challenge the legality of them in the federal court system. For example, in 2014, the Supreme Court considered a challenge to regulations issued requiring the inclusion of contraception in employer-sponsored health insurance plans under the Affordable Care Act. In the case, *Hobby Lobby v. Kathleen Sebelius, Secretary of Health and Human Services et al.*, the Court ruled in favor of Hobby Lobby being able to opt out of the guidelines in the final regulations for some forms of contraception (see Chapter 4, Civil Liberties, for more on this case). In addition to court action, the House or Senate can pass appropriations bills with language that prevents an agency or department from using federal money to implement the regulations. However, the president typically threatens to veto the bill if this type of language is included because it undermines his policy priorities and, more broadly, his executive power to implement laws. As a result, legislative leaders usually remove such language in the final version of appropriations bill sent to the president (see Chapter 10 for more on the appropriations process).

State Governments and Public Policy

As we noted in Chapter 3, it is important to understand how the federal government interacts with state government in implementing policy and, at the same time, how states interact with each other. In this section, we will take a closer look at how states can influence each other through processes referred to as policy diffusion and the race to the bottom.

Policy Diffusion. In a 1932 opinion, Supreme Court Justice Louis Brandeis wrote, "It is one of the happy incidents of the federal system that a single courageous State may, if its citizens choose, serve as a laboratory; and try novel social and economic experiments without risk to the rest of the country."[4] The main benefit of states serving as laboratories of change is that other states can learn about successful programs and copy them or learn what not to do if an experimental program fails. This takes place through a process known as **policy diffusion**, and it typically starts with states that border one another. Examples are numerous, including the Children's Health Insurance Program,[5] regulation of air pollution,[6] school choice plans (allowing students to choose which school in a district to attend),[7] health care reform,[8] and Indian gambling casinos.[9] States learn not only from neighboring states but also from their local governments. Such was the case with antismoking ordinances, which cities and towns successfully adopted before states did.[10]

The federal system of government requires cooperation between the national and state governments, and federal policy is frequently implemented by state governments. Here governors meet to discuss proposed changes to federal educational guidelines during a meeting of the National Governors Association.

★ **policy diffusion:** *Process by which policy ideas and programs initiated by one state spread to other states.*

The Race to the Bottom. If diffusion is the good side of policy making in a federal system, the race to the bottom can, depending on one's point of view, potentially involve negative consequences. A race to the bottom exists when states compete against each other to reduce taxes, environmental protections, or welfare benefits in order to create incentives for businesses to come to the state or disincentives for poor people to come. For example, lower tax rates draw people to a state, yet to keep people there, the state cannot raise taxes even when the public might desire more spending.[11] When states compete economically with one another, if one state decreases environmental enforcement, a neighboring state may be forced to do so as well.[12] In terms of welfare benefits, individuals seeking benefits move to the most generous states. This situation led states to establish residency requirements for welfare until the Supreme Court prohibited them.[13] Consequently, states that want to increase welfare benefits for their own citizens hesitate to do so unless neighboring states also do so, lest they attract an overload of recipients from those other states.[14] Alternatively, the Obama administration established a "Race to the Top" (RTTP) in education, whereby states that implement education reforms, such as increasing the number of charter schools, receive more federal aid. This action coincides with increasing federal involvement in education over the past fifty years.

→ KEY QUESTIONS:
How does policy diffusion serve as an example of policy making in a federal system?

Checkpoint

CAN YOU:

- Identify the steps in the policy-making process
- Summarize the stages of the regulatory process
- Describe how regulations can be blocked from taking effect
- Explain what is meant by policy diffusion

14.2 Domestic Policy

> Identify the key federal programs that comprise domestic policy

The term domestic policy covers a wide range of policy areas in which the government plays a role, at the federal, state, and local levels, in the lives of average citizens. Table 14.1 lists the major federal programs generally considered under the category of domestic policy, when they were originally enacted into law at the federal level, and a brief description of what they do.

Throughout the book, we have covered major issues in domestic policy, including public education (see Chapter 3), affirmative action (Chapter 13, The Judiciary), and workplace equality (Chapter 5, Civil Rights). In this chapter, we explore three major areas of domestic policy that are sparking intense debate today: entitlement programs, income security, and health care; immigration; and energy and environmental policy. In each of these issue areas, we will provide an overview of public policy and then analyze an example of how a specific policy has been crafted and implemented (see Public Policy features).

Table 14.1 **Major Federal Programs**

Names	Year	Description
Social Security	1935	Old age retirement insurance program that pays a monthly amount to retired workers
Unemployment Insurance	1935	Temporary replacement income for job loss
Social Security Disability Insurance	1935	Payments to individual who can no longer work due to disability
Supplemental Security Income	1972	Subsidy for low-income individuals who are over 65, or blind, or disabled
Medicare	1965	Health care insurance for elderly and disabled
Medicaid	1965	Health care insurance for low-income individuals
Temporary Aid to Needy Families	1935	Subsidy for low-income individuals with children; originally known as Aid to Families with Dependent Children but replaced in 1996 by TANF
Food Stamps	1964	Subsidy for low-income individuals for food purchase
Public Housing Assistance	1937	Subsidy for low-income individuals for housing
Immigration and Nationality Act	1952	Laws governing documented entry and citizenship into the United States
Clean Air Act	1963/1970	Laws requiring minimum standards for air quality; amended in 1970 to create the Environmental Protection Agency
Clean Water Act	1972	Regulations for the discharge of potential contaminants into water sources
Affordable Care Act	2010	Mandate requiring every individual to have health insurance coverage and providing access and subsidies through exchanges and expanded Medicaid

Entitlement Programs, Income Security, and Health Care Overview

During the twentieth century, the federal government enacted laws to create a social safety net to provide income stability for the elderly and disabled, and assistance with food, health care, and housing for the poor. **Social Security** is one of the largest and likely best-known federal domestic policy programs; it is essentially a federally guaranteed pension program funded by taxes imposed by employers and workers. Social Security was created in 1935 as part of the set of policy programs known as the New Deal proposed by President Franklin Delano Roosevelt (1933–45) (see Chapter 11, The Presidency). The New Deal represented a major change in the relationship between the federal government and individuals by establishing a set of programs that would guarantee payment to an individual if he or she met certain criteria, for example, age, children, low income, or disability. This type of program is commonly known as an **entitlement program**, which means that an individual is "entitled" to receive the benefit as long as they qualify under these criteria. The passage of the Social Security Act marked the beginning of the transformation of the role of the federal and state governments in providing a social safety net for individuals in need of financial assistance as well as aid to secure food, housing, and health care.

Social Security itself is a mandatory retirement account for all workers that is funded by taxes paid by both employers and workers. The amount of Social Security retired workers receive is calculated based on the amount of time they worked while paying into the program; when they retire, they receive a monthly payment direct from the federal government. The drive to provide this kind of income security for individuals was in large part a response to the dire effects of the Great Depression, which left millions of people without jobs and income. At the same time, the federal government created Unemployment Insurance, which is run by state governments according to federal guidelines; it provides short-term payments to workers who lose their jobs and is funded by taxes imposed on employers.

In addition to these programs, which are targeted at the working population, the Social Security Act of 1935 and its subsequent legislative expansions have created several other programs that are designed to help individuals who need assistance supporting themselves or their families. Two of these, Social Security Disability Insurance and Supplemental Security Insurance, are designed to help those who are no longer able to work, or who have a disability that prevents them from working full time. Another major program is Temporary Aid to Needy Families (TANF), which is a program to provide payments to women in poverty with children (it was originally called Aid to Families with Dependent Children). The majority of this program's costs are funded by the federal government through a single amount of funding per year, known as a block grant, although states are expected to contribute a minimum amount of money to help administer the program.

In addition to income security, as part of the New Deal, the federal government also put in place sets of programs to help individuals get mortgages to buy housing through the Fannie Mae Corporation and to build affordable housing by offering subsidies to developers. These programs were aimed at helping people buy houses because that was believed to help ensure financial stability and help the economy through new housing construction.[15]

In the 1960s, under President Johnson's Great Society initiative (see Chapter 11), these types of income security programs were expanded to include health care, food security, and expanded

Social Security: *Federal pension program that makes a monthly payment to retired elderly workers and disabled persons.*

entitlement programs: *Federal programs, such as Social Security, Medicare, or Medicaid, that pay out benefits to individuals based on a specified set of eligibility criteria.*

COMPARE WITH YOUR PEERS
MindTap™ for American Government

Access the Economic Policy Forum: Polling Activity—Reforming Social Security.

→ KEY QUESTIONS:
What policy goals do entitlement programs address?

AP IMAGES/J. SCOTT APPLEWHITE

Senior citizens who are recipients of Social Security and Medicare are very vocal in seeking to protect their benefits. Here a group of elderly activists traveled to Capitol Hill in Washington D.C. to oppose proposed cuts to those programs.

★ **Medicare:** *Federal health insurance program for the elderly and disabled.*

★ **Medicaid:** *Shared Federal and state health insurance program for low-income persons.*

→ KEY QUESTIONS:
Why has the implementation of the Affordable Care Act been so complicated?

housing assistance. In terms of health care, **Medicare** was created as a federal program, funded through a payroll tax that provided health insurance to people over the age of 65. **Medicaid** was created as a shared program between the federal and state governments, funded through general taxation, to provide health care coverage for low-income people.[16] The Food Stamp Program, today known as Supplemental Nutritional Assistance Program, was designed to provide money to low-income families to purchase food and household items and is fully funded through general taxation. Lastly, federal housing assistance was expanded under the Section 8 program to provide payments to housing developers to cover the rental costs of housing for low-income individuals who typically must pay a minimum of $25 or 30 percent of their income toward rent under the program.[17]

It has been nearly eighty years since the passage of the Social Security Act, and the federal government has expanded many of the programs the Act first established, but not without controversy and opposition. When the Social Security Act was first passed, opponents claimed it was an overreach of federal power to take money from individuals only to give it back to them in their later years. Moreover, establishing other anti-poverty subsidies that would be paid directly to lower income individuals might create a dependency on that payment that would discourage them from securing independent financial security. Lastly, opponents of expanding the role of the federally guaranteed safety net have argued that as the population expands and lives longer, the cost of these programs is unsustainable. Currently, the net cost of entitlement programs is $1.22 trillion, which is nearly 34 percent of the federal budget for fiscal year 2014.

The federal bureaucracy, specifically the Department of Health and Human Services (HHS), is largely responsible for administering these programs in conjunction with state and local government. We provide a brief overview of HHS in Chapter 12 (The Bureaucracy), but here we embed it in the larger context of the expansion of the federal role in health care over the past decade. The most recent such expansion came with the Affordable Care Act, which was enacted in 2010 and requires all individuals to purchase health insurance, either on their own, or if they are low-income, with subsidies from the federal government.

The American health care system includes private and public health care insurance components. Most Americans receive health insurance through their employment or purchase it independently from private insurance companies; as noted previously, federal programs are available to help cover the costs of health insurance. At the federal level, the Department of Health and Human Services is responsible for overseeing these programs, as well as implementing new ones. Each state also has a department of health, as do many cities and counties, and, importantly, states also have the power to regulate insurance providers who provide coverage there.

The process by which the Affordable Care Act (ACA), otherwise known as Obamacare, moved from proposal to bill to law was long and winding, as lawmaking always is, and it was especially complicated because of the fragmented nature of America's health care system, party politics and partisanship, and the heightened political rhetoric that surrounded the effort (see Chapter 10 for details). Ultimately, the Democrats used their majority party power in the House and Senate to pass the law, with no Republican support.

The primary impetus of the law was to provide access to health insurance to the nearly 10 percent of Americans who did not have it. They did not have health insurance for a range of reasons: their employer did not offer it; they were self-employed and could not afford to purchase it; they were unemployed but not poor or old enough to qualify for a government program; or they were deemed ineligible by private insurance companies because they had health conditions that made them high risk and expensive to cover.[18]

The ACA established a number of new programs, the most notable of which extended access to health insurance coverage to uninsured citizens and legal immigrants through an expansion of Medicaid eligibility and the provision of federal subsidies to workers to purchase private health insurance through health insurance exchanges that would be set up by states, or if the states refused, by the federal government directly.[19] The act provided for increased regulation of the medical services covered by private health insurance companies, mandated that individuals carry health insurance, required that young adults under the age of 26 be able to stay on a parent's insurance policy, and banned the denial of health insurance or an increase in premiums based on a preexisting condition. The act also increased payment levels to doctors who participate in the Medicaid program and helped senior citizens by closing a loophole in Medicare coverage for prescription drugs. The ACA is an important example of how the domestic policy process works, from the passage of the law to its implementation.

The Affordable Care Act (ACA)

The implementation of the act came in stages, with some of the regulations issued very soon after the bill passed, and others taking much longer to finalize. Part of the delay was attributable to a key lawsuit filed against the bill claiming that provisions included in it were unconstitutional. Twenty-six state attorneys general signed onto a lawsuit challenging the constitutionality of the federal health insurance mandate included in the law. The lawsuit made its way to the Supreme Court, which ruled in June 2012 and upheld the mandate (see Chapter 10).

The Court case cleared the way for implementation of the insurance provision through health care exchanges under ACA. However, only fourteen states set up their own health insurance exchanges; the federal government established exchanges in the remaining thirty-six states. The federal government established a six-month sign-up period to obtain coverage through the federal website, www.Healthcare.gov, or state websites that linked to the federal site. The federal website opened for business on October 1, 2013, but there were major problems from the start. The website crashed frequently, and concerns were raised about the security of the information people entered into the website. Ultimately, the problems with the website were resolved, but in the meantime, consumers had become wary of both the website and the program. Opponents of the program kept up a relentless attack both at the state and federal levels, and the negative communications were thought to have depressed enrollment numbers.[20] At the same time, and despite President Obama's oft-repeated declaration, "If you like your health insurance, you can keep it," health insurance policies for millions of Americans were canceled by insurance companies because these policies did not meet the minimum standards of coverage mandated by the ACA. In response to the public outcry over these cancelations, the Obama administration extended the timeline for switching to more comprehensive policies.

The ACA also encourages states to expand Medicaid to cover individuals at or below 138 percent of poverty because the federal government will pay the extra costs of the expansion for up to three years. As of September 2014, twenty-seven states agreed to the Medicaid expansion, with twenty-one refusing it, and two states still considering it.[21] Additionally, individuals who make between 100 percent and 400 percent of poverty level are eligible for subsidies where the federal government will help pay for part of the cost of their premiums.[22] Traditionally underserved communities, such as Latinos, are estimated to comprise nearly 25 percent of those eligible for coverage under ACA, and the Obama administration made it a point to engage in targeted outreach to encourage enrollment among them.[23]

In terms of overall costs of health insurance premiums under the ACA, Figure 14.4 shows how the costs can vary across states, income levels, and the extent of available federal

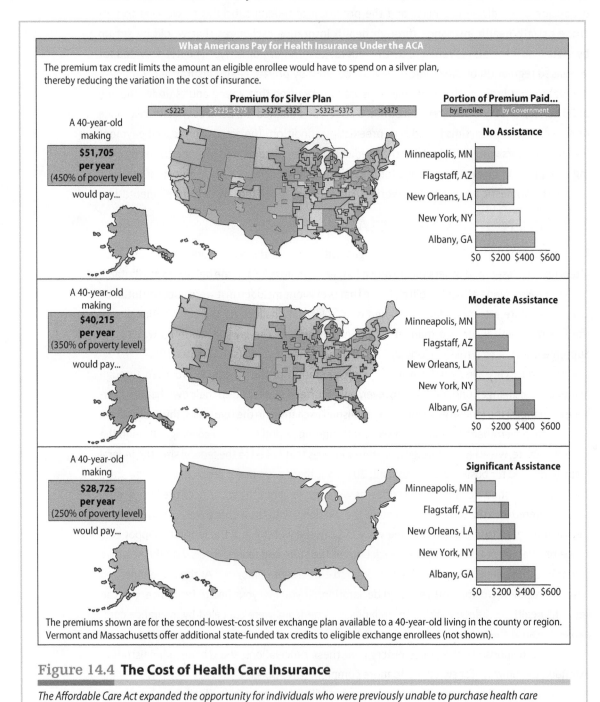

Figure 14.4 The Cost of Health Care Insurance

The Affordable Care Act expanded the opportunity for individuals who were previously unable to purchase health care insurance to buy it through state or federal run insurance exchanges. Figure 14.4 shows the estimated costs of health care insurance to individuals depending on personal circumstances.

Source: Kaiser Family Foundation, "Visualizing Health Policy: What Americans Pay for Health Insurance under the ACA," March 19, 2014, accessed March 19, 2014, http://kff.org/infographic/visualizing-health-policy-what-americans-pay-for-health-insurance-under-the-aca/.
© 2016 CENGAGE LEARNING

subsidies.[24] The dynamics surrounding the ACA reflect the complexity of implementing health care policy for millions of Americans across states. At the end of the first enrollment period, as we noted in Chapter 8, Political Parties, more than 8 million people had signed up to get health insurance through the ACA, a number which was above the Obama administration's target. Despite the rollout pitfalls and intense opposition, the program was up and running in 2014. However, Secretary of Health and Human Services Kathleen Sebelius ultimately took the blame for all the problems surrounding the initial implementation of the ACA; she resigned her post in April 2014 after serving for five and a half years and was replaced by Sylvia Mathews Burwell (our vignette subject in Chapter 11). The ACA brings up the larger question of whether major policy overhauls can be accomplished without bipartisan support in the American federalism structure because states are so vital in the implementation process. Without their full cooperation, it becomes much more difficult for a federal program to succeed.

Immigration Policy Overview

Another very important and often contentious issue in the public policy sphere is immigration policy—for both legal and unauthorized immigration. The Department of Homeland Security, the Department of Justice, and the Department of State share jurisdiction over immigration policy. Immigration has fueled U.S. population growth since the nation's founding, and the United States now comprises citizens with ancestries from many different foreign lands. In 2012, there were 13.3 million legal permanent residents in the United States—people born outside of the United States who have been granted legal status and reside in the United States.[25] The largest percentage of foreign-born people come from Latin America (mostly Mexico), followed by Asia and then Europe. Immigration laws serve simultaneously as gates regulating entry into the United States and as gateways to eventual citizenship. For those individuals who entered the United States without authorization and have put down roots, there is no current pathway to legal citizenship available. However, children who are born to unauthorized immigrants living in the United States are legal citizens because of the Fourteenth Amendment to the Constitution.

The Legal Immigration Process.   The legal immigration process is jointly administered by the Department of State and the U.S. Citizenship and Immigration Services (USCIS), an agency of the Department of Homeland Security. Immigrants seeking to come to the United States apply for visas, which are granted by the Department of State; once they arrive, their journey toward citizenship is overseen by USCIS.[26]

To come to the United States with the intention of staying on a permanent basis, individuals can apply for a general immigration visa, a family relations visa, or an employment visa. The Immigration and Nationality Act of 1990 sets an annual limit of between 416,000 and 675,000 on these types of visas; in addition, 50,000 visas are set aside for people born in countries that have recently had the lowest numbers of immigrants to the United States.[27] In 2013, 459,751 individuals entered the United States as legal permanent residents.[28]

→ KEY QUESTIONS:
How do immigrants become naturalized citizens?

To become a naturalized citizen, an immigrant must first apply to be a legal permanent resident (LPR) of the United States, a step known as getting a green card, which is the permanent resident card issued to those who are eligible. (The green card is no longer green, but the name has remained.) To get a green card, an individual must secure a sponsor who will attest that the individual has some means of financial support. The individual must also take a medical

DOMESTIC POLICY   **467**

Immigrants go through a long and complex process to become a naturalized U.S. citizen. In this photo, immigrants who have come from many different nations are sworn in as U.S. citizens.

exam and secure proof of employment if he or she intends to hold a job in the United States. This criterion can present a significant barrier to permanent residency: The federal government requires an individual seeking permanent residence to have talents or skills for a particular job that a current U.S. citizen could not provide. Marriage to an American citizen can also serve as a gateway to a green card, although the federal government has imposed stricter oversight on such marriages to counteract fraud. In 2013, the federal government also extended this gateway to apply to same-sex marriages, in response to the Supreme Court ruling in the DOMA case, which struck down discrimination against same-sex partners under federal law.[29] To become a fully naturalized U.S. citizen, a green card holder must reside in the United States continuously for at least five years; be able to read, write, and speak English; pass a citizenship test on the history and government of the United States (see Chapter 5); and pledge support for the United States.[30]

The Debate over Unauthorized Immigration.

In recent years, pressure to reform immigration laws to address the issue of unauthorized immigration has mounted because of the millions of individuals who have entered the United States outside the legal immigration process.[31] Proponents of reform argue that individuals who arrived illegally but have since established productive lives should be legally incorporated into society and have the opportunity to be full and active citizens, a position that opponents refer to as "amnesty." Opponents tend to counterargue that individuals who broke the law to enter the United States must be forced to return to their country of origin and apply for legal immigration status, and that without stronger border security, the hope of amnesty will just drive greater unauthorized immigration. The Republican and Democratic Parties are split along these lines as well; Democrats are stronger supporters of immigration reform that includes amnesty, while Republicans support a stronger border enforcement program with no amnesty.

The last major piece of legislation to deal specifically with unauthorized immigration was the 1986 Immigration Reform and Control Act, which passed with bipartisan support and was signed into law by President Ronald Reagan (1981–89). The act granted amnesty, or forgiveness, to almost 2.8 million individuals who had entered the country without authorization and wished to stay as legal residents.[32] The 1986 reform bill did not stem the flow of unauthorized immigrants to the United States. In 2007, President George W. Bush (2001–2009), a Republican, and the Democratic-controlled Congress tried to produce a new immigration reform bill that would give unauthorized immigrants who were already in the United States an opportunity to become citizens but would, at the same time, discourage future unauthorized immigration. They failed to reach agreement.

→ KEY QUESTIONS:
Why is immigration the responsibility of the federal government? Should that change—why or why not?

One reform bill that gained traction was the Development, Relief, and Education for Alien Minors proposal, known as the DREAM Act, which would allow children who entered the country illegally with their parents to get on a path to legal citizenship at age 16 if they have been in the country for five years, have graduated from high school, and have no criminal record.[33] In his first term, President Obama announced his support for the DREAM Act. By June 2012, Congress had not passed it, so, using his authority over border control and national security, President Obama ordered the Department of Homeland Security to stop the deportation of young people who met the criteria of the DREAM Act and allow them to apply for temporary work permits. Although it did not create a full path to citizenship, President Obama's action did partially implement the policy goals of the DREAM Act.[34]

Local and Federal Action on Unauthorized Immigration.   States and localities, especially those along the border with Mexico, have tried to address unauthorized immigration in their own ways and in opposite policy directions. States with Republican-dominated legislatures have taken more punitive action than those controlled by Democrats. The most publicized effort took place in Arizona, where in April 2010 then-Governor Jan Brewer signed a law, S.B. 1070, that allowed police officers to ask about immigration status when they stopped individuals for any other police inquiry. Under the law, it was a crime to fail to show documentation establishing legal residence in the United States, and police officers could hold someone until their immigration status was verified.[35] Later that year, the U.S. Justice Department sued to get the law struck down in federal court on the basis that the state was infringing on the proper role of the federal government on immigration. The case made its way to the Supreme Court in 2012, and in *Arizona v. United States*, the court struck down the law because it assumed state powers over immigration that are granted to the federal government.

Not all state responses to unauthorized immigration have been punitive. For example, California, Texas, and New Mexico each adopted policies that allow unauthorized immigrants to receive private and public aid to attend state colleges and universities. Their justification is that it is better to educate residents who are in the United States so that they can contribute to society than it is to put up gates against their educational and economic advancements.

Ultimately it will be a major challenge for policy makers in both major political parties to construct a holistic immigration policy that is both fair and practical. Although there is general agreement within the core membership of each party, there are enough dissenting voices on how to best cope with illegal immigration that a clear policy position may not emerge. One factor that might affect the future of immigration reform is the growing number of Latinos in the United States who typically express strong opposition to punitive measures on unauthorized immigration. As the number of Latino voters grows, the United States may see more convergence on a single policy position by the parties in an effort to win this increasingly important voting bloc.

Energy, Environmental Policy, and Climate Change Overview

The public policy sphere of energy and environmental issues is ever expanding, from the domestic production of energy in the coal, oil, and natural gas sectors, to the protection of clean air and water, to the cleanups of toxic waste, to the global concern over climate change. Over the course of the twentieth century, these issues became ever more important with the expansion

supreme court cases

Arizona v. United States (2012)

QUESTION: Does the supremacy clause prevent the state of Arizona from supplementing federal immigration law?

ORAL ARGUMENT: April 25, 2012 (listen at http://www.oyez.org/cases/2010-2019/2011/2011_11_182)

DECISION: Decided June 25, 2012 (read at http://caselaw.lp.findlaw.com/scripts/getcase.pl?court=US&vol=000&invol=11-182)

OUTCOME: 5–3. The Supreme Court struck down three restrictions in the law.

As noted in Chapter 3, the national government has only those powers granted to it in the Constitution. While the remaining powers remain with the states, the supremacy clause declares that where federal and state laws conflict, federal law is supreme.

In response to a large influx of undocumented persons across the border with Mexico into Arizona, the Arizona State Legislature passed S.B. 1070. The United States believed that the law encroached on federal power to regulate immigration and sought to prohibit enforcement of its provisions. A federal district court found four provisions to be beyond the constitutional authority of Arizona to regulate: (1) creating a state-law crime for being unlawfully present in the United States, (2) creating a state-law crime for working or seeking work while not authorized to do so, (3) requiring state and local officers to verify the citizenship or alien status of anyone who was lawfully arrested or detained, and (4) authorizing warrantless arrests of aliens believed to be removable from the United States.

All eight of the justices hearing the case (Justice Kagan did not participate due to her prior work

on issues related to the case while in the Justice Department) agreed that the provision requiring local police officers to check the immigration status of anyone lawfully arrested was constitutional. With Justices Scalia, Thomas, and Alito dissenting in part, a majority of the justices held that the rest of the provisions violated the supremacy clause given Congress's regulation of the subject.

The Court, in an opinion by Justice Kennedy, held that the Constitution's grant to Congress to "establish an uniform Rule of Naturalization," combined with Congress's extensive regulation of immigration deprives states of the authority to 1) make it illegal under state law for people to enter the United States without legal documentation, 2) make it illegal under state law for people without proper documentation to find employment, or 3) allow warrantless arrests of people believed to be in the United States without proper documentation. In all three provisions, the Court ruled that Congress's regulation of those facets of immigration were so extensive that states were "preempted" from adding to those regulations.

1. Why do you think the Arizona legislature might have passed the law in question?

2. Do you think any of the Arizona provisions were in fact unconstitutional; that is, they would be invalid even if Congress had not extensively regulated the areas in question?

of manufacturing, population growth, geographic mobility, technology, and consumer consumption of natural resources. In the 1960s, however, Americans became increasingly concerned about the impact of new energy and other technologies on the environment. Rachel Carson's epic study of the effects of pesticides on the bird population, called *Silent Spring*, provoked an intense debate between large chemical companies and the scientific community and created national concern that gave rise to the environmental movement. The United States took sweeping steps to regulate the effects of energy use on the environment in 1963, when Congress passed the **Clean Air Act** to reduce pollution in response to growing public concerns and calls for stricter government controls.[36] However, in order to effectively oversee the government's role in regulating the environment, it became necessary to create an agency with jurisdiction specifically designed to protect the environment. Consequently, Congress revisited the Clean Air Act in 1970 and created the Environmental Protection Agency (EPA) to implement the Act.

Since that time, the federal government has grappled with balancing the need to protect the environment and the nation's need for energy sources to fuel the economy and everyday living. Over the past forty years, the nation has experienced several energy crises where the demand and cost of energy, for example, gasoline prices, rose so high that businesses and consumers suffered. In response, the government has encouraged alternative sources of energy as well as the expanded development of fossil fuels in the United States. Today, the nation is almost to the point where it is entirely energy self-sufficient, which somewhat reduces the reliance on foreign nations for energy and at the same time, decreases the chances of getting involved in international conflicts waged over energy.[37]

Just as the United States depends on energy to drive its economy, developing nations around the world also require energy as their economies grow. As nations around the world expand their economies and increase the standard of living for their residents, pressure builds on both the supply of energy that is required to fuel that economic growth and the environmental impact of that growth. Fears regarding global climate change are fueled not only by the continued reliance of developed countries on fossil fuels but also by the increased consumption of fossil fuels by nations such as India and China in their efforts to develop industrialized economies.[38] There is an inherent tension between industrialized nations that have used the world's energy resources freely for more than a hundred years and more recently developed nations that are seeking to industrialize their economies. Now that more advanced nations are concerned about the environment—and climate change in particular—they want to encourage, even require, all nations to use energy-efficient technology. However, this type of technology can be expensive and add to the costs of production, which developing nations fear would slow their economic growth. Although the international community has tried to forge agreements with developing nations to limit pollution and other damage to the environment, those efforts have not been widely successful.

The United States has had more success pursuing domestic energy policies. Within the federal government, the EPA shares jurisdiction with the Department of Energy and the Department of Interior over federal energy and environmental policy from regulating carbon emissions and auto fuel efficiency, to granting leases to drill for oil and natural gas both on- and offshore of the continental United States. In rare instances, the Department of State might also be involved in environmental policy if it will have an international impact. We discuss one such case in this chapter (see Public Policy and the Environment: Keystone XL Pipeline). Once an agency has been created, it is responsible for policy implementation within its jurisdiction. When the federal government proposes a policy change in an issue area whether

Clean Air Act: *Broad federal legislation that expanded the federal government's ability to monitor and protect the environment against pollution.*

→ KEY QUESTIONS:
What is the federal government's role in protecting the environment?

Checkpoint

CAN YOU:

■ Define entitlement and identify two federal programs as examples

■ Explain the process by which the Affordable Care Act passed and how it is being implemented

■ Describe the arguments for and against immigration reform

■ Outline the development of energy and environmental policy

■ Evaluate the Keystone XL Pipeline debate in the context of U.S. energy policy

independently, or as a response to a new law passed by Congress, the agency with jurisdiction in that issue area issues regulations to guide implementation.

Domestic policy, such as health care, immigration, and environmental protection, has several important layers. Congress and the president enact laws, which are then implemented by the executive branch through the regulatory process. At the same time, state and local governments are also helping to implement federal policies, as well as put in place policies that fall under their own set of powers (see Chapter 3). There are advantages and disadvantages to this layering; on the one hand, layering acts as a gateway for a wide range of voices to be heard in the policy process, but on the other hand, layering can serve as a gate that stands in the way of quickly and efficiently addressing important policy issues.

14.3 Economic Policy

> Explain how the federal government intervenes in the economy

Ever since the founding, Americans have debated about whether and how the federal government should intervene in the economy. For the first 100 years of the nation's existence, the major source of government intervention in the economy was to impose taxes (known as tariffs) on goods imported from outside the country. Tariffs served as both a way to protect domestic industries and to raise revenues. But as the economy grew in the late 1800s, pressure mounted to regulate the growth of big business and working conditions, which resulted in a series of laws ranging from antitrust (against big monopolies) to laws designed to guarantee safety in the workplace. In the twentieth century, the federal income tax replaced tariffs as the key financing mechanism for federal government spending. The reality in today's world is that the government is heavily involved in the economy and that U.S. fiscal and monetary policy has a major impact in the national and international arena. The federal government intervenes in the economy to support economic development, regulate business practices, oversee banking and finance, and maintain a safety net of retirement, unemployment, and disability benefits.

An Overview: Intervention in the Economy

Beginning with Theodore Roosevelt (1901–1909), presidents have overseen the federal role in the nation's economy; some have wanted more intervention, and some have wanted less. Republican presidents typically want to lower all taxes, a policy that provides less revenue to the federal government and subsequently decreases federal spending. Democratic presidents have typically wanted to cut taxes for individuals with lower incomes and to raise taxes on wealthier citizens to support federal programs. The key advisors to the president on economic policy are the Secretary of the Treasury, the National Economic Council, and the Council of Economic Advisers. The president also appoints the chairman of the Federal Reserve (discussed later in this section), which has a major role in monetary policy. The set of stakeholders in federal economic policy includes the president, Congress, business interests, and consumers (see Figure 14.5).

When the economy is weak, there is pressure on the president to take extraordinary steps to strengthen it. This is what President Franklin Roosevelt did during the Great Depression and what President Obama did in response to the 2007–2009 recession. A **recession** is typically

recession: *A period of time marked by successive quarters of lower economic output.*

defined as a downturn in economic activity, with declines in employment levels, income, retail spending, and industrial production. The 2007–2009 recession was attributed largely to inflated housing prices, irresponsible lending by banks, and excessive borrowing by consumers, all of which led to widespread foreclosures and the collapse of major sectors of the financial and construction industries. When people lose jobs, consumer spending declines, forcing business and industry to cut back production and lay off workers, potentially leading to a vicious circle in which consumer spending declines even further, forcing businesses and industry to cut back production even more and lay off ever more workers.

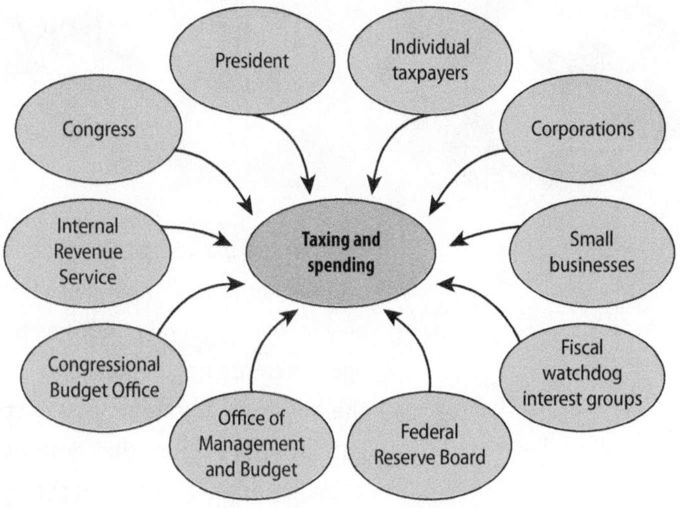

President Obama responded to the economic crisis by adopting a mixed strategy on taxes and spending. He continued President George W. Bush's program, which effectively bailed out banks, and he instituted a bailout program for the auto industry; the majority of those funds have been paid back to the government with interest. Additionally, he worked with Congress to enact a nearly $800 billion stimulus bill that was a combination of spending increases favored by Democrats and tax credits (which amount to tax cuts) favored by Republicans to boost the economy. Because raising taxes during a recession is widely believed to have a negative impact on consumer spending and job growth, Obama and Congress extended tax cuts in 2010 and 2012.

Just as there are specific stakeholders that often participate in the formation and implementation of economic policy, there are also specific tools that have been developed over time that are used to achieve specific economic goals.

Figure 14.5 **Stakeholders in Federal Economic Policy**

A diverse set of public and private organizations and individuals impact economic policy.

© CENGAGE LEARNING

→ KEY QUESTIONS:
How can the federal government intervene in the economy during periods of economic recession?

Fiscal Policy

Government can use fiscal policy to intervene in the economy through taxing and spending. Fiscal policy can also be used to manipulate the money supply to avoid recession. More spending or lower taxes increase the money supply, while lower spending or more taxes decrease the money supply. In times of severe economic crises, the president may support a policy of increasing the money supply to ward off a recession. Alternatively, an increase in prices can cause workers to demand raises. Higher wages will lead to even larger increases in prices, setting off inflation. In this case, the president may support a decrease in the money supply to ward off or reduce the extent of inflation. It also remains true in the American economic system that there is a business cycle, based on innovation, production, and consumer demand, which operates independently but simultaneous to the implementation of government economic policy. In other words, both the private and public sector shape the direction of the economy.

Monetary Policy

The president is limited in his power to directly influence the nation's economic conditions because monetary policy is under the control of the **Federal Reserve Board**, an independent

Federal Reserve Board: *Independent regulatory commission that affects the money supply by setting the reserve requirements of member banks, establishing a discount rate for loans to member banks, and buying or selling government securities.*

Public Policy and the Environment:
Keystone XL Pipeline

Against the backdrop of higher energy costs, projects such as the Keystone XL oil pipeline, a Canadian-funded pipeline that would run from Canada to the Texas coast, underscore the way in which federal policy has to balance the nation's demand for energy and employment against competing demands to live in a clean and safe environment. Energy projects such as the Keystone XL can act as a gateway for Americans today in terms of jobs, but it can be a gate against a future that ensures a clean environment in which to live and work. It serves as an important example of the dynamics of domestic policy making because it involves the executive branch, Congress, interest groups, private industry, and even a foreign nation.

In 2008, the energy company TransCanada submitted an application to the State Department to build a 1,700-mile oil pipeline from Alberta, Canada, to Nederland, Texas.[39] Because the project crossed over the border from a foreign nation, it fell under the jurisdiction of the U.S. State Department, which does not normally have a role in this policy area; the State Department required TransCanada to submit an application for a presidential permit.[40] The State Department also conducted a study for an Environmental Impact Statement (EIS) to see if the pipeline would have any adverse environmental effects on the regions through which the pipeline would run. Although the State Department was designated as the lead agency for the review of the project, the EPA was also involved and reviewed the environmental impact of the project.[41]

Almost two years later, the State Department released a draft of its EIS, which stated that the construction and operation of the pipeline would have minimal environmental impacts. The State Department then solicited public comment on the draft. By the time the opportunity for public comment closed, it had received thousands of public comments from interest groups and industry members on the proposal. In 2011, the State Department released its final EIS, which concluded that the project was in line with President Obama's environmental policies.[42]

Although the State Department gave the go-ahead for the project, the EPA and numerous environmental interest groups were not persuaded by the State Department's findings. Congress also reflected the division over the pipeline, where representatives from both sides of the aisle struggled over the project and its merits. Proponents of the project saw it as key to economic growth in the United States, while opponents had serious concerns about the potential for environmental damage from a pipeline leak. The Republican majority in the House of Representatives wanted to push President Obama into making a final decision on the project, so, as part of a bill to extend the payroll tax cut (see Chapter 11), they attached a provision requiring that the president issue a decision within sixty days. Obama responded by denying TransCanada the permit to build the pipeline, citing inadequate information to gauge its full environmental impact. One major concern was the pipeline's proximity to the Sand Hills region that covers the Ogallala Aquifer, which provides most of the drinking and irrigation water for the Midwest. In response, TransCanada reapplied for the permit proposing a route that avoided the Sand Hills region in Nebraska[43] (see Figure 14.6).

Throughout the presidential permit process, numerous interest groups, including labor unions, environmental activists, and energy producers, stated their positions on the Keystone

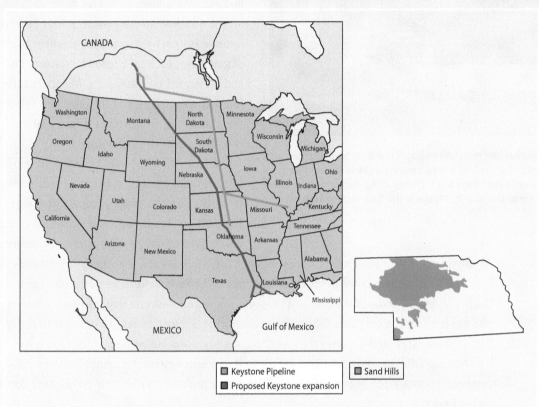

Keystone Pipeline
Proposed Keystone expansion

Sand Hills

Figure 14.6 **Keystone Pipeline Map**

© Cengage Learning, *Source:* Laris Karklis/The Washington Post. http://www.washingtonpost.com/national/health-science/canadian-firm-to-push-ahead-with-part-of-keystone-pipeline/2012/02/27/glQAvJftdR_story.html/; for the state of Nebraska, http://www.montrealgazette.com/technology/route+Keystone+pipeline+proposed+through+Nebraska/6486974/story.html.

XL Pipeline. In an interesting twist, labor and energy interest groups were allies, as both supported the construction of the pipeline. Environmental groups vigorously voiced their objections against the pipeline. In contrast, both the House and Senate passed resolutions calling for the approval of the pipeline. In fact, the amount of public response was so great that President Obama announced in 2014 that he had to delay his final decision on the Keystone XL Pipeline because the public comments on the project numbered in the millions, and the administration needed more time to consider all the views expressed on both sides of this issue.

▶ **Construct Your Own Policy**

1. Propose a policy review process for energy-related proposals that you believe is more efficient than current practice.
2. Suggest alternative routes for the delivery of oil from Canada that would address environmentalists' concerns.

A number of Federal Reserve chairmen have served multiple terms, and under different presidents. The chair of the Federal Reserve is Janet Yellen, who was nominated by President Obama in October 2013, confirmed by the Senate, and took office in January 2014; she is the first female Federal Reserve chair in history.

agency that serves as the nation's central bank, increasing or decreasing the money supply by changing the reserve requirements—the amount of cash reserves that banks must keep on hand. To control the flow of money in the economy, Congress created the Federal Reserve in 1913 as a system of twelve regional banks in one national banking system. The Federal Reserve System is led by a seven-member board of governors, each nominated by the president and confirmed by the Senate. Members serve fourteen-year terms, and the president selects the board chair, who serves a four-year term, with the option of reappointment.

When the Federal Reserve increases reserve requirements, banks have less money to lend, and the money supply decreases. This action tends to raise interest rates. When the Federal Reserve decreases reserve requirements, banks have more money to lend, and thus the money supply increases (see Table 14.2). This move tends to lower interest rates. The Federal Reserve Board also controls the money supply through the discount rate, which is the interest rate that the Federal Reserve charges other banks on loans. When the discount rate is lower, banks are not able to charge high interest rates on the money they lend to consumers and businesses.

Although the president can name people to the Federal Reserve, he cannot fire them if they promote monetary policy that differs from his policy preferences. His only power over them comes from the nomination process.

The power of the federal government to steer the economy has been debated since our nation's founding. In times of crisis, the president and Congress can enact programs that target specific problems, as in the case of the auto industry bailout and stimulus

→ KEY QUESTIONS:
What roles do fiscal and monetary policy play in the economy?

Table 14.2 Comparison of Fiscal and Monetary Policy

Actions by Congress and the president affect fiscal policy, while actions by the Federal Reserve Board affect monetary policy.

Type of Policy	Policy Maker	Action	Direct Effect	Effect on Money Supply
Fiscal	Congress, president	Increase spending or cut taxes	Consumers have more money to spend.	Increases
	Congress, president	Decrease spending or increase taxes	Consumers have less money to spend.	Decreases
Monetary	Federal Reserve Board	Increase reserve requirement	Banks have less money to loan.	Decreases
	Federal Reserve Board	Decrease reserve requirement	Banks have more money to loan.	Increases
	Federal Reserve Board	Increase the discount rate	Loans are more expensive.	Decreases
	Federal Reserve Board	Decrease the discount rate	Loans are less expensive.	Increases

package. But more generally, it is the Federal Reserve that has a strong role in setting monetary policy by setting interest rates, which in turn controls the flow of money to businesses and individuals seeking to take out loans.

Trade Policy

International trade—the exchange of commerce with other nations—is also an integral component of our nation's economic policy. In the twenty-first century, trade remains an important gateway to economic, political, and cultural relationships with other nations, though in recent years the nation has begun to import more goods than it exports.

Protectionism versus Free Trade. Trade policy has long been aligned with foreign policy and has been used by the United States to export both capitalism and democracy. International trade policy is complex because each nation wants to negotiate deals that give its industries the greatest advantages either to sell their goods abroad or to be protected from cheaper imports from foreign nations. A policy that protects against foreign imported goods more than it promotes exports is known as **protectionist**, and a policy that strikes down barriers on imported foreign goods is known as **free trade**. A third and relatively recent policy, **fair trade**, encourages foreign trade as long as there are comparable working conditions and wages within the industries in the trading nations. Environmental regulation has also become increasingly important in trade negotiations. If one nation exploits its workers with long hours, unsafe conditions, environmental pollution, and low pay to produce and sell goods more cheaply than another, it violates fair trade practices. When a nation violates fair trade practices, individuals may boycott its products, or, more significantly, other nations may refuse to trade with it.

The president takes the lead in negotiating international trade agreements, either bilaterally (with one other country) or multilaterally through the office of the United States Trade Representative (USTR), an office created within the Executive Office of the President by President John F. Kennedy (1961–63) in 1963. The USTR is responsible for negotiating the terms of international trade agreements. To present a balanced position on behalf of the U.S. government, the USTR solicits information and feedback about the potential impact of the trade agreement from import- and export-related industries, cabinet departments, and members of Congress. Gathering such information is helpful not only in crafting an agreement that benefits U.S. industries but also in building the necessary support to get the trade agreement ratified by Congress.

During the late nineteenth and twentieth century, protectionist trade policies enabled U.S. industries to corner the consumer market and make huge profits. Businesses reinvested those profits in developing technology and in expanding so that the United States became the major supplier of manufactured goods throughout the world. It did not face strong competition in the world marketplace until the late 1980s, when Japan, China, and India developed their industrial capacity sufficiently to become competitive in a number of economic sectors. They replicated the U.S. policy of exporting their goods while maintaining trade barriers against the import of U.S. goods.

In the decades since, the United States has forged multilateral trade agreements designed both to expand export markets for U.S. goods and to allow more imported goods. The Canada Free Trade agreement, followed by the **North American Free Trade Agreement (NAFTA)**, created a free trade zone of goods and services across the northern and southern borders of the United States, creating jobs nationwide. However, some industries, such as the domestic textile

protectionist: *Policy designed to raise import barriers for goods that are domestically produced.*

free trade: *Policy designed to lower import barriers to encourage trade across nations.*

fair trade: *Policy designed to make sure that the working conditions are relatively equal in nations that trade with each other.*

→ KEY QUESTIONS:
What are the advantages and disadvantages of free trade over protectionism?

NAFTA: *Comprehensive multi-nation trade agreement ratified in 1994 that knocked down trade barriers among Canada, the United States, and Mexico.*

globalgateways

The Rise of the European Union

The European Union today consists of twenty-eight member nations that cooperate on economic and political issues such as monetary policy, trade subsidies, immigration, and international criminal justice. Although each EU member nation retains its own separate government and control over its military, all member nations agree to abide by the decisions of the European Union. In joining together under a single formal institution, these nations now constitute a powerful trading partner. Many of the EU nations also share a common currency, the euro, although the United Kingdom, Sweden, and Denmark are among those that have retained their own currencies.[44] By adopting a common currency that is not tied to a single nation's economy, the EU has achieved a greater role in shaping international monetary policy. However, when one EU member nation suffers a major financial crisis, as Greece and Spain recently did, there can be widespread negative effects on financial markets across the globe.

For the United States, the expansion of the European Union means that it must now consider the effects of its trade and monetary policies on a number of countries simultaneously, rather than working out agreements with each nation separately or in smaller groups. Indeed, in 2014, the United States forged ahead with a proposed trade agreement, known as the Transatlantic Trade and Investment Partnership (TTIP), which treats the EU as a single collective trading partner.

1. What is the European Union and why was it formed? Does it have its own currency?

2. Is the formation of the European Union as a trading bloc a good development for the United States' economy? Why or why not?

Legend:
- 1952
- 1973
- 1981
- 1986
- 1995
- 2007
- 2013

© 2016 CENGAGE LEARNING

and steel industries, were adversely affected and lost jobs. Many business executives moved their production facilities to Mexico, where it was less expensive to produce goods. These goods could then be sold cheaply in the United States because, under the free trade agreement, no import duties could be charged. The impact of NAFTA is an example of the consequences of policies that are designed to integrate the U.S. economy into the global world of trade.

Six years after the passage of NAFTA, the United States normalized trade status with China, which reduced trade barriers and opened up Chinese markets to U.S. goods; in doing so, it also encouraged American producers of goods such as textiles, apparel, steel, and electronics to relocate their production facilities to China. More than a decade later, the United States has a large trade imbalance with China; for the first seven months of 2014, U.S. imports exceeded exports to China by nearly $186 billion.[45] A large trade imbalance means that the American consumers are buying far more goods made in China than Chinese consumers are buying goods made in the United States. Such an imbalance in trade can harm U.S. manufacturers who are trying to compete with Chinese imported goods (see Figure 14.7).

Figure 14.7 U.S. Balance of Trade, 1995–2014

Source: Adapted from Economic Research from the Federal Reserve Bank of St. Louis.

The increase in the number of economically developed nations as producers and consumers of goods, combined with the presence of U.S.-owned industries in these nations, has created a strong incentive for the United States to be a supportive partner in the international economy in order to encourage other countries to allow U.S. goods to be sold there.

Trade and International Economic Organizations. In addition to the unilateral trade agreements that it has struck with other nations, the United States also participated in the General Agreement on Tariffs and Trade (GATT), which governed multinational trade agreements between 1948 and 1994. In 1994, during the eighth round of GATT, the **World Trade Organization (WTO)** was created to deal with the explosive expansion of the global trade community and to establish a single international organization with the authority to resolve trade disputes.[46] If one country claims that another country is engaged in unfair trading practices, it can bring its case to the WTO; each party to the dispute must abide by the WTO's ruling or face monetary fines and trade limitations. For example, in 2009, China imposed a ban on broiler products, which covers chicken, from the United States, and the United States lodged a formal complaint with the WTO citing unfair trade practices, and the WTO formed a panel to resolve the issue.

 **World Trade Organization (WTO):** *International organization that considers and resolves trade disputes among member nations.*

It took nearly four years for the WTO to return a decision, and it ruled that China had violated fair trade practices and had to remove the barriers to imported chicken from the United States.[47] The slow pace of the WTO deliberation illustrates how an international organization can serve as a gate or obstacle to efficient resolution of economic disputes. Entering the WTO was a major change in U.S. trade policy because it required the United States to relinquish its right to act unilaterally in trade disputes. At the same time, by agreeing to abide by WTO rulings, the United States gave assurance to foreign nations that it would respect international rules and would be a fair and reliable trading partner while expecting other nations to do the same.

Public Policy and the Economy:
Federal Deficit and the Debt Ceiling

Although many experts credit President Obama's policies with warding off an even deeper recession, or depression, they temporarily increased the federal deficit, which in turn increased the federal debt. As we noted in Chapter 10, the federal deficit is the difference between the amount of money that the government takes in and the amount of money that the government spends. When the federal government runs a deficit, it must borrow money to make up the shortfall. Consequently, the federal government pays interest on this borrowed money, and the combined amount of the borrowed money and the interest that accumulates over time constitutes the national debt.

As the federal debt has risen in recent years, Americans have become increasingly concerned about burdening future generations with the task of paying it back. There are two components to the federal debt: public debt, which is the money that comes from issuing debt instruments, such as U.S. Treasury bonds, that investors buy with a promise of getting a set amount of interest on the bonds at a later date; and intragovernment held debt, which is the amount of money that the federal government borrows from itself when it transfers money from one program to another or uses built-up reserves in one program as collateral for borrowing. The **debt ceiling** is a cap on the amount of money that Congress authorizes the president to borrow to pay the federal government's bills. Before 1917, there was no legal limit on the government's ability to issue such debt. However, to fund operations for World War I, Congress passed the Second Liberty Bond Act, which allows the federal government to issue longer-term debt as long as Congress issues its approval for doing so.[48] Consequently, today the president must ask to raise the debt ceiling and cannot do so without congressional approval.

The issue of the debt ceiling has become a major source of contention between the president and Congress. When President Obama first took office, he inherited a federal deficit of $1.4 trillion and a total national debt of $11.9 trillion dollars (see Figure 14.8); both were the cumulative effect of past presidential policy making, including the Bush tax cuts and the Iraq and Afghanistan wars. But during the first two years of the Obama administration, the national debt climbed to $13.5 trillion.[49] In the 2010 midterm congressional elections, the Tea Party movement became active within the Republican Party in order to strengthen the GOP's existing commitment to reduce taxes and federal spending. When the Republicans won control of the House of Representatives, those members who were elected with Tea Party support stayed adamant in their position against raising the debt ceiling. As noted in Chapter 10, the majority of those members were reelected in 2012, as was President Obama, which maintained divided party control between Congress and the presidency. Since then, the Tea Party factions in the House and the Senate have maintained their opposition to increased federal spending.

In September 2014, the end of fiscal year 2014, the projected federal deficit stood at $486 billion, which was less than half the size of what President Obama inherited in 2009, but the national debt had risen to $17.9 trillion. During his term, the issue of the federal debt ceiling caused standoffs with Congress on two separate occasions.

In 2011 President Obama proposed a "grand bargain" that would have cut the debt by $4 trillion over ten years with a combination of spending reductions and increased taxes. Republicans in

debt ceiling:
The congressionally authorized limit on federal borrowing.

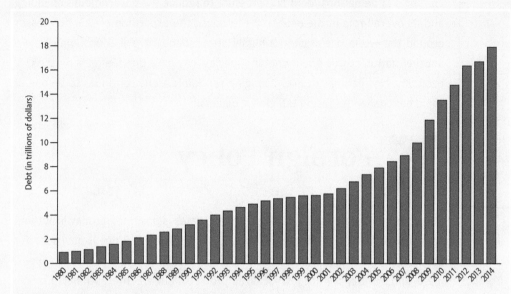

Figure 14.8 **U.S. National Debt, 1980–2014**

Source: The White House, Office of Management and Budget, Table 7.1, Federal Debt at the End of Year: 1940–2019, U.S. Budget for FY 2015, http://www.whitehouse.gov/omb/budget/Historicals/.

© CENGAGE LEARNING

the House rejected any plan that included tax increases. Eventually, the president, Senate leaders, and Speaker Boehner agreed to raise the debt ceiling in exchange for cutting $900 billion over ten years from the federal budget.

In October 2013, a similar scenario repeated itself, but this time, the Republicans in the House tied all government spending to the debt ceiling and refused to act unless implementation of the Affordable Care Act was delayed or repealed. This action resulted in a government shutdown that lasted sixteen days, and the United States came close to the brink of defaulting on its debt obligations. The public outcry over the government shutdown was so strong that Congress and the president came to a longer term agreement about the federal budget to try to avoid future shutdowns.

As this sequence of events reveals, the president does not have sole power over any element of the national economy; he shares power with Congress. This shared power arrangement can be a gate against efficient and responsive policy making in these areas, especially in times of divided party government.

Construct Your Own Policy

1. Devise a set of tax increases and budget cuts that you believe are fair and would reduce the federal deficit.
2. Create a mechanism for raising the federal debt ceiling that does not create conflict between Congress and the president.

European Union (EU): *Association of European nations formed in order to facilitate economic and political interactions across their borders.*

Checkpoint

CAN YOU:

- Describe the role of the federal government in times of economic crisis
- Identify the key tools of fiscal, monetary, and trade policy
- Define the federal deficit and debt and explain how they are related

Another significant development in international trade relations was the creation of the **European Union (EU)**, a major expansion of a preexisting European economic organization known as the European Community[50] (see the Global Gateways feature).

Economic policy is an enormously complicated arena in which the U.S. government tries to implement policies that will encourage stability and growth. In the past two decades especially, continuous deficit spending and severe swings in the economy have created a large national debt and pressure to reduce the government's spending and its overall role in the economy. Moreover, the expansion of U.S. businesses around the world has created a highly interdependent global economy, where another nation's trade and monetary policies may have direct effects on the U.S. economy. Navigating this ever-changing economic arena continues to be one of the great challenges facing U.S. policy makers.

14.4 Foreign Policy

> Evaluate the effectiveness of U.S. foreign policy

The international arena in which the United States is positioned today is nothing like the world in which the Framers wrote the Constitution. Travel to Europe is now a matter of hours instead of months; communication with all parts of the world is instantaneous. Conflict, disease, and poverty are not just localized problems but are international in scope. In this section, we examine how the United States came to its position as global leader and discuss the constitutional gates and international conditions that constrain its actions. As we noted in Chapter 11, the conduct of foreign policy is the purview of the executive branch led by the president as commander in chief but with significant input from Congress; the Department of Defense, the Department of State, the Department of Homeland Security, and the National Security Agency all play vital roles in our foreign and military policy.

An Overview: International Relations and U.S. Foreign Policy Goals

→ KEY QUESTIONS:
How has globalization changed the types of political challenges the United States must overcome?

globalization: *The interconnectedness of nations around the world on economic, political, cultural, social, and military dimensions.*

When the Framers wrote the Constitution, the United States, as a democracy, stood virtually alone in a world ruled by monarchs. Though independent and isolated by geography, the new nation was still vulnerable, and in its first years, it was caught up in European rivalries. In 1796, when he was leaving the presidency, George Washington (1789–97) warned against foreign entanglements: "The great rule of conduct for us in regard to foreign nations," he wrote in his farewell address, "is in extending our commercial relations, to have with them as little political connection as possible."[51] More than two hundred years later, Washington's isolationist tendencies have been swamped by the evolution of **globalization**, which intertwines the fate of the United States with hostilities, health crises and epidemics such as the Ebola virus, and natural disasters and environmental degradation wherever they occur.

With globalization, regional economies, societies, and cultures have become increasingly integrated through trade, capital investment, labor flows, migration, travel, and, most strikingly, the World Wide Web and instantaneous communication (for example, Twitter). In one sense, these changes opened the economic and political gates that long kept nations apart. People are today interconnected on multiple levels. Citizens of China drink Coke and eat McDonald's hamburgers, and Americans wear clothing with "made in China" on the label. Over the course of the late twentieth century and through today, developed nations have found it cheaper to manufacture goods in developing countries, and free trade is seen as a gateway to more open and democratic societies in nations previously closed to outside influences.

The interdependence of the new globalized world might sound like a formula for peace, but in fact the connections are complex. Being connected does not mean sharing political systems and religions, or even cultures below the level of popular culture. The differences that do exist have intensified in the new global age and have produced political, social, and military conflict. America has objective strategic interests that it must protect, such as maintaining its energy supplies from abroad, but it also has a strong commitment to human rights and democratic principles of government, and sometimes these guiding principles clash. As a leading military, diplomatic, and economic power, the United States has to balance the need to preserve its own interests against the benefits that arise from working with other nations under an international framework of laws and policies. To recognize the challenges the United States faces in achieving its goals today, we must first understand the nature of the international system and how it evolved.

The Origins of U.S. Foreign Policy.

In Russia, a **Communist** revolution installed a political and economic system that used government management of the economy to prevent large concentrations of private wealth. A long-term goal of this system was economic security and equality for all citizens. The Communist Party was the only political party in the new Soviet Union, stifling virtually all dissent. In Germany, a new democracy struggled such that voters elected Adolf Hitler and the Nazi Party who promised to restore Germany's economic and military power. Under Hitler's dictatorship, Germany became an aggressor once again, and in 1939, its invasion of Poland triggered the Second World War. In Asia, Japan had launched a similar course of aggression, and its air assault on Pearl Harbor on December 7, 1941, led President Franklin Delano Roosevelt (1933–45) to ask Congress for a declaration of war against Japan the next day (and against Germany and Italy on December 11, 1941, after those nations, in alliance with Japan, had declared war on the United States).

When WWII ended in 1945, Europe was on the brink of collapse. The United States emerged as a leading world power and could no longer sustain its isolationist policies. New weapons technologies, especially airpower, expanded the reach and level of destruction that one nation could impose on another. Roosevelt envisioned a peace in which an international organization could prevent aggression and meet humanitarian needs. The **United Nations** (UN) was founded in April 1945, and Congress ratified U.S. membership in December. Its headquarters was built along the East River in New York City, and it became a gateway for nations to interact with each other and try to resolve disputes in a neutral environment.

Hopes for a peaceful world were shortly shattered, however, as rivalry between the United States with its Western democratic allies and the Soviet Union and Eastern European states provoked a **Cold War**. As new nations emerged from the aftermath of the war, they were forced to align themselves with the forces of democracy or Communism. On March 12, 1947, President Harry Truman (1945–53) spoke to a joint session of Congress convened to consider a growing economic crisis in Greece. He clearly stated his belief that the economic stability of Greece was essential to keeping it from falling to the Communists. During

Frequently residents of foreign nations complain about the "Americanization" of their food and culture, but at the same time, American businesses are very successful internationally. Here we see customers at a McDonald's in Beijing, China.

Communist: *Government management and ownership of key elements of a nation's economy.*

CONNECT WITH YOUR CLASSMATES
MindTap™ for American Government

Access the Foreign Policy and National Security Forum: Discussion—Developing Foreign Policy.

United Nations (UN): *Organization formed after World War II to mediate disputes among nations around the world.*

Cold War: *An era in history marked by conflict and distrust between the United States and Communist nations.*

this speech, Truman set forth the policy that the United States would take active steps to preserve democracy and contain Communism throughout the world, a policy that became known as the Truman Doctrine or the policy of containment.

For the next decades, U.S. efforts to contain Communism involved the nation in military interventions, most notably in Korea and Vietnam but also in the Middle East and Latin America. As we saw in Chapter 11, these military interventions were undertaken by the president in his role as commander in chief. Presidential power grew in accord with America's commitment to world leadership. In an age when atomic bomb capabilities called for split-second decisions, the president's authority to command military response went mostly unchallenged.

Beginning in 1989, facing enormous economic difficulties and organized political dissent, the Communist regimes of Eastern Europe began to fall, which was symbolically represented by the collapse of the Berlin Wall which separated East (Communist) and West (democratic) Germany. In 1991, the Soviet Union itself disintegrated into separate states. Thus the United States could declare victory in the Cold War but now faced the challenge of winning and keeping the peace (see Figure 14.9).

The context for international relations at the end of the Cold War was vastly different from earlier eras. After that struggle ended, the old bipolar world of the two superpowers quickly became **multipolar**, with numerous centers of power competing for regional dominance and

→ KEY QUESTIONS:
What lessons can we take from the past and apply to foreign policy today?

⭐ **multipolar:** *A world system where there are distinct centers of political and military power.*

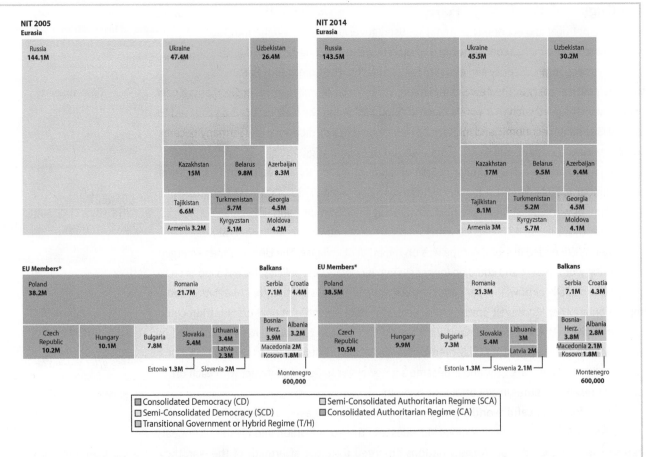

Figure 14.9 Chart of Nations that Used to Be Included in the Soviet Union

The Soviet Union consisted of a base country, Russia, and a number of other nations that had been brought under Russian control after World War II. Here we see the current level of democracy in those countries and whether they are more aligned economically with Russia or the European Union.

© 2016 CENGAGE LEARNING

with numerous regional conflicts. Since the end of WWII, many nations in addition to Vietnam and Iran had gained independence from such former colonial powers as France and the United Kingdom. Some of these nations—India and Indonesia, for example—had risen to prominence by attempting to remain neutral in the superpower struggle, forming the nonaligned movement (NAM). Modernization in China gave that huge nation new international stature. In the Middle East, tensions between Israel and the Arab states went unresolved. In Africa, decolonization had created a patchwork of new states across tribal lines struggling against corruption, poverty, and disease. And in the old Soviet bloc, especially in central Asia, new states struggled to suppress regional, religious, and ethnic hostilities and to resist Russian dominance. As we saw in 2014, Cold War tensions still resonate when issues of sovereignty emerge as they did with the Russian takeover of the Crimean peninsula, which was part of the country of Ukraine. In that case, the majority of residents in Crimea were of Russian descent and welcomed the aggressive takeover by the Putin-led government. Western nations responded by imposing economic sanctions on Russia, but tensions only escalated when Russian sympathizers in Eastern Ukraine waged war against the government. Russia kept control of Crimea, but a tentative cease fire was imposed in September 2014, in the eastern part of Ukraine.

CONNECT WITH YOUR CLASSMATES
MindTap° for American Government

Access the Foreign Policy and National Security Forum: Polling Activity—U.S. as the World's Superpower.

Foreign Policy Tools

Nations have a wide array of policy tools available to them. Some involve cooperation through bilateral or multilateral treaties, diplomatic relations, and aid; others entail conflict through the use of force or the threat of military action. In this section, we will examine how the United States uses these tools.

Military Action.   The president, as commander in chief, has always made the decision to engage in military action. Although Congress has formally declared war only five times, U.S. troops have been sent into conflicts and potential conflicts about 250 times since the beginning of the nation.[52] Today, in making the decision to engage in military action, the president is heavily influenced by the recommendations of the secretary of defense, the national security adviser, and the director of the Central Intelligence Agency.

For military missions that are publicized, not secret, a president usually enjoys widespread support if the mission can be clearly tied to preserving national security. In cases in which the United States is attacked on its own soil, support for a military response is even higher. This so-called **rally-around-the-flag effect** is a surge in patriotic sentiment that translates into presidential popularity.[53] For example, when President George H. W. Bush commenced the first Gulf War, his approval ratings shot up to 89 percent.[54] His son, President George W. Bush, experienced a similar spike in popularity after 9/11; his job approval ratings went from 52 percent to 90 percent, and they remained above 70 percent for almost an entire year.[55]

rally-around-the-flag effect: *Surge of public support for the president in times of international crisis.*

The public's influence on the president's decision to engage in military action is always limited because the amount of information available to the public is purposely restricted, both to ensure the safety of the troops involved and to preserve military advantages in conflict. Simply put, the president and his military advisers have access to far greater amounts of information than does the average citizen, and in turn, the average citizen expects the president to act on this information in a way that preserves national security. Even when Congress debates sending troops or funding military action, most classified information is held in secret and not revealed to the public (but see Chapter 4 on the Snowden NSA revelations).

⭐ **nonstate actors:** *Individuals or groups that do not represent any specific national government and may take action across borders.*

The fundamental imbalance of information held by the government and what the general public understands poses a major problem for the assumptions of a democracy because the people cannot hold the government fully accountable if they are not fully informed. Nevertheless, when a president decides to send troops, he has to anticipate public reaction and hope that the public maintains its trust and confidence in his decision to take such action.

The twenty-first century had ushered in new weaponry and new levels of violence committed by nations and **nonstate actors**, such as terrorist groups who take up violence against civilians as a means of attacking the United States and other Western nations.

The Bush administration used this new reality to justify military action against the Taliban regime in Afghanistan. President George W. Bush went one step further to launch a preemptive attack—that is, an attack prior to an act of aggression by another—against Iraq in 2003 to remove Saddam Hussein from power and dismantle alleged weapons of mass destruction that might be used against the United States and its allies (see Chapter 11 for more on the Iraq and Afghanistan wars). In invading Afghanistan and Iraq, Bush was trying to leverage the full strength of the U.S. military to combat terrorism.

However, many critics argue that in conflicts between a state and nonstate actors, traditional military weapons and strategies are ineffective, and new tools, such as surveillance, intelligence gathering and analysis, and the use of unmanned drones, are the only way to prevent future attacks. The policy infrastructure dedicated to addressing terrorism has grown dramatically over the past decade, with a greater reliance on cooperation among the Department of Homeland Security (see Chapter 12), Department of Defense, Department of Justice, and the president's National Security Council. Coordinating across such a vast portion of the federal government can produce both gates and gateways to effective antiterrorism policies, both at home and abroad (see Chapter 4 and Chapter 6, Public Opinion and the Media, for more on U.S. anti-terrorism policy).

Anti-Nuclear Proliferation Measures. Compounding the challenges of fighting terrorism is the fear of nuclear proliferation among established nations and nonstate terrorist groups. In addition to the United States and Russia, the United Kingdom, France, China, India, North Korea, Pakistan, and Israel have nuclear capabilities. Because India and Pakistan have experienced border clashes and are generally unfriendly toward each other, their possession of nuclear weapons poses a threat to the stability of Southeast Asia. Most recently, the United States has focused intense concern on nuclear weapons development in Iran (see Figure 14.10).

As the preeminent international peacekeeping organization, the United Nations has long led efforts to curb nuclear proliferation through treaties that would ban the testing of nuclear weapons and set up an official verification system whereby countries would be regularly inspected to make sure they were not developing nuclear capabilities. The Nuclear Non-Proliferation Treaty that went into effect in 1970 was designed to discourage nations from developing nuclear weapons technology; currently, 190 nations are signatories.[56] The key element of this treaty is the use of the International

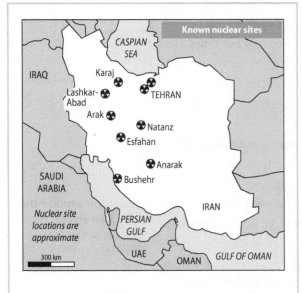

Figure 14.10 Map of Nuclear Facilities in Iran

Iran has been developing the capability to produce nuclear weapons, but has not yet finished the process. Here we see the sites in Iran that are believed to contain components in nuclear weapons production.

Source: http://cdn2-b.examiner.com/sites/default/files/styles/image_content_width/hash/38/44/1359993295_5197_AFP_Iran_Nuclear_Program(1).jpg?itok=_QZsnNy-.
© 2016 CENGAGE LEARNING

Atomic Energy Commission to monitor and inspect nations' weapons capability. The United States and the rest of the international community rely on this organization and its powers to monitor nuclear facility development in countries that do not currently have nuclear weapons, such as Iran. To that end, President Obama instructed his Secretary of State, John Kerry, to participate in multilateral negotiations with Iran to limit their progress toward acquiring a nuclear weapon.

Diplomacy and Humanitarian Assistance.

In addition to military actions, another cornerstone of U.S. foreign policy is diplomacy. The Department of State is responsible for formulating foreign policy using nonmilitary methods; these efforts

The U.S. Agency for International Development provides humanitarian assistance around the world. In 2014, USAID workers were sent to the front lines of the effort to treat and contain the Ebola virus in West Africa.

are conducted by diplomatic personnel in U.S. missions, consulates, and embassies around the world. There are also agencies within the Department of State that oversee a key component of our foreign policy—the provision of humanitarian assistance. The interdependence of nations today provides an opportunity for Americans, from the average citizen to the president, to participate on a wider level and improve living conditions everywhere. A world with more stable nations that treat their citizens equally and with dignity benefits the United States because it means that fewer internal conflicts will emerge that warrant military intervention. Governmental and nongovernmental organizations that provide funds for economic, health, and educational development provide an avenue for the U.S. government, groups, and individual citizens to take an active role in international life.

For example, within the U.S. federal government, the U.S. Agency for International Development (USAID) is an independent agency with the mission of providing gateways for the provision of training, education, and materials to developing nations and of promoting democracy.[57] It is led by an administrator appointed by the president who works closely with other federal departments, including the Department of State, on international aid issues. USAID was created by President John F. Kennedy in 1961 as part of the Foreign Assistance Act. Today its activities include disaster relief, child health and nutrition, and disease treatment and prevention. For example USAID Disaster Assistance Response Teams were very involved in fighting the Ebola virus in West Africa. In fiscal year 2014, USAID had an operating budget of $1.57 billion.[58]

In addition to unilaterally promoting economic development, the United States is also a member of the World Bank and the International Monetary Fund, two global economic organizations. The **World Bank** was founded in 1944 as an international aid and reconstruction organization to help rebuild nations that had been badly damaged during WWII.[59] Today it has 186 members, known as shareholders, and five divisions that work together to provide low-interest loans, grants, and investment capital to build and improve infrastructure and

→ KEY QUESTIONS:
What goals can the United States accomplish through humanitarian aid?

★ **World Bank:**
International organization that distributes grants and low-income loans in developing countries.

Public Policy and International Relations: Promotion of Democracy

President Woodrow Wilson's idea was that the United States should make the world "safe for democracy," and President Truman's view was that the United States should intervene militarily to promote and defend against Communist takeovers. Truman's approach drew strength from the theory of "democratic peace," which holds that the world is a safer place if nations are democratic. The core contention is that democracies, reflecting the will of the people, have almost never gone to war against other each other.[62] The public's desire for peace simply makes that outcome rare.

The federal government attempts to export democratic values through diplomatic and cultural programs. The Voice of America broadcasts news and programming in more than forty different languages across the world and cooperates with private organizations, such as Radio Free Asia, that provide a forum for democratic activists in Myanmar, China, and other nondemocratic states. American interest groups and nonprofit organizations also promote democracy abroad. Freedom House supports nonviolent civil initiatives in societies where freedom is denied or threatened. Since 1972, the organization has issued reports on every country around the world, classifying countries as free, partially free, or not free based on a freedom index that takes into account the electoral process, civil liberties, and human rights (see Figure 14.11).

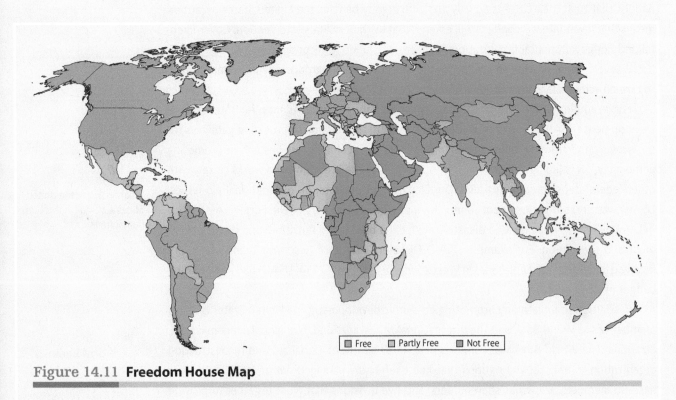

Figure 14.11 **Freedom House Map**

Today, the question of what is justified in the name of preserving and promoting the American form of democracy remains unresolved, especially in the face of old and new conflicts in nations such as Iraq, Egypt, and Syria where internal forces are battling for control of their governments. Making the case to the American people that direct U.S. intervention is necessary in distant regions with long histories of conflict, such as the Middle East, is difficult to do, as we saw with the debate over punishing Syria for its use of chemical weapons. America's international reputation was tarnished by its unilateralism in the Iraq War, making it more difficult for the United States to gain cooperation from the international community for intervention.

For these and other reasons, President Obama tried to reshape U.S. foreign policy by becoming more reliant on international organizations such as the United Nations, and using the international economic system to impose financial penalties and block trade with nations that violate international law or harbor terrorist groups. In an address to West Point, Obama made it clear that the United States would intervene when its interests were directly threatened, but that it could not be expected to send forces to engage in every military action occurring around the world. However, as the upheaval in Iraq shows, the United States remains involved in military conflicts even after the formal cessation of its role in war. The promotion of democracy is a long and unstable process, and when countries in which the United States has had a military presence devolve into civil war, there is enormous pressure to reengage to prevent further bloodshed.

Construct Your Own Policy

1. Outline guidelines for active U.S. engagement in foreign conflicts.
2. Devise a policy that only allows peaceful or nonmilitary U.S. involvement in promoting democracy.

alleviate poverty. The United States is the largest shareholder in the World Bank and consequently has leadership responsibilities; the president nominates the head of the bank, who serves a five-year renewable term.[60] The World Bank funds specific projects to improve transportation, provide clean water, build energy utilities, modernize medical care, initiate crop development programs, and provide start-up money for new businesses in poor and developing countries. In fiscal year 2014, the World Bank provided $39.6 billion in grants, loans, and investment capital to nations around the world.[61]

The **International Monetary Fund (IMF)** was created alongside the World Bank in 1944 with a different mission. The IMF focuses on preserving economic stability, including currency values, among nations and makes short-term loans to nations that cannot balance their budgets or are in need of immediate funds.[63] The IMF also works with nations to try to reduce their government debt by renegotiating loans or by providing loans on better terms. The IMF has the same set of members as the World Bank, and each member makes a financial contribution to the fund based on its share of the global economy. The IMF has a board of governors, which includes a governor from each member nation, but the daily operations of the fund are overseen by a managing director and a twenty-four-member executive board. In contrast to its role in the World Bank, the United States does not play a prominent role in directing IMF operations and does not nominate the managing director. However, the United States pays the largest single share (17 percent) of the IMF's fund, so it wields significant influence over lending decisions. In 2014, the IMF had $87.3 billion in outstanding loans to countries around the world.[64]

The United States supports organizations that send individuals to foreign nations for peacekeeping, educational, and cultural purposes. The **Peace Corps** is perhaps the best known of these organizations. The Peace Corps was established in 1961; since then, more than 195,000 U.S. citizen volunteers have lived and worked in seventy-six countries all over the world.[65] The mission of the Peace Corps is to help train citizens of other nations in essential skills, establish communication about Americans with other nations, and bring more knowledge about foreign peoples back to America through the volunteers. Today the Peace Corps operates on a budget of $378.8 million, and it still attracts recent college graduates and others who work in seventy-six countries in wide ranging fields, including teaching, agriculture, HIV/AIDS prevention, medicine, engineering, communications, environmental conservation, and construction.[66] The model of the Peace Corps has spurred the creation of domestic volunteer organizations including AmeriCorps and Teach for America, which operate within the United States but pursue similar goals of education and economic development in underserved areas.

However, the fact that nations are more connected to each other in our global world does not mean that they share political systems, religions, or culture. The differences that do exist have come into the forefront through regime change in recent years, which has resulted in political, social, and military conflict. America has objective strategic interests that it must protect, but it also has a strong commitment to human rights and democratic principles of government, and sometimes these guiding principles clash in the formulation of our foreign and military policy. Where the line should be drawn in international relations is decided by each presidential administration, in consultation with Congress; in that way, every presidential election is a gateway through which the American voters have the opportunity to render their opinions on whether to reset the boundaries of engagement.

International Monetary Fund (IMF): *International organization that works to stabilize currency values and government debt for nations in economic difficulty.*

Peace Corps: *U.S. government-funded organization that sends individuals on educational and cultural missions around the world.*

Checkpoint

CAN YOU:

- Describe the goals of U.S. foreign policy
- Assess the roles of military and diplomatic actions in U.S. foreign policy
- Evaluate U.S. efforts to promote democracy around the world

Public Policy and Democracy

Public policy covers a lot of territory in the language of American politics. It is essentially the set of outputs by federal, state, and local governments that address the interests and opinions of citizens. In this chapter, we have presented an overview of the federal regulatory system that serves as the main vehicle to implement the laws that Congress and the president enact. Once a law is passed, the executive branch produces a set of guidelines for how the law will work, and the public has a chance to comment on those regulations before they are finally put into place.

The three broad policy areas discussed in this chapter—domestic, economic, and foreign—all differ in the ways that policy outcomes can be directly controlled by policy makers. In domestic policy, our federal system of government has expanded over the past century to provide direct and indirect assistance to individuals in the area of income security, food security, housing, and health care. Our system of federalism allows states some leeway in how they implement federal law, especially when the policy overlaps with areas that are solely controlled by the states. The different ways that the Affordable Care Act has been implemented or blocked at the state level illustrate the variation in the potential impact of federal policy.

In the economic sphere, the president, Congress, and the Federal Reserve all have a role to play in how much money the government spends and how cheaply consumers can borrow money, but the independent business cycle also has a strong impact on whether those policies succeed in contributing to economic growth and stability.

In the area of foreign policy, the United States has always had to balance its own principles regarding human rights and freedoms with its military and economic self-interest around the world. Additionally, military and humanitarian crises emerge frequently and fall out of direct U.S. control; however, the United States is still faced with the choice of whether to intervene and to what extent. As recent events in Libya, Syria, and the Ukraine have shown, choosing the right policy is no easy task.

At times, it seems that there are more gates to influencing public policy in our system of government than there are gateways. Policy makers can be well intentioned and sincerely interested in reflecting the interests and concerns of the majority of the people, but the process itself can be slower and less inefficient than most of us would like. The policy-making process is complicated because it involves elected officials in multiple branches of government at all levels (federal, state, and local), the business community, interest groups, and private citizens who choose to make their opinions heard. Our system has about as much participation as James Madison would have expected; the question remains as to whether it is enough to address the pressing needs of the twenty-first century.

CONNECT WITH YOUR CLASSMATES
MindTap® for American Government

Access the Domestic Policy Forum: Discussion—The Public's Impact on Policy Making.

Master the Concept
of Economic, Domestic, and Foreign Policy with MindTap® for American Government

 REVIEW MindTap® for American Government
Access Key Term Flashcards for Chapter 14.

 STAY CURRENT MindTap® for American Government
Access the KnowNow blog and customized RSS for updates on current events.

 TEST YOURSELF MindTap® for American Government
Take the Wrap It Up Quiz for Chapter 14.

 STAY FOCUSED MindTap® for American Government
Complete the Focus Activities for Economic, Domestic, and Foreign Policy.

⭐ Key Concepts

Clean Air Act (p. 471) What role does the Clean Air Act play in U.S. environmental policy history?

Cold War (1946–91) (p. 483) What were the causes of the beginning and end of the Cold War?

Communism (p. 483) What is Communism?

debt ceiling (p. 480) What is the relationship between the debt ceiling and the federal deficit?

entitlement programs (p. 463) What is the definition of an entitlement program?

European Union (p. 482) What is the European Union, and what role does it play in international economics?

fair trade (p. 477) How does fair trade try to promote economic equality around the world?

Federal Register (p. 459) Where are all official federal government regulations published?

Federal Reserve Board (p. 473) When was the Federal Reserve created, and what does it do?

free trade (p. 477) What is the definition of free trade?

globalization (p. 482) How has globalization emerged as an international process over time?

International Monetary Fund (IMF) (p. 487) How does the IMF help stabilize nations that are in economic difficulty?

Medicaid (p. 464) Who is eligible for Medicaid, and what does it do?

Medicare (p. 464) Who is typically served through the Medicare program?

multipolar (p. 484) What does it mean to have a multipolar world?

NAFTA (p. 477) How did NAFTA affect trade among Canada, the United States, and Mexico?

nonstate actors (p. 486) How do nonstate actors complicate international peacemaking efforts?

Peace Corps (p. 490) When and why was the Peace Corps created?

policy agenda (p. 457) How do issues get on the policy agenda?

policy diffusion (p. 461) How do policy ideas spread across states?

policy enactment (p. 458) What does it mean when a policy is enacted?

policy evaluation (p. 458) What is the role of evaluation in the policy process?

policy formulation (p. 457) How does formulation work as the third step in the policy-making process?

policy implementation (p. 458) How does the executive branch implement public policy?

protectionist (p. 477) Who benefits from protectionist trade policy?

problem identification (p. 457) How does identification work as the first step in the policy-making process?

public policy (p. 456) Define public policy.

rally-around-the-flag effect (p. 485) Why do citizens tend to increase their support for government when facing a military threat?

recession (p. 472) How did the government react when the economy went into a recession in 2007–2008?

regulations (p. 459) How do regulations help government officials and individuals follow federal law?

regulatory process (p. 459) How would you describe the role of the regulatory process in our public policy system?

Social Security (p. 463) How is Social Security funded?

United Nations (p. 483) When and why was the United Nations created?

World Bank (p. 487) What function does the World Bank serve in international economic development?

World Trade Organization (WTO) (p. 479) When was the WTO created and why?

Learning Outcomes: What You Need . . .

To Know	To Test Yourself	To Participate

 Outline the steps in the policy-making process

To Know	To Test Yourself	To Participate
The path from idea to a policy involves five key steps. First a problem has to be identified, then it has to be on the congressional and executive agenda, then it has to be formulated into a policy according to federal guidelines, then it has to be enacted into law, then it has to be implemented (put into practice), and finally it has to be evaluated to see if the policy is accomplishing its stated goals.	• Describe how an idea becomes a policy proposal. • Identify the three key parts of the regulatory process. • Explain how the judiciary can be used to block implementation of policy. • Outline the role of state governments in implementing federal policies.	• Evaluate how the average citizen can get an idea on the policy agenda. • Design a way to streamline policy implementation.

To Know	To Test Yourself	To Participate

▶ Identify the key federal programs that comprise domestic policy

The federal government oversees a wide range of programs designed to address the income, health, and environmental safety of its citizens. These programs include Social Security, Medicaid, Medicare, Temporary Aid to Needy Families, Unemployment Compensation, and the Affordable Care Act. The federal government also takes responsibility for ensuring that citizens have clean air and clean water. Immigration is also a responsibility of the federal government both to regulate the documented process and to address the situations of longtime undocumented residents.

- Describe what it means to be an entitlement program, and identify two key programs that meet this description.
- Explain the costs and benefits of the Affordable Care Act in terms of domestic policy.
- Evaluate federal immigration policy.
- Identify the key agency designated to oversee environmental protection.

- Devise a way of controlling the costs of entitlement programs.
- Explain how you would improve the Affordable Care Act.
- Create a new system of immigration, and state whether you would include remedies for undocumented residents.
- Propose two steps that individual citizens could take to reduce carbon emissions.

▶ Explain how the federal government intervenes in the economy

The federal government intervenes in the economy through its fiscal, monetary, and trade policy. The federal government has the constitutional power to impose taxes to raise revenues, and the power to spend those revenues for the general welfare. The balancing of taxing and spending is known as fiscal policy. Monetary policy is not directly controlled by the federal government but rather by the Federal Reserve, which is a private/public banking institution that controls the flow of money by raising or lowering interest rates. The president appoints the chairman of the Federal Reserve. Trade policy uses a combination of tariffs and trade agreements with individual nations and trading blocs to sell U.S. goods abroad and maintain fair competition between U.S. domestically produced and imported goods.

- Explain the relationship between federal taxes and the federal deficit.
- Describe the lever of control that the federal government has over the Federal Reserve.
- Explain why trade agreements are so important for the U.S. economy.

- Propose a strategy for reducing the federal deficit.
- Devise a means of giving the average citizen more control over the Federal Reserve.
- Write a trade agreement with China that opens up new markets for U.S. goods but also protects existing U.S. industries.

▶ Evaluate the effectiveness of U.S. foreign policy

U.S. foreign policy has undergone tremendous change since the beginning of the twentieth century. The United States first became engaged in global military conflict in World War I, and then became involved in World War II, the Korean War, the Vietnam War, the Gulf War, and at the start of the twenty-first century, wars in Iraq and Afghanistan. Given the recent financial and human costs of the wars in Iraq and Afghanistan, Americans have begun to question the effectiveness of military intervention, and U.S. foreign policy has shifted toward relying more on economic sanctions, international agencies, and when necessary, the use of unmanned drones to engage in targeted actions against perceived enemies.

- Describe the evolution of U.S. foreign policy over the past 100 years.
- Explain the limitations of military action as a foreign policy tool.
- Evaluate the effectiveness of U.S. efforts to limit the spread of nuclear weapons.
- Identify two key international agencies that the U.S. works with to engage in diplomacy and address humanitarian concerns.

- Which nation do you believe is more important strategically, China or Russia?
- Devise a way of reducing the U.S. military role in conflict around the world but at the same time, fighting human rights abuses.
- State whether and why you would increase U.S. reliance on the United Nations as an international peace-keeping organization in order to reduce military engagement in foreign conflicts.

The Declaration of Independence

In Congress, July 4, 1776

The Unanimous Declaration of the Thirteen United States of America

When, in the course of human events, it becomes necessary for one people to dissolve the political bands which have connected them with another, and to assume, among the powers of the earth, the separate and equal station to which the laws of nature and of nature's God entitle them, a decent respect to the opinions of mankind requires that they should declare the causes which impel them to the separation.

We hold these truths to be self-evident: That all men are created equal; that they are endowed by their Creator with certain unalienable rights; that among these are life, liberty, and the pursuit of happiness; that, to secure these rights, governments are instituted among men, deriving their just powers from the consent of the governed; that whenever any form of government becomes destructive of these ends, it is the right of the people to alter or to abolish it, and to institute new government, laying its foundation on such principles, and organizing its powers in such form, as to them shall seem most likely to effect their safety and happiness. Prudence, indeed, will dictate that governments long established should not be changed for light and transient causes; and accordingly all experience hath shown that mankind are more disposed to suffer, while evils are sufferable, than to right themselves by abolishing the forms to which they are accustomed. But when a long train of abuses and usurpations, pursuing invariably the same object, evinces a design to reduce them under absolute despotism, it is their right, it is their duty, to throw off such government, and to provide new guards for their future security. Such has been the patient sufferance of these colonies; and such is now the necessity which constrains them to alter their former systems of government. The history of the present King of Great Britain is a history of repeated injuries and usurpations, all having in direct object the establishment of an absolute tyranny over these states. To prove this, let facts be submitted to a candid world.

He has refused to assent to laws, the most wholesome and necessary for the public good.

He has forbidden his governors to pass laws of immediate and pressing importance, unless suspended in their operation till his assent should be obtained; and, when so suspended, he has utterly neglected to attend to them.

He has refused to pass other laws for the accommodation of large districts of people, unless those people would relinquish the right of representation in the legislature, a right inestimable to them, and formidable to tyrants only.

He has called together legislative bodies at places unusual, uncomfortable, and distant from the depository of their public records, for the sole purpose of fatiguing them into compliance with his measures.

He has dissolved representative houses repeatedly, for opposing, with manly firmness, his invasions on the rights of the people.

He has refused for a long time, after such dissolutions, to cause others to be elected; whereby the legislative powers, incapable of annihilation, have returned to the people at large for their exercise; the state remaining, in the mean time, exposed to all dangers of invasions from without and convulsions within.

He has endeavored to prevent the population of these states; for that purpose obstructing the laws for naturalization of foreigners; refusing to pass others to encourage their migration hither, and raising the conditions of new appropriations of lands.

He has obstructed the administration of justice, by refusing his assent to laws for establishing judiciary powers.

He has made judges dependent on his will alone, for the tenure of their offices, and the amount and payment of their salaries.

He has erected a multitude of new offices, and sent hither swarms of officers to harass our people and eat out their substance.

He has kept among us, in times of peace, standing armies, without the consent of our legislatures.

He has affected to render the military independent of, and superior to, the civil power.

He has combined with others to subject us to a jurisdiction foreign to our constitution, and unacknowledged by our laws, giving his assent to their acts of pretended legislation;

For quartering large bodies of armed troops among us;

For protecting them, by a mock trial, from punishment for any murders which they should commit on the inhabitants of these states;

For cutting off our trade with all parts of the world;

For imposing taxes on us without our consent;

For depriving us, in many cases, of the benefits of trial by jury;

For transporting us beyond seas, to be tried for pretended offenses;

For abolishing the free system of English laws in a neighboring province, establishing therein an arbitrary government, and enlarging its boundaries, so as to render it at once an example and fit instrument for introducing the same absolute rule into these colonies;

For taking away our charters, abolishing our more valuable laws, and altering fundamentally the forms of our governments;

For suspending our own legislatures, and declaring themselves invested with power to legislate for us in all cases whatsoever.

He has abdicated government here, by declaring us out of his protection and waging war against us.

He has plundered our seas, ravaged our coasts, burned our towns, and destroyed the lives of our people.

He is at this time transporting large armies of foreign mercenaries to complete the works of death, desolation, and tyranny already begun with circumstances of cruelty and perfidy scarcely paralleled in the most barbarous ages, and totally unworthy the head of a civilized nation.

He has constrained our fellow-citizens, taken captive on the high seas, to bear arms against their country, to become the executioners of their friends and brethren, or to fall themselves by their hands.

He has excited domestic insurrections among us, and has endeavored to bring on the inhabitants of our frontiers the merciless Indian savages, whose known rule of warfare is an undistinguished destruction of all ages, sexes, and conditions.

In every stage of these oppressions we have petitioned for redress in the most humble terms; our repeated petitions have been answered only by repeated injury. A prince, whose character is thus marked by every act which may define a tyrant, is unfit to be the ruler of a free people.

Nor have we been wanting in our attentions to our British brethren. We have warned them, from time to time, of attempts by their legislature to extend an unwarrantable jurisdiction over us. We have reminded them of the circumstances of our emigration and settlement here. We have appealed to their native justice and magnanimity; and we have conjured them, by the ties of our common kindred, to disavow these usurpations, which would inevitably interrupt our connections and correspondence. They, too, have been deaf to the voice of justice and of consanguinity. We must, therefore, acquiesce in the necessity which denounces our separation, and hold them, as we hold the rest of mankind, enemies in war, in peace friends.

We, therefore, the representatives of the United States of America, in General Congress assembled, appealing to the Supreme Judge of the world for the rectitude of our intentions, do, in the name and by the authority of the good people of these colonies, solemnly publish and declare, that these United Colonies are, and of right ought to be, FREE AND INDEPENDENT STATES; that they are absolved from all allegiance to the British crown, and that all political connection between them and the state of Great Britain is, and ought to be, totally dissolved; and that, as free and independent states, they have full power to levy war, conclude peace, contract alliances, establish commerce, and do all other acts and things which independent states may of right do. And for the support of this declaration, with a firm reliance on the protection of Divine Providence, we mutually pledge to each other our lives, our fortunes, and our sacred honor.

John Hancock, *President and delegate from Massachusetts*

Georgia
- Button Gwinnett
- Lyman Hall
- George Walton

North Carolina
- William Hooper
- Joseph Hewes
- John Penn

South Carolina
- Edward Rutledge
- Thomas Heyward Jr.
- Thomas Lynch Jr.
- Arthur Middleton

Maryland
- Samuel Chase
- William Paca
- Thomas Stone
- Charles Carroll of Carrollton

Virginia
- George Wythe
- Richard Henry Lee
- Thomas Jefferson
- Benjamin Harrison
- Thomas Nelson Jr.
- Francis Lightfoot Lee
- Carter Braxton

Pennsylvania
- Robert Morris
- Benjamin Rush
- Benjamin Franklin
- John Morton
- George Clymer
- James Smith
- George Taylor
- James Wilson
- George Ross

Delaware
- Caesar Rodney
- George Read
- Thomas McKean

New York
- William Floyd
- Philip Livingston
- Francis Lewis
- Lewis Morris

New Jersey
- Richard Stockton
- John Witherspoon
- Francis Hopkinson
- John Hart
- Abraham Clark

New Hampshire
- Josiah Bartlett
- William Whipple
- Matthew Thornton

Massachusetts
- Samuel Adams
- John Adams
- Robert Treat Paine
- Elbridge Gerry

Rhode Island
- Stephen Hopkins
- William Ellery

Connecticut
- Roger Sherman
- Samuel Huntington
- William Williams
- Oliver Wolcott

We the People of the United States, in Order to form a more perfect Union, establish Justice, insure domestic Tranquility, provide for the common defence, promote the general Welfare, and secure the Blessings of Liberty to ourselves and our Posterity, do ordain and establish this Constitution for the United States of America.

Article I.

Section 1.   All legislative Powers herein granted shall be vested in a Congress of the United States, which shall consist of a Senate and House of Representatives.

Section 2.   The House of Representatives shall be composed of Members chosen every second Year by the People of the several States, and the Electors in each State shall have the Qualifications requisite for Electors of the most numerous Branch of the State Legislature.

No Person shall be a Representative who shall not have attained to the age of twenty five Years, and been seven Years a Citizen of the United States, and who shall not, when elected, be an Inhabitant of that State in which he shall be chosen.

Changed by the Fourteenth Amendment, Section 2.

Representatives and direct Taxes shall be apportioned among the several States which may be included within this Union, according to their respective Numbers, which shall be determined by adding to the whole Number of free Persons, including those bound to Service for a Term of Years, and excluding Indians not taxed, three fifths of all other Persons. The actual Enumeration shall be made within three Years after the first Meeting of the Congress of the United States, and within every subsequent Term of ten Years, in such Manner as they shall by Law direct. The Number of Representatives shall not exceed one for every thirty Thousand, but each State shall have at Least one Representative; and until such enumeration shall be made, the State of New Hampshire shall be entitled to chuse three, Massachusetts eight, Rhode-Island and Providence Plantations one, Connecticut five, New-York six, New Jersey four, Pennsylvania eight, Delaware one, Maryland six, Virginia ten, North Carolina five, South Carolina five, and Georgia three.

When vacancies happen in the Representation from any State, the Executive Authority thereof shall issue Writs of Election to fill such Vacancies.

The House of Representatives shall chuse their Speaker and other Officers; and shall have the sole Power of Impeachment.

Section 3.   The Senate of the United States shall be composed of two Senators from each State, chosen by the Legislature thereof, for six Years; and each Senator shall have one Vote.

Changed by the Seventeenth Amendment.

Immediately after they shall be assembled in Consequence of the first Election, they shall be divided as equally as may be into three Classes. The Seats of the Senators of the first class shall be vacated at the Expiration of the second Year, of the second Class at the Expiration of the fourth Year, and of the third Class at the Expiration of the sixth Year, so that one third may be chosen every second Year; and if Vacancies happen by Resignation, or otherwise, during the Recess of the Legislature of any State, the Executive thereof may make temporary Appointments until the next Meeting of the Legislature, which shall then fill such Vacancies.

Changed by the Seventeenth Amendment.

No Person shall be a Senator who shall not have attained to the Age of thirty Years, and been nine Years a Citizen of the United States, and who shall not, when elected, be an Inhabitant of that State for which he shall be chosen.

The Vice President of the United States shall be President of the Senate, but shall have no Vote, unless they be equally divided.

The Senate shall chuse their other Officers, and also a President pro tempore, in the Absence of the Vice President, or when he shall exercise the Office of President of the United States.

The Senate shall have the sole Power to try all Impeachments. When sitting for that Purpose, they shall be on Oath or Affirmation. When the President of the United States is tried the Chief Justice shall preside: And no Person shall be convicted without the Concurrence of two thirds of the Members present.

Judgment in Cases of Impeachment shall not exceed further than to removal from Office, and disqualification to hold and enjoy any Office of honor, Trust or Profit under the United States: but the Party convicted shall nevertheless be liable and subject to Indictment, Trial, Judgment and Punishment, according to Law.

Section 4.   The Times, Places and Manner of holding Elections for Senators and Representatives, shall be prescribed in each State by the Legislature thereof; but the Congress may at any time by Law make or alter such Regulations, except as to the Places of chusing Senators.

The Congress shall assemble at least once in every Year, and such Meeting shall be on the first Monday in December, unless they shall by Law appoint a different Day.

Changed by the Twentieth Amendment, Section 2.

Section 5.   Each House shall be the Judge of the Elections, Returns and Qualifications of its own Members, and a Majority of each shall constitute a Quorum to do Business; but a smaller number may adjourn from day to day, and may be authorized to compel the Attendance of absent Members, in such Manner, and under such Penalties as each House may provide.

Each House may determine the Rules of its Proceedings, punish its Members for disorderly Behaviour, and, with the Concurrence of two thirds, expel a Member.

Each House shall keep a Journal of its Proceedings, and from time to time publish the same, excepting such Parts as may in their Judgment require Secrecy; and the Yeas and Nays of the Members of either House on any question shall, at the Desire of one fifth of those Present, be entered on the Journal.

Neither House, during the Session of Congress, shall, without the Consent of the other, adjourn for more than three days, nor to any other Place than that in which the two Houses shall be sitting.

Section 6.   The Senators and Representatives shall receive a Compensation for their Services, to be ascertained by Law, and paid out of the Treasury of the United States. They shall in all Cases, except Treason, Felony and Breach of the Peace, be privileged from Arrest during their Attendance at the Session of their respective Houses, and in going to and returning from the same; and for any Speech or Debate in either House, they shall not be questioned in any other Place.

Amplified by the Twenty-Seventh Amendment.

No Senator or Representative shall, during the Time for which he was elected, be appointed to any civil Office under the Authority of the United States, which shall have been created, or the Emoluments whereof shall have been encreased during such time; and no Person holding any Office under the United States, shall be a Member of either House during his Continuance in Office.

Section 7. All Bills for raising Revenue shall originate in the House of Representatives; but the Senate may propose or concur with Amendments as on other Bills.

Every Bill which shall have passed the House of Representatives and the Senate, shall, before it become a Law, be presented to the President of the United States; If he approve he shall assign it, but if not he shall return it, with his Objections to that House in which it shall have originated, who shall enter the Objections at large on their Journal, and proceed to reconsider it. If after such Reconsideration two thirds of that House shall agree to pass the Bill, it shall be sent, together with the Objections, to the other House, by which it shall likewise be reconsidered, and if approved by two thirds of that House, it shall become a Law. But in all such Cases the Votes of both Houses shall be determined by yeas and Nays, and the Names of the Persons voting for and against the Bill shall be entered on the Journal of each House respectively. If any Bill shall not be returned by the President within ten Days (Sundays excepted) after it shall have been presented to him, the Same shall be a Law, in like Manner, as if he had signed it, unless the Congress by their Adjournment prevent its Return, in which Case it shall not be a Law.

Every Order, Resolution, or Vote to which the Concurrence of the Senate and House of Representatives may be necessary (except on a question of Adjournment) shall be presented to the President of the United States; and before the Same shall take Effect, shall be approved by him, or being disapproved by him, shall be repassed by two thirds of the Senate and House of Representatives, according to the Rules and Limitations prescribed in the Case of a Bill.

Section 8. The Congress shall have Power To lay and Collect Taxes, Duties, Imposts and Excises, to pay the Debts and provide for the common Defence and general Welfare of the United States; but all Duties, Imposts and Excises shall be uniform throughout the United States.

General welfare clause gives Congress the power to tax to provide for the general welfare.

To borrow Money on the credit of the United States;

Commerce clause gives Congress the power to regulate commerce with foreign nations, with Indian tribes, and among the various states.

To regulate Commerce with foreign Nations, and among the several States, and with the Indian Tribes;

To establish an uniform Rule of Naturalization, and uniform Laws on the subject of Bankruptcies throughout the United States;

To coin Money, regulate the Value thereof, and of foreign Coin, and fix the Standard of Weights and Measures;

To provide for the Punishment of counterfeiting the Securities and current Coin of the United States;

To establish Post Offices and post Roads;

To promote the Progress of Science and useful Arts, by securing for limited Times to Authors and Inventors the exclusive Right to their respective Writings and Discoveries;

To constitute Tribunals inferior to the Supreme Court;

To define and punish Piracies and Felonies committed on the high Seas, and Offences against the Law of Nations;

To declare War, grant Letters of Marque and Reprisal, and make Rules concerning Captures on Land and Water;

To raise and support Armies, but no Appropriation of Money to that Use shall be for a longer Term than two Years;

To provide and maintain a Navy;

To make Rules for the Government and Regulation of the land and naval Forces;

To provide for calling forth the Militia to execute the Laws of the Union, suppress Insurrections and repel Invasions;

To provide for organizing, arming, and disciplining, the Militia, and for governing such Part of them as may be employed in the Service of the United States, reserving to the States respectively, the Appointment of the Officers, and the Authority of training the Militia according to the discipline prescribed by Congress;

To exercise exclusive Legislation in all Cases whatsoever, over such District (not exceeding ten Miles square) as may, by Cession of Particular States, and the Acceptance of Congress, become the Seat of the Government of the United States, and to exercise like Authority over all Places purchased by the Consent of the Legislature of the State in which the Same shall be, for the Erection of Forts, Magazines, Arsenals, dock-Yards and other needful Buildings;—And

To make all Laws which shall be necessary and proper for carrying into Execution the foregoing Powers, and all other Powers vested by this Constitution in the Government of the United States, or in any Department or Officer thereof.

Necessary and proper clause gives Congress the power to pass all laws necessary and proper to the powers enumerated in Section 8.

Section 9. The Migration or Importation of such Persons as any of the States now existing shall think proper to admit, shall not be prohibited by the Congress prior to the Year one thousand eight hundred and eight, but a Tax or duty may be imposed on such Importation, not exceeding ten dollars for each Person.

The Privilege of the Writ of Habeas Corpus shall not be suspended, unless when in Cases of Rebellion or Invasion the public Safety may require it.

No bill of Attainder or ex post facto Law shall be passed.

No Capitation, or other direct, Tax shall be laid, unless in Proportion to the Census or Enumeration herein before directed to be taken.

Changed by the Sixteenth Amendment.

No Tax or Duty shall be laid on Articles exported from any State.

No Preference shall be given by any Regulation of Commerce or Revenue to the Ports of one State over those of another; nor shall Vessels bound to, or from, one State, be obliged to enter, clear or pay Duties in another.

No Money shall be drawn from the Treasury, but in Consequence of Appropriations made by Law; and a regular Statement and Account of the Receipts and Expenditures of all public Money shall be published from time to time.

No Title of Nobility shall be granted by the United States: And no Person holding any Office of Profit or Trust under them, shall, without the Consent of the Congress, accept of any present, Emolument, Office, or Title, of any kind whatever, from any King, Prince, or foreign State.

Section 10. No State shall enter into any Treaty, Alliance, or Confederation; grant Letters of Marque and Reprisal; coin Money; emit Bills of Credit; make any Thing but gold and silver Coin a Tender in Payment of Debts; pass any Bill of Attainder, ex post facto Law, or Law impairing the Obligation of Contracts, or grant any Title of Nobility.

No State shall, without the Consent of the Congress, lay any Imposts or Duties on Imports or Exports, except what may be absolutely necessary for executing its inspection Laws; and the net Produce of all Duties and Imposts, laid by any State on Imports or Exports, shall be for the Use of the Treasury of the United States; and all such Laws shall be subject to the Revision and Control of the Congress.

No State shall, without the Consent of Congress, lay any Duty of Tonnage, keep Troops, or Ships of War in time of Peace, enter into any Agreement or Compact with another State, or with a foreign Power, or engage in War, unless actually invaded, or in such imminent Danger as will not admit of delay.

Article II.

Vesting clause gives the president the executive power.

Section 1. The executive Power shall be vested in a President of the United States of America. He shall hold his Office during the term of four Years, and, together with the Vice President, chosen for the same Term, be elected, as follows

Each State shall appoint, in such Manner as the Legislature thereof may direct, a Number of Electors, equal to the whole Number of Senators and Representatives to which the State may be entitled in the Congress: but no Senator or Representative, or Person holding an Office of Trust or Profit under the United States, shall be appointed an Elector.

Changed by the Twelfth Amendment.

The Electors shall meet in their respective States, and vote by Ballot for two Persons, of whom one at least shall not be an Inhabitant of the same State with them-selves. And they shall make a List of all the Persons voted for, and of the Number of Votes for each; which List they shall sign and certify, and transmit sealed to the Seat of the Government of the United States, directed to the President of the Senate. The President of the Senate shall, in the Presence of the Senate and House of Representatives, open all the Certificates, and the Votes shall then be counted. The Person having the greatest Number of Votes shall be the President, if such Number be a Majority of the whole Number of Electors appointed; and if there be more than one who have such Majority, and have an equal Number of Votes, then the House of Representatives shall immediately chuse by Ballot one of them for President; and if no Person have a Majority, then from the five highest on the List the said House shall in like Manner chuse the President. But in chusing the President, the Votes shall be taken by States, the Representation from each State having one Vote; a quorum for this Purpose shall consist of a Member or Members from two thirds of the States, and a Majority of all the States shall be necessary to a Choice. In every Case, after the Choice of the President, the Person having the greatest Number of Votes of the Electors shall be the Vice President. But if there should remain two or more who have equal Votes, the Senate shall chuse from them by Ballot the Vice President.

The Congress may determine the Time of chusing the Electors, and the Day on which they shall give their Votes, which Day shall be the same throughout the United States.

No Person except a natural born Citizen, or a Citizen of the United States, at the time of the Adoption of this Constitution, shall be eligible to the Office of President; neither shall any person be eligible to that Office who shall not have attained to the Age of thirty five Years, and been fourteen Years a Resident within the United States.

Changed by the Twenty-Fifth Amendment.

In Case of the Removal of the President from Office, or of his Death, Resignation, or Inability to discharge the Powers and Duties of the said Office, the Same shall devolve on the Vice President, and the Congress may by Law provide for the Case of Removal, Death,

Resignation or Inability, both of the President and Vice President, declaring what Officer shall then act as President, and such Officer shall act accordingly, until the Disability be removed, or a President shall be elected.

The President shall, at stated Times, receive for his Services, a Compensation, which shall neither be encreased nor diminished during the Period for which he shall have been elected, and he shall not receive within that Period any other Emolument from the United States, or any of them.

Before he enter on the Execution of his Office, he shall take the following Oath or Affirmation:—"I do solemnly swear (or affirm) that I will faithfully execute the Office of President of the United States, and will to the best of my Ability, preserve, protect and defend the Constitution of the United States."

Section 2.   The President shall be Commander in Chief of the Army and Navy of the United States, and of the Militia of the several States, when called into the actual Service of the United States; he may require the Opinion, in writing, of the principal Officer in each of the executive Departments, upon any Subject relating to the Duties of their respective Offices, and he shall have Power to grant Reprieves and Pardons for Offences against the United States, except in Cases of Impeachment.

He shall have Power, by and with the Advice and Consent of the Senate, to make Treaties, provided two thirds of the Senators present concur; and he shall nominate, and by and with the Advice and Consent of the Senate, shall appoint Ambassadors, other public Ministers and Consuls, Judges of the supreme Court, and all other Officers of the United States, whose Appointments are not herein otherwise provided for, and which shall be established by Law: but the Congress may by Law vest the Appointment of such inferior Officers, as they think proper, in the President alone, in the Courts of Law, or in the Heads of Departments.

The President shall have Power to fill up all Vacancies that may happen during the Recess of the Senate, by granting Commissions which shall expire at the End of their next Session.

Section 3.   He shall from time to time give to the Congress Information of the State of the Union, and recommend to their Consideration such Measures as he shall judge necessary and expedient; he may, on extraordinary Occasions, convene both Houses, or either of them, and in Case of Disagreement between them, with Respect to the Time of Adjournment, he may adjourn them to such Time as he shall think proper; he shall receive Ambassadors and other public Ministers; he shall take Care that the Laws be faithfully executed, and shall Commission all the Officers of the United States.

Take care clause requires the president to make sure that the laws are "faithfully executed."

Section 4.   The President, Vice President and all civil Officers of the United States, shall be removed from Office on Impeachment for, and Conviction of, Treason, Bribery, or other high Crimes and Misdemeanors.

Article III.

Section 1.   The judicial Power of the United States, shall be vested in one supreme Court, and in such inferior Courts as the Congress may from time to time ordain and establish. The Judges, both of the supreme and inferior Courts, shall hold their Offices during good Behaviour, and shall, at stated Times, receive for their Services, a Compensation, which shall not be diminished during their Continuance in Office.

Section 2.   The judicial Power shall extend to all Cases, in Law and Equity, arising under this Constitution, the Laws of the United States, and Treaties made, or which shall be made, under their Authority;—to all Cases affecting Ambassadors, other public Ministers and Consuls;—to all Cases of admiralty and maritime Jurisdiction;—to Controversies to which the United States shall be a Party;—to Controversies between two or more States;—between a State and Citizens of another State;—between Citizens of different States;—between Citizens of the same State claiming Lands under Grants of different States, and between a State, or the Citizens thereof, and foreign States, Citizens or Subjects.

Changed by the Eleventh Amendment.

In all Cases affecting Ambassadors, other public Ministers and Consuls, and those in which a State shall be Party, the supreme Court shall have original Jurisdiction. In all the other Cases before mentioned, the supreme Court shall have appellate Jurisdiction, both as to Law and Fact, with such Exceptions, and under such Regulations as the Congress shall make.

The Trial of all Crimes, except in Cases of Impeachment, shall be by Jury; and such Trial shall be held in the State where the said Crimes shall have been committed; but when not committed within any State, the Trial shall be at such Place or Places as the Congress may by Law have directed.

Section 3.   Treason against the United States, shall consist only in levying War against them, or in adhering to their Enemies, giving them Aid and Comfort. No Person shall be convicted of Treason unless on the Testimony of two Witnesses to the same overt Act, or on Confession in open Court.

The Congress shall have Power to declare the Punishment of Treason, but no Attainder of Treason shall work Corruption of Blood, or Forfeiture except during the Life of the Person attainted.

Article IV.

Section 1.   Full Faith and Credit shall be given in each State to the public Acts, Records, and judicial Proceedings of every other State. And the Congress may by general Laws prescribe the Manner in which such Acts, Records and Proceedings shall be proved, and the Effect thereof.

Full faith and credit clause requires states to accept civil proceedings from other states.

Section 2.   The Citizens of each State shall be entitled to all Privileges and Immunities of Citizens in the several States.

Privileges and immunities clause requires states to treat nonresidents equally to residents.

A person charged in any State with Treason, Felony, or other Crime, who shall flee from Justice, and be found in another State, shall on Demand of the executive Authority of the State from which he fled, be delivered up, to be removed to the State having Jurisdiction of the Crime.

No Person held to Service or Labour in one State, under the Laws thereof, escaping into another, shall, in Consequence of any Law or Regulation therein, be discharged from such Service or Labour, but shall be delivered up on Claim of the Party to whom such Service or Labour may be due.

Fugitive slave clause required states to return runaway slaves; negated by the Thirteenth Amendment.

Section 3.   New States may be admitted by the Congress into this Union; but no new State shall be formed or erected within the Jurisdiction of any other State; nor any State be formed by the Junction of two or more States, or Parts of States, without the Consent of the Legislatures of the States concerned as well as of the Congress.

The Congress shall have Power to dispose of and make all needful Rules and Regulations respecting the Territory or other Property belonging to the United States; and nothing in this Constitution shall be so construed as to Prejudice any Claims of the United States, or of any particular State.

Section 4. The United States shall guarantee to every State in this Union a Republican Form of Government, and shall protect each of them against Invasion; and on Application of the Legislature, or of the Executive (when the Legislature cannot be convened) against domestic Violence.

Guarantee clause provides a federal government guarantee that the states will have a republican form of government.

Article V.

The Congress, whenever two thirds of both Houses shall deem it necessary, shall propose Amendments to this Constitution, or, on the Application of the Legislatures of two thirds of the several States, shall call a Convention for proposing Amendments, which, in either Case, shall be valid to all Intents and Purposes, as Part of this Constitution, when ratified by the Legislatures of three fourths of the several States, or by Conventions in three fourths thereof, as the one or the other Mode of Ratification may be proposed by the Congress; Provided that no Amendment which may be made prior to the Year One thousand eight hundred and eight shall in any Manner after the first and fourth Clauses in the Ninth Section of the first Article; and that no State, without its Consent, shall be deprived of its equal Suffrage in the Senate.

Article VI.

All Debts contracted and Engagements entered into, before the Adoption of this Constitution, shall be as valid against the United States under this Constitution, as under the Confederation.

This Constitution, and the Laws of the United States which shall be made in Pursuance thereof; and all Treaties made, or which shall be made, under the Authority of the United States, shall be the Supreme Law of the Land; and the Judges in every State shall be bound thereby, any Thing in the Constitution or Laws of any State to the Contrary notwithstanding.

Supremacy clause makes federal law supreme over state laws.

The Senators and Representatives before mentioned, and the Members of the several State Legislatures, and all executive and judicial Officers, both of the United States and of the several States, shall be bound by Oath or Affirmation, to support this Constitution; but no religious Test shall ever be required as a Qualification to any Office or public Trust under the United States.

Article VII.

The Ratification of the Conventions of nine States, shall be sufficient for the Establishment of this Constitution between the States so ratifying the Same.

Done in Convention by the Unanimous Consent of the States present the Seventeenth Day of September in the Year of our Lord one thousand seven hundred and Eighty seven and of the Independence of the United States of America the Twelfth In witness whereof We have hereunto subscribed our Names,

George Washington, *President and deputy from Virginia*

Delaware
George Read
Gunning Bedford Jr.
John Dickinson
Richard Bassett
Jacob Broom

Maryland
James McHenry
Daniel of St. Thomas Jennifer
Daniel Carroll

Virginia
John Blair
James Madison Jr.

North Carolina
William Blount
Richard Dobbs Spaight
Hugh Williamson

South Carolina
John Rutledge
Charles Cotesworth Pinckney
Charles Pinckney
Pierce Butler

Georgia
William Few
Abraham Baldwin

New Hampshire
John Langdon
Nicholas Gilman

Massachusetts
Nathaniel Gorham
Rufus King

Connecticut
William Samuel Johnson
Roger Sherman

New York
Alexander Hamilton

New Jersey
William Livingston
David Brearley
William Paterson
Jonathan Dayton

Pennsylvania
Benjamin Franklin
Thomas Mifflin
Robert Morris
George Clymer
Thomas FitzSimons
Jared Ingersoll
James Wilson
Gouverneur Morris

[The first ten amendments, known as the Bill of Rights, were ratified in 1791.]

First Amendment

Congress shall make no law respecting an establishment of religion, or prohibiting the free exercise thereof; or abridging the freedom of speech, or of the press; or the right of the people peaceably to assemble, and to petition the Government for a redress of grievances.

Establishment clause prohibits governmental establishment of religion.

Free exercise clause protects the free exercise of religion.

Second Amendment

A well regulated Militia, being necessary to the security of a free State, the right of the people to keep and bear Arms, shall not be infringed.

Third Amendment

No Soldier shall, in time of peace be quartered in any house, without the consent of the Owner, nor in time of war, but in a manner prescribed by law.

Fourth Amendment

The right of the people to be secure in their persons, houses, papers, and effects, against unreasonable searches and seizures, shall not be violated, and no Warrants shall issue, but upon probable cause, supported by Oath or affirmation, and particularly describing the place to be searched, and the persons or things to be seized.

Fifth Amendment

No person shall be held to answer for a capital, or otherwise infamous crime, unless on a presentment or indictment of a Grand Jury, except in cases arising in the land or naval forces, or in the Militia, when in actual service in time of War or public danger; nor shall any person be subject for the same offence to be twice put in jeopardy of life or limb; nor shall be compelled in any criminal case to be a witness against himself, nor be deprived of life, liberty, or property, without due process of law, nor shall private property be taken for public use, without just compensation.

Double jeopardy clause prevents the government from retrying someone for a crime after an initial acquittal.

Self-incrimination clause protects people from having to testify against themselves at trial.

Due process clause prevents the federal government from denying any person due process of law.

Takings clause requires just compensation when the government seizes private property for a public purpose.

Sixth Amendment

In all criminal prosecutions, the accused shall enjoy the right to a speedy and public trial, by an impartial jury of the State and district wherein the crime shall have been committed, which district shall have been previously ascertained by law, and to be informed of the nature and cause of the accusation; to be confronted with the witnesses against him; to have compulsory process for obtaining witnesses in his favor, and to have Assistance of Counsel for his defence.

Seventh Amendment

In Suits at common law, where the value in controversy shall exceed twenty dollars, the right of trial by jury shall be preserved, and no fact tried by a jury, shall be otherwise reexamined in any Court of the United States, than according to the rules of the common law.

Eighth Amendment

Excessive bail shall not be required, nor excessive fines imposed, nor cruel and unusual punishments inflicted.

Cruel and unusual punishment clause prohibits cruel and unusual punishments.

Ninth Amendment

The enumeration in the Constitution, of certain rights, shall not be construed to deny or disparage others retained by the people.

Tenth Amendment

The powers not delegated to the United States by the Constitution, nor prohibited by it to the States, are reserved to the States respectively, or to the people.

Reserve powers clause reserves to the states or to the people those powers not delegated to the United States.

Eleventh Amendment (1798)

The Judicial power of the United States shall not be construed to extend to any suit in law or equity, commenced or prosecuted against one of the United States by Citizens of another State, or by Citizens or Subjects of any Foreign State.

Twelfth Amendment (1804)

The Electors shall meet in their respective states and vote by ballot for President and Vice President, one of whom, at least, shall not be an inhabitant of the same state with themselves; they shall name in their ballots the person voted for as President, and in distinct ballots the person voted for as Vice President, and they shall make distinct lists of all persons voted for as President, and of all persons voted for as Vice President, and of the number of votes for each, which lists they shall sign and certify, and transmit sealed to the seat of the government of the United States, directed to the President of the Senate;—The President of the Senate shall, in the presence of the Senate and House of Representatives, open all the certificates and the votes shall then be counted;—The person having the greatest number of votes for President, shall be the President, if such number be a majority of the whole number of Electors appointed; and if no person have such majority, then from the persons having the highest numbers not exceeding three on the list of those voted for as President, the House of Representatives shall choose immediately, by ballot, the President. But in choosing the President, the votes shall be taken by states, the representation from each state having one vote; a quorum for this purpose shall consist of a member or members from two-thirds of the states, and a majority of all the states shall be necessary to a choice. And if the House of Representatives shall not choose a President whenever the right of choice shall devolve upon them, before the fourth day of March next following, then the Vice President shall act as President, as in the case of the death or other constitutional disability of the President.—The person having the greatest number of votes as Vice President, shall be the Vice President, if such number be a majority of the whole number of Electors appointed, and if no person have a majority, then from the two highest numbers on the list, the Senate shall choose the Vice President; a quorum for the purpose shall consist of two-thirds of the whole number of Senators, and a majority of the whole number shall be necessary to a choice. But no person constitutionally ineligible to the office of President shall be eligible to that of Vice President of the United States.

Changed by the Twentieth Amendment, Section 3.

Thirteenth Amendment (1865)

Section 1.   Neither slavery nor involuntary servitude, except as a punishment for crime whereof the party shall have been duly convicted, shall exist within the United States, or any place subject to their jurisdiction.

Section 2.   Congress shall have power to enforce this article by appropriate legislation.

Fourteenth Amendment (1868)

Citizenship clause makes all persons born in the United States citizens of the United States and of the state in which they reside.

Privileges or immunities clause prohibits states from abridging certain fundamental rights.

Due process clause prevents state governments from denying any person due process of law.

Equal protection clause prevents states from denying any person the equal protection of the laws.

Section 1.   All persons born or naturalized in the United States and subject to the jurisdiction thereof, are citizens of the United States and of the State wherein they reside. No State shall make or enforce any law which shall abridge the privileges or immunities of citizens of the United States; nor shall any State deprive any person of life, liberty, or property, without due process of law; nor deny to any person within its jurisdiction the equal protection of the laws.

Section 2.   Representatives shall be apportioned among the several States according to their respective numbers, counting the whole number of persons in each State, excluding Indians not taxed. But when the right to vote at any election for the choice of electors for President and Vice President of the United States, Representatives in Congress, the Executive and Judicial officers of a State, or the members of the Legislature thereof, is denied to any of the male inhabitants of such State, being twenty-one years of age, and citizens of the United States, or in any way abridged, except for participation in rebellion, or other crime, the basis of representation therein shall be reduced in the proportion which the number of such male citizens shall bear to the whole number of male citizens twenty-one years of age in such State.

Changed by the Nineteenth and Twenty-Sixth Amendments.

Section 3.   No person shall be a Senator or Representative in Congress, or elector of President and Vice President, or hold any office, civil or military, under the United States, or under any State, who, having previously taken an oath, as a member of Congress, or as an officer of the United States, or as a member of any State legislature, or as an executive or judicial officer of any State, to support the Constitution of the United States, shall have engaged in insurrection or rebellion against the same, or given aid or comfort to the enemies thereof. But Congress may by a vote of two-thirds of each House, remove such disability.

Section 4.   The validity of the public debt of the United States, authorized by law, including debts incurred for payment of pensions and bounties for services in suppressing insurrection or rebellion, shall not be questioned. But neither the United States nor any State shall assume or pay any debt or obligation incurred in aid of insurrection or rebellion against the United States, or any claim for the loss or emancipation of any slave; but all such debts, obligations and claims shall be held illegal and void.

Section 5.   The Congress shall have power to enforce, by appropriate legislation, the provisions of this article.

Fifteenth Amendment (1870)

Section 1.   The right of citizens of the United States to vote shall not be denied or abridged by the United States or by any State on account of race, color, or previous condition of servitude.

Section 2.   The Congress shall have power to enforce this article by appropriate legislation.

Sixteenth Amendment (1913)

The Congress shall have power to lay and collect taxes on incomes, from whatever source derived, without apportionment among the several States, and without regard to any census or enumeration.

Seventeenth Amendment (1913)

The Senate of the United States shall be composed of two Senators from each State, elected by the people thereof, for six years; and each Senator shall have one vote. The electors in each State shall have the qualifications requisite for electors of the most numerous branch of the State legislatures.

When vacancies happen in the representation of any State in the Senate, the executive authority of such State shall issue writs of election to fill such vacancies: *Provided*, That the legislature of any State may empower the executive thereof to make temporary appointments until the people fill the vacancies by election as the legislature may direct.

This amendment shall not be so construed as to affect the election or term of any Senator chosen before it becomes valid as part of the Constitution.

Eighteenth Amendment (1919)

Section 1.   After one year from the ratification of this article the manufacture, sale, or transportation of intoxicating liquors within, the importation thereof into, or the exportation thereof from the United States and all territory subject to the jurisdiction thereof for beverage purposes is hereby prohibited.

Repealed by the Twenty-First Amendment.

Section 2.   The Congress and the several States shall have concurrent power to enforce this article by appropriate legislation.

Section 3.   This article shall be inoperative unless it shall have been ratified as an amendment to the Constitution by the legislatures of the several States, as provided in the Constitution, within seven years from the date of the submission hereof to the States by the Congress.

Nineteenth Amendment (1920)

The right of citizens of the United States to vote shall not be denied or abridged by the United States or by any State on account of sex.

Congress shall have power to enforce this article by appropriate legislation.

Twentieth Amendment (1933)

Section 1. The terms of the President and Vice President shall end at noon on the 20th day of January, and the terms of Senators and Representatives at noon on the 3rd day of January, of the years in which such terms would have ended if this article had not been ratified; and the terms of their successors shall then begin.

Section 2. The Congress shall assemble at least once in every year, and such meeting shall begin at noon on the 3d day of January, unless they shall by law appoint a different day.

Section 3. If, at the time fixed for the beginning of the term of the President, the President elect shall have died, the Vice President elect shall become President. If a President shall not have been chosen before the time fixed for the beginning of his term, or if the President elect shall have failed to qualify, then the Vice President elect shall act as President until a President shall have qualified; and the Congress may by law provide for the case wherein neither a President elect nor a Vice President elect shall have qualified, declaring who shall then act as President, or the manner in which one who is to act shall be selected, and such person shall act accordingly until a President or Vice President shall have qualified.

Section 4. The Congress may by law provide for the case of the death of any of the persons from whom the House of Representatives may choose a President whenever the right of choice shall have devolved upon them, and for the case of the death of any of the persons from whom the Senate may choose a Vice President whenever the right of choice shall have devolved upon them.

Section 5. Sections 1 and 2 shall take effect on the 15th day of October following the ratification of this article.

Section 6. This article shall be inoperative unless it shall have been ratified as an amendment to the Constitution by the legislatures of three-fourths of the several States within seven years from the date of its submission.

Twenty-First Amendment (1933)

Section 1. The eighteenth article of amendment to the Constitution of the United States is hereby repealed.

Section 2. The transportation or importation into any State, Territory, or possession of the United States for delivery or use therein of intoxicating liquors, in violation of the laws thereof, is hereby prohibited.

Section 3. This article shall be inoperative unless it shall have been ratified as an amendment to the Constitution by conventions in the several States, as provided in the Constitution, within seven years from the date of the submission hereof to the States by the Congress.

Twenty-Second Amendment (1951)

Section 1.   No person shall be elected to the office of the President more than twice, and no person who has held the office of President, or acted as President, for more than two years of a term to which some other person was elected President shall be elected to the office of the President more than once. But this Article shall not apply to any person holding the office of President when this Article was proposed by the Congress, and shall not prevent any person who may be holding the office of President, or acting as President, during the term within which this Article becomes operative from holding the office of President or acting as President during the remainder of such term.

Section 2.   This Article shall be inoperative unless it shall have been ratified as an amendment to the Constitution by the legislatures of three-fourths of the several States within seven years from the date of its submission to the States by the Congress.

Twenty-Third Amendment (1961)

Section 1.   The District constituting the seat of Government of the United States shall appoint in such manner as the Congress may direct:

A number of electors of President and Vice President equal to the whole number of Senators and Representatives in Congress to which the District would be entitled if it were a State, but in no event more than the least populous State; they shall be in addition to those appointed by the States, but they shall be considered, for the purposes of the election of President and Vice President, to be electors appointed by a State; and they shall meet in the District and perform such duties as provided by the twelfth article of amendment.

Section 2.   The Congress shall have power to enforce this article by appropriate legislation.

Twenty-Fourth Amendment (1964)

Section 1.   The right of citizens of the United States to vote in any primary or other election for President or Vice President, for electors for President or Vice President, or for Senator or Representative in Congress, shall not be denied or abridged by the United States or any State by reason of failure to pay any poll tax or other tax.

Section 2.   Congress shall have power to enforce this article by appropriate legislation.

Twenty-Fifth Amendment (1967)

Section 1.   In case of the removal of the President from office or of his death or resignation, the Vice President shall become President.

Section 2.   Whenever there is a vacancy in the office of the Vice President, the President shall nominate a Vice President who shall take office upon confirmation by a majority vote of both Houses of Congress.

Section 3.   Whenever the President transmits to the President pro tempore of the Senate and the Speaker of the House of Representatives his written declaration that he is unable to discharge the powers and duties of his office, and until he transmits to them a written declaration to the contrary, such powers and duties shall be discharged by the Vice President as Acting President.

Section 4.   Whenever the Vice President and a majority of either the principal officers of the executive departments or of such other body as Congress may by law provide, transmit to the President pro tempore of the Senate and the Speaker of the House of Representatives their written declaration that the President is unable to discharge the powers and duties of his office, the Vice President shall immediately assume the powers and duties of the office as Acting President.

Thereafter, when the President transmits to the President pro tempore of the Senate and the Speaker of the House of Representatives his written declaration that no inability exists, he shall resume the powers and duties of his office unless the Vice President and a majority of either the principal officers of the executive department[s] or of such other body as Congress may by law provide, transmit within four days to the President pro tempore of the Senate and the Speaker of the House of Representatives their written declaration that the President is unable to discharge the powers and duties of his office. Thereupon Congress shall decide the issue, assembling within forty-eight hours for that purpose if not in session. If the Congress, within twenty-one days after receipt of the latter written declaration, or, if Congress is not in session, within twenty-one days after Congress is required to assemble, determines by two-thirds vote of both Houses that the President is unable to discharge the powers and duties of his office, the Vice President shall continue to discharge the same as Acting President; otherwise, the President shall resume the powers and duties of his office.

Twenty-Sixth Amendment (1971)

Section 1. The right of citizens of the United States, who are eighteen years of age or older, to vote shall not be denied or abridged by the United States or by any State on account of age.

Section 2. The Congress shall have power to enforce this article by appropriate legislation.

Twenty-Seventh Amendment (1992)

No law varying the compensation for the services of the Senators and Representatives shall take effect, until an election of Representatives shall have intervened.

Federalist Papers 10 and 51

10

James Madison
November 22, 1787

To the People of the State of New York

Among the numerous advantages promised by a well constructed Union, none deserves to be more accurately developed than its tendency to break and control the violence of faction. The friend of popular governments, never finds himself so much alarmed for their character and fate, as when he contemplates their propensity to this dangerous vice. He will not fail therefore to set a due value on any plan which, without violating the principles to which he is attached, provides a proper cure for it. The instability, injustice and confusion introduced into the public councils, have in truth been the mortal diseases under which popular governments have every where perished; as they continue to be the favorite and fruitful topics from which the adversaries to liberty derive their most specious declamations. The valuable improvements made by the American Constitutions on the popular models, both ancient and modern, cannot certainly be too much admired; but it would be an unwarrantable partiality, to contend that they have as effectually obviated the danger on this side as was wished and expected. Complaints are every where heard from our most considerate and virtuous citizens, equally the friends of public and private faith, and of public and personal liberty; that our governments are too unstable; that the public good is disregarded in the conflicts of rival parties; and that measures are too often decided, not according to the rules of justice, and the rights of the minor party; but by the superior force of an interested and over-bearing majority. However anxiously we may wish that these complaints had no foundation, the evidence of known facts will not permit us to deny that they are in some degree true. It will be found indeed, on a candid review of our situation, that some of the distresses under which we labor, have been erroneously charged on the operation of our governments; but it will be found, at the same time, that other causes will not alone account for many of our heaviest misfortunes; and particularly, for that prevailing and increasing distrust of public engagements, and alarm for private rights, which are echoed from one end of the continent to the other. These must be chiefly, if not wholly, effects of the unsteadiness and injustice, with which a factious spirit has tainted our public administrations.

By a faction I understand a number of citizens, whether amounting to a majority or minority of the whole, who are united and actuated by some common impulse of passion, or of interest, adverse to the rights of other citizens, or to the permanent and aggregate interests of the community.

There are two methods of curing the mischiefs of faction: the one, by removing its causes; the other, by controlling its effects.

There are again two methods of removing the causes of faction: the one by destroying the liberty which is essential to its existence; the other, by giving to every citizen the same opinions, the same passions, and the same interests.

It could never be more truly said than of the first remedy, that it is worse than the disease. Liberty is to faction, what air is to fire, an aliment without which it instantly expires. But it could not be a less folly to abolish liberty, which is essential to political life, because it nourishes faction, than it would be to wish the annihilation of air, which is essential to animal life, because it imparts to fire its destructive agency.

The second expedient is as impracticable, as the first would be unwise. As long as the reason of man continues fallible, and he is at liberty to exercise it, different opinions will be formed. As long as the connection subsists between his reason and his self-love, his opinions and his passions will have a reciprocal influence on each other; and the former will be objects to which the latter will attach themselves. The diversity in the faculties of men from which the rights of property originate, is not less an insuperable obstacle to a uniformity of interests. The protection of these faculties is the first object of Government. From the protection of different and unequal faculties of acquiring property, the possession of different degrees and kinds of property immediately results: and from the influence of these on the sentiments and views of the respective proprietors, ensues a division of the society into different interests and parties.

The latent causes of faction are thus sown in the nature of man; and we see them every where brought into different degrees of activity, according to the different circumstances of civil society. A zeal for different opinions concerning religion, concerning Government and many other points, as well of speculation as of practice; an attachment to different leaders ambitiously contending for pre-eminence and power; or to persons of other descriptions whose fortunes have been interesting to the human passions, have in turn divided mankind into parties, inflamed them with mutual animosity, and rendered them much more disposed to vex and oppress each other, than to co-operate for their common good. So strong is this propensity of mankind to fall into mutual animosities, that where no substantial occasion presents itself, the most frivolous and fanciful distinctions have been sufficient to kindle their unfriendly passions, and excite their most violent conflicts. But the most common and durable source of factions, has been the various and unequal distribution of property. Those who hold, and those who are without property, have ever formed distinct interests in society. Those who are creditors, and those who are debtors, fall under a like discrimination. A landed interest, a manufacturing interest, a mercantile interest, a monied interest, with many lesser interests, grow up of necessity in civilized nations, and divide them into different classes, actuated by different sentiments and views. The regulation of these various and interfering interests forms the principal task of modern Legislation, and involves the spirit of party and faction in the necessary and ordinary operations of Government.

No man is allowed to be a judge in his own cause; because his interest would certainly bias his judgment, and, not improbably, corrupt his integrity. With equal, nay with greater reason, a body of men, are unfit to be both judges and parties, at the same time; yet, what are many of the most important acts of legislation, but so many judicial determinations, not indeed concerning the rights of single persons, but concerning the rights of large bodies of citizens; and what are the different classes of legislators, but advocates and parties to the causes which they determine? Is a law proposed concerning private debts? It is a question to which the creditors are parties on one side, and the debtors on the other. Justice ought to hold the balance between them. Yet the parties are and must be themselves the judges; and the most numerous party, or, in other words, the most powerful faction must be expected to prevail. Shall domestic manufactures be encouraged, and in what degree, by restrictions on foreign manufactures? are questions which would be differently decided by the landed and the manufacturing classes; and probably by neither, with a sole regard to justice and the public good. The apportionment of taxes on the various descriptions of property, is an act which seems to require the most exact impartiality; yet, there is perhaps no legislative act in which greater opportunity and temptation are given to a predominant party, to trample on the rules of justice. Every shilling with which they over-burden the inferior number, is a shilling saved to their own pockets.

It is in vain to say, that enlightened statesmen will be able to adjust these clashing interests, and render them all subservient to the public good. Enlightened statesmen will not always be at the helm: Nor, in many cases, can such an adjustment be made at all, without taking into view indirect and remote considerations, which will rarely prevail over the immediate interest which one party may find in disregarding the rights of another, or the good of the whole.

The inference to which we are brought, is, that the *causes* of faction cannot be removed; and that relief is only to be sought in the means of controlling its *effects*.

If a faction consists of less than a majority, relief is supplied by the republican principle, which enables the majority to defeat its sinister views by regular vote: It may clog the administration, it may convulse the society; but it will be unable to execute and mask its violence under the forms of the Constitution. When a majority is included in a faction, the form of popular government on the other hand enables it to sacrifice to its ruling passion or interest, both the public good and the rights of other citizens. To secure the public good, and private rights, against the danger of such a faction, and at the same time to preserve the spirit and the form of popular government, is then the great object to which our enquiries are directed: Let me add that it is the great desideratum, by which alone this form of government can be rescued from the opprobrium under which it has so long labored, and be recommended to the esteem and adoption of mankind.

By what means is this object attainable? Evidently by one of two only. Either the existence of the same passion or interest in a majority at the same time, must be prevented; or the majority, having such co-existent passion or interest, must be rendered, by their number and local situation, unable to concert and carry into effect schemes of oppression. If the impulse and the opportunity be suffered to coincide, we well know that neither moral nor religious motives can be relied on as an adequate control. They are not found to be such on the injustice and violence of individuals, and lose their efficacy in proportion to the number combined together; that is, in proportion as their efficacy becomes needful.

From this view of the subject, it may be concluded, that a pure Democracy, by which I mean, a Society, consisting of a small number of citizens, who assemble and administer the Government in person, can admit of no cure for the mischiefs of faction. A common passion or interest will, in almost every case, be felt by a majority of the whole; a communication and concert results from the form of Government itself; and there is nothing to check the inducements to sacrifice the weaker party, or an obnoxious individual. Hence it is, that such Democracies have ever been spectacles of turbulence and contention; have ever been found incompatible with personal security, or the rights of property; and have in general been as short in their lives, as they have been violent in their deaths. Theoretic politicians, who have patronized this species of Government, have erroneously supposed, that by reducing mankind to a perfect equality in their political rights, they would, at the same time, be perfectly equalized and assimilated in their possessions, their opinions, and their passions.

A republic, by which I mean a government in which the scheme of representation takes place, opens a different prospect, and promises the cure for which we are seeking. Let us examine the points in which it varies from pure democracy, and we shall comprehend both the nature of the cure and the efficacy which it must derive from the union.

The two great points of difference, between a democracy and a republic, are, first, the delegation of the government, in the latter, to a small number of citizens, elected by the rest; secondly, the greater number of citizens, and greater sphere of country, over which the latter may be extended.

The effect of the first difference is, on the one hand, to refine and enlarge the public views, by passing them through the medium of a chosen body of citizens, whose wisdom may best discern the true interest of their country, and whose patriotism and love of justice, will be least likely to sacrifice it to temporary or partial considerations. Under such a regulation, it may well happen, that the public voice, pronounced by the representatives of the people, will be more consonant to the public good, than if pronounced by the people themselves, convened for the purpose. On the other hand the effect may be inverted. Men of factious tempers, of local prejudices, or of sinister designs, may by intrigue, by corruption, or by other means, first obtain the suffrages, and then betray the interest of the people. The question resulting is, whether small or extensive republics are most favorable to the election of proper guardians of the public weal, and it is clearly decided in favor of the latter by two obvious considerations.

In the first place, it is to be remarked that, however small the republic may be, the representatives must be raised to a certain number, in order to guard against the cabals of a few; and that however large it may be, they must be limited to a certain number, in order to guard against the confusion of a multitude. Hence, the number of representatives in the two cases not being in proportion to that of the constituents, and being proportionally greatest in the small republic, it follows, that if the proportion of fit characters be not less in the large than in the small republic, the former will present a greater option, and consequently a greater probability of a fit choice.

In the next place, as each Representative will be chosen by a greater number of citizens in the large than in the small Republic, it will be more difficult for unworthy candidates to practise with success the vicious arts, by which elections are too often carried; and the suffrages of the people being more free, will be more likely to center on men who possess the most attractive merit, and the most diffusive and established characters.

It must be confessed, that in this, as in most other cases, there is a mean, on both sides of which inconveniences will be found to lie. By enlarging too much the number of electors, you render the representatives too little acquainted with all their local circumstances and lesser interests; as by reducing it too much, you render him unduly attached to these, and too little fit to comprehend and pursue great and national objects. The Federal Constitution forms a happy combination in this respect; the great and aggregate interests being referred to the national, the local and particular, to the state legislatures.

The other point of difference is, the greater number of citizens and extent of territory which may be brought within the compass of Republican, than of Democratic Government; and it is this circumstance principally which renders factious combinations less to be dreaded in the former, than in the latter. The smaller the society, the fewer probably will be the distinct parties and interests composing it; the fewer the distinct parties and interests, the more frequently will a majority be found of the same party; and the smaller the number of individuals composing a majority, and the smaller the compass within which they are placed, the more easily will they concert and execute their plans of oppression. Extend the sphere, and you take in a greater variety of parties and interests; you make it less probable that a majority of the whole will have a common motive to invade the rights of other citizens; or if such a common motive exists, it will be more difficult for all who feel it to discover their own strength, and to act in unison with each other. Besides other impediments, it may be remarked, that where there is a consciousness of unjust or dishonorable purposes, communication is always checked by distrust, in proportion to the number whose concurrence is necessary.

Hence it clearly appears, that the same advantage, which a Republic has over a Democracy, in controlling the effects of factions, is enjoyed by a large over a small Republic—is enjoyed by the Union over the States composing it. Does this advantage consist in the substitution of Representatives, whose enlightened views and virtuous sentiments render them superior to local prejudices, and to schemes of injustice? It will not be denied, that the Representation of the Union will be most likely to possess these requisite endowments. Does it consist in the greater security afforded by a greater variety of parties, against the event of any one party being able to outnumber and oppress the rest? In an equal degree does the increased variety of parties, comprised within the Union, increase this security? Does it, in fine, consist in the greater obstacles opposed to the concert and accomplishment of the secret wishes of an unjust and interested majority? Here, again, the extent of the Union gives it the most palpable advantage.

The influence of factious leaders may kindle a flame within their particular States, but will be unable to spread a general conflagration through the other States: a religious sect, may degenerate into a political faction in a part of the Confederacy but the variety of sects dispersed over the entire face of it, must secure the national Councils against any danger from that source: a rage for paper money, for an abolition of debts, for an equal division of property, or for any other improper or wicked project, will be less apt to pervade the whole body of the Union, than a particular member of it; in the same proportion as such a malady is more likely to taint a particular county or district, than an entire State.

In the extent and proper structure of the Union, therefore, we behold a Republican remedy for the diseases most incident to Republican Government. And according to the degree of pleasure and pride, we feel in being Republicans, ought to be our zeal in cherishing the spirit, and supporting the character of Federalists.

PUBLIUS

51

James Madison
February 6, 1788

To the People of the State of New York

To what expedient then shall we finally resort for maintaining in practice the necessary partition of power among the several departments, as laid down in the constitution? The only answer that can be given is, that as all these exterior provisions are found to be inadequate, the defect must be supplied, by so contriving the interior structure of the government, as that its several constituent parts may, by their mutual relations, be the means of keeping each other in their proper places. Without presuming to undertake a full development of this important idea, I will hazard a few general observations, which may perhaps place it in a clearer light, and enable us to form a more correct judgment of the principles and structure of the government planned by the convention.

In order to lay a due foundation for that separate and distinct exercise of the different powers of government, which to a certain extent, is admitted on all hands to be essential to the preservation of liberty, it is evident that each department should have a will of its own; and consequently should be so constituted, that the members of each should have as little agency as possible in the appointment of the members of the others. Were this principle rigorously adhered to, it would require that all the appointments for the supreme executive, legislative, and judiciary magistracies, should be drawn from the same fountain of authority, the people, through channels, having no communication whatever with one another. Perhaps such a plan of constructing the several departments would be less difficult in practice than it may in contemplation appear. Some difficulties however, and some additional expense, would attend the execution of it. Some deviations therefore from the principle must be admitted. In the constitution of the judiciary department in particular, it might be inexpedient to insist rigorously on the principle; first, because peculiar qualifications being essential in the members, the primary consideration ought to be to select that mode of choice, which best secures these qualifications; secondly, because the permanent tenure by which the appointments are held in that department, must soon destroy all sense of dependence on the authority conferring them.

It is equally evident that the members of each department should be as little dependent as possible on those of the others, for the emoluments annexed to their offices. Were the executive magistrate, or the judges, not independent of the legislature in this particular, their independence in every other would be merely nominal.

But the great security against a gradual concentration of the several powers in the same department, consists in giving to those who administer each department, the necessary constitutional means, and personal motives, to resist encroachments of the others. The provision for defense must in this, as in all other cases, be made commensurate to the danger of attack. Ambition must be made to counteract ambition. The interest of the man must be connected with the constitutional rights of the place. It may be a reflection on human nature, that such devices should be necessary to control the abuses of government. But what is government itself but the greatest of all reflections on human nature? If men were angels, no government would be necessary. If angels were to govern men, neither external nor internal controls on government would be necessary. In framing a government which is to be administered by men over men, the great difficulty lies in this: You must first enable the government to control the governed; and in the next place, oblige it to control itself. A dependence on the people is no doubt the primary control on the government; but experience has taught mankind the necessity of auxiliary precautions.

This policy of supplying by opposite and rival interests, the defect of better motives, might be traced through the whole system of human affairs, private as well as public. We see it particularly displayed in all the subordinate distributions of power; where the constant aim is to divide and arrange the several offices in such a manner as that each may be a check on the other; that the private interest of every individual, may be a sentinel over the public rights. These inventions of prudence cannot be less requisite in the distribution of the supreme powers of the state.

But it is not possible to give each department an equal power of self defense. In republican government the legislative authority, necessarily, predominates. The remedy for this inconveniency is, to divide the legislature into different branches; and to render them by different modes of election, and different principles of action, as little connected with each other, as the nature of their common functions, and their common dependence on the society, will admit. It may even be necessary to guard against dangerous encroachments by still further precautions. As the weight of the legislative authority requires that it should be thus divided, the weakness of the executive may require, on the other hand, that it should be fortified. An absolute negative, on the legislature, appears at first view to be the natural defense with which the executive magistrate should be armed. But perhaps it would be neither altogether safe, nor alone sufficient. On ordinary occasions, it might not be exerted with the requisite firmness; and on extraordinary occasions, it might be prefidiously abused. May not this defect of an absolute negative be supplied, by some qualified connection between this weaker department, and the weaker branch of the stronger department, by which the latter may be led to support the constitutional rights of the former, without being too much detached from the rights of its own department?

If the principles on which these observations are founded be just, as I persuade myself they are, and they be applied as a criterion, to the several state constitutions, and to the federal constitution, it will be found, that if the latter does not perfectly correspond with them, the former are infinitely less able to bear such a test.

There are moreover two considerations particularly applicable to the federal system of America, which place that system in a very interesting point of view.

First. In a single republic, all the power surrendered by the people, is submitted to the administration of a single government; and usurpations are guarded against by a division of the government into distinct and separate departments. In the compound republic of America, the power surrendered by the people, is first divided between two distinct governments, and then the portion allotted to each, subdivided among distinct and separate departments. Hence a double security arises to the rights of the people. The different governments will control each other; at the same time that each will be controlled by itself.

Second. It is of great importance in a republic, not only to guard the society against the oppression of its rulers; but to guard one part of the society against the injustice of the other part. Different interests necessarily exist in different classes of citizens. If a majority be united by a common interest, the rights of the minority will be insecure. There are but two methods of providing against this evil: The one by creating a will in the community independent of the majority, that is, of the society itself, the other by comprehending in the society so many separate descriptions of citizens, as will render an unjust combination of a majority of the whole, very improbable, if not impracticable. The first method prevails in all governments possessing an hereditary or self appointed authority. This at best is but a precarious security; because a power independent of the society may as well espouse the unjust views of the major, as the rightful interests, of the minor party, and may possibly be turned against both parties. The second method will be exemplified in the federal republic of the United States. While all authority in it will be derived from and dependent on the society, the society itself will be broken into so many parts, interests and classes of citizens, that the rights of individuals or of the minority, will be in little danger from interested combinations of the majority. In a free government, the security for civil rights must be the same as for religious rights. It consists in the one case in the multiplicity of interests, and in the other, in the multiplicity of sects. The degree of security in both cases will depend on the number of interests and sects; and this may be presumed to depend on the extent of country and number of people comprehended under the same government. This view of the subject must particularly recommend a proper federal system to all the sincere and considerate friends of republican government: Since it shows that in exact proportion as the territory of the union may be formed into more circumscribed confederacies or states, oppressive combinations of a majority will be facilitated, the best security under the republican form, for the rights of every class of citizens, will be diminished; and consequently, the stability and independence of some member of the government, the only other security, must be proportionally increased. Justice is the end of government. It is the end of civil society. It ever has been, and ever will be pursued, until it be obtained, or until liberty be lost in the pursuit. In a society under the forms of which the stronger faction can readily unite and oppress the weaker, anarchy may as truly be said to reign, as in a state of nature where the weaker individual is not secured against the violence of the stronger: And as in the latter state even the stronger individuals are prompted by the uncertainty of their condition, to submit to a government which may protect the weak as well as themselves: So in the former state, will the more powerful factions or parties be gradually induced by a like motive, to wish for a government which will protect all parties, the weaker as well as the more powerful. It can be little doubted, that if the state of Rhode Island was separated from the confederacy, and left to itself, the insecurity of rights under the popular form of government within such narrow limits, would be displayed by such reiterated oppressions of factious majorities, that some power altogether independent of the people would soon be called for by the voice of the very factions whose misrule had proved the necessity of it. In the extended republic of the United States, and among the great variety of interests, parties and sects which it embraces, a coalition of a majority of the whole society could seldom take place on any other principles than those of justice and the general good; and there being thus less danger to a minor from the will of the major party, there must be less pretext also, to provide for the security of the former, by introducing into the government a will not dependent on the latter; or in other words, a will independent of the society itself. It is no less certain than it is important, notwithstanding the contrary opinions which have been entertained, that the larger the society, provided it lie within a practicable sphere, the more duly capable will be of self government. And happily for the *republican cause,* the practicable sphere may be carried to a very great extent, by a judicious modification and mixture of the *federal principle.*

PUBLIUS

Glossary

A

adversary process Confrontational legal process under which each party presents its version of events.

affirmative action Policies that support greater equality, often by granting racial or gender preferences in hiring, education, or contracting.

agenda setting Ability of the media to affect the way people view issues, people, or events by controlling which stories are shown and which are not.

amendment Formal process of changing the Constitution.

amicus curiae Latin term meaning "friend of the court" that is used to describe individuals or interest groups who have an interest in a lawsuit but are not themselves direct parties to the suit.

Antifederalists Those who opposed the new proposed Constitution during the ratification period.

appeal Legal proceeding whereby the decision of a lower court on a question of law can be challenged and reviewed by a higher court.

appropriate Congress's power to allocate a set amount of federal dollars for a specific program or agency.

Articles of Confederation Initial governing authority of the United States, 1781–88.

Australian ballot Voting system in which state governments run elections and provide voters the option of choosing candidates from multiple parties; also called the secret ballot.

authorize Congress's power to create a federal program or agency and set levels of federal funds to support that program or agency.

autocracy System of government in which the power to govern is concentrated in the hands of an individual ruler.

B

ballot List of candidates who are running for elected office; used by voters to make their choice.

battleground state State in which the outcome of the presidential election is uncertain and in which both candidates invest much time and money, especially if its votes are vital for a victory in the Electoral College.

Bill of Rights First ten amendments to the Constitution, which provide basic political rights.

Brown v. Board of Education The 1954 Supreme Court decision striking down segregated schools.

bully pulpit Nickname for the power of the president to use the attention associated with the office to persuade the media, Congress, and the public to support his policy positions.

bureaucracy Executive branch departments, agencies, boards, and commissions that carry out the responsibilities of the federal government.

C

cabinet Set of executive departments responsible for carrying out federal policy in specific issue areas.

cabinet secretaries Heads of cabinet departments and chief advisers to the president on the issues under their jurisdiction.

capitalism Economic system in which businesses and key industries are privately owned and in which individuals, acting on their own or with others, are free to create businesses.

career civil servants Federal employees who are hired through a merit-based system to implement federal programs and who are expected to be neutral in their political affiliations.

caucus Meeting of party members in town halls, schools, and private homes to select a presidential nominee.

checks and balances Government structure that authorizes each branch of government (executive, legislative, and judicial) to share powers with the other branches, thereby holding some scrutiny of and control over the other branches.

chief of staff Person who coordinates and oversees interactions among the president, his personal staff, and his cabinet secretaries.

citizens' groups Groups that form to draw attention to purely public issues that affect all citizens equally.

citizenship Full-fledged membership in a nation.

civil liberties Those rights, such as freedom of speech and religion, that are so fundamental that they are outside the authority of government to regulate.

civil rights Set of rights centered around the concept of equal treatment that government is obliged to protect.

Civil Rights Act Prohibits discrimination in employment, education, and places of public accommodation (1964).

civil service The nonpartisan federal workforce employed to carry out government programs and policies.

Civil Service Commission Created by the Pendleton Act to administer entrance exams for the federal civil service and set standards for promotion based on merit.

civil society Voluntary organizations that allow communities to flourish.

civil suit Lawsuit by a person, organization, or government against another person, organization, or government.

class action lawsuit Lawsuit filed by one person on behalf of that person plus all similarly situated people.

Clean Air Act Broad federal legislation that expanded the federal government's ability to monitor and protect the environment against pollution.

clear and present danger test First Amendment test that requires the state to prove that there is a high likelihood that the speech in question would lead to a danger that Congress has a right to prevent.

cloture Vote that can stop a filibuster and bring debate on a bill to end.

Cold War An era in history marked by conflict and distrust between the United States and Communist nations.

commander in chief Leader of the armed forces of the United States.

commerce clause Gives Congress the power to regulate commerce with foreign nations, with Indian tribes, and among the various states (Article I, Section 8).

common law Judge-made law in England and the United States that results from gaps in statutory law.

Communist Government management and ownership of key elements of a nation's economy.

compelling interest test Standard frequently used by the Supreme Court in civil liberties cases to determine whether a state has a compelling interest for infringing on a right and whether the law is narrowly drawn to meet that interest.

compulsory voting Practice that requires citizens to vote in elections or face punitive measures such as community service, fines, or imprisonment.

concurrent budget resolution Congressional blueprint outlining general amounts of funds that can be spent on federal programs.

concurrent powers Powers held by both the national and state governments in a federal system.

concurring opinion Opinion that agrees with the results of the majority opinion (that is, which party wins) but sets out a separate rationale.

confederal system System of government in which ultimate authority rests with the regional (for example, state) governments.

confidence interval Statistical range with a given probability that takes random error into account.

Connecticut Compromise Compromise on legislative representation whereby the lower chamber is based on population, and the upper chamber provides equal representation to the states.

conservatives Individuals who distrust government, believing that free markets offer better ways than government involvement to improve people's livelihood. In the social sphere, conservatives have more faith in government's ability to enforce traditional values.

constitution Document or set of documents that establish the basic rules and procedures for how a society shall be governed.

constitutional system System of government in which people set up and agree on the basic rules and procedures that will govern them.

content-neutral Free speech doctrine that allows certain types of regulation of speech, as long as the restriction does not favor one side or another of a controversy.

continuing resolution Measure passed to fund federal programs when the appropriations process has not been completed by September 30, the end of the fiscal year.

countermajoritarian difficulty Alexander Bickel's phrase for the tension that exists for representative government when unelected judges have the power to strike laws passed by elected representatives.

Court-packing plan President Franklin Roosevelt's proposal to add new justices to the Supreme Court so that the Court would uphold his policies.

courts of appeals Intermediate federal courts that are above the district courts and below the Supreme Court.

criminal case Government prosecution of an individual for breaking the law.

D

debt ceiling The congressionally authorized limit on federal borrowing.

Declaration of Independence 1776 document declaring American independence from Great Britain and calling for equality, human rights, and citizen participation.

democracy System of government in which the supreme power is vested in the people and exercised by them either directly or indirectly through elected representatives.

direct democracy Form of democracy in which political power is exercised directly by citizens.

dissenting opinion Opinion that disagrees with the majority opinion as to which party wins.

district courts Federal trial courts at the bottom of the federal judicial hierarchy.

divided government Situation in which one party controls the executive branch, and the other party controls the legislative branch.

Dred Scott v. Sandford The 1857 Supreme Court decision declaring that blacks could not be citizens and Congress could not ban slavery in the territories.

dual federalism Doctrine holding that state governments and the federal government have almost completely separate functions.

E

earmark Federal dollars devoted specifically to a local project in a congressional district or state.

economic interest group Group formed to advance the economic status of its members.

efficacy Extent to which people believe their actions can affect public affairs and the actions of government.

Electoral College The presidential electors, selected to represent the votes of their respective states, who meet every four years to cast the electoral votes for president and vice president.

en banc Decision by an entire Court of Appeals circuit, typically following an original judgment by a three-judge panel of the circuit.

entitlement programs Federal programs, such as Social Security, Medicare, or Medicaid, that pay out benefits to individuals based on a specified set of eligibility criteria.

enumerated powers Powers expressly granted to Congress by the Constitution.

equality Idea that all individuals are equal in their moral worth and so must be equal in treatment under the law and have equal access to the decision-making process.

equality of opportunity Expectation that citizens may not be discriminated against on account of race, gender, or national background and that every citizen should have an equal chance to succeed in life.

equality of outcome Expectation that equality is achieved if results are comparable for all citizens regardless of race, gender, or national background or that such groups are proportionally represented in measures of success in life.

Equal Pay Act Prohibits different pay for males and females for the same work (1963).

equal protection clause Prevents states from denying any person the equal protection of the laws (Fourteenth Amendment).

establishment clause First Amendment clause prohibiting governmental establishment of religion.

European Union (EU) Association of European nations formed in order to facilitate economic and political interactions across their borders.

exclusionary rule Supreme Court rule declaring that evidence found in violation of the Fourth Amendment cannot be used at trial.

executive branch The branch of the federal government that executes the laws.

executive order Presidential directive that usually involves implementing a specific law.

executive privilege President's right to engage in confidential communications with his advisers.

exit polls Polls that survey a sample of voters immediately after exiting the voting booth to predict the outcome of the election before the ballots are officially counted.

expectation of privacy test Supreme Court test for whether Fourth Amendment protections apply.

F

faction Defined by Madison as any group that places its own interests above the aggregate interests of society.

fair trade Policy designed to make sure that the working conditions are relatively equal in nations that trade with each other.

federal budget deficit Difference between the amount of money the federal government spends in outlays and the amount of money it receives from revenues.

federalism System of government in which sovereignty is constitutionally divided between national and state governments.

Federalist Papers Series of essays written by James Madison, Alexander Hamilton, and John Jay arguing for the ratification of the Constitution; today a leading source for understanding the Constitution.

Federalists Initially, those who supported the Constitution during the ratification period; later, the name of the political party established by supporters of Alexander Hamilton.

Federal Register Official published record of all executive branch rules, regulations, and orders.

federal regulatory commission Federal agency typically run by a small number of officials, known as commissioners, who are appointed by the president for fixed terms and oversee economic or political issues.

Federal Reserve Board Independent regulatory commission that affects the money supply by setting the reserve requirements of member banks, establishing a discount rate for loans to member banks, and buying or selling government securities.

filibuster Tactic of extended speech designed to delay or block passage of a bill in the Senate.

501(c)(3) organizations Tax-exempt groups that are prohibited from lobbying or campaigning for a party or candidate.

Founders The people who were involved in establishing the United States, whether at the time of the Declaration of Independence or the writing of the Constitution.

Framers The people who were involved in writing the Constitution.

framing Ability of the media to influence public perception of issues by constructing the issue or discussion of a subject in a certain way.

free exercise clause First Amendment clause protecting the free exercise of religion.

free rider problem Problem faced by interest groups when a collective benefit they provide is so widespread and diffuse that members and nonmembers alike receive it, reducing the incentive for joining the group.

free trade Policy designed to lower import barriers to encourage trade across nations.

G

gender gap Differences in the political attitudes and behavior of men and women.

general election Election in which voters choose their elected officials.

general welfare clause Gives Congress the power to tax to provide for the general welfare (Article I, Section 8).

generational replacement Cycle whereby younger generations replace older generations in the electorate.

gerrymandering Redistricting that blatantly benefits one political party over the other or concentrates (or dilutes) the voting impact of racial and ethnic groups.

globalization The interconnectedness of nations around the world on economic, political, cultural, social, and military dimensions.

grandfather clauses Election rules that exempted people from difficult literacy and interpretation tests for voting if their grandfathers had been eligible to vote.

grassroots movement Group that forms in response to an economic or political event but does not focus on only one issue.

graveyard voting Corrupt practice of using a dead person's name to cast a ballot in an election.

Great Society Lyndon Johnson's program for expanding the federal social welfare programs in health care, education, and housing and for ending poverty.

H

hard news Political news coverage, traditionally found in the printed press, that is more fact-based, opposed to more interpretive narratives and commentary.

head of state Title given to the president as national leader.

hold Power available to a senator to prevent the unanimous consent that allows a bill or presidential nomination to come to the Senate floor, which can be broken by invoking cloture (sixty votes).

home style The way in which incumbents portray themselves to constituents.

House majority leader Leader of the majority party in the House and second in command to the Speaker.

House minority leader Leader of the minority party in the House.

I

ideological interest groups Groups that form among citizens with the same beliefs about a specific issue.

impeachment Process whereby the House brings charges against the president or another federal official that will, upon conviction by the Senate, remove him or her from office.

imperial presidency Power of the president to speak for the nation on the world stage and to set the policy agenda at home.

implied powers Powers not expressly granted to Congress but added through the necessary and proper clause.

incorporate Process of applying provisions of the Bill of Rights to the states.

independent agency Federal organization that has independent authority and does not operate within a cabinet department.

individualism Set of beliefs holding that people, and not government, are responsible for their own well-being.

inside strategy A strategy employed by interest groups to pursue a narrow policy change and influence legislators directly rather than using a wider grassroots approach.

institutional model Model of voting that focuses on the context of the election, including whether it is close and whether the rules encourage or discourage participation.

interest groups Groups of citizens who share a common interest—a political opinion, a religious or ideological belief, a social goal, or an economic characteristic—and try to influence public policy to benefit themselves.

International Monetary Fund (IMF) International organization that works to stabilize currency values and government debt for nations in economic difficulty.

invisible primary Period just before the primaries begin during which candidates attempt to capture party support and media coverage.

iron law of oligarchy Theory that leaders in any organization eventually behave in their own self-interest, even at the expense of rank-and-file members; the larger the organization, the greater the likelihood that the leader will behave this way.

iron triangle Insular and closed relationship among interest groups, members of Congress, and federal agencies.

issue network View of the relationship among interest groups, members of Congress, and federal agencies as more fluid, open, and transparent than that described by the term iron triangle.

J

judicial activism Decisions that go beyond what the law requires made by judges who seek to impose their own policy preferences on society through their judicial decisions.

judicial branch The branch of the federal government that interprets the laws.

judicial independence Ability of judges to reach decisions without fear of political retribution.

judicial restraint Decisions by judges respecting the decisions of other branches or, through the concept of precedent, the decisions of earlier judges.

judicial review Authority of courts to declare laws passed by Congress and acts of the executive branch to be unconstitutional.

jurisdiction Lawful authority of a court to hear a case.

L

lame duck Term-limited official in his or her last term of office.

Lawrence v. Texas 2003 Supreme Court case extending the right to privacy to homosexual behavior.

legislative branch The branch of the federal government that makes the laws.

Lemon test Test for determining whether aid to religion violates the establishment clause.

levels of conceptualization Measure of how ideologically coherent individuals are in their political evaluations.

liberals Individuals who have faith in government to improve people's lives, believing that private efforts are insufficient. In the social sphere, liberals usually support diverse lifestyles and tend to oppose any government action that seeks to shape personal choices.

libertarians Those who generally believe that government should refrain from acting to regulate either the economy or moral values.

liberty Political value that cherishes freedom from an arbitrary exercise of power that constricts individual choice.

lobbying Act of trying to persuade elected officials to adopt a specific policy change or maintain the status quo.

M

majority opinion Opinion of a court laying out the official position of the court in the case.

majority rule Idea that a numerical majority of a group should hold the power to make decisions binding on the whole group; a simple majority.

majority vote Vote in which the winner needs to win 50 percent plus 1 of the votes cast.

Marbury v. Madison An 1803 Supreme Court decision that established the Supreme Court's power of judicial review.

marketplace of ideas Idea that the government should not restrict the expression of ideas because the people are capable of accepting good ideas and rejecting bad ones.

markup Process by which bills are literally marked up, or written, by the members of the committee.

mass media News sources, including newspapers, television, radio, and the Internet, whose purpose is to provide a large audience with information about the nation and the world.

McCulloch v. Maryland 1819 Supreme Court decision upholding the right of Congress to create a bank.

median voter theorem Theory that, in a two-party race, if voters select candidates on the basis of ideology and everyone participates equally, the party closer to the middle will win.

Medicaid Shared Federal and state health insurance program for low-income persons.

Medicare Federal health insurance program for the elderly and disabled.

merit system System of employment under which employees are chosen and promoted based on merit.

microtargeting Gathering detailed information on cross sections of the electorate to track potential supporters and tailor political messages for them; also called narrowcasting.

Miller test Supreme Court test for determining whether material is obscene.

minimal effects model View of the media's impact as marginal because most people seek news reports to reinforce beliefs already held rather than to develop new ones.

minority rights Idea that majority should not be able to take certain fundamental rights away from those in the minority.

moderates Individuals who are in the middle of the ideological spectrum and do not hold consistently strong views about whether government should be involved in people's lives.

monarchy System of government that assigns power to a single person who inherits that position and rules until death.

multipolar A world system where there are distinct centers of political and military power.

N

NAFTA Comprehensive multi-nation trade agreement ratified in 1994 that knocked down trade barriers among Canada, the United States, and Mexico.

national committee Top level of national political parties; coordinates national presidential campaigns.

national debt Sum of loans and interest that the federal government has accrued over time to pay for the federal deficit.

natural (unalienable) rights Rights that every individual has and that government cannot legitimately take away.

necessary and proper clause Gives Congress the power to pass all laws necessary and proper to the powers enumerated in Article I, Section 8.

negativity Campaign strategy of telling voters why they should not vote for the opponent and of highlighting information that raises doubts about the opponent.

New Deal Franklin Delano Roosevelt's program for ending the Great Depression through government intervention in the economy and development of a set of safety-net programs for individuals.

news media Subset of the mass media that provides the news of the day, gathered and reported by journalists.

nonattitudes Sources of error in public opinion polls in which individuals feel obliged to give opinions when they are unaware of the issue or have no opinions about it.

nongovernmental organizations (NGOs) Organizations independent of governments that monitor and improve political, economic, and social conditions throughout the world.

nonstate actors Individuals or groups that do not represent any specific national government and may take action across borders.

not-so-minimal effects model View of the media's impact as substantial, occurring by agenda setting, framing, and priming.

O

Office of Management and Budget (OMB) Federal agency that oversees the federal budget and all federal regulations.

oligarchy System of government in which the power to govern is concentrated in the hands of a powerful few, usually wealthy individuals.

omnibus bill One very large bill that encompasses many separate bills.

order Political value in which the rule of law is followed and does not permit actions that infringe on the well-being of others.

override Congress's power to overturn a presidential veto with a two-thirds vote in each chamber.

oversight Powers of Congress to monitor how the executive branch implements the laws.

P

pardon Full forgiveness for a crime.

party alignment Voter identification with a political party in repeated elections.

party caucus Group of party members in a legislature.

party identification Psychological attachment to a political party; partisanship.

party platform Document that lays out a party's core beliefs and policy proposals for each presidential election.

patronage system Political system in which government programs and benefits are awarded based on political loyalty to a party or politician.

Peace Corps U.S. government-funded organization that sends individuals on educational and cultural missions around the world.

Pendleton Act 1883 act that established a merit- and performance-based system for federal employment.

permanent campaign Charge that presidents and members of Congress focus more on winning the next election than on governing.

petition for a writ of certiorari Request to the Supreme Court that it review a lower court case.

plea bargain Agreement by a criminal defendant to plead guilty in return for a reduced sentence.

pluralist View of democratic society in which interest groups compete over policy goals, and elected officials are mediators of group conflict.

plurality vote Vote in which the winner needs to win more votes than any other candidate.

pocket veto Automatic veto that occurs when Congress goes out of session within ten days of submitting a bill to the president and the president has not signed it.

polarization Condition in which differences between parties and/or the public are so stark that disagreement breaks out, fueling attacks and controversy.

policy agenda The second step in the policy-making process, in which a problem that has been identified gets the attention of policy makers.

policy diffusion Process by which policy ideas and programs initiated by one state spread to other states.

policy enactment The fourth step in the policy-making process, in which Congress passes a law that authorizes a specific governmental response to the problem.

policy evaluation The final step in the policy-making process, in which the policy is evaluated for its effectiveness and efficiency; if changes are needed, the issue is placed back on the policy agenda, and the cycle starts again.

policy formulation The third step in the policy-making process, in which those with a stake in the policy area propose and develop solutions to the problem.

policy implementation The fifth step in the policy-making process, in which the executive branch develops the rules that will put the policy into action.

political action committees (PACs) Groups formed to raise and contribute funds to support electoral candidates and that are subject to campaign finance laws.

political appointees Federal employees appointed by the president with the explicit task of carrying out his political and partisan agenda.

political culture A shared way of thinking about community and government and the relationship between them.

political equality The idea that people should have equal amounts of influence in the political system.

political ideology Set of coherent political beliefs that offers a philosophy for thinking about the scope of government.

political tolerance Willingness of people to put up with ideas with which they disagree.

political trust Extent to which people believe the government acts in their best interests.

politics Process by which people make decisions about who gets what, when, and how.

populists Those who oppose concentrated wealth and adhere to traditional moral values.

position issues Political issues that offer specific policy choices and often differentiate candidates' views and plans of action.

power elite Small handful of decision makers who hold authority over a large set of issues.

precedent Practice of reaching decisions based on the previous decisions of other judges.

presidential directive Official instructions from the president regarding federal policy.

primary election Election in which voters select the candidates who will run on the party label in the general election; also called direct primary.

priming Process whereby the media influence the criteria the public uses to make decisions.

prior restraint Government restrictions on freedom of the press that prevent material from being published.

private discrimination Discrimination by private individuals or businesses.

private goods Goods or benefits provided by government in which most of the benefit falls to the individuals, families, or companies receiving them.

problem identification The first step in the policy-making process, in which a problem in politics, the economy, or society is recognized as warranting government action.

propaganda model Extreme view of the media's role in society, arguing that the press serves the interest of the government only, driving what the public thinks about important issues.

proportional representation An electoral system that assigns party delegates according to vote share in a presidential primary election or that assigns seats in the legislature according to vote share in a general election.

protectionist Policy designed to raise import barriers for goods that are domestically produced.

public discrimination Discrimination by national, state, or local governments.

public goods Goods or benefits provided by government from which everyone benefits and from which no one can be excluded.

public opinion Aggregate of individual attitudes or beliefs about certain issues or officials.

public policy Intentional actions of government designed to achieve a goal.

push polls Polls that are designed to manipulate the opinions of those being polled.

R

rally-around-the-flag effect Surge of public support for the president in times of international crisis.

random sample Method of selection that gives everyone who might be selected to participate in a poll an equal chance to be included.

ranking member Leader of the minority party members of a committee.

rational voting Economic model of voting wherein citizens weigh the benefits of voting against the costs in order to take the most personally beneficial course of action.

realignment Long-term shift in voter allegiance from one party to another.

recession A period of time marked by successive quarters of lower economic output.

reconciliation A measure used to bring all bills that contain changes in the tax code or entitlement programs in line with the congressional budget.

Reconstruction The period from 1865 to 1877 in which the former Confederate states gained readmission to the Union and the federal government passed laws to help the emancipated slaves.

redistricting Process whereby state legislatures redraw the boundaries of congressional districts in the state to make them equal in population size.

regulations Guidelines issued by federal agencies for administering federal programs and implementing federal law.

regulatory process System of rules that govern how a law is implemented; also called the rule-making process.

representative democracy Form of democracy in which citizens elect public officials to make political decisions and formulate laws on their behalf.

republic Form of government in which power derives from citizens, but public officials make policy and govern according to existing law.

reserve powers Powers retained by the states under the Constitution.

responsible parties Parties that take responsibility for offering the electorate a distinct range of policies and programs, thus providing a clear choice.

responsiveness Idea that government should implement laws and policies that reflect the wishes of the public and any changes in those wishes.

revolving door Movement of members of Congress, lobbyists, and executive branch employees into paid positions in each other's organizations.

right of association Right to freely associate with others and form groups, as protected by the First Amendment.

right of petition Right to ask the government for assistance with a problem or to express opposition to a government policy, as protected by the First Amendment.

right to privacy Constitutional right inferred by the Court that has been used to protect unlisted rights such as sexual privacy and reproductive rights, plus the right to end life-sustaining medical treatment.

Roe v. Wade 1973 Supreme Court case extending the right to privacy to abortion.

rule Guidelines issued by the House Rules Committee that determine how many amendments may be considered for each bill.

rule of four Supreme Court rule that grants review to a case if as few as four of the justices support review.

rule of law Legal system with known rules that are enforced equally against all people.

S

safe seat Seat in Congress considered to be reliably held by one party or the other.

Schedule C appointees Federal employees appointed by the president to oversee civil service employees.

secession Act of seceding, or formally withdrawing, from a nation-state.

selective benefits Benefits offered exclusively to members of an interest group.

selective exposure Process whereby people secure information from sources that agree with them, thus reinforcing their beliefs.

selective incorporation Doctrine used by the Supreme Court to make those provisions of the Bill of Rights that are fundamental rights binding on the states.

selective perception Process whereby partisans interpret the same information differently.

self-government Rule by the people.

Senate majority leader Leader of the majority party in the Senate.

Senate minority leader Leader of the minority party in the Senate.

Senior Executive Service (SES) Senior management personnel in the federal government appointed by the president.

separate-but-equal doctrine Supreme Court doctrine that upheld segregation as long as there were equivalent facilities for blacks.

separation of powers Government structure in which authority is divided among branches (executive, legislative, and judicial), with each holding separate and independent powers and areas of responsibility.

signing statements Written remarks issued by the president when signing a bill into law that often reflect his interpretation of how the law should be implemented.

single-issue groups Groups that form to present one view on a highly salient issue that is intensely important to members, such as gun control or abortion.

single-member plurality system Electoral system that assigns one seat in a legislative body to represent citizens who live in a defined area (a district) based on which candidate wins the most votes.

social contract Theory that government has only the authority accorded it by the consent of the governed.

Social Security Federal pension program that makes a monthly payment to retired elderly workers and disabled persons.

socialism Economic system in which the government owns major industries.

soft news News stories focused less on facts and policies than on sensationalizing secondary issues or on less serious subjects of the entertainment world.

solicitor general Official in the Justice Department who represents the president in federal court.

Speaker of the House Constitutional and political leader of the House.

special interests Set of groups seeking a particular benefit for themselves in the policy process.

state action Action by a state, as opposed to a private person, that constitutes discrimination and therefore is an equal protection violation.

State of the Union address Speech on the condition of the country given by the president to Congress every January.

Stonewall riots Street protest in 1969 by gay patrons against a police raid of a gay bar in New York; the protest is credited with launching the gay rights movement.

suffrage Right to vote; also called franchise.

Super PACs Independent groups that can raise unlimited amounts of money from individuals, labor unions, and corporations and can spend it to support or oppose political candidates but cannot coordinate directly with candidates or political parties.

supremacy clause Makes federal law supreme over state laws (Article VI).

swing states States that are not clearly pro-Republican or pro-Democrat and therefore are of vital interest to presidential candidates, as they can determine election outcomes.

swing voters Voters who are neither reliably Republican nor reliably Democratic and who are pursued by each party during an election, as they can determine which candidate wins.

symbolic speech Actions, such as burning the flag, that convey a political message without spoken words.

T

term limits Rule restricting the number of terms an elected official can serve in a given office.

third parties Minor political parties that present a third alternative to the two dominant political parties in the American political system.

three-fifths compromise Compromise over slavery at the Constitutional Convention that granted states extra representation in the House of Representatives based on their number of slaves at the ratio of three-fifths.

tracking polls Polls that seek to gauge changes of opinion of the same sample size over a period of time, common during the closing months of presidential elections.

U

unanimous consent agreement Agreement among all 100 senators on how a bill or presidential nomination will be debated, changed, and voted on in the Senate.

unions Interest groups of individuals who share a common type of employment and seek better wages and working conditions through collective bargaining with employers.

unitary system System of government in which ultimate authority rests with the national government.

United Nations (UN) Organization formed after World War II to mediate disputes among nations around the world.

V

valence issues Noncontroversial or widely supported campaign issues that are unlikely to differ among candidates.

valid secular purpose Supreme Court test that allows states to ban activities that infringe on religious practices as long as the state has a nonreligious rationale for prohibiting the behavior.

vanishing marginals Trend marking the decline of competitive congressional elections.

veto Authority of the president to block legislation passed by Congress. Congress can override a veto by a two-thirds majority in each chamber.

vote-by-mail (VBM) system Method of voting in an election whereby ballots are distributed to voters by mail, and voters complete and return the ballots by mail.

voting-age population (VAP) Used to calculate the rate of participation by dividing the number of voters by the number of people in the country who are 18 and over.

voting-eligible population (VEP) Used to calculate the rate of participation by dividing the number of voters by the number of people in the country who are eligible to vote rather than just of voting age.

Voting Rights Act Gives the federal government the power to prevent discrimination in voting rights (1965).

W

War Powers Act The 1973 act which provides that the president cannot send troops into military conflict for more than a total of ninety days without seeking a formal declaration of war, or authorization for continued military action, from Congress.

watchdog Role of the press in monitoring government actions.

wedge issue Divisive issue focused on a particular group of the electorate that candidates use to gain more support by taking votes away from their opponents.

whistleblowers Employees who report mismanagement, corruption, or illegal activity within their agencies.

winner-take-all system Electoral system in which whoever wins the most votes in an election wins the election.

women's suffrage movement Movement to grant women the right to vote.

World Bank International organization that distributes grants and low-income loans in developing countries.

World Trade Organization (WTO) International organization that considers and resolves trade disputes among member nations.

writ of habeas corpus Right of individuals who have been arrested and jailed to go before a judge, who determines whether their detention is legal.

Endnotes

Chapter 1

1. International Social Survey Program, as cited in Russell Dalton, *The Good Citizen* (Washington, D.C.: CQ Press, 2007), 144; Morley Winograd and Michael D. Hais, *Millennial Makeover: MySpace, YouTube and the Future of American Politics* (New Brunswick, N.J.: Rutgers University Press, 2008), 260–63. The caption for the photo on page 5 is drawn from this source.

2. Dalton, *Good Citizen*, 153.

3. Larry Bartels, *Unequal Democracy* (Princeton, N.J.: Princeton University Press, 2008); David Cay Johnston, "The Gap between Rich and Poor Grows in the United States," *New York Times*, March 29, 2007. The caption for the photo on page 5 is drawn from these sources: U.S. census data; Merrill Goozner, "Top 1 Percent Got Lion's Share of Income," *Fiscal Times*, March 5, 2012, http://www.thefiscaltimes.com/Blogs/Gooz-News/2012/03/05/Top-1-Percent-Got-Lions-Share-of-Income-Gains-in-2010.aspx; and Emmanuel Saez, "Striking It Richer: The Evolution of Top Incomes in the United States (Updated with 2009 and 2010 Estimates)," *Pathways Magazine* (Winter 2008): 6–7, http://www.stanford.edu/group/scspi/_media/pdf/pathways/winter_2008/Saez.pdf.

4. "Americans' Approval of Congress Drops to Single Digits," *New York Times*, October 25, 2011, http://www.nytimes.com/interactive/2011/10/25/us/politics/approval-of-congress-drops-to-single-digits.html.

5. Kerem Ozan Kalkan, Geoffrey C. Layman, and Eric M. Uslaner, "Attitudes toward Muslims in Contemporary American Society," *Journal of Politics* 69 (2009): 847–62. Brett Benson, Jennifer Merolla, and John Geer, "Two Steps Forward, One Step Back?" *Electoral Studies* 30 (2011): 607–620.

6. "Obama Ratings Historically Polarized," Gallup Politics, January 27, 2012, accessed April 10, 2012, http://www.gallup.com/poll/152222/Obama-Ratings-Historically-Polarized.aspx.

7. See http://www.usdebtclock.org, accessed September 15, 2014.

8. See http://www.cnbc.com/id/101025377.

9. Charles Beard, *American Government and Politics* (New York: Macmillan Company, 1915), 18.

10. Edmund Burke, *Reflections on the Revolution in France*, in *The Portable Edmund Burke*, ed. Isaac Kramnick (New York: Viking, 1999), 32.

11. John Adams to John Taylor, April 15, 1814, in *The Political Writings of John Adams: Representative Selections*, ed. George Peek Jr. (New York: Hackett Publishing, 2003), 67.

12. Quoted in David McCullough, *John Adams* (New York: Simon and Schuster, 2001), 68.

13. Jonathan Grossman, "Fair Labor Standards Act of 1938: Maximum Struggle for a Minimum Wage," United States Department of Labor, accessed April 1, 2014, http://www.dol.gov/dol/aboutdol/history/flsa1938.htm.

14. Oregon State University, accessed April 1, 2014, http://oregonstate.edu/instruct/anth484/minwage.html.

15. Staff, "Wages and Hours Worked: Minimum Wage and Overtime Pay," Department of Labor, accessed April 1, 2014, http://www.dol.gov/compliance/guide/minwage.htm.

16. President Barack Obama, State of the Union Address 2014, http://www.whitehouse.gov/the-press-office/2014/01/28/president-barack-obamas-state-union-address.

17. Ibid.

18. See Josiah Ober, *Mass and Elite in Democratic Athens* (Princeton, N.J.: Princeton University Press, 1991).

19. Harold Lasswell, *Politics: Who Gets What, When, How* (New York: McGraw-Hill, 1936).

20. President Barack Obama, Inaugural Address, January 20, 2009, http://www.whitehouse.gov/blog/inaugural-address.

21. Winograd and Hais, *Millennial Makeover*; Morley Winograd and Michael D. Hais, "The Boomers Had Their Day. Make Way for the Millennials," *Washington Post*, February 3, 2008, http://www.washingtonpost.com/wp-dyn/content/article/2008/02/01/AR2008020102826.html.

22. See https://www2.ed.gov/about/overview/budget/history/edhistory.pdf.

23. Darrell M. West, Grover J. Whitehurst, and E. J. Dionne Jr., "Invisible: 1.4 Percent Coverage for Education Is Not Enough," Brookings.edu, December 2, 2009, accessed April 10, 2012, http://www.brookings.edu/research/reports/2009/12/02-education-news-west.

24. James Madison to W. T. Barry, "Epilogue: Securing the Republic," August 4, 1822, in *The Founders' Constitution*, ed. Philip B. Kurland and Ralph Lerner (Chicago: University of Chicago Press, 1986), accessed April 25, 2012, http://press-pubs.uchicago.edu/founders/documents/v1ch18s35.html.

Chapter 2

1. Cited in Lupe S. Salinas, "Gus Garcia and Thurgood Marshall: Two Legal Giants Fighting for Justice," *Thurgood Marshall Law Review* 28, (2003): 145–173.

2. *Delgado et al. v. Bastrop Independent School District* Civil No. 388, W.D. Texas (1948).

3. Michael A. Olivas (ed.). *Colored Men and Hombres Aqui:* Hernandez v. Texas *and the Emergence of Mexican-American Lawyering*. (Houston, TX: Arte Público Press, 2006).

4. *Hernandez v. Texas*, 347 U.S. 475 (1954).

5. *Hernandez v. Texas*, at 475.

6. *Hernandez v. Texas* at 479.

7. Edmund Burke, "Speech to the Electors of Bristol," November 3, 1774, in *The Founders' Constitution* ed. Philip B. Kurland and Ralph Lerner (Chicago: University of Chicago Press, 1986), accessed April 25, 2012, http://press-pubs.uchicago.edu/founders/documents/v1ch13s7.html.

8. Robert Middlekauff, *The Glorious Cause: The American Revolution, 1763–1789* (New York: Oxford University Press, 1982), 231.

9. Thomas Paine, *Common Sense* (Philadelphia, 1776), USHistory.org, accessed April 10, 2012, http://www.ushistory.org/paine/commonsense/sense4.htm.

10. Articles of Confederation, Article IX, Paragraph 5, U.S. Constitution Online, accessed April 10, 2012, http://www.usconstitution.net/articles.html#Article9.

11. See "Variant Texts of the Plan Presented by William Patterson," in *Debates in the Federal Convention of 1787 Reported by James Madison*, ed. Gaillard Hunt and James B. Scott (New York: 1920), 102–4, quoted by the Avalon Project, Yale University, Lillian Goldman Law Library, accessed April 10, 2012, http://avalon.law.yale.edu/18th_century/patexta.asp.

12. "1790 Census of Slave and Free Population," U.S. Census of Population and Housing, Historical Census Browser, University of Virginia, Geospatial and Statistical Data Center, accessed April 10, 2012, http://mapserver.lib.virginia.edu/.

13. Quoted in Max Farrand, *The Framing of the Constitution of the United States* (New Haven, Conn.: Yale University Press, 1913), 1:486–87.

14. Garry Wills, *Negro President: Jefferson and the Slave Power* (Boston: Houghton Mifflin, 2003), 5–6.

15. Wendy J. Schiller and Charles Stewart III, *Electing the Senate: Indirect Democracy before the 17th Amendment* (Princeton, NJ: Princeton University Press, 2014).

16. See Allison M. Martens, "Reconsidering Judicial Supremacy: From the Counter-Majoritarian Difficulty to Constitutional Transformations," *Perspectives on Politics* 5 (2007): 447–59.

17. James Madison, "*Federalist 47,*" in *The Federalist Papers,* U.S. Constitution Online, accessed April 10, 2012, http://www.constitution.org/fed/federa47.htm.

18. James Madison, "*Federalist 39,*" in *The Federalist Papers,* U.S. Constitution Online, accessed May 3, 2012, http://www.constitution.org/fed/federa39.htm.

19. Brutus, "Antifederalist 1," U.S. Constitution Online, accessed May 10, 2012, http://www.constitution.org/afp/brutus01.htm.

20. James Madison, "*Federalist 41,*" in *The Federalist Papers,* U.S. Constitution Online, accessed April 10, 2012, http://www.constitution.org/fed/federa41.htm.

21. *Furman v. Georgia*, 408 U.S. 238 (1972).

22. *Gregg v. Georgia*, 428 U.S. 153 (1976).

23. "States with and without the Death Penalty," Death Penalty Information Center, accessed February 24, 2014, http://www.deathpenaltyinfo.org/states-and-without-death-penalty.

24. See http://www.gallup.com/poll/1606/death-penalty.aspx.

25. "Federal Death Penalty," Death Penalty Information Center, accessed April 10, 2012, http://www.deathpenaltyinfo.org/federal-death-penalty?scid=29&did=147.

26. Matt Apuzzo, "U.S. Is Seeking Death Penalty in Boston Case," *New York Times,* January 31, 2014, A1.

27. David Baldus, Charles A. Pulaski Jr., and George Woodworth, *Equal Justice and the Death Penalty* (Boston: Northeastern University Press, 1990).

28. *McCleskey v. Kemp*, 481 U.S. 279 (1987).

29. *Roper v. Simmons*, 543 U.S. 551 (2005); *Kennedy v. Louisiana,* 554 U.S. 407 (2008).

30. See http://www.innocenceproject.org/know/, accessed March 12, 2014.

31. *District Attorney's Office v. Osborne*, 174 L. Ed. 2d 38 (2009).

32. *Wickard v. Filburn,* 317 U.S. 111 (1942).

33. *National Federation of Independent Business v. Sebelius*, 11–393 (2012).

Chapter 3

1. This story was written by Dana K. Glencross of Oklahoma City Community College and compiled from information on the Oklahoma County website, http://www.oklahomacounty.org; Bryan Painter, "Local community service project helps area SHINE," *The Oklahoman,* October 11, 2010, 1A; Bryan Painter, "Community Service Project helps area SHINE," *The Oklahoman,* November 14, 2010, 9J; and telephone and e-mail interviews with Brian Maughan, February 29, March 28, and April 5, 2012, conducted for this textbook; chapter-opening quotation from March 13, 2012, e-mail.

2. Colin Bonwick, *The American Revolution* (Charlottesville: University of Virginia Press, 1991), 194.

3. "The First Political Cartoons," Archiving Early America, accessed April 13, 2012, http://www.earlyamerica.com/earlyamerica/firsts/cartoon/.

4. William Riker, *Federalism: Origin, Operation, Significance* (Boston: Little Brown, 1964), 5.

5. Article 6, the Virginia Plan, accessed August 7, 2014, http://avalon.law.yale.edu/18th_century/vatexta.asp

6. *Revenues and Expenditures for Public Elementary and Secondary Education: School Year 2010-11 (Fiscal Year 2011)* (Washington, D.C.: National Center for Education Statistics, 2014), accessed March 22, 2014, http://nces.ed.gov/pubs2013/2013344/findings.asp.

7. Michael B. Berkman and Eric Plutzer, *Ten Thousand Democracies* (Washington D.C.: Georgetown University Press, 2005).

8. 247 U.S. 483 (1954)

9. 404 U.S. 1211 (1971).

10. Joy Resmovits, "No Child Left Behind Waivers Granted to 33 U.S. States, Some with Strings Attached," *Huffington Post,* July 19, 2012, accessed July 20, 2012, http://www.huffingtonpost.com/2012/07/19/no-child-left-behind-waiver_n_1684504.html.

11. Alan Greenblatt, "Q and A with Paul Posner: July/August 2010," National Conference of State Legislators, 2010, accessed June 6, 2014, http://www.ncsl.org/bookstore/state-legislatures-magazine/q-and-a-with-paul-posner.aspx.

12. See http://www.ed.gov/news/press-releases/education-department-announces-next-rounds-race-top-including-another-key-invest.

13. James Madison, "*Federalist* 39," in *The Federalist Papers,* U.S. Constitution Online, accessed April 13, 2012, http://www.constitution.org/fed/federa39.htm.

14. *Cohens v. Virginia*, 19 U.S. 264 (1821).

15. *Chisolm v. Georgia*, 2 U.S. 419 (1793).

16. Elinor Ostrom, *Governing the Commons: The Evolution of Institutions for Collective Action* (New York: Cambridge University Press, 1990), 106–10.

17. *United States v. Windsor*, 133 S. Ct. 2675 (2013).

18. "Gay Marriage." ProCon.org., 2014, accessed April, 4, 2014, http://gaymarriage.procon.org/view.resource.php?resourceID=004857.

19. Chrissie Thompson, "Ohio Will Have to Recognize Gay Marriages, Judge Says." *USA Today,* April 4, 2014, accessed April 5, 2014, http://www.usatoday.com/story/news/nation/2014/04/04/ohio-gay-marriage/7304753/.

20. *McCulloch v. Maryland*, 17 U.S. 316 (1819).

21. *Gibbons v. Ogden*, 22 U.S. 1 (1824).

22. *Dred Scott v. Sandford,* 60 U.S. 393 (1857).

23. "Confederate States of America—Declaration of the Immediate Causes Which Induce and Justify Secession of South Carolina from the Federal Union," December 24, 1860, Avalon Project, Yale University, Lillian Goldman Law Library, accessed April 30, 2012, http://avalon.law.yale.edu/19th_century/csa_scarsec.asp.

24. See http://www.civil-war.net/pages/ordinances_secession.asp.

25. Andrew Johnson, "Veto of the Civil Rights Bill," March 27, 1866, Teaching American History, accessed April 13, 2012, http://teachingamericanhistory.org/library/document/veto-of-the-civil-rights-bill/.

26. Morton Grodzins, *The American System: A New View of the Government of the United States* (New York: Rand McNally, 1966), 8.

27. Wendy J. Schiller, "Building Careers and Courting Constituents: U.S. Senate Representation, 1889–1924," *Studies in American Political Development* 20 (2006): 1.

28. *Carter v. Carter Coal Co.*, 298 U.S. 238 (1936).

29. *National Labor Relations Board v. Jones & Laughlin Steel Corporation*, 301 U.S. 1 (1937).

30. *United States v. Darby Lumber Company*, 312 U.S. 100 (1941).

31. Grodzins, *American System*, 8–9.

32. "American Independent Party Platform of 1968," October 13, 1968, online by Gerhard Peters and John Woolley, The American Presidency

Project, accessed April 13, 2012, http://www.presidency.ucsb.edu/ws//index.php?pid=29570#axzz1rwnAcK5P.

33. Sean Nicholson-Crotty, "Rational Election Cycles and the Intermittent Political Safeguards of Federalism," *Publius: The Journal of Federalism* 38 (2008): 295–314.

34. Timothy Conlon, *New Federalism: Intergovernmental Reform from Nixon to Reagan* (Washington D.C.: Brookings Institution, 1988).

35. "Ronald Reagan, First Inaugural Address," January 20, 1981, American Rhetoric, accessed April 13, 2012, http://www.americanrhetoric.com/speeches/ronaldreagandfirstinaugural.html.

36. Tim Conlan and John Dinan, "Federalism, the Bush Administration, and the Transformation of American Conservatism," *Publius: The Journal of Federalism* 37 (2007): 279–303.

37. Scott F. Abernathy, *No Child Left Behind and the Public Schools* (Ann Arbor: University of Michigan Press, 2007), 23.

38. John Schwartz, "Obama Seems to Be Open to a Broader Role for States," *New York Times,* January 29, 2009, http://www.nytimes.com/2009/01/30/us/politics/30federal.html/; "DEA Pot Raids Go On; Obama Opposes," *The Washington Times,* February 5, 2009, http://www.washingtontimes.com/news/2009/feb/05/dea-led-by-bush-continues-pot-raids/?page=1.

39. *Younger v. Harris,* 401 U.S. 37 (1971).

40. *United States v. Lopez,* 514 U.S. 549 (1995).

41. *South Dakota v. Dole,* 483 U.S. 203 (1987) at 211.

42. *National Federation of Independent Business v. Sebelius,* 132 S. Ct. 2566 (2012).

43. *Gonzales v. Raich,* 545 U.S. 1 (2005).

44. *National Federation of Independent Business v. Sebelius,* 183 L. Ed 2d 450 (2012).

45. U.S. Census Bureau, "Local Government and Public School Systems by Type and State: 2012," accessed March 21, 2014, http://www.census.gov/govs/go/index.html.

46. See http://www.washingtonpost.com/blogs/the-fix/post/arizona-recall-why-russell-pearce-lost/2011/11/09/gIQALj6a5M_blog.html.

47. National Conference of State Legislatures, "Initiative, Referendum, and Recall," NCSL.org, http://www.ncsl.org/legislatures-elections/elections/initiative-referendum-and-recall-overview.aspx.

48. *Hollingsworth v. Perry,* 133 S. Ct. 2652 (2013).

49. http://www.iandrinstitute.org/BW%202014-2%20Election%20results%20(v1)%202014-11-04.pdf, and http://www.iandrinstitute.org/BW%202014-1%20Preview%20(v1)%202014-10-15.pdf. Accessed November 5, 2014.

50. Colorado Marijuana-Legalization Amendment Spending Tops $3 Million," *The Denver Post,* accessed April 6, 2014, http://www.denverpost.com/ci_21820068/colorado-marijuana-legalization-amendment-spending-tops-3-million.

51. Reid Wilson, "The Most Expensive Race of 2014 Could Be This California Ballot Measure," *The Washington Post,* March 25, 2014, accessed April 6, 2014. http://www.washingtonpost.com/blogs/govbeat/wp/2014/03/25/the-most-expensive-race-of-2014-could-be-this-california-ballot-measure/.

Chapter 4

1. Brutus, "*Antifederalist* 2," U.S. Constitution Online, accessed May 9, 2012, http://www.constitution.org/afp/brutus02.htm.

2. *West Virginia Board of Education v. Barnette,* 319 U.S. 624 (1943).

3. Annals of Congress, H439 (June 8, 1789), American Memory, Library of Congress, accessed May 18, 2012, http://memory.loc.gov/cgi-bin/ampage?collId=llac&fileName=001/llac001.db&recNum=221.

4. *Schenck v. United States,* 249 U.S. 47 (1919).

5. Judith A. Baer, *Equality under the Constitution* (Ithaca, N.Y.: Cornell University Press, 1983).

6. *Chicago B & Q Railway Company v. Chicago,* 166 U.S. 226 (1897).

7. *Gitlow v. New York,* 268 U.S. 652 (1925).

8. *Palko v. Connecticut,* 302 U.S. 319 (1937).

9. *Schenck v. United States,* 249 U.S. 47 (1919); *Debs v. United States,* 249 U.S. 211 (1919).

10. *Hirota v. MacArthur,* 338 U.S. 197 (1948).

11. *Hamdan v. Rumsfeld,* 548 U.S. 557 (2006).

12. See http://www.fas.org/irp/agency/doj/fisa/#rept.

13. Robin Toner and Neil A. Lewis, "A NATION CHALLENGED: CONGRESS; House Passes Terrorism Bill Much Like Senate's, but with 5-Year Limit, *New York Times,* October 12, 2011. accessed April 27, 2014, http://www.nytimes.com/2001/10/13/us/nation-challenged-congress-house-passes-terrorism-bill-much-like-senate-s-but.html.

14. Robert McMillan, "Obama Administration Defends Bush Wiretapping," *PC World,* July 15, 2009, http://www.pcworld.com/article/168502/obama_administration_defends_bush_wiretapping.html.

15. *Al Haramain Islamic Foundation v. Obama* 690 F.3d 1089 (2012), accessed April 28, 2014, http://cdn.ca9.uscourts.gov/datastore/opinions/2012/08/07/11-15468.pdf.

16. *Smith v. Maryland,* 442 U.S. 735 (1979).

17. See http://www.nytimes.com/2013/06/08/us/mining-of-data-is-called-crucial-to-fight-terror.html?nl=todaysheadlines&emc=edit_th_20130608&_r=0.

18. See http://www.nytimes.com/2014/03/25/us/obama-to-seek-nsa-curb-on-call-data.html.

19. See http://epic.org/privacy/wiretap/stats/fisa_stats.html.

20. See http://afgeneralcounsel.dodlive.mil/2014/01/14/u-s-judiciary-weighs-in-on-special-advocates-before-fisa-court/.

21. Charlie Savage, "U.S. Law May Allow Killings, Holder Says," *New York Times,* March 5, 2012.

22. See http://www.foxnews.com/politics/2014/04/21/federal-court-obama-administration-must-release-targeted-killings-memo/.

23. *Brandenburg v. Ohio,* 395 U.S. 444 (1969).

24. *Chaplinsky v. New Hampshire,* 315 U.S. 568 (1942).

25. David L. Hudson Jr., "Hate Speech and Campus Speech Codes," First Amendment Center, September 13, 2002, accessed May 9, 2012, http://www.firstamendmentcenter.org/hate-speech-campus-speech-codes.

26. Alan Charles Kors and Harvey Silvergate, *The Shadow University: The Betrayal of Liberty on America's Campuses* (New York: Free Press, 1998).

27. "Warning: College Students, this editorial may upset you," *Los Angeles Times,* March 31, 2014, http://www.latimes.com/opinion/editorials/la-ed-trigger-warnings-20140331,0,6700908.story#ixzz2yaSoYsXi.

28. See http://chronicle.com/blogs/conversation/2014/03/10/trigger-warnings-trigger-me.

29. *Virginia v. Black,* 538 U.S. 343 (2003).

30. *Tinker v. Des Moines School District,* 393 U.S. 503 (1969). The quotation in the caption on page 99 is from this decision, at 506.

31. *Bland et al. v. Roberts,* E.D. Va. (Apr. 24, 2012).

32. *United States v. O'Brien,* 391 U.S. 367 (1968).

33. *Hill v. Colorado,* 530 U.S. 703 (2000). The pro-protest decision in 2014 is *McCullen v. Coakley* (citation not yet available).

34. *West Virginia Board of Education v. Barnette*, 319 U.S. 624 (1943).

35. *Texas v. Johnson*, 491 U.S. 397 (1989).

36. *Morse v. Frederick*, 551 U.S. 393 (2007).

37. *Grayned v. City of Rockford*, 408 U.S. 104 (1972).

38. William Blackstone, *Commentaries on the Laws of England*, 1769 (Chicago: University of Chicago Press, 2002), 4:151–53.

39. *New York Times v. United States*, 403 U.S. 713 (1971).

40. *United States v. Progressive*, 467 F. Supp. 990 (1979).

41. See http://www.wikileaks.org.

42. Adam Liptak and Brad Stone, "Judge Shuts Down Web Site Specializing in Leaks," *New York Times*, February 20, 2008.

43. *Hustler Magazine v. Falwell*, 485 U.S. 46 (1988).

44. Anna Badkhen, "Web Can Ruin Reputation with Stroke of a Key," *San Francisco Chronicle*, May 6, 2007.

45. *Miller v. California*, 413 U.S. 15 (1973).

46. See http://thecolbertreport.cc.com/videos/49r39y/pussy-riot-pt--1.

47. *Ibid.*

48. Joe Nocera, "Pussy Riot Tells All," *New York Times*, February 7, 2014, http://www.nytimes.com/2014/02/08/opinion/nocera-pussy-riot-tells-all.html?_r=0.

49. *Jenkins v. Georgia*, 418 U.S. 153 (1974).

50. *New York v. Ferber*, 458 U.S. 747 (1982).

51. *Ashcroft v. Free Speech Coalition*, 535 U.S. 234 (2002).

52. *Reno v. American Civil Liberties Union*, 521 U.S. 844 (1997).

53. *Brown v. Entertainment Merchants Association*, 131 S. Ct. 2729 (2011).

54. *United States v. Stevens*, 559 U.S. 460 (2010).

55. Ontario Consultants on Religious Tolerance, "Religious Laws," ReligiousTolerance.org, accessed May 9, 2012, http://www.religioustolerance.org/lawmenu.htm.

56. *Rosenberger v. University of Virginia*, 515 U.S. 819 (1995).

57. *Church of Lakumi Babalu Aye v. City of Hialeah*, 508 U.S. 520 (1993).

58. *Reynolds v. United States*, 98 U.S. 145 (1878).

59. Bill Mears,"Judge Strikes Down Part of Utah Polygamy Law in 'Sister Wives' Case," *CNN*, December 16, 2013, http://www.cnn.com/2013/12/14/justice/utah-polygamy-law/.

60. *Clay, aka, Ali v. United States*, 403 U.S. 698 (1971).

61. *Employment Division v. Smith*, 494 U.S. 872 (1990).

62. *City of Boerne v. Flores*, 521 U.S. 507 (1997), at 536.

63. *Hosanna-Tabor Evangelical Lutheran Church and School v. Equal Employment Opportunity Commission*, 132 S. Ct. 694 (2012).

64. See "Rethinking the Incorporation of the Establishment Clause: A Federalist View," *Harvard Law Review* 105 (1992): 1700.

65. *Everson v. Board of Education*, 330 U.S. 1 (1947).

66. *Lemon v. Kurtzman*, 403 U.S. 602 (1971).

67. *Engel v. Vitale*, 370 U.S. 421 (1962) (prayer); *Abington School District v. Schempp*, 374 U.S. 203 (1963) (Bible reading).

68. *Epperson v. Arkansas*, 393 U.S. 97 (1968).

69. *Edwards v. Aguillard*, 482 U.S. 578 (1987).

70. *Lee v. Weisman*, 505 U.S. 577 (1992).

71. *Santa Fe Independent School District v. Doe*, 530 U.S. 290 (2000).

72. *Board of Education v. Allen*, 392 U.S. 236 (1968).

73. *Meek v. Pittenger*, 421 U.S. 349 (1975).

74. *District of Columbia v. Heller*, 554 U.S. 570 (2008).

75. *McDonald v. Chicago*, 561 U.S. 3025 (2010).

76. *Florence v. County of Burlington*, 10-945 (2012).

77. *Riley v. California*, 134 S. Ct. 999 (2014).

78. *Schneckloth v. Bustamonte*, 412 U.S. 218 (1973).

79. *Missouri v. McNeely* 133 S. Ct. 1552 (2013).

80. *Maryland v. King*, 133 S. Ct. 1958 (2013).

81. See Jeffrey A. Segal, "Predicting Supreme Court Decisions Probabilistically: The Search and Seizure Cases, 1962–1981," *American Political Science Review* 78 (1984): 801.

82. *California v. Ciraolo*, 476 U.S. 207 (1986).

83. *Florida v. Jardines*, 133 S. Ct. 1409 (2013).

84. *Kyllo v. United States*, 533 U.S. 27 (2001).

85. *Virginia v. Moore*, 553 U.S. 164 (2008).

86. *Prado Navarette v. California*, accessed April 28, 2014. http://www.supremecourt.gov/opinions/13pdf/12-9490_3fb4.pdf.

87. *United States v. Jones, 132 S. Ct. 945 (2012)*.

88. *Vernonia School District 47J v. Acton*, 515 U.S. 646 (1995); *National Treasury Union v. Von Raab*, 489 U.S. 656 (1989); *Chandler v. Miller*, 520 U.S. 305 (1997).

89. *Mapp v. Ohio*, 367 U.S. 643 (1961).

90. Priscilla H. Machado Zotti, *Injustice for All: Mapp v. Ohio and the Fourth Amendment* (New York: Peter Lang, 2005).

91. *United States v. Leon*, 468 U.S. 897 (1984).

92. *Nix v. Williams*, 467 U.S. 431 (1984).

93. *Miranda v. Arizona*, 384 U.S. 436 (1966).

94. *Dickerson v. United States*, 530 U.S. 428 (2000).

95. *Powell v. Alabama*, 287 U.S. 45 (1932).

96. *Gideon v. Wainwright*, 372 U.S. 335 (1963).

97. *Argersinger v. Hamlin*, 407 U.S. 25 (1972).

98. *Williams v. Florida*, 399 U.S. 78 (1970); *Johnson v. Louisiana*, 406 U.S. 356 (1972).

99. *Georgia v. McCollum*, 505 U.S. 42 (1992); *J. E. B. v. Alabama*, 511 U.S. 127 (1994).

100. Peter Johnson, "Decisions Uncertain in Civil Rights Charges against Zimmerman," ABC News, March 19, 2014, http://www.abc57.com/news/national-world/Decision-uncertain-in-civil-rights-charges-against-Zimmerman-251100481.html.

101. Akhil Amar, *The Bill of Rights* (New Haven, Conn.: Yale University Press, 1998), 82.

102. *Rummel v. Estelle*, 445 U.S. 263 (1980).

103. *Furman v. Georgia*, 408 U.S. 238 (1972).

104. *Gregg v. Georgia*, 428 U.S. 153 (1976).

105. *District Attorney's Office v. Osborne*, 557 U.S. 52 (2009).

106. *Herrera v. Collins*, 506 U.S. 390 (1993).

107. *Griswold v. Connecticut*, 381 U.S. 479 (1965).

108. *Eisenstadt v. Baird*, 405 U.S. 438 (1972).

109. Gerald Rosenberg, *The Hollow Hope* (Chicago: University of Chicago Press, 1991), 262.

110. *Roe v. Wade*, 410 U.S. 113 (1973).

111. *Planned Parenthood of Southeastern Pennsylvania v. Casey*, 505 U.S. 833 (1992).

112. *Bowers v. Hardwick*, 478 U.S. 186 (1986).

113. National Opinion Research Center, General Social Survey, University of Chicago.

114. *Lawrence v. Texas*, 539 U.S. 558 (2003).

115. *Cruzan v. Director, Missouri Department of Health*, 497 U.S. 261 (1990), at 278.

116. *Washington v. Glucksberg*, 521 U.S. 702; *Vacco v. Quill*, 521 U.S. 793 (1997).

117. *West Virginia State Board of Education v. Barnette*, 319 U.S. 624 (1943).

118. Robert Dahl, "Decision-Making in a Democracy: The Supreme Court as a National Policy-Maker," *Journal of Public Law* 6 (1957): 279–95.

119. Anthony Lewis, *Freedom for the Thought That We Hate: A Biography of the First Amendment* (New York: Basic Books, 2007).

120. John L. Sullivan, James Pierson, and George Marcus, *Political Tolerance and American Democracy* (Chicago: University of Chicago Press, 1973); James L. Gibson, "Enigmas of Intolerance: Fifty Years after Stouffer's *Communism, Conformity, and Civil Liberties*," *Perspectives on Politics* 4 (March 2006): 22.

Chapter 5

1. Information for this vignette came from Anna Fifieild, "Tough Talk over Illegal Immigrants Leaves 'Dreamers' Disillusioned," *Financial Times*, February 27, 2012, accessed April 29, 2014 via LexisNexis Academic Universe; Lawrence Downes, "Questions for a Young Immigration-Rights Activist," *New York Times*, April 10, 2013, http://www.nytimes.com/2013/04/11/opinion/questions-for-a-young-immigration-rights-activist.html?_r=0;http://www.youtube.com/watch?v=FVZKfoXsMxk; http://freedomfromfearaward.com/celebrate/erikaandiola; https://www.facebook.com/erika.andiola; http://unitedwedream.org/press-releases/dream-youth-and-supporters-denounce-home-raid-and-detention-of-erika-andiolas-family-by-ice/; Julia Preston, "Report Finds Deportation Focus on Criminal Records, *New York Times*, April 29, 2014, p. A16, http://www.nytimes.com/2014/04/30/us/report-finds-deportations-focus-on-criminal-records.html?_r=0; "Erika Andiola Slams Obama over Deportations," accessed April 30, 2014, http://video.foxnews.com/v/3430812515001/erika-andiola-slams-obama-over-deportations/#sp=show-clips.

2. See Alexander Keyssar, *The Right to Vote* (New York: Basic Books, 2000), 17 (women) and 164 (Native Americans).

3. Senator Lyman Trumbull, quoted in Judith Baer, *Equality under the Constitution* (Ithaca, N.Y.: Cornell University Press, 1983), 96.

4. Quoted in Steven M. Gillon and Cathy D. Matson, *The American Experiment*, 2nd ed. (Boston: Houghton Mifflin, 2006), 61.

5. *Dred Scott v. Sandford*, 60 U.S. 393 (1857).

6. Peter H. Schuck and Rogers M. Smith, *Citizenship without Consent* (New Haven, Conn.: Yale University Press, 1985), 1–2.

7. *Johnson v. M'Intosh*, 21 U.S. 543 (1823), at 569.

8. *Elk v. Wilkins*, 112 U.S. 94 (1884).

9. Institute for Texan Cultures, *The Tejanos*, accessed June 3, 2014, http://www.texancultures.com/assets/1/15/Texans_One_and_All%20-%20The%20Tejanos.pdf.

10. Kevin R. Johnson, "The Forgotten Repatriation of Persons of Mexican Ancestry and Lessons for the War on Terror," *Pace L. Rev.* 26, 1 (2005): 104.

11. Texas State Historical Association, *Operation Wetback*, accessed June 3, 2014, http://www.tshaonline.org/handbook/online/articles/pqo01.

12. Johnson, 111.

13. Johnson, 110.

14. California Alien Land Law (1913).

15. *Korematsu v. United States,* 323 U.S. 214 (1944).

16. Anne McDermott, "Orphans Tell of World War II Internment," March 24, 1997, CNN, http://www.cnn.com/US/9703/24/interned.orphans.

17. Immigration Act of 1907, 43 Statutes at Large 153.

18. Rogers M. Smith, *Civic Ideals* (New Haven, Conn.: Yale University Press, 1997), 16; Siobhan B. Sommerville, "Queer Alienage: The Racial and Sexual Logic of the 1952 U.S. Immigration and Nationality Act," Working Paper Series on Historical Systems, Peoples and Cultures (No. 12), 2002, 8, accessed June 6, 2014, http://www2.bgsu.edu/downloads/cas/file46880.pdf.

19. "Immigration Restriction," eHistory @ The Ohio State University, accessed May 12, 2012, http://ehistory.osu.edu/osu/mmh/clash/Imm_KKK/Immigration%20Pages/Immigration-page1.htm.

20. Smith, *Civic Ideals*, 17.

21. Immigration Act of 1924, 43 Statutes at Large 153.

22. *United States v. Cruikshank*, 92 U.S. 542 (1876).

23. Ronald Walters, "'The Association Is for the Direct Attack': The Militant Context of the NAACP Challenge to *Plessy*," *Washburn Law Journal* 43 (Winter 2004): 329.

24. *Plessy v. Ferguson*, 163 U.S. 537 (1896).

25. Vicki L. Ruiz, "South by Southwest: Mexican Americans and Segregated Schooling, 1900–1950," *OAH Magazine of History* 15 (Winter 2001): 23–27.

26. *Westminster School District v. Mendez*, 161 F.2d 774 (1947).

27. Ruiz, "South by Southwest."

28. Quoted in Renata Fengler, "Abigail and John Adams Discuss Women and Republican Government: 1776," part of the "Documenting American History" project, University of Wisconsin–Green Bay, last modified July 29, 2009, accessed April 25, 2012, http://www.historytools.org/sources/Abigail-John-Letters.pdf.

29. Keyssar, *Right to Vote*.

30. E. Susan Barber, comp., "One Hundred Years toward Suffrage: An Overview," Library of Congress, National American Woman Suffrage Association Collection, accessed May 14, 2012, http://memory.loc.gov/ammem/naw/nawstime.html.

31. Survey conducted by the Office of Public Opinion Research, July 1945, retrieved May 14, 2012, from the iPOLL Databank, The Roper Center for Public Opinion Research, University of Connecticut.

32. "The Law: Up from Coverture," *Time Magazine*, March 20, 1972, http://www.time.com/time/magazine/article/0,9171,942533,00.html.

33. *Kirchberg v. Feenstra*, 450 U.S. 455 (1981), at 456.

34. Richard Kluger, *Simple Justice* (New York: Knopf, 1975), 376.

35. See Laurence H. Tribe, *American Constitutional Law* (Mineola, N.Y.: Foundation Press, 1988), 1561–65.

36. Ibid.

37. Baer, *Chains of Protection*, 111–21.

38. *Hoyt v. Florida*, 368 U.S. 57 (1961).

39. *Civil Rights Cases*, 109 U.S. 3 (1883); *Shelley v. Kraemer*, 334 U.S. 1 (1948).

40. *Missouri ex rel. Gaines v. Canada*, 305 U.S. 337 (1938); *Sipuel v. Board of Regents of University of Oklahoma*, 332 U.S. 631 (1948); *Sweatt v. Painter*, 339 U.S. 629 (1950).

41. *Bolling v. Sharpe*, 347 U.S. 497 (1954).

42. *Brown v. Board of Education*, 349 U.S. 294 (1955).

43. *Cooper v. Aaron*, 358 U.S. 1 (1958).

44. Gerald N. Rosenberg, *The Hollow Hope: Can Courts Bring about Social Change* (Chicago: University of Chicago Press, 1991), 46–54.

45. *Alexander v. Holmes County Board of Education*, 396 U.S. 1218 (1969).

46. *Browder v. Gayle*, 352 U.S. 903 (1956).

47. *Jackson v. Alabama*, 348 U.S. 888 (1954).

48. Quoted in Walter F. Murphy, *Elements of Judicial Strategy* (Chicago: University of Chicago Press, 1964), 193.

49. *Loving v. Virginia*, 388 U.S. 1 (1967).

50. David Fankhauser, "Freedom Rides: Recollections by David Fankhauser," last modified May 13, 2011, accessed April 25, 2012, http://biology.clc.uc.edu/fankhauser/society/freedom_rides/freedom_ride_dbf.htm.

51. Martin Luther King Jr., "Letter from Birmingham Jail," April 16, 1963, The King Center, accessed April 25, 2012, http://www.thekingcenter.org/archive/document/letter-birmingham-city-jail-0.

52. Martin Luther King Jr., "The I Have a Dream Speech," August 28, 1963, U.S. Constitution Online, accessed April 25, 2012, http://www.usconstitution.net/dream.html.

53. *Heart of Atlanta Motel v. United States*, 379 U.S. 241 (1964); *Katzenbach v. McClung*, 379 U.S. 294 (1964).

54. *Guinn v. United States*, 238 U.S. 347 (1915); *Smith v. Allwright*, 321 U.S 649 (1944).

55. Martin Luther King Jr., "Civil Right No. 1: The Right to Vote," *New York Times Magazine*, March 14, 1965, 26.

56. Pew Hispanic Center, "Dissecting the 2008 Electorate: Most Diverse in U.S. History," Pew Research Center, April 30, 2009, accessed April 25, 2012, http://www.pewhispanic.org/2009/04/30/dissecting-the-2008-electorate-most-diverse-in-us-history/.

57. *Northwest Austin Municipal Utility District No. One v. Holder* 557 U.S. 193 (2009).

58. Rachel Weiner, "Black Voters Turned Out at Higher Rate Than White Voters in 2012 and 2008," *The Washington Post,* April 29, 2013, http://www.washingtonpost.com/blogs/the-fix/wp/2013/04/29/black-turnout-was-higher-than-white-turnout-in-2012-and-2008.

59. *Shelby County v. Holder* 133 S. Ct. 2612 (2013).

60. Adam Liptak, "Supreme Court Invalidates Key Part of Voting Rights," *The New York Times*, June 25, 2013, http://www.nytimes.com/2013/06/26/us/supreme-court-ruling.html?pagewanted=all&_r=0›.

61. *Hernandez v. Texas*, 347 U.S. 475 (1954).

62. *Cisneros v. Corpus Christi Independent School District*, 404 U.S. 1211 (1970).

63. A. Reynaldo Contreras and Leonard A. Valverde, "The Impact of *Brown* on the Education of Latinos" *Journal of Negro Education* (1994) 63: 471–72.

64. *Plyler v. Doe*, 457 U.S. 202 (1982).

65. Library of Congress. *Hispanic Americans in Congress, 1822-1995*, http://www.loc.gov/rr/hispanic/congress/gonzalez.html; Molly Ivins, November 30, 2000, http://www.creators.com/opinion/molly-ivins/molly-ivins-november-30-2000-11-30.html.

66. *Katzenbach v. Morgan*, 384 U.S. 641 (1966), *Cardona v. Power*, 384 U.S. 672 (1966).

67. 42 USC sec. 203 (1975)

68. *White v. Regester*, 412 U.S. 755 (1973). See also *Graves v. Barnes*, 405 U.S. 1201 (1972).

69. Charles L. Cotrell and R. Michael Stevens, "The 1975 Voting Rights Act and San Antonio, Texas: Toward a Federal Guarantee of a Republican Form of Government," *Publius* (1977): 79–99; United States Commission on Civil Rights, "Using the Voting Rights Act" (Washington, D.C.: U.S. Government Printing Office, 1975).

70. Guadalupe San Miguel, Jr.,"'Let All of Them Take Heed': Mexican Americans and the Campaign for Educational Equality in Texas, 1910-1981" (University of Texas Press, 1987).

71. United Farm Workers, "Successes Through the Years," http://www.ufw.org/_page.php?menu=research&inc=history/02.html.

72. Steven Yaccino and Lizette Alvarez, "New G.O.P. Bid to Limit Voting in Swing States," *New York Times*, March 29, 2014, http://www.nytimes.com/2014/03/30/us/new-gop-bid-to-limit-voting-in-swing-states.html?hp&_r=1&assetType=nyt_now.

73. Cesar Chavez, *1984 Commonwealth Club Address*, http://www.ufw.org/_page.php?menu=research&inc=history/12.html.

74. U.S. Bureau of Labor Statistics, *Highlights of Women's Earnings in 2012* (Washington, D.C., October 2013), Table 1, accessed June 6, 2014, http://www.bls.gov/cps/cpswom2012.pdf.

75. Ibid.

76. *Burlington Northern and Santa Fe Railway Co. v. White*, 548 U.S. 53 (2006).

77. *Ledbetter v. Goodyear Tire and Rubber Co.*, 550 U.S. 618 (2007).

78. Ibid., 645.

79. Lilly Ledbetter Fair Pay Act of 2009, Pub. L. No. 111-2, 42 USC 2000e-5 (2009), http://www.gpo.gov/fdsys/pkg/PLAW-111publ2/html/PLAW-111publ2.htm.

80. ABA Section of Labor & Employment Law, *Survey of Recent Cases under the Lily Ledbetter Fair Pay Act,* March 2011, accessed May 23, 2012, http://www2.americanbar.org/calendar/ll0322-2011-midwinter-meeting/Documents/08_complexlitigation.pdf (on new cases), and U.S. Bureau of Labor Statistics, *Highlights of Women's Earnings*, on continuing pay disparity.

81. http://beta.congress.gov/bill/113th-congress/senate-bill/84, accessed April 29, 2014.

82. Wesley Lowery, "Senate Falls Six Votes Short of Passing Paycheck Fairness Act," *Washington Post*, April 9, 2014, http://www.washingtonpost.com/blogs/post-politics/wp/2014/04/09/senate-falls-six-votes-short-of-passing-paycheck-fairness-act/.

83. Juliet Eilpern, "Obama to Sign Two Executive Orders Aimed at Narrowing Gender Gap in Wages," *Washington Post,* April 7, 2014, http://www.washingtonpost.com/politics/obama-to-sign-two-executive-orders-aimed-at-narrowing-gender-gap-in-wages/2014/04/07/3f0ce4a8-be74-11e3-bcec-b71ee10e9bc3_story.html.

84. *Bowers v. Hardwick*, 478 U.S. 186 (1986).

85. *Romer v. Evans*, 517 U.S. 620 (1996).

86. *Lawrence v. Texas*, 539 U.S. 558 (2003).

87. *Hollingsworth v. Perry*, 133 S.Ct. 2652 (2013).

88. 133 S. Ct. 2675 (2013).

89. A March 2014 Bloomberg National poll found by 55–36 that Americans support allowing same-sex couples to get married; data accessed April 28, 2014, from http://www.pollingreport.com/civil.htm.

90. U.S. Equal Employment Opportunity Commission, *The Americans with Disabilities Act: A Primer for Small Business*, last modified February 4, 2004, accessed May 15, 2012, http://www.eeoc.gov/eeoc/publications/adahandbook.cfm.

91. "Employers Say OFCCP Disabilities Proposal Would Be Overly Burdensome," *Bloomberg BNA*, April 16, 2012, accessed May 14, 2012, http://www.bna.com/employers-say-ofccp-n12884908933.

92. Gustave Valdes, "Undocumented Immigrant Population on the Rise in the U.S.," *CNN*, September 25, 2013, accessed April 15, 2014, http://www.cnn.com/2013/09/24/us/undocumented-immigrants-population.

93. "32% Say Child Born in U.S. to Illegal Immigrant Should Receive Automatic Citizenship," accessed June 6, 2014, http://www.rasmussenreports.com/public_content/politics/current_events/immigration/august_2013/32_say_child_born_in_u_s_to_illegal_immigrant_should_receive_automatic_citizenship.

94. Poll conducted by Quinnipiac University, October 2011, retrieved March 18, 2012, from the iPOLL Databank, The Roper Center for Public Opinion Research, University of Connecticut.

95. *Plyler v. Doe*, 457 U.S. 202 (1982).

96. King, "Civil Right No. 1."

97. M. V. Hood, Quentin Kidd, and Irwin L. Morris, "The Key Issue: Constituency Effects and Southern Senators' Roll-Call Voting on Civil Rights," *Legislative Studies Quarterly* 26 (2001): 599–621.

98. Royce Carroll, Jeff Lewis, James Lo, Nolan McCarty, Keith Poole, and Howard Rosenthal, "'Common Space' DW-NOMINATE Scores with Bootstrapped Standard Errors (Joint House and Senate Scaling)," Voteview.com, last modified January 22, 2011, accessed May 14, 2012, http://www.voteview.com/dwnomjoint.asp.

Chapter 6

1. Chad Livengood, "Armed with His Delaware-based 'Anonymous Shell Corporation,' Colbert Seeks 'Massive' Donations," *Dialogue Delaware*, last modified October 7, 2011, accessed April 14, 2014, http://blogs.delawareonline.com/dialoguedelaware/2011/10/07/armed-with-his-anonymous-delaware-shell-corporation-colbert-seeks-massive-donations/.

2. Survey for Pew Research Center for the People & the Press, conducted by Princeton Survey Research Associates International, May 9 – June 3, 2012, retrieved April 23, 2014.

3. Cynthia Littleton, "Stephen Colbert's Rise: From South Carolina to Second City to Pop Culture Player," *Variety*, April 10, 2014, accessed April 14, 2014, http://variety.com/2014/tv/news/stephen-colberts-rise-from-south-carolina-to-second-city-to-pop-culture-player-1201155535/.

4. See http://www.hsc.edu/About-H-SC.html.

5. Littleton, "Stephen Colbert's Rise;" Ken P., "An Interview with Stephen Colbert," *IGN*, August 11, 2003, accessed April 14, 2014, http://www.ign.com/articles/2003/08/11/an-interview-with-stephen-colbert?page=1.

6. Ken P., "An Interview with Stephen Colbert;" Littleton, "Stephen Colbert's Rise."

7. "Truthiness," *Wikipedia*, last modified April 9, 2014, accessed April 14, 2014, https://en.wikipedia.org/wiki/Truthiness.

8. See http://www.merriam-webster.com/info/06words.htm.

9. James H. Fowler, "The Colbert Bump in Campaign Donations: More Truthful Than Truthy," *PS: Political Science & Politics* 41 (3) (2008): 533–39, http://jhfowler.ucsd.edu/colbert_bump.pdf.

10. "Stephen Colbert: 2010 Congressional Testimony," *Wikipedia*, last modified April 13, 2014, accessed April 14, 2014, https://en.wikipedia.org/wiki/Stephen_Colbert#2010_Congressional_testimony.

11. KrayolaTop, "Stephen Colbert to Congress 'migrant workers suffer and have no rights'," *YouTube*, uploaded September 24, 2010, access April 14, 2014, https://www.youtube.com/watch?v=nxeIO4pW05s&noredirect=1.

12. See http://www.mediaite.com/online/limbaugh-blasts-colbert-pick-cbs-has-just-declared-war-on-the-heartland-of-america/, accessed April 28, 2014.

13. Quoted in Harry Jaffa, *The Crisis of the House Divided*, 2nd ed. (Chicago: University of Chicago Press, 1959), 10.

14. See James Bryce, *The American Commonwealth* (New York: MacMillan, 1895), 239.

15. Survey conducted by Quinnipiac University Polling Institute, January 15–19, 2014, retrieved April 7, 2014, from the iPOLL Databank, The Roper Center for Public Opinion Research, University of Connecticut.

16. See 2012 American National Election Studies, http://electionstudies.org/.

17. Survey for Pew Research Center for the People & the Press, conducted by Princeton Survey Research Associates International, February 14–23, 2014, retrieved April 7, 2014, through The Roper Center for Public Opinion Research, University of Connecticut.

18. It is hard to know the exact share of people who would support overthrowing the American government because pollsters almost never ask that question. We say "almost never," but in our search of questions asked over the past seventy-five years, we have not found one such question. A database at the Roper Center at the University of Connecticut contains nearly five hundred thousand questions, allowing a detailed search.

19. Robert Erikson and Kent Tedin, *American Public Opinion*, 6th ed. (New York: Longman, 2003), 7.

20. George Gallup, *The Pulse of Democracy* (New York: Simon and Schuster, 1940).

21. Survey for *60 Minutes, Vanity Fair*, conducted by CBS News, March 27–30, 2013, accessed on April 7, 2014, through The Roper Center for Public Opinion Research, University of Connecticut.

22. Erikson and Tedin, *American Public Opinion*, 26.

23. Joshua D. Clinton, and Steven Rogers, "Robo-Polls: Taking Cues from Traditional Sources?" *PS: Political Science & Politics* 46, 2 (2013): 333–337.

24. Alicia C. Shepard, "How They Blew It," *American Journalism Review* (January/February 2001).

25. Kathy Frankovic, "The Truth about Push Polls," *CBS News*, February 11, 2009, http://www.cbsnews.com/2100-250_162-160398.html.

26. These data come from 2003 polls retrieved April 15, 2012, from the iPOLL Databank, The Roper Center for Public Opinion Research, University of Connecticut.

27. See Philip E. Converse, "Nonattitudes and American Public Opinion: Comment: The Status of Nonattitudes," *American Political Science Review* 68 (June 1974): 650–60.

28. Pew Research Center for the People & the Press, "Cell Phones and the 2008 Vote: An Update," Pew Research Center, July 17, 2008, accessed April 27, 2012, http://pewresearch.org/pubs/901/cell-phones-polling-election-2008.

29. See also Pew Research Center for the People & the Press, "Polls Face Growing Resistance, but Still Representative," Pew Research Center, April 20, 2004, accessed April 27, 2012, http://people-press.org/2004/04/20/polls-face-growing-resistance-but-still-representative/.

30. The classic book that lays out the argument about party identification is Angus Campbell, Philip Converse, Warren Miller, and Donald Stokes, *The American Voter* (New York: Wiley, 1960).

31. See American National Election Studies, "Party Identification 7- Point Scale 1952–2008," *ANES Guide to Public Opinion and Electoral Behavior*, last modified August 5, 2010, accessed April 27, 2012, http://www.electionstudies.org/nesguide/toptable/tab2a_1.htm.

32. David Brooks, "What Independents Want," *New York Times*, November 5, 2009, A31.

33. John Sides, "Three Myths about Political Independents," *The Monkey Cage* (blog), December 17, 2009, http://www.themonkeycage.org/blog/2009/12/17/three_myths_about_political_in/.

34. Survey for Associated Press, conducted by GfK Knowledge Networks, March 20–24, 2014, retrieved April 7, 2014, from the iPOLL Databank, The Roper Center for Public Opinion Research, University of Connecticut.

35. This way of thinking about the public comes from Philip Converse, "Nature of Belief Systems in Mass Publics," in *Ideology and Discontent*, ed. David Apter (New York: Free Press, 1964).

36. The exact percentage of the public that was literate at the time of the founding is unclear. This percentage reflects the best guess of some historians.

37. *CIA World Factbook*, https://www.cia.gov/library/publications/the-world-factbook/geos/us.html.

38. These data all come from Erikson and Tedin, *American Public Opinion*, 8th ed., 61.

39. See John Zaller, "Monica Lewinsky and the Mainsprings of American Politics," in *Mediated Politics: Communication in the Future of Democracy*, ed. W. Lance Bennett and Robert M. Entman (Cambridge, U.K.: Cambridge University Press, 2001).

40. Stanley Kelley, *Interpreting Elections* (Princeton, N.J.: Princeton University Press, 1983).

41. Christopher Achen, "Mass Political Attitudes and the Survey Response," *American Political Science Review* 69 (1975): 1218–31.

42. Sam Popkin developed this concept in his book *The Reasoning Voter* (Chicago: University of Chicago Press, 1991).

43. "The Polarization of the Congressional Parties," Voteview.com, last modified March 6, 2012, accessed April 27, 2012, http://voteview.com/political_polarization.asp.

44. "The Abu Ghraib Files," *Salon*, March 14, 2006, http://www.salon.com/2006/03/14/introduction_2/.

45. Sarah Mendelson, "The Guantanamo Countdown," *Foreign Affairs*, October 1, 2009.

46. Survey from Associated Press, conducted by National Opinion Research Center, University of Chicago, August 12–29, 2013, retrieved April 17, 2014, from the iPOLL Databank, The Roper Center for Public Opinion Research, University of Connecticut.

47. Survey conducted by Quinnipiac University Polling Institute, January 4–7, 2014, retrieved May 4, 2014, from the iPOLL Databank, The Roper Center for Public Opinion Research, University of Connecticut.

48. See http://www.people-press.org/2013/12/03/public-sees-u-s-power-declining-as-support-for-global-engagement-slips/, accessed May 4, 2014.

49. For a comprehensive account of these data, see Alan Abramowitz and Kyle Saunders, "Is Polarization a Myth?," *Journal of Politics* 70 (2008): 542–55.

50. "Polarization of the Congressional Parties."

51. See Morris Fiorina, *Culture War?* (New York: Longman, 2008).

52. Morris Fiorina, Samuel Abrams, and Jeremy Pope, "Polarization in the American Public," *Journal of Politics* 70 (2008): 558.

53. See Alan Abramowitz, *The Disappearing Center* (New Haven, Conn.: Yale University Press, 2010).

54. The data from 2000 are from the CBS/*New York Times* polls conducted during the presidential campaigns and available through the iPOLL Databank, The Roper Center for Public Opinion Research, University of Connecticut.

55. The data for 2012 are from a survey by the Associated Press, conducted by Gfk Roper Public Affairs & Corporate Communications, by the Associated Press. Methodology: Conducted by Gfk Roper Public Affairs & Corporate Communications, September 13–17, 2012, and based on 1,512 telephone interviews.

56. Erikson and Tedin, *American Public Opinion, 8th ed.*, 193.

57. Survey conducted for CBS News/*New York Times*, February 19–23, 2014, retrieved April 7, 2014, from the iPOLL Databank, The Roper Center for Public Opinion Research, University of Connecticut.

58. Ibid., 208.

59. Pew Research Center, "Muslim Americans: Middle Class and Mostly Mainstream," Pew Research Center, May 22, 2007, accessed April 27, 2012, http://pewresearch.org/pubs/483/muslim-americans.

60. Susan Page, "Swing States Poll: A Shift by Women Puts Obama in Lead," *USA Today*, last modified April 2, 2012, http://www.usatoday.com/news/politics/story/2012-04-01/swing-states-poll/53930684/1.

61. Center for American Women and Politics, Eagleton Institute of Politics, Rutgers University, "The Gender Gap: Voting Choices in Presidential Elections," December 2008, accessed May 23, 2012, http://www.cawp.rutgers.edu/fast_facts/voters/documents/GGPresVote.pdf.

62. Survey for United Technologies, National Journal, conducted by Princeton Survey Research Associates International, October 3–6, 2013, retrieved April 8, 2014, from the iPOLL Databank, The Roper Center for Public Opinion Research, University of Connecticut.

63. Survey conducted for CNN by ORC International, May 17–18, 2013, retrieved April 8, 2014, from the iPOLL Databank, The Roper Center for Public Opinion Research, University of Connecticut.

64. Data from American National Election Studies, "Aid to Blacks/Minorities 1970–2008," *ANES Guide to Public Opinion and Electoral Behavior*, last modified August 5, 2010, accessed May 12, 2012, http://www.electionstudies.org/nesguide/2ndtable/t4b_4_1.htm.

65. Data from the March 2012 General Social Survey conducted by the National Opinion Research Center (NORC) at The University of Chicago.

66. Carole Jean Uhlaner and F. Chris Garcia, "Latino Public Opinion," in *Understanding Public Opinion*, ed. Barbara Norrander and Clyde Wilcox (Washington, D.C.: CQ Press, 2002).

67. Rodolfo De la Garza, Louis DeSipio, F. Chris Garcia, John Garcia, and Angelo Falcon, *Latino Voices: Mexican, Puerto Rican, and Cuban Perspectives on American Politics* (Boulder, Colo.: Westview Press, 1992).

68. That figure combines identifiers with "leaners."

69. Pew Research Hispanic Trends Project, December 28, 2011, http://www.pewhispanic.org/2011/12/28/vii-views-of-the-political-parties-and-party-identification/.

70. David L. Leal, "Latino Public Opinion," Texas A&M University, Department of Political Science: Project for Equity, Representation, and Justice, accessed April 27, 2012, http://perg.tamu.edu/lpc/Leal.pdf.

71. Alexander Kuo, Neil Malhotra, and Cecilia Hyunjung Mo, Why Do Asian Americans Identify as Democrats? Testing Theories of Social Exclusion and Intergroup Solidarity, working paper, Vanderbilt University, February 25, 2014.

72. Pew Research Center for the People & the Press, "Where the Public Stands on Immigration Reform," Pew Research Center, November 23, 2009, accessed April 27, 2012, http://pewtrusts.org/our-work-report-detail.aspx?id=56203.

73. See Norman H. Nie, Jane Junn, and Kenneth Stehlik-Barry, *Education and Democratic Citizenship in America* (Chicago: University of Chicago Press, 1996).

74. Herbert Gans, *Democracy and the News* (New York: Oxford University Press, 2003), 1.

75. Thomas Jefferson to Edward Carrington, "Volume 5, Amendment I (Speech and Press), Document 8," January 16, 1787, *The Founders' Constitution*, ed. Philip B. Kurland and Ralph Lerner (Chicago: University of Chicago Press, 1986), accessed May 27, 2012, http://press-pubs.uchicago.edu/founders/documents/amendI_speechs8.html.

76. Pew Research Center's Project for Excellence in Journalism, "A Year in the News," *The State of the News Media 2009: An Annual Report on American Journalism*, accessed May 27, 2012, http://stateofthemedia.org/2009/a-year-in-the-news. See, especially, the section titled, "The Economy Finally Emerges as a Major Story."

77. See http://www.journalism.org/media-indicators/top-20-network-news-stories-of-2013/, accessed April 20, 2014.

78. Bob Woodward and Carl Bernstein, *All the President's Men* (New York: Simon and Schuster, 1994).

79. Thomas E. Patterson, *Out of Order* (New York: Knopf, 1993), 82.

80. See http://stateofthemedia.org/2013/overview-5/key-findings/, accessed April 20, 2014.

81. "Clear Channel Media + Entertainment," Clear Channel, accessed June 25, 2014 http://clearchannel.com/CCME/Pages/default.aspx.

82. Shanto Iyengar, *Media Politics: A Citizen's Guide,* 2nd ed. (New York: W.W. Norton, 2011), 51.

83. See Pew Research Center's Project for Excellence in Journalism's *The State of the News Media 2012: An Annual Report on American Journalism,* http://stateofthemedia.org/2012/, for a range of data documenting this point.

84. Michael Schudson and Susan Tifft, "American Journalism in Historical Perspective," in *The Press,* ed. Geneva Overholser and Kathleen Hall Jamieson (New York: Oxford University Press, 2005), 26.

85. See http://www.pewinternet.org/2014/02/27/summary-of-findings-3/, accessed on April 20, 2014.

86. Charlie Sorrel, "Apple's iPad Sales Accelerate: Three Million Sold in 80 Days," *Gadget Lab* (blog), Wired, June 23, 2010, http://www.wired.com/gadgetlab/2010/06/apples-ipad-sales-accelerate-three-million-sold-in-80-days.

87. See http://www.statista.com/statistics/183585/adult-twitter-users-in-the-us-since-2009/, accessed on April 20, 2014.

88. See http://www.pewinternet.org/, accessed State of the News Media 2014 on April 20, 2014.

89. Data available at "Report: Community Journalism in the United States," Bill Lane Center for the American West, Stanford University, last modified August 7, 2011, accessed May 27, 2012, http:// www.stanford.edu/group/ruralwest/cgi-bin/drupal/projects /newspapers.

90. For data on news consumption, see *The State of the News Media 2014* report available from the Pew Research Center's Project for Excellence in Journalism at http://www.journalism.org/packages /state-of-the-news-media-2014/

91. Alex Jones, *Losing the News* (New York: Oxford University Press, 2009).

92. The data come from a study conducted for the Newspaper Association of America. See "Study: Newspapers Attract 102.8 million U.S. Internet Users," *SFN Blog,* World Association of Newspapers and News Publishers, http://www.sfnblog.com/2010/10/14/study -newspapers-attract-1028-million-us-internet-users.

93. Geoffrey Cowan, "Leading the Way to Better News" (Discussion Paper Series, Joan Shorenstein Center on the Press, Politics, and Public Policy, Harvard University, 2008), 7.

94. Ibid.

95. See http://www.journalism.org/2014/03/26/the-losses-in-legacy/, accessed April 28, 2014.

96. See Jones, *Losing the News.*

97. See Bill Mitchell, "Clues in the Rubble: Finding a Framework to Sustain Local News" (Discussion Paper Series, Joan Shorenstein Center on the Press, Politics, and Public Policy, Harvard University, 2010).

98. Pew Research Center's Project for Excellence in Journalism, "Audio: How Far Will Digital Go?," *The State of the News Media 2012,* Pew Research Center, accessed May 27, 2012, http://stateofthemedia. org/2012/audio-how-far-will-digital-go/.

99. See David Barker, *Rushed to Judgment* (New York: Columbia University Press, 2002).

100. Pew Research Center's Project for Excellence in Journalism, "Talk Radio," *The State of the News Media 2012,* Pew Research Center, accessed May 28, 2012, http://stateofthemedia.org/2012 /audio-how-far-will-digital-go/#talk-radio.

101. No one has studied reasons why liberal talk radio has failed, but we offer some hypotheses here. Thank you to Markus Prior of Princeton University for brainstorming with us on this topic.

102. See http://www.journalism.org/media-indicators/evening-network-news -share-over-time/, accessed April 20, 2014.

103. Most of the data presented here came from Pew Research Center's Project for Excellence in Journalism, "Journalism, Satire or Just Laughs? 'The Daily Show with Jon Stewart,' Examined," Journalism .org, May 8, 2008, http://www.journalism.org/node/10961.

104. http://www.thefutoncritic.com/ratings/2013/04/04/the-daily-show -and-the-colbert-report-finish-1q-2013-as-number-1-and-number-2 -among-adults-18-49-and-all-key-young-demos-795303/20130404 comedycentral01/, accessed April 21, 2014.

105. eBizMBA's ranking of the top fifteen blogs is available at http://www .ebizmba.com/articles/blogs. The rankings shown here were retrieved in April 2014.

106. Eric Lawrence, John Sides, and Henry Farrell, "Self-Segregation or Deliberation? Blog Readership, Participation, and Polarization in American Politics," *Perspectives on Politics* 8, 1 (2010): 146.

107. See http://www.drudgereport.com and http://www.rushlimbaugh .com/.

108. See Dylan Tweney, "Controlled Chaos: An Interview with Kos," *Epicenter* (blog), Wired, May 8, 2007, http://blog.wired.com/business /2007/05/controlled_chao.html.

109. https://www.facebook.com/facebook/info, accessed June 25, 2014.

110. http://www.businessweek.com/articles/2014-01-29/facebook -quiets-skeptics-with-member-growth-and-mobile-money, accessed April 21, 2014. In an informal survey of high school kids in middle Tennessee, Olivia Alpert found that 80 percent of her classmates also use Snapchat.

111. http://mashable.com/2014/02/24/snapchat-study-college-stu-dents/, accessed on April 21, 2014.

112. The authors confirmed this fact through their own Facebook accounts.

113. "ABC News Joins Forces with Facebook," *ABC News,* December 18, 2007, http://abcnews.go.com/Technology/Politics/story?id=3899006& page=1#.T7J9ccXtMVA.

114. For example, in a local county election for a judgeship in Tennessee, Vince Wyatt had a twitter feed: @Wyatt4Judge. This is hardly unusual in 2014.

115. See http://tvbythenumbers.zap2it.com/2013/05/22/telemundo-delivers -best-season-ever-up-9-vs-2011-2012-season/183980/ and http://www .deadline.com/2013/05/cbs-wins-season-abc-tops-adults-18-49-in -seasons-final-week/.

116. Mark Hugo Lopez and Anna Gonzalez-Barrera, "A Growing Share of Latinos Get Their News in English," *Pew Research Hispanic Trends Project,* July 23, 2013, http://www.pewhispanic.org/2013/07/23/a -growing-share-of-latinos-get-their-news-in-english/.

117. Thomas E. Patterson, *Young People and News* (Cambridge, MA: Joan Shorenstein Center on the Press, Politics, and Public Policy, Harvard University, July 2007).

118. Morley Winograd and Michael D. Hais, *Millennial Makeover: MySpace, YouTube and the Future of American Politics* (New Brunswick, N.J.: Rutgers University Press, 2008).

119. Paul Lazarsfeld, Bernard Berelson, and Hazel Gaudet, *The People's Choice* (New York: Columbia University Press, 1944). It is worth noting that the 1940 campaign was probably the worst campaign

in which to look for possible media effects. It was the only presidential election in U.S. history in which a sitting president, Franklin Roosevelt, was running for a third term. The stability of preference surely reflected the fact that people had opinions about Roosevelt and that not much would change them one way or the other. In contrast, Senator Obama was not a well-known figure in the 2008 presidential campaign.

120. Angus Campbell et al., *The American Voter* (New York: Wiley, 1960).

121. http://www.gallup.com/poll/170750/despite-enrollment-success-healthcare-law-remains-unpopular.aspx

122. Bernard Cohen, *The Press and Foreign Policy* (Princeton, N.J.: Princeton University Press, 1963), 13.

123. Darrell M. West, Grover J. Whitehurst, and E. J. Dionne Jr., "Invisible: 1.4 Percent Coverage for Education Is Not Enough," Brookings.edu, December 2, 2009, accessed May 28, 2012, http://www.brookings.edu/research/reports/2009/12/02-education-news-west.

124. Shanto Iyengar and Jennifer A. McGrady, *Media Politics: A Citizen's Guide* (New York: W.W. Norton, 2007), 216.

125. These scholars have reshaped how we think about framing. In fact, Kahneman won a Nobel Prize for this work in 2003. See http://psych.hanover.edu/classes/cognition/papers/tversky81.pdf.

126. W. Lance Bennett, Regina C. Lawrence, and Steven Livingston, *When the Press Fails: Political Power and the News Media from Iraq to Katrina* (Chicago: University of Chicago Press, 2007).

127. See Jonathan Ladd, *Why Americans Hate the Media* (Princeton, N.J.: Princeton University Press, 2012). Ladd also kindly provided us updated figures for this trend line.

128. See Jonathan Ladd, *Why Americans Hate the Media* (Princeton, N.J.: Princeton University Press, 2012). Ladd also kindly provided us updated figures for this trend line.

129. See Michael Schudson, *The Sociology of News* (New York: W.W. Norton, 2003), 33.

130. See the Accuracy in Media website at http://www.aim.org.

131. Conducted by Gallup Organization, September 5–8, 2013, retrieved from the iPOLL Databank, The Roper Center for Public Opinion Research, University of Connecticut accessed April 14, 2014.

132. Thomas Patterson, "Political Roles of the Journalist," in *The Politics of the News*, ed. Doris Graber, Denis McQuail, and Pippa Norris (Washington, D.C.: CQ Press, 2000), 3.

133. For a thoughtful discussion of soft news, see Matthew Baum, *Soft News Goes to War: Public Opinion and American Foreign Policy in the New Media Age* (Princeton, N.J.: Princeton University Press, 2003), 6–7.

134. Gary Bunker, *From Rail-Splitter to Icon: Lincoln's Image in Illustrated Periodicals, 1860–1865* (Kent, Ohio: Kent State University Press, 2001).

135. CB Presidential Research Services, "Presidential Campaign Slogans," PresidentsUSA.net, accessed May 28, 2012, http://www.presidentsusa.net/campaignslogans.html.

136. Pew Research Center for the People & the Press, "Public Knowledge of Current Affairs Little Changed by News and Information Revolutions," Pew Research Center, April 15, 2007, accessed May 28, 2012, http://www.people-press.org/2007/04/15/public-knowledge-of-current-affairs-little-changed-by-news-and-information-revolutions/.

137. http://www.pewinternet.org/data-trend/mobile/cell-phone-and-smartphone-ownership-demographics/, accessed April 21, 2014.

138. http://www.pewinternet.org/three-technology-revolutions/, accessed April 21, 2014.

139. The argument presented over the next few paragraphs is inspired by the work of Markus Prior, *Post Broadcast Democracy* (New York: Cambridge University Press, 2007).

140. Ibid.

141. Robert S. Erikson, Michael B. MacKuen, and James A. Stimson, *The Macro Polity* (Cambridge, U.K.: Cambridge University Press, 2002).

142. Richard Pérez-Peña, "Group Plans to Provide Investigative Journalism," *New York Times,* October 15, 2007, http://www.nytimes.com/2007/10/15/business/media/15publica.html.

Chapter 7

1. This story was compiled from information on the Common Sense Action's website, http://www.commonsenseaction.org; Andrew Kaplan and Sam Gilman, "Repairing Politics the Millennial Way," *Switch and Shift,* March 1, 2014: http://switchandshift.com/repairing-politics-the-millennial-way; and an in-person interview with Andrew Kaplan and Sam Gilman, April 9, 2014, conducted for this textbook, which is the source of Gilman's quotation.

2. Alexis de Tocqueville, *Democracy in America*, ed. J. P. Mayer, trans. George Lawrence (New York: Doubleday & Company, 1969), 193.

3. William C. DiGiacomantonio, "Petitioners and Their Grievances," in *The House and Senate in the 1790s: Petitioning, Lobbying, and Institutional Development*, ed. Kenneth R. Bowling and Donald R. Kennon (Columbus: Ohio University Press, 2002), 29–56.

4. Interest groups at the state level have even been involved in elections for state judges. See Clive S. Thomas, Michael L. Boyer, and Ronald J. Hrebenar, "Interest Groups and State Court Elections: A New Era and Its Challenges," *Judicature* 87 (2003): 135–49.

5. Elizabeth Cady Stanton, Susan B. Anthony, and Matilda J. Gage, eds., *History of Woman Suffrage* (Rochester, N.Y.: Charles Mann Publishers, 1887), 1:70.

6. "141 Men and Girls Die in Waist Factory Fire; Trapped High Up in Washington Place Building; Street Strewn with Bodies; Piles of Dead Inside," *New York Times*, March 26, 1911, 1.

7. Office of the Secretary, United States Department of Labor, "Our Mission," accessed May 23, 2012, http://www.dol.gov/opa/aboutdol/mission.htm.

8. National Labor Relations Act, 29 U.S.C. §§ 151–169 (1935), http://www.nlrb.gov/national-labor-relations-act.

9. Beth L. Leech, Frank R. Baumgartner, Timothy M. La Pira, and Nicholas A. Semanko, "Drawing Lobbyists to Washington: Government Activity and the Demand for Advocacy," *Political Research Quarterly* 58, no. 1 (2005): 19–30.

10. Elizabeth Ashack, Bureau of Labor Statistics, "Profiles of significant collective bargaining disputes of 2012." May 2013, accessed March 16, 2015, http://www.bls.gov/opub/mlr/2013/article/profiles-of-significant-collective-bargaining-disputes-of-2012.htm.

11. Rachel Weiner, "Issue 2 Falls, Ohio Collective Bargaining Law Repealed," *The Fix* (blog), *Washington Post,* November 8, 2011, http://www.washingtonpost.com/blogs/the-fix/post/issue-2-falls-ohio-collective-bargaining-law-repealed/2011/11/08/gIQAyZ0U3M_blog.html; the information in the caption on page 205 is from Becket Adams, "Ohio Votes to Overturn Collective Bargaining Law, Votes 'No' to Forced Health Care," *Blaze,* November 8, 2011, http://www.theblaze.com/stories/ohio-votes-to-overturn-collective-bargaining-bill.

12. John Helton and Tom Cohen, "Walker's Wisconsin Win Big Blow to Unions, Smaller One to Obama," CNN, June 6, 2012, http://www.cnn.com/2012/06/05/politics/wisconsin-recall-vote/index.html?hpt=hp_t1.

13. National Right to Work Legal Defense Foundation, Inc., "Right to Work States," accessed August 20, 2014, http://www.nrtw.org/rtws.htm.

14. U.S. Bureau of Labor Statistics, "Union Members Summary," January 24, 2014, accessed March 16, 2014, http://www.bls.gov/news.release/union2.nr0.htm.

15. MoveOn.org, http://front.moveon.org/.

16. American Israel Public Affairs Committee, accessed June 4, 2014, http://www.aipac.org/.

17. Mark R. Amstutz, "Faith-Based NGOs and U.S. Foreign Policy," in *The Influence of Faith: Religious Groups and Foreign Policy*, ed. by Elliot Abrams, 175–87 (Lanham, Md.: Rowman and Littlefield Publishers, 2001); National Council of the Churches of Christ in the USA, http://www.ncccusa.org.

18. American Civil Liberties Union, *Report: Blocking Faith, Freezing Charity*, June 16, 2009, accessed May 23, 2012, http://www.aclu.org/human-rights/report-blocking-faith-freezing-charity.

19. Sierra Club, "Tell President Obama You Support Strong Climate Action!" accessed June 4, 2014, https://secure.sierraclub.org/site/Advocacy?cmd=display&page=UserAction&id=13709&s_src=614ESCHT01.

20. For more information on general lobbying, see Anthony J. Nownes, *Total Lobbying* (New York: Cambridge University Press, 2006).

21. Center for Responsive Politics, "Lobbying Database," OpenSecrets.org, accessed March 14, 2014, http://www.opensecrets.org/lobby/.

22. Ibid.

23. Bart Jansen, "Legislative Summary: Congressional Affairs: Lobbying Practices and Disclosures," *CQ Weekly Online*, January 7, 2008, 39.

24. Gregory Koger and Jennifer N. Victor, "Polarized Agendas: Campaign Contributions by Lobbyists," *PS: Political Science and Politics* 42 (2009): 485–88.

25. Bureau of the Census, "NAIS 2011 – Oil and Gas Extraction" http://thedataweb.rm.census.gov/TheDataWeb_HotReport2/econsnap-shot/snapshot.hrml?NAICS=211&IND=%3DCOMP%28C2%2FC3*1000%29&STATE=ALL&COUNTY=ALL.

26. Environmental Protection Agency, "EPA's Study of Hydraulic Fracturing and Its Potential Impact on Drinking Water Resources," accessed June 4, 2014, http://www2.epa.gov/hfstudy.

27. ANGA "About Us," http://anga.us/about-us#.UycJCfldWCk; NRDC "Consolidated Financial Statements" June 30, 2013, http://www.nrdc.org/about/NRDC_auditedfinancialstatements_FY2013.pdf.

28. ANGA, "Washington County Pennsylvania Retrospective Case Study Characterization Report," February, 2013, http://anga.us/media/content/F7BDA298-DFF6-686B-2DF23939F9838B75/files/13%20Feb%2022%20FinalWashingtonCountyReport_clean%2021.pdf.

29. Natural Resources Defense Council, "Fracking: Community Defense," http://www.nrdc.org/land/fracking-community-defense/.

30. Natural Resource Defense Council, http://www.nrdc.org/land/fracking-community-defense/.

31. Citizens for Responsibility and Ethics in Washington, "About CREW," accessed March 14, 2014, http://www.citizensforethics.org/pages/about; http://www.citizensforethics.org/pages/under-investigation/.

32. U.S. Internal Revenue Service, "Exemption Requirements—Section 501(c)(3) Organizations," accessed June 4, 2014, http://www.irs.gov/Charities-&-Non-Profits/Charitable-Organizations/Exemption-Requirements-Section-501(c)(3)-Organizations.

33. James Oliphant, "Remember the IRS Tea-Party Scandal? Get Ready for Round Two," *National Journal*, February 5, 2014, accessed March 14, 2014, http://www.nationaljournal.com/white-house/remember-the-irs-tea-party-scandal-get-ready-for-round-two-20140205.

34. *Buckley v. Valeo*, 424 U.S. 1 (1976).

35. See John R. Wright, *Interest Groups and Congress: Lobbying, Contributions, and Influence* (Boston: Allyn & Bacon, 1995, reprinted in Longman Classics Series, 2009); Michelle L. Chin, Jon R. Bond, and Nehemia Geva, "A Foot in the Door: An Experimental Study of PAC and Constituency Effects on Access," *Journal of Politics* 62 (2000): 534–49.

36. *Federal Election Commission v. Wisconsin Right to Life, Inc.*, 551 U.S. 449 (2007).

37. *McCutcheon et. al. v. Federal Election Commission*, decided April 2, 2014, http://www.supremecourt.gov/opinions/13pdf/12-536_e1pf.pdf.

38. Tocqueville, *Democracy in America*, 514.

39. David Truman, *The Governmental Process: Political Interests and Public Opinion* (New York: Alfred Knopf, 1971).

40. Mancur Olson, *The Logic of Collective Action* (Cambridge, Mass.: Harvard University Press, 1971).

41. Robert Dahl, *A Preface to Democratic Theory* (Chicago: University of Chicago Press, 1956). Also see Robert Dahl, *Who Governs?*, 2nd ed. (New Haven, Conn.: Yale University Press, 2005).

42. C. Wright Mills, *The Power Elite* (New York: Oxford University Press, 1956).

43. Theodore J. Lowi, *The End of Liberalism: Ideology, Policy, and the End of Public Authority* (New York: Norton, 1969).

44. E. E. Schattschneider, *The Semi-Sovereign People* (New York: Holt, Rinehart, and Winston, 1960). Also see E. E. Schattschneider, *Politics, Pressures, and the Tariff* (New York: Prentice-Hall, 1935).

45. Center for Climate and Energy Solutions, "Federal Vehicle Standards," accessed March 16, 2014, http://www.c2es.org/federal/executive/vehicle-standards#timeline.

46. Dwight D. Eisenhower, "Farewell Radio and Television Address to the American People," January 17, 1961; Gerhard Peters and John T. Woolley, The American Presidency Project, accessed May 23, 2012, http://www.presidency.ucsb.edu/ws/index.php?pid=12086&st=&st1=#axzz1uPYslFQG.

47. Thom Shankar and Helene Cooper, "Pentagon Plans to Shrink Army to pre-World War II Level," *New York Times*, February 23, 2014, http://www.nytimes.com/2014/02/24/us/politics/pentagon-plans-to-shrink-army-to-pre-world-war-ii-level.html.

48. Hugh Heclo, "Issue Networks and the Executive Establishment," in *The New American Political System*, ed. Anthony King (Washington, D.C.: American Enterprise Institute, 1978), 87–124.

49. Shane Goldmacher, "The Long Arm (and Hidden Hand) of Jim DeMint" *National Journal*, October 1, 2013, accessed March 15, 2014, http://www.nationaljournal.com/politics/the-long-arm-and-hidden-hand-of-jim-demint-20131001.

50. Americans for Tax Reform, "About Americans for Tax Reform," accessed May 23, 2012, http://www.atr.org/about.

51. Robert H. Salisbury, "An Exchange Theory of Interest Groups," *Midwest Journal of Political Science* 13 (1969):1–32.

52. In *Logic of Collective Action*, Olson labels these *selective incentives* (p. 51).

53. Ibid., pp. 50–51.

54. DeWayne Wickham, "Group Loses Another Leader, and More Luster," *USA Today*, March 6, 2007, A13; Krissah Thompson, "100 Years Old, NAACP Debates Its Current Role," *Washington Post*, July 12, 2009.

55. AARP, "AARP Annual Report 2013," p. 53, accessed August 20, 2014, http://www.aarp.org/content/dam/aarp/about_aarp/annual_reports/2014-06/2013-Annual-Report-AARP.pdf.

56. Ibid., p. 51.

57. Staff, "The Numbers," *National Journal*, February 16, 2008, 1–45.

Chapter 8

1. This story has been compiled from "McKoon State Senate 29," on Georgia State Senator Josh McKoon's website, accessed April 3, 2014, http://www.senate.ga.gov/senators/en-US/Member.aspx?Member=749; http://www.joshmckoon.com; Larry Gierer, "Local GOP Elects New Chairman, Officers: Attorney Josh McKoon to Take Helm of Party," *Columbus Ledger-Enquirer*, March 31, 2007; Brian Mc Dearmon, "Attorney to Run for GOP Chair: McKoon Seeks Top Post

Vacated by Rob Doll," *Columbus Ledger-Enquirer*, February 26, 2007; Chuck Williams, "Republican Josh McKoon Running for Senate District 29 Seat with Abandon, Even with No Opposition Yet," *Columbus Ledger-Enquirer*, March 28, 2010; Liz Buckthorpe, "Inside Story: Senator Josh McKoon," WRBL News, February 15, 2012, http://www.wrbl.com/story/21339655/inside-story-senator-josh-mckoon; phone interview with Josh McKoon, January 28, 2008, and e-mail interview with Josh McKoon, April 29, 2010, both conducted for this textbook. The chapter-opening quotation is from the April 29 e-mail interview.

2. V. O. Key Jr., *Politics, Parties, and Pressure Groups*, 5th ed. (New York: Thomas Y. Crowell Company, 1964).

3. Center for Responsive Politics, "Political Parties," accessed August 20, 2014, http://www.opensecrets.org/parties/index.php?cmte=&cycle=2014.

4. Center for Responsive Politics, "Political Parties," accessed November 5, 2014, http://www.opensecrets.org/parties/index.php?cmte=&cycle=2014.

5. For more information on the informal networking that occurs among party activists, see Gregory Koger, Seth Masket, and Hans Noel, "Partisan Webs: Information Exchange and Party Networks," *British Journal of Political Science* 39 (2009): 633–53.

6. Marjorie Hershey, *Party Politics in America*, 12th ed. (New York: Pearson-Longman, 2007), 159.

7. In the 2008 Democratic nomination contest between Senator Barack Obama (D-Ill.) and then Senator Hillary Clinton (D-N.Y.), superdelegates played the most important role since their creation. By the end of the regular primary season, Obama led in the primary and caucus delegate count, but not by enough to win the nomination outright. The nomination would be determined by the 823 superdelegates, only about half of whom had committed to one or the other candidate early in the process. As it became clear that Obama had more support among party members generally, many of the remaining superdelegates swung their support to him.

8. Republican National Committee, "New Timing Rules for 2012 Republican Presidential Nominating Schedule" as cited by Josh Putnam, "An Update on the 2012 Republican Delegate Selection Rules," *FrontloadingHQ* (blog), February 27, 2011, http://frontloading.blogspot.com/2011/02/update-on-2012-republican-delegate.html.

9. Peter Hamby, "GOP adopts changes to 2016 presidential primary process," CNN.com, January 24, 2014, accessed April 3, 2014. http://politicalticker.blogs.cnn.com/2014/01/24/gop-adopts-changes-to-2016-presidential-primary-process/.

10. George Washington, "Washington's Farewell Address," reprinted in Randall E. Adkins, *The Evolution of Political Parties, Campaigns, and Elections* (Washington, D.C.: CQ Press, 2008), 47–50.

11. John F. Bibby and Brian F. Schaffner, *Politics, Parties and Elections in America*, 6th ed. (Boston: Thomson-Wadsworth, 2008), 24.

12. United States Senate, Office of the Historian, *Biographical Directory of the United States Congress*, http://bioguide.congress.gov.

13. U.S. Census Bureau, "1990 Population and Housing Unit Counts: United States," Table 2, in *1990 Census of Population and Housing*, accessed May 31, 2012, http://www.census.gov/population/www/censusdata/files/table-2.pdf.

14. Quoted in James L. Sundquist, *Dynamics of the Party System* (Washington, D.C.: Brookings Institution Press, 1973), 65.

15. Sean M. Theriault, *The Power of the People* (Columbus: Ohio State University Press, 2005), Chapter 3.

16. Douglas W. Jones, "The Australian Paper Ballot," in "A Brief Illustrated History of Voting," University of Iowa, Department of Computer Science, 2003, accessed May 31, 2012, http://www.divms.uiowa.edu/~jones/voting/pictures/.

17. Erik J. Engstrom and Samuel Kernell, "Manufactured Responsiveness: The Impact of State Electoral Laws on Unified Party Control of the Presidency and the House of Representatives, 1840–1940," *American Journal of Political Science* 49 (July 2005): 531–49, see 535.

18. Anthony Downs, *An Economic Theory of Democracy* (New York: Harper, 1957).

19. Stuart Elaine Macdonald and George Rabinowitz, "Solving the Paradox of Nonconvergence: Valence, Position, and Direction in Democratic Politics," *Electoral Studies* 17, no. 3 (1998): 281–300.

20. Maurice Duverger, "Public Opinion and Political Parties in France," *American Political Science Review* 46, no. 4 (1952): 1069–78, especially 1071.

21. See https://www.lp.org/candidates/elected-officials.

22. Texas State Historical Association, *Raza Unida Party*, http://www.tshaonline.org/handbook/online/articles/war01.

23. Kate Zernike, Kitty Bennett, Ford Fessenden, Kevin Quealy, Amy Schoenfeld, Archie Tse, and Derek Willis, "Where Tea Party Candidates Are Running," *New York Times*, October 14, 2010, accessed April 4, 2014, http://www.nytimes.com/interactive/2010/10/15/us/politics/tea-party-graphic.html.

24. For an expanded analysis of the Tea Party, see Theda Skocpol and Vanessa Williams, *The Tea Party and the Remaking of Republican Conservatism* (New York: Oxford University Press, 2013).

25. Jonathan Martin, "For Many Republican Incumbents, Challenge from Right Fizzles," *New York Times*, April 4, 2014, http://www.nytimes.com/2014/04/05/us/politics/tea-party-challenge-to-republican-incumbents-fizzles.html.

26. For a detailed discussion of how interest groups interact with parties in campaigning, see Matthew J. Burbank, Ronald J. Hrebenar, and Robert C. Benedict, *Parties, Interest Groups, and Political Campaigns* (Boulder, Colo.: Paradigm Publishers, 2008).

27. Gallup.com, "U.S. Remains Divided over Passing Stricter Gun Control," October 2013, accessed April 7, 2014, http://www.gallup.com/poll/165563/remains-divided-passing-stricter-gun-laws.aspx.

28. Pew Research Center, "Wide Partisan Gap on Gun Policy Proposals – Except Background Checks" May 2013, accessed April 7, 2014, http://www.pewresearch.org/key-data-points/gun-control-key-data-points-from-pew-research/.

29. Democratic National Committee, "2012 Democratic National Platform," http://www.democrats.org/democratic-national-platform#protecting-rights.

30. Republican National Committee, "Republican Platform: We Believe in America,"http://www.gop.com/2012-republican-platform_We/#Item10.

31. Center for Responsive Politics, "Political Action Committees," accessed August 20, 2014, http://www.opensecrets.org/pacs/

32. Cornell Belcher and Donna Brazile, "The Black and Hispanic Vote in 2006," *Democratic Strategist*, March 29, 2007, http://www.thedemocraticstrategist.org/ac/2007/03/the_black_and_hispanic_vote_in.php.

33. "Election Results 2008," *New York Times*, December 9, 2008, http://elections.nytimes.com/2008/results/president/map.html.

34. "Campaign 2010," CBS News, November 2, 2010, http://www.cbsnews.com/election-results-2012/exit.shtml.

35. The Roper Center, "US Elections: How Groups Voted in 2012," http://www.ropercenter.uconn.edu/elections/how_groups_voted/voted_12.html.

36. *Engel v. Vitale*, 370 U.S. 421 (1962).

37. For a broad discussion of the resurgence of Republican conservatives, see Mark A. Smith, *The Right Talk: How Conservatives Transformed the Great Society into the Economic Society* (Princeton, N.J.: Princeton University Press, 2007).

38. Scholar Tasha Philpot pointed to underlying shifts as early as 2004. See Tasha S. Philpot, "A Party of a Different Color? Race, Campaign Communication, and Party Politics," *Political Behavior* 26 (2004): 249–70.

39. Greg Giroux, "Final Tally Shows Obama First Since '56 to win 51% Twice, "Bloomberg News, accessed April 4, 2014, http://www.bloomberg.com/news/2013-01-03/final-tally-shows-obama-first-since-56-to-win-51-twice.html; Roper Center, accessed April 28, 2014, http://www.ropercenter.uconn.edu/elections/how_groups_voted/voted_12.html.

40. "Party Affiliation," Gallup.com, accessed May 31, 2012, http://www.gallup.com/poll/15370/party-affiliation.aspx.

Chapter 9

1. See Michael Barone, and Chuck McCutcheon, "Arizona," in *The Almanac of American Politics 2014* (Chicago: University of Chicago Press, 2013). Also, "Kyrsten Sinema's Biography," *Project Vote Smart*, accessed April 20, 2014, http://votesmart.org/candidate/biography/28338/kyrsten-sinema#.U1SPgscmCZw.

2. http://www.washingtonpost.com/lifestyle/style/kyrsten-sinema-a-success-story-like-nobody-elses/2013/01/02/d31fadaa-5382-11e2-a613-ec8d394535c6_story.html, accessed May 16, 2014.

3. http://www.washingtonpost.com/lifestyle/style/kyrsten-sinema-a-success-story-like-nobody-elses/2013/01/02/d31fadaa-5382-11e2-a613-ec8d394535c6_story.html, accessed May 16, 2014.

4. Barone and McCutcheon, "Arizona."

5. http://kyrstensinema.com/record/, accessed May 15, 2014.

6. Quoted in Jeff Broadwater, *George Mason, Forgotten Founder* (Chapel Hill: University of North Carolina Press, 2006), 178.

7. http://www.eiu.com/FileHandler.ashx?issue_id=411847425&mode=pdf (U.S.);http://www.eiu.com/FileHandler.ashx?issue_id=191787003&mode=pdf (Russia), accessed July 1, 2014.

8. For more on the differences between indirect and direct elections of U.S. senators, see Wendy J. Schiller and Charles Stewart III, *Electing the Senate: Indirect Democracy before the 17th Amendment*, (Princeton, NJ: Princeton University Press, 2014).

9. For a longer discussion of redistricting, see Bernard Grofman, Lisa Handley, and Richard G. Niemi, *Minority Representation and the Quest for Voting Equality* (New York: Cambridge University Press, 1992).

10. 478 U.S. 30 (1986).

11. 548 U.S. 399 (2006).

12. Survey conducted by CBS News/*New York Times*, September 8–12, 2012, retrieved September 29, 2012, from the iPOLL Databank, The Roper Center for Public Opinion Research, University of Connecticut.

13. Michael McGerr, *The Decline of Popular Politics* (New York: Oxford University Press, 1986).

14. Sidney Blumenthal, *The Permanent Campaign* (New York: Simon and Schuster, 1982).

15. Federal Election Commission, "The FEC and Federal Campaign Finance Law: Historical Background," February 2004, accessed June 4, 2012, http://www.fec.gov/pages/brochures/fecfeca.shtml.

16. Federal Election Commission, "How Much Can I Contribute?," FEC.gov, accessed May 1, 2014, http://www.fec.gov/ans/answers_general.shtml#How_much_can_I_contribute.

17. Federal Election Commission, "*McCutcheon*, et al. *v. FEC Case Summary*," FEC.gov, accessed May 1, 2014, http://www.fec.gov/law/litigation/McCutcheon.shtml.

18. See Federal Election Commission, http://www.fec.gov.

19. Richard Briffault, "Super PACs" (Working Paper 12-298, Columbia Law School, April 16, 2012).

20. Kevin Quealy and Derek Willis, "Independent Spending Totals," *New York Times*, http://elections.nytimes.com/2012/campaign-finance/independent-expenditures/totals.

21. http://www.opensecrets.org/outsidespending/summ.php?cycle=2012&chrt=V&type=S, accessed May 2, 2014.

22. Steven J. Rosenstone and John Mark Hansen, *Mobilization, Participation, and Democracy in America* (New York: Macmillan, 1993).

23. This insightful observation was made by Senator Lamar Alexander to one of the authors on March 16, 2012.

24. Lynn Vavrek, "The A-Little-Bit-Less Undecided," *Campaign Stops* (blog), *The New York Times*, September 20, 2012, http://campaignstops.blogs.nytimes.com/2012/09/20/the-a-little-bit-less-undecided/.

25. http://www.nytimes.com/2014/04/23/upshot/the-myth-of-swing-voters-in-midterm-elections.html?_r=0, accessed May 2, 2014.

26. Daron R. Shaw, *The Race to 270: The Electoral College and the Campaign Strategies of 2000 and 2004* (Chicago: University of Chicago Press, 2006); figures for 2008 provided by Daron R. Shaw.

27. Total population in the U.S in 2012 was 313,914,040. The population in the battleground states was 66,867,548, constituting 21 percent of the total. See http://www.census.gov/popest/data/state/totals/2012/index.html, accessed May 2, 2014.

28. Chris Cillizza, "Romney's Data Cruncher," *Washington Post*, September 7, 2007, A1.

29. Mark J. Penn with E. Kinney Zalesne, *Microtrends: The Small Forces Behind Tomorrow's Big Changes* (New York: Twelve, Hatchett Book Group USA, 2007), xiii.

30. Thomas B. Edsall, "Let the Nanotargeting Begin," *Campaign Stops* (blog), *New York Times*, April 15, 2012, http://campaignstops.blogs.nytimes.com/2012/04/15/let-the-nanotargeting-begin/.

31. See http://www.thevictorylab.com/ for an account of revolution in campaigns that is often called "micro-targeting."

32. http://www.targetmarketingmag.com/article/election-2012-barack-obama-mitt-romney-microtargeting-retargeting-mobile-marketing-social-media-voter-databases/1, accessed May 2, 2014.

33. John G. Geer, *In Defense of Negativity* (Chicago: University of Chicago Press, 2006), 59–60.

34. Lynn Vavreck, *The Message Matters* (Princeton, N.J.: Princeton University Press, 2009).

35. Donald Stokes, "Spatial Models of Party Competition," *American Political Science Review* 57 (1963): 368–77.

36. Geer, *In Defense of Negativity*, 105.

37. Sunshine Hillygus and Todd Shields, *The Persuadable Voter* (Princeton, N.J.: Princeton University Press, 2008), 36.

38. Mark Z. Barabak, "Wedge Issues May Boost Obama's Prospects," *Los Angeles Times*, April 27, 2012, http://www.latimes.com/news/nationworld/nation/la-na-campaign-2012-wedge-issues-20120428,0,2706316.story.

39. Kathleen Jamieson, *Dirty Politics* (New York: Oxford University Press, 1992).

40. Erika Franklin Fowler and Travis N. Ridout, "Negative, Angry and Ubiquitous: Political Advertising in 2012," *The Forum, A Journal of Applied Research in Contemporary Politics* 10, no. 4 (2012): 51–61.

41. Geer, *In Defense of Negativity*.

42. Federal Election Commission, *Federal Election Campaign Laws* (Washington, D.C.: Federal Election Commission, April 2008), 56–60, http://www.fec.gov. Note that the contribution levels have been increased slightly to adjust for inflation.

43. https://www.opensecrets.org/overview/topraces.php; https://www.opensecrets.org/overview/cost.php, accessed November 5, 2014.

44. Albert Cover, "One Good Term Deserves Another: The Advantage of Incumbency in Congressional Elections," *American Journal of Political Science* 21, no. 3 (1977): 523–41.

45. See Gary C. Jacobson, *The Politics of Congressional Elections*, 8th ed. (Upper Saddle River, N.J.: Prentice Hall, 2012).

46. Richard F. Fenno Jr., *Home Style: Home Members in Their Districts* (Boston: Little, Brown, 1978).

47. See Jacobson, *Politics of Congressional Elections*.

48. Poll conducted by Fox News, September 9–11, 2012, retrieved on September 29, 2012, from the iPOLL Databank, The Roper Center for Public Opinion Research, University of Connecticut.

49. Morris Fiorina, *Congress: Keystone to the Washington Establishment* (New Haven, Conn.: Yale University Press, 1977).

50. John Zaller, "Politicians as Prize Fighters," in *Politicians and Party Politics*, ed. John G. Geer (Baltimore: Johns Hopkins University Press, 1998), 128–85.

51. Bruce Oppenheimer, "Deep Red and Blue Congressional Districts: The Causes and Consequences of Declining Party Competitiveness," in *Congress Reconsidered*, 8th ed., ed. Lawrence Dodd and Bruce Oppenheimer (Washington, D.C.: CQ Press, 2005), 135–58.

52. Kevin Corder and Christina Wolbrecht, "Political Context and the Turnout of New Women Voters after Suffrage," *Journal of Politics* 68 (2006): 34–49.

53. Samuel Huntington, "The United States," in *The Crisis of Democracy*, ed. Michael Crozier, Samuel Huntington, and Joji Watanuki (New York: NYU Press, 1975), 59–115.

54. Steven E. Finkel "Reciprocal Effects of Participation and Political Efficacy: A Panel Analysis," *American Journal of Political Science* 29, no. 4 (1985): 891–913; Steven E. Finkel, "The Effects of Participation on Political Efficacy and Political Support: Evidence from a West German Panel," *Journal of Politics* 49, no. 2 (1987): 441–64. These articles provide empirical evidence that supports the arguments of Carol Pateman, *Participation and Democratic Theory* (New York: Cambridge University Press, 1970).

55. This section draws heavily on Alexander Keyssar, *The Right to Vote: The Contested History of Democracy in the United States* (New York: Basic Books, 2001).

56. 42 USC 203 §1973 to 1973bb.

57. Voting Rights Act Language Assistance Amendments of 1992: Hearings on S. 2236 before the Subcomm. on the Constitution of the Senate Comm. on the Judiciary [1992 hearings], 102d Cong., 2d Sess., S. Hrg. 102-1066, at 134 (1992).

58. M. Hugo Lopez, S. Motel, and E. Patten, "A Record 24 Million Latinos Are Eligible to Vote, But Turnout Rate Has Lagged That of Whites, Blacks," Washington, DC: Pew Hispanic Center, 2012, http://www.pewhispanic.org/files/2012/10/trends_in_Latino_voter_participation_FINALREVISED.pdf.

59. See Marisa Abrajano and Michael Alvarez, *New Faces, New Voices: The Hispanic Electorate in America* (Princeton, N.J.: Princeton University Press, 2010); Matt A. Barreto, Gary M. Segura, and Nathan D. Woods, "The Mobilizing Effect of Majority-Minority Districts on Latino Turnout," *American Political Science Review* 98, no. 1 (2004): 65–75; Matt A. Barreto, Loren Collingwood, and Sylvia Manzano, "A New Measure of Group Influence in Presidential Elections: Assessing Latino Influence in 2008," *Political Research Quarterly* 63 (2010): 908–21.

60. *Voter Identification Requirements*, National Conference of State Legislatures, April 30, 2014, http://www.ncsl.org/research/elections-and-campaigns/voter-id.aspx.

61. *Crawford v. Marion County Election Board*, 553 U.S. 181 (2008). See also Bill Mears, "High Court Upholds Indiana's Voter ID Law," CNN, April 28, 2008, http://articles.cnn.com/2008-04-28/politics/scotus.voter.id_1_voter-impersonation-voter-id-laws-voter-fraud?_s=PM:POLITICS; Linda Greenhouse, "In a 6-to-3 Vote, Justices Uphold a Voter ID Law," *New York Times*, April 29, 2008.

62. American Civil Liberties Union, "Applewhite et al. v. Commonwealth of Pennsylvania, et al.," ACLU, accessed May 19, 2012, http://www.aclupa.org/our-work/legal/legaldocket/applewhite-et-al-v-commonwealth-pennsylvania-et-al/. Rick Lyman, "Pennsylvania Voter ID Law Struck Down as Judge Cites Burden on Citizens," *New York Times*, January 17, 2014, http://www.nytimes.com/2014/01/18/us/politics/pennsylvania-voter-id-law-struck-down.html.

63. Wade Goodwin, "Texas Voter ID Law Creates a Problem for Some Women," October 20, 2013, http://www.npr.org/2013/10/30/241891800/texas-voter-id-law-creates-a-problem-for-some-women.

64. Matt Barreto, "Latino Decisions Research Critical to Overturning Wisconsin Voter-ID Law," *Latino Decisions*, April 30, 2014, http://www.latinodecisions.com/blog/2014/04/30/latino-decisions-research-critical-to-overturning-wisconsin-voter-id-law/.

65. 42 USC 203 §1973 to 1973bb.

66. http://elections.gmu.edu/Turnout_2012G.html, accessed June 3, 2014.

67. Michael P. McDonald, "2012 Presidential Nomination Contest Turnout Rates," United States Elections Project, last modified April 25, 2012, accessed June 7, 2012, http://elections.gmu.edu/Turnout_2012P.html.

68. See Jan Leighley, "Attitudes, Opportunities, and Incentives," *Political Research Quarterly* 48 (1995): 184.

69. Stanley and Niemi, *Vital Statistics on American Politics 2013–2014*.

70. http://www.pewresearch.org/fact-tank/2013/05/08/six-take-aways-from-the-census-bureaus-voting-report/, accessed June 3, 2014.

71. Jan E. Leighley and Jonathan Nagler, *Who Votes Now?* (Princeton: Princeton University Press, 2014).

72. http://www.pewresearch.org/fact-tank/2013/05/08/six-take-aways-from-the-census-bureaus-voting-report/, accessed June 3, 2014.

73. Thom File and Sarah Crissey, *Voting and Registration in the Election of November 2008* (Washington, D.C.: U.S. Census Bureau, May 2010), http://www.census.gov/prod/2010pubs/p20-562.pdf.

74. See, for instance, Raymond Wolfinger and Steven Rosenstone, *Who Votes?* (New Haven, Conn.: Yale University Press, 1980). There has been much research since the publication of this book, but it remains a leading source on this topic.

75. File and Crissey, *Voting and Registration in the Election of November 2008*.

76. Cindy D. Kam and Carl L. Palmer, "Reconsidering the Effects of Education on Political Participation," *Journal of Politics* 70, no. 3 (2008): 612–31.

77. Howard Gillman, *The Votes That Counted* (Chicago: University of Chicago Press, 2001), 77.

78. William Riker and Peter Ordeshook, "A Theory of the Calculus of Voting," *American Political Science Review* 62 (1968): 25–42.

79. For other efforts to solve this problem, see John H. Aldrich, "Rational Choice and Turnout," *American Journal of Political Science* 37, no. 1 (1993): 246–78; Robert Grafstein, "An Evidential Decision Theory of Turnout," *American Journal of Political Science* 35 (1991): 989–1010.

80. These data are from a survey by Pew Research Center for the People & the Press, conducted by Princeton Survey Research Associates International, April 4–April 15, 2012, retrieved June 3, 2014, from the iPOLL Databank, The Roper Center for Public Opinion Research, University of Connecticut.

81. Allyson Holbrook and Jon Krosnick, "Vote Over-Reporting: Testing the Social Desirability Hypothesis in Telephone and Internet Surveys" (paper presented at the annual meeting of the American Association for Public Opinion Research, Miami Beach, Florida, 2009).

82. David Campbell, *Why We Vote* (Princeton, N.J.: Princeton University Press, 2006).

83. See G. Bingham Powell Jr., "American Voter Turnout in Comparative Perspective," *American Political Science Review* 80 (1986): 17–43; and Henry Brady, Sidney Verba, and Kay Schlozman, "Beyond SES: A Resource Model of Political Participation," *American Political Science Review* 89 (1995): 271–94.

84. John Zipp, "Perceived Representativeness and Voting: An Assessment of the Impact of 'Choices' vs. 'Echoes,'" *American Political Science Review* 79 (1985): 50–61.

85. Alan Gerber, Donald Green, and David Nickerson, "Getting Out the Vote in Local Elections: Results from Six Door-to-Door Canvassing Experiments," *Journal of Politics* 65 (2003): 4.

86. Allison Dale and Aaron Strauss, "Don't Forget to Vote: Text Message Reminders as a Mobilization Tool," *American Journal of Political Science* 53 (2009): 787–804.

87. Steven J. Rosenstone and John Mark Hansen, *Mobilization, Participation, and Democracy in America* (New York: Macmillan, 1993).

88. James H. Fowler, Laura A. Baker, and Christopher T. Dawes, "Genetic Variation in Political Participation," *American Political Science Review* 102, no. 2 (2008): 233–48.

89. James H. Fowler and Christopher T. Dawes, "Two Genes Predict Voter Turnout," *Journal of Politics* 70 (2008): 579–94.

90. Fances Fox Piven and Richard A. Cloward, *Why Americans Still Don't Vote: And Why Politicians Want It That Way* (Boston: Beacon Press, 2000); Martin P. Wattenberg, *Where Have All the Voters Gone?* (Boston: Harvard University Press, 2002); Thomas E. Patterson, *The Vanishing Voter: Public Involvement in an Age of Uncertainty* (New York: Alfred A. Knopf, 2003).

91. See http://www.electproject.org/2014g, accessed November 5, 2014; http://elections.gmu.edu/Turnout_2012G.html, accessed June 3, 2013.

92. Ibid.

93. www.idea.int.

94. Powell, "American Voter Turnout," 17–37.

95. This "puzzle of participation" was first discussed by Richard Brody in *The New American Political System,* ed. Anthony King (Washington, D.C.: American Enterprise Institute for Public Policy Research, 1978).

96. Warren Miller, "Puzzle Transformed," *Political Behavior* 14 (1992): 1–43.

97. Rosenstone and Hansen, *Mobilization, Participation, and Democracy in America.*

98. Ibid.

99. Keena Lipsitz, Christine Trost, Matthew Grossman, and John Sides, "What Voters Want from Campaign Communication," *Political Communication* 22 (2005): 337–54.

100. Steven Ansolabehere and Shanto Iyengar, *Going Negative* (New York: Free Press, 1995).

101. John G. Geer, *In Defense of Negativity* (Chicago: University of Chicago Press, 2006).

102 See, for example, Joshua Clinton and John Lapinski, "'Targeted' Advertising and Voter Turnout: An Experimental Study of the 2000 Presidential Election," *Journal of Politics* 66 (2004): 69–96.

103. Richard R. Lau, Lee Sigelman, and Ivy Brown Rovner, "A New Meta-Analysis," *Journal of Politics* 69 (2007): 1176–1209.

104. Julia Preston, "Immigrants Number 11.5 Million," *New York Times,* March 24, 2012, http://www.nytimes.com/2012/03/24/us/illegal-immigrants-number-11-5-million.html. http://cnsnews.com/news/article/ali-meyer/latest-estimate-illegal-alien-population-exceeds-unemployed, accessed June 3, 2014.

105. Pew Safety Performance Project, *One in 100: Behind Bars in America 2008* (Washington, D.C.: Pew Center on the States, February 2008), http://www.pewtrusts.org/en/research-and-analysis/reports/0001 /01/01/one-in-100; http://www.nytimes.com/2013/07/26/us/us-prison-populations-decline-reflecting-new-approach-to-crime.html?pagewanted=all, accessed June 3, 2014.

106. Michael P. McDonald and Samuel L. Popkin, "The Myth of the Vanishing Voter," *American Political Science Review* 95 (2001): 963–74.

107. See Larry Bartels, *Unequal Democracy* (Princeton, N.J.: Princeton University Press, 2008).

108. Task Force on American Inequality, "American Democracy in an Age of Rising Inequality," American Political Science Association, 2004.

109. See Dayton McKean, *The Boss: The Hague Machine in Action* (New York: Russell and Russell Publishers, 1967), for an account of the corrupt practices of machine politicians.

110. See James Bryce, *The American Commonwealth* (New York: MacMillan, 1895).

111. For the best account of the importance and impact of registration, see Benjamin Highton, "Voter Registration and Turnout in the United States," *Perspectives on Politics* 2 (2004): 507–15.

112. See Nonprofit Vote at http://www.NonProfitVote.Org.

113. Read about the National Voter Registration Act of 1993 at http://www.justice.gov/crt/about/vot/nvra/activ_nvra.php.

114. Texas Secretary of State Hope Andrade's official website, http://www.sos.state.tx.us/.

115. http://www.oregonlive.com/mapes/index.ssf/2013/03/in_last_presidential_election.html, accessed June 3, 2014.

116. https://www.sos.state.co.us/pubs/rule_making/written_comments/2009/111009_commoncause_votebymailproject.pdf, accessed June 30, 2014.

117. *Absentee and Early Voting*, National Conference of State Legislatures, February 26, 2014, http://www.ncsl.org/research/elections-and-campaigns/absentee-and-early-voting.aspx.

118. Paul Gronke, Eva Galanes-Rosenbaum, and Peter A. Miller, "Early Voting and Turnout," *PS: Political Science and Politics* (October 2003) 639–645.

119. Steven Yaccino and Lizette Alvarez, "New G.O.P. Bid to Limit Voting in Swing States," *New York Times*, March 29, 2014.

120. V. O. Key, *The Responsible Electorate* (Cambridge, Mass.: Harvard University Press, 1966).

121. See Jeff Manza and Christopher Ugge, *Locked Out: Felon Disenfranchisement and American Democracy* (Oxford, U.K.: Oxford University Press, 2007).

Chapter 10

1. This story was compiled from information on Representative Joaquin Castro's congressional website, http://castro.house.gov/; Georgia Park "Castro Highlights Importance of Public Service Work, Leadership," *The Chronicle*, April 2, 2014, http://www.dukechronicle.com/articles/2014/04/02/castro-highlights-importance-public-service-work-leadership; "Interview with Representative Joaquin Castro," *The Situation Room*, CNN, January 4, 2013, http://www.realclearpolitics.com/articles/2013/01/04/interview_with_representative_joaquin_castro_116607.html#ixzz2yDth5yUN; Office of the Secretary of State of Texas, "Race Summary Report, 2012 General Election" November 6, 2012, http://elections.sos.state.tx.us, "Congressman Castro Visits Afghanistan," KSAT-San Antonio, April 7, 2014, http://www.ksat.com/news/Congressman-Castro-visits-Afghanistan/25370616.

2. Totals do not include House Delegates or the Resident Commissioner; see Jennifer E. Manning, *Membership of the 113th Congress: A Profile*, CRS Report for Congress, R42964 (Washington, D.C.: Congressional Research Service, March 14, 2014), accessed April 16, 2014, http://www.fas.org/sgp/crs/misc/R42964.pdf; census.gov, "Age and Sex Composition in the United States: 2012, http://www.census.gov/population/age/data/2012comp.html.

3. Manning, *Membership.*

4. Ibid. For a broader discussion of the careers of women legislators in the House, see Jennifer Lawless and Sean Theriault, "Will She Stay or Will She Go? Career Ceilings and Women's Retirement from the U.S. Congress," *Legislative Studies Quarterly* 30 (2005): 581–96.

5. See Wendy J. Schiller and Charles Stewart III. 2014. *Electing the Senate: Indirect Democracy before the Seventeenth Amendment.* (Princeton: Princeton University Press), and Lana R. Slack, *Senate Manual: Standing Rules, Orders, Laws, and Resolutions Affecting the Business of the United States Senate* (Washington, D.C.: U.S. Government Printing Office, 1988), 684–85.

6. United States Senate, "Senate Classes," Senate.gov, accessed June 21, 2012, http://www.senate.gov/artandhistory/history/common/briefing/Constitution_Senate.htm#3.

7. In rare cases in which a senator dies or resigns, an interim replacement is typically chosen by the governor of the state until an election is held to fill the seat.

8. U.S Census Bureau, Kristen D. Burnett, "Congressional Apportionment," November 2011, http://www.census.gov/prod/cen2010/briefs/c2010br-08.pdf, accessed April 16, 2014; Census.gov, "Annual Population Estimates," http://www.census.gov/popclock/.

9. After the first census of the new federal government under the Constitution, Congress grew to 105 members in 1792. See Brian Frederick, *Congressional Representation and Constituents: The Case for Increasing the Size of the U.S. House of Representatives* (New York: Routledge, 2010), 23–24.

10. U.S. House of Representatives, "Historical Highlights: The Permanent Apportionment Act of 1929," June 11, 1929, accessed June 21, 2012, http://artandhistory.house.gov/highlights.aspx?action=view&intID=200.

11. For a discussion of representation by Latino members, see Jason P. Casellas, "The Institutional and Demographic Determinants of Latino Representation," *Legislative Studies Quarterly* 34, no. 3 (2009): 399–426; see also David Leal and Frederick M. Hess, "Who Chooses Experience? Examining the Use of Veteran Staff by House Freshmen," *Polity* 36 (2004): 651–64.

12. U.S. Bureau of the Census, "Fast Facts for Congress," My Congressional District (the American Community Survey), http://www.census.gov/fastfacts/, accessed online April 16, 2014.

13. See *Shaw v. Reno*, 509 U.S. 630 (1993); *Miller v. Johnson*, 515 U.S. 900 (1995); and *Easley v. Cromartie*, 532 U.S. 234 (2001). *Thornburg v. Gingles*, 478 U.S. 30 (1986) provides plaintiffs with a right to force a state to create a majority-minority district. If the minority community is large and concentrated enough to form a majority in the district, the minority community votes cohesively, and white voting prevents the minority community from electing its preferred candidate. For a longer discussion of redistricting, see Bernard Grofman, Lisa Handley, and Richard G. Niemi, *Minority Representation and the Quest for Voting Equality* (New York: Cambridge University Press, 1992).

14. Frances E. Lee and Bruce I. Oppenheimer, *Sizing up the Senate: The Unequal Consequences of Equal Representation* (Chicago: University of Chicago Press, 1999).

15. Two prominent works on this point are Richard F. Fenno Jr., *The Power of the Purse: Appropriations Politics in Congress* (Boston: Little, Brown, 1966), and Aaron B. Wildavsky, *The New Politics of the Budgetary Process* (Boston: Addison-Wesley Educational, 1992).

16. Fiona McGillivray, "Trading Free and Opening Markets," in *International Trade and Political Institutions,* ed. Fiona McGillivray, Iain McLean, Robert Pahre, and Cheryl Schonhardt-Bailey (Cheltenham, U.K.: Edward Elgar, 2001), 80–98.

17. United States Courts: Federal Courts, http://www.uscourts.gov/FederalCourts.aspx.

18. Sarah A. Binder and Forrest Maltzman, "Senatorial Delay in Confirming Federal Judges, 1947–1998," *American Journal of Political Science* 46, no. 1 (2002): 190–99.

19. Sarah A. Binder, *Majority Rights, Minority Rule* (New York: Cambridge University Press, 1997); Eric Schickler, *Disjointed Pluralism: Institutional Innovation and the Development of the U.S. Congress* (Princeton, N.J.: Princeton University Press, 2001).

20. Sean Gailmard and Jeffery A. Jenkins, "Minority-Party Power in the Senate and the House of Representatives," in *Why Not Parties? Party Effects in the United States Senate,* ed. Nathan W. Monroe, Jason M. Roberts, and David W. Rohde (Chicago: University of Chicago Press, 2008), 181–97.

21. Randall Strahan, *Leading Representatives: The Agency of Leaders in the Politics of the U.S. House* (Baltimore: Johns Hopkins University Press, 2007).

22. Ibid., 79–126.

23. David W. Rohde, *Parties and Leaders in the Postreform House* (Chicago: University of Chicago Press, 1991).

24. Gary W. Cox and Mathew D. McCubbins, *Legislative Leviathan: Party Government in the House* (Berkeley: University of California Press, 1993).

25. Gallup.com, "Congressional Job Approval at 12% in February," http://www.gallup.com/poll/167375/congressional-job-approval-february.aspx, accessed April 16, 2014.

26. Barry C. Burden and Tammy M. Frisbee, "Preferences, Partisanship, and Whip Activity in the U.S. House of Representatives," *Legislative Studies Quarterly* 29 (2004): 569–90.

27. Ralph Huitt, "Democratic Party Leadership in the Senate," *American Political Science Review* 55 (1961): 333–44.

28. E. Scott Adler and John Wilkerson, "Intended Consequences: Jurisdictional Reform and Issue Control in the U.S. House of Representatives," *Legislative Studies Quarterly* 33, no. 1 (2008): 85–112.

29. For a list of current caucuses, see Committee on House Administration, "112th Congress Congressional Member Organizations (CMO)," updated April 11, 2012, accessed June 21, 2012, http://cha.house.gov/sites/republicans.cha.house.gov/files/documents/cmo_cso_docs/cmo_112th_congress.pdf.

30. Daily Digest, "Resume of Congressional Activity, First Session of the One Hundred Twelfth Congress," *Congressional Record D210,* March 7, 2012; Daily Digest, "Resume of Congressional Activity, Second Session of the One Hundred Twelfth Congress," *Congressional Record D196,* March 13, 2013, http://thomas.loc.gov.

31. For an extended discussion of the right of recognition and the powers it affords senators, see Floyd Riddick, *Senate Procedure,* ed. Alan Frumin (Washington D.C.: U.S. Government Printing Office, 1992), 1091–99.

32. Sarah A. Binder and Steven S. Smith, *Politics or Principle: Filibustering in the U.S. Senate* (Washington, D.C.: Brookings Institution Press, 1997). For a discussion of the use of the filibuster by retiring senators, see Martin Overby, L. Overby, and Lauren Bell, "Rational Behavior or the Norm of Cooperation? Filibustering among Retiring Senators," *Journal of Politics* 66 (2004): 906–24.

33. For more details on the cloture rules and recent changes, see Valerie Heitshusen, Congressional Research Service, "Majority Cloture for Nominations: Implications and the 'Nuclear' Proceedings," December 6, 2013, R43331, accessed April 16, 2014, http://www.fas.org/sgp/crs/misc/R43331.pdf.

34. David Stout, Carl Hulse, and Sheryl Gay Stolberg, "Senate Backs Disputed Judicial Nomination," *New York Times,* October 27, 2007, A21.

35. Wendy J. Schiller, "Resolved the Filibuster Should Be Abolished—Con," in *Debating Reform,* 2nd ed., ed. Richard J. Ellis and Michael Nelson (Washington, D.C.: CQ Press, 2012).

36. Wendy J. Schiller, "Senators as Political Entrepreneurs: Using Bill Sponsorship to Shape Legislative Agendas," *American Journal of Political Science* 1 (1995): 186–203.

37. Glen Krutz, *Hitching a Ride: Omnibus Legislating in the U.S. Congress* (Columbus: Ohio State University Press, 2001).

38. For a general discussion on committees, see Keith R. Krehbiel, *Information and Legislative Organization* (Ann Arbor: University of Michigan Press, 1991).

39. For a few examples of this work, see Aage Clausen, *How Congressmen Decide* (New York: St. Martin's Press, 1973); John Kingdon, *Congressmen's Voting Decisions* (New York: Harper & Row, 1989); David W. Brady, *Critical Elections and Congressional Policy Making* (Stanford, Calif.: Stanford University Press, 1988); Stanley Bach and Steven S. Smith, *Managing Uncertainty in the U.S. House of Representatives* (Washington, D.C.: Brookings Institution Press, 1989). For examples of the ideological examination of roll call voting, see Keith T. Poole and Howard Rosenthal, *Ideology and Congress* (New Brunswick, N.J.: Transaction Publishers, 2009).

40. Humberto Sanchez, "2012 Vote Studies: Party Unity," *CQ Weekly*, January 21, 2013, 132; Staff, "Party Unity Background," *CQ Annual Report*, January 21, 2013, 137.

41. C. Lawrence Evans and Walter J. Oleszek, "Message Politics and Senate Procedure," in *The Contentious Senate: Partisanship, Ideology and the Myth of Cool Judgment,* ed. Colton C. Campbell and Nicol C. Rae (Lanham, Md.: Rowman and Littlefield, 2000).

42. Barbara Sinclair, *Unorthodox Lawmaking: New Legislative Processes in the U.S. Congress,* 3rd ed. (Washington, D.C.: CQ Press, 2007).

43. Congressional Budget and Impoundment Control Act of 1974 (Public Law 93-344). For additional background on budget history, see the Senate Budget Committee's website at http://www.budget .senate.gov/democratic/public/index.cfm/history-of-the-budget -committee.

44. Balanced Budget and Emergency Deficit Control Act of 1985 (Public Law 99-177). For historical tables on the U.S. federal budget, see Congressional Budget Office, "The Budget and Economic Outlook Fiscal Years 2012 to 2022," January 31, 2012, accessed June 21, 2012, http://www.cbo.gov/publication/42905. The Fiscal 1985 budget deficit number is taken from Table F-1, http://www.cbo.gov /publication/42911.

45. See Walter J. Oleszek, *Congressional Procedures and the Policy Process*, 6th ed. (Washington, D.C: CQ Press, 2004), especially 63–69. For a more comprehensive look at the history of budget politics and deficits, see Jasmine Farrier, *Passing the Buck: Congress, Budgets, and Deficits* (Lexington: University of Kentucky Press, 2004).

46. Kathleen Hunter, "GOP Readies Procedural Salvo against Reconciliation Play," *CQ Weekly Online*, March 8, 2010, 568.

47. Charles M. Cameron, *Veto Bargaining: Presidents and the Politics of Negative Power* (New York: Cambridge University Press, 2000).

48. Bureau of Labor Statistics, "Labor Force Statistics from the Current Population Survey," http://data.bls.gov/timeseries/LNS14000000.

49. Department of Labor, "Unemployment Insurance 75th Anniversary," accessed April 17, 2014, http://www.dol.gov/ocia/pdf/75th-Anniversary -Summary-FINAL.pdf.

50. Staff, Department of Labor, "Chronology of Federal Unemployment Compensation Laws, February 2014," accessed April 17, 2014, http:// workforcesecurity.doleta.gov/unemploy/pdf/chronfedlaws.pdf.

51. Albert D. Cover and Bruce S. Brumberg, "Baby Books and Ballots: The Impact of Congressional Mail on Constituent Opinion," *American Political Science Review* 76 (1982): 347–59.

52. Richard L. Hall, *Participation in Congress* (New Haven, Conn.: Yale University Press, 1998).

53. Tracy Sulkin, *Issue Politics in Congress* (New York: Cambridge University Press, 2005).

54. Daily Digest, "Resume of Congressional Activity, First Session of the One Hundred Twelfth Congress," *Congressional Record D210*, March 7, 2012; Daily Digest, "Resume of Congressional Activity, Second Session of the One Hundred Twelfth Congress," *Congressional Record D196*, March 13, 2013, http://thomas.loc.gov.

55. For a comprehensive look at this congressional activity, see Diana Evans, *Greasing the Wheels: Using Pork Barrel Projects to Build Majority Coalitions in Congress* (New York: Cambridge University Press, 2004).

56. Jennifer A. Dlouhy, "Alaska 'Bridge to Nowhere' Funding Gets Nowhere; Lawmakers Delete Project after Critics Bestow Derisive Moniker," *San Francisco Chronicle*, November 17, 2005, A7.

57. Citizens Against Taxpayer Waste, "2010 Pig Book Summary," accessed June 21, 2012, http://www.cagw.org/content/2010-pig-book-summary.

58. Richard F. Fenno Jr., *Home Style: House Members in Their Districts* (Boston: Little, Brown, 1978).

59. David R. Mayhew, *Congress: The Electoral Connection* (New Haven, Conn.: Yale University Press, 1974).

60. For an extended discussion of how senators from the same state interact, see Schiller, *Partners and Rivals.*

61. Charles Mahtesian, "2012 Reelection Rate: 90 percent" Politico.com, December 13, 2012, accessed April 16, 2014, http://www .politico.com/blogs/charlie-mahtesian/2012/12/reelection-rate -percent-151898.html.

Chapter 11

1. Sylvia Mathews Burwell, "Testimony before the Senate Health, Education, Labor, and Pensions Committee" May 8, 2014, accessed May 15, 2014, http://www.help.senate.gov/imo/media/doc/Burwell .pdf.

2. This story was compiled from the Office of Management and Budget's website: http://www.whitehouse.gov/omb; President Barack Obama, transcript of "Remarks by the President in Nominating Sylvia Mathews Burwell as Secretary of Health and Human Services," October 9, 2013, http://www.whitehouse.gov; Dylan Matthews, "Sylvia Mathews Burwell: Six Things to Know about the New White House Budget Director," Wonkblog, *Washington Post*, March 3, 2013; "Q&A: Sylvia Mathews, President of the Gates Foundation Global Development Program," *The Seattle Times*, March 17, 2007; Jennifer Haberkorn, "Sylvia Mathews Burwell's Hurdles," *Politico*, April 11, 2014; Sarah Plummer, "Obama Taps Hinton Native for Budget Chief," *The Register-Herald*, March 5, 2013.

3. See Hedrick Smith, "Bush Says He Sought to Avoid Acting Like Surrogate President," *New York Times*, April 12, 1981, A1, http: //www.nytimes.com/1981/04/12/us/bush-says-he-sought-to-avoid -acting-like-surrogate-president.html.

4. Bruce G. Peabody and Scott E. Grant, "The Twice and Future President: Constitutional Interstices and the Twenty-Second Amendment," *Minnesota Law Review* 83 (1999): 565–94.

5. "The Presidents," The White House, accessed June 22, 2012, http: //www.whitehouse.gov/about/presidents.

6. Arthur Schlesinger Jr., *The Imperial Presidency* (New York: Mariner Books, 2004; first published 1973).

7. U.S. Department of Justice, Office of the Pardon Attorney, "Clemency Statistics," accessed May 1, 2014, http://www.justice.gov/pardon /statistics.htm.

8. Robert Wielaard, "Kosovo Recognition Irritates Russia and China," *Herald-Tribune*, February 19, 2008, A11, http://www.heraldtribune .com/article/20080219/NEWS/802190626.

9. Charles M. Cameron, *Veto Bargaining: Presidents and the Politics of Negative Power* (New York: Cambridge University Press, 2000).

10. Glenn S. Krutz, *Hitching a Ride: Omnibus Legislating in the U.S. Congress* (Columbus: Ohio State University Press, 2001). Also see Cameron, *Veto Bargaining.*

11. William W. Lammers and Michael A. Genovese, *The Presidency and Domestic Policy* (Washington, D.C.: CQ Press, 2000), 315–24.

12. Wilson delivered the speech on December 2, 1913. See John T. Woolley and Gerhard Peters, "Length of State of the Union Messages and Addresses (in words), Washington–Obama," The American Presidency Project, accessed June 22, 2012, http://www.presidency.ucsb.edu/sou_words.php#axzz1yaTY1UIo.

13. Jeff Cummins, "State of the Union Addresses and the President's Legislative Success," *Congress and the Presidency* 37 (2010): 176–99.

14. The chronology that follows is taken from the *Washington Post*'s history of Watergate, available online at http://www.washingtonpost.com/wp-srv/onpolitics/watergate/chronology.htm.

15. Ibid.

16. William G. Howell, *Power without Persuasion: The Politics of Direct Presidential Action* (Princeton, N.J.: Princeton University Press, 2003).

17. Harold C. Relyea, *Presidential Directives: Background and Overview*, CRS Report for Congress, 98-611 (Washington, D.C.: Congressional Research Service, 2007).

18. Kenneth R. Mayer, "Executive Orders and Presidential Power," *Journal of Politics* 61 (1999): 445–66, especially 448.

19. Ibid.

20. Harry S. Truman, "Memo 'Concerning the Interpretation of the President's Order. . . ,' Harry S. Truman Library & Museum, ca. 1948, accessed June 22, 2012, http://www.trumanlibrary.org/whistlestop/study_collections/desegregation/large/documents/index.php?documentdate=1948-00-00&documentid=5-20&studycollectionid=&pagenumber=1&sortorder=.

21. Christopher S. Kelley and Bryan W. Marshall, "The Last Word: Presidential Power and the Role of Signing Statements," *Presidential Studies Quarterly* 38 (2008): 248–67; Michael J. Berry, "Controversially Executing the Law: George W. Bush and the Constitutional Signing Statement," *Congress and the Presidency* 36 (2009): 244–71.

22. The White House, "Memorandum for the Heads of Executive Departments and Agencies: Subject: Presidential Signing Statements," news release, March 9, 2009, http://www.whitehouse.gov/the-press-office/memorandum-presidential-signing-statements.

23. Gerhard Peters, "Executive Orders Washington–Obama," The American Presidency Project, ed. John T. Woolley and Gerhard Peters, updated September 6, 2014, accessed September 6, 2014, http://www.presidency.ucsb.edu/data/orders.php; John T. Woolley, "Presidential Signing Statements, Hoover–Obama," The American Presidency Project, ed. John T. Woolley and Gerhard Peters, updated September 6, 2014, http://www.presidency.ucsb.edu/signingstatements.php?year=2012&Submit=DISPLAY#axzz1uKYKvi91.

24. Joseph A. Pika and John Anthony Maltese, *The Politics of the Presidency*, 8th ed. (Washington, D.C.: CQ Press, 2012), 14–16.

25. "Bully Pulpit," C-SPAN Congressional Glossary, accessed June 22, 2012, http://legacy.c-span.org/guide/congress/glossary/alphalist.htm.

26. George C. Edwards III, *On Deaf Ears: The Limits of the Bully Pulpit* (New Haven, Conn.: Yale University Press, 2006).

27. John T. Woolley and Gerhard Peters, "Presidential News Conferences, Hoover–Obama," The American Presidency Project, updated May 1, 2014, accessed May 1, 2014, http://www.presidency.ucsb.edu/news_conferences.php?year=2012&Submit=DISPLAY.

28. See Zachary A. Goldfarb and Juliet Eilperin, "White House looking for new ways to penetrate polarized media," *Washington Post*, May 6, 2014, accessed online May 7, 2014, http://www.washingtonpost.com/politics/white-house-looking-for-new-ways-to-penetrate-polarized-media/2014/05/06/ebd39b6c-d532-11e3-aae8-c2d44bd79778_story.html; Melvin C. Laracey, *Presidents and People: The Partisan Story of Going Public* (College Station, Tex.: Texas A&M University Press, 2002); Reed L. Welch, "Presidential Success in Communicating with the Public through Televised Addresses," *Presidential Studies Quarterly* 33 (2003): 347–65; Samuel Kernell and Laurie L. Rice, "Cable and the Partisan Polarization of the President's Audience," *Presidency Studies Quarterly* 41, no. 4 (2011): 693–711.

29. Richard E. Neustadt, *Presidential Power and the Modern Presidents* (New York: Free Press, 1990).

30. Jon R. Bond, Richard Fleisher, and B. Dan Wood, "The Marginal and Time Varying Effect of Public Approval on Presidential Success in Congress," *Journal of Politics* 65 (2003): 92–110.

31. Andrew Barrett and Matthew Eshbaugh-Soha, "Presidential Success on the Substance of Legislation," *Political Research Quarterly* 60 (2007): 100–12.

32. Joint Resolution of Congress, House Joint Resolution 1145, August 7, 1964, *Department of State Bulletin*, August 24, 1964, reprinted in Henry Steele Commager and Milton Cantor, eds., *Documents of American History*, 10th ed. (Englewood Cliffs, N.J.: Prentice Hall, 1988), 2: 690.

33. Louis Fisher, *Presidential War Power*, 2nd ed. (Lawrence: University Press of Kansas, 2004), 128–33.

34. Ibid., 144–51.

35. For a longer discussion of this struggle for power over the conduct of war, see William G. Howell and Jon C. Pevenhouse, *Congressional Checks on Presidential War Powers* (Princeton, N.J.: Princeton University Press, 2007).

36. For more on presidential decisions to engage in military conflicts, see James Meernick, "Domestic Politics and the Political Use of Military Force by the United States," *Political Research Quarterly* 54 (2001): 889–904.

37. U.S. House of Representatives, House Joint Resolution, 114 Section 3 (a) 1, Library of Congress, http://thomas.loc.gov.

38. John J. Kruzel, "Afghanistan Troop Level to Eclipse Iraq by Midyear," United States Army, March 25, 2010, http://www.army.mil/article/36297/.

39. Afghanistan International Security Assistance Force, ISAF, NATO, http://www.isaf.nato.int/troop-numbers-and-contributions/index.php.

40. This paragraph is based on "Libya–Revolution and Aftermath," *New York Times*, updated June 11, 2012, http://topics.nytimes.com/top/news/international/countriesandterritories/libya/index.html.

41. This section is based on "Syria," *New York Times*, updated June 18, 2012, http://topicsnytimes.com/top/news/international/countriesandterritories/syria/index.html.

42. Scott Shane and Thom Shanker, "Yemen Strike Reflects U.S. Shift to Drones as Cheaper War Tool," October 2, 2011, *New York Times*, accessed May 6, 2014, http://www.nytimes.com/2011/10/02/world/awlaki-strike-shows-us-shift-to-drones-in-terror-fight.html?_r=0.

43. Craig Whitlock, "U.S. Airstrike that Killed American Teen in Yemen Raises Legal, Ethical Questions," *Washington Post*, October 22, 2011, accessed May 6, 2014, http://www.washingtonpost.com/world/national-security/us-airstrike-that-killed-american-teen-in-yemen-raises-legal-ethical-questions/2011/10/20/gIQAdvUY7L_story.html.

44. White House, Office of the Press Secretary, "Remarks by the President at the National Defense University, May 23, 2013," http://www.whitehouse.gov/the-press-office/2013/05/23/remarks-president-national-defense-university.

45. Bruce Drake, "Report Questions Drone Use, Widely Unpopular Globally, But Not in the U.S," Pew Research Center, October 23, 2013, accessed May 15, 2014, http://www.pewresearch.org/fact-tank/2013/10/23/report-questions-drone-use-widely-unpopular-globally-but-not-in-the-u-s/.

46. See "Public Sees U.S. Power Declining as Support for Global Engagement Slips," accessed May 4, 2014, http://www.people-press.org/2013/12/03/public-sees-u-s-power-declining-as-support-for-global-engagement-slips/.

47. *Hamdi v. Rumsfeld*, 542 U.S. 507 (2004).

48. *Rasul v. Bush*, 542 U.S. 466 (2004).

49. *Hamdan v. Rumsfeld*, 548 U.S. 557 (2006).

50. *Boumediene v. Bush*, 553 U.S. 723 (2008)

51. Fred I. Greenstein, *Presidential Difference*, 3rd ed. (Princeton, N.J.: Princeton University Press, 2009).

52. Mondale wrote a detailed memorandum to President Carter outlining his views of the office of vice president. For a broader discussion of Mondale's vice presidential tenure, see Richard Moe, "The Making of the Modern Vice Presidency: A Personal Reflection," *Minnesota History* 60 (2006): 88–99.

53. Joel K. Goldstein, "The Rising Power of the Modern Vice Presidency," *Presidential Studies Quarterly* 38, no. 3 (2008): 389.

54. Stephen Skowronek, *The Politics Presidents Make: Leadership from John Adams to Bill Clinton* (Cambridge, Mass.: Harvard University Press, 1997). Also see Stephen Skowronek, *Presidential Leadership in Political Time: Reprise and Reappraisal* (Lawrence: University Press of Kansas, 2008).

55. Aaron Wildavsky, "The Two Presidencies" in *The Presidency*, ed. Aaron Wildavsky (Boston: Little, Brown, 1969), 231–43.

56. For a more recent test of this theory, see Brandes Canes-Wrone, William G. Howell, and David E. Lewis, "Toward a Broader Understanding of Presidential Power: A Reevaluation of the Two Presidencies Thesis," *Journal of Politics* 69 (2007): 1–16.

57. Lammers and Genovese, *Presidency and Domestic Policy*. See also Neustadt, *Presidential Power and the Modern Presidents*.

58. Samuel Kernell, *Going Public: New Strategies of Presidential Leadership*, 4th ed. (Washington, D.C.: CQ Press, 2007), 131.

59. Ibid., 87–88.

60. Lammers and Genovese, *Presidency and Domestic Policy*.

61. Robert A. Caro, *The Years of Lyndon Johnson: The Passage of Power* (New York: Alfred A. Knopf, 2012), 487. Also see Lyndon Johnson's commencement address at Howard University, "To Fulfill These Rights," June 4, 1965, accessed June 22, 2012, http://www.lbjlib.utexas.edu/johnson/archives.hom/speeches.hom/650604.asp.

62. Lynn Rosellini, "'Honey, I Forgot to Duck,' Injured Reagan Tells Wife," *New York Times*, March 21, 1981, http://www.nytimes.com/1981/03/31/us/honey-i-forgot-to-duck-injured-reagan-tells-wife.html.

63. American Rhetoric, "Top 100 Speeches," accessed June 22, 2012, http://www.americanrhetoric.com/newtop100speeches.htm.

64. Hank C. Jenkins-Smith, Carol L. Silva, and Richard W. Waterman, "Micro- and Macro-level Models of the Presidential Expectations Gap," *Journal of Politics* 67 (2005): 690–715.

Chapter 12

1. Mike M. Ahlers, "Fired Air Marshal Loses Battle in Job Fight," *CNN.com*, August 5, 2011, http://www.cnn.com/2011/US/08/05/air.marshal.fired/index.html.

2. This story was compiled from the Transportation Security Administration website, http://www.tsa.gov/careers/; Jacob Gershman, "U.S. Takes Whistleblower Case against Air Marshal to Supreme Court," *The Wall Street Journal*, January 28, 2014, http://blogs.wsj.com/law/2014/01/28/u-s-takes-whistleblower-case-against-air-marshal-to-supreme-court/; Peter Van Buren, "The Next Battleground in the War on Whistleblowers," *The Nation*, March 4, 2014; Dan Weikel, "Air Marshal Whistle-blower Fired in 2006 Claims Big Win in Court," *Los Angeles Times*, May 25, 2013; The Government Accountability Project, "Robert MacLean, Air Marshal Whistleblower," http://www.whistleblower.org/robert-maclean-air-marshal-whistleblower; Laurence Hurley, "Supreme Court Agrees to Hear Air Marshal Whistleblower Case," Reuters News Service, printed in *Chicago Tribune*, May 19, 2014, http://www.chicagotribune.com/news/nationworld/la-na-nn-air-marshal-whistleblower-20140519,0,6366235.story.

3. Max Weber, *Economy and Society*, ed. Guenther Roth and Claus Wittich (Berkeley, Calif.: University of California Press, 1978).

4. The White House, Office of Management and Budget, Fiscal Year 2015 *Analytical Perspectives, Budget of the U.S. Government* (Washington, D.C.: U.S. Government Printing Office, 2014), Table 8-3, Total Federal Employment, p. 81, accessed May 19, 2014, http://www.whitehouse.gov/sites/default/files/omb/budget/fy2015/assets/spec.pdf; Note that the total number of federal employees cited above does not include active and reserve members of the National Guard.

5. "President Jefferson in the White House," EyeWitness to History, 2006, accessed June 27, 2012, http://www.eyewitnesstohistory.com/jeffersonwhitehouse.htm.

6. "The Cabinet," The White House, accessed May 19, 2014, http://www.whitehouse.gov/administration/cabinet.

7. A.P. staff, "United Nations Trims Staff and Spending," *New York Times*, December 27, 2013, http://www.nytimes.com/2013/12/28/world/un-budget-trims-staff-and-spending.html.

8. The White House, Office of Management and Budget, *Analytical Perspectives, Budget*, Table 8.2; The White House, Office of Management and Budget, *FY 2015 Analytical Perspectives, Budget*, Table 25-11, "Budget Authority by Agency in the Adjusted Baseline", p. 392, accessed May 19, 2014, http://www.whitehouse.gov/sites/default/files/omb/budget/fy2015/assets/spec.pdf.

9. Department of Health and Human Services, "HHS Programs and Services," accessed May 19, 2014, http://www.hhs.gov/about/programs/index.html

10. The White House, Office of Management and Budget, Fiscal Year 2015, *Analytical Perspectives, Budget*, Table 8.2.

11. Transportation Security Administration, "About TSA" accessed May 19, 2014, http://www.tsa.gov/about-tsa/layers-security; Transportation Security Administration, "About Us: Workforce" accessed May 19, 2014, http://www.tsa.gov/about-tsa/our-workforce.

12. U.S. Department of Health and Human Services, "About HHS," http://www.hhs.gov/about/.

13. James Q. Wilson, *Bureaucracy* (New York: Basic Books, 1989), 91.

14. Donald F. Kettl, *System under Stress: Homeland Security and American Politics*, 2nd ed. (Washington, D.C.: CQ Press, 2007), 37–39.

15. Matt Egan, "BP, Oil Plaintiffs Hammer Out Settlement," FOXBusiness, April 18, 2012, http://www.foxbusiness.com/industries/2012/04/18/bp-oil-spill-plaintiffs-hammer-out-settlement/.

16. Ian Urbina, "U.S. Said to Allow Drilling without Needed Permits," *New York Times*, May 13, 2010, http://www.nytimes.com/2010/05/14/us/14agency.html?pagewanted=all.

17. NPR staff, "White House Lifts Ban on Offshore Drilling," NPR, October 12, 2010, http://www.npr.org/templates/story/story.php?storyId=130512541.

18. Egan, "BP, Oil Plaintiffs Hammer Out Settlement."

19. Daniel P. Carpenter, *The Forging of Bureaucratic Autonomy: Reputations, Networks, and Policy Innovation in Executive Agencies, 1862–1928* (Princeton, N.J.: Princeton University Press, 2001).

20. United States Postal Service, Office of the Postmaster, *The United States Postal Service: An American History, 1775–2006* (Washington, D.C.: Government Relations, United States Postal Service, 2007), 6–7, http://about.usps.com/publications/pub100.pdf.

21. Michael Moss, "E. Coli Path Shows Flaws in Beef Inspection," *New York Times*, October 3, 2009, A1; Michael Moss, "E. Coli Outbreak Traced to Company That Halted Testing of Ground Beef Trimmings," *New York Times*, November 12, 2009, A16; Bill Tomson, "Tuna Blamed

in Salmonella Outbreak is recalled," *Wall Street Journal*, April 17, 2012, A3.

22. U.S. Consumer Product Safety Commission, http://www.cpsc.gov.

23. "The Consumer Financial Protection Bureau," The White House, September 17, 2010, http://www.whitehouse.gov/photos-and-video /video/2010/09/17/consumer-financial-protection-bureau.

24. Lewis, *Politics of Presidential Appointments*, 12–13.

25. Theda Skocpol, *Protecting Soldiers and Mothers* (Cambridge, Mass.: Harvard University Press, 1992).

26. Sean M. Theriault, *The Power of the People* (Columbus: Ohio State University Press, 2005), Chapter 3.

27. Davis Polk, "Dodd-Frank Progress Report," accessed September 9, 2014 http://www.davispolk.com/Dodd-Frank-Rulemaking-Progress-Report/.

28. Lewis, *Politics of Presidential Appointments*, 19–20, especially Figure 2.1.

29. U.S. Office of Personnel Management, "Federal Employment Statistics: Federal Civilian Employment," September 2010, accessed June 27, 2012, http://www.opm.gov/feddata/html/geoagy10.asp.

30. Department of Labor, Bureau of Labor Statistics, accessed May 30, 2014, http://www.bls.gov/ooh/about/ooh-faqs.htm.

31. For more on political appointees, see Jeff Gill and Richard Waterman, "Solidary and Functional Costs: Explaining the Presidential Appointment Contradiction," *Journal of Public Administration Research and Theory* 14 (2004): 547–69.

32. Lewis, *Politics of Presidential Appointments*, 11.

33. Ibid., 100, Figure 4.3.

34. Juliet Eilperin, "Obama Cabinet Picks Add Diversity, But Still Frustrate White House Allies," *Washington Post*, March 4, 2013, http://www. washingtonpost.com/national/health-science/obama-cabinet-picks -add-diversity-but-still-frustrate-white-house-allies/2013/03/04/7e 2030a6-84fe-11e2-98a3-b3db6b9ac586_story.html.

35. Office of Personnel Management, "Diversity and Inclusion: Federal Workforce At-a-glance," accessed May 19, 2014, http://www.opm .gov/policy-data-oversight/diversity-and-inclusion/federal -workforce-at-a-glance/.

36. For an in-depth example of private contracting in Medicaid in New York State, see Nina Bernstein, "Medicaid Shift Sees Rush for Profitable Clients," *New York Times*, May 8, 2014, http://www .nytimes.com/2014/05/09/nyregion/medicaid-shift-fuels-rush-for -profitable-clients.html.

37. U.S. Office of Special Counsel, "Hatch Act," updated October 6, 2011, http://www.osc.gov/hatchact.htm, and "Political Activity and the Federal Employee," http://www.osc.gov/documents/hatchact /ha_fed.pdf, both accessed June 27, 2012.

38. For more on the relationships among bureaucrats, members of Congress, and interest groups, see Anthony M. Bertelli and Christian R. Grose, "Secretaries of Pork? A New Theory of Distributive Public Policy," *Journal of Politics* 71 (2009): 926–45; and Sanford C. Gordon and Catherine Hafer, "Corporate Influence and the Regulatory Mandate," *Journal of Politics* 69 (2007): 300–19.

39. http://public.tableausoftware.com/views/Veterans_VA_mobile/Vetera nsAffairs?amp%3B:embed=y&:display_count=no&:showVizHome=no#, accessed May 25, 2014.

40. Scott Bronstein and Drew Griffin, "A Fatal Wait: Veterans Languish and Die on a VA Hospital's Secret List," CNN, April 30, 2014, accessed May 19, 2014, http://www.cnn.com/2014/04/23/health/veterans -dying-health-care-delays/index.html?iid=article_sidebar.

41. Chelsea J. Carter, Greg Seaby, and Greg Botelho, "Rights Group Calls VA Official 'Scapegoat' in Scandal over Wait Times, Care," CNN, May 16, 2014, accessed May 19, 2014, http://www.cnn.com/2014/05/16 /politics/va-scandal/.

42. Daniel P. Carpenter, "Groups, the Media, Agency Waiting Costs, and FDA Drug Approval," *American Journal of Political Science* 46, no. 3 (2002): 490–505. Also see Susan L. Moffitt, "Promoting Agency Reputation through Public Advice: Advisory Committee Use in the FDA," *Journal of Politics* 72, no. 3 (2010): 1–14. For a longer discussion of the history and effectiveness of the FDA, see Daniel P. Carpenter, *Reputation and Power: Organizational Image and Pharmaceutical Regulation at the FDA* (Princeton, N.J.: Princeton University Press, 2010).

43. U.S. Food and Drug Administration, "FDA Safety Communication: Shasta Technologies GenStrip Blood Glucose Test Strips May Report False Results," issued April 29, 2014, accessed May 8, 2014, http:// www.fda.gov/MedicalDevices/Safety/AlertsandNotices/ucm395180 .htm.

44. L. Paige Whitaker, "The Whistleblower Protection Act: An Overview," CRS Report for Congress, RL33918 (Washington, D.C.: Congressional Research Service, March 12, 2007).

Chapter 13

1. Material for this vignette taken from Justice Sotomayor's memoir, *My Beloved World* (2013); the Supreme Court case *Schuette v. Coalition to Defend Affirmative Action*, 134 S.Ct. 1623 (2014) http://www .supremecourt.gov/opinions/13pdf/12-682_j4ek.pdf; and an interview on National Public Radio (http://www.npr.org/2013/01/14/167699633 /a-justice-deliberates-sotomayor-on-love-health-and-family).

2. "Federal Judgeships," Administrative Office of the United States Courts, accessed May 12, 2014, http://www.uscourts.gov /JudgesAndJudgeships/FederalJudgeships.aspx.

3. *Steelworkers v. Weber*, 443 U.S. 193 (1979).

4. *Firefighters Local Union No. 1784 v. Stotts*, 467 U.S. 561 (1984).

5. *Johnson v. Transportation Agency*, 480 U.S. 616 (1987).

6. *Fullilove v. Klutznick*, 448 U.S. 448 (1980).

7. *Richmond v. J. A. Croson Co.*, 488 U.S. 469 (1989).

8. *Metro Broadcasting, Inc. v. FCC*, 497 U.S. 547 (1990); *Adarand Constructors, Inc. v. Pena*, 515 U.S. 200 (1995).

9. *Regents v. Bakke*, 438 U.S. 265 (1978).

10. *Hopwood v. Texas*, 78 F.3d 932 (1996).

11. http://www.nbcnews.com/news/latino/more-latinos-whites-admitted -university-california-n85511, accessed June 5, 2014.

12. 134 S.Ct. 1623 (2014).

13. Federal litigation data can be found at "Judicial Facts and Figures 2012," Administrative Office of the U.S. Courts, accessed May 7, 2014, http://www.uscourts.gov/Statistics/JudicialFactsAndFigures/Judicial -Facts-Figures2012.aspx.

14. "Judicial Facts and Figures 2012," Administrative Office of the U.S. Courts, table 4.10, accessed June 10, 2014, http://www.uscourts.gov /Statistics/JudicialFactsAndFigures/judicial-facts-figures-2012.aspx.

15. Paul M. Collins Jr., "Friends of the Court: Examining the Influence of *Amicus Curiae* Participation in U.S. Supreme Court Litigation," *Law and Society Review* 38 (2004): 807–32.

16. Rebecca Salokar, *The Solicitor General: The Politics of Law* (Philadelphia: Temple University Press, 1992).

17. Lisa Solowiej and Paul Collins Jr., "Counteractive Lobbying in the U.S. Supreme Court," *American Politics Research* 37 (2009): 670–99.

18. *Regents of the University of California v. Bakke*, 438 U.S. 265 (1978).

19. Federal Bureau of Investigation, *Crime in the United States 2012*, Fall 2013, accessed May 7, 2014, http://www.fbi.gov/about-us/cjis /ucr/crime-in-the-u.s/2012/crime-in-the-u.s.-2012/offenses-known -to-law-enforcement/clearances.

20. Mark Motivans, "Federal Justice Statistics 2010," United States Department of Justice, Office of Justice Programs, Bureau of Justice

Statistics, accessed May 7, 2014, http://www.bjs.gov/content/pub/pdf/fjs10.pdf.

21. Gregory Caldeira and John R. Wright, "Organized Interests and Agenda Setting in the U.S. Supreme Court," *American Political Science Review* 82 (1988): 1109–28.

22. *Hopwood v. Texas*, 78 F.3d 932 (1996).

23. Timothy Johnson, Paul Wahlbeck, and James Spriggs, "The Influence of Oral Arguments on the U.S. Supreme Court," *American Political Science Review* 100 (2006): 99.

24. Alexander Bickel, *The Least Dangerous Branch: The Supreme Court at the Bar of Politics* (Indianapolis: Bobbs-Merrill, 1963).

25. Harold J. Spaeth, Sara Benesh, Lee Epstein, Andrew D. Martin, Jeffrey A. Segal, and Theodore J. Ruger, Supreme Court Database, Version 2013, Release 01, accessed May 10, 2014, http://supremecourtdatabase.org.

26. *Gonzalez v. Raich*, 545 U.S. 1 (2005).

27. Segal and Spaeth, *Supreme Court and the Attitudinal Model*.

28. Ibid.

29. Lee Epstein and Jack Knight, *The Choices Justices Make* (Washington, D.C.: CQ Press, 1998); Forrest Maltzman, James F. Spriggs II, and Paul J. Wahlbeck, *Crafting Law on the Supreme Court: The Collegial Game* (New York: Cambridge University Press, 2000).

30. See Lawrence Baum, *The Puzzle of Judicial Behavior* (Ann Arbor: University of Michigan Press, 1997).

31. Jeffrey A. Segal and Robert M. Howard, "How Supreme Court Justices Respond to Litigant Requests to Overturn Precedent," *Judicature* 85 (2001): 148–57.

32. Jeffrey A. Segal and Robert M. Howard, "A Preference for Deference? The Supreme Court and Judicial Review," *Political Research Quarterly* 57 (2004): 131–43. See also Lori Ringhand, "The Changing Face of Judicial Activism: An Empirical Examination of Voting Behavior on the Rehnquist Natural Court," *Constitutional Commentary* 24 (2007): 43.

33. Gerald Rosenberg, *The Hollow Hope* (Chicago: University of Chicago Press, 1991).

34. "Samuel Chase—The Samuel Chase Impeachment Trial," Law Library, accessed May 10, 2012, http://law.jrank.org/pages/5151/Chase-Samuel-Chase-Impeachment-Trial.htm.

35. Lee Epstein and Jeffrey A. Segal, *Advice and Consent: The Politics of Judicial Appointments* (New York: Oxford University Press, 2006).

36. Denis Steven Rutkus and Mitchel A. Sollenberger, *Judicial Nomination Statistics: U.S. District and Circuit Courts, 1977–2003*, CRS Report for Congress, RL31635 (Washington, D.C.: Congressional Research Service, February 23, 2004), Table 2(b), accessed July 1, 2014, http://www.senate.gov/reference/resources/pdf/RL31635.pdf.

37. Russell Wheeler, "Judicial Nominations and Confirmations: Fact and Fiction." *Brookings*, accessed May 7, 2014, http://www.brookings.edu/blogs/fixgov/posts/2013/12/30-staffing-federal-judiciary-2013-no-breakthrough-year.

38. Ibid.

39. Richard Nixon, "Transcript of President's Announcement," *New York Times*, October 22, 1971.

40. "Robert Bork's Position on Reproductive Rights," *New York Times*, September 13, 1987, B9.

41. Jonathan P. Kastellec, Jeffrey R. Lax, and Justin H. Phillips, "Public Opinion and Senate Confirmation of Supreme Court Nominees," *Journal of Politics* 72 (2010): 767–84.

42. Charlie Savage, "A Judge's View of Judging Is on the Record," *New York Times*, May 14, 2009, p. A21, http://www.nytimes.com/2009/05/15/us/15judge.html.

43. Charles M. Cameron, Albert D. Cover, and Jeffrey A. Segal, "Senate Voting on Supreme Court Nominees: A Neoinstitutional Model," *American Political Science Review* 84 (1990): 525–34.

44. Christina Boyd, Lee Epstein, and Andrew D. Martin, "Untangling the Causal Effects of Sex on Judging," *American Journal of Political Science* 54 (2010): 389–411.

45. See, e.g., Karen O'Connor and Jeffrey A. Segal, "Justice Sandra Day O'Connor and the Supreme Court's Reaction to Its First Female Member," *Women and Politics* 10 (1990): 95–104.

46. John J. Szmer, Tammy A. Sarver, and Erin B. Kaheny, "Have We Come a Long Way, Baby? The Influence of Attorney Gender on Supreme Court Decision Making," *Politics and Gender* 6 (2010): 1–36.

47. *McCulloch v. Maryland,* 4 Wheaton 316 (1819); *Gibbons v. Ogden,* 9 Wheaton 1 (1824); and *Cohens v. Virginia,* 6 Wheaton 264 (1821).

48. 60 U.S. 393 (1857).

49. *Slaughterhouse Cases,* 83 U.S. 36 (1873).

50. *United States v. Cruikshank,* 92 U.S. 542 (1876).

51. *Civil Rights Cases,* 109 U.S. 3 (1883).

52. *Brandenburg v. Ohio,* 395 U.S. 444 (1969) (speech rights); *New York Times v. Sullivan,* 376 U.S. 254 (1964) (press rights); *Memoirs v. Massachusetts,* 383 U.S. 413 (1966) (obscenity); and *Engel v. Vitale,* 370 U.S. 421 (1962); *Abington Township School District v. Schempp,* 374 U.S. 203 (1963) (prayer and Bible reading).

53. *Brown v. Board of Education,* 347 U.S. 483 (1954); *Wesberry v. Sanders,* 376 U.S. 1 (1964); *Reynolds v. Sims,* 377 U.S. 533 (1964).

54. *Griswold v. Connecticut,* 381 U.S. 479 (1965) (birth control); *Roe v. Wade,* 410 U.S. 113 (1973).

55. *Mapp v. Ohio,* 367 U.S. 643 (1961); *Miranda v. Arizona,* 384 U.S. 436 (1966).

56. *Swann v. Charlotte-Mecklenburg Board of Education,* 402 U.S. 1 (1971) (busing); *Roe v. Wade,* 410 U.S. 113 (1973) (abortion); *Furman v. Georgia,* 408 U.S. 238 (1972) (death penalty); *Reed v. Reed,* 404 U.S. 71 (1971) (sex discrimination); and *Regents of the University of California v. Bakke,* 438 U.S. 265 (1978) (affirmative action).

57. *San Antonio Independent School District v. Rodriguez,* 411 U.S. 1 (1973) (school funding); *United States v. Leon,* 468 U.S. 897 (1984) (limiting the exclusionary rule); and *New York v. Quarles,* 467 U.S. 649 (1984) (limiting *Miranda*).

58. *Lawrence v. Texas,* 539 U.S. 558 (2003).

59. *Planned Parenthood v. Casey,* 505 U.S. 833 (1992); *United States v. Lopez,* 514 U.S. 549 (1995); *Gratz v. Bollinger,* 539 U.S. 244 (2003); and *Grutter v. Bollinger,* 539 U.S. 306 (2003).

60. *Bush v. Gore,* 531 U.S. 98 (2000).

61. Adam Liptak, "Justices Offer Receptive Ear to Business Interests," *New York Times,* December 19, 2010, p. A1.

62. *Wal-mart Stores v. Dukes,* 131 S. Ct. 2541 (2011).

63. *Citizens United v. Federal Election Commission,* 558 U.S. 310 (2010).

64. *National Federation of Independent Business et al. v. Sebelius,* 132 S. Ct. 2566 (2012).

65. *United States v. Windsor,* 570 U.S. 12 (2013).

66. *Schuette v. Coalition to Defend Affirmative Action,* 133 S. Ct. 1653 (2014).

67. Robert Dahl, "Decision Making in a Democracy: The Supreme Court as a National Policy-Maker," *Journal of Public Law* 6 (1957): 179–295.

68. Herbert M. Kritzer, "Federal Judges and Their Political Environments: The Influence of Public Opinion," *American Journal of Political Science* 23 (1979): 194–207.

69. *West Virginia State Board of Education v. Barnette*, 319 U.S. 624 (1943), 638.

Chapter 14

1. This story has been compiled from a series of news items as follows: Marilyn Adams, "Pair of Flier Advocates Fight for Airline Passengers' Rights," *USA Today*, May 19, 2008; Joan Lowy, "Government Asking Why Passengers Were Stranded," Associated Press, August 12, 2009, http://www.realclearpolitics.com/news/ap/politics/2009/Aug/12/gov_t_asking_why_airline_passengers_were_stranded.html; Jeff Bailey, "An Air Travel Activist Is Born," *New York Times*, September 20, 2007; Matthew L. Wald, "Stiff Fines Are Set for Long Wait on the Tarmac," *New York Times*, December 21, 2009; Coalition for an Airline Passengers' Bill of Rights, "An Early Christmas Present for the Flying Public," December 23, 2009, http://FlyersRights.org; Bureau of Transportation Statistics, "Airlines Report Seven Tarmac Delays Longer Than Three Hours On Domestic Flights, 11 Longer Than Four Hours on International Flights in October." For more general information about airline delays on tarmacs, see the Department of Transportation website, http://www.dot.gov/briefingroom. An e-mail interview with Kate Hanni was conducted for this textbook, from which the chapter-opening quotation is taken.

2. Bryan D. Jones and Frank M. Baumgartner, *The Politics of Attention* (Chicago: University of Chicago Press, 2005).

3. Kate Sheppard, "North Carolina Coal Ash Spill Renews Push For Long-Delayed Federal Regulations" HuffPost.com, February 5, 2014, accessed May 24, 2014, http://www.huffingtonpost.com/2014/02/05/coal-ash-spill-north-carolina_n_4733164.html.

4. *New State Ice Co. v. Liebmann*, 285 U.S. 262 (1932) at 311. See Andrew Karch, *Democratic Laboratories: Policy Diffusion among the American States* (Ann Arbor: University of Michigan Press, 2007).

5. Craig Volden, "States as Policy Laboratories: Emulating Success in the Children's Health Insurance Program," *American Journal of Political Science* 50 (2006): 294–312.

6. Chris Koski, "Greening America's Skylines: The Diffusion of Low-Salience Policies," *Policy Studies Journal* 38 (2010): 93–117.

7. Michael Mintron and Sandra Vergari, "Policy Networks and Innovations Diffusion: The Case of State Education Reforms," *Journal of Politics* 60 (1998): 126–48.

8. Christopher Stream, "Health Reform in the States: A Model of State Small Group Health Insurance Market Reforms," *Political Research Quarterly* 52 (1999): 499–525.

9. Frederick J. Boehmke and Richard Witmer, "Disentangling Diffusion: The Effects of Social Learning and Economic Competition on State Policy Innovation and Expansion," *Political Research Quarterly* 57 (2004): 39–51.

10. Charles R. Shipan and Craig Volden, "Bottom-Up Federalism: The Diffusion of Antismoking Policies from U.S. Cities to States," *American Journal of Political Science* 50 (2006): 825–43.

11. Robert R. Preuhs, "State Policy Components of Interstate Migration in the United States," *Political Research Quarterly* 52 (1999): 527–47.

12. David M. Konisky, "Regulatory Competition and Environmental Enforcement: Is There a Race to the Bottom?," *American Journal of Political Science* 51 (2003): 853.

13. *Shapiro v. Thompson*, 394 U.S. 618 (1969); *Saenz v. Roe*, 526 U.S. 489 (1999).

14. Craig Volden, "The Politics of Competitive Federalism: A Race to the Bottom in Welfare Benefits?," *American Journal of Political Science* 46 (2006): 352–63.

15. Department of Housing and Urban Development, "HUD Historical Background," http://www.hud.gov/offices/adm/about/admguide/history.cfm.

16. For details on these programs, see the U.S. Department of Health and Human Services, Centers for Medicare and Medicaid Services (CMS), http://www.cms.hhs.gov.

17. See http://www.hud.gov/offices/adm/about/admguide/history.cfm#1960; also see Center on Budget and Policy Priorities, "Policy Basics: Section 8 Project-Based Rental Assistance," accessed March 22, 2014, http://www.cbpp.org/cms/?fa=view&id=3891.

18. Centers for Disease Control and Prevention, "Early Release of Selected Estimates Based on Data from the 2010 National Health Interview Survey," CDC.gov, updated and accessed June 22, 2012, http://www.cdc.gov/nchs/nhis/released201106.htm.

19. Henry J. Kaiser Family Foundation, "Summary of Coverage Provisions in the Patient Protection and Affordable Care Act," *Focus on Health Reform*, updated April 14, 2011, accessed June 21, 2012, http://kff.org/health-costs/issue-brief/summary-of-coverage-provisions-in-the-patient/.

20. Phil Galewitz, "10 States Are Critical To Administration's Efforts to Enroll 6 Million in New Health Plans." Kaiser Health News, accessed March 20, 2014, http://www.kaiserhealthnews.org/Stories/2014/March/19/10-States-Are-Critical-To-Administrations-Efforts-To-Enroll-6-Million-In-New-Health-Plans.aspx.

21. Kaiser Family Foundation, "State Health Facts, Status of State Action on the Medicaid Expansion 2014," accessed September 18, 2014, http://kff.org/health-reform/state-indicator/state-activity-around-expanding-medicaid-under-the-affordable-care-act/.

22. Centers for Medicare and Medicaid Services, "Affordable Care Act," http://www.medicaid.gov/AffordableCareAct/Affordable-Care-Act.html.

23. Department of Health and Human Services, "The Affordable Care Act and Latinos," accessed March 10, 2014, http://www.hhs.gov/healthcare/facts/factsheets/2012/04/aca-and-latinos04102012a.html; Tamara Keith, "Obama Pitches Health Care Law to Latinos in a Bid to Boost Enrollment," National Public Radio, March 6, 2014, http://www.npr.org/blogs/codeswitch/2014/03/06/286859961/obama-pitches-health-care-law-to-latinos-in-bid-to-boost-enrollment.

24. Kaiser Family Foundation, "Visualizing Health Policy: What Americans Pay for Health Insurance Under the ACA," accessed March 19, 2014. http://kff.org/infographic/visualizing-health-policy-what-americans-pay-for-health-insurance-under-the-aca/.

25. Nancy Rytina, "Estimates of the Permanent Legal Immigrant Population in 2012," Office of Immigration Statistics, Department of Homeland Security, July 2013, https://www.dhs.gov/sites/default/files/publications/ois_lpr_pe_2012.pdf.

26. U.S. Citizenship and Immigration Services, "About Us," accessed May 31, 2012, http://www.uscis.gov/aboutus.

27. Randall Monger and James Yankay, *Annual Flow Report: U.S. Legal Permanent Residents: 2012* (Washington, D.C.: Office of Immigration Statistics, Department of Homeland Security, March 2013), 1, http://www.dhs.gov/sites/default/files/publications/ois_lpr_fr_2012_2.pdf.

28. Randall Monger and James Yankay, Annual Flow Report: *U.S. Lawful Permanent Residents: 2013* (Washington, D.C.: Office of Immigration Statistics, Department of Homeland Security, May 2014), 2.

29. U.S. Citizenship and Immigration Services, "Statement from Secretary of Homeland Security Janet Napolitano on July 1, 2013," accessed June 13, 2014, http://www.uscis.gov/family/same-sex-marriages.

30. U.S. Citizenship and Immigration Services, "A Guide to Naturalization," http://www.uscis.gov/us-citizenship/citizenship-through-naturalization/guide-naturalization.

31. Michael Hoefer, Nancy Rytina, and Bryan Baker, "Estimates of the Unauthorized Immigrant Population Residing in the United States: January 2011," Office of Immigration Statistics Department of Homeland Security, March 2012, http://www.dhs.gov/xlibrary/assets/statistics/publications/ois_ill_pe_2011.pdf.

32. U.S. Immigration Support: Your Online Guide to U.S. Visas, Green Cards and Citizenship, http://www.usimmigrationsupport.org.

33. Luis Miranda, "Get the Facts on the DREAM Act," *The White House Blog,* December 1, 2010, http://www.whitehouse.gov/blog/2010/12/01/get-facts-dream-act.

34. The White House, Office of the Press Secretary, "Remarks by the President on Immigration," last modified on June 15, 2012, accessed July 2, 2012, http://www.whitehouse.gov/the-press-office/2012/06/15/remarks-president-immigration.

35. Randal C. Archibold, "Arizona Enacts Stringent Law on Immigration," *New York Times*, April 23, 2010, A1.

36. Jack Lewis, "The Birth of the EPA," *EPA Journal* (Washington, D.C.: U.S. Environmental Protection Agency, 1985), http://www.epa.gov.

37. Bruce Jones, "Despite Growing Energy Independence, U.S. Cannot Escape Global Risks," The Brookings Institution, May 27, 2014, accessed July 2, 2014, http://www.brookings.edu/blogs/planetpolicy/posts/2014/05/27-energy-independence-us-global-risks-jones.

38. U.S. Energy Information Administration, "International Energy Outlook 2013 ," July 25, 2013, http://www.eia.gov/forecasts/ieo/

39. Lachlan Markay and Jay Lucas, "Timeline: Keystone's Three Years in Limbo," *The Foundry* (blog), January 19, 2012, http://blog.heritage.org/2012/01/19/timeline-keystones-three-years-in-limbo/.

40. "Keystone XL Pipeline Project," TransCanada, accessed May 22, 2012, http://www.transcanada.com/keystone.html.

41. House Energy and Commerce Committee, "Waiting for the Keystone XL Pipeline," accessed May 22, 2012, http://energycommerce.house.gov/keystonexl.shtml.

42. Pierre Bertrand, "Keystone Pipeline: 5 Things You Need to Know," *International Business Times,* January 19, 2012, http://www.ibtimes.com/keystone-pipeline-5-things-you-need-know-397928; House Energy and Commerce Committee, "Waiting for Keystone XL, Waiting for Jobs," January 4, 2012, accessed May 22, 2012, http://energycommerce.house.gov/news/

43. John M. Broder, "TransCanada Renewing Request to Build Keystone Pipeline," *New York Times*, February 27, 2012, http://www.nytimes.com/2012/02/28/science/earth/keystone-pipeline-permit-request-to-be-renewed.html?_r=2&hp.

44. European Central Bank, http://www.ecb.int/.

45. U.S. Census Bureau, "Trade in Goods with China," http://www.census.gov/foreign-trade/balance/c5700.html.

46. Information in this paragraph is from World Trade Organization, http://www.wto.org.

47. See http://www.ustr.gov/US-Wins-Trade-Enforcement-Case-American-Farmers-Proves-Export-Blocking-Chinese-Duties-Unjustified-Under-WTO-Rule.

48. D. Andrew Austin and Mindy R. Levit, *The Debt Limit: History and Recent Increases*, CRS Report for Congress, RL31967 (Washington, D.C.: Congressional Research Service, January 20, 2011), http://www.fas.org/sgp/crs/misc/RL31967.pdf.

49. The White House, Office of Management and Budget, Historical Tables, Table 1.1—Summary of Receipts, Outlays, and Surpluses or Deficits (–): 1789–2017; The White House, Office of Management and Budget, Historical Tables, Table 7.1—Federal Debt at the End of Year:–2017. Both tables are available at http://www.whitehouse.gov/omb/budget/Historicals/.

50. Europa: Gateway to the European Union, http://europa.eu/.

51. Washington's Farewell Address, 1796, Yale Law School Avalon Project, http://avalon.law.yale.edu.

52. Ellen C. Collier, "Instances of Use of United States Forces Abroad, 1798–1993," Naval Historical Center, last modified September 12, 1997, accessed May 12, 2012, http://www.history.navy.mil/wars/foabroad.htm.

53. John Mueller, *War, Presidents, and Public Opinion* (New York: Wiley, 1970).

54. Presidential Approval Ratings, Gallup Historical Statistics, accessed May 12, 2012, http://www.gallup.com/poll/124922/presidential-approval-center.aspx.

55. "Presidential Approval Ratings," George W. Bush, Gallup.com, accessed May 12, 2012, http://www.gallup.com/poll/124922/presidential-approval-center.aspx.

56. United Nations Office for Disarmament Affairs (UNODA), Treaty on the Non-Proliferation of Nuclear Weapons (NPT), http://www.un.org.

57. United States Agency for International Development, http://www.usaid.gov.

58. See http://www.state.gov/documents/organization/208292.pdf.

59. World Bank, http://www.worldbank.org.

60. World Bank, Archives, http://www.worldbank.org.

61. World Bank, Projects and Operations, http://www.worldbank.org.

62. Michael W. Doyle, "Liberalism and World Politics," *American Political Science Review* 80 (1986): 1151–69.

63. Information in this and the next paragraphs from International Monetary Fund, http://www.imf.org.

64. See http://www.imf.org/external/np/fin/tad/extcred1.aspx.

65. Information in this and subsequent paragraphs is from Peace Corps, http://www.peacecorps.gov.

66. Fiscal Year 2014 budget number taken from the U.S. State Department, http://www.state.gov/documents/organization/208292.pdf.

Index

Note: Page numbers followed by an "f" indicate figures. Page numbers followed by a "t" indicate tables.

A

AARP, 203, 226
Abortion, 111–13, 207–8, 257, 448, 449
    public opinion on, 162–63
Adams, John, 6–7, 241, 242, 361
Adams, John Quincy, 242
Administrative Procedures Act (APA), 459
Adversary process, 420
Advice and consent, 317–19, 356–57, 438–40
Advocacy caucuses, 329
Affirmative action, 419–20, 424–25, 432–33, 448, 450. *See also Gratz* and *Grutter* cases
Affordable Care Act (ACA), 462t, 464–67
    contraception and, 104f, 111, 460
    as election issue, 279, 283
    Hobby Lobby and, 104f, 460
    implementation of, 393–94, 460, 491
    insurance costs under, 466–67, 466f
    mandate for insurance, 111, 318, 465
    Medicaid expansion and, 77, 465–66
    overview, 465–67
    passage through Congress, 260, 464
    Sebelius, Kathleen and, 460, 467
    Supreme Court ruling on, 78, 450, 460, 465
Afghanistan War, 370–71, 486
African Americans
    civil rights movement and, 134–39, 256
    segregation and. *See* Racial segregation and discrimination
    voting rights, 126, 126–27, 138–39, 139f, 284–85
    voting turnout, 287, 287f
Agenda, policy making and, 457, 458f
Agenda setting, 187–88
    by president, 367–68
    in Senate, 330–33
Air pollution, 412
Air travel
    federal air marshals, 387–88, 414
    NTSB and, 395
    TSA and, 387–88, 395, 414
Amendments (to the Constitution), 51f
    amendment process, 41–42, 42f
    amendments expanding public participation, 50, 51f
    amendments on civil liberties, 90f
    amendments on civil rights, 123f
    amendments on federalism, 65f
    amendments on presidency, 352f
    amendments on right to vote, 285f
    amendments overturning Supreme Court decisions, 440t
    Bill of Rights (First through Tenth), 48–50
    Civil War Amendments (Thirteenth through Fifteenth), 50, 73, 121
    incorporated provisions of, 91f
    First Amendment, 50, 91, 96–103
    Second Amendment, 50, 106, 252
American Revolution, events leading to, 31–33, 32f
Americans for Tax Reform, 224, 226
Amicus curiae briefs, 427, 430, 431
Amnesty International, 209

Andiola, Erika, 117f, 118–19, 142
Annapolis Convention, 34
Antifederalists, 46–48, 47f, 241–42, 242t
Appeals, 111, 421
Appeals courts, 421, 423f, 428–29, 429f, 441
Appointments, 317–19, 357–59, 390
    judicial, 438–44
    political appointees, 404, 405–6
    recess appointments, 357
Appropriate, 316–17
Arizona v. United States, 469, 470
Articles of Confederation, 33–35, 39t
Asian Americans, 124–25, 174, 287f
    wartime internment of, 125
Assange, Julian, 100–101
Assault weapons ban, 252–53
Association, right of, 201–2
Attainder, bills of, 45, 65, 68
Australia, compulsory voting in, 297
Australian ballot, 245, 246f
Authorize, 317, 320
Autocracy, 15
Automobiles, fuel efficiency standards, 221, 221f
Awlaki, Anwar al, 96, 372

B

Bakke case (*Regents v. Bakke*), 424, 427, 434, 435, 449t
Ballot, 237, 245
Ballot reform, 245, 246f
Bank bailout, 473
Barron v. Baltimore, 91
Battleground states, 277–78
Bicameral, 40, 310–11
Biden, Joseph, 377
Bill of Rights, 38, 48–50, 88
    English, 49
    incorporation to states, 90–92, 91f
    not included in original Constitution, 38–39, 47–48
bin Laden, Osama, death of, 371
Birth control, 104f, 111–13
Black codes, 125–26
Blogs, 175, 182–83, 367
Boehner, John, 323, 324–25, 325f
Bork, Robert, 442
Boston Massacre, 32, 32f
Boston Tea Party, 32, 32f
Bowers v. Hardwick, 158
Branches of government, 10–11, 11f
Breyer, Stephen, 432, 432f, 437
British constitution, 30
Brown v. Board of Education, 30, 66, 75, 134, 135, 435, 437, 443, 448, 449t
Buckley v. Valeo, 216
Budget, federal, 335–37. *See also* Debt, national
    Byrd rule, 336–37
    concurrent budget resolution, 336
    continuing resolution, 336
    federal budget deficit, 335–36, 480–81
    national debt and, 336
    reconciliation process, 336–37
Bully pulpit, 365, 365f
Bureaucracy, 386–417
    accountability and responsiveness, 410–14
    bureau analogy for, 389
    cabinet, 389–90, 406–7
    civil service, 404–5, 404f
        reforms, 409
    components of, 396–98
        bureaucratic culture, 397–98

Bureaucracy (*continued*)
　　decision-making process, 396–97
　　expertise, 397
　　mission, 396
　constitutional foundations, 390
　defined, 389
　democracy and, 415
　diversity in, 406–7, 407f
　efficiency and transparency, 411–14
　executive departments, 392–94, 392t, 399–400
　failures of, 398, 414
　federal regulatory commission, 395
　federal workforce, 404f, 407f
　historical evolution of, 399–409
　impact of, 388–89
　independent agencies, 394–96, 394t
　iron triangles and issue networks and, 409
　legislative and judicial branches and, 410–11
　organizational chart, 393f
　oversight and, 400
　patronage system and, 401–4
　political appointees, 404, 405–6
　politics and, 408–9
　private-sector contract workers, 407–8
　regulations, 389, 392, 458, 459
　regulatory agencies, 400–401
　regulatory process, 458, 459–60, 459f
　reputation of, 388
　Senior Executive Service, 406
　structure of, 390–96
　United Nations bureaucracy, 391
　whistleblowing and, 387–88, 414
Burger Court, 448, 449t
Burwell, Sylvia Mathews, 348f, 349–50, 376, 467
Bush, George H. W., 249, 351, 356, 400, 441
　cost of milk statement, 166–67
Bush, George W., 258, 357, 364
　approval ratings of, 188
　bank bailout of, 473
　Cheney and, 376–77
　election of (2000), 161, 162, 269
　immigration reform and, 468
　Iraq and Afghanistan Wars and, 370–71, 486
　No Child Left Behind Act and, 67, 76
　press conferences of, 367
　private contractors and, 408
　War on Terror and, 76–77, 93, 168, 375
Bush, Jeb, 273
Bush v. Gore, 269, 449, 449t
Byrd rule, 336–37

C

Cabinet, 389–90, 405
　departments, 392–94, 392t
　secretaries, 390, 405
California Democratic Party v. Jones, 238
Campaign finance, 275–77
　Citizens United case, 218, 276, 444
　corporations and, 218
　Federal Election Commission and, 275–76, 408
　limits on, 275, 276
　McCain-Feingold Act, 216–17
　political action committees and Super PACs, 216–19, 217t, 276–77
　political parties and, 281
　top spending by presidential candidates, 276f
Campaigns, 273–83. *See also* Campaign finance; Elections
　battleground states, 277–78
　congressional, 280–83
　democracy and, 303–4

　fundraising/money, 275–77, 281
　incumbency advantage, 281–83, 281f
　interest groups and, 215–19
　issues in, 275–83
　microtargeting and, 278
　negativity in, 279–80, 280f
　permanent, 273
　presidential, 273–80
　swing states/voters, 277–78
Cantor, Eric, 344
Capitalism, 13
Career civil servants, 404–5
Carter, Jimmy, 257, 353, 406, 409
Castro, Joaquín, 250, 309–10, 309f, 341f
Castro, Julián, 250, 309, 405, 407
Castro, Rosie, 250
Caucuses, 239, 274
　advocacy, 329
　party caucus, 234, 274
Census, 271
Certiorari (petition for a writ of), 426, 430
Chavez, Cesar, 141–42
Checks and balances, 11, 42–44, 45f
Cheney, Richard (Dick), 376–77
Chevron U.S.A. v. Natural Resources Defense Council, 412
Chief of staff, 376
Christie, Chris, 273
Cisneros v. Corpus Christi Independent School District, 66, 128t, 139
Citizen involvement, 4, 18–21
　specific examples of. *See first pages of each chapter*
Citizens' groups, 207
Citizens United v. Federal Election Commission, 218, 276, 444, 449t
Citizenship, 123–25
　immigration issues and, 467–68
　Native Americans, 121, 123
　naturalization, 123, 467–68
Civic interest, 10, 18
Civil liberties, 86–117
　American values and, 96
　balancing liberty and order, 89–90
　Bill of Rights, 88, 90–92
　civil rights and, 88–89, 89f, 120
　compelling interest test, 92
　constitutional rights, 90, 90f
　criminal procedure, 106–11
　defined, 88
　democracy and, 114
　First Amendment, 50, 91, 96–103
　　freedom of speech, 96–100
　　freedom of the press, 100–103
　　religious freedom, 103–5
　homosexual behavior, 113
　increased protections for, 448–50
　right to die, 114
　right to keep and bear arms, 106
　right to privacy, 111–14, 112f
　Supreme Court and, 448–50
　in times of crisis, 92–96, 365
Civil procedure, 426–27
Civil rights, 74–75, 118–53. *See also* Discrimination
　citizenship restrictions, 123–25
　civil liberties and, 89f, 120
　civil rights movement, 134–39, 256
　Constitution and, 120–21, 123f
　defined, 120
　democracy and, 150–51
　equal protection, expansion of, 132–33, 133t, 135
　ethnic discrimination, 127, 139–42
　frontiers in, 146–50
　　disability rights, 149

sexual orientation and same-sex marriage, 146–48
undocumented immigrants, 149–50
gender discrimination, 127–32, 142–45
immigration limits, 125
increased protections for, 448–50
judicial review and, 133, 133t
legal restrictions on, 121–32
end of, 134–45
private discrimination, 120, 132–33, 141–42
public discrimination, 120, 134–36, 139–40
racial segregation and discrimination, 125–27, 134–39
racial voting barriers, 127, 138–39
slavery and, 122
Supreme Court and, 448–50
women's suffrage, 127–29
workplace equality, 144–45
Civil Rights Act (1866, 1875), 73, 126
Civil Rights Act (1964), 75, 138, 256, 379
Civil Rights Cases (1883), 73, 132–33, 446
Civil service, 404–5, 404f
reforms, 409
Civil Service Commission, 404
Civil society, 18
Civil War, 73, 244
Civil War Amendments, 50, 73, 121
Class action lawsuits, 426
Clean Air Act, 462t, 471
Clean Water Act, 462t
Clear and present danger test, 97
Climate change, overview, 469–72
Clinton, Bill, 76, 167, 249, 278, 290
Defense of Marriage Act and, 70, 147
diversity in administration of, 406
"don't ask, don't tell" policy and, 98
impeachment of, 362
Clinton, Hillary, 190
Cloture, 332, 332f
Cohens v. Virginia, 446, 449t
Colbert, Stephen, 154f, 155–56, 182, 182f
Cold War, 483–84
Collective bargaining, 205
College. *See* Education
Commerce, regulation of, 69, 71, 75, 317, 318
Commerce clause, 69
Committee system, 326–29, 328t, 340–41
lawmaking and, 334
ranking member, 329
Common law, 421
Common Sense (Paine), 33
Common Sense Action (CSA), 199–200
Communism, containment of, 369, 483–84
Compelling interest test, 92
Concurrent powers, 64, 65f
Concurring opinion, 431
Confederal system, 61, 62f
Confidence interval, 162
Conformity costs, 82–83
Congress, 308–47. *See also* House of Representatives; Senate
advocacy caucuses, 329
approval rating of, 343, 343f
bicameralism, 40, 310–11
budget and reconciliation, 335–37
committee system, 326–29, 328t, 340–41
constituencies, 314
democracy and, 344–45
demographics of 113th, 313f
differences between House and Senate, 311–16, 312f
elections for, 271–72, 280–83, 312–13
next election, 342–44, 343f
safe seats, 281

filibuster and cloture, 331–33, 332f
House of Representative, 323–25
incumbents, voter opinion of, 343, 343f
interest groups and, 222, 222f
lawmaking process, 330–37. *See also* Lawmaking
legislative authority, 47, 356t
as legislative branch, 10, 11f, 40–41, 310–16
member at work, 337–40
communication with constituents, 342
federal funds, 341–42
legislative responsibilities, 340–42
next election, 342–44, 343f
offices and staff, 337–40
roll call votes, 341
omnibus bills, 333–34, 336, 359–60
organization of, 322–29
party leadership in, 323–25, 326, 327f
political parties and, 322–23
powers of, 47, 64, 78, 316–22, 356t
advice and consent, 317–19, 356–57
appointments and treaties, 317–19
authorization of courts, 320
checks and balances on, 44, 45f
commerce regulation, 69, 317
enumerated powers, 64, 71
impeachment and removal from office, 40–41, 319, 361–63
implied powers, 47, 69
lawmaking, 47, 319–20
limits on, 44–45, 65–68
override of veto, 40, 337, 359
oversight, 320–22, 400
taxation and appropriation, 40, 47, 51, 71, 74–75, 316–17
war powers, 317
powers of , 47, 64, 78, 316–22
qualifications for office, 311–12
redistricting and, 271–72, 314–16
representation and, 310–11
Senate, 325–26
terms of office, 282, 313–14
Connecticut Compromise, 36
Conservatives, 12, 12f, 164–65
Reagan and, 257–59
Constitution, 28–57. *See also* Amendments; Constitutional Convention
amendment process, 41–42, 42f
Bill of Rights, 48–50
British constitution, 30
defined, 30
democracy and, 54–55
executive authority under, 46–47
federal authority under, 46
federalism and, 64–70
Framers of, 7
as gatekeeper, 7–11
gates against popular influence, 38
government before, 30–35
government under, 40–45
implied powers, 47, 69
interpretation of, 50–54, 320
legislative authority under, 47, 310, 356t
power, partition of, 42–45
preamble to, 15
ratification debates, 45–48
ratification process, 38–39
responsiveness of, 48–54
text of, 498–513
Constitutional Convention, 35–39
Bill of Rights not included, 38–39, 47–48
Connecticut Compromise, 36
large vs. small states, 35–36
nation vs. state, 36

Constitutional Convention (*continued*)
  New Jersey Plan, 36, 37t
  North vs. South (slavery issues), 36–38
  remedies to the Articles of Confederation, 39t
  three-fifths compromise, 37
  Virginia Plan, 35, 37t
Constitutional system, 7
Consumer financial protection, 402–3
Consumer Financial Protection Bureau, 400, 402–3
Consumer Product Safety Commission, 400
Content-neutral, 99
Continental Congresses, 32–33, 32f
Continuing resolution, 336
Contraception, 104f, 111, 460
Contract workers, private sector, 407–8
Cooper v. Aaron, 439
Cordray, Richard, 357, 402–3
Corporations, 204–5, 449–50
  campaign finance and, 218
  federal, 395
Countermajoritarian difficulty, 433
Court-packing plan, 74, 378, 447–48
Courts. *See* Judiciary
Coverture, 128–29, 130
Criminal cases, 421
Criminal procedure, 50, 51f, 106–11, 428, 448
Cruel and unusual punishment, 52
Cruz, Ted, 273

D

Daily Show, The, 181–82
Death penalty, 52–53, 52f
Debs, Eugene V., 92–93, 93f
Debt
  national, 5, 20–21, 336, 480–81
    in 2014, 20, 481f
    growth of, 481f
    in other countries, 14, 14f
    as percentage of GDP, 14, 14f
  public, 14, 14f
  student, 19f
Debt ceiling, 480–81
Declaration of Independence, 3–4, 33
  text of, 494–97
Defense of Marriage Act, 69f, 70, 147–48, 450
Deficit, federal, 335–36, 480–81
DeMint, James, 223, 223f
Democracy
  alternative models of government, 15
  constitutional system and, 6–11
  defined, 6
  demands and responsibilities in, 16–21
  direct, 10, 68, 80–82
  evaluating, 4–6, 13–16
  gateways to, 2–27
  promotion of, 488–89, 488f, 490–91
  pure, 10
  representative, 10, 16
  successes and problems of, 4–5
Democracy in America (de Tocqueville), 200
Democratic Party, 242–43, 254–55. *See also* Political parties
  ideology of, 254–56
  presidential nominating process, 239–40
  realignment of, 256–57
Democratic-Republicans, 242–43
Denny's restaurant, 147f
Department of Health and Human Services (HHS), 392–94, 393f, 464
Department of Homeland Security, 392t, 397, 400, 467

Departments, 392–94, 392t
Desegregation, 75, 134–36, 437–38, 439
Diplomacy, 487–90
Direct democracy, 10, 68, 80–82
Disability rights, 149
Discrimination
  ethnic, 127, 139–41
  gender-based, 127–32
  private, 120, 132–33, 137–38, 141–42
  public, 120, 134–36
  racial, 125–27, 134–39
  state action and, 132–33
Dissenting opinion, 431–32
District courts, 421, 423f, 426–28, 429f, 440–41
District of Columbia, gun ownership in, 106
Divided government, 320, 409
Dodd-Frank Act, 400, 402–3
Domestic policy, 462–72. *See also* Economic policy
  energy, environmental policy, and climate change, 469–72
  entitlement programs, income security, and health care, 463–65
  immigration, 467–69
  layers in, 472
  major federal programs, 462t
"Don't ask, don't tell policy," 98
Double jeopardy, 109–10
DREAM Act, 119, 128t, 469
Dred Scott v. Sandford, 73, 122, 126, 440t, 446, 449t
Drinking age, 76, 77
Drones, 372–73, 372t
Drug approval process, 413

E

Earmarks, 341–42
Economic interest groups, 204–6
Economic model of voting, 293–94
Economic opportunity, 20–21, 20f
Economic policy, 472–82
  fiscal policy, 473, 476t
  interest rates, 476
  International Monetary Fund and, 487–90
  minimum wage and, 8–9, 8t
  monetary policy, 473–77, 476t
  overview, 472–73
  stakeholders in, 473f
  trade policy, 477–82
Economy. *See also* Economic policy
  debt ceiling, 480–81
  federal deficit, 480–81
  intervention in, 472–73
  national debt, 480–81, 481f
  as political issue, 188, 280
  recession, 472–73
  regulation of, 74, 378, 447–48, 472–77
Education, 66–67. *See also* Schools
  affirmative action and, 424–25
  costs of college, 18–19, 19f
  educational opportunity, 18–20, 19f
  equal access to, 135, 139
  federal policy and, 66–67
  future earnings and, 20f
  Head Start programs, 67
  No Child Left Behind, 67, 76
  political opinions and, 174, 174f
  public education, 66–67
  Race to the Top, 67, 461
  student debt, 19f
  voter turnout and, 292–93, 293f
Efficacy, 157–59, 295

Eisenhower, Dwight D., 134–35, 222, 369
Elections, 264–72. *See also* Campaigns; Voting
    ballot reform, 245, 246f
    battleground states, 277–78
    campaigns for. *See* Campaigns
    caucuses, 234, 239, 274
    congressional, 271–72, 280–83, 342–44
        redistricting and, 271–72
    constitutional requirements for, 266–72
    decision to run and invisible primary, 273
    democracy and, 303–4
    Electoral College and, 38, 267–68, 268f
    Federal Election Commission (FEC), 275–76, 408
    general, 237
    gerrymandering and, 272, 272f
    incumbency advantage, 281–83, 281f
    microtargeting and, 278
    negativity in, 279–80, 280f
    presidential, 266–69
        of 2000, 161, 162, 269
        of 2012, 190
        campaign and issues, 273–80
        fundraising and money, 275–77
        national convention, 274
        nomination process, 237–41, 239f
        turnout rates for, 290, 290f–93f
        votes by demographic group, 259f
    primary, 237, 238, 274
    safe seats, 281
    swing states/voters, 277–78
Electoral College, 38, 267–68
    defined, 38, 267
    functioning of, 268f
    problems and reform, 268–69
    winner-take-all system, 239
Elites, 13, 219–20
Emancipation Proclamation, 73, 122
Enemy combatants, 93
Energy and energy policy, 469–72
England. *See* United Kingdom
English language
    literacy tests, 286
    requirement for voting, 140
Entitlement programs, 360, 380–81, 463–64
Enumerated powers, 64, 71
Environment
    environmental policy, 469–72
    fracking, 212–13
    Keystone XL Pipeline, 474–75
Environmental Protection Agency (EPA), 212–13, 390, 394, 412, 460, 471
Equal Employment Opportunity Commission (EEOC), 144
Equal Pay Act, 142, 144–45
Equal protection clause, 126, 149
Equal protection under law, 121, 132–33, 133t, 135, 448
Equal Rights Amendment (ERA), 129–30, 143, 143f
Equality, 15, 120–21
    constitutional amendments on, 51f
    Declaration of Independence and, 3–4
    equal protection, 121, 132–33, 133t, 135
    of opportunity, 16, 121
    of outcome, 16, 121
    political, 16
    state action and, 132–33
    in workplace, 144–45
Establishment clause, 104–5
Ethnicity
    discrimination based on, 127, 139–42
    political attitudes and, 172–74, 172f
    voting barriers, 140–41
European Union, 478, 482

Evidence, exclusionary rule for, 108
Ex post facto laws, 45, 65, 68
Exclusionary rule, 108, 448
Executive authority, 46–47, 356t
Executive branch, 10, 11f, 41. *See also* Presidency
    checks and balances, 44, 45f
Executive order, 364
Executive privilege, 362–63
Extralegal approach, 435–37

F

Facebook, 183–84, 210
Factions, 10, 83, 201, 241–42
Fair pay, 9
Fair trade, 477
Federal aid
    to public schools, 75
    to state and local governments, 76f
Federal budget. *See* Budget, federal
Federal Communications Commission (FCC), 176–77
Federal corporation, 395
Federal deficit. *See* Deficit, federal
Federal Election Campaign Act (FECA), 275
Federal Election Commission (FEC), 275–76, 408
Federal funds (earmarks), 341–42
Federal government. *See* Government
Federal Register, 364, 392, 459–60
Federal regulatory commission, 395
Federal Reserve Board, 473–76
Federal Trade Commission (FTC), 400
Federalism, 56–85
    across the world, 63
    Antifederalists and, 78
    changing nature of, 70–78
    Civil War and, 73
    confederal and unitary systems vs., 61–62, 62f, 82
    constitutional amendments on, 65f
    constitutional framework for, 64–70
    cooperative, 74–75, 74f
    defined, 11, 42, 61–62
    democracy and, 82–83
    direct democracy and, 68, 80–82
    dual, 74, 74f
    founding generation and, 71
    Framers and, 60–63, 83
    local governments and, 76f, 80
    nation-centered, 71, 74–75
    New Federalism, 75–78
    nullification and, 71–73
    power, grants of, 64
    power, limits on, 44–45, 65–68
    power, partition of, 42, 44
    reasons for, 60–63
    relationships in, 68–70
    self-government and, 62
    state-centered, 75–76
    state governments and, 79–82, 83
Federalist Papers, 46
    text of, 514–21
Federalists, 46–48, 47f, 241–42, 242t
Fifth Amendment, 50
Fighting words, 97–99
Filibuster, 331–33, 441
Financial sector, oversight and regulation, 400–403
First Amendment, 50, 91, 96–103, 448
FISA courts, 94–95, 95f, 421
Fiscal policy, 473, 476t
501(c)(3) organizations, 215

501(c)(4) organizations, 215–16
Food and Drug Administration (FDA), 400, 413
Food safety, 400
Food stamps, 462t, 464
Ford, Gerald R., 166, 166f, 351, 363
Foreign Intelligence Surveillance Courts, 94–95, 95f, 421
Foreign policy, 482–90
    anti-nuclear proliferation, 486–87
    diplomacy and humanitarian assistance, 487–90
    interest groups on, 208–9
    military action and, 485–86
    multipolar world system, 484–85
    origins of, 483–84
    overview, 482–85
    promotion of democracy, 488–89, 489f, 490–91
Founders, 4, 7
Fracking, 212–13
Framers, 7
Framing, 188–89
Franklin, Benjamin, 32
    "Join or Die" cartoon of, 59–60, 60f
Free enterprise, 14, 14f
Free exercise clause, 103–4
Free rider problem, 225
Free trade, 477–79
Freedom, balance with order, 38f
Freedom of religion, 103–5
Freedom of speech, 50, 96–100
    advocacy of unlawful activities, 97
    fighting words and hate speech, 97–99
    symbolic speech, 99, 99f
    time, place, and manner regulations, 99–100
Freedom of the press, 100–103, 176–77, 448
    prior restraint and, 100–101
    subsequent punishment and, 101–3
Friedan, Betty, 142
Fuel efficiency standards, 221, 221f
Full faith and credit clause, 70
Funerals, protests at, 98

G

Gallup Poll, 160, 160f
Garcia, Gus, 28f, 29–30
Garfield, James A., 401
Gatekeeper, Constitution as, 7–11
Gates, 4, 38
Gateways to American democracy, 2–27
GATT (General Agreement of Tariffs and Trade), 358, 479
Gender, 171
Gender discrimination, 129–32
    dismantling, 142–45
    voting rights (suffrage), 127–29
Gender gap, 171
General election, 237
General welfare clause, 47
Generational replacement, 298
Gerrymandering, 272, 272f
Gibbons v. Ogden, 446, 449t
Gideon v. Wainright, 109
Gilman, Sam, 198f, 199–200
Gingrich, Newt, 240, 240f, 277, 323–24, 360
Ginsburg, Ruth Bader, 142–43, 142f, 145, 443
    ideology and votes of, 432f, 436f
Globalization, 482–83
Goldwater, Barry, 257, 279–80
Gonzales, Henry B., 139, 140f
Good, R. Stephanie, 86f, 87–88
Gore, Albert, Jr., 357
    election of 2000 and, 161, 269

Government
    before the Constitution, 30–35
    branches of, 10–11, 11f
    divided, 320, 409
    powers of, 64–68, 65f
    public's support of, 157–59
    shutdown, 360, 481
    structure of, 40–41
    under the Constitution, 40–45
Grand jury, 109
Grandfather clauses, 138
Grassroots movements, 202, 203–4, 226
Gratz and *Grutter* cases, 419, 421, 425, 426–27, 427f, 429
    Supreme Court on, 430–34, 432f, 437, 448, 449t, 451
Graveyard voting, 300
Great Depression, 255, 377, 378f, 447, 463
Great Society program, 75, 379–80, 463–64
Griswold v. Connecticut, 111, 449t
Grutter, Barbara. See *Gratz* and *Grutter* cases
Guantanamo Bay facility, 375
Guarantee clause, 68
Guns
    assault weapons ban, 252–53
    gun control, 252–53, 254
    Second Amendment rights, 50, 106, 252

H

Habeas corpus, writ of, 45, 90, 450
    suspension of, 65, 365, 374
Hagel, Chuck, 390
Hamdi v. Rumsfeld, 168, 375
Hamilton, Alexander, 46, 71, 241
    Federalist Papers of, 46–47, 48, 444
Hamiltonian model of participation, 283–84, 283f, 304
Hanni, Kate, 454f, 455–56
Hastert, Dennis, 324
Hatch Act, 408
Hate speech, 97–99
Head Start programs, 67
Health care, 464–65. See also Affordable Care Act (ACA)
    Affordable Care Act, 462t, 464–67
        insurance costs under, 466–67, 466f
        insurance mandate under, 111, 318, 465
    health maintenance organizations (HMOs), 408
Health and Human Services, Department of (HHS), 392–94, 393f
Henry, Patrick, 31, 46
Hernandez v. Texas, 29, 30, 128t, 135, 448, 449t
Highway funds, 76, 77
Hill, Anita, 443f
Hobby Lobby, 104f, 460
Hold(s), 333, 441
Holder, Eric, 96, 110, 322
Home style, 342
Homosexual behavior, 102, 113, 158, 448–49. See also
    Same-sex marriage
House of Representatives, 323–25. See also Congress
    composition and election of, 40, 271–72, 311–12
    constituencies, 314
    differences from Senate, 311–16, 312f
    diversity in, 312
    impeachment power of, 40, 361
    majority/minority leader, 325
    redistricting and, 271–72, 314–16
    Reed's Rules, 323
    Rules Committee, 330
    Speaker of, 323–25
Human rights, 208–9
Humanitarian assistance, 487–90
Hussein, Saddam, 370, 486

I

Ideological interest groups, 207–8
Ideology. *See* Political ideology
Immigration, 467–69
    citizenship issues and, 468
    green card, 467–68
    Immigration Act (1924), 125
    Immigration Reform and Control Act (1986), 468
    legal process of, 467–68
    limits/quotas, 125
    naturalization and, 467–68
    reform, 468–69
    unauthorized immigration, 468–69
    undocumented immigrants, 141f, 149–50
        children of, 17, 119, 150, 469
        DREAM Act and, 119, 128t, 469
Impeachment, 319, 361–63
Implied powers, 47, 69
Income
    gap between rich and poor, 5f
    income security programs, 463–64
    voter turnout and, 292, 292f
Incorporation, 90–92, 91f, 448
Incumbency advantage, 281–83, 281f
Independent agencies, 394–96, 394t
Independents, 164, 164f, 251–54
Individualism, 13
Informed public, 165–67, 193–94
Infotainment, 181–82
Initiative(s), 81–82, 81f
Inside strategy, 214
Institutional model, 295–96
Interest groups, 198–229
    association and petition, rights of, 201–2
    campaign activities, 215–19
    defined, 200–201
    democracy and, 227
    economic, 204–6
    economic and political change and, 225–26
    factions, 201
    501(c)(3) organizations, 215
    foreign policy and international, 208–9
    free rider problem, 225
    functions of, 210–19
    ideological and issue-oriented, 207–8
    impact of, 82, 219–23, 226
    iron triangle, 222, 222f, 409
    issue networks and, 223, 409
    lobbying by, 202, 210–15, 214t
    natural balance vs. disproportionate power, 219–20
    open vs. closed routes of influence, 222–23
    political action committees (PACs), 216–19, 217t
    political parties, pressure on, 254
    revolving door and, 223
    self-service vs. public service, 220–21
    special interests, 220
    successful, characteristics of, 224–26
    types of, 204–9
International interest groups, 208–9
International Monetary Fund (IMF), 487–90
Internet, 192–93. *See also* Blogs
    access, 178, 178f, 192–93
    news and, 178, 178f, 182–83, 192–93
    polls, 161
    social networking on, 183–84
    voting and, 302
Interrogations, 108, 109f
    harsh techniques of, 168, 169f
Interstate commerce, regulation of, 69, 71, 75, 77

Investigations, 107–8
Investigative reporting, 176, 176f, 194, 362
Iran, nuclear facilities in, 486f, 487
Iran-contra scandal, 381–82
Iraq War, 370, 486
Iron law of oligarchy, 224
Iron triangle, 222, 222f, 409
Issue networks, 223, 409

J

Jackson, Andrew, 191–92, 242f, 243, 401
Japanese-Americans, WWII internment of, 125, 365, 374
Jay, John, 46
Jefferson, Thomas, 2f, 3–4, 7, 34, 71, 175, 241–43
    Declaration of Independence and, 3–4, 33, 88
    on separation of church and state, 104–5
Jeffersonian model of participation, 283–84, 283f, 304
Jim Crow laws, 127
Johnson, Andrew, 73, 359, 362
Johnson, Lyndon Baines, 75, 256–57, 352–53, 369, 379f
    Great Society program of, 75, 379–80, 463–64
    greatness of, 379–80
    legislation of, 75, 138, 256, 379–80
"Join or Die" cartoon, 59–60, 60f
Journalism. *See* News media
Judicial independence, 440
Judicial review, 41, 43, 51, 133, 422
Judiciary, 418–53. *See also* Judicial review; Supreme Court
    adversary process, 420
    amicus curiae, 427, 430, 431
    appeals courts, 421, 423f, 428–29, 429f
        appointments to, 441
    appointment process, 438–44
    Article I courts, 422, 422f
    authorization of courts, 320
    checks and balances, 44, 45f
    class action lawsuits, 426
    common law, 421
    constitutional grants of power, 421–22
    countermajoritarian difficulty, 433
    criminal cases vs. civil suits, 421
    decision making, 433–38
    democracy and, 450–51
    district courts, 421, 423f, 426–28, 429f
        appointments to, 440–41
        civil procedure, 426–27
        criminal procedure, 428
    en banc review, 423f
    English legal traditions, 420–21
    extralegal approach, 435–37
    female judges, worldwide, 445
    judicial activism and restraint, 433–37
    judicial branch of government, 10, 11f, 41
    jurisdiction, 422
    as "least dangerous branch," 444
    majority opinion, 429
    nominations, 359
    organization of (U.S.), 423f
    precedents, 421
    president and, power struggles, 374–75
    responsiveness of, 114, 450–51
    role and powers of, 420–22
    state and lower federal courts, 423–29, 423f
    Supreme Court, 430–38, 441–50
        appointments to, 441–43
    trial by jury, 50, 109, 420, 428
Judiciary Act (1789), 421
Jurisdiction, 422

K

Kagan, Elena, 436f, 444
Katzenbach v. Morgan, 128t, 140
Kennedy, John F., 138, 367f, 369
Keystone XL Pipeline, 474–75
King, Martin Luther, Jr., 137, 150, 151, 379f
   "I Have a Dream Speech" of, 137
Korematsu v. United States, 125
Kosovo, recognition of, 357
Ku Klux Klan, 97–99, 125, 126
Kyoto Protocol, 357

L

La Raza Unida Party (LRUP), 249–50
Lame duck, 352
Latinos, 29–30, 123–24, 139–40, 172–74
   appointees of Obama, 406–7, 444
   civil rights and, 127, 128t
   La Raza Unida Party (LRUP), 249–50
   LULAC, 29, 133, 139, 203
   MALDEF, 139, 141
   news media and, 184–85, 185f
   political opinions, 172–74, 173f
   segregation and, 66, 139
   on Supreme Court, 444
   targeted by presidential candidates, 278
   terminology, Latino vs. Hispanic, 173
   voting and, 140–41, 184–85, 272, 285–87, 287f
Lawmaking, 319–20, 330–37
   agenda-setting (Senate), 330–33
   bill sponsorship, 341
   budget and reconciliation, 335–37
   committee action, 334
   conference committee, 335
   filibuster and cloture, 331–33, 332f
   floor action and vote, 334–35
   hold, 333
   House Rules Committee, 330
   legislative proposals, 333–34
   markup, 329
   omnibus bills, 333–34, 336, 359–60
   presidential signature or veto, and override, 337, 359
   roll call vote, 334–35, 341
   unanimous consent agreement, 333
Lawrence v. Texas, 113, 146, 449t
Lawsuits
   civil vs. criminal, 421
   class action, 426
Ledbetter v. Goodyear Tire and Rubber Co., 145
Legislative authority, 47, 356t
Legislative branch, 10, 11f, 40–41, 310–16. *See also* Congress; Lawmaking
   checks and balances, 44, 45f
Lemon test, 105
Levels of conceptualization, 165
Libel, 101
Liberals, 11–12, 12f, 164–65, 165f
Libertarians, 12f, 13, 249
Liberty, 6–7. *See also* Civil liberties
   balancing with order, 38f, 89–90
   "Give me liberty or give me death," 31
Libya, 371
Limbaugh, Rush, 180, 180t
Lincoln, Abraham, 73, 122, 156, 191, 192f, 244, 374
Literacy (in 2014), 166
Literacy tests, 140
Little Rock, Arkansas, school desegregation in, 134–36
Lobbying, 202, 210–15
   top spenders on, 214t
Local governments, 76f, 80
Local party organization, 235–36, 235f
Loving v. Virginia, 136, 136f
LULAC, 29, 133, 139, 203
LULAC v. Perry, 272

M

Machine politics, 244–45
MacLean, Robert, 386f, 387–88, 414, 415
Madison, James, 7, 10, 21, 34, 35–36, 44, 46, 83, 103, 104, 165–66, 219, 242
   Federalist Papers of, 7, 46, 68, 241, 311
Majority opinion, 429
Majority rule, 6
Majority vote, 247
MALDEF, 139, 141
Marbury v. Madison, 41, 43, 51, 103, 320, 422, 446, 449t
Marijuana
   criminalization of, 77–78
   legalization of, 82
   medical, 82–83, 435
Markup, 329
Marriage
   Defense of Marriage Act, 69f, 70, 147–48, 450
   same-sex, 69f, 146–48, 148f, 468
Marshall, John, 71, 134
Marshall, Thurgood, 443
Marshall Court, 446, 449t
Martin, Trayvon, 110
Mass media, 175, 177–86. *See also* News media
Maughan, Brian, 58f, 59–60, 80
McCain, John, 162, 190, 276
McCain-Feingold Act, 216–17
McCulloch v. Gibbons, 71
McCulloch v. Maryland, 71, 72, 446, 449t
McKoon, Josh, 229f, 230–31, 258
Media. *See* News media
Median voter theorem, 247
Medicaid, 75, 77, 380, 408, 462t, 464
   Affordable Care Act and, 77, 465–66
Medical marijuana, 82–83, 435
Medicare, 75, 360, 380, 393–94, 462t, 464
   administration of, 408
Merit system, 404
Microtargeting, 278
Mikulski, Barbara, 313f
Military
   don't ask, don't tell policy, 98
   military action, 485–86
   military-industrial complex, 222
Millennials, 18, 178, 185–86, 192, 194, 199–200
Miller test, 101–3
Minimal effects model, 187
Minimum wage, 8–9, 8t
Minority rights, 7
Miranda v. Arizona, 108, 109f, 449t
Miranda warnings, 108, 109f, 448
Missouri Compromise, 122
Mob rule, 6–7
Moderates, 12–13, 165
Mohammed, Khalid Sheikh, 93f
Monarchy, 15
Mondale, Walter, 376
Monetary policy, 473–77, 476t
Mortgages, 463
   loan crisis, 402
MoveOn.org, 207, 220
Multipolar world system, 484–85

N

NAACP, 133, 202, 225
Nader, Ralph, 249
NAFTA (North American Free Trade Agreement), 477–79
NARAL, 207–8
National Bank, 71, 72
National committees, 234
National convention, 274
National debt. *See* Debt, national
National endowment, 396
National Federation of Independent Business et al. v. Sebelius, 318, 449t
National law, supremacy over state law, 68–69
National Organization for Women (NOW), 142
National power, 64, 65f
    expansion of, 71–75, 446
    federalist/antifederalist views on, 46–48
    limits on, 65–68, 446–47
    public opinion on, 78, 78f
    reduction in, 71, 75–78
    strengthened, 447–50
    Supreme Court rulings and, 446–50
National Rifle Association (NRA), 203, 207, 215, 252–53, 254
National Security Agency (NSA), 94–95
National Transportation Safety Board (NTSB), 395
Native Americans, 103, 121, 123
Natural (unalienable) rights, 4, 7, 88
Naturalization, 123, 467–68
Nazi Germany, 186–87, 483
Necessary and proper clause, 47, 64, 69, 78, 319
Negativity in campaigns, 279–80, 280f
New Deal, 74–75, 255, 377–79, 463
New Jersey Plan, 36, 37t
New York Times v. Sullivan, 449t
New York Times v. United States, 100, 449t
News media, 175–94
    agenda setting and, 187–88
    bias in, 189–90
    blogs, 175, 182–83
    changing environment of, 178, 178f
    choice: era of media choice, 193
    defined, 175
    democracy and, 193–94
    evaluating, 189–93
    FCC and, 176–77
    freedom of the press, 176–77
    functions of, 175–76
    hard news, 179
    impact of, 186–89
    information, 175
        quality of, 190–92
    infotainment, 181–82
    Internet and, 178, 178f, 192–93
    investigating, 176, 176f, 194, 362
    Latino voters and, 184–85, 185f
    mass media, 175, 177–86
    Millenials and, 185–86, 194
    models of, 186–89
    news sources, by age, 185f
    newspapers, 179–80, 179f
    ownership of, 177
    partisanship and, 190, 191f
    public confidence in, 189, 189f
    radio, 178, 178f, 180–81, 180t
    selective exposure/perception and, 187
    social networking and, 183–84
    soft news, 181–82, 193
    sound bites, 192
    television, 178, 178f, 181, 182f, 193
    watchdog role of, 175, 180, 194

Newspapers, 179–80, 179f
Nixon, Richard M., 71, 75, 351, 376
    impeachment threat and, 319, 361–63
    pardon of, 363
    resignation of, 176, 176f, 362–63, 362f
    Supreme Court nominees, 441
    Watergate scandal and, 176, 176f, 362
No Child Left Behind Act (2002), 67, 76
Nomination process, 237–41, 239f
Nonattitudes, 163
Nongovernmental organizations (NGOs), 208–9
Nonstate actors, 486
Norquist, Grover, 226
Northwest Ordinance, 37–38
Not-so-minimal effects model, 187–88
Nuclear anti-proliferation, 486–87
Nullification, 71–73

O

Obama, Barack, 16
    cabinet of, 390, 405, 406–7
    climate change policies of, 411
    Congress, lack of cooperation in, 324
    Congressional Black Caucus and, 329
    consumer financial protection and, 400, 402–3
    on Defense of Marriage Act, 70
    district court judges and, 441
    on DREAM Act, 119, 469
    drones and, 372–73, 372t
    economic policies of, 472–73, 480–81
    economic problems inherited by, 480
    on equal pay, 145, 459
    foreign policy of, 489
    fuel efficiency standards and, 221
    fundraising and campaign spending, 276, 276f
    health care act and, 71
    Iraq and Afghanistan Wars and, 370–71
    Keystone XL Pipeline and, 474, 475
    on marijuana, 78
    on minimum wage, 9
    nominees, Senate approval of, 332
    on offshore drilling, 398
    pardons by, 356
    political appointees, 405, 406
    presidential election (2008), 5, 171, 190, 257, 259, 259f
    presidential election (2012), 188, 260, 267, 298
        campaign for, 273, 277, 279, 280
            targeting strategy, 278
    press conferences of, 367
    Race to the Top, 67
    recess appointments of, 357, 403
    on signing statements, 365
    state-centered federalism and, 77
    on unemployment insurance, 338–39
    White House blog, 367
    women appointees of, 406–7, 444
Obscenity, 101–3
O'Connor, Sandra Day, 425, 432–33, 443
    ideology and votes of, 432, 432f, 436f, 437, 451
Office of Management and Budget (OMB), 390, 394, 459, 460
Office of Personnel Management (OPM), 409
Oil
    fracking and, 212–13
    Keystone XL Pipeline, 474–75
    offshore drilling regulations, 398
    spill in Gulf of Mexico (Deepwater Horizon), 398, 415
Oligarchy, 15
Omnibus bills, 333–34, 336, 359–60

Opinion. *See* Public opinion
Order, 6–7
  balancing with liberty, 38f, 89–90
Override of veto, 40, 337, 359
Oversight, 320–22, 400

P

Padilla, Jose, 93
Paine, Thomas, 33
Panetta, Leon, 371, 376
Pardon, 355–56
Parks, Rosa, 136
Parliamentary System (U.K.), 321
Participation, 4, 18–21, 54, 303–4. *See also* Voting
  constitutional amendments expanding, 50, 51f
  examples of. *See first pages of each chapter*
  Hamiltonian and Jeffersonian models of, 283–84, 283f, 304
Partisanship, 164. *See also* Political parties
  news media and, 190, 191f
Party. *See* Political parties
PATRIOT Act. *See* USA PATRIOT Act
Patronage system, 244–45, 401–4
Paul, Rand, 251f, 273, 330f
Peace Corps, 490
Pelosi, Nancy, 323, 324–25, 324f
Pendleton Act, 401
Perot, Ross, 249
Petition for a writ of *certiorari*, 426, 430
Petition, right of, 201–2
Plea bargain, 428
Plessy v. Ferguson, 127
Pluralism, 13, 219
Plurality vote, 247
Plyer v. Doe, 19, 128t, 139, 449t
Polarization, 167–70, 167f
Policy/policies, 454–93
  constitutional system and, 456–61
  domestic policy, 462–72
  economic policy, 472–82
  foreign policy, 482–90
  policy agenda, 457, 458f
  policy diffusion, 461
  policy enactment, 458, 458f
  policy evaluation, 458, 458f
  policy formulation, 457–58, 458f
  policy implementation, 458, 458f
    blocking, 460
  policy-making process, 457–59, 458f
  problem identification, 457, 458f
  regulatory process, 458, 459–60, 459f
  stakeholders in, 457–58, 457f
  state governments and, 460–61
Policy diffusion, 461
Political action committees (PACs), 216–19, 276–77
  Super PACs, 155, 240, 276–77
  top contributors to, 217t
Political appointees, 404, 405–6
Political culture, 11–13
Political equality, 16
Political ideology, 11–12, 12f, 164. *See also* Political parties
Political machines, 244–45
Political parties, 230–63. *See also* Democratic Party; Republican Party
  alignment and ideology, 254–60
    realignment, 256–59
  campaign finance/support, 281
  challenges to party power, 254
  Congress, role in, 322–23
  defined, 232–33
  democracy and, 260–61

development of, 241–45
  Democratic Party, 242–43
  Democratic-Republicans, 242–43
  erosion of party control, 245
  Federalist vs. Antifederalist factions, 241–42
  Republican Party, 243–44
  third parties, 243–44, 247–54
functions of, 233–37
interest groups and, 254
machine politics and, 244–45
national committees, 234
nomination process, 237–41, 239f
party alignment, 255
party caucuses, 234, 274
party identification, 11, 164
party in government, 234
party in the electorate, 233–34
party organization, 234–37, 235f
party platform, 232–33
patronage system and, 244–45
polarization of, 167–70, 167f
proportional representation and, 239, 240
realignment of, 256–59
responsible parties, 260
role of, 232–41
state and local organization, 235–36, 235f
two-party system, 71, 246–54
  third parties and, 247–50
Political polarization, 167–70, 167f
Political tolerance, 114
Political trust, 5, 157–59
Politics, 11, 15–16, 18–21
Poll taxes, 127, 138
Polls, 159–63
  error in, 162–63
  exit polls, 161–62
  push polls, 162
  sample/random sample, 160
  scientific polling, 159–60
  tracking polls, 161
  types of, 160–62
Polygamy, 103–4
Populists, 12f, 13, 82
Position issues, 279
Powell v. Alabama, 109
Power(s), 42–45. *See also* National power; States; *and specific branches of government*
  checks and balances, 44, 45f
  concurrent, 64, 65f
  of Congress, 316–22
  enumerated, 64, 71
  grants of (by Constitution), 64
  implied, 47, 69
  limits on, 44–45, 65–68
  partition of, 42–45
  of president, 41, 355–63
  separation of, 10–11, 42–44
Power elite, 13, 219–20
Precedents, 421
Presidency, 348–85
  agenda setting by, 367–68
  constitutional amendments on, 352f
  democracy and, 382–83
  directives and signing statements, 363–65
  elections, 266–69. *See also* Elections, presidential
  executive authority, 46–47, 356t
  executive branch functions, 10, 11f, 41
  executive office of, 375–76
  executive orders, 364
  executive privilege and, 362–63

expansion of, 354–55
greatness in (examples), 377–82
growth of executive influence, 363–68
head of state, 368
impeachment of president, 361–63
imperial presidency, 354–55
lame duck president, 352
list of presidents, 353–54t
New Federalism and, 76–77
nomination process, 237–41, 239f
organization of White House, 375–77
powers of, 41, 355–63
    appointments/nominations, 357–59, 390
    checks and balances, 44, 45f
    commander in chief, 355
    executive power, 41, 46–47, 355
    pardon, 355–56
    persuasion, 365–67
    treaties/recognition of nations, 356–57
    veto, 40, 337, 359–60, 360t
press conferences, 365–67, 367f
qualifications for, 350–55
    background and experience, 352–53
    constitutional eligibility, 350–52
staff of, 375–76
State of Union address, 361, 368
succession, line of, 350–51, 351t
take care clause and, 363
temporary transfer of power, 351
term limit for, 79, 351–52
in wartime, 368–75
President pro tempore (Senate), 326, 351
Press. See also News media
freedom of, 100–103, 176–77
watchdog role of, 175, 180, 194
Press conferences, presidential, 365–67, 367f
Primary elections, 237, 274
blanket primaries, 237, 238
invisible, 273
white primary, 138
Priming, 188
Prior restraint, 100–101
Privacy
expectation of, 107–8
right to, 111–14, 112f
Private discrimination, 120, 137–38, 141–42
state action and, 132–33
Private goods, 15
Private-sector contract workers, 407–8
Privatization of federal services, 407–8
Privileges and immunities clause, 70, 446–47
Progressives, 245, 249, 300
Promotion of democracy, 488–89, 488f, 490–91
Propaganda model, 186–87
Proportional representation, 239, 240, 248
Protectionism, 477
Psychological model of voting, 294–95
Public discrimination, 120, 134–36, 139–40
Public goods, 15, 225
Public opinion, 154–74
on antiterrorism measures, 168–69
defined, 157
democracy and, 193–94
group differences, 170–74
    age, 171
    education, 174, 174f
    gender, 171
    race and ethnicity, 172–74, 172f
    religion, 171
    socioeconomic status, 170–71

ideology and, 164
informed public, 165–67, 193–94
partisanship and, 164
polarization of, 167–70, 167f
polls, 159–63
power of, 156–59
shape of, 163–70
support of government, 157–59
Public policy, 5–6, 454–93. See also Policy/policies
competing interests in, 456
Constitutional system and, 456–61
defined, 456
policy-making process, 457–59, 458f
promotion of democracy, 490–91
state governments and, 460–61
Push polls, 162
Pussy Riot, 102
Putin, Vladimir, 102, 270

R
Race (ethnicity), 139–40
political attitudes and, 172–74, 172f
Race to the bottom, 461
Race to the Top, 67, 461
Racial segregation and discrimination, 125–27, 134–39. See also
    Discrimination
black codes, 125–26
civil rights movement and, 134–39
desegregation, 75, 134–36, 437–38, 439
dismantling of, 134–39
Jim Crow laws, 127
private discrimination, 120, 132–33, 137–38
public discrimination, 120, 134–36, 139–40
school segregation, 66–67, 66f, 75, 126f, 134, 135, 139
separate-but-equal doctrine, 127, 134, 135
voting barriers, 126–27
voting barriers, dismantling, 126, 138–39, 139f
Radio, 178, 178f, 180–81, 180t
Rally-around-the-flag effect, 485
Random sample, 160
Ranking member, 329
Reagan, Ronald, 171, 257–59, 351, 468
as "Great Communicator," 381
greatness of, 380–82
New Federalism and, 75–76
press conferences of, 367
Supreme Court nominees, 441–42
Recall, 80–81, 81f, 205
Recess appointments, 357
Recession, 472–73
Reconciliation, 336–37
Reconstruction, 126
Redistricting, 271–72, 314–16
Referendum, 81f
Regents v. Bakke, 424, 427, 434, 435, 449t
Regulations, 389, 392, 458, 459
Regulatory agencies, 400–401
Regulatory process, 458, 459–60, 459f
Rehnquist, William, 77, 432, 432f, 433, 448
Rehnquist Court, 77, 448–49, 449t
Reid, Harry, 332
Religion
church and state, separation between, 105
opinions and voting and, 171
religious tolerance, 5
Religious freedom, 103–5
establishment of religion, 50, 104–5
free exercise, 103–4

Representation
  proportional, 239, 240, 248
  three-fifths compromise and, 37
Representative democracy, 10, 16
Republic, 10, 38, 83
Republican form of government, 44, 68
Republican Party, 243–44, 254–55. *See also* Political parties
  antislavery movement and, 243–44
  conservative ideology and, 257–59
  Contract with America, 323
  presidential nominating process, 239–41
  Reagan and, 380–82
  realignment of, 256, 257–59
  states' rights and, 76
  Tea Party and, 250–51
Reserve powers, 64
Responsible parties, 260
Responsiveness, 13–16, 450
  of bureaucracy, 410–14
  of Constitution, 48–54
  of judiciary, 114, 450–51
Revolving door, 223
Right-to-work laws, 205
Rights. *See also* Bill of Rights
  of association, 200–201
  civil. *See* Civil rights
  to die, 114
  natural (unalienable), 4, 7, 88
  of petition, 200–201
  of privacy, 107–8, 111–14, 112f
Roberts, John, 441, 442, 443f
Roberts Court, 78, 449–50, 449t
Roe v. Wade, 113, 257, 449t
Roll call vote, 334–35, 341
Romney, Mitt, 188, 267, 273, 277, 279, 280
  campaign finance, 276
  targeting strategy, 278
Roosevelt, Franklin Delano, 8, 71, 159, 255f, 338, 357, 367, 483
  court-packing plan of, 74, 378, 447–48
  greatness of, 377–79
  New Deal of, 74–75, 255, 377–79, 447, 463
  political appointees, 406
  terms in office, 351
Roosevelt, Theodore "Teddy," 249, 365, 365f, 472
Rubio, Marco, 278f
Rule, 330
Rule of four, 430
Rule of law, 7
Rumsfeld, Donald, 405f
Russia, 102, 357, 374
  elections in, 270
  nations in former Soviet Union, 484f
  Pussy Riot, 102
  Ukraine and, 374

S

Safe seats, 281
Same-sex marriage, 69f, 70, 82, 146–48, 148f, 468
  public opinion on, 148, 149f
Sample/sampling, 160
Sampling error, 162
Sanders, Bernie, 251
Santorum, Rick, 240, 277
Scalia, Antonin, 435, 436f, 442
Schenck, Charles, 92
Schools. *See also* Education
  desegregation of, 75, 134–36, 437–38, 439
  public, federal aid to, 75

  segregation of, 66–67, 66f, 75, 126f, 134, 135, 139
  separate-but-equal doctrine, 127, 134
Schuette v. Coalition to Defend Affirmative Action, 425
Searches and seizures, 107–8, 435, 448
Sebelius, Kathleen, 460, 467
Secession, 73, 244
Second Amendment, 50, 106, 252
Securities and Exchange Commission (SEC), 395
Sedition Act, 92–93
Segregation. *See* Racial segregation and discrimination
Selective benefits, 225
Selective exposure, 187
Selective incorporation, 92
Selective perception, 187
Self-government, 6, 7–10, 62
Self-interest, 18
Senate, 325–26. *See also* Congress
  advice and consent, 317–19, 319f, 356–57, 438–40
  agenda-setting tools, 330–33
  composition and election of, 38, 40, 271, 311–13
  confirmation of appointments, 317–19, 406
  differences from House, 311–16, 312f
  filibuster and cloture, 331–33, 332f, 441
  holds in, 333, 441
  majority/minority leader, 326
  president pro tempore, 326, 351
  presidential nominees and, 332
  representation in, 315f
  vice president and, 326
Senior Executive Service (SES), 406
Sentencing, 110
Separate-but-equal doctrine, 127, 134, 135
Separation of powers, 10–11, 42–44
September 11, 2001, attacks. *See* Terrorism
Sexual orientation, 146–48, 151
Shay's Rebellion, 34f, 35
Shinseki, Eric, 411, 411f
Sierra Club, 202, 203, 215, 225, 254
Signing statements, 364–65
Sinema, Kyrsten, 264f, 265–66
Single-issue groups, 207
Single-member plurality system, 247
Slaughterhouse Cases, 446
Slavery, 71–73, 122
  abolitionists, 202–3, 202f, 243
  Constitution and, 37–38
  constitutional amendments concerning, 50
  Dred Scott decision, 73, 122, 126, 440t, 446
  Emancipation Proclamation, 73, 122
  Missouri Compromise, 122
  states' rights, 83
  three-fifths compromise, 37
Snowden, Edward, 94, 100, 168–69
Snyder v. Phelps, 98
Social contract, 7
Social networking, 183–84, 210
Social Security, 338, 462t, 463
Social Security Disability Insurance (SSDI), 59, 462t, 463
Social welfare, 14, 14f
Socialism, 13, 82, 92
Socioeconomic status, 170–71
Solicitor General, 427
Sotomayor, Sonia, 418f, 443–44
  background and career of, 419–20
  district court nomination of, 441
  ideology and votes of, 432f, 436f
  Supreme Court nomination of, 442, 443f
Speaker of the House, 323–25
Special interests, 220. *See also* Interest groups
Speech, freedom of. *See* Freedom of speech

Speech codes, of colleges, 97
Stakeholders, 457–58, 457f
Stamp Act of 1765, 31, 31f, 32f
Standing committees, 328t
State action, 132–33
State-centered federalism, 75–76
State courts, 423–26, 423f
State of Union address, 361, 368
States. *See also* Interstate commerce
  Bill of Rights, incorporation to, 90–92, 91f, 448
  federalism and, 75–76, 79–82
  immigration laws in, 469
  judicial selection in, 79
  policy diffusion and, 461
  policy implementation and, 460–61
  political parties and, 235, 235f, 236f
  by population (2013), 315f
  powers of, 64, 65f, 75–76
    limits on, 44–45, 68
    reserve powers, 64
  race to the bottom, 461
  relationship with nation, 68–69
  relationships among, 69–70
  republican form of government, 44, 68
  supremacy of national law over, 68–69
  veto power in, 79
States' rights, 83
  nullification and, 71–73
Steel Seizure case, 364, 366
Steelworkers v. Weber, 424
Stewart, Jon, 181–82, 182f
Stonewall riots, 146
Sub-prime mortgage crisis, 402
Subsequent punishment, 101–3
Suffrage, 283. *See also* Voting
Sugar Act of 1764, 32f
Super PACs, 155, 240, 276–77
Supremacy clause, 68–69, 470
Supreme Court, 430–38, 441–50
  amicus curiae, 430, 431
  appointments to, 441–43, 443f
  constitutional interpretation by, 50–54, 320
  court-packing plan, 74, 378, 447–48
  decision making, 433–38
    decision/opinions, 431–33
    decisions overturned, 438
    decisions overturned by constitutional amendments, 438, 440t
    extralegal approach, 435–37
    judicial activism/restraint, 433–37
    legal approach, 434–35
  discuss list, 430
  federal court system and, 423f
  federal laws declared unconstitutional by, 433, 434f
  historical trends in rulings, 444–50, 449t
    Burger Court, 448, 449t
    expansion of national power, 446
    increased protections for civil liberties and rights, 448–50
    limits on national power, 446–47
    Marshall Court, 446, 449t
    Rehnquist Court, 448–49, 449t
    Roberts Court, 449–50, 449t
    strengthened national power, 447–50
    Taney Court, 449t
    Warren Court, 448, 449t
  impact of rulings, 437–38
  judicial independence of, 440
  judicial review and, 41, 43, 51, 133, 422
  jurisdiction of, 44, 422
  Justices
    demographic diversity, 443–44

    ideology and votes of, 432, 432f, 435–37, 436f
    impeachment of (Chase), 440
    preferences of, 435–36
    strategic considerations, 437
    women, 443–44
  New Federalism and, 77–78
  nominations to, 359
  Opinion of the Court, 431–33
    concurring opinion, 431
    dissenting opinion, 431–32
  petitions for writs of *certiorari*, 426, 430
  procedures
    decision, 431–33
    granting review, 430
    oral arguments, 431
  responsiveness of, 114, 450–51
  rule of four, 430
  tests used by, 133t
Supreme Court cases, 449t. *See also specific cases by name*
  Arizona v. United States, 470
  Bowers v. Hardwick, 158
  Brown v. Board of Education, 135
  California Democratic Party v. Jones, 238
  Chevron U.S.A. v. Natural Resources Defense Council, 412
  Citizens United v. Federal Election Commission, 218
  Cooper v. Aaron, 439
  Hernandez v. Texas, 135
  Lawrence v. Texas, 113
  Marbury v. Madison, 43, 422
  McCulloch v. Maryland, 72
  National Federation of Independent Business et al. v. Sebelius, 318
  Plyer v. Doe, 19
  Roe v. Wade, 113
  Snyder v. Phelps, 98
  United States v. Windsor, 158
  Youngstown Sheet and Tube Co. v. Sawyer, 366
Surveillance, national security, 94–95
Survey research, 159–60
Swing states/voters, 277–78
Symbolic speech, 99, 99f
Syria, conflict in, 371–72

T

Take care clause, 363
Taliban, 370–71, 486
Talk radio, 180–81, 180t
Taxation
  Americans for Tax Reform, 224, 226
  power of Congress, 40, 47, 51, 71, 74–75, 316–17
  Reagan and, 380–81
  without representation, 31, 32
Tea Party movement, 164, 167, 215, 250–51, 480
Television, 178, 178f, 181, 182f, 193
Term limits, 79, 282
Terrorism
  al-Qaeda and Taliban, 370–71
  antiterrorism measures, 168–69
  September 11, 2001, attacks, 93–94, 96, 168, 188, 370–71, 397
    national power strengthened after, 76–77
    public opinion after, 95
  USA PATRIOT Act and, 93, 94
  War on Terror, 76–77, 93, 168–69, 375
Tests
  clear and present danger, 97
  compelling interest, 92
  equal protection, 133t
  Lemon test, 105
  Miller test, 101–3

Third parties, 243–44, 247–54
  obstacles to, 251–54
  role of, 247–50
Thomas, Clarence, 435, 443
  Anita Hill and, 443f
  ideology and votes of, 432f, 436f
Three-fifths compromise, 37
Tocqueville, Alexis de, 200, 219
Tolerance
  political, 114
  religious, 5
Townshend Acts, 31, 32f
Trade, 477–82
  agreements, 358
  associations and organizations, 204, 358, 479–82
  balance of, U.S., 479, 479f
  European Union, 478, 482
  global, 358
  international agreements, 477–82
  NAFTA, 477–79
  protectionism vs. free trade, 477–79
Transparency in government, 411–14
Transportation Security Administration (TSA), 387–88, 395
Treaties, 319, 356–57
Trial by jury, 50, 109, 420, 428
Trial procedures, 109
Trigger warnings, 97
Truman, Harry S., 125, 162f, 364, 366, 379, 483–84, 488
Trust, political, 5, 157–59
Turnout. *See* Voting
Tweed, William Marcy "Boss," 244f
Twitter, 178, 184, 210
Two-party system, 246–54

U

Ukraine, 374
Unanimous consent agreements, 333, 441
Undocumented immigrants. *See* Immigration
Unemployment insurance, 338–39
Unions, 203, 205–6, 206f, 207t
Unitary system, 61, 62f, 82
United Farm Workers, 141–42
United Kingdom (U.K.)
  Constitution in, 30
  English Bill of Rights, 49
  legal traditions, 30, 420–22
  Parliamentary system of, 321
United Nations, 483
  bureaucracy of, 391
United States v. Cruikshank, 447
United States v. Nixon, 449t
United States v. Windsor, 148, 158, 449t
Unlawful activities, advocacy of, 97
Uprisings in foreign lands, 371–74
USA PATRIOT Act, 93, 94
USAID, 487

V

Valence issues, 279
Valid secular purpose, 103–4
Vanishing marginals, 281
Verdict, punishment, and appeal, 109–11
Veterans Administration, 400, 411, 411f
Veto, 40, 79, 337, 359–60, 360t
  line-item, 79
  override of, 40, 337
  pocket, 359

Vice president, 376–77
  election of, 268–69
  succession of presidency and, 350–51
  tie-breaking power of, 326
Vietnam War, 369–70, 380, 450
Virginia Plan, 35, 37t
Voting, 283–304. *See also* Elections
  African American suffrage, 126, 138–39, 139f
  Australian ballot, 245, 246f
  ballot, 237, 245
  ballot reform, 245, 246f
  competing views of participation, 283–84, 283f
  compulsory (in Australia), 297
  Constitution and, 283, 285f
  democracy and, 303–4
  demographics of, 287–93, 291f
  early voting, 301, 302f
  efficacy and, 295
  generational replacement and, 298
  grandfather clauses and, 138
  graveyard voting, 300
  history in America, 284–87
  language requirements, 140, 285, 286
  literacy tests and, 140, 286
  models of, 293–96
      economic model, 293–94
      genes and, 296
      institutional model, 295–96
      psychological model, 294–95
  new forms of, 301–3
  plurality vs. majority vote, 247
  poll taxes and, 127, 138
  racial barriers, 284–87
      dismantling, 126, 138–39, 139f
  rational, 294
  turnout, 290–93, 296–300
      age and, 291–92, 291f
      assessment of, 296–300
      dangers to democracy (potential), 303–4
      demographics of, 291–93, 291f–93f
      education and, 292–93, 293f
      income and, 292, 292f
      inequality and, 299–300, 303–4
      low level of, perceived, 296–99
      sex and, 291
      trends in, 297–98
      U.S. vs. other democracies, 297
  vote-by-mail system, 301
  voter registration, 300–301
  voting age population (VAP), 298–99, 299f
  voting eligible population (VEP), 299, 299f
  white primary and, 138
  women's suffrage, 127–29, 202–3
Voting laws and regulations, 300–303
  National Voter Registration Act, 301
  reforms in 1890s, 300–301
  voter ID laws, 139, 288–89, 289f
  Voting Rights Act (1965), 75, 138–39, 256, 285, 316, 379

W

Walker, Scott, 205
Wallace, George, 75, 138, 249
War(s)
  Afghanistan, 370–71, 486
  Cold War, 483–84
  drones and, 372–73, 372t
  enemy combatants and, 93
  Iraq, 370, 486
  presidency and, 368–75

uprisings in foreign lands, 371–74
Vietnam, 369–70, 380
War on Terror, 76–77, 93, 168–69, 375
war powers, 317, 369–70
World Wars, 92–93
War Powers Act, 369–70
Warrants, 107–8
Warren Court, 448, 449t
Washington, George, 33, 71, 241, 273, 351, 361, 482
Watchdog role of press, 175, 180, 194
Watergate scandal, 176, 176f, 362
Wedge issue, 279
Welfare system, 76
Whig Party, 243
Whistleblowing, 387–88, 414
White primary, 138
White v. Regester, 128t, 140–41
Wikileaks, 100–101
Wilson, Woodrow, 361, 488
Winner-take-all system, 239
Wiretapping, 93, 168, 365
Women
  appointees of Obama, 406–7, 444
  coverture, 128–29, 130
  discrimination against, 129–32
    dismantling, 142–45

Equal Pay Act, 142, 144–45
Equal Rights Amendment (ERA), 129–30, 143, 143f
equal treatment, worldwide, 131, 131f
equality in workplace, 144–45
female judges, worldwide, 445
National Organization for Women (NOW), 142
Supreme Court Justices, 443–44
Violence Against Women Act, 77
voting trends, 171
Women's suffrage, 127–29, 202–3
Workplace equality, 144–45
World Bank, 487
World Trade Organization (WTO), 358, 479
Writ of *certiorari*, 426, 430
Writ of *habeas corpus*. *See Habeas corpus*

Y

Yellin, Janet, 476f
Youngstown Sheet and Tube Co. v. Sawyer, 364, 366

Z

Zimmerman, George, 110